COMMUNITY-ORIENTED POLICING

A Systemic Approach to Policing

WILLARD M. OLIVER

GLENVILLE STATE COLLEGE

Prentice Hall
Upper Saddle River, New Jersey 07458

Library of Congress Cataloging-in-Publication Data

OLIVER, WILLARD M.
    Community-oriented policing: a systemic approach to policing
/ Willard M. Oliver.
      p. cm.
    Includes bibliographical references and index.
    ISBN 0-13-524869-8
    1. Community policing—United States.   2. Police—United
States—Attitudes.   I. Title.
    HV7936.C83044   1998
    363.2'0973—dc21   97-23651
                                          CIP

Production Supervision and Interior Design: *Eileen M. O'Sullivan*
Managing Editor: *Mary Carnis*
Acquisitions Editor: *Neil Marquardt*
Director of Manufacturing and Production: *Bruce Johnson*
Manufacturing Manager: *Ed O'Dougherty*
Page Layout: *Stephen Hartner*
Marketing Manager: *Frank Mortimer, Jr.*
Editorial assistant: *Rose Mary Florio*
Printer/Binder: *RR Donnelley & Sons Company*

©1998 by Prentice-Hall, Inc.
A Simon & Schuster Company
Upper Saddle River, New Jersey 07458

Printed in the United States of America

10 9 8 7 6 5 4 3 2 1

ISBN   0-13-524869-8

Prentice-Hall International (UK) Limited, *London*
Prentice-Hall of Australia Pty. Limited, *Sydney*
Prentice-Hall Canada Inc., *Toronto*
Prentice-Hall Hispanoamericana, S.A., *Mexico*
Prentice-Hall of India Private Limited, *New Delhi*
Prentice-Hall of Japan, Inc., *Tokyo*
Simon & Schuster Asia Pte. Ltd., *Singapore*
Editora Prentice-Hall do Brasil, Ltda., *Rio de Janeiro*

Dedicated to my beloved wife Judy,
who most importantly is my best friend,
       and
To Paul, who in death, through God, gave life

CONTENTS

FOREWORD

No doubt, the concept of community policing has been riding a tidal wave of popularity in recent years. Nor has that momentum been overlooked in textbook publishing. Authors eager to join the community policing bandwagon have been churning out a proliferation of books. But just as there may be as many different variations of community policing as there are departments implementing it, the quality of publications on this topic also varies widely.

It is no exaggeration to state that this book stands out among a very few of the community policing efforts that have captured my highest levels of praise and admiration. In over thirty years of reviewing and editorial advising for Prentice Hall, I have rarely seen a manuscript surface and survive that measures up to the standards which this author sets. Not only is the subject an extremely timely one, but more importantly, the author addresses the uniqueness of community-oriented policing, while still acknowledging that it also embraces many "common sense" and "traditional" ingredients. While some would promote community policing as the virtual panacea for all social ills, Professor Oliver takes a more rational, balanced approach. He teaches, but does not preach, the message.

Moreover, he has done a masterful job of explaining community policing's historical evolution, rationale, strategies, pilot programs, areas of responsibility, implementation techniques, ideals to be accomplished, and even how to evaluate these programs to determine when and if we are succeeding. Simply put, no other text on the topic is as comprehensive.

This book combines the best of all worlds—for those who require historical perspective, it is precise; . . . for those who want an update on progress, it is detailed and illustrative; . . . for those who ask "So what else is new?", it firmly speaks to an inventive philosophy that is interwoven into the efficient but often unbending institution that we have all come to know as our modern police structure.

Police departments are to many of us the same as our young children were as they were maturing. We care deeply about them, we have learned to live with their shortcomings, and we have tried hard to grasp the adjustments they have had to make as society molded them. They, in turn, worked to adapt themselves to outside pressures, changing environments, and higher expectations. This textbook grasps how those changes occur, without ever losing sight of the many diverse roles of the police and how the community never quite agrees on how they should be accomplished.

In my manuscript reviews, I typically have commented that the material is fine for a practitioner, but lacks the academic rigor or the proper level of references to serve as a textbook. On the other hand, manuscripts often lack realism and relevance, even though they might be heavy with research citations. Or even more frequently, the narrative lacks the thoroughness and breadth of scope to truly address the subject completely. None of these drawbacks are found in this text. In Professor Oliver's *Community-Oriented Policing*, one finds all of the necessary ingredients to state without hesitation that this book combines knowledge, understanding, insights, and realism. It provides an encyclopedia of information about this most significant and widely heralded development in law enforcement.

If community-oriented policing accomplishes everything that its advocates anticipate, its current tidal wave of popularity may well stabilize to become a solid foundation underlying the transition of American policing into the twenty-first century. But perhaps most significant is the promise it holds for propelling the momentum to raise policing to the status of professionalism that has been so elusively sought during the last half of the twentieth century.

James D. Stinchcomb
Director (retired)
School of Justice and Safety
Administration
Miami-Dade Community College

PREFACE

Community-oriented policing is truly an idea whose time has come. Research and application over the past twenty years have moved the idea from explaining the past failures of team policing, to a method that could avoid these past pitfalls, to a viable, but crude method in the 1980s, to the successful and detailed practices of the 1990s that have caused many to deem this the community-oriented policing decade. There is little doubt that this paradigm in policing has captured the attention of both citizen and police, mayors and police chiefs, state government and national government officials, and has worked its way into becoming a household name. The dilemma of understanding arises in how community-oriented policing is defined and what the paradigm entails. It is to this end that we must now set our sights.

Perhaps one of the first debates over this approach lies in questioning if it is "old wine in a new bottle" Critics of this paradigm have thus argued it is early-twentieth century policing glorified and that turning back the policing clock would prove detrimental to both the profession and the citizens served. These critics seem to miss the fact that it is more than just making a new case for the methods, practices, and procedures utilized by the police today, but rather, it is argument for changing the way we think about policing, both from the perspectives of the police and the community. Abraham Lincoln perhaps said it best, "As our case is new, so we must think and act anew." We recognize that the current case for promulgating community-oriented policing is new, what we on many occasions have failed to do, both from an academic and practical standpoint, is allow ourselves to think and act anew. Although the nostalgia, a consistent trend in all organizations, may exist in policing, community-oriented policing is not a push backward, but rather a rapid movement forward regarding the mission of the police and how they perform their duties. Yet, despite this realization, the questions continue to linger as to what specifically is community-oriented policing?

A key debate within the central understanding of the systemic approach to policing is whether community-oriented policing is a philosophy or a program. The argument on the side of a philosophy is rooted in the premise that in order for the systemic approach to be fully functional it must grow from a conceptual framework from which all the actors can adhere to mutual principles, but retain the freedom to ad-lib. The argument on the programmatic side is rooted in the understanding that methods employed by the actors must be more substantive and should therefore be put forth in a script with written parts for each actor. The argument can be further broken down into whether or not community-oriented policing is a concept for the way we think about the police or for actions garnering the policing. It is an argument between the theoretical and the practical.

In order to delineate between the importance of the two, it is important to reach an age-old method of issue resolution: compromise. Theory, often in its true form, ignores the practical application, thus negating the possible benefits derived from a theory. Practical application, in turn, often ignores theory, thus negating the benefits that can be derived from a guiding theoretical construct. The consensus lies in the commitment for both the theoretical and practical to coalesce into a synthesis that supersedes the ontological perspectives, thus creating a mutually beneficial relationship. The synthesis can then be utilized for the proposition of a conceptual framework, from which to guide the systemic application from the theoretical to the practical.

Community-oriented policing, as a systemic approach to policing, is in fact the realization of this synthesis. It incorporates both the theoretical and the practical into the overall framework, thus allowing for the maximization of benefits. It must start as a new philosophy, a new way of thinking about the role of the police in society, and it must be enacted through new and various programs that adhere to the philosophical premise. This, then, is the primary emphasis of this book. It is an attempt to weave both the theoretical and the practical, as well as combine the various interpretations of the systemic approach, into one concept under the banner of community-oriented policing.

OVERVIEW OF THE BOOK'S CONTENTS

The first chapter is a historical review of police and community relations since the formation of the United States. Although other authors have attempted to analyze the eras of policing from a strict police perspective, this chapter analyzes the relationship between the two parties and places them into eras indicative of the type of relationship occurring at the time. A review of history from this perspective, it is largely historical, and that is acceptable, for it allows the reader a better understanding of the different relationships we are now entering into under the auspices of community-oriented policing.

Chapter 2 is then the guiding chapter for the rest of the book in that it attempts to provide a clear understanding of what community-oriented policing is and how it is defined, in both theoretical and practical terms. The construct of the chapter shares a three-pronged process that was assembled to reach a definition of community-oriented policing. It reflects the multitude of definitions and explanations that have surfaced in the academic literature for the past fifteen years, which covers both theoretical constructs and research methodologies. It reflects the practical applications covered in various journals and magazines, and synthesizes the definitions and actions implemented by police departments across the United States under the auspices of community-oriented policing. And finally, it would not be a factual representation if I were not to state that the third prong is the inclusion of this author's understanding and definition of the systemic approach based upon my experiences as a police officer and the community-oriented policing programs I have had the fortune to witness. The culmination of this three-pronged approach has revealed many consistent themes throughout the academic literature, the practical literature, and my own experiences. Community-oriented policing can then be defined as:

> . . . a systemic approach to policing with the paradigm of instilling and fostering a sense of community, within a geographical neighborhood, to improve the quality of life. It achieves this through the decentralization of the police and the implementation of a synthesis of three key components: 1) strategic-oriented policing—the redistribution of traditional police resources; 2) neighborhood-oriented policing—the interaction of police and all community members to reduce crime and the fear of crime through indigenous proactive programs; and 3) problem-oriented policing—a concerted effort to resolve the causes of crime, rather than the symptoms.

The next four chapters then concentrate on expanding the definition, by breaking down each component into its own chapter, along with one additional chapter that explains how the three become synthesized into one framework: community-oriented policing. Chapter 3 is a more detailed explanation of strategic-oriented policing and all of the potential methods the police can employ to achieve this component. Chapter 4 is an overview of the many types of police and community programs that can promote interaction and communication between the two actors to understand the quality-of-life benefits that can be derived from this cooperation. Chapter 5 defines the component of problem-oriented policing and draws heavily from the works of Herman Goldstein (academic) and John E. Eck and William Spelman (practical). Chapter 6 is then an overview of how the three components are integrated into the systemic approach of community-oriented policing. Chapter 6 also includes three case studies of a large-, medium-, and small-sized police department and demonstrates how they have implemented the three components as they relate to the systemic approach.

Chapter 7 then provides an understanding of how the systemic approach to policing will mandate systemic changes to both the organization of the police department and the management methods employed. It specifically details how the police department must decentralize by geography, personnel, and by its structure to achieve the true benefits of community-oriented policing, and it reviews the varying types of management practices that complement the systemic approach, specifically Total Quality Management (TQM).

The next three chapters detail the role of the three key actors involved in ensuring the success of community-oriented policing: the police, the community, and the police chief. Chapter 8, on the role of the police, gives wide coverage to the changes that must be made to move traditional police officers to community-oriented police officers. As the police are the street level implementors of the philosophy and programs under the systemic approach, they are a key link to the overall success of community-oriented policing. However, because the systemic approach is geared toward the community, it is readily apparent that the community's role in community-oriented policing is equally important. Their role is detailed in Chapter 9 and provides an understanding of what is meant by "community" and how past attitudes of not getting involved in police matters can be overcome. Chapter 10 then provides the key link to the relationship between the police and the community and that is the role of the police chief in community-oriented policing. This role, as a result of changes in the police, community, and organizational and management structures, must also change to accommodate the synthesis of philosophy and practical applications. It is important that the chief become a dynamic member of the community and that the chief's office provide the impetus for the systemic approach.

Chapter 11 then sketches a rough outline for implementing the systemic approach to policing. Community-oriented policing is a profound change to police practices of the past, therefore it is not a "program" that can be implemented overnight, but rather one that must see a gradual and incremental form of implementation to ensure its success. Each department will see variations on their community-oriented policing methods as a result of endogenous variables, exogenous variables, and the differences that account for both space (location of the police department) and time (the current development of the police department); each department will then see a different time line for their implementation of the systemic approach.

Chapter 12 proves to be the most daunting of the chapters, but it highlights the fact that evaluations under community-oriented policing are crucial to the success of this paradigm. The evaluation process must not be limited to one actor, but made a part of the everyday duties of the police and can include surveys of local citizens, police officers, and local government employees. As the systemic approach is implemented in an incremental fashion, these surveys become part of the evaluation process and provide the necessary information for the police, citizens, and police chief to make the determination as to whether a particular program or policing method should be continued, deleted, or altered in some way.

Chapter 13 covers many of the "caveats" that go with implementing community-oriented policing. These caveats are based upon the various failures of past policing experiments and recent failures with community-oriented policing. In reviewing this information, it provides an insight into why certain programs have failed in the hopes that these methods will not be repeated in future implementations of the systemic approach. Hence, these are not in actuality problems for the implementation process, but rather caveats, making the police department that decides to shift to this new paradigm aware of the many possibilities for failure.

In turn, Chapter 14 speaks of the future benefits that police departments may receive when implementing community-oriented policing, as well as the overall benefits that have already been achieved. It also delves further into the future to discuss many of the potential benefits and provides some discussion for how police departments can plan for the future, today.

Chapter 15 is then a summary conclusion that discusses further why community-oriented policing should be implemented and why it is considered a systemic approach to policing. It is at the same time a review and a preview of what lies in the future for policing regarding both the philosophy and practical application of community-oriented policing.

ACKNOWLEDGMENTS

I must say I was stunned to discover how long the process of writing and producing a textbook takes. By the time you are able to read these words, it will have taken almost three years of my life. What is perhaps even more stunning is the number of people who have allowed me to get where I am. In thinking about everyone who assisted me either overtly or covertly, I am overwhelmed by their generosity and hope that I can satisfactorily name them all, and I must immediately apologize to those I fail to mention . . . you are not forgotten.

I must once again thank the one person who has allowed me to grasp hold of every dream and has endured the consequences of these endeavors, quietly behind the scene, my wife, Judy Ilaria Oliver. She has managed to be my wife, the mother of my child, my mentor, my role model, my reality check, my godparent, but most of all my friend. It is to her that this book is dedicated for her love, guidance, and assistance.

In addition, this book is also dedicated to three Pauls, Paulo Ponzi, who died saving a child trapped in a well, a life of giving cut short; Paul Fellers, a man I would have loved to have known, whose life was also cut far too short; and to Paul Oliver, my son, who was born during the writing of this book and has renewed my confidence in life. Judy and Paul, despite my many dreams, you two are the most important dream come true.

I would also like to thank everyone at Prentice Hall, Inc., who has made this book a reality. Bryce Dodson, whom I absentmindedly queried for a textbook on community-oriented policing—and then I ended up writing one. To Robin Baliszewski, acquisitions editor, who was perhaps even more dedicated to the project than I was and to Neil Marquardt who entered as the acquisitions editor half-way through the project and continued charging on where Robin left off, demonstrating that Prentice Hall, Inc., only hires the best. And to Rose Mary Florio, whom one day I'd like to meet in person and thank her for answering the thousand questions, patiently, that a college professor has in the unknown world of publishing.

I must also thank those individuals who served as reviewers of my manuscript. The hints, ideas, and constructive criticism that was provided served to elevate this manuscript to a far superior product than I could have ever made alone. Thank you for your time and effort and please know I am indebted to you for your assistance. I would like to specifically thank them individually and in person, but for now this must suffice. My appreciation goes especially to James D. Stinchcomb of Miami-Dade Community College for his kind criticism, thoughtful insights, and for agreeing to write the Foreword of this book. My thanks is extended to the other reviewers who include, Lois A. Wims of Salve Regina University; Richard R. Becker of North Harris College; and Leslie W. Parks of the University of Texas, Brownsville.

In moving to many of the other people that have made this possible, I must thank Glenville State College as a whole for making this a reality. Specifically, I must thank Jim Hilgenberg, who provided a police officer with the opportunity he so desired and for serving as a role model and mentor along the way. I must also thank two other individuals who were instrumental in my hiring: Dolores Mysliwiec, a friend I find more in common with everyday and Tom Todd, a friend with many dreams. I must also thank two people who hold the position of secretary at Glenville State College, who are in actuality miracle workers: Mary Alltop, who assisted in some of the early work and computer problems, a hard worker, a true friend, and someone who always has a smile on her face; and Patty Knicely, who did most of the illustrations for this textbook and never complained, and, like Mary, always had a smile on her face. Thank you both for putting up with me.

Although Glenville State College has allowed me the opportunity to work in an academic environment, I owe a great deal to two other colleges: one that has shaped me and one that continues to do so. I must thank Radford University, Radford, Virginia, for shaping me through the many people that touched my life. Specifically, I must thank Dr. Paul Lang, who supported me in obtaining my Master's degree and who still serves as a role model for me; Dr. Jack E. Call, who awoke the analytical process in me; Dr. Vernon Rich, who diligently guided me through my Bachelor's degree; Dr. James N. Gilbert, who set the standard for all good professors my freshman year of college; and a special thanks goes out to Dr. James Unnever, who unknowingly managed to turn on that imaginary light bulb and take an average student and make him a straight-A student ever since. Thank you. All of you and all of Radford University have made me who I am today, both academically and personally.

I must also thank the university that continues to mold and shape me today, West Virginia University. I must thank all of the political science department for allowing a criminal justice major and professor to explore the political world of crime and allowing me the opportunity to advance. Specifically, I must thank Dr. Robert Duvall for supporting my acceptance into the program; Dr. Kevin Leyden for showing as strong an interest in my ideas as I have, and hence serving as my advisor; and Dr. John Kilwein, who has pushed my thinking to a much higher level. Thank you for your continued support in my future endeavors.

I must also thank several other organizations that have shaped me in a different way, and they are the organizations that have provided me with a background in policing. I must first thank Wildwood Police Department, Wildwood, New Jersey, for that first taste of being a cop; Fairfax Security and Ron Miller for demonstrating that policing is not just a public venture; the United States Army Reserves and the Military Police Corp, for providing a different perspective on policing; and finally Arlington County Police Department, Arlington, Virginia, an organization that provided me with all the realities of policing. I would like to specifically thank several fellow officers at Arlington for their friendships that have lasted beyond the world of policing: Jackson Hunter Miller, Bruce Silvernale, Don Fortunato, Jim Daly, and Bob Barnett.

I would also like to thank several people who have contributed directly to this book: to Bruce Cameron, editor of *Law & Order* magazine for allowing me reprint rights and to all of the staff and authors who produced each article; Carol Gibeson and all the staff of the Community Policing Consortium for their help in securing reprint rights; and to all of the police departments that provided me with photographs and literature for assistance in my book, especially the Parkersburg Police Department, Parkersburg, West Virginia (specifically Chief Rick W. Modesitt and Lt. J. R. Harvey). Thank you for your time, patience, and reprint rights, it is greatly appreciated and has greatly enhanced this book.

As I started with family, so I must end with family. I would like to thank two people that are greatly important to me and my love for them should go without saying. To my Mom, Carol R. Oliver for her love and support of her "little boy," of which I now understand the love of a son as I see myself, and our relationship, in Paul. And to my Dad, Charles J. Oliver, who has managed to succeed in perhaps one of the highest goals of Fatherhood, making his son's life better than his. I would also like to thank my sisters Nadine and Debbie for their love and support over the years. And I would like to thank my "other family," for that is how I have come to see them, mom and dad, Ilaria and Donald Fellers, and my brother and sister, David and Kathy Fellers; thank you for your love and support through the years as well. And a final, and very special thanks, goes out to two wonderful people I have come to consider "my guardian angels," Gene and Julia Oliver, an aunt and uncle who have always managed to be there when I needed them most. Although there are so many other people I would like to thank, I must end here. But although not mentioned, as I stated before, they are not forgotten.

Willard M. Oliver
Glenville, West Virginia

CHAPTER 1

The Evolution of Community-Oriented Policing

History in illuminating the past illuminates the present and in illuminating the present illuminates the future.

-Benjamin N. Cardozo-

Policing in the United States is currently undergoing a period of rapid change. Police departments in the United States at any point during the twentieth century bear little resemblance to those existing today. This evolution of the way police departments perform their mission can primarily be attributed to the concept of community-oriented policing. This new method of police-provided services to the public, whether focused on crime fighting or order maintenance, has initiated a revolution that will alter the way policing is conducted well into the twenty-first century.

Community-oriented policing is not a new philosophy. Its roots can be traced as far back as the first conceptual model of policing and the first police department in the free world. Historically, it is firmly established in the founding and evolution of a new nation with the expansion westward, the Industrial Revolution, and the more recent transformation into an information age. Community-oriented policing is found in past policy and procedure regarding the police and in past literature from both the practitioner and academic fields. The concept started with a simple premise and through many successes and failures pushed itself into the well-established doctrine we see and recognize today as part of community-oriented policing.

In order to understand the concept's development throughout the 1980s and 1990s, it is important to examine these past concepts that have developed into community-oriented policing. What has gone before is important for understanding this theoretical framework that has no standard definition and

A Dallas police officer from the Dallas, Texas Police Department teaches students at a local elementary school. (Courtesy of the Dallas Police Department, Dallas, Texas.)

often lacks a standard method of implementation. Although there are varying thoughts as to the history of policing and the eras from which it has progressed, the majority run along consistent themes that provide the clarity necessary to understanding the evolution. In other cases, the lineage of today's concept is clearly evident within the past literature regarding the police. The culmination of these historical approaches to the modern doctrine provides many answers to the philosophy we so highly regard today.

"CRIME FILES"

Throughout this textbook, reference will be made to a series of tapes sponsored by the National Institute of Justice. This series is an innovative group of VHS tapes focusing on America's most critical criminal justice issues. There are currently 42 tapes in the series: tapes one through ten were created in 1990; tapes eleven through twenty were produced in 1987; and tapes twenty-one through forty-two were made in 1985. Each of the tapes is approximately twenty minutes in length and all are hosted by James Q. Wilson, Collins Professor of Management at the University of California, Los Angeles, and who is also one of the creators of community-oriented policing.

These tapes provide a complementary method of understanding the issues of community-oriented policing and pull on many of the items discussed throughout this textbook. The "Crime Files" tapes and complementary study guide can be ordered through the National Institute of Justice by calling them toll free at 1-800-851-3420.

THE HISTORICAL ROOTS OF POLICING

Policing dates back to the early days of man, and is usually dated by historians in the pre-2100 B.C. timeframe. In the year 2100 B.C., the first record of a "police" force that enforced written laws and their punishments was the Code of Hammurabi in ancient Babylon (Sullivan 1977, 2). The police at this time, as is common throughout most of civilization's history, was the military. Prior to the 2100 B.C. timeframe, it is largely believed that the practices of policing were left to the individual tribes who utilized either the warriors or the elders (Sullivan 1977, 1).

The first true method of "community" policing is found in the Anglo-Saxon period when King Alfred established the Frank-Pledge system in England (Sullivan 1977, 3). The Frank-Pledge system emphasized rudimentary community policing to implement most forms of social control. If a crime or serious matter was at hand the people raised the "hue and cry" and the other members of the community were required to render assistance (Dempsey 1994, 3). The community was divided up along the power of ten, with groups of ten families known as tithings (Dempsey 1994, 2). Each tithing was responsible for the actions of its group members and any criminal act or order-maintenance issue was handled within the tithing (Dempsey 1994, 3). The leader of the tithing was known as the tithingman (Sullivan 1977, 3). The next level of responsibility was the ten-tithing, which was the collection of 100 families, who answered to a constable (Sullivan 1977, 3). The collection of several ten-tithings were organized along geographical lines and were under the control of the king (Dempsey 1994, 3). Although the king was in control of the geographical area, he generally placed a man to govern this collection of various ten-tithings. This man was known as the shire-reeve or, in today's terms, the sheriff (Dempsey 1994, 3).

The system was perhaps the first in the history of policing that fully integrated the policing of a community with the members of the community. Despite the fact that there were appointed individuals such as the tithingman, the constable, or the shire-reeve, no formal police force existed separate from the citizens. This system is then the first rudimentary element of the concept of community-oriented policing. This system remained in effect from its implementation by King Alfred in 899 A.D. until the Duke of Normandy conquered England in the year 1066 A.D., at which time the function of policing returned to the hands of the military (Sullivan 1977, 5).

In the year 1215, the rebel barons succeeded in forcing King John to sign the Magna Carta, granting certain rights and concessions to the people (Sullivan 1977, 5). This cleared the way for the Statute of Winchester to pass in 1285 which essentially revised the majority of policing practices that had been successful in the past (Sullivan 1977, 6). These successful practices included the "hue and cry," the use of the "watch and ward," the night and day patrol, respectively, and required all males from 15 to 60 to retain arms in their residence (Sullivan 1977, 6). These practices remained in effect for the next 500 years and reflected the only other community-oriented philosophy of policing until the first official police department was formed.

At the turn of the 18th century, England experienced its Industrial Revolution. During this time period, major social change occurred within every fabric of society, of which crime was no exception. The rising crime rates necessitated a response in the form of an advanced method of social control. Although previously pursued by Patrick Colquhoun, a London magistrate in 1789, the concept of a metropolitan police force was not received well by the citizenry at that time (Gilbert 1986, 9). However, Patrick Colquhoun planted a seed of possibility in the minds of the citizens and with the new social conditions this seed began to take shape.

In 1829, Sir Robert Peel, utilizing Patrick Colquhoun's ideas, drafted and promoted the Metropolitan Police Act of 1829 (Sullivan 1977, 11). Although still a hotly contested concept, it passed parliament and became law. The first large-scale and official police department was now a reality and the parliament chose Sir Robert Peel to lead the new organization (Sullivan 1977, 11).

The organization was not military in nature, however it was organized along military lines (Dempsey 1994, 5). The police were uniformed with "three-quarter-length royal blue coats, white trousers, and top hats," were armed with a truncheon (nightstick), and walked a beat (Dempsey 1994, 5). They were housed in an old palace that originally housed Scottish royalty, hence the name "Scotland Yard," and they were affectionally known as "Bobbies," named in reference to their founder, Sir Robert Peel (Dempsey 1994, 5). Although this was clearly the first formally organized police department, it was also the first formalized method of community policing.

This is clearly evident in the premise of policing by Sir Robert Peel, when he stated that "...the police are the public and the public are the police" (Braiden 1992, 108). This was the foundation of Peel's beliefs of what an effective police department should be like, specifically, community oriented. This was also evident when Sir Robert Peel condensed his theory of basic policing principles into "Peel's Principles" (Sullivan 1977, 11). The following are the twelve basic principles as put forth by Sir Robert Peel:

1. The police must be stable, efficient, and organized along military lines.
2. The police must be under government control.
3. The absence of crime will best prove the efficiency of police.
4. The distribution of crime news is essential.
5. Proper deployment of police strength, by both time and area, is essential.
6. No quality is more indispensable to a policeman than a perfect command of temper. A quiet, determined manner has more effect than violent action.

7. Good appearance commands respect.

8. The selection and training of proper persons are at the root of efficient law enforcement.

9. Public security demands that every police officer be given an identifying number.

10. Police headquarters should be centrally located and easily accessible to people.

11. Policemen should be hired on a probationary basis before permanent assignment.

12. Police crime records are necessary for the best distribution of police strength. (Sullivan 1977, 11).

These principles, although not definitively aimed at community policing, do provide some insight into the fact that the police should be responsive to the community's needs. Peel's principles attempted to take into account that to a large degree the police must be well-trained, committed, and ethical organizations that are under the control of the government must be accountable to the people. Although there is a strong demand for a centralized police force within Peel's principles, there is also the demand for community relations, something largely missing throughout most of policing's history.

"CRIME FILES"

WHAT WORKS—PART 20

This edition of the "Crime Files," hosted by James Q. Wilson, features Richard A. Staufenberger, Department of Labor; George L. Kelling, Professor of Criminal Justice Northeastern University; and Joel Garner, National Institute of Justice. The discussion revolves around three police experiments in Kansas City, Minneapolis, and San Diego, and the panelists discuss both old and new ways the police can prevent crime by tracing the evolution to Community-Oriented Policing.

POLICING IN THE NEW FRONTIER

The development of the police in the new frontier known as America was slow in its evolution. Although the first city, Jamestown, Virginia, was established in 1607, it would be over 200 years before the first police department was established. This period of American history, prior to the signing of the Declaration of Independence and the passage of the Constitution, was largely policed by the sheriff. The sheriff at this time was generally a political appointee who performed multiple tasks in his jurisdiction to include overseeing elections. Night watches were a common method of policing, borrowed from the old country for nighttime security, and were usually staffed by volunteers, but in some areas they were paid meager wages (Dempsey 1994, 6).

In 1776, the Declaration of Independence was signed and the United States commenced its journey toward the path of freedom, creating a government whose authority was vested in the people. Thomas Jefferson managed to convey multiple theories of the rights of man, the ideology of community, and the institution of government within this document. When Jefferson explained that "All men are created equal" and that they enjoy certain "unalienable rights," he set the stage for the inherent ideology of the American people that still exerts its influence today. He also detailed that these rights included "Life, Liberty, and the pursuit of Happiness," thereby enumerating those particular rights that Americans hold so dear. When Jefferson spoke of government existing to protect those rights and that the government was created by "the consent of the governed" he alluded to the power of the government to protect the people and that the government is made up of those people. The philosophy of the "police are the public and the public are the police" resurfaces into the "government are the people and the people are the government," all very central to the tenets of community-oriented policing.

In the long hot summer of 1787, the Constitutional Convention convened to determine the organization of a new government, predicated on the beliefs that Jefferson spoke so eloquently of in the Declaration of Independence. Presented on September 17, 1787, the Constitution became the form of government by the people with a system of checks and balances to prevent dictatorial rule and despotism. Although the Constitution addresses little in the way of specifics for the organization of the police, it speaks tenfold to the police in the greatest mission statement ever written.

The preamble to the Constitution of the United States is essentially the mission statement of the country. Within this superbly articulated sentence, the role of the government is dictated and the inferences to the relationship of the police within the community can easily be extracted. Police power is not specifically dictated within the Constitution, but rather juxtaposed by those rights reserved to the people and the requirements of "due process."

The preamble states:

> We the People of the United States of America, in Order to form a more perfect Union, establish Justice, insure domestic Tranquility, provide for the common defence, promote the general Welfare, and secure the Blessings of Liberty to ourselves and our Posterity, do ordain and establish this Constitution for the United States of America.

Because the preamble commences with the word "We," there is no distinction along the lines of government and the common person, and this is perhaps the ultimate sense of community. The goal of these "people" to "form a more perfect Union" provides the purpose for the organization. However, it is the statement "establish Justice" that stands out most clearly for the police. The police do not exist in a vacuum and are an essential part of this clause. The government, via the police, must ensure that justice is served in our society for the purposes of order maintenance. Through this, the American people can "insure domestic Tranquility."

Another clause that gives credence to the power of the police is the goal to "promote the general Welfare." The police services oriented on law enforcement and order maintenance provide for the overall welfare of the American people. The ability for people to live without fear in their communities is important to the overall health of the nation, and the founding fathers understood this important concept. The police are often tasked with overseeing the ideology found in this clause and, through past orientation, have not been as successful in its implementation.

And finally, the emphasis can be placed heavily upon the police ability to "secure the Blessings of Liberty to ourselves and our Posterity" for the purpose of their role in society. The ability of the police to maintain order and to reduce crime intrinsically provides for a better America today as well as for our children. The ultimate goal of the police mission should perhaps be focused primarily upon providing a better place to live for our "posterity," for it is every parent's dream to provide a better world for their children. The police and the community have that chance to fulfill this goal. They have that chance through the implementation of community-oriented policing, upon which the "Blessings of Liberty to ourselves and our Posterity" is the cardinal goal.

The power of the government was not lost upon any of the founding fathers, especially Alexander Hamilton. Although no statement as to the authority of the police is stated within the Constitution, there is little argument that the function of the police is a necessary deed. Hamilton realized the full potential of the system of justice, or in today's terms the criminal justice system, of which policing is an integral part. Hamilton stated succinctly:

> There is one transcendent advantage belonging to the province of the State governments, which alone suffices to place the matter in a clear and satisfactory light—I mean the ordinary administration of criminal and civil justice. This, of all others, is the most powerful, most universal, and most attractive source of popular obedience and attachment. It is this which, being the immediate and visible guardian of life and property, having its benefits and its terrors in constant activity before the public eye, regulating all those personal interests and familiar concerns to which the sensibility of individuals is more immediately awake, contributes more than any other circumstances to impressing upon the minds of the people affection, esteem, and reverence towards the government. This great cement of society, which will diffuse itself almost wholly through the channels of the particular governments, independent of all other causes of influence, would insure them so decided an empire over their respective citizens as to render them at all times a complete counterpoise...to the power of the union (Rossiter 1961, 120)

Alexander Hamilton could easily have spoken of the one component of the criminal justice system we are concerned with here—the police. The introduction of the American citizen to not only the police, but the criminal justice system and government itself is often wrapped up within that simple contact of the citizen with a police officer. This contact can be as simple as the introduction of the citizen to the officer or as complex as the interaction between a rape victim and the investigating officer. In either case, it is this contact that formulates the perception the public has of the police, the criminal justice system, and the government. The weight of this is often lost on those who work the street. Through the concepts of community-oriented policing, this concept that Hamilton spoke of over 200 years ago is an overall focus to this systemic approach to policing.

COP IN ACTION

POLICE MUSEUMS OFFER OPPORTUNITIES TO TEACH, RECRUIT

It's difficult to believe that shortly over a decade ago there was no Houston Police Department Museum. Today, the two-storied treasury of historical artifacts is an impressive teaching and recruiting tool. Its director, Officer Denny Hair, displays interesting memorabilia which recounts the days of Houston's growth, both as a city and a police department. Visitors come in droves. Hair said the facility has greeted more than 180,000 people to date, with many of those coming from both public and private schools. "It's a wonderful recruiting tool for the department," Hair said.

The museum is nestled in a corner of the city's police academy. The setting is both operational and architecturally attractive. It is a grouping of several buildings surrounding a display of water fountains and reflection pools. Visitors see cadets walking and visiting as they change classes, enjoying lunch and break times, and crossing to buildings housing the firing range. An interesting aspect of the museum is its ability to teach adults and children about police officers and their jobs.

With the birth of the museum, Hair went out in the community soliciting assistance. Financial aid in the form of donations from area businesses and the 100 Club of Houston, Inc. provided funding for the necessary display cases to begin the massive project. Then Hair began purchasing mat board, glue, and cutting tools with his own money and began preparation of the displays. Items for the exhibits come from a variety of sources. Donations of family memorabilia-pictures, old uniforms, badges, letters and scrapbooks—are filled with historical interest. Other displays have been begged for and pieced together.

Hair is proud of his efforts with the museum and wants to ensure that the facility is around long after he is gone. "This is a great recruiting tool. I see the positive impact that officers have on the community because of those who come to visit the museum."

Along with the two-hour tours conducted twice weekly, preparations of exhibits and other job assignments linked directly to the operation of the facility, Hair also teaches classes on the history of the police department to cadets going through the academy. While his job assignment might be out of the ordinary for the normal uniformed officer on patrol, Hair has proven his point that Houston needed a museum.

Source: Adapted with permission from Worrell, Ann. "Police Museums Offer Opportunities to Teach, Recruit." *Law and Order*, December 1993, p. 32-35.

POLICING IN A YOUNG AMERICA

The nineteenth century was truly the century that witnessed the early formulation of the concepts of modern-day policing. The sheriff remained the primary law enforcement officer throughout the land although various forms of night-watchmen remained in effect. It was not until 1838 that the first organized police department was created in Boston, Massachusetts (Dempsey 1994, 7). The department consisted of eight members who patrolled the streets of Boston during daylight hours (Dempsey 1994, 7). Similar police departments began formulating across the country with New York City's first in 1845 and Philadelphia in 1854 (Dempsey 1994, 7). The growth of police departments was largely seen in the major urban areas and most of the appointments were entrenched in politics (Walker 1980, 63).

The Lynchburg Police Department, Lynchburg, Virginia DARE Van which was refurbished by the local high school shop class (featured) at the request of Officer James J. Stapleton III. (Courtesy of the City of Lynchburg Police Department, Lynchburg, Virginia.)

Eventually Congress passed the Pendleton Act of 1883, which created the establishment of a civil service for the police in order to prevent political appointments, corruption, and scandals (Sullivan 1977, 19). The states, counties, and cities soon followed suit and appointments and promotions were eventually based primarily upon merit and not politics (Sullivan 1977, 19). This became one of the first movements toward police reform, but it would not reach fruition until well into the twentieth century. It was then, at the turn of the century, with the advent of the Industrial Revolution, that policing became the established institution that we recognize today and the evolution to community-oriented policing became self-evident.

POLICING IN THE TWENTIETH CENTURY

Policing, like the rest of the country, was dramatically changed at the start of the twentieth century by the arrival of the Industrial Revolution. The movement toward technology, the increase in urban populations, and a move toward scientific management principles all promoted progressive changes within the police. However, two key events had the most dramatic effect on the police, both curiously occurring within the same year: the Boston Police Strike of 1919 and the passage of the Volstead Act in 1919.

The Boston police strike was a direct result of the Industrial Revolution which witnessed the organization of labor unions. The police coexisted with various industries and organizations that were unionizing and obtaining increased salaries, improved working conditions, and various forms of collective bargaining; while the police were losing ground and becoming one of the least respectable institutions in society (Dempsey 1994, 13). A handful of police departments across the country were allowing their officers to unionize; however, in Boston, Massachusetts, the city refused to allow the American Federation of Labor (AFL) to establish a union (Cole 1995, 246). This conflict came to a head on September 9, 1919, when over 1,000 policemen went on strike (Dempsey 1994, 13). Riots broke out in the community and the state militia was mobilized by then-Governor Calvin Coolidge (Dempsey 1994, 13). The strike terminated the ability of police officers to unionize for several decades and launched Calvin Coolidge into the White House (Dempsey 1994, 13).

The second significant event during this period was the passage of the Volstead Act in 1919 which became law through the Eighteenth Amendment to the Constitution of the United States, outlawing the sale, transportation, and manufacture of liquor. Prohibition saw the rise in both organized crime and street crime before the amendment was repealed in 1933 by the Twenty-First Amendment. This time period was marked by an increased demand upon the police as well as an increase in police corruption. President Calvin Coolidge appointed J. Edgar Hoover to the director's position within the Federal Bureau of Investigation (FBI) and the use of federal, state, and local police dramatically increased (Dempsey 1994, 13–15). These two events helped launch the police into a new era of policing, which allowed for the police to modify their practices and procedures to the familiar aspects we recognize today.

This time period of policing is often recognized as the political era (Kelling and Moore 1988, 6). The specific dates of 1840 through 1930 are easily recognizable as a period of policing in its rudimentary stages (Kelling and Moore 1988, 6). Politics were largely responsible for the authority of the police, and as described previously, their function in society served multiple purposes (Kelling and Moore, 1988, 7). The police were clearly decentralized, were close to the community, and were well-entrenched in the politics of the locale, despite the passage of the Pendleton Act (Kelling and Moore 1988, 7–9). However, many problems surfaced with policing during this time period, necessitating an evolutionary change and a period of reform.

Kelling and Moore (1988, 6–17) describe the period of 1930 through the 1970s and partially into the 1980s as the reform era. This era is clearly marked by the Wickersham Commission's 1931 report on the criminal justice system (Dempsey 1994, 13), the professionalization of policing through great leaders such as August Vollmer and O. W. Wilson (Kelling and Moore 1988, 9–10), as well as the reform-minded J. Edgar Hoover who, in his early years, overtook a corrupt organization and changed both the abilities of the agency and the perceptions of the agency on the part of the people (Kelling and Moore 1988, 10). The Supreme Court decisions revolving around police standards also contributed to this reformation of the police (Dempsey 1994, 16) as did the Johnson administration's passage of the Omnibus Crime Control and Safe Streets Act of 1968 and the creation of the Law Enforcement Assistance Administration (LEAA) which existed from 1969 to 1980 (Dempsey 1994, 21). A dramatic change in the way police perform their duties was then a direct result of a concerted effort between these individuals, Supreme Court decisions, and various public policies.

The reform era was essentially the professionalization of the police and a concentration of their effectiveness on laws, through laws (Kelling and Moore 1988, 14). The majority of police departments across the country moved toward centralization to establish better command and control, effectively isolating themselves from the communities, thus functioning in a detached manner (Kelling and Moore 1988, 14–15). This mode of policing remained the predominate method of providing services to the community for the greater part of the twentieth century.

In a collective sense of determining the role of the police, one author, Malcolm K. Sparrow (1988, 8–9), sees the combination of these two eras as "traditional policing." The police are largely seen as "principally responsible for law enforcement" and are "highly centralized, governed by rules, regulations, and policy directives" and are "accountable to the law" (Sparrow 1988, 8–9). The simplicity of this analysis allows comparison of community policing to the traditional methods of policing and provides clarity on the changing philosophy (See Sparrow, 1988, Appendix, p. 8–9, Traditional vs. Community Policing: Questions and Answers).

The methods of analyzing the eras of policing are conducive to understanding police practices and procedures prevalent within our society. However, the issue focusing on the relationship between the community and the police is often lost in the overview of policing as an institution within our society, but not as a part of society. Unfortunately there was a time period in American policing where this was clearly the case. Occurring during the period that Kelling and Moore (1988, 12) discuss as the reform era, the police were described as "impersonal or oriented toward crime solving rather than responsive to the emotional crisis of the victim." Although the police have migrated through these eras associated with their overall institutions, they have also migrated through eras of community relations.

TABLE 1.1   TRADITIONAL VS. COMMUNITY POLICING: QUESTIONS AND ANSWERS

Question	Traditional	Community Policing
Who are the police?	A government agency principally for law enforcement.	Police are the public and the public are the police: The police officers are those who are paid to give full-time attention to the duties of every citizen.
What is the relationship of the police force to other public service departments?	Priorities often conflict.	The police are one department among many responsible for improving the quality of life.
What is the role of the police?	Focusing on solving crimes.	A broad problem-solving approach.
How is police efficiency measured?	By detection and arrest rates.	By the absence of crime and disorder.
What are the highest priorities?	Crimes that are high value (e.g., bank robberies) and those involving violence.	Whatever problems disturb the community most.
What, specifically, do police deal with?	Incidents.	Citizens' problems and concerns.
What determines the effectiveness of police?	Response times.	Public cooperation.
What view do police take of service calls?	Deal with them only if there is no real police work to do.	Vital function and great opportunity.
What is police professionalism?	Swift effective response to serious crime.	Keeping close to the community.
What kind of intelligence is most important?	Crime intelligence (study of particular crimes or series of crimes).	Criminal intelligence (information about the activities of individuals or groups).

What is the essential nature of police accountability?	Highly centralized; governed by rules, regulations, and policy directives; accountable to the law.	Emphasis on local accountability to community needs.
What is the role of headquarters?	To provide the necessary rules and policy directives.	To preach organizational values.
What is the role of the press liaison department?	To keep the "heat" off operational officers so they can get on with the job.	To coordinate an essential channel of communication with the community.
How do the police regard prosecutions?	As an important goal.	As one tool among many.

Source: Sparrow, Malcolm K., Implementing Community Policing, *Perspectives on Policing,* U.S. Department of Justice, p. 8-9, November 1988.

HISTORICAL APPROACHES RELATED TO COMMUNITY POLICING

The early history of policing in the United States, dating back to the colonial period, is heavily marked by politics as previously demonstrated. From the founding of this nation to the early twentieth century, police relations with the community were intertwined with politics. The relationship was solely based upon the dominant power within a community, and it was to this power that the police were appointed and beholden. Although the Pendleton Act was intended to provide relief from these political ties, it did not solve the inherent problems of widespread corruption at the time. The period of the Wickersham Commission's investigation into the criminal justice system is perhaps the best time period to show the transition of the relationship between the police and the community. Like the Kelling and Moore analysis, the political era of policing is closely related to the relationship between the police and the community, tied into politics from the founding of the new nation in 1776 through the year 1930. The political relations era is then self-evident from the literature.

The new mode of thinking focused on the relationship between the police and the community in terms of public relations. The idea of public relations entailed a separation of the police and community, although the police still remained somewhat beholden to the community they served. As Richard L. Holcomb described (1954, 6) "the fundamental principle of good public relations can be summed up very briefly. It amounts to doing a good, efficient job in a courteous manner and then letting the public know about the job." The police had little desire to integrate with the public during this time period and distanced themselves from any ties to the community. The public relations era was marked by simply responding to the public's demands only to that degree which satisfied the immediate problems and in turn the community. The police distanced themselves from the public and an "us versus them" attitude surfaced which marked the police for many decades to come. This period of relationship existed between the years 1930 and 1960.

TABLE 1.2   COMMUNITY-ORIENTED POLICING VS. POLICE–COMMUNITY RELATIONS

Community Policing	Police–Community Relations
Goal: Solve problems—improved relations with citizens is a welcome by-product.	Goal: Change attitudes and project positive image—improved relations with citizens is main focus.
Line Function: Regular contact of officer with citizen.	Staff Function: Irregular contact of officer with citizen.
A department-wide philosophy and department-wide acceptance.	Isolated acceptance often localized in the PCR unit.
Internal and external influence and respect for officers.	Limited influence and respect for officers.
Well-defined role—does both proactive and reactive policing —a full-service officer.	Loose role definitions; focus on dealing with problems of strained relations between police and citizens; crime prevention encouraged.
Direct service—same officer takes complaints and gives crime prevention tips.	Indirect service—advice on crime prevention from PCR officer but "regular" officers respond to complaints.
Citizens identify problems and cooperate in setting police agenda.	"Blue Ribbon" committees identify the problems and "preach" to police.
Police accountability is insured by the citizens receiving the service in addition to administrative mechanisms.	Police accountability is insured by civilian review boards and formal police supervision.
Officer is the leader and catalyst for change in the neighborhood to reduce fear, disorder, decay, and crime.	Officer provides consultation on crime issues without having identified beat boundaries of "field of responsibilities."
Chief of police is an advocate and sets the tone for the delivery of both law enforcement and social services in the jurisdiction.	Chief of police reacts to only the law enforcement concerns of special interest groups.

Officers educate public about issues (like response time or preventive patrol) and the need to prioritize services.

Officers focus on racial and ethnic tension issues and encourage increased services.

Increased trust between the police officer and citizens because long-term, regular contact results in an enhanced flow of information to the police.

Cordial relationship between police officer and citizens but often superficial trust with minimum information flow to prevent and solve crime.

Officer is continually accessible in person, by telephone, or in a decentralized office.

Intermittent contact with the public because of city-wide responsibility; contact is made through central headquarters.

Regular visibility in the neighborhood.

Officer seldom seen "on the streets."

Officer is viewed as having a "stake in the community."

Officer is viewed as an "outsider."

Officer is a role model because of regular contact with citizens (especially youth role model).

Citizens do not get to know officer on an intense basis.

Influence is from "the bottom up." Citizens receiving service help set priorities and influence police policy.

Influence is from "the top down"— those who "know best" have input and make decisions.

Meaningful organizational change and departmental restructuring— ranging from officer selection to training, evaluations, and promotions.

Traditional organization stays intact with "new" programs periodically added; no fundamental organizational change.

When intervention is necessary, informal social control is the first choice.

When intervention is necessary, formal means of control is typically the first choice.

Officer encourages citizens to solve many of their own problems and volunteer to assist neighbors.

Citizens are encouraged to volunteer but are told to request and expect more government (including law enforcement) services.

Officer encourages other service providers like animal control, firefighters, and mail carriers to become involved in community problem solving.

Service providers stay in traditional roles.

TABLE 1.2   *(continued)*

Community Policing	Police–Community Relations
Officer mobilizes all community resources, including citizens, private and public agencies, and private businesses.	Officers do not have mobilization responsibility because there is no specific beat area for which they are responsible.
Success is determined by the reduction in citizen fear, neighborhood disorder, and crime.	Success is determined by traditional measures, i.e., crime rates and citizen satisfaction with the police.
All officers are sworn personnel.	Most staff members are sworn personnel but some are non-sworn.

Source: Reprinted with permission from Trojanowicz, Robert and Bonnie Bucqueroux. *Community Policing: How to Get Started.* Cincinnati, Ohio: Anderson Publishing Company, 1994.

The movement from public relations to police–community relations has a far more distinct progression than the previous evolution from political relations. This is evident in Radelet's (1973, 12) discussion of the National Institute of Police and Community Relations conference, first held in 1955 at Michigan State University. This five-day conference provided the impetus for police departments across the nation to begin encouraging and fostering a sense of police and community partnership (Radelet 1973, 13). The predominant method of carrying out this partnership was generally through the development of special units within police departments often known as "community resources" or "community relations" divisions. The other key component to this philosophy was developing some understanding between the police and the community. The police had to understand the various sociological aspects of the groups they dealt with on a daily basis, and the community had to understand what police officers were tasked to perform and how they carried out these duties. The overall assumption then, was to provide for a special unit and create an understanding between the police and the community (See Cohn and Viano 1976; Johnson, Misner, and Brown 1981; Radelet 1973; Watson 1966).

Some debate still exists as to the evolution of public relations to police–community relations. Although Radelet points to the 1955 conference, some argue that the call for police-community relations was a direct result of the civil unrest of the 1960s and a response to Supreme Court laws reigning in police power such as *Mapp* v. *Ohio* (1961), *Escobedo* v. *Illinois* (1964) and *Miranda* v. *Arizona* (1966). Regardless of the catalyst for the movement to police–community relations, this era of relations began taking shape in 1960 and remained the predominate ideology of policing into the 1980s.

A large proportion of the police–community relations programs were conducted for nothing more than public relations purposes and in some cases political purposes. One primary method of delivering police–community relations services was the concept of "team policing" implemented in various communities across the nation in the early 1970s (Greene 1987; Radelet 1973).

Although touted as one of the more prominent police–community relations programs, it was also relegated to failure (Greene 1987). The premise of team policing was to make the "team" of police officers part of the community and in turn make the community they policed more valuable to them on a personal level. According to Lawrence Sherman (1975), team policing failed because management created the teams and controlled them, but failed to provide the proper support. The summation of why team policing failed is perhaps best stated by Jack R. Greene (1987, 3), when he wrote it "required a rethinking of the social and formal organization of policing on a massive scale," something that was not conducive with the climate of the times.

TABLE 1.3 KEY ASPECTS OF THE STRATEGIES FOR IMPLEMENTING TEAM POLICING VS. COMMUNITY-ORIENTED POLICING.

Characteristics	Team Policing	Community-Oriented Policing
Planning and training	Limited to start-up phase	Significant at all stages
Role of chief	Critical at initial stage	Involved at all stages
Statement of values	Implicit	Explicit
Involvement of middle management	Unclear and undefined	Substantial—considerable ownership
Involvement of patrol division	Tangential	Total
Involvement of investigative division	Non-Existent	Gradual
Measurement tools	Traditional	More responsive and creative

Source: Reprinted with permission from Geller, William A., *Local Government Police Management,* 3rd edition. Washington, D.C.: International City Management Association (ICMA), 1991.

Other programs during this era were aimed at various aspects of creating an alliance with the community. The programs were divided into different aspects of the police–community relations ideology. The division consisted of the public relations programs such as "wave at a cop" and "ride-a-longs"; crime prevention and safety education programs such as "theft prevention lectures" and "neighborhood watch"; youth programs such as "community–police service corps" and "law enforcement explorers"; and core police–community relations programs such as "community service units" and various "volunteer committees" oriented on key social issues (see Johnson, Misner, and Brown 1981, 329–363). All of these programs combined were a demonstration of the police–community relations ideology.

Officer James J. Stapleton III and DARE officer Kevin Shroyer, both of the Lynchburg Police Department, Lynchburg, Virginia, with students during a neighborhood clean-up. (Courtesy of the City of Lynchburg Police Department, Lynchburg, Virginia.)

The Era of Community Policing

The evolution from police–community relations is cited as commencing in the mid-1980s (Kelling and Moore 1988, 6). Some say it began with the writings of Herman Goldstein on the topic of problem-oriented policing (see Goldstein 1979; Goldstein 1987; Goldstein 1990) and an article titled "Broken Windows: The Police and Neighborhood Safety" by James Q. Wilson and George L. Kelling (1982) published in the *Atlantic Monthly*. Through their writings, the ideology and the majority of writings on policing shifted to a community-oriented approach which, unlike the reason for the failure of the team policing concept, called for a systemic approach to policing. The entire system of policing was questioned, rethought, and new methods of police practices and procedures were implemented.

Kelling and Moore (1988, 18–23) detailed an era of policing revolving around the decentralization of the police, with a wider commitment to providing services, and a closer relationship with the community. Malcolm K. Sparrow also detailed similar circumstances of policing in the community policing era, one of which returned to the philosophy that Sir Robert Peel spoke of so long ago, that the "police are the public and the public are the police" (See Sparrow 1988, Appendix, 8–9, Traditional vs. Community Policing: Questions and Answers). The literature continued to accumulate in the community-oriented

FIGURE 1.1   Mainstream Popularity of Community-Oriented Policing.

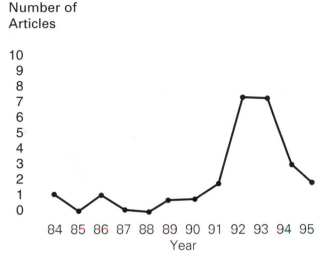

Source: Reader's Guide to Periodical Literature, The H.H. Wilson Co., 1985–1996.Note: The listings for 1993 and 1994 fall under "Community Policing" while the listings for 1984–1992 fall under the listing of "Police Public Relations."

policing field throughout the 1980s and well into the 1990s, filling three anthologies (see Greene and Mastrofski 1988; Kratcoski and Dukes 1995; Rosenbaum 1994), two books entitled *Community Policing* (Miller and Hess 1994; Trojanowicz and Bucqueroux 1989); several specialized topic books (Goldstein 1990; Eck and Spelman 1987), and filling up both journals (e.g., *Crime & Delinquency* and *Criminology*) and practitioner's magazines (e.g. *The Police Chief* and *Law & Order*).

In order to understand the growing trend of community-oriented policing, one only has to look to the mainstream literature to see the public's expanding awareness of the systemic approach. As the concept took shape in the early 1980s, only a few articles were published in the mainstream journals as recorded by the *Readers' Guide to Periodical Literature*, and until 1993 it still fell under the heading of police-community relations (see Figure 1.1). In 1992, seven articles on community-oriented policing were published and when seven more were published in 1993, a new category under "Police" was added to the *Readers' Guide.* However, the true gauge of literature on community-oriented policing can be found in the *Criminal Justice Abstracts* which listed an average of six articles per year from 1989 to 1992, followed by a dramatic increase to 14 articles in 1993 and 23 articles in 1994 (see Figure 1.2). However, despite the growing trend in community-oriented policing literature, a central question continued to surface: What exactly is community-oriented policing?

Community-oriented policing, despite winning over the hearts and minds of both academic and practitioner, has rarely seen a common definition or witnessed the same exact implementation in various communities. It has suffered

FIGURE 1.2   Popularity of Community-Oriented Policing from Criminal Justice Specific Literature.

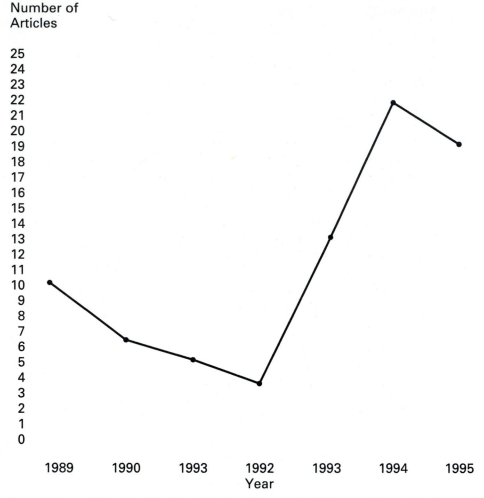

Number of
Articles

Year

Source: Allinson, Richard S., Ed., *Criminal Justice Abstracts,* The Willow Tree Press, Inc., Monsey, NY 1990–1996.

the fate of many concepts lacking a standard definition in the confusion over what it entails and how to implement the ideology. A strong need exists for a standard definition of community-oriented policing in order for it to continue to grow, expand, and be evaluated on its successes and failures. Although there is little dispute over the fact we have entered the era of community-oriented policing, there is a strong call for a standard definition and understanding of the concept.

TABLE 1.4 STATE AND LOCAL LAW ENFORCEMENT AGENCIES

Type of Agency	Number
Local	12,502
State	49
Sheriff	3,086
Special police	1,721
TOTAL	17,358

Source: Maguire, Kathleen, and Ann L. Pastore. *Bureau of Justice Statistics Sourcebook of Criminal Justice Statistics—1994.* Washington, D.C.: Bureau of Justice Statistics, 1995.

THE EVOLUTION OF COMMUNITY-ORIENTED POLICING

The evolution of community-oriented policing is rooted in the relationship between the police and the community throughout the history of the United States. From the period of 1776, with the founding of a new nation, to the year 1930, the relationship between the police and the community was one of politics. This period existed then as the political era of relations. The period from 1930 to 1960 saw a transformation to the public relations era of cooperation, when the police isolated themselves and only interacted when it was necessary to appease the public. The period of 1960 to 1985 saw a transformation in the relationship to what is now known as police–community relations. This era was marked largely by various programs aimed at providing services to the community and at the same time providing some contact between the police and the citizens. In the mid-1980s, the police–community relations concept gave way to community-oriented policing as the main philosophical approach to policing relations with the public. Although this remains the current ideology of policing and has seen widespread implementation across the country, there is a consensus that the term has no concrete definition.

TABLE 1.5 POLICE AND COMMUNITY RELATIONS OVER TIME IN THE UNITED STATES

Eras of policing	Premise	Years
Political relations	Political	1776–1930
Public relations	Objectivity	1930–1960
Police-community relations	Advocacy	1960–1985
Community-oriented policing	Partnerships	1985–Present

REFERENCES

BRAIDEN, CHRIS. "Enriching Traditional Police Roles." *Police Management: Issues and Perspectives*. Washington, D.C.: Police Executive Research Forum, 1992.

COHN, ALVIN W. and EMILIO C. VIANO, eds. *Police Community Relations: Images, Roles, Realities*. Philadelphia: Lippincott, 1976.

COLE, GEORGE F. *The American System of Criminal Justice,* 7th ed. Belmont, CA: The Wadsworth Publishing Company, 1995.

DEMPSEY, JOHN S. *Policing: An Introduction to Law Enforcement*. St. Paul: West Publishing Company, 1994.

ECK, JOHN E. and WILLIAM SPELMAN. *Problem-Solving: Problem-Oriented Policing in Newport News*. Washington, D.C.: Police Executive Research Forum, 1987.

GILBERT, JAMES N. *Criminal Investigation,* 2nd ed. Columbus, OH: Charles E. Merrill Publishing Company, 1986.

GOLDSTEIN, HERMAN. "Improving Policing: A Problem-Oriented Approach." *Crime & Delinquency* 25, no. 2 (1979): 236–258.

———— "Toward Community-Oriented Policing: Potential, Basic Requirements, and Threshold Questions." *Crime & Delinquency* 33, no. 1 (1987): 6–30.

————. *Problem-Oriented Policing*. New York, New York: McGraw Hill Publishing Co., 1990.

GREENE, JACK R. "Foot Parol and Community Policing: Past Practices and Future Prospects." *American Journal of Police* 6, no. 1: 1–15, 1987.

GREENE, JACK R. and STEPHEN D. MASTROFSKI. *Community Policing: Rhetoric or Reality*. Jack R. Greene and Stephen D. Mastrofski, eds. New York: Praeger Publishers, 1988.

HOLCOMB, RICHARD L. *The Police and the Public*. Springfield, IL: Charles C. Thomas Publishing, 1954.

JOHNSON, THOMAS A., GORDON E. MISNER, and LEE P. BROWN. *The Police and Society: An Environment for Collaboration and Confrontation*. Englewood Cliffs, N.J.: Prentice-Hall, Inc., 1981.

KELLING, GEORGE L. "Police and Communities: the Quiet Revolution." *Perspective on Policing*. Washington, D.C.: U.S. Department of Justice, June, 1988.

KELLING, GEORGE L. and MARK H. MOORE. "From Political to Reform to Community: The Evolving Strategy of Police." In *Community Policing: Rhetoric or Reality,* ed. Jack R. Greene and Stephen D. Mastrofski. New York: Praeger Publishers, 1988.

KRATCOSKI, PETER C. and DAVID DUKES. *Issues in Community Policing,* ed. Peter C. Kratcoski and David Dukes. Cincinnati: Anderson Publishing Company, 1995.

MILLER, LINDA S. and KAREN M. HESS. *Community Policing: Theory and Practice*. St. Paul: West Publishing Company, 1994.

RADELET, LOUIS A. *The Police and the Community*. Beverly Hills: Glencoe Press, 1973.

ROSENBAUM, DENNIS P. *The Challenge of Community Policing: Testing The Promises,* ed. Dennis P. Rosenbaum. Thousand Oaks, CA: SAGE Publications, Inc., 1994.

ROSSITER, CLINTON. *The Federalist Papers*. New York, New York: New American Library, 1961.

SHERMAN, LAWRENCE W. "Middle Management and Democratization: A Reply to John E. Angell." *Criminology* 12, no. 4: 363–377, 1975.

SPARROW, MALCOLM K. "Implementing Community Policing." *Perspectives on Policing*. Washington, D.C.: National Institute of Justice and the Program in Criminal Justice Policy and Management (November 1988).

SULLIVAN, JOHN L. *Introduction to Police Science*. 3rd ed. New York: McGraw-Hill Book Company, 1977.

TROJANOWICZ, ROBERT and BONNIE BUCQUEROUX. *Community Policing: A Contemporary Perspective*. Cincinnati: Anderson Publishing Company, 1989.

WALKER, SAMUEL. *Popular Justice: History of American Criminal Justice*. New York: Oxford University Press, 1980.

WATSON, NELSON A. *Police-Community Relations*. Washington, D.C.: International Association of Chiefs of Police, 1966.

WILSON, JAMES Q. and GEORGE L. KELLING. "Broken Windows: The Police and Neighborhood Safety." *The Atlantic Monthly*. March 1982, 29–38.

CHAPTER 2

Community-Oriented Policing Defined

There is nothing more difficult to take in hand, more perilous to conduct,
or more uncertain in its success, than to take the lead in the
introduction of a new order of things.

- Machiavelli-

Community-oriented policing has sparked the most fundamental change in policing and promises to carry policing well into the twenty-first century. Community-oriented policing has reevaluated the role of the police and its central goal is reducing fear. The fear of crime is one of the most pervasive concerns of the American people and there is a demand to control what has seemingly spiraled out of control. The media constantly reminds the American people of the increasingly high levels of urban violence and the problems of gangs, drugs, juvenile crime, and a host of other social problems causing the epidemic proportions of crime. Community-oriented policing has become the American panacea for crime, supported not only by the public, but by a rapidly growing number of police departments across the country. This is apparent in the fact that "in cities with populations of 50,000 or more, 50 percent of the police officials responding to a recent survey...said that they had implemented community policing, and another 20 percent anticipated doing so within the next year" (Grinc 1994, 437).

The ideas of community-oriented policing are relatively simplistic. The police take on a role of being more "community oriented" and the citizens become more involved by assisting the police with information. Typically, people conjure up images of the police officer walking a beat, greeting people in the neighborhood as they go about their daily routines, and deterring crime

Officer Pecoraro of the Montgomery County Police Department,
Montgomery County, Maryland, during law enforcement/fire safety
day at a local elementary school. (Courtesy of Montgomery
County Department of Police, Montgomery County, Maryland.)

by his or her presence. There is generally the overall idea that the police will be able to solve the community's problems, which will reduce crime and restore social order. The ideas seem simple enough; however, because they are ideas, herein lies the problem.

The concept of community-oriented policing is essentially a philosophy of policing that is often difficult to transform into policy. Although foot patrols are an easily implemented policing tool, the concept goes far beyond the police officer walking the beat. Police departments across the United States hold the philosophy in high esteem, but wrestle with the task of implementation. This is most apparent when discussing the positions of police chiefs who want to implement community-oriented policing, but they have no framework for actually implementing the systemic approach. This creates a most frustrating situation for everyone involved in the process, but this even cuts a little deeper.

The most difficult aspect of understanding community-oriented policing is attempting to arrive at a standard definition. Theorists and practitioners both have the same ideas overall; however, when it comes to defining and implementing the concept, they often diverge. While one organization may implement the concept throughout the entire police department, another may place one police officer on foot patrol in an area of high pedestrian traffic. Both can now lay claim to implementing community-oriented policing. This variance results in a multitude of interpretations on what community policing entails. The term then, when invoked, conjures up just as many ideas and programs as there are people contemplating what community-oriented policing involves. This is most clearly seen in the recent call by President Clinton for the "Community Policing" bill which focuses on placing 100,000 additional police officers on the streets of America. As one author points out, "Community policing was not intended simply to put more foot patrol officers on the street; and it was not seen as a quick-fix crime reduction strategy. Many of the current advocates of community policing, such as the Times and Bill Clinton, have got it all wrong" (Walker 1994, 136). The meaning of the term *community-oriented policing*, then, is critical to any discussion about the concept.

The purpose of this chapter is to review the current literature from both theorists and practitioners and analyze it for consistent themes. The goal is to derive an identifiable definition of what has become known as community-oriented policing in order to advance its theoretical aspects as well as determining the methods of implementation. As the term has no standard definition, community-oriented policing will remain the philosophy's term out of reverence for its immediate capture of the ideological advancement of the police.

"CRIME FILES"

DRUGS: COMMUNITY RESPONSES—PART 3

This edition of the "Crime Files," hosted by James Q. Wilson, features Herman Wrice, of Mantua Against Drugs, Philadelphia, Pennsylvania; Wesley Skogan, Professor of Urban Affairs, Northwestern University; and Captain Gordon Harrison, Director, Operation Cul-De-Sac, Los Angeles Police Department, California. The discussion revolves around community-oriented policing actions taken by both the police and the community to stem the tide of drugs in the nation's neighborhoods.

THE ABSENCE OF A DEFINITION

It is readily apparent there is no shared definition of community-oriented policing among the theorists and practitioners of law enforcement. This is clear from the research by key proponents of the community-oriented policing philosophy, such as Herman Goldstein (1990, 24), who wrote, "We now make wide use of 'community policing' to categorize these efforts, but the term does not yet have a uniform meaning." A more recent statement by Dennis P. Rosenbaum (1994, xii) claims, "At this moment in the history of policing, there is no simple or commonly shared definition of community policing, either in theory or practice." It is common to find a lack of definition in most of the literature, and while some try, many are resolved to conclude that the term means many different things to many different people (Bayley 1994, 278; Greene and Mastrofski 1988, 45; Murphy 1988, 49; and Oliver 1992, 46).

Community-oriented policing is an intangible concept based on intangible ideas (Oliver 1992). Theorists have attempted to define the term as a precursor to the implementation of the concept. However there is often disagreement within the proposed definitions (Grinc 1994) and, as is often the case, the definition itself becomes contradictive (Weisheit, Wells, and Falcone 1994). The definitions are often unclear and intangible, thereby not allowing for the concept to be implemented. This in turn has left many practitioners wondering how not only to define community-oriented policing, but how to implement it as well.

As the conceptual definitions can find no standard definition, many researchers look to the organizations that have implemented community-oriented policing in order to develop a clear and concise definition based on the actual application of these practices and procedures. Unfortunately, the theorists fare no better in reviewing what the practitioners have implemented to

The Berkeley Police Department, Berkeley, California, Twilight Basketball Team during the winter of 1994. (Courtesy of the Berkeley Police Department, Berkeley, California.)

arrive at a definition. As Herman Goldstein (1994, viii) states, "In many quarters today, 'community policing' is used to encompass practically all innovations in policing, from the most ambitious to the most mundane, from the most carefully thought through to the most casual." The term has become an interchangeable phrase, utilized to describe nearly any change or upgrade in a police department's services (Goldstein, 1987; Goodstein, 1991; and McElroy, Cosgrove, and Sadd, 1993). Although this term and the concept have remained strong within the literature of both theorists and practitioners, there is clearly the need for a standard definition, to avoid the debasement of the term *community-oriented policing*.

COP IN ACTION

COMMUNITY POLICING: A PHILOSOPHY—NOT A PROGRAM

Of the variety of concepts in police science, community policing is perhaps the oldest, most controversial and least understood. Community policing in its best sense is a philosophy and not just a program. It is a philosophy of police and community cooperating with one another to ascertain the problems and needs of a community and working in harmony to address those needs. In order for the philosophy to work, there must be total immersion of management and rank-and-files; there must be total commitment. An agency cannot compartmentalize a community-policing program. That model is doomed to failure because of its internal divisiveness and lack of career path for the officers involved.

The philosophic approach to community policing encourages, aids and abets community cooperation. It means motivating citizens to participate in auxiliary police activities, block watching, police-support volunteer units, community crisis-intervention teams, quality-of-life action groups, neighborhood councils and town meetings. And all of this cannot be the work of one or two officers dedicated to "community affairs." It must be the work of an entire department and each of its subdivisions.

Critics who say that the philosophy of community policing takes away from the enforcement role of the police officer and makes him or her a "social worker" fail to perceive its underlying effectiveness. The true practice of community policing may well save a cop's life. It may well provide solutions that change a community, once written off as too dangerous to patrol, into a productive, safe neighborhood. It may well provide information previously not available on perpetrators of crime, gang members, and drug dealers. And it may well change the quality of life for both the police practitioner and the public. One need not be a social worker, but one should be aware of the social and economic dimensions of crime.

Over the past three decades, we have seen a marked change in the dynamics of street law enforcement. American society, with its variety of cultural, religious, ethnic, and racial groups, is a phenomenon unequalled anywhere on this planet. This diversity makes our nation strong; yet, ironically, it can also divide us. We are all in a learning curve about understanding and accepting one another. This is what the philosophy of community policing is all about. It is understanding, helping, and supporting one another to build communities and programs that will enhance the quality of life for citizens and officers. This philosophy and methodology does not make any officer less of a "cop." But it does provide new ways to be more effective as a law enforcement professional. It does provide training to defuse neighborhood situations before they became crises. And it does make for a breed of officers who can serve as role models for youth.

Some departments still shy away from a community policing model or from total immersion in its philosophy. A successful model will first assess the community to be served by analyzing demographics and neighborhood composition. It would further assess the department's capability to serve the diverse needs of the community. The next steps include identifying missions and goals, training personnel, reaching out to the community, analyzing budget and resources, targeting neighborhoods for concentration, mobilizing the "grass-roots" forces of the community and establishing community participation. Once in place, the department should evaluate the model every six to twelve months for effectiveness. Indications of success include a decrease in the incidence of crime, improved cooperation with police, improved quality of life and, of course, an improved community image of the police. But no model is absolute or permanently structured. Each model will change as a particular community's needs change. That's the essence of community policing—it's a living, breathing, changing phenomenon.

I am convinced that the community policing model is the most effective method of delivering police services efficiently, cost-effectively, and humanely. I am also convinced that if we are to create greater harmony and understanding in our society and defuse the ugliness brought on by frustration, hate, and ignorance, the philosophy of community policing is a step in that direction. However, it can only be effective if the philosophy pervades the department and if the cynics and nay-sayers give it an opportunity to blossom.

Source: Gentile, John R. "Community Policing: A Philosophy—Not a Program." Community Policing Exchange. Washington, D.C.: The Community Policing Consortium, November/December, 1995.

Community-Oriented Policing, Not Police-Community Relations

In attempting to define community-oriented policing, it must be clarified that community-oriented policing and police–community relations are two separate entities. Although community-oriented policing was born of the police–community relations theory, the two have become philosophies unto themselves. This is apparent through a slow evolutionary process, as detailed in chapter one, that has spanned nearly six decades, with slightly altered and advanced ideas.

The 1930s and 1940s were essentially the public relations era, marked by little to no literature in the law enforcement field discussing the relationship between the police and community (Trojanowicz and Dixon 1974, 49). The concept of police–community relations was explored in 1955 at the National

Institute of Police–Community Relations at Michigan State University (Trojanowicz and Dixon 1974, 49). Over the next several decades, the majority of police departments developed special units dealing in community relations programs. However, much akin to the situation today, the theorists and practitioners could not determine a standard definition for the term (Trojanowicz and Dixon 1974, 52).

The problem of defining the police–community relations concept was caused by the enormous amount of literature being published on the philosophy (see Brandstatter and Radelet 1968; Earle 1967; Pomrenke 1966). As Trojanowicz and Dixon (1974, 52) stated, "Police–community relations have been defined in many similar and some quite different ways." A concrete definition of the concept was never found, but many agreed it was predicated on an interwoven trilogy of ideas: efficiency, responsiveness, and representativeness (Trojanowicz and Dixon, 1974, 54). The increased efficiency and responsiveness of the police to the community and an increased representation on the part of the community in dealing with the crime problem formed the nexus of police–community relations.

The literature on this philosophy explored the trilogy of ideas and analyzed the police officer's relationship with the community. The police officer's interaction with various groups in society was explored, ranging from the youth to the elderly, the deaf to the mentally ill, and from gangs to the media. All of these issues were detailed, explored, and policy was derived from the analysis to make the police–community relationship stronger. Community relations sections became well-entrenched within the hierarchy of police organizations and programs such as Neighborhood Watch were implemented.

At the beginning of the 1980s, the concept of police–community relations, still without a definitive definition, was beginning to see a divergence away from the profound relationship between the police and community. The literature began exploring variations on police–community relations in order to advance the concept (see Johnson, Misner, and Brown, 1981). The publication of "Broken Windows: The Police and Neighborhood Safety" by James Q. Wilson and George L. Kelling (1982), caused a shift in the thinking relative to the role of the police, from crime control to order maintenance, specifically focusing on the issue of public fear. Around the same time Herman Goldstein (1979) was advancing his ideas on problem-oriented policing, an attempt to solve the root cause of crime, rather than repetitively responding to the symptoms. It is a combination of these advanced ideas that would collectively become known and touted as community-oriented policing.

BROKEN WINDOWS

In February 1982, James Q. Wilson and I published an article in *The Atlantic Monthly* known popularly as "Broken Windows." We made three points.

1. Neighborhood disorder—drunks, panhandling, youth gangs, prostitution, and other urban incivilities—creates citizen fear.

2. Just as unrepaired broken windows can signal to people that nobody cares about a building and lead to more serious vandalism, untended disorderly behavior can also signal that nobody cares about the community and lead to more serious disorder and crime. Such signals—untended property, disorderly persons, drunks, obstreperous youth, etc.—both create fear in citizens and attract predators.

3. If police are to deal with disorder to reduce fear and crime, they must rely on citizens for legitimacy and assistance.

   "Broken Windows" gave voice to sentiments felt both by citizens and police. It recognized a major change in the focus of the police. For them, it not only suggested changes in the focus of police work (disorder, for example), it also suggested major modifications in the overall strategy of police departments.

Source: Kelling, George L. "Police and Communities: the Quiet Revolution." *Perspectives on Policing*. Washington, D.C.: National Institute of Justice, June 1988.

Today's literature often blends the two concepts of community-oriented policing and problem-oriented policing together without any distinction between the two philosophies. Several publications still analyze the police–community relations concept and include a chapter discussing the community–policing model (See Mayhall, Barker, and Hunter 1995; Radelet and Carter 1994). Other publications lay claim to advancing the community–policing philosophy, but are repackaged police–community relations texts (see Miller and Hess 1994). The current publications on community–oriented policing are few, but steadily growing in number (see Greene and Mastrofski 1988; Rosenbaum 1994). As the concept continues to advance and expand, there is a clear need for a concrete definition.

The attempt to define community–oriented policing must then avoid recapitulating the police–community relations philosophy and instead advance its own ideas. Trojanowicz and Dixon (1974, 53) explained that, "Although police–community relations is very different from public relations, public relations is a part of police–community relations programs." Consistent with this statement, community–oriented policing is very different from police–community relations, yet it too is a part of the community-oriented policing concept.

COP IN ACTION

PROMISES VS. REALITY IN COMMUNITY POLICING

The concept and practice of community policing has affected police departments from coast to coast over the last fifteen years. It has been touted as the next generation of policing, the model that will replace traditional policing. Its supporters claim it reduces crime, improves police/community relations and makes neighborhoods livable once again. Countless books and articles have been written on the subject, but like many seemingly good ideas or theories which garner widespread publicity and support, it sometimes takes awhile before reality catches up with the rhetoric. That may be the case with community policing.

The practice of community policing must start in the minds of line officers. It is an attitude that the job of a patrol officer goes beyond the immediate resolution of a radio call. Officers must "feel" a sense of ownership of the community, have some understanding of community problems, and possess a desire and ability to look beneath the immediate issue and evaluate the underlying causes of neighborhood problems.

Most community policing and problem-solving efforts require resources not normally found inside a police station or patrol car. Without the participation of the city's building and safety departments, health departments, zoning officials and city attorney's offices, and even some non-profit organizations, the police alone will be unable to resolve neighborhood problems. Whether other city departments will want to become involved or have the resources to assist their police is an open question. All of the targeted cities except one were unable to establish an adequate link between their police problem-solving strategies and other city departments.

The final component required to support the community policing model is the community's willingness to become involved in cooperative partnerships with the police. Here, too, the study showed that achieving widespread community support and involvement was extremely difficult. Community policing remains a high abstraction concept for police officers, public officials, and community members. But an even bigger problem facing decision makers is how to overcome the formidable obstacles to the successful implementation of community policing.

However, we must not be so enamored with the promises of community policing that we fail to recognize the formidable obstacles to its implementation and the fact that some of the largest departments in the country have tried and failed. It is much too soon to claim community policing a failure. More research and experimentation needs to be conducted. But at least we are beginning to recognize the causes of past failures and, thus, the future challenges.

Source: Adapted with permission from Berg, Gregory R. "Promises vs. Reality in Community Policing." *Law and Order.* September 1995. 147–140.

COMMON THEMES

As we recognize that the police officer's role within the community he or she serves has evolved from public relations, to police–community relations, to community-oriented policing, we must come to an understanding of where we are before we analyze where we are heading. Importantly, establishing some groundwork on this conceptual model to understand the foundation on which this concept has evolved can avoid any unnecessary anomalies. It is from the current literature in community-oriented policing that we must derive our definition, pulling the common themes together, to establish the premise upon which all else will be predicated.

The primary theme originating from all definitions, dealing in both theory and practice, is the use of the term "community." As Buerger argues:

> Nowhere in this scheme is there an articulated substantive role for the community. Little attention has been given to a definition of the community commensurate with the vast promise imbedded in the rhetoric of community policing. Even less has been spared for defining the role that can be reasonably expected of the community, howsoever it should be defined. (Buerger 1994a, 415)

Since the current philosophy consistently evokes the term "community," understanding this central tenet is important to the overall definition.

A common sociological definition of community is "a group of people who share three things: They live in a geographically distinct area; they share cultural characteristics, attitudes, and lifestyles; and they interact with one another on a sustained basis" (Farley 1994, 506). Utilizing this definition with present-day American society, it is easy to see why community is a key component within the new policing philosophy. The interaction of the community and the shared culture, attitudes, and lifestyles has declined and continues to decline. The issues of order maintenance, quality-of-life, and the complexities of crime all call upon the community as well as the police for improvement. It is Buerger again who

Montgomery County Police Department, Montgomery County, Maryland, Central Business District Bike Patrol. Featured left to right are Sgt. Crumpler, Lt. Bodie, and Officer Parlon who initiated the bike patrol. (Courtesy of Montgomery County Department of Police, Montgomery County, Maryland.)

states, "the rhetoric of community policing ascribes to 'the community' a great power to regulate itself, shake off its fear of crime by forming 'partnerships' with the police, and reestablish community norms that regulate behavior and successfully resist the encroachments of the criminal element" (Buerger 1994b, 270). Although it sounds like an unattainable goal, reestablishing community is possible with some directed guidance on the part of the police.

Instilling a sense of community then becomes the police officer's lot. Where a small town may have established customs to deal with order maintenance, many towns and cities do not have these mechanisms in place. The juvenile who attempts to spray paint a building may find this difficult in a town where witnesses will call the juvenile's parents. In other aspects, the officer may have the time and leisure to help improve the quality of life of the community, perhaps by rattling doors at night or playing softball with the local children. In many jurisdictions, there is no time or sense of community to conduct these types of events. These events instill a sense of community that "suggests a fundamental paradox of community policing—in many ways it is the formalization of informal customs and the routinization of spontaneous events" (Weisheit, Wells, and Falcone 1994, 565). Community-oriented policing essentially takes the small-town method of handling problems, much like the fictional town of Mayberry from the "Andy Griffith Show," and makes it formal policy within a police department.

The definition of community within community-oriented policing then revolves around the citizens. The interaction between the citizens and police must develop and foster the sense of community spirit. The community must open up to the police and assist them in controlling crime, maintaining order within the community, and forming a working partnership. This relationship must also allow police officers to think of themselves as members of the community and not have what is considered the standard police mentality of "us versus them." As former Speaker of the House, Tip O'Neil once stated, "All politics are local," so too is all crime. Each community has its own type of criminal element, local problems, and order maintenance issues. The highly affluent area may have problems with burglaries, suspicious solicitors, and vehicles driving over the posted speed limit in their neighborhoods. The lower income, subsidized housing area may have problems with prostitution, an open-air drug market, and old abandoned cars lining their streets. Both communities perceive their "crime" problems as high. Each community feels their problems are the most important and deserve the most attention. Both are presumably right. However, each community's inherent problems call for different methods of response.

COMMUNITY POLICING AND THE FEAR OF CRIME

When crimes occur, society's attention is naturally focused on the victims and their material losses. Their wounds, bruises, lost property, and inconvenience can be seen, touched, and counted. These are the concrete signs of criminal victimization. Behind the immediate, concrete losses of crime victims, however, is a different, more abstract crime problem—that of fear. For victims, fear is often the largest and most enduring legacy of their victimization.

Of course, fear is not totally unproductive. It prompts caution among citizens and thereby reduces criminal opportunities. Too, it motivates citizens to shoulder some of the burdens of crime control by buying locks and dogs, thereby adding to general deterrence. And fear kindles enthusiasm for publicly supported crime control measures. Thus, reasonable fears, channeled in constructive directions, prepare society to deal with crime. It is only when fear is unreasonable, or generates counterproductive responses, that it becomes a social problem.

It is possible that fear might be attacked by strategies other than those that directly reduce criminal victimization. Fear might be reduced even without changes in levels of victimization by using the communications within social networks to provide accurate information about risks of criminal victimization and advice about constructive responses to the risk of crime; by eliminating the external signs of physical decay and social disorder; and by more effectively regulating group conflict between young and old, whites and minority groups, rich and poor. The more intriguing possibility, however, is that if fear could be rationalized and constructively channeled, not only would fear and its adverse consequences be ameliorated, but also real levels of victimization reduced. In this sense, the conventional understanding of this problem would be reversed: instead of controlling victimization to control fear, we would manage fear to reduce victimization.

If it is true that fear is a problem in its own right, then it is important to evaluate the effectiveness of police strategies not only in terms of their capacity to control crime, but also in terms of their capacity to reduce fear. And if fear is affected by more factors than just criminal victimization, then there might be some special police strategies other than controlling victimization that could be effective in controlling the fear of crime.

The current police strategy, which relies on motorized patrol, rapid response to calls for service, and retrospective investigations of crime, seems to produce little reassurance to frightened citizens, except in unusual circumstances when the police arrest a violent offender in the middle of a crime spree. Moreover, a focus on controlling crime rather than increasing security (analogous to the medical profession's focus on curing diseases rather than promoting health) leads the police to miss opportunities to take steps that would reduce fear independently of reducing crime. Consequently, the current strategy of policing does not result in reduced fear. Nor does it leave much room for fear reduction programs in the police department.

This is unfortunate, because some fear reduction programs have succeeded in reducing citizens' fears. Two field experiments showed that foot patrol can reduce fear and promote security. Programs which enhance the quantity and quality of police contacts with citizens through neighborhood police stations and through required regular contacts between citizens and police have been successful in reducing fear in Houston and Newark. These examples illustrate the security-enhancing potential of problem-solving and community approaches to policing. By incorporating fear reduction as an important objective of policing, by changing the activities of the police to include more frequent, more sustained contacts with citizens, and by consultation and joint planning, police departments seem to be able not only to reduce fear, but to transform it into something that helps to build strong social institutions. That is the promise of these approaches.

Source: Moore, Mark H. and Robert C. Trojanowicz. "Policing and the Fear of Crime." *Perspectives on Policing*. Washington, D.C.: National Institute of Justice, June 1988.

The literature consistently states that the police and community must work closely together (Brown 1992; Brown 1985; Community Policing Consortium 1994; Eck and Rosenbaum 1994; Grinc 1994; Miller and Hess 1994; Murphy 1988; Roberg 1994; Rosenbaum and Lurigio 1994; Rush 1994; Sadd and Grinc 1994; Skogan 1994; Trojanowicz and Bucqueroux 1990). Through community-oriented policing, one group of authors states, "police will become more connected with and integrated into their communities, which means that police will interact with citizens on a personal level, will be familiar with community sentiments and concerns, and will work with the community to address those concerns" (Weisheit, Wells, and Falcone 1994, 551). Several authors also note that police will work with all members of the community and not just certain selected elements (Brown 1985; Community Policing Consortium 1994; Lurigio and Skogan 1994).

FIGURE 2.1   Percentage of Response to the "Most Important Problem" Regarding Crime and Drugs.

Source: Gallup, George. *The Gallup Poll; Public Opinion.* Wilmington, Delaware: Scholarly Resources, Inc., 1964–1994.

TABLE 2.1   "MOST IMPORTANT PROBLEM" OVER TIME, 1964–1994

Question: "What do you think is the most important problem facing this country today?"

YEAR	Most Important	2nd Most Important	3rd Most Important
1964	Racial Problems	Foreign Problems	Unemployment
1965	Vietnam	Civil Rights	Threat of War
1966	Vietnam	Cost of Living	Civil Rights
1967	Vietnam	Civil Rights	Cost of Living
1968	Vietnam	Race Relations	**CRIME**
1969	Vietnam	**CRIME**	Race Relations
1970	Campus Unrest	Vietnam	Foreign Problems
1971	Vietnam	Economy	Foreign Problems
1972	Vietnam	Inflation	**DRUGS**
1973	Cost of Living	**DRUGS**	**CRIME**
1974	Energy Crisis	Cost of Living	Government Corruption
1975	Cost of Living	Unemployment	Government Corruption
1976	Cost of Living	Unemployment	**CRIME**
1977	Cost of Living	Unemployment	Energy Problems
1978	Cost of Living	Energy Problems	Unemployment
1979	Cost of Living	Foreign Problems	Energy Problems
1980	Foreign Problems	Cost of Living	Energy Problems
1981	Cost of Living	Unemployment	**CRIME**
1982	Cost of Living	Unemployment	Budget Cuts
1983	Unemployment	Inflation	Fear of War
1984	Threat of War	Unemployment	Government Spending
1985	Threat of War	Unemployment	Government Spending
1986	Foreign Tensions	Unemployment	Federal Deficit
1987	Unemployment	Federal Deficit	Economy
1988	Federal Deficit	Economy	**DRUGS**
1989	Economy	**DRUGS**	Poverty
1990	**DRUGS**	Federal Deficit	Poverty
1991	Economy	**DRUGS**	Poverty
1992	Economy	Unemployment	Poverty
1993	Economy	Unemployment	Poverty
1994	**CRIME**	Economy	Unemployment

Source: Adapted from Gallup, George. *The Gallup Poll: Public Opinion*. Wilmington, Delaware: Scholarly Resources, Inc., 1964–1994.

Once the citizens and police start coming together, their first goal is defining those problems indigenous to the community (Capowich and Roehl 1994; Community Policing Consortium 1994; Grinc 1994; Roberg 1994; Wilson and Kelling 1989). Once the problems are identified, the cooperatively developing solutions become the second goal (Capowich and Roehl 1994; Community Policing Consortium 1994; Grinc 1994; Roberg 1994; Wilson and Kelling 1989). The third goal is to develop programs from those solutions that could be implemented by both the police and community and fall within acceptable criteria, such as state law and local norms. And the fourth and final goal is implementation, where "at the operational level, these concepts translate into specific practices that are expected from the police officers engaged in such programs" (Lurigio and Rosenbaum 1994, 147). These programs could include: community meetings, neighborhood watch programs, bike patrols, police-youth softball leagues, and police mini-stations in the community and in the malls. Although individually these programs may not solve the community's problems, collectively they can steer the community in the right direction.

COP IN ACTION

COMMUNITY-ORIENTED POLICING IN DENTON, TEXAS

The Denton Police Department's approach to C.O.P.S. is significantly different than the approach presented in most literature on community policing. The philosophy of C.O.P.S. must permeate the entire organization. This truth is not disputed. The difference, however, is in the assignment of personnel. Every field officer is expected to become involved in the community rather than assigning that responsibility to selected individual officers. Individuals are part of a team rather than supporting a specialist. This approach requires every field officer to think in terms of C.O.P.S. The division between officers performing traditional functions and community officers does not exist. Eventually every employee will be a member of a team and will therefore have some responsibility for direct service delivery.

This change in philosophy does not come easily. There is no definitive, "cookie cutter" plan for implementation and maintenance of community-oriented policing. This lack of definition accounts for the ambiguity about roles and responsibilities. During the almost six years that have been invested in C.O.P.S., roles and responsibilities have undergone continual modification. Roles can be expected to continue to be altered as we define C.O.P.S. for Denton, Texas.

The front line officer is the key player in C.O.P.S.. It is the duty and responsibility of the front line officer to consult with the community, to identify neighborhood problems, to adapt strategies to deal with problems and ultimately to mobilize the resources within the community and within the department to solve the problems. Front line officers are officers of all ranks or positions who are in daily contact with the community. Dispatchers and other civilians are also front-line personnel.

The greatest part the employees who are not direct-service providers play is in support and planning. These employees include investigators, other non-field officers, dispatchers, and civilian employees. The organization has not consistently included anyone but patrol personnel in the consultation and planning process. It is paramount that all personnel become directly involved if we are to continue our success. For these reasons, a great deal of this plan is dedicated to training and the improvement of communication processes.

Source: Denton Police Department. *Community Oriented Policing: A Strategy.* Denton, Texas: Denton Police Department, 1995.

Another consistent theme within community-oriented policing, that is also based in this cooperative effort between the police and the community, is problem solving. Problem solving is closely associated with the decision-making process described in the cooperative effort between the citizens and the police. The problems indigenous to a community are defined and solutions are generated to solve the cause of the crime or public disorder, rather than the symptoms. This problem-solving process can be a collaborative effort between the citizens and the police, or it can be conducted solely by the police officer in the course of his or her duties. "A problem-oriented approach," as Eck and Rosenbaum (1994, 9) explain, "does not start with a tactical solution to a problem and seek to apply it to all occurrences of the problem. Instead, it begins with the peculiar circumstances that give rise to the problem and then looks for a situational solution."

TABLE 2.2 ATTITUDES TOWARD CRIME RATE IN OWN AREA, 1967–1993

Question: "In the past year, do you feel the crime rate in your area has been increasing, decreasing, or has it remained the same as it was before?"

Year	Increasing	Decreasing	Remained Same	Not Sure
1967	46%	4%	43%	7%
1970	62%	3%	30%	5%
1973	48%	7%	40%	5%
1975	70%	3%	24%	3%
1978	46%	7%	42%	5%
1981	68%	4%	27%	1%
1982	59%	6%	34%	1%
1983	41%	15%	43%	1%
1984	33%	21%	44%	2%
1985	40%	17%	42%	1%
1991	55%	5%	39%	1%
1993	54%	5%	39%	2%

Source: Maguire, Kathleen, and Ann L. Pastore. *Bureau of Justice Statistics Sourcebook of Criminal Justice Statistics–1994.* Washington, D.C.: Bureau of Justice Statistics, 1995.

Although originally put forth as its own individualistic philosophy on policing by founder Herman Goldstein, problem-oriented policing has become an integral part of community-oriented policing (Eck and Spelman 1987; Goldstein 1994; Goldstein 1990; Goldstein 1987; Goldstein 1979). Problem-oriented policing, as policy, can stand alone; however, "it is believed...that in order for community policing to be a truly effective approach the police must do both" (Roberg 1994, 249). Therefore, problem-oriented policing can be implemented without community-oriented policing, but community-oriented policing cannot be implemented without problem-oriented policing.

TABLE 2.3   ATTITUDES OF UNEASINESS ON THE STREETS, 1966–1993

Question: "Compared to a year ago, do you personally feel more uneasy on the streets, less uneasy, or not much different?"

Year	More Uneasy	Less Uneasy	Not Much Different	
1966	49%	3%	44%	4%
1968	53%	4%	42%	1%
1969	55%	4%	39%	2%
1970	62%	3%	30%	5%
1971	55%	5%	39%	1%
1975	55%	2%	42%	1%
1977	49%	4%	46%	1%
1978	40%	5%	53%	2%
1981	48%	6%	45%	1%
1982	41%	7%	51%	1%
1983	26%	9%	63%	2%
1984	24%	10%	65%	1%
1985	32%	7%	60%	1%
1991	38%	5%	57%	<0.5%
1993	42%	5%	51%	2%

Source: Maguire, Kathleen, and Ann L. Pastore. *Bureau of Justice Statistics Sourcebook of Criminal Justice Statistics–1994.* Washington, D.C.: Bureau of Justice Statistics, 1995.

An additional aspect of community-oriented policing is the use of standard police tactics, such as patrols, arrests, and the use of specialized units, in a slightly different manner. It entails redistributing police sources, directing an excessive amount of resources toward particular problems, and dispersing the criminal element from a particular community. Police Chief Reuben Greenburg utilized this technique in Charleston, South Carolina with much success, and he coined the term "strategic policing" to describe this innovative use of standard police resources (Greenburg and Gordon, 1989). Taking high-quality, standard police practices and procedures, the police flood a high-crime area in the hopes of disrupting the entrenched criminal element. The goal is to drive out the cause of the crime and replace it with some type of neighborhood program to keep the community free of crime and disorder (Greenburg and Gordon, 1989). This type of policing is usually directed at highly visible elements such as open-air drug markets and street prostitutes, but it can be directed toward less visible criminal elements such as crack houses. The federal government has also attempted similar strategies in a program known as "weed and seed" (U.S. Dept. of Justice 1992).

TABLE 2.4   RESPONDENTS REPORTING FEAR OF WALKING ALONE AT NIGHT AND FEELING UNSAFE AT HOME, 1965–1993

Question: "Is there any area near where you live—that is, within a mile—where you would be afraid to walk alone at night? How about at home at night—do you feel safe and secure, or not?"

Year	Afraid to Walk Alone at Night	Feel Unsafe at Home
1965	34%	NA
1967	31%	NA
1972	42%	17%
1975	45%	20%
1977	45%	15%
1981	45%	16%
1983	45%	16%
1989	43%	10%
1990	40%	10%
1992	44%	11%
1993	43%	NA

Source: Maguire, Kathleen, and Ann L. Pastore. *Bureau of Justice Statistics Sourcebook of Criminal Justice Statistics–1994.* Washington, D.C.: Bureau of Justice Statistics, 1995.

The important standard when utilizing strategic policing is putting something in place of the criminal element. Common sense dictates that when the police remove themselves en masse, the criminal element will simply return. This, then, necessitates using neighborhood programs and problem-solving cooperation with the members of the community to determine what will and will not work. These three concepts then become components of an integral web known as community-oriented policing.

However, in order for any of these concepts to translate into police practices, there is an overwhelming call for the decentralization of the police hierarchy (Geller 1991; Goldstein 1990; Greene, Bergman, and McLaughlin 1994; Rosenbaum and Lurigio 1994; Skogan 1994; Wilkinson and Rosenbaum 1994). For the police to become a part of a community, they must be permanently assigned to that community. Rotating beats and rotating shifts do not foster a sense of community. There is no time to develop ties to the community, to discover the problems indigenous to any segment of the community, or to implement possible solutions because of the organizational commitment to a bureaucracy. The police officers must be given the freedom to interact with the community, develop solutions to problems, and have the freedom to implement, fail, and discover the benefits of their programs. In the current centralized form of police organization, that capability is not there. "It is an organizational strategy that redefines the goals of policing," Skogan explains, and "community policing relies upon organizational decentralization" to achieve these new goals (Skogan 1994, 167).

TABLE 2.5   HIGH SCHOOL SENIORS REPORTING THAT THEY WORRY
ABOUT CRIME AND VIOLENCE, 1982–1994.

Question: "Of all the problems facing the nation today, how often do you worry about...crime and violence?"[*]

Class of:	Total:
1982	86.3%
1983	85.4%
1984	83.9%
1985	82.3%
1986	79.4%
1987	81.9%
1988	83.9%
1989	86.3%
1990	88.8%
1991	88.1%
1992	91.6%
1993	90.8%
1994	92.7%

[*]Percentage responding "often" or "sometimes."

Source: Maguire, Kathleen, and Ann L. Pastore. *Bureau of Justice Statistics Sourcebook of Criminal Justice Statistics–1994.* Washington, D.C.: Bureau of Justice Statistics, 1995.

TABLE 2.6   ATTITUDES TOWARD EFFECTIVENESS OF MEASURES TO
REDUCE VIOLENCE IN PUBLIC SCHOOLS.

Question: "How effective do you think each of the following measures would be in reducing violence in the public schools—very effective, somewhat effective, not very effective, or not at all effective?"

Measure	Very Effective	Somewhat Effective	Not Very Effective	Not at All Effective
Stronger penalties for possession of weapons by students	86%	8%	3%	2%
Training school staffs in how to deal with student violence	72%	20%	5%	2%
More vocational or job-training courses in public schools	67%	25%	7%	1%
Drug and alcohol abuse programs for students	66%	23%	7%	3%
Values and ethics education for students	60%	27%	9%	3%
Education designed to reduce racial and ethnic tensions	57%	27%	10%	4%
Courses offered by the public schools in how to be a good parent	51%	28%	15%	5%
Conflict education for students	45%	35%	11%	3%

Source: Maguire, Kathleen, and Ann L. Pastore. *Bureau of Justice Statistics Sourcebook of Criminal Justice Statistics–1994.* Washington, D.C.: Bureau of Justice Statistics, 1995.

The organizational decentralization, thus called for by the literature, in turn details the fact that community-oriented policing is not a temporary program, but a long-term, systemic philosophy that must permeate the entire police organization. By decentralizing an entire police department for the components of community-oriented policing to work, all of the fundamentals of policing must change as well. The mission statement, job descriptions, and goals of the police department must change. The role of the police chief, leadership, management style, and management structure must change. The recruitment, training, and requirements of the police officers must change. The expectations, roles, and actions of the community must change.

All of these societal structures, collective thoughts, and individuals must change to reflect the community-oriented approach. It is not enough to change one division or to create a new program. The true implementation of community-oriented policing must go from philosophical concept to practical applications throughout the entire police department in order for its goals and the goals of the community to be achieved.

COP IN ACTION

COMMUNITY POLICING IS ALIVE AND WELL

A commander in a big-city department invites the community to help him design an effective drug-gang strategy that avoids the inequity—and the danger—of stigmatizing and harassing minority youth. In a small town in Arizona, the police and the community together launch a curfew incentive program that allows youngsters who play by the rules to earn points toward a bicycle. A chief from the "new" South explores ways to lure other service providers back into the community to work alongside the police in troubled neighborhoods. In an economically depressed New England town, the police open a substation in an experimental school to encourage greater collaboration between public housing residents and their more affluent—and fearful—neighbors. An enterprising captain out West cuts the bureaucratic red tape that had long kept the sidewalks in a poor neighborhood unpaved, thereby ending the corrosive ridicule that the neighborhood's fragile youngsters faced each time they showed up at school with muddy shoes.

With a nod to Mark Twain, these successes, large and small, confirm that reports of the death of community policing are greatly exaggerated. No doubt there will always be the occasional, high-profile casualty—a promising effort that implodes or explodes for a variety of complex reasons. Yet for every widely reported flame-out, there are innumerable unheralded success stories in law enforcement agencies nationwide.

The "no definition" myth

Indeed, surveys done by the Police Executive Research Forum and the National Center for Community Policing in conjunction with the FBI confirm that roughly two out of three police agencies in major jurisdictions report that they have adopted some form of community policing or plan to do so in the near future. If that sounds too good to be true, at least in part, it is; the NCCP/FBI research showed that three out of four police agencies that claim to be doing community policing do not allow the community a voice in identifying, prioritizing, and solving problems.

Sadly, some would use that finding to define community policing, insisting that any definition must derive from quantifying what is happening in the field. Yet that ignores the clear and concise definition of community policing in widespread use for more than a decade, which has served as the ideal toward which progressive police have aspired: Community policing is a philosophy based on forging a partnership between the police and the community, so that they can work together on solving problems of crime, and fear of crime and disorder, thereby enhancing the overall quality of life in community neighborhoods.

Its academic underpinnings blend the wisdom of power sharing and decentralized decision-making contained in the ten Principles of Community Policing, as proposed by the late Dr. Robert Trojanowicz, with the effectiveness of strategic thinking in problem-oriented policing (POP), as envisioned by Dr. Herman Goldstein. While each man's vision independently advanced policing far beyond business as usual, combining these powerful approaches together under the rubric of community policing dramatically reinvents the role and function of the police.

Changing the policing paradigm

The Trojanowicz legacy underscores the importance of bringing key stake-holders together as equals, since solutions always benefit from including as many perspectives as possible. The police alone cannot make communities safe, and tapping the eyes, ears, minds, and energies of law-abiding citizens increases the likelihood of success. Add to that the Goldstein contribution of the S.A.R.A. (Scanning, Analysis, Response, Assessment) model, which elevates policing from catching the bad guys to exploring the underlying dynamics that allow problems to persist—as profound a shift as from checkers to chess.

Operationalizing the philosophy can differ in terms of specific strategies and tactics, as part of tailoring the approach to local resources and needs, but the major challenge facing police managers lies in harnessing the full power of this potent new paradigm. In this climate, the allegation that community policing has yet to be defined threatens its future. For one thing, it blurs the standards by which we can hold departments accountable, allowing any police agency that jumps on the community policing bandwagon the potential to dilute what it stands for. For another, it allows police a tempting loophole to avoid the hard work of fundamental change, particularly the daunting challenge of engaging the community fully in the following steps: determining the vision, values, and mission of the department; recruiting, selecting, training, evaluating, promoting, and rewarding personnel; and participating directly in problem solving and assessment.

How sad if community policing ends up tagged as a failure without receiving a fair trial on its own merits. *Newsweek* columnist George Will treated community policing as synonymous with "saturation policing" as if the goal is simply to flood neighborhoods with police officers as a visible deterrent to crime. Another challenge now comes from "crime-specific" policing, touted as superior to community policing in reducing target crimes.

The illusion of "crime-specific" policing

The most famous of the current crime-specific policing sites is Houston, with its 655 Program (which refers to the goal of using overtime to add the equivalent of an additional full-time officer to each of the city's 655 square miles). This approach again narrows the mission of the police to a primary focus on crime, which it addresses by "proactive, aggressive" patrol and investigation, with interaction between the police and the community limited to communication about security concerns.

Conceptually, it differs little from traditional policing, albeit with more sworn personnel and greater fervor for making arrests for minor infractions. In Houston, reports of Part I "suppressible" crimes declined, while arrests for Part II curfew violations and loitering increased.

Mark Twain also warned us about lies, damn lies, and statistics. Even the advocates of crime-specific policing admit that the Houston results are ambiguous, since reductions in crimes such as robberies and burglaries mirrored decreases in neighboring jurisdictions that have not adopted this approach.

Keep in mind as well that only one out of every three crimes is ever reported to the police. By fostering trust, community policing can actually produce an initial increase in crime rates, as people share information about incidents that would otherwise have gone unreported (and surveys confirm that people feel safer). Crime-specific policing, in contrast, may well do a better job of suppressing crime reporting than suppressing crime itself. And if minority communities in particular perceive "aggressive" as "harassing," this approach could elevate the threat of civil unrest, whereas community policing is widely perceived as reducing this risk.

Community policing is about both means and ends. Targeting disorder could be part of a community policing problem-solving initiative, but only as a result of the direct participation and support of the community. It is easy to see the appeal of an alternative strategy that allows police to remain the independent and autonomous experts. Yet crime-specific policing suffers from fostering dependence on government to make communities safe, at a time when there is growing consensus that voters support empowering people to do more for themselves.

The reality is that the choice is not among the four concepts of traditional, community, problem-oriented, or crime-specific policing, but between public and private policing. Community policing did not emerge because it is easy to implement and to do, but because the traditional system is failing. Where a decade ago there were three private security guards for each police officer, there are now four to one. As those who can afford to do so increasingly isolate themselves in high-rise fortresses and walled suburban communities, the public police find themselves left to protect "consumers" who cannot "shop" elsewhere for their safety. What will happen if frustrated taxpayers lose their taste for supporting an unresponsive system that they themselves no longer use?

The question is not whether any new strategy can effect a temporary decline in a handful of selected crime rates, but whether a philosophy of policing helps to inform the use of existing police resources as the catalyst in making troubled neighborhoods safer. As Bob Trojanowicz used to remind us, community policing recognizes that until we are all safe, no one is safe.

Source: Adapted with permission from Bucqueroux, Bonnie. "Community Policing is Alive and Well." *Community Policing Exchange.* Washington, D.C.: The Community Policing Consortium, May/June 1995.

FROM PHILOSOPHY TO STRATEGIC APPLICATION

An extensive part of the literature consistently identifies community-oriented policing as a policing philosophy (Bennett 1994; Geller 1991; Goodstein 1991; Miller and Hess 1994; Rush 1994; Trojanowicz and Bucqueroux 1990). The issue that subsequently arises is whether or not community-oriented policing can be strategically applied in a real-world setting. As the definitions of community-oriented policing often specifically detail either the philosophical side or the practical side, there exists much debate on whether these two definitions are truly oriented on the same goal. The debate over practical application of theory has always plagued both the academic and practical worlds. The application of the community-oriented policing philosophy is no different.

As Commissioner Norman D. Inkster of the Royal Canadian Mounted Police stated, "We have been discussing the concept of community policing for more than ten years; a few of us have actually been practicing it. Some claim to have implemented community policing but—apart from a few discreet programs—their organization continues as before" (Inkster 1992, 28). The disparity over the concept of community-oriented policing has caused much confusion and false promises. Focusing on current and past literature on the community-oriented policing concept helps us move toward a common goal. So too does the development of a workable definition of the concept. It is again Norman Inkster who stated, "I think the essence of community-based policing still eludes some of us and many of our efforts do not yield results because we have not properly understood the concept we are trying to apply" (Inkster 1992, 28). The first step to understanding a concept is to understand what is intended by way of the definition.

REPORT OF THE INDEPENDENT COMMISSION OF THE LOS ANGELES POLICE DEPARTMENT: COMMUNITY POLICING

In the wake of the Rodney King incident, the trial of the four police officers, and the Los Angeles riots following the decision; the Christopher Commission was created as an independent commission to review the causes of excessive force complaints with the LAPD. One of the responses to addressing the problems within the police department was a call for Community-oriented policing. The following is an excerpt from the report:

Community Policing

The LAPD has an organizational culture that emphasizes crime control over crime prevention and that isolates the police from the communities and the people they serve. With the full support of many, the LAPD insists on aggressive detection of major crimes and a rapid, seven-minute response time to calls for service. Patrol officers are evaluated by statistical measures (for example, the number of calls handled and arrests made) and are rewarded for being "hardnosed." This style of policing produces results, but it does so at the risk of creating a siege mentality that alienates the officer from the community.

Witness after witness testified to unnecessarily aggressive confrontations between LAPD officers and citizens, particularly members of minority communities. From the statements of these citizens, as well as many present and former LAPD officers, it is apparent that too many LAPD patrol officers view citizens with resentment and hostility; too many treat the public with rudeness and disrespect. LAPD officers themselves seem to recognize the extent of the problem: nearly two-thirds (62.9 percent) of the 650 officers who responded to the recent LAPD survey expressed the opinion that "increased interaction with the community would improve the Department's relations with citizens."

A model of community policing has gained increased acceptance in other parts of the country during the past ten years. The community policing model places services to the public and prevention of crime as the primary role of the police in society and emphasizes problem solving, with active citizen involvement in defining those matters that are important to the community, rather than arrest statistics. Officers at the patrol level are required to spend less time in their cars communicating with other officers and more time on the street communicating with citizens. Proponents of this style of policing insist that addressing the causes of crime makes police officers more effective crime-fighters, and at the same time enhances the quality of life in the neighborhood.

The LAPD made early efforts to incorporate community policing principles and has continued to experiment with those concepts. For example, the LAPD's nationally recognized DARE program has been viewed by officers and the public alike as a major achievement. The LAPD remains committed, however, to its traditional style of law enforcement with an emphasis on crime control and arrests. LAPD officers are encouraged to command and confront, not to communicate. Community policing concepts, if successfully implemented, offer the prospect of effective crime prevention and substantially improved community relations. Although community-based policing is not a panacea for the problem of crime in society, the LAPD should carefully implement this model on a city-wide basis. This will require a fundamental change in matters that affect local neighborhoods, development of programs to gain an adequate understanding of what is important to particular communities, and learning to manage departmental affairs in ways that are consistent with the community views expressed. Above all, the department must understand that it is accountable to all segments of the community.

Source: Christopher, William, et. al. "Summary Report." Report of the Independent Commission on the Los Angeles Police Department. Los Angeles, California: City of Los Angeles, 1991.

COMMUNITY POLICING DEFINED

As the review of the literature revealed, a standard definition is lacking for what has become known as community-oriented policing. There are common themes from both the philosophical side and practical side of the concept. The predominant themes consist of the police and community working together, creating solutions to the indigenous problems that plague their community, and implementing programs to solve these problems. It is through this cooperation that communities will be able to actualize the true sense of the term "community."

In order to actually implement community-oriented policing, there must be a method of transferring theory and ideas into action and workable programs. In extracting the philosophy's common themes, we can categorize all of the concepts into three components.

The first component of community-oriented policing is strategic-oriented policing. Here the police utilize traditional police practices and procedures, by redistributing their resources toward identified problem areas. The goal of this component is to drive out the criminal element or cause of social disorder, to allow the community the chance to establish some type of groundwork in reclaiming their community.

The second key component discussed in the literature is neighborhood-oriented policing. This would be any and all programs that help open the lines

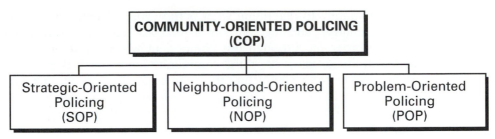

FIGURE 2.2   The Three Components of Community Oriented Policing.

of communication between the police and the citizens, to work toward fostering the true sense of community. This could include the creation of police-youth softball leagues, mini-police stations in the community, or having police officers move into the communities they serve.

The third component revealed in the literature is the problem-policing method. This method includes a concerted effort on the part of both the police

A local youth enjoying the festivities during "National Night Out" sponsored by the Montgomery County Police Department, Montgomery County, Maryland. (Courtesy of Montgomery County Department of Police, Montgomery County, Maryland.)

and the community to determine what is the cause of crime and social disorder in a community, creating solutions to the problems, and implementing the most viable program. Although this component will predominantly be implemented with the cooperation of the community members, it does not preclude the police officer from conducting this type of analysis during a routine shift. This component must be an ongoing process, and the success or failure of the programs should be determined, with updated or alternative programs then implemented.

This trilogy of components however, is really an interconnected web of programs that must be implemented together. The strategic policing component clears the way for the neighborhood-oriented and problem-oriented components to be set in motion. Many of the neighborhood-oriented programs that are implemented are determined via the problem-oriented process. And in many cases to achieve the community's support in problem solving, the communication between the police and the community must be opened up through the neighborhood-oriented policing component. The three components, therefore, depend upon each other for the successful implementation of community-oriented policing.

TABLE 2.7   PROFESSIONAL SERVICE VERSUS COMMUNITY CARE

* Communities have more commitment to their members than service delivery systems have to their clients.
* Communities understand their problems better than service professionals.
* Professionals and bureaucracies deliver services; communities solve problems.
* Institutions and professionals offer "service"; communities offer "care."
* Communities are more flexible and creative than large service bureaucracies.
* Communities are cheaper than service professionals.
* Communities enforce standards of behavior more effectively than bureaucracies or service professionals.
* Communities focus on capacities; service systems focus on deficiencies.

Source: Adapted with permission from Osborne, David and Ted Gaebler. *Reinventing Government: How the Entrepenuerial Spirit is Transforming the Public Sector From Schoolhouse to Statehouse, City Hall to the Pentagon.* Reading, Massachusetts: Addison-Wesley Publishing Company, Inc., 1992.

The concept, however must go further than this to achieve its end. The true concept must also deal with those common themes found in the literature that detail a department-wide implementation of the philosophy. Community-oriented policing must be a systemic approach to policing, with a decentralized organizational structure, and all members of the police force, including officers, supervisors, and civilians must be behind the philosophy. And this philosophy, this way of thinking, must be carried over into the implementing programs that complement these ideas.

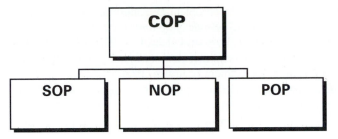

FIGURE 2.3

Therefore, through a consensus of the past and present literature, as well as a combination of the philosophical and practical concepts, community-oriented policing can be defined as:

> A systemic approach to policing with the paradigm of instilling and fostering a sense of community, within a geographical neighborhood, to improve the quality of life. It achieves this through the decentralization of the police and the implementation of a synthesis of three key components: 1) strategic-oriented policing–the redistribution of traditional police resources; 2) neighborhood-oriented policing–the interaction of police and all community members to reduce crime and the fear of crime through indigenous proactive programs; and 3) Problem-oriented policing–a concerted effort to resolve the cause of crime, rather than the symptoms.

REFERENCES

Bayley, David H. "International Differences in Community Policing." In *The Challenge of Community Policing: Testing the Promises*. ed. Dennis P. Rosenbaum. Thousand Oaks, CA: SAGE Publications, Inc., 1994.

Bennett, Trevor. "Community Policing on the Ground." In *The Challenge of Community Policing: Testing the Promises*. ed. by Dennis P. Rosenbaum. Thousand Oaks, CA: SAGE Publications, Inc., 1994.

Brandstatter, A. F. and Louis A. Radelet. *Police and Community Relations: A Sourcebook*. Beverly Hills: Glencoe Press, 1968.

Brown, Lee P. "Police-Community Power Sharing." In *Police Leadership in America*. ed. William A. Geller. Chicago: American Bar Foundation, Praeger Publishers, 1985.

——. "Community Policing: A Partnership with Promise." *The Police Chief*. (October 1992): 45—48.

Buerger, Michael. "A Tale of Two Targets: Limitations of Community Anticrime Actions." *Crime & Delinquency*. 40 no. 3 (July 1994a): 411—436.

Buerger, Michael E. "The Limits of Community." In *The Challenge of Community Policing: Testing the Promises*. ed. Dennis P. Rosenbaum. Thousand Oaks, CA: SAGE Publications, Inc., 1994b.

Capowich, George E. and Janice A. Roehl. "Problem-Oriented Policing: Actions and Effectiveness in San Diego." In *The Challenge of Community Policing: Testing the Promises*. ed. Dennis P. Rosenbaum. Thousand Oaks, CA: SAGE Publications, Inc., 1994.

Community Policing Consortium. *Understanding Community Policing: A Framework for Action*. Washington D.C.; U.S. Department of Justice, 1994.

Earle, Howard H. *Police-Community Relations: Crisis in Our Times*. Springfield, IL: Charles C. Thomas, Publishers, 1967.

Eck, John E. and Dennis P. Rosenbaum. "The New Police Order." *The Challenge of Community Policing: Testing the Promises*. ed. Dennis P. Rosenbaum. Thousand Oaks, California: SAGE Publications, Inc., 1994.

Eck, John E. and William Spelman. *Problem-Solving: Problem-Oriented Policing in Newport News*. Washington, D.C.: Police Executive Research Forum, 1987.

Farley, John E. *Sociology*. 3rd ed. Englewood Cliffs, N.J.: Prentice-Hall, Inc., 1994.

Geller, William A., ed. *Local Government Police Management*. 3rd ed. Washington, D.C.: International City/County Management Association, 1991.

Goldstein, Herman. "Improving Policing: A Problem-Oriented Approach." *Crime & Delinquency*. Vol. 25, no. 2, 1979: 236–258.

——. "Toward Community-Oriented Policing: Potential, Basic Requirements, and Threshold Questions." *Crime & Delinquency* 33, no. 1, (January 1987): 6—30.

——. *Problem-Oriented Policing*. New York: McGraw Hill Publishing Co., 1990.

——. "Foreword." *The Challenge of Community Policing: Testing the Promises*. ed. Dennis P. Rosenbaum. Thousand Oaks, CA: SAGE Publications, Inc., 1994.

Goodstein, Laurie. "New Philosophy of Policing." *Washington Post*. (December 23, 1991): A1–A7.

Greenburg, Reuben and Arthur Gordon. *Let's Take Back Our Streets!* Chicago: Contemporary Books, Inc., 1989.

Greene, Jack R., William T. Bergman, and Edward J. McLaughlin. "Implementing Community Policing." In *The Challenge of Community Policing: Testing the Promises*. ed. Dennis P. Rosenbaum. Thousand Oaks, CA: SAGE Publications, Inc., 1994.

Greene, Jack R. and Stephen D. Mastrofski, eds. "Preface." *Community Policing: Rhetoric or Reality?* New York: Praeger Publishers, 1988.

Grinc, Randolph M. "'Angels in Marble': Problems in Community Involvement in Community Policing." *Crime & Delinquency*. 40, no. 3 (July 1994): 437–468.

Inkster, Norman D. "The Essence of Community Policing." *The Police Chief*, March 1992, 28–31.

Johnson, Thomas A., Gordon E. Misner, and Lee P. Brown. *The Police and Society: An Environment for Collaboration and Confrontation*. Englewood Cliffs, N.J.: Prentice-Hall, Inc., 1981.

Lurigio, Arthur J. and Dennis P. Rosenbaum. "The Impact of Community Policing on Police Personnel." In *The Challenge of Community Policing: Testing the Promises*. ed. Dennis P. Rosenbaum. Thousand Oaks, CA: SAGE Publications, Inc., 1994.

Lurigio, Arthur J. and Wesley G. Skogan. "Winning the Hearts and Minds of Police Officers: An Assessment of Staff Perceptions of Community Policing in Chicago." *Crime & Delinquency* 40, no. 3 (July 1994): 315–330.

Mayhall, Pamela D., Thomas Barker, and Ronald D. Hunter. *Police-Community Relations and the Administration of Justice*. 4th ed. Englewood Cliffs, N.J.: Prentice-Hall, Inc., 1995.

McElroy, Jerome E., Colleen A. Cosgrove, and Susan Sadd. *Community Policing: The CPOP in New York.* Newbury Park, CA: SAGE Publications, Inc., 1993.

Miller, Linda S. and Karen M. Hess. *Community Policing: Theory and Practice.* St. Paul: West Publishing Company, 1994.

Murphy, Chris. "The Development, Impact, and Implications of Community Policing in Canada." In *Community Policing: Rhetoric or Reality?* ed. Jack R. Greene and Stephen D. Mastrofski. New York: Praeger Publishers, 1988.

Oliver, Willard M. "Community Policing Defined." *Law & Order,* August 1992, 46, 56–58.

Pomrenke, Norman E. *Police Community Relations.* Norman E. Pomrenke. Chapel Hill, N.C.: University of North Carolina Press, 1966.

Radelet, Louis A. and David L. Carter. *The Police and the Community.* 5th ed. Englewood Cliffs, New Jersey: Prentice-Hall, Inc., 1994.

Roberg, Roy. "Can Today's Police Organizations Effectively Implement Community Policing?" *The Challenge of Community Policing: Testing the Promises.* Dennis P. Rosenbaum (ed.). Thousand Oaks, CA: SAGE Publications, Inc., 1994.

Rosenbaum, Dennis P. *The Challenge of Community Policing: Testing The Promises.* ed. Dennis P. Rosenbaum. Thousand Oaks, CA: SAGE Publications, Inc., 1994.

Rosenbaum, Dennis P. and Arthur J. Lurigio. "An Inside Look at Community Policing Reform: Definitions, Organizational Changes, and Evaluation Findings." *Crime & Delinquency* 40, no. 3 (July 1994): 299–314.

Rush, George E. *The Dictionary of Criminal Justice.* 4th ed. Guilford, CT.: The Dushkin Publishing Group, Inc., 1994.

Sadd, Susan and Randolph Grinc. "Innovative Neighborhood Oriented Policing." In *The Challenge of Community Policing: Testing the Promises.* ed. Dennis P. Rosenbaum. Thousand Oaks, CA: SAGE Publications, Inc., 1994.

Skogan, Wesley G. "The Impact of Community Policing on Neighborhood Residents." A Cross-Site Analysis." In *the Challenges of Community Policing: Testing the Promises,* ed. Dennis P. Rosenbaum. Thousand Oaks, CA: SAGE Publications, Inc., 1994.

Trojanowicz, Robert and Bonnie Bucqueroux. *Community Policing: How to Get Started.* Cincinnati: Anderson Publishing Company, 1990.

Trojanowicz, Robert C. and Samuel L. Dixon. *Criminal Justice and the Community.* Englewood Cliffs, N.J.: Prentice-Hall, Inc., 1974.

U.S. Department of Justice. Office of Justice Programs. *Drugs, Crime, and the Justice System.* Washington, D.C.: GPO, December 1992.

Walker, Samuel. *Sense and Nonsense About Crime and Drugs 3/e.* Belmont, CA: Wadsworth Publishing Company, 1994.

Weisheit, Ralph A., L. Edward Wells, and David N. Falcone. "Community Policing in Small Town and Rural America." *Crime & Delinquency.* 40, no. 4 (October 1994): 549–567.

Wilkinson, Deanna L. and Dennis P. Rosenbaum. "The Effects of Organizational Structure on Community Policing: A Comparison of Two Cities." In *The Challenge of Community Policing: Testing the Promises.* ed. Dennis P. Rosenbaum. Thousand Oaks, CA: SAGE Publications, Inc., 1994.

Wilson, James Q. and George L. Kelling. "Broken Windows: The Police and Neighborhood Safety." *The Atlantic Monthly,* March 1982, 29–38.

——. "Making Neighborhoods Safe." *The Atlantic Monthly,* February 1989, 46–52.

CHAPTER 3

Strategic-Oriented Policing

Let's take back our streets!
-Reuben Greenberg-

The first component of community-oriented policing, as previously described, is strategic-oriented policing. The concept broadens traditional police practices and procedures into a more beneficial model conducive to the goals of establishing all of community-oriented policing's tenets. It is the catalyst for all of the ideas that eventually will unfold within the community and it allows for a smooth transition into the other components. Utilizing a slightly altered method of past policing procedures, the police do not have to adapt immediately to a new policing philosophy. Implementing the move from traditional reactive patrolling to community-oriented policing allows this to become the transition stage for not only the police, but the community as well.

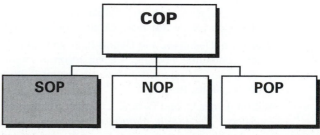

FIGURE 3.1

As Herman Goldstein (1990, 132) stated, "The police always have available to them the option of increasing their enforcement of laws that might bear on a specific problem, although they may not routinely enforce them because they lack the resources, the problem has low priority, or enforcement is judged to be ineffective." Strategic policing enforces laws oriented on a specific problem as Goldstein states. However, it realizes and accepts the three problems Goldstein raises.

"CRIME FILES"

REPEAT OFFENDERS—PART 38

This edition of the "Crime Files," hosted by James Q. Wilson, features Peter Gilchrist, District Attorney, Charlotte, North Carolina; Leslie Harris, Former Director, Washington Chapter, American Civil Liberties Union; and Edward Spurlock, Commander, Repeat Offender Project, Washington, D.C. Police Department. The discussion revolves around strategic methods dealing with criminals who commit serious crimes, frequently and over long periods of time.

First, the police throughout history lacked the necessary resources to accomplish their mission. There is always a need for additional personnel, equipment, and training. The police never have enough staffing manpower due to increased crime rates in specific geographical areas or because too many officers would like their summer vacations at the same time. This is not news to any police administrator. Nor is utilizing statistical crime data to allocate resources to high-crime areas. However, when these resources are allocated, they are generally limited to only a handful of additional beat-cops and perhaps one or two non-uniform officers. The concept of strategic policing recommends the temporary use of multiple officers from various divisions in various ways. This may include a single officer assigned to check on a single problem to upwards of twenty officers assigned to a specific area for a week or two, of which some may be street officers, tactical officers, detectives, and motor officers, all temporarily assigned for the purposes of a show of force. However, the police department cannot maintain this extended use of resources for any long duration of time, therefore something else must be put in place of the physical presence of the police. This comes later in the form of neighborhood-oriented policing and problem-oriented policing techniques.

Second, strategic policing recognizes that often many of these "problems" have extremely low priority within the police department. Determining what has priority is often a difficult task. One area may appear to need immediate attention, despite crime statistics for the area that place it in a low priority category. Another area may not appear to be a high priority area, but may in fact reflect this need in the crime statistics. The goal then is to determine which

DARE students trying on SWAT equipment during a DARE picnic
sponsored by the St. Petersburg Police Department, St. Petersburg,
Florida. (Courtesy of St. Petersburg Police Department, St.
Petersburg, Florida.)

area is in the greatest need, not just by crime statistics but by talking with the
officers who work the areas in need and finding out where the members of
the local community feel the stepped-up police presence is necessary. This
consensus of the allocation of resources will determine exactly what has priority, what necessitates a limited response, and what can wait.

Third, the idea of judging the police presence to be ineffective has generally in the past been based upon arrest statistics going up and crime rates
going down. In a community sense, this can no longer be the sole basis for
determining if the police enforcement was "effective." The quality of living for
the community must also be explored, along with the reduced fear and crime
perception of the community. This must be done throughout the various
stages of implementing community-oriented policing services in a time series
analysis. Determining these elements before the use of strategic policing techniques, after the techniques, and at the commencement of neighborhood/
problem-oriented policing can be helpful. Only then can a true assessment of
the community's fear, crime rates, and quality of living be fully understood. Only
then can the success rates of community-oriented policing be documented.

There are no limitations on the methods that can be employed under
strategic policing. It is only important that "the basic goal remains the effective
control of crime" (Moore and Trojanowicz 1988, 6). The techniques however can

be categorized into the determination of where strategic policing will be implemented and three types of patrols. The determination of where strategic policing is to be implemented is known in the literature as "targeting" and will remain so here (e.g., Fleissner et. al. 1992; Tien and Rich 1994). The three types of patrols are 1) directed, 2) aggressive, and 3) saturation. These three concepts will be explored further as will those jurisdictions where particular techniques have been successful and some of the problems that may arise from implementation.

STRATEGIC-ORIENTED POLICING AND VARIOUS DRUG ENFORCEMENT TACTICS

Mail-in Coupons: Police place newspaper advertisements that contain forms for readers to fill in with information on suspected or observed drug activity; readers then mail the form to the department.

Taxi Connection: Undercover police officers ride in taxis and ask the driver to connect them with a drug dealer; if the driver sets up or handles a drug transaction, the undercover officer arrests the driver.

Hotel Managers: Police train managers of hotels and motels to spot signs of drug activity and to call the police.

Package Interdiction: Working with parcel-shipping companies, police in some communities are examining and intercepting packages that may contain drugs.

Clone Beepers: Drug dealers, sellers, runners, and buyers who use beepers may learn that police are tuned to their frequency and can, through new electronic capability, identify telephones from which calls are made; arrests may follow.

Child Abuse and Neglect: Pregnant women who use drugs may be charged with child abuse by police. Parents of juvenile drug offenders may be charged with child neglect.

Traffic Checkpoints: Signs put up by a state highway patrol along interstate highways warn of a drug checkpoint a few miles ahead; motorists who drive off at the next exit, however, learn that the checkpoint is actually on the exit.

Source: National Institute of Justice. *Searching for Answers: Annual Evaluation Report on Drugs and Crime: 1992*. Washington D.C.: National Institute of Justice, 1993.

TARGETING

Targeting is a term utilized in many jurisdictions and in the literature to give credence to the fact the police are not randomly conducting proactive patrol, but are focusing in on specific problems. Police resources are directed at these targets to alleviate specific problems indigenous to a particular area. There are multiple ways to arrive at what should be targeted, as well as multiple ways to derive a solution for the problems. However, because this is a process to foster a sense of "community," the community must be involved.

The determination of what to target, what has precedence, and how the strategic policing should be carried out, should not be directed in only downward communication, but in lateral communication with the police officers who patrol the areas being discussed, other public agencies, community leaders, as well as citizens who live in the area. It is important to include all of these in a targeting committee and a majority should be derived from the employees of these agencies and the common citizens of the community.

Some may argue the point of having the employees and common citizens as members of this focal group is pointless, because those persons in leadership positions in the agencies and in the community are better equipped to handle the problem analysis and solve the problems through their various administrations. As James Q. Wilson and George L. Kelling (1989, 51) respond to this premise, "Forcing them to cooperate by knocking heads together at the top rarely works; what department heads promise the mayor they will do may bear little relationship to what their rank-and-file employees actually do." They then conclude that "you have to get the neighborhood-level supervisors from each agency together in a 'district cabinet' that meets regularly and addresses common concerns" (Wilson and Kelling 1989, 51). It should include not only rank-and-file employees from the various agencies, but also a cross-section of the community, from the police to those citizens without credentials, living in the community.

Inclusion of the police officers is extremely important simply because they are there in the community, day in and day out, dealing with the problems indigenous to a particular community. They have a perspective related to the overall picture of what plagues a particular community and can communicate in organizational terms. The patrol officer can provide not only the facts of the problems, but an educated insight into the problems as well. The key revolves around the fact that officers are members of the community who are tapped into the pulse of crime and social problems that plague the community.

Additional public agencies can also provide information on the problems plaguing a community. Any additional police agency that has concurrent jurisdiction is an obvious choice to provide a different interpretation of the crime problems in a specific area. Other public safety organizations such as the fire department and emergency medical services can provide a particularly helpful analysis of the community's problems such as areas of frequent drug overdoses, areas prone to multiple assault calls, or areas that could be deemed hazardous to public health, welfare, and safety. The departments of social services or social work can provide input into what specific social problems an area incurs, ranging from domestic violence to difficulties with area landlords. The housing authority could also provide this insight to housing areas that may be deemed hazardous to the health of its residents or where multiple landlord–tenant disputes occur. Any office of business or economic development can provide information on commercial establishments that may be a magnet for various types of crime and social disorders. Finally, the government's public works division can provide a vast amount of knowledge concerning areas that may sustain high crime rates or societal problems from the number of calls they receive to a specific area or the type of request they receive for their services. All of these resources are generally within the reach of the police department and most can easily provide a representative to attend the meetings regarding the crime, social disorders, and quality of life in a particular community.

The community leaders are also important for the roundtable meeting that should be established to determine what will be primary and secondary targets in strategic policing. These leaders can originate from any of the community's established organizations. There is no organization that could not provide some understanding of the crime problems indigenous to a local community. Business leaders or members of the local chamber of commerce are the key personnel to provide information on problems associated with commercial establishments located in a particular neighborhood or area. A member of the local school board, parent-teacher association, or housing association can provide information on problems associated with residential areas located in the community. And finally the various political, social, and religious associations should be considered to provide information on specific community problems from their perspectives as members of the community.

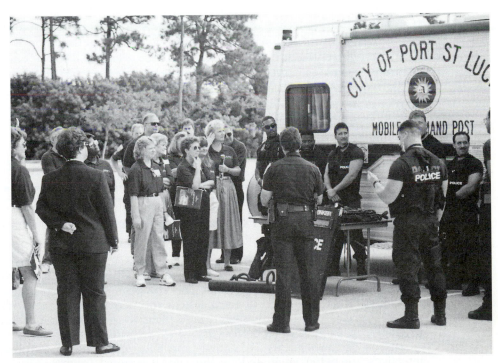

Officers from the City of Port St. Lucie Police Department's
Special Response Team demonstrate equipment to the leadership
group of the St. Lucie County Chamber of Commerce, Florida.
(Courtesy of City of Port St. Lucie Police Dept., City of Port St.
Lucie, Florida.)

It is also extremely important to move away from the governmental and organizational aspect of community members and look to individuals who represent the common man or common woman of a community. This should include members of the community who represent the community or area being focused on for targeting. A middle-class banker would not be appropriate for discussing quality-of-life problems in the lower-class, subsidized housing projects, any more than a member from this community would be sitting in on a targeting group for the upper-class neighborhood. The members can be drawn from all walks of life to include the unemployed, those family members who stay home during the day, or a teenager who lives in the neighborhood. There should be no real criteria for the selection of common citizens, only that they can articulate what they perceive as the crime, social, or quality-of-life problems.

As Wilson and Kelling had stated, they should then meet regularly in a roundtable to discuss the various types of problems concerning them. They should develop lists of all the potential problems, brainstorm over possible solutions, and prioritize the most serious concerns necessitating immediate action and those that could do with less police response or needing a different course of action separate from the actions available from the police. The group, in their regular meetings, can assess the success of varying methods in both subjective and objective terms, develop new courses of action, and re-prioritize as necessary. New members to the committee, perhaps on a rotating basis or through simple attrition, will be extremely beneficial to the committee, contributing fresh ideas and innovative methods not previously discussed.

The ultimate goal of targeting is the inclusion of the community in making policy decisions as to where police resources will be allocated. Allowing this voice will help target the most real and perceived threats to the community, allow the community to exercise some power in goal setting, and will open a direct line of communications with the community, fostering a strong relationship.

STRATEGIC-ORIENTED POLICING AND MODERN TECHNOLOGY UTILIZED TO ADDRESS DRUG PROBLEM IN JERSEY

Jersey City's Drug Market Analysis Project (DMAP) uses a location-based computer information system to help police identify drug markets and develop crime prevention and control programs. This computer system links the police department's computer-aided dispatch system and personal computer technology so that data can be represented both visually—on computer-generated geographic maps—and in report format.

Data on narcotics arrests and activity and interviews with narcotics squad detectives are being integrated by the DMAP system. To determine what information the community could provide on drug dealing, a one-day narcotics "phone-in" and a community survey of 500 Jersey City residents were conducted during the first phase of the project.

The program differs from conventional enforcement strategies in three ways:

- First, it has changed the management style of the experimental narcotics team by giving responsibility for particular markets to individual officers. The aim is to generate a sense of ownership for each market so that officers can develop close contacts with residents and businesses in their area, and sustain long-term maintenance programs within the market boundaries.
- Second, it classifies the different types of drug markets into categories depending on the situations and physical environments that prevail within market boundaries.
- Third, crackdowns are now developed after intensive surveillance of market areas and advance preparations of arrest warrants for dealers frequenting the market. These crackdowns may involve as many as 45 officers in a single evening or day, or may involve a dozen officers executing arrest warrants in a one-hour sweep through the area.

Source: National Institute of Justice. *Searching for Answers: Annual Evaluation Report on Drugs and Crime: 1992*. Washington, D.C.: National Institute of Justice, 1993.

DIRECTED PATROLS

The first method of strategic policing is the technique known as directed patrol. This is the easiest of the patrols to conduct, as it is easily implemented and has the least drain on police resources. Directed patrols can be implemented for criminal activity and traffic violations. They can be based on officers' discretion, crime analysis, or from a specific complaint received by the community or the community committee. The officers are required to simply check on the area involved in their designated assignment in between the calls they receive during a normal tour of duty.

In Arlington County, Virginia, police officers are required to pick one criminal- and one traffic-directed patrol each month. They then record the number of times they check the area and any contacts or arrests they make during their shift. Additional directed patrols are signed out at the beginning of a shift to particular beats where either a crime analysis has shown a high crime or traffic problem or through the complaint of a citizen. The information is recorded on the log sheet and passed along to the next shift if it is a recurring problem not unique to a particular time. Some of the directed patrols may include walks through local parks, patrols of areas where the homeless urinate and defecate, or patrols in the vicinity of known crack houses.

One of the common complaints among officers assigned to directed patrols is the inability to perform the checks or being pulled away from the directed patrol assignment to answer various calls for services, 911 calls, and to attend to administrative duties that may tie up the officer for an entire shift. One method that has been implemented is a split-force patrol (Tien, Simon, and Larson 1977). This method splits the patrol shift into two segments. One is responsible for responding to calls and the other is responsible solely for the directed patrols, unless an emergency arises. In this manner those working the directed patrols have the understanding that they will be able to conduct these patrols without constant interruptions. However, effective management must insure that the directed patrols are conducted in this method and that the split is rotated daily or weekly to prevent any friction between the officers working the directed patrol split and those tied to a potential backlog of calls in the standard patrol split.

Studies conducted on the success of directed patrols have generally found that crime does decrease in the targeted area when this type of patrol is utilized (Cordner 1981; Cordner and Trojanowicz 1992; Roncek and Maier 1991; Warren, Forst, and Estrella 1979). A dedicated patrol, where the police are continually present, whether at varying intervals or for long periods of time, can clearly be seen as beneficial in stopping criminal activity or in helping various forms of social problems.

AGGRESSIVE PATROLS

The second method of strategic-oriented policing utilizes methods that have come to be known as aggressive patrol or aggressive order maintenance. This is an increased pressure on specific criminal or social order problems, as well as on specific criminal elements, by the police. According to Stephen D. Mastrofski (1988, 53), "aggressive order maintenance strategies include rousing or arresting people thought to cause public disorder, field interrogations and roadblock checks, surveillance of suspicious people, vigorous enforcement of public order and nuisance laws, and, in general, much greater attention to the minor crimes and disturbances thought to disrupt and displease the civil public." The tactics, although aggressive in nature, must still abide by all legal and societal controls upon the police. Aggressive patrols merely increase the quantity of contacts for a particular situation in an attempt to alleviate the problem. The various forms of aggressive patrols may be categorized as follows: field stops, traffic stops, use of plainclothes officers, habitual offender programs, sting operations, and stakeouts.

Field stops, field interviews, or field investigations, regardless of the name used, have always been a method for police to question and record suspicious persons information. Although the individual may not be committing a crime in violation of a criminal statute, his or her actions may be inappropriate for the surrounding community, which can easily label the individual as "suspicious" or "out of place." The police record their contact with the individual, by conducting a pat-down, noting personal identification information, and taking a Polaroid photograph, thereby maintaining a record of all individuals encountered in a particular neighborhood. This may serve as a deterrent or it may serve as a future means of identifying the perpetrator of a crime. An increased use of these field interrogations can have a profound effect on crime and should not necessarily be limited to any particular time, place, or circumstances.

James Q. Wilson (1994, 47) wrote that this particular method could be utilized more often by the police with individuals who are thought to be carrying concealed or unlicensed weapons. He believes this would be more effective in reducing crime than the continued passage of new laws attempting to ban these weapons. Additionally, a study conducted in San Diego tested the effects of these field interviews on crime and found field interviews have a substantial effect on area crime rates specifically as a deterrent for crimes committed by youths in groups (Boydstun 1975). Implementing a common police practice in a more intensified program has a profound effect on crime. This is just as clear on the street as it is in the research.

Traffic enforcement has always been a key mission of the police. Their primary function is to maintain the flow of traffic in a safe and expedient manner by monitoring and directing the traffic, as well as enforcing all state and local traffic laws. Randomly issuing citations for traffic violations may or may not have a deterrent effect upon the individual driver and it is very doubtful that it has any effect on the general population of motorists. However, the use of aggressive patrol techniques at a particular intersection or road subject to either accidents or traffic violations can have this desired overall effect, if the presence and sincerity of the police function in these instances is felt by the public. Essentially the enforcement of traffic laws "contributes to the maintenance of order, educates the public in safe driving habits, and provides a visible community service" (Cole 1995, 197). Additionally, a significant amount of criminal activity is discovered during traffic stops which may not have been discovered otherwise, and this is further testimony to the successful use of this form of aggressive patrol.

Aggressive patrol used in traffic enforcement is distinctly different from that of a directed patrol. In the traffic directed patrol, officers are encouraged to check on a previously specified area for traffic violations in between their calls or during their tour of a split-force patrol. The use of aggressive patrol is for a dedicated officer, specifically assigned to monitor the specified area, to issue citations to violators without the broad use of discretion. Although the police retain their discretionary abilities in these tours, they should attempt to minimize the overall use.

Despite the fact this form of aggressive patrol is oriented on traffic, it significantly impacts the criminal element and not just by reducing traffic problems. The research conducted specifically on the use of aggressive patrol in traffic enforcement has found that those areas utilizing this technique have lower crime rates (Wilson and Boland 1978; Wilson and Boland 1979). Another study on the use of aggressive patrols in traffic enforcement discovered that those police departments implementing this technique had lower robbery rates in their jurisdictions (Sampson and Cohen 1988). The advantage of increasing aggressive patrols in the area of traffic enforcement is then not for the sole purpose of reducing traffic problems, but criminal problems as well.

Another method that mixes field stops and traffic stops in a different manner is the use of plainclothes officers. Most jurisdictions have varying names for these types of officers, sometimes called "felony cars" when operating in unmarked vehicles, and "tactical teams" or "undercover officers" while

Officer John Boyd of the Phoenix Police Department, Phoenix, Arizona, teaches a local youth how to ride a bicycle safely. (Courtesy of Phoenix Police Department, Phoenix, Arizona, and Mr. Bob Rink.)

on foot in the communities. Regardless of the name, this is the use of officers in street clothes who attempt to blend into the community to observe those crimes or order maintenance problems that may not be visible to a uniformed police officer. This allows officers to follow possible offenders and observe their behavior or follow potential victims. The police are then in a position to either prevent a crime from occurring or react to the crime as it occurs. It is also a method of dealing with known criminal problems or a specific area that is suffering an order maintenance problem that would disappear, only to reappear again, if a police officer in uniform was observed. The key however, just like in the rest of strategic policing methods, is to curtail, drive away, or abolish some behavior that is a criminal or order maintenance problem.

Another method that has gained popularity over the past decade is the use of habitual-offender or repeat-offender programs. The habitual offender can be tracked in various ways: by tracking known criminals who are considered by certain factors to be a high risk for future crime; by tracking the number of arrests of an individual by crime type and presenting the past history in court; and by a preventative method through cooperation with the district/commonwealth's attorney's office where certain individuals can be declared "habitual offenders" and sentenced in a manner where, if committing the act again, they will receive tougher sentences. The key to most habitual offender programs is the relationship between the police and the district/commonwealth's attorney's office, who can reach an agreement as to what is deemed a habitual/repeat offender and can determine the type of sentence the offender will receive for this type of specific violation. Actual programs of habitual/repeat offenders have been utilized for robberies, larcenies from retail establishments, and for local prostitutes or drunken offenders.

The habitual/repeat offender programs have been very successful where implemented and have seen many of these offenders removed from the street for long periods of time. Following the theory that the police spend most of their time with a small number of the community, by removing this small element from the community, this in turn frees the police from this restrictive fact of policing. This form of aggressive patrol, through research, has been found to be an effective method, but is also considered to be costly because of the drain on police resources (Martin 1986; Martin and Sherman 1986). Although this may be true initially, the goal is for the offenders to receive longer sentences, preventing those officers assigned to this type of enforcement from having to spend any obtrusive amount of time in this endeavor.

The final two types of aggressive patrols are old friends to the police: the sting and the stakeout. In the sting, the police establish some type of false front to capture a large portion of a specific criminal element. In many cases, the police may pose as a storekeeper who collects fenced property in order to catch those committing larcenies, burglaries, and robberies. The police have established similar fronts in dealing with stolen vehicles, combatting the war on drugs, and attempting to serve warrants. One famous case involved several suspects wanted on outstanding warrants, who were called and told they had won tickets to a baseball game and could meet the local team players for photographs and autographs. The wanted individuals arrived on the day of the baseball game to receive their prizes and were arrested on the outstanding warrants.

The other old friend is the stakeout. Although there is no specific formula for this tactical method, the police essentially establish a hidden position in a store, bank, or crime-prone area, wait for a crime to occur and then react. Utilizing this technique in an arbitrary manner is generally considered a waste of resources and should only be employed when there are tips that a crime is to occur or where a pattern of crimes has developed. Either way, this method is a drain on police resources and should be used on a limited basis.

The purpose for raising the awareness of these two common police techniques is to show that there is a use for them in strategic policing. It is often the case that old techniques are good techniques and should not be dismissed by the police under the auspices of community-oriented policing. Rather, they should be utilized in new and innovative ways.

COP IN ACTION

CODE ENFORCEMENT TEAMS

Seeking new ways to cope with crime-ridden troubled areas, the Albuquerque Police Department set up an interagency team to enforce city codes against delinquent properties. These properties are often focal points for crime, with the knowledge, connivance, or apathy of their owners.

The Code Enforcement Team is an innovation originally pioneered by the Fort Lauderdale, Florida, Police Department. Albuquerque's adaptation of the concept resulted in a team including a police detective, a housing inspector from Albuquerque Family and Community Services, a zoning inspector and a fire inspector performing comprehensive inspections for violations in all spheres.

The advantages of a team approach are that a law enforcement presence deters intimidation of inspectors and all necessary inspections on a single property are carried out simultaneously. The team approach results in quicker action against violators, who are often absentee landlords who allow their properties to be used for criminal activities.

Abandoned buildings serve as rendezvous points, not only for squatters, but people involved in illegal drugs. Because of their neglected condition, abandoned properties often constitute safety hazards. A typical trouble spot might include debris, littering, insufficient fire extinguishers, inoperative smoke alarms, exposed electrical wiring, and inadequate drainage. The location might have had police called to it many times and reports of gunshots.

The team gives the property owner thirty days to begin corrective action and schedules a reinspection at the end of this period to monitor progress. If the owner is cooperative, the team may grant an extension, but lacking this, enforcement action is initiated.

Initially, the emphasis was against motels lining old Route 66 (Central Avenue), long a trouble area. Some motels had holes in walls, plumbing defects such as inoperative toilets, insect infestation, and inadequate fire protection. Route 66 motels catered to prostitutes by renting rooms by the hour. These are often substandard rooms, because working prostitutes don't require the amenities that legitimate motel guests expect. One Central Avenue motel, for example, had nine rooms out of forty with no toilets.

Private residences can also become targets for collaborative inspections. One apartment complex was notorious for its violations, and the owner had only nine out of its twenty-one units leased. All apartments were occupied, however, by squatters, drug dealers, and other people.

With private residences, sometimes the owner of record is not immediately available or even visible. In these cases, a title search usually produces a name, and the team serves papers on the responsible individual.

Condemnation of an abandoned building is a further step. The team requires the owner to secure and board up an abandoned building within five to ten days, and failure to comply results in a condemnation resolution from the city council. While final action can take six months, the threat of condemnation usually motivates the owner to comply.

Support from the community's courts was necessary to the team's efforts. Some judges commonly passed lenient sentences on violators, apparently because of their unfamiliarity with the seriousness of the situations surrounding code violations. Code Team personnel conducted a slide show and presentation for judges who regularly deal with code violations, to show them how serious the ramifications can be for related crime in the community. This approach required no new legislation, only stricter and more thorough enforcement of existing laws and regulations, including national housing, construction, electrical, health, and plumbing codes.

With more personnel, code enforcement in Albuquerque will become more intense, making it more difficult for criminal elements to obtain and retain a foothold in the community.

Source: Adapted with permission from Lesce, Tony. "Code Enforcement Teams." *Law and Order.* September 1995, 93–95.

SATURATION PATROLS

The third form of patrol under strategic-oriented policing is the use of the saturation patrol. This is the most difficult of the three patrols as it is the largest drain on police resources and is the greatest show of force, which can often have a negative effect on the community. However, if implemented with the cooperation of the community, there is generally a more positive show of support for this type of patrol.

Saturation patrol is forming a collection of officers from various shifts, tactical units, traffic units, and investigators, who, all in uniform, saturate a predesignated area in a show of force. The initial actions on the part of the police in this form of patrol is to establish their presence in the area, whether the target is an entire neighborhood or a street corner near two or three crack houses. This can be conducted through multiple arrests, investigative stops, or traffic stops of people going into and coming from the designated area. Once the initial impact of the arrests is made, generally over a three-day period, the police must maintain the show of force for an additional period of time, approximately one week to one month. The goal is to drive the criminal element out of the area by temporarily displacing or eliminating the criminal or order maintenance problem.

This technique has multiple applications in the community. Actions against the criminal element are the most obvious with the ability to drive away users and dealers of drugs from an open-air drug market or to prevent the buyers of prostitution from driving into an area because of the police presence and displacing the prostitutes themselves. Additional applications could involve specific problems such as homosexual activity on children's playgrounds or general problems such as communities with extremely high overall crime rates. Saturation patrols can be utilized in order maintenance issues, working in areas known for aggressive panhandlers, homeless people, and drunks that citizens avoid out of fear created by their presence.

Chief Reuben Greenburg, the police chief of Charleston, South Carolina has had much success with this technique against drug dealers and prostitutes

(Greenburg and Gordon, 1989). Research has also proven this particular type of patrol is an effective method against criminal and order maintenance issues by having an initial deterrent effect (Sherman 1990a, 1990b). Lawrence Sherman (1990a, 1990b) conducted an analysis of eighteen police "crackdowns," most of which utilized the police saturation patrol. The study included a drug crackdown in Washington, D.C. against an open-air drug market that utilized sixty police officers assigned to the area each day. In another Washington D.C. use of the saturation patrol, a project known as "Operation Clean Sweep", used an additional 100 to 200 officers to target 59 drug markets by using various tactics of police presence that netted over 60 arrests a day (Sherman 1990a, 1990b).

OPERATION PRESSURE POINT

In early 1984, a newly appointed New York City police commissioner launched "Operation Pressure Point," a two-year crackdown on the Lower East Side drug markets. Prior to the crackdown, the area had offered many blatant drug bazaars, with customers attracted from all over the New York area. Heroin buyers could be seen standing in long lines stretching around street corners.

The crackdown, at a cost of $12 million per year, used more than 150 uniformed officers, most of them rookies. The crackdown began with a high volume of drug arrests—65 per day for the first 6 weeks, then dropping to 20 per day. This rate continued until at least August 1986, by which time the police had made 21,000 drug-related arrests in the target area.

Tactics included observation-of-sale arrests, undercover buys, raids on dealing locations, arrests for unrelated misdemeanors and violations, tips from informers, and a "hotline" phone number.

The initial deterrent effect was a 47 percent reduction in robberies in 1984 compared to 1983, and a 62 percent reduction (from 34 to 13) in homicides during the same period. This initial effect was maintained until at least the first 8 months of 1986, with a 40 percent reduction in robbery and a 9 percent reduction in homicide compared to the first 8 months of 1983. While no displacement to the immediate vicinity was found, other parts of Manhattan experienced a growth in drug markets.

Source: Sherman, Lawrence. *Police Crackdowns*. Washington, D.C.: National Institute of Justice Research in Action, March/April 1990.

Another such operation occurred in New York City, where "Operation Pressure Point" utilized 240 additional police officers to combat a high-drug area (Zimmer 1990). The operation was a success because the result was the reduction of drug trafficking and an increased sense of community (Zimmer 1990). Another success story of the saturation patrol was found in the New York City subway system where the number of officers patrolling was increased from 1,200 to 3,100 officers, placing essentially one officer per train and station, and the crime rates fell for approximately two years (Sherman 1990a, 1990b).

The use of the saturation patrol is effective for both criminal and order maintenance issues. If implemented with the agreement of the community and targeted at a specific problem, rather than in a shotgun method, it can have a substantial deterrent effect necessary for community-oriented policing.

EXAMPLES OF POLICE CRACKDOWNS

Police crackdowns can target specific neighborhoods or specific offenses, and their duration can range from a few weeks to several years. The following, selected from the eighteen case studies reviewed for this article, illustrate this range. Initial and residual deterrent effects varied, sometimes based on factors outside the scope of the crackdowns themselves.

Drug crackdown, Washington, D.C. A massive police presence—sixty police officers per day and a parked police trailer—in the Hanover Place neighborhood open-air drug market provided an effective initial deterrent.

Lynn, Massachusetts, open-air heroin market. A four-year crackdown using four to six police officers led to 140 drug arrests in the first ten months and increased demand for drug treatment.

Operation Clean Sweep, Washington D.C. The city allocated 100 to 200 officers—many on overtime—to 59 drug markets, making 60 arrests a day. Tactics included roadblocks, observation of open-air drug markets, "reverse buy" sell-and-bust by undercover officers, and seizure of cars.

Repeat Call Address Policing (REAP) Experiment, Minneapolis. A special unit of five police officers attempted to reduce calls for service from 125 residential addresses by increasing their presence with landlords and tenants. This short-term targeting of resources led to a 15-percent drop in calls from these addresses, compared to 125 control addresses.

Nashville, Tennessee, patrol experiment. A sharp increase in moving patrol at speeds under twenty miles per hour in four high-crime neighborhoods netted a measurable decrease in Part I Index crime during two short crackdowns (eleven days and fifteen days).

Disorder crackdown in Washington, D.C. Massive publicity accompanied a crackdown on illegal parking and disorder that was attracting street crime to the Georgetown area of the city. Police raised their weekend manpower 30 percent and installed a trailer at a key intersection to book arrestees.

New York City subway crackdown. This massive crackdown involved increasing the number of police officers from 1,200 to 3,100, virtually guaranteeing an officer for every train and every station. Crime fell during the first two years of the crackdown but rose again during the following six years.

Source: Sherman, Lawrence W. *Police Crackdowns*. Washington, D.C.: National Institute of Justice Research in Action, March/April 1990.

ASSESSMENT

The current literature on community-oriented policing often cites examples of strategic-oriented policing as being the sole method for implementing this concept. The literature details various implementations of directed, aggressive, and saturation patrols, and shows that it has a positive result in reducing crime rates, order maintenance problems, and the fear of community members. Whether it has been used to control drug problems (Younce 1992) or to deal with the ever-increasing problem of gangs (Bassett 1993), strategic policing has been found to be a well-regarded policing technique by the police administration, the police officers, and the community. However, despite the immediate benefits of this component of community-oriented policing, there are several problems that must be addressed.

There are essentially three problems with the implementation of strategic policing: The issue of the duration of success for these programs, the effect strategic policing has on the community, and the perception that this component in and of itself is community-oriented policing. The first issue is the fact that although the majority of police "crackdowns" in the literature demonstrated a strong deterrent effect on crime, it is important to focus in on the fact that this effect was only found to be temporary (Sherman 1990a, 1990b). In the New York study, crime rates rose after the initial two-year period, and continued to do so for the next six years (Sherman 1990a, 1990b). The research demonstrates this reduction in the initial effect of strategic policing, especially in the use of saturation patrols, after a certain time period is not uncommon. As Lawrence Sherman pointed out, the effects of the police saturation patrols "began to decay after a short period, sometimes despite continued dosage of police presence or even increased dosage of police sanctions" (Sherman 1990b). This issue must be examined or, in the long term, the attitudes toward the effectiveness of these programs will diminish and future implementation is highly unlikely.

Another problem that can arise is the perception that these strategic policing methods can exact on the public's attitude toward the police. As Herman Goldstein (1990, 132) explains "too often they constitute the only response that the police make to a worsening situation—reflecting a narrowly limited concept of what the police can do and, more generally, a lack of imagination and initiative." This can in turn lead to resentment or direct hostility toward the police from residents in minority areas, because they often feel they are the true targets of these forms of patrol tactics, which can spark an unnecessary fire (Siegel 1995; Sherman 1986). The goal of the patrols utilized in strategic policing would then be negated by this reaction, because the overall goal is that of fostering a better relationship with the community, not alienating them from the police. As George L. Kelling (1985, 307) summarizes, "these are short-term, unwise, and potentially dangerous approaches. They continue to rely on remote professional and centralized political authority. Moreover, they fail to recognize the inherent normative pluralism of communities and neighborhoods and will likely be perceived as police acting against, rather than on behalf of, localities."

Officer James Olsen of the City of Port St. Lucie Police Department, Florida, demonstrates some of the Special Response Team's (SRT) equipment during a citizen's Police Academy. (Courtesy of City of Port St. Lucie Police Dept., City of Port St. Lucie, Florida.)

The final problem is the fact that many of these strategic policing strategies are implemented under the auspices of community-oriented policing. The concept becomes a new method of utilizing police "crackdowns" on the criminal and order maintenance problems in the community, of which the only difference in regard to past policing methods is the fact the community at large may support this technique. There is no regard for the fact that this is a short-term solution to a long-term problem, which, as the literature has proven, is not successful in the long term.

The community-oriented policing model takes all of these problems into consideration and responds to them when the entire concept is implemented. This model recognizes the fact that displacing or temporarily eliminating the criminal element or order maintenance problems with these techniques will only work while they are in effect. Once the police scale back, the problem itself creeps back. Remove the police entirely, and the element returns in full force.

COP IN ACTION

CRACKING DOWN ON CRACK

In the spring of 1995, fifteen crack houses were destroyed in Indianapolis during a two-day demolition project. City officials hope to destroy 200 abandoned houses used for dealing crack. The demolition is part of Indianapolis' new "Crackdown on Crack" campaign, a multifaceted approach to fighting crack cocaine in the nation's twelfth largest city. The mass demolition of crack houses was intended not only as a way to reduce crime at targeted locations, but also as a way to send a powerful message. The dealers would be somewhere nearby as bulldozers throughout the city were rumbling over crack houses. The "customers" would see their supply sites in ruins.

Indianapolis Mayor Stephen Goldsmith took the controls of a bulldozer for the first bash of the mass crack demolition. Goldsmith, a former prosecutor, said police had responded to 3,088 calls in areas immediately surrounding the crack houses targeted for demolition. "These abandoned structures are the home of crack cocaine in Indianapolis," Goldsmith said. "We can no longer tolerate their presence in our community. They endanger the lives of neighborhood residents, public safety officers, and passersby."

Source: Adapted with permission from Begovich, Ray. "Cracking Down on Crack." *Law and Order*. October 1995, 80–81.

Under community-oriented policing, the strategic-oriented policing component is only implemented as a short-term solution until long-term solutions, through neighborhood-oriented policing and problem-oriented policing, can be developed. The community can have more freedom for decision making and implementation if the elements they are to address have been removed from the community or temporarily driven underground. This allows time to get certain programs established in the community, for criminal and civil court hearings to be heard, and for a sense of community pride to return to those law-abiding members of the community. Once the police presence is reduced by removing the saturation and aggressive patrols, as the criminal element returns, they find a different community than the one they left. In turn, the goal is for the new community and the police to prevent the returning element from thriving again.

CONCLUSION

Strategic-oriented policing is then the catalyst for all other community-oriented policing programs. Implementing the saturation and aggressive patrol tactics in

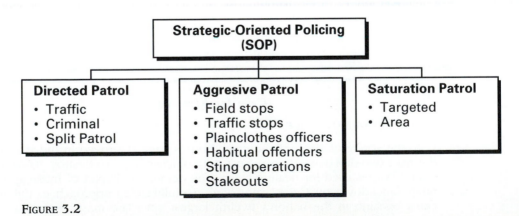

FIGURE 3.2

high-crime areas displaces the criminal element through their deterrent effects. This allows the community to establish innovative programs within the community that will not tolerate the return of the criminal or order maintenance problems. These programs must be put in place in order for the community to retain its social control of happenings and events within that same community. Neighborhood-oriented policing and problem-oriented policing are those programs that help the community analyze, create, and implement these programs that address the specific needs of the community. These methods will be described in the following two chapters and their relationship with each other is discussed in chapter six. It is only with this complete implementation of the three components that community-oriented policing can be truly implemented within a community and subsequently evaluated on these merits.

REFERENCES

Bassett, Adele. "Community-Oriented Gang Control." *The Police Chief,* February 1993, 20–23.

Boydstun, John E. *San Diego Field Interrogations: Final Report.* Washington, D.C.: The Police Foundation, 1975.

Cole, George F. *The American System of Criminal Justice.* Belmont, CA.: Wadsworth Publishing Company, 1995.

Cordner, Gary W. "The Effects of Directed Patrol: A Natural Quasi-Experiment in Pontiac." In *Contemporary Issues in Law Enforcement.* ed. by James J. Fyfe. Beverly Hills: Sage Publications, 1981: 242–261.

Cordner, Gary W. and Robert C. Trojanowicz. "Patrol." In *What Works in Policing? Operation and Administration Examined.* ed. Gary W. Cordner and Donna C. Hale. Cincinnati: Anderson Publishing, 1992.

Fleissner, Dan, Nicholas Fedan, David Klinger, and Ezra Stotland. "Community Policing in Seattle: A Model Partnership Between Citizens and Police." In *National Institute of Justice: Research in Brief.* Washington, D.C.: National Institute of Justice, August 1992.

Goldstein, Herman. *Problem-Oriented Policing.* New York: McGraw Hill Publishing Co., 1990.

Greenburg, Reuben and Arthur Gordon. *Let's Take Back Our Streets!* Chicago: Contemporary Books, Inc., 1989.

Kelling, George L. "Order Maintenance, the Quality of Urban Life, and Police: A Line of Argument." *Police Leadership In America.* ed. William A. Geller. New York: American Bar Foundation, 1985.

————. "Police and Communities: the Quiet Revolution." *Perspectives on Policing.* No. 1. Washington, D.C.: U.S. Department of Justice June, 1988.

Martin, Susan E. "Policing Career Criminal: An Examination of an Innovative Crime Control Program." *Journal of Criminal Law and Criminology* 77, (Winter 1986): 1159–1182.

Martin, Susan E. and Lawrence W. Sherman. "Selective Apprehension: A Police Strategy for Repeat Offenders." *Criminology* 24, (February 1986): 155–173.

Mastrofski, Stephen D. "Community Policing As Reform: A Cautionary Tale." In *Community Policing: Rhetoric or Reality.* ed. Jack R. Greene and Stephen D. Mastrofski. New York: Praegar Publishers, 1988: 47–67.

Moore, Mark H. and Robert C. Trojanowicz. "Corporate Strategies for Policing." *Perspectives on Policing.* Washington, D.C.: National Institute of Justice, November, 1988.

Roneck, Dennis and Pamela Maier. "Bars, Blocks, and Crime Revisited: Linking the Theory of Routine Activities to the Empiricism of 'Hot Spots.'" *Criminology* 29, 1991: 725–753.

Sampson, Robert and Jacqueline Cohen. "Deterrent Effects of the Police on Crime: A Replication and Theoretical Extension." *Law and Society Review* 22, 1988: 163–191.

Sherman, Lawrence. "Policing Communities: What Works." In *Crime and Justice: A Review of Research*. vol. 8. ed. A.J. Reiss and Michael Tonry. Chicago: University of Chicago Press, 1986: 366–379.

————. "Police Crackdowns." *National Institute of Justice Reports,* March/April, 1990a.

————. "Police Crackdowns: Initial and Residual Deterrence." In *Crime and Justice: A Review of Research*. vol. 12. Edited by Michael Tonry and Norval Morris. Chicago: University of Chicago Press, 1990b: 1–48.

Siegel, Larry. *Criminology*. 5th ed. St. Paul: West Publishing Company, 1995.

Tien, James M. and Thomas F. Rich. "The Hartford COMPASS Program: Experiences With a Weed and Seed-Related Program." In *The Challenge of Community Policing: Testing the Promises*. ed. Dennis P. Rosenbaum. Thousand Oaks, CA: SAGE Publications Inc., 1994.

Tien, James M., James W. Simon, and Richard C. Larson. *An Alternative Approach in Police Patrol: The Wilmington Split-Force Experiment*. Cambridge, MA: Public Systems Evaluation, 1977.

Warren, J.W., M.L. Forst, and M. M. Estrella. "Directed Patrol: An Experiment That Worked." *The Police Chief,* July 1979, 48–49.

Williams, Hubert. "Retrenchment, the Constitution, and Policing." In *Police Leadership in America*. ed. William A. Geller. Chicago: American Bar Foundation, 1985.

Williams, Hubert and Antony M. Pate. "Returning to First Principles: Reducing the Fear of Crime in Newark." *Crime & Delinquency* 33, No. 1 (January 1987): 53–70.

Wilson, James Q. "Just Take Away Their Guns." *The New York Times Sunday Magazine,* March 20, 1994: p. 47.

Wilson, James Q. and Barbara Boland. "The Effect of Police on Crime." *Law and Society Review*. 12, 1978: 367–384.

————. *The Effects of Police on Crime*. Washington, D.C.: U.S. Government Printing Office, 1979

Wilson, James Q. and George L. Kelling. "Making Neighborhoods Safe." *The Atlantic Monthly*. February 1989, 46–52.

Younce, Thomas C. "'Broken Window' Stops Drug Sales." *Law & Order,* April 1992, 67–70.

Zimmer, Lynn. "Proactive Policing Against Street-Level Drug Trafficking." *American Journal of Police,* 9, 1990: 43–65.

CHAPTER 4

Neighborhood-Oriented Policing

Crime and bad lives are the measure of a State's failure, all crime in the end is the crime of the community.

-H.G. Wells-

The second component of community-oriented policing is neighborhood-oriented policing. This component entails the interaction of police and all community members to reduce crime and the fear of crime through indigenous proactive programs. It is an integration of the police and the community working together, opening up the lines of communication and establishing responses to the criminal and social problems in a community. It is through this cooperative effort that the goals of reducing crime and reducing the fear of crime can be achieved.

The literature often details this component as the core of community policing or often as being the entire and sole concept of community-oriented

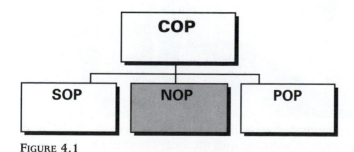

FIGURE 4.1

75

policing (e.g., Cole 1995; Moore and Trojanowicz 1988; Schmalleger 1995; Skogan 1994). The practitioners implementing neighborhood-oriented programs often refer to these programs in a general sense as community-oriented policing as well (e.g., Bloom 1992; Fleissner et al. 1992; Hamilton 1993; Perez 1993). However, despite the varying use of the term *neighborhood-oriented policing*, all are focused on the integration of the police and the community. Although this is the overall goal of community-oriented policing, when discussing neighborhood-oriented policing the focus should be on the various types of patrols and programs that bring the community and the police together.

As revealed in the chapter on the history of community-oriented policing, the past model of policing known as police–community relations was concerned with establishing police units to address various groups and concerns within the community. A prime example is the importance of children in any community and the establishment under police–community relations of special juvenile or youth units to work with children both in and out of the schools. However, it is imperative that we remember the police officers assigned to these units were dedicated solely to this function and this function alone.

Under the neighborhood-oriented policing component of community-oriented policing, every police officer should be involved in some form or fashion in establishing relations with the community. The mentality that because a police officer is not assigned to the juvenile section of the police department, he or she should not have to deal with juveniles, is a mentality that must be dismissed in order for neighborhood-oriented policing techniques to be successful.

Sgt. Scott D. Morgan of the Parkersburg Police Department, Parkersburg, West Virginia, working with the local community from the DARE trailer at the Annual Homecoming Event. (Courtesy of the Parkersburg Police Dept., Parkersburg, West Virginia.)

In the same way, the community must give up the mentality that crime fighting and even order maintenance is a police officer's job and of no concern to them. Police officers easily recognize they have an impossible job, because they cannot be everywhere at once. The common citizen recognizes this fact as well in the oft-heard statement, "There's never a cop around when you need one." However, this mentality must change. The statement is always heard in a negative sense. However, if the citizen recognizes that there is never a cop around when you need one because there are so few officers and they legitimately cannot be everywhere at once, then it is the citizen's responsibility to assist the police and make them aware of situations that impact on the community in both criminal and order maintenance areas.

Changing the mentality of the police and the community and bringing them together to address these issues is the key to a successful neighborhood-oriented policing program. The success also depends largely on the participation of the entire neighborhood or community and not just segments. Those institutions that we find in any community include the family, schools, churches, retail establishments, neighborhood associations, professionals such as doctors, dentists, and lawyers, as well as social/community groups such as the Elks, local historical societies, and the Veterans of Foreign Wars. It is important that all of these institutions pull their resources together and participate in the neighborhood-oriented policing programs and help develop the bonds between the police and the community at large.

In order to accomplish a reduction in crime and the fear of crime, the neighborhood must create some form of committee or coalition that consists of a cross section of the neighborhood. It should consist of both the formal leadership, informal leadership, and the "average" citizen in the neighborhood. This committee must then become the representatives of the community and bring to the attention of all the members what problems exist in the neighborhoods both on a criminal and order maintenance level. They must prioritize these concerns and develop courses of actions that will abolish the problem or at a minimum alleviate some of the symptoms. These problems must then be brought to the attention of the police, along with the solutions to the problems, and those programs that are viable should then be implemented by both the police and the neighborhoods.

"CRIME FILES:

NEIGHBORHOOD SAFETY—PART 34

This edition of the "Crime Files," hosted by James Q. Wilson, features Lawrence W. Sherman, University of Maryland; Lucy Gerold, Director of Minneapolis Community Crime Prevention; and C. Robin Kirk, Houston Police Department. The discussion revolves around the effectiveness of neighborhood-oriented policing strategies.

INITIATING NEIGHBORHOOD-ORIENTED POLICING

It is here that a subtle issue arises that can have a major impact on the success of not only neighborhood-oriented policing, but the overall concept of community-oriented policing as well. The issue arises as to who implements these programs and policies in addressing criminal and order maintenance concerns. If the community does not have a committee in place or some system for addressing the local concerns, then neighborhood-oriented policing programs must be initiated by the police. The police must then do everything possible to draw in the support of the community in assisting them and supporting the programs implemented. The police become the catalyst for a "community" program and must lead members of the neighborhood down the road to a fully implemented concept of community-oriented policing.

If the community has some form of system in place, then it becomes possible to work together with the police and create programs and policies initiated by both the police and the neighborhood. These programs are generally more oriented on what the community desires of its police and are more in line with the community concept. However, there will always be a problem with power and determining who is in power and who has more power when the community and the police disagree on a course of action.

In order for neighborhood-oriented policing to be fully implemented and operational, it should, in actuality, be initiated solely by the community or neighborhood. The community should no longer be viewed as simply a political ally or functional partner in fighting crime, but rather as the head of an institution for which the police work, namely the community. The police have powers to enforce laws, use deadly force, and with reasonable suspicion can invade our lives; therefore, community supervision must be in place and ultimately, the police should be run by the community. Just as the founding fathers placed the United States military under civilian control, so should the police be under civilian control. This is not to say that the police have no input into the decisions the neighborhood coalition makes or into the programs they wish to see implemented, only that they are initiated primarily by the neighborhood.

Herein lies one fundamental problem with the concept of community-oriented policing. Under the concept of neighborhood-oriented policing, it is the neighborhood that makes the decisions. The same revolves around all of the tenets of community-oriented policing. Once these programs are fully functional and have become a part of the local community's method of policing, then it is the community and the neighborhood that make the decisions for what is of concern and what is not a concern on the part of the police. These citizens decide where the police place their resources, which high crime areas should be targeted, and in many cases how they will be targeted. The citizens essentially become one of the two leaders of the police. The leadership that determines the overall mission of the police and the programs that should be implemented is the community. The leadership that carries out the mission and sees to the day-to-day operations is the police chief. It is a concept of leadership that works and has worked in large institutions.

Captain David Smith of the Cincinnati Police Department, Cincinnati, Ohio, instructs local citizens participating in the Cincinnati Police Division's Citizen's Police Academy. (Courtesy of Cincinnati Police Division, Cincinnati, Ohio.)

A simple and clearcut example of this concept can be found in the United States Army. One of the smallest collections of personnel in the military that resembles a small neighborhood is the platoon. The platoon generally consists of three to four squads of approximately ten soldiers each. The leadership of the platoon is handled by the platoon leader and the platoon sergeant. The platoon leader is an officer, generally with the rank of lieutenant. The platoon sergeant is a non-commissioned officer and generally holds the rank of sergeant first class. Both are the leaders of this small neighborhood, but each has fundamentally different responsibilities, roles, and functions in this setting. The platoon leader is what the military classifies as an instrumental leader whose chief responsibility is helping to define the job or task at hand and how best to accomplish this task. The platoon sergeant is the expressive leader and his responsibility is to maintain unit cohesion and insure that the platoon has everything it needs to accomplish the task, both physically and mentally.

In the concept of community-oriented policing and predominantly in the area of neighborhood-oriented policing, the community must take on the role of the instrumental leader. The community and neighborhoods must determine what the job, roles, and responsibilities of the police should be and determine how they could best do their job. Under neighborhood-oriented policing, that may consist of determining if bike patrols or foot patrols would be of any benefit to the area as well as the type of programs that should be implemented to lower crime and create better living conditions for all the members of the community.

Using the army analogy, the police chief is the expressive leader, responsible for the police officers' welfare and instilling a sense of unit cohesion to create a police force that is capable of carrying out the tasks or jobs determined by the community. The police chief, in this same line, insures that the police are highly trained, well educated, and well equipped for the variety of missions that may be dictated by the instrumental leader. The police chief, however, is not relegated to only following orders, but is responsible for challenging those tasks which are not feasible for the department, or police officers, to conduct; he is responsible for becoming an advocate not only for the police, but for the community as well; and he must set the example for the police department, and by default, for the entire community.

Through this cooperative effort, the concept of neighborhood-oriented policing can be successful in both areas of order maintenance and crime reduction. The citizens of the local community have a clear and established role in the policing of the neighborhood by directing where police resources should be dedicated through the concerns of those living in the neighborhoods. This empowerment helps citizens become more concerned for their neighborhoods, causing them to work closer with the police and assisting them in restoring order and in the arrest and prosecution of criminals.

EXAMPLES OF NEIGHBORHOOD-ORIENTED POLICING

Reducing crime in Norfolk, Virginia   This city has cut homicides by more than 10 percent in each of the last three years and, even more impressive, has reduced overall crime rates citywide by 26 percent and in some neighborhoods by as much as 40 percent. A good share of the credit goes to Police-Assisted Community Enforcement (PACE), a crime prevention initiative that works neighborhood by neighborhood in conjunction with teams of social, health, and family services agencies (the Family Assistance Services Team, or FAST) and public works and environmental agencies (Neighborhood Environmental Assistance Team, or NEAT) to cut through red tape and help residents reclaim their neighborhoods.

Campaigning against youth violence in Minnesota   The Minnesota Crime Prevention Officers' Association enlisted the support of families, public officials, and forty-five statewide and local organizations, including schools and churches, to wage a campaign against youth violence. Actions ranged from encouraging children and parents to turn off violent television shows to providing classroom training in violence prevention.

Providing safe havens after school in Trenton, New Jersey   A partnership of schools, parents, city leaders, and others led to a Safe Haven program in which the schools in the neighborhood became multipurpose centers after school hours for youth activities including sports, crafts, and tutoring. Children have flocked to the centers as a positive alternative to being at home alone after school or being at risk on the streets.

Helping parents get drug treatment in Ohio A congregation was the focus for efforts to reach addicted parents and their children. Tutoring for children, courtesy of the local college, courses on black history taught by church members, and recreational activities helped the spirits and self-esteem of the children rise. The addicted parents were counseled and supported by church members both during and after treatment. The majority of the parents are now holding steady jobs and reaching out to help others.

Preventing campus crime in Columbus, Ohio Crime near a college campus became an opportunity for a partnership formed by the city of Columbus, the state of Ohio, Ohio State University, the Franklin County Sheriff, and the Columbus Police Department. The Community Crime Patrol puts two-person, radio-equipped teams of observers into the neighborhoods near the campus during potential high-crime hours. A number of these paid, part-time observers are college students interested in careers in law enforcement.

Source: National Crime Prevention Council. *Working as Partners with Community Groups.* Washington, D.C.: Bureau of Justice Assistance, September 1994.

NEIGHBORHOOD-ORIENTED POLICING PROGRAMS

There are essentially five types of neighborhood-oriented policing programs. These programs include:

1) community patrols;
2) community crime prevention;
3) communication programs;
4) community social control programs; and
5) problem-oriented policing.

The last program is almost always included under community-oriented policing and is essentially a neighborhood-oriented policing program as it is primarily a part of the neighborhood coalition decision-making process. However, it can also stand alone as has been previously discussed and will be reviewed in the next chapter. Therefore, our concern for the rest of this chapter will be the first four types of programs under this component of community-oriented policing.

These four programs are the practitioner's method of implementing neighborhood-oriented policing. Each program serves a different purpose in addressing the criminal and order maintenance issues of a particular community. The types of programs are general in what they set out to accomplish and the actual programs listed are by no means inclusive. As each neighborhood is different, so too should the programs utilized be different. And all of the programs should be community-driven with the assistance of the community coalition and the police.

COMMUNITY PATROLS

Community patrols are those types of police patrols that create a strong police presence and allow the police to be more accessible to the public. Although the police cannot be everywhere at once, community patrols allow them to be in areas of high traffic and where they are generally most needed. They often serve a specific purpose with their presence or they may be available for any type of citizen request or complaint. Regardless, the main concern for community patrols is high visibility.

Perhaps the most well-known community patrol is the use of foot patrols. Foot patrols have not only come to symbolize community-oriented policing, but in and of themselves have a long and colorful history. The cop on the beat was an early American icon which had grown out of the early watch system. With the advent of automobiles, the police left the limitations of foot patrols behind for the more efficient and faster response time automobiles afforded. The foot patrol became almost totally extinct by the 1960s, but was occasionally brought back by some police departments under special programs. By the 1980s, the foot patrol had come to represent a change in the way police performed their duties and subsequently became the shining star of community-oriented policing.

Although foot patrols are easily recognizable under community-oriented policing, they are not the sole program for determining whether or not a police department has implemented community-oriented policing. As foot patrols are obviously best established in high-density commercial and residential areas with large populations, it is equally obvious that they would not be feasible or practical in a rural setting. Again, each neighborhood is unique in its problems and must design programs accordingly.

Those cities that have not only implemented foot patrols under the auspices of community-oriented policing, but have studied its effects as well, have all shown positive signs for this type of patrol (See Greene and Taylor 1988; Skogan 1994; Wycoff 1988). The literature shows strong evidence that the public feels safer when foot patrols are implemented; the level of fear decreases and citizen satisfaction with the police increases (Kelling 1987). There is also additional evidence that when the foot patrols are removed from a neighborhood, regardless of the reason, the community refuses to allow them to leave (Geller 1991, 202). And, not only are foot patrols received well by the neighborhoods, they are received well by the police officers who work the patrols. Officers have a greater appreciation of the neighborhoods they patrol and they show greater job satisfaction and higher morale (Kelling 1987).

The only issue on foot patrols currently debated is whether or not they are successful at reducing the actual numbers of crimes. There is little to no dispute that foot patrols reduce fear, even when based solely on anecdotal evidence; however, in some studies, foot patrols show no affect on crime rates (Kelling 1987). One study showed significant decreases in the crime rates in a variety of areas that were targeted with foot patrols; however, it must be kept in mind that the study was based solely on police department data

(Trojanowicz 1986). And some actually argue, through anecdotal evidence again, that crime rates actually increase because the police are spread far too thin and do not have the fast response times they have in the automobile.

Another form of community patrol similar to the foot patrol, but slightly more mobile, is the bike patrol. Placing police officers on bicycles and sending them on patrol has increased as a mode of getting police officers out of motor vehicles, but allowing them to remain somewhat mobile. Arlington County Police Department in Arlington, Virginia, implemented this program in the early 1990s. The department took those officers assigned to the juvenile division who work in the schools and essentially have no job during the summer months, and placed them on mountain bikes. The officers generally patrol high-density areas, housing projects, and bike paths. The community and police response to these patrols has been very similar to those demonstrated in the studies of foot patrols.

Additional methods of community patrol include police officers patrolling on horseback, such as those conducted in New Orleans during Mardi Gras. These patrols allow the police to see from above the crowds and allow citizens to be able to quickly pick out the police. Motorcycle patrols have also increased with the advent of community-oriented policing, despite the fact they have existed in most police departments for several decades.

Other successful types of community patrols are police ministations or storefronts in a variety of settings. One form of the police substation is to utilize

"Skyway Community Resource Center: Volunteer Staffed, Community Funded." St. Petersburg, Florida. (Courtesy of St. Petersburg Police Dept., St. Petersburg, Florida.)

a storefront in a business/retail area or an apartment/community center in a residential area. The police utilize this as a simple office where the public may make incident reports, report or discuss criminal and order maintenance issues, or it may be utilized for meetings, neighborhood programs, and as a place for both adults and children to leave their homes for a short respite in a safe environment. The literature has shown these to be viable types of community patrols as the substations are "associated with reductions in fear of personal victimization, lowered perceptions of the amounts of personal and property crime in the area, and lowered perceptions of the amount of social disorder in the area" (Brown and Wycoff 1987, 84). Once again, this form of community patrol may or may not reduce the numbers of actual crimes, but it changes the perceptions of crime on the part of the public and increases the accessibility and contact with the police officers.

COP IN ACTION

THE EAST DALLAS POLICE STOREFRONT

The East Dallas Storefront is one of five stations in the central patrol division. It covers eight square miles just outside of the central business district in a unique neighborhood—a mixture of Asians, Hispanics, Blacks, and Anglos, who live in everything from a public housing project to rundown apartment buildings to tidy blue-collar homes to mansions worth hundreds of thousands of dollars. The staff of four sworn officers and three civilian employees handles everything from bike patrols to community liaisons to after-school sports programs to traditional law enforcement. It has been a success both in terms of community relations and reduced crime almost from its inception in 1985.

The officers and civilians assigned to the storefront do not stay in their cars or behind their desks, hidden from the public. They patrol on bikes. They speak in schools. They speak to church groups. They offer the storefront building for community meetings. Several community-oriented functions are assigned to the storefront, including central patrol's crime prevention unit and its liaison to the city's gay and lesbian community. Again, these are outreach programs, where the officers are active among neighborhood residents. In addition, a separate mobile unit, commanded by a sergeant and with its own staff, is based at the storefront.

The storefront doesn't operate on a regular eight-hour shift schedule. It's open from 7 A.M. to 7 P.M., making it easier for neighborhood residents to stop by. Also, there is usually someone at the storefront on duty who can speak one of the neighborhood's languages, English, Spanish, or Cambodian.

Among the non-traditional functions embraced by the storefront:

- Social services. Although this is not as important as it was when the storefront opened, officers and staff still handle requests for food, clothing, translation services, and the like. They also refer requests to the proper agencies.

- Fingerprinting. The storefront may be the only place in the Dallas metropolitan area that still fingerprints immigrants, who need the procedure as part of the naturalization process.

- Meeting rooms. Community groups are welcome at the storefront, even at night. A number of programs, including citizenship classes and after-school tutoring, are held there.

- Youth activities.

Source: Adapted with permission from Siegel, Jeff. "The East Dallas Police Storefront." *Law and Order*, May 1995, 53–55.

Another variation of the police substation has begun cropping up in malls across the United States. From Prince William County, Virginia to the CNN Center in Atlanta to Roswell, New Mexico; police substations located in local malls have created an additional avenue of accessibility to the police by the citizen. They have also helped decrease the fear of crime on the part of the patrons. Regardless of where the substations have been placed, the overall concept has demonstrated to be very successful in all of the cities in which it has been implemented (Skogan 1994).

COP IN ACTION

ROPE: THE RESIDENT OFFICER PROGRAM OF ELGIN

If you can't beat 'em, join 'em

This phrase could sum up the Resident Officer Program of Elgin (ROPE), a program instituted in Elgin, Illinois, where officers live and work in a problem neighborhood. Together with their neighbors, they are helping the area get back on its feet. The program works proactively to eliminate crime and other local problems at their roots by improving the status of life in a neighborhood to the degree that crime and related problems are not produced.

ROPE officers are unique in that they work and reside in a specific neighborhood, dealing only with problems affecting their neighborhood and its residents. Living in donated or subsidized homes or apartments, ROPE officers normally work an eight-hour day, but for all practical purposes are on twenty-four-hour call.

The city provides ROPE officers and their families (many are bachelors) with a residence, utilities (not including long distance phone calls), a bicycle and squad car for patrol, answering machine, and whatever expenses are necessary for special needs in the neighborhood. In return, the officers must meet every resident in their areas, work with tenant and neighborhood groups and attend their meetings, and oversee newsletters that are disseminated to residents regularly, in addition to interacting with the residents to learn their concerns and then working to alleviate them.

The program's effectiveness can be seen by the change in answers to a survey distributed to one area's residents. When ROPE first started in their neighborhood, a questionnaire asked what problems concerned the residents. "Drugs and gangs" were the major problems then. Two years later, the same residents answered another survey with "loud stereos and speeding cars."

Source: Adapted with permission from Schmitt, Sheila. "ROPE: The Resident Officer Program of Elgin." *Law and Order*, May 1995, 52, 56–58.

COMMUNITY CRIME PREVENTION

Community crime prevention programs are an important part of neighborhood-oriented policing, despite the fact many of the programs have been around since the mid- to late-1960s. A large portion of these programs were born out of the police–community relations era and have seen some modifications in the way they are presented, but for all intents and purposes, they are the same programs. The main goal or focus in community crime prevention is reaching out to those institutions, groups, and individuals that may be targets of crime or future perpetrators of crime and preventing either of these from occurring. It also includes the awareness and markings of those objects that are potential targets for crime. In most of the community crime prevention programs, the police become the facilitators of the programs, but the community must at a minimum participate in order for the programs to remain viable and have any chance at success.

The primary community crime prevention programs are Block Watch (Neighborhood Watch, Apartment Watch, etc.), Operation ID, and home security surveys. These, according to Feins (1983), are known as the "Big Three." Widespread use of these three programs across the United States by a majority of police departments, positive opinion on the part of the communities, and evidence that demonstrates these programs have reduced crime and assisted in solving crimes have contributed to these three programs being labeled as the most successful in community crime prevention.

Neighborhood Watch programs, depending upon where one lives, will have a variety of names. Some of the names used are Block Watch, Crime Watch, and Community Alert, just to name a few. However, all of these programs have one thing in common and that is to have neighbors watch out for each other, to be alert to day-to-day happenings in the neighborhood, and to call the police when anything suspicious occurs (Garofalo and McLeod 1988). This is generally accomplished by meetings with members of the community, usually once a month or once a quarter, where local crime problems are addressed, crime prevention strategies are shared, and planning for community patrols or surveillance is arranged (Rosenbaum 1987, 104). This allows for not only a chance to share information and make plans, but it also allows for community contact and enhances the feelings of community commitment. It provides some feeling of empowerment, thereby allowing for a stronger sense of social control.

COP IN ACTION

RESTAURANTS AS POLICE OUTPOSTS

Through a privately funded program offered by a popular fast-food restaurant chain, Phoenix area police officers now have seventy telephone-equipped "substations" where they can interview subjects, conduct follow-up investigations, and dictate reports to their precinct stations. The specially designated "law enforcement booths" are located in the dining rooms of Jack in the Box® restaurants within the greater Phoenix area.

The program, begun early in 1993, was the result of several meetings between Sergeant Bill Schemers of the Phoenix Police Department and Ed Dubiel, area manager for Jack in the Box, a division of Foodmaker, Inc. With concerns such as officer safety, noisy or unavailable telephone booths, and the fact that officers can sometimes spend over an hour for each report during a ten-hour shift, Jack in the Box management decided to outfit two restaurants as test sites for the police booth program. One of the sites was in the roughest patrol beat—an intersection where drug deals, shootings, and random gang violence were regular occurrences in and around the twenty-four-hour restaurant.

"Shortly after officers began using the police booths, we noticed that the type of people coming to the locations was changing," Dubiel said. "Troublemakers and other suspicious types were moving on, and neighborhood families, feeling more secure, began to come in for meals." By November 1994, the program had expanded to include all seventy of the Phoenix area locations, as well as Jack in the Boxes in nearby jurisdictions.

The program is still too new to pinpoint a direct impact on crime at Jack in the Box locations, but Dubiel believes that the program is developing into an obvious crime deterrent in and around his restaurants. "I haven't been getting as many late at night 'problem calls' from my managers," Dubiel said. Dubiel added that his office has received positive support for the program from community groups and local families, including the parents of neighborhood teenagers who eat at the restaurants or work for Jack in the Box.

Source: Adapted with permission from Bragg, Mike. "Restaurants as Police Outposts." *Law and Order*, October 1995, 77–78.

These programs are generally established by the police in the initial formation of the program; however, they are primarily a community program and must be run by the community, not dictated by the police. This, however, is not to say that once they are up and running, the police should no longer be involved. As research has clearly demonstrated, Neighborhood Watch programs occasionally need some guidance and sometimes a structure that is facilitated by the police (Garofalo and McLeod 1988; Rosenbaum 1987; Rosenbaum and Lurigio 1994). As with most community prevention programs the police may establish the program, but it is the community that must at least participate in, if not manage, these programs in order for them to be successful.

The other two programs under the "Big Three" are Operation ID and home security surveys. Operation ID is the program where a citizen's property is engraved for future identification in the event it is stolen. In some police departments, the police officer will actually respond to a requesting citizen's home and perform the engraving with a scribe. In other departments the scribe can be checked out by local citizens for them to conduct their own engraving. The general recommendation is the owner engrave the state's abbreviation followed by his or her social security number for the easiest identification. This number can then be entered into the local and state computer as well as the National Crime Information Center (NCIC) when the owner's property is stolen. There is some evidence that citizens who do utilize this program stand a greater chance of not being victimized and recovering their property in the event it is stolen (Geller 1991, 118).

The final program of the "Big Three" is the use of home security surveys. Police departments across the United States often offer this service to the victim of a crime after it is too late. The police should advertise this service or notify

A Phoenix Police Department, Phoenix, Arizona Neighborhood Patrol officer educates a resident on home security. (Courtesy of the Phoenix Police Dept., Phoenix, Arizona, and Mr. Bob Rink.)

citizens through the local government that this service is available free of charge. The police will then dispatch an officer upon request with a checklist on crime prevention techniques that can be utilized inside and outside the home in order to harden the target. The home security survey should be tailored to the needs of the citizen and should be conducted in a positive manner.

Another community crime prevention program that has gained nationwide attention and is viewed as a very favorable program by the public is Drug Abuse Resistance Education or DARE. First conducted under the leadership of Chief Daryl Gates of the Los Angeles Police Department in 1983, the DARE program has become a nationwide program attempting to prevent the children of today from becoming the drug users and drug dealers of tomorrow. The DARE program achieves this by training veteran police officers to teach a structured, sequential curriculum in the schools (Bureau of Justice Assistance 1992). The program is seventeen weeks long and "uses a variety of techniques including lectures, exercises, audiovisual material, and role playing to teach students to say no to drugs" (Bureau of Justice Statistics 1992, 104). It is estimated that, as of 1991, nearly 10,000 police officers had been trained to teach in the DARE program and an estimated 5 million students participated in the program that year (Bureau of Justice Statistics 1992, 104 and 153).

Although the program presents an admirable crime prevention technique to our young children in a country plagued by drugs, the success of the program has not been as positive. A recent study conducted by Dennis P. Rosenbaum and co-workers (1994) found no statistical significance on the use of drugs or on attitudes and beliefs about drugs in a longitudinal study on children who had participated in the DARE program. Despite the overall data, there was the possibility that the program was effective with specific populations such as females, urban residents, and Hispanic students (Rosenbaum et al. 1994). Regardless of the actual effects, in looking at the intent of neighborhood-oriented policing and the category of community crime prevention, there still exists the unquantifiable elements of social control and order maintenance in which a community can benefit from these programs.

One program with demonstrated benefits to the community is the Outreach program. Primarily focused on reducing fear in the community, Outreach programs accomplish this by going door-to-door in a selected neighborhood to solicit information on crime, determine what the local problems are, and attempt to form a neighborhood coalition. The first police department to utilize and study this method of police–citizen contact was the Baltimore Police Department in what they called the Citizen-Oriented Police Enforcement (COPE) (Cordner 1988; Greene and Taylor 1988; and Skogan 1994). The COPE teams were able to determine what the citizens considered to be local problems and in some cases they discovered problems where they thought none existed, and in other cases they found content communities in places they had perceived as crime-ridden. In the end, with the information obtained from the citizens, the Baltimore Police Department was able to address those problems identified, succeed in reducing the fear of crime and was able to expand the capabilities of the program at the same time (Cordner 1988).

COP IN ACTION

OPERATION BLUE: COPS BECOME BANKERS TO AID ELDERLY CITIZENS

"I had never paid much attention to the elderly," Adrian L. "Windy" Miller admitted. "I was not aware how trusting they are. Many of them go to a nearby store or bank to cash their monthly checks, and walk away from the counter holding the cash in plain view." These actions, coupled with the somewhat slowed and helpless nature of the elderly, have made them prey for those in need of quick cash. "We had a ring of crooks preying on the elderly," Miller, a member of the San Antonio Police Officers' Association, said. San Antonio is one of Texas' most attractive tourist cities, providing dining, theme parks, outdoor Mexican markets, and the historic Alamo.

Nearly a decade ago, the officers answered a plea for help from the Alamo Area Council of Government, which operated the city's housing projects. In co-sponsorship with Frost National Bank, they began a program known as Operation Blue. The program is activated once a month, as officers gather to transport a temporary banking facility to the elderly who reside in the city-owned housing projects. The officers cash government checks for the residents and assist in purchasing money orders to pay bills.

While Operation Blue is a great service to San Antonio's senior citizens, Miller is quick to point out that the program is also rewarding to the officers involved. "We have become a form of family to them. They are excited to see us and visit with us. Real friendships have developed over the years. There's lots of teasing, and we have a lot of fun. There's a satisfaction in providing someone a little help," he said. "You're providing a potential victim with a safe environment. It gives me a good feeling."

The bank became a co-sponsor in the program as a public service and to show its commitment to the elderly and community. They have co-sponsored the program from its inception, without any financial benefit. The bank's participation actually bears some expense, with its staff preparing for the event and tallying up the results. After nine years the program works very smoothly. The seniors receive their government checks the third of each month; a date known to many crooks. That fact alone was making the seniors victims as the crooks knew where to look and when. The first working day following the third, the officers receive approximately $66,000 from a special account set up at the bank. Miller, who now coordinates the program, divides the cash up according to the needs of each location served. To that he adds a predetermined number of money orders.

The San Antonio Police Officer's Association guarantees the program and is responsible for any losses. The association makes no monetary profit from the system, but the rewards are great. "It's wonderful to see those smiling faces lined up when we get there," Miller said. "Both the elderly and officers really enjoy the program," Detective Corn said, "Its rewards are too great to count. It helps the elderly, cuts down on crime, and provides us with a feeling of doing something really positive for others."

Source: Adapted with permission from Worrell, Ann. "Operation Blue: Cops Become Bankers to Aid Elderly Citizens." *Law and Order*, December 1993, 27–30.

Other police departments that have attempted outreach programs have reported similar results. A fear reduction project, which was evaluated by the Police Foundation and conducted by the Houston Police Department and Newark Police Department, was successful in establishing a strong perception by the residents of restored social order and a more positive evaluation of the police (Brown and Wycoff 1987; Pate et al. 1986; Skogan 1994). And a study conducted by the Vera Institute on New York City's implementation of the Community Patrol Officer Program (CPOP) found that opening the lines of communication in this outreach manner resulted in enhanced community relations and problem solving of both order maintenance and criminal issues (See Farrell 1988; McElroy, Cosgrove, and Sadd 1993; Weisburd and McElroy 1988).

Additional community crime prevention programs can include, but are not limited to, various types of programs aimed at educating children on the values of respecting one's community and the law. These programs may include a police–school liaison, such as exists in Arlington County Police Department, where one police officer is assigned to each school in the county and that becomes the officer's "community." There are also youth camp outings, wilderness programs, and any sport program that integrates the police and the children. These programs serve to open the lines of communication with the children, teach the children that the police are also members of the community, and allows for a subtle form of social control. Other programs may consist of stolen property prevention, such as a registration drive for children to register their bicycles with the police; establishing a Combat Auto Theft (CAT) program where citizens sign a form saying they will not drive their car between the hours of midnight and 6 A.M., and if the car is seen on the road by the police, marked by a CAT sticker, it may be stopped; or the establishment of hotlines and cash rewards for stolen property.

The programs available under community crime prevention are too numerous to list, but they are only limited by the imagination of the police and the community. These programs, whether addressing the prevention of future victims and future criminals or the targets for possible crime, should be an important part of neighborhood-oriented policing as it promotes, assists, and is often the catalyst for a complete community-oriented policing program in a community.

COMMUNICATION PROGRAMS

Communication programs stand out from community patrols and community crime prevention because the main goal in these programs is to directly open the lines of communication between the police and the community. Although in the programs previously described in this chapter, there seems to be a consistent theme of communication, their goals are separate. Community patrols attempt to make the police more visible and accessible, community crime prevention programs attempt to do just that, prevent crime, while community control programs, which follow, attempt to establish a strong sense of social control within the community. Communication programs are just simple methods of communicating to the citizens who the police are, what they do, and how they can assist. They are what a police officer would consider "feel-good" programs.

A large portion of these programs also originated out of the police–community relations era, but have been updated to fill a community-oriented policing approach. The ride-along program where citizens can ride a shift with a police officer is perhaps the best program to open communications with the public. This is a golden opportunity for the police to demonstrate to citizens what a large part of their job entails and why they need the support of the public. The ride-along can also assist the police by advertising to specific segments of the community that may feel alienated by the police such as new immigrants or by requesting ride-alongs that speak another language to assist in translations.

Another communication program that was implemented at one time for the spouses of police officers, and more recently for the local community, is a miniacademy. Fairfax County Police Department, Fairfax, Virginia, created a spouses' academy in the 1980s to create a sense of understanding of the police officer's job. The academy consisted of firearms safety and training, courtroom testimony, classes on the law and officer safety, and culminated in the ride-along program. This form of communication has recently been implemented in several police departments across the nation with anecdotal success.

Officer Kay Shelly of the St. Petersburg Police Department working for the downtown Community Policing Squad. (Courtesy of St. Petersburg Police Dept., St. Petersburg, Florida.)

With the advent of cable television, local police programs have gained wide acceptance. Many of these programs, such as the ones in Arlington County, Fairfax County, Prince William County, and the cities of Alexandria and Manassas, Virginia, are taped each week and aired as many as a dozen times during the week. The show is able to explain what the police department is currently doing, detail accounts of recent crimes, explain safety/crime prevention tips, and provide an overall method of communicating a plethora of information to the public. Other programs that follow along similar lines are brochures, newsletters, and attendance at local community events such as fairs, community meetings, and parades.

Once again, these programs are only limited by the ingenuity of the police and community, which is demonstrated in the DARE card program. Through the sponsorship of the DARE program, trading cards can be printed up and given to children while the police work the street. They feature a police officer from the local police department with his or her picture on the front and a short biography and safety tip on the back. The children can then collect them and trade them like any other trading cards. In the Washington Metropolitan area the DARE program sponsors DARE trading cards featuring the members of the Washington Redskins football team. Anecdotal evidence suggests these programs are received extremely well by the children; they will often approach the officer on the street and ask for a trading card, thereby offering an excellent communication opportunity.

COMMUNITY SOCIAL CONTROL PROGRAMS

The community social control programs are those programs based on social control theory as articulated by Travis Hirschi and transformed into hands-on programs that allow the police and community to exert influence over various segments that commit or cause criminal activity or acts against order maintenance. In order to understand the community social control programs, one must have a simple understanding of social control theory.

Social control theory was born in the 1969 book, *Causes of Delinquency*, written by Travis Hirschi. Hirschi used social control theory to explain not just why criminals commit crime, but rather why most people do not commit crime (for a review of social control theory see Siegel 1995 and Vold and Bernard 1986). Hirschi believed that generally, if left to our own devices, we would all commit crime, but it is our attachments, commitments, involvements, and beliefs that prevent us from committing these crimes (Hirschi 1969). The attachments to our peers, schools, parents, and spouses all keep us from committing criminal behavior. Our commitments to our education, careers, and future plays an equal impact, as do our involvement in the community through church, sports, and social groups; and our beliefs in honesty, morality, and caring for others (Hirschi, 1969). If these four factors are in place, then the individual is far less likely to commit a crime than those individuals who are lacking in one or more areas. Although this is a theory on crime causation, we can utilize this concept within neighborhood-oriented policing in the development of community social control programs.

These programs consist of not only utilizing the police, but once again integrating the police and the community to establish and exert social control on those groups possibly lacking in one of the four areas. This also returns to the "Broken Windows" theory which essentially states that if the community allows a broken window in a building to be tolerated, then the community will also allow for further destruction and eventually allow crime to enter the neighborhood, losing any form of social control over the community (See Wilson and Kelling 1982). Therefore, it is the goal of the police and the community to either maintain, enhance, or restore a strong sense of social control over the entire community. They must do this though strengthening the bonds of those groups in a position to exert social control and they must work with those groups that fail to abide by the societal norms.

COP IN ACTION

LAW CAMPS: A NEW TWIST ON AN OLD FAVORITE

In times past, when a kid went to summer camp, he or she slept in a tent or cabin, did a little nature study, worked on lots of crafts, and went swimming in a lake. Not any more. Now there are special camps: computer camps, soccer camps, music camps, and even weight-loss camps, to name just a few. Many of them are held on college campuses, and the kids sleep in dormitories and swim in an indoor pool.

One organization that has kept up on these trends, and uses them to its advantage, is the Indiana State Police Youth Services Division. This unique series of summer camps, each geared to a different grade level from 6th through 12th, was developed in cooperation with several service organizations focused on youth. The Optimists help with the 6th and 7th grade Respect for Law (RFL) Camp, the Lions work with 7th, 8th, and 9th graders at Law Camp, and Kiwanis team up with the police for Career Camp. At RFL Camp, kids get a chance to take a close look at how law enforcement and the legal system work. The three-day weekend's schedule keeps kids hopping, balancing presentations by officers from various police departments with cookouts, swimming, sports, pizza parties, and Sunday morning church services. The kids hear about DARE and the "dangers of strangers." There's a talk on gun safety, a trip to the Huntington jail, and a recreational swim in the pool where scuba divers "attack" swimmers' feet.

A SWAT team, fully dressed in fatigues and camouflage makeup, sets booby traps in the woods for the kids to find (flares go off). Railroad detectives, hazardous materials crews, K-9 Corps, an equestrian regiment, and karate experts also attend. Motorcycle, helicopter, and police, fire, and ambulance divisions are there, complete with equipment and vehicles. The kids have marching drills, flag ceremonies, and are assigned push-ups for misbehaving. An impressive graduation and awards ceremony climaxes the weekend. At the ceremony, two scholarships to Law Camp are bestowed, one to a boy, and one to a girl, a "Best Camper" award is given, and medals for excellence in sports activities are presented.

The Lion's Law Camp is an outgrowth of the RFL Camps. It was developed for a slightly older group of kids who had attended the RFL camps and wanted to come back. There is less "show and tell," and the Law Camp does not repeat the RFL curriculum. There are classroom lectures on AIDS, cults, teen stress and suicide, lung disease, and cancer. These are interspersed with activities such as swimming, basketball, and a day-long field trip to Grissom Air Force Base or Crane Naval Ammunitions Center, where campers fire revolvers at the pistol range. The staff also arranges a mock trial, using a real judge and public defender, with a police officer dressed as a person caught trafficking cocaine. Kids act as jurors.

Attendees at Career Camp, a week-long, in-depth program for high school students interested in pursuing law enforcement careers, attend a heavy lecture schedule during which all phases of the criminal justice system are presented. A defense attorney, prosecutor, street patrol officer, judge, narcotics specialist, and a legislator give presentations. Movies and videotapes play an important role and topics range from the history of law enforcement to police training films dealing with patrol techniques, arrest procedures, accident and crime prevention theories, and investigation methods. Sandwiched between lectures are recreational activities.

The application for the camps states: "Besides introducing the kids to our legal system in general, and law enforcement in particular, the camps teach students that discipline is a prerequisite in gaining self-respect, and self-respect is the first step in gaining the respect of others. The programs demonstrate the rewards of hard work and dedication. They promote teamwork, while instilling self-confidence."

Source: Adapted with permission from Abella, Mary. "Law Camps: A New Twist on an Old Favorite." *Law and Order*, December 1994, 30–32.

The police and community can work together in a number of ways to strengthen the bonds of those who can exert their influence on other members of the community, but often they need some assistance on the part of the police. In some communities those who abide by the law and rules are often scared to say something to a juvenile spray-painting a building for fear of their personal safety, fear of retribution on their property such as a slashed tire, fear of a civil suit, or fear of just getting involved. If the police can strengthen these law-abiding community members, then the element of fear may be removed and the community would be more likely to get involved.

A program could be created for police officers to live in those crime-ridden communities, such as the one started in Alexandria, Virginia. Several police officers were offered the ability to buy a home at a reduced price and low interest rate if they would move into a troubled neighborhood. This program assists the neighborhood in a variety of ways. The police officer has a more vested interest in the community he or she patrols, the majority of citizens in these neighborhoods are good hard-working people who suffer with the crime, and it provides some feeling of security which may in turn enhance the social control by these neighborhood members. In Charleston, West Virginia, Chief Dallas Staples achieved this in a retirement home setting by establishing a low rent apartment in the retirement home for a police officer. This assisted the police officer in cost of housing and provided a reduction in fear on the part of the senior citizens and their ability to exert some community social control.

Another group the police can work with to exert some forms of community social control is the media. Whether it is through television or print, the media can provide an avenue for communicating the social control measures and reinforce the bonds of the community.

The police must also work with those groups that violate the social control of the community and create the order maintenance issues that arise, by attempting to create an atmosphere of zero tolerance for certain behaviors that the community finds reprehensible. If the community dictates that gang graffiti is a key concern, then the police must work with the gangs and develop programs to eradicate this problem. If the order maintenance issue is the homeless aggressively panhandling, then programs that prevent aggressive panhandling or stop citizens from giving money to the homeless in this setting must be put in place. The same can be said for those areas that are known for drug dealing or by singling out individual crack houses and shutting down the operation through various means and, once gone, never allowing a crack house to return.

One method of exerting community social control has been though the development of code enforcement teams. The city of Fort Lauderdale, Florida, created a code enforcement team that consisted of a member of the police, fire, building, and zoning departments to target these order maintenance issues

FIGURE 4.2

(Donsi 1992). The team, from 1987 to 1991, tore down 124 crack houses, boarded up 587, and reduced the drug activity by 57 percent (Donsi 1992). Additionally, during this time, the team collected $600,000 in fines and forced landlords to spend nearly $6 million dollars repairing property that did not meet code specifications (Donsi 1992). This is a prime example of how attacking the order maintenance issues and attacking the criminal activity in a variety of ways can restore a sense of social control to the community.

Conclusion

Neighborhood-oriented policing consists of the programs that the police and community can utilize to address criminal problems as well as order maintenance issues. These programs should be utilized based on the community's needs and their perceptions of the local problems. Whether implemented on their own or with the assistance of strategic policing techniques, these programs are the core of community-oriented policing. They must be created, implemented, and maintained with the assistance and cooperation of the community in order for them to be viable under the community-oriented policing philosophy. Through the implementation of these four programs: community patrols, community crime prevention programs, communication programs, and community social control programs, along with the concepts of problem-oriented policing detailed in the next chapter, community-oriented policing can be achieved.

References

Bloom, Lynda. "Community Policing Nips Gang Problem In The Bud." *Law & Order,* September 1992, 67–70.

Brown, Lee P. and Mary Ann Wycoff. "Policing Houston: Reducing Fear and Improving Service." *Crime and Delinquency.* Beverly Hills: Sage Publications, Inc., 1987: 71–89.

Bureau of Justice Assistance. *An Introduction to DARE: Drug Abuse Resistance Education.* Washington, D.C.: U.S. Department of Justice, Bureau of Justice Administration, 1992.

Bureau of Justice Statistics. *Drugs, Crime, and the Justice System.* Washington, D.C.: U.S. Department of Justice, December 1992.

Cole, George F. *The American System of Criminal Justice.* 7th ed. Belmont, CA.: Wadsworth Publishing Company, 1995.

Cordner, Gary W. "A Problem-Oriented Approach to Community-Oriented Policing." In *Community Policing: Rhetoric or Reality.* ed. Jack R. Greene and Stephen D. Mastrofski. New York: Praegar Publishers, 1988.

Donsi, Joseph M. "Police Practices: Ft. Lauderdale's Code Enforcement Team." *FBI Law Enforcement Bulletin,* March 1992, 24–25.

Farrell, Michael J. "The Development of the Community Patrol Officer Program: Community-Oriented Policing in the New York City Police Department." *Community Policing: Rhetoric or Reality.* ed. Jack R. Greene and Stephen D. Mastrofski. New York: Praegar Publishers, 1988.

Feins, J.D. *Partnerships For Neighborhood Crime Prevention*. Washington, D.C.: The
    National Institute of Justice, 1983.

Fleissner, Dan, Nicholas Fedan, David Klinger, and Ezra Stotland. "Community Policing in
    Seattle: A Model Partnership Between Citizens and Police." *National Institute of Justice,
    Research in Brief*. Washington, D.C.: U.S. Department of Justice, August 1992.

Garafalo, James and Maureen McLeod. "Improving the Use and Effectiveness of
    Neighborhood Watch Programs." *National Institute of Justice/Research in Action*.
    Washington, D.C.: The National Institute of Justice, April, 1988.

Geller, William A. ed. *Local Government Police Management*. 3rd ed. Washington, D.C.:
    International City Management Association, 1991.

Greene, Jack R. and Ralph B. Taylor. "Community-Based Policing and Foot Patrol: Issues of
    Theory and Evaluation." In *Community Policing: Rhetoric or Reality*. ed. Jack R. Greene
    and Stephen D. Mastrofski. New York: Praegar Publishers, 1988.

Hamilton, Sandra. "The Saskatoon Experience." *Law & Order*, December 1993, 20–26.

Hirschi, Travis. *Causes of Delinquency*. Berkeley, CA.: University of California Press, 1969.

Kelling, George. *Foot Patrol*. Washington, D.C.: The National Institute of Justice, 1987.

McElroy, Jerome E., Colleen A. Cosgrove, and Susan Sadd. *Community Policing: The CPOP
    in New York*. Newbury Park, CA.: SAGE Publications, Inc., 1993.

Moore, Mark H. and Robert C. Trojanowicz. "Corporate Strategies for Policing." *Perspectives
    on Policing* Washington, D.C.: National Institute of Justice and the Program in Criminal
    Justice Policy and Management, November 1988.

Pate, Anthony M., Mary Ann Wycoff, Wesley G. Skogan, and Lawrence Sherman. *Reducing
    Fear of Crime in Houston and Newark: A Summary Report*. Washington, D.C.: The Police
    Foundation, 1986.

Perez, Marta Brito. "IACP Offers Training in Community-Oriented Policing." *The Police
    Chief*, May 1993, 39–40.

Rosenbaum, Dennis P. "The Theory and Research Behind Neighborhood Watch: Is It a
    Sound Fear and Crime Reduction Strategy?" *Crime & Delinquency* 33, no. 1 (January
    1987): 103–134.

Rosenbaum, Dennis P., Robert Flewelling, Susan Bailey, Chris Ringwalt, and Deanna
    Wilkinson. "Cops in the Classroom: A Longitudinal Evaluation of Drug Abuse Resistance
    Education (DARE)." *Journal of Research in Crime and Delinquency* 31 (1994): 3–31.

Rosenbaum, Dennis P. and Arthur J. Lurigio. "An Inside Look at Community Policing
    Reform: Definitions, Organizational Changes, and Evaluation Findings." *Crime &
    Delinquency* 40 no. 3 (July 1994): 299–314.

Schmalleger, Frank. *Criminal Justice Today*. 3rd ed. Englewood Cliffs, N.J.: Prentice-Hall
    Inc., 1995.

Siegel, Larry J. *Criminology*. 5th ed. St. Paul: West Publishing Company, 1995.

Skogan, Wesley G.. "The Impact of Community Policing on Neighborhood Residents." In
    The Challenge of Community Policing: Testing the Promises. ed. Dennis P. Rosenbaum.
    Thousand Oaks, CA: SAGE Publications Inc., 1994.

Trojanowicz, Robert C. "Evaluating a Neighborhood Foot Patrol Program: The Flint Michigan
    Project." In *Community Crime Prevention: Does it Work?* ed. Dennis P. Rosenbaum.
    Beverly Hills: Sage Publications, 1986.

Vold, George B. and Thomas J. Bernard. *Theoretical Criminology*. 3rd ed. New York:
    Oxford University Press, 1986.

Weisburd, David and Jerome E. McElroy. "Enacting the CPO Role: Findings From the New York City Pilot Program in Community Policing." In *Community Policing: Rhetoric or Reality*. ed. Jack R. Greene and Stephen D. Mastrofski. New York: Praegar Publishers, 1988.

Wilson, James Q. and George L. Kelling. "Broken Windows: The Police and Neighborhood Safety." *The Atlantic Monthly,* March 1982, 29–38.

Wycoff, Mary Ann. "The Benefit of Community Policing: Evidence and Conjecture." In *Community Policing: Rhetoric or Reality*. ed. Jack R. Greene and Stephen D. Mastrofski. New York: Praegar Publishers, 1988.

CHAPTER 5

Problem-Oriented Policing

A problem well stated is a problem half solved.
-Charles Kettering-

The final component of community-oriented policing is problem-oriented policing. This component is a concerted effort on the part of the police and the community to resolve the causes of criminal activity and order maintenance issues, rather than the symptoms. Problem-oriented policing addresses a particular problem, analyzes the problem, determines a course of action, implements the program, then follows up in an evaluative manner. If the problem is resolved, then the police and community must only keep the problem in check. If it is not resolved, alternative solutions are generated and implemented. The goal of problem-oriented policing is for the police and community to work together in solving those particular problems that cannot be solved by traditional police work or need special attention for their resolution, by developing a tailor-made response for the particular problem and situation.

The concept of problem-oriented policing was not created within the parameters of community-oriented policing, but rather separate and at relatively the same time. Herman Goldstein, the Evjue-Bascom Professor of Law at the Law School, University of Wisconsin in Madison, studied the police response to various types of crimes in the mid-1970s and developed an alternative to improve the police response. The results were first revealed in his 1979 article in *Crime & Delinquency* entitled "Improving Policing: A Problem-Oriented Approach" (Goldstein 1979). The article detailed Goldstein's concept for creating a more

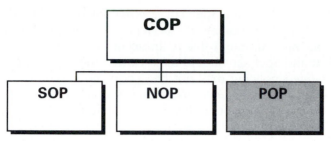

FIGURE 5.1

efficient police response to repetitive problems and would later be expounded upon in his 1990 book entitled *Problem-Oriented Policing* (Goldstein 1990).

As this new concept of problem-oriented policing began to take shape, another article appeared in 1982 in *The Atlantic Monthly* by James Q. Wilson and George L. Kelling entitled "Broken Windows: The Police and Neighborhood Safety," which would be the catalyst for the concept of community-oriented policing. Although these two concepts evolved at roughly the same time, the question continues to be raised on the issue of whether or not community-oriented policing and problem-oriented policing are the same concept. In much of the literature, the two concepts are presented as consisting of the same philosophy and the same ideas (See Cordner 1988; Goldstein 1987; Lurigio and Rosenbaum 1994; and Wilson and Kelling 1989). In other literature, the two concepts are considered different philosophies and therefore translate into two distinct programs (Eck and Spelman 1987a; Eck and Spelman 1987b; Trojanowicz and Bucqueroux 1989). In light of this disparity over the two concepts, it is clear that some relationship exists between the

A Dallas police officer talks with local residents. (Courtesy of the Dallas Police Dept., Dallas, Texas.)

two concepts. John Eck and William Spelman (1987b) stated, "Problem-oriented policing relies on and supports community policing, but it is not synonymous with community policing." Although this is an accurate representation based on the literature, Eck and Spelman should have carried the statement one step further. Problem-oriented policing may not be synonymous with community-oriented policing, but community-oriented policing is synonymous with problem-oriented policing. Problem-oriented policing was designed on its own and can operate and function in a police department on its own without the implementation of community-oriented policing. However, community-oriented policing cannot be implemented without the assistance of the problem-oriented policing approach. Therefore, community-oriented policing **is** synonymous with problem-oriented policing.

As the key literature on problem-oriented policing has developed based on its own merits and programs, this chapter will review the evolution of problem-oriented policing, detail the methods of implementation, and review the literature for details of both evaluative and anecdotal evidence of its success and failure.

"CRIME FILES"

CRIME AND PUBLIC HOUSING—PART 9

This edition of the "Crime Files," hosted by James Q. Wilson, features Vincent Lane, Chicago Housing Authority; Major Carolyn Robison, Tulsa Police Department; and Hattie Dudley, Tenants' Task Force, Alice Taylor Apartments, Boston. The discussion revolves around a comparison between two Boston housing projects: one run-down and crime-ridden, the other orderly and law-abiding, and the problem-oriented policing approaches utilized to address these concerns.

THE EVOLUTION

As previously stated, the evolution of problem-oriented policing commenced with the research of Herman Goldstein. As a result of the policing styles in the 1960s and the demand for changing the way the police conducted their business during that time period, Goldstein raised the issue in an article on public policy formation as it applies to the police (Goldstein 1967). He would eventually expound on the public policy issue and discuss the police and their role in a book entitled *Policing a Free Society* (Goldstein 1977). He then developed his theory, as a result of his extensive research on how police respond to various calls, into his 1979 article entitled "Improving Policing: A Problem-Oriented Approach" (Goldstein 1979). The article successfully showed that police focus on how to deal with the means of a situation, rather than the end.

By dealing with the ends, the police would have a better rate of success in the multitude of problems they face on any given shift. This theory became the basis for all the literature that followed on problem solving and it would be known as problem-oriented policing.

The same problems that existed with problem-oriented policing became readily apparent with community-oriented policing. Many of the police programs attempted to change over to a problem-solving style of policing while some only remotely changed the way they performed their duties, but all of them were utilizing the title "problem-oriented policing" to describe their programs. As Goldstein stated in his 1990 book, "Problem-oriented policing,…use of the phrase also creates the great risk that, when the concept is widely broadcast under the abbreviated label, it will be drained of much of its meaning" (Goldstein 1990). He then cites this as one reason for writing the book that expounded further and updated his original policy proposal for the way police carry out their duties.

As Herman Goldstein explained, there were many reasons for the development of problem-oriented policing, but he cites five concerns as strongly influencing its creation:

1. The police field is preoccupied with management, internal procedures, and efficiency to the exclusion of appropriate concern for effectiveness in dealing with problems.
2. The police devote most of their resources to responding to calls from citizens, reserving too small a percentage of their time and energy for acting on their own initiative to prevent or reduce community problems.
3. The community is a major resource with an enormous potential, largely untapped, for reducing the number and magnitude of problems that otherwise become the business of the police.
4. Within their agencies, police have readily available to them another huge resource: their rank-and-file officers, whose time and talent have not been used effectively.
5. Efforts to improve policing have often failed because they have not been adequately related to the overall dynamics and complexity of the police organization. Adjustments in policing and organizational structure are required to accommodate and support change. (Goldstein 1990, 14–15)

The philosophy and implementation of problem-oriented policing across the nation closely followed the concepts as dictated by Herman Goldstein, yet several other programs developed during the 1980s that also influenced the creation of the concept. The first to appear, one evaluated through a pre/post-research methodology, was the previously mentioned Citizen-Oriented Police Enforcement (COPE) program in Baltimore County, Maryland, which commenced in 1981 (Cordner 1985; Cordner 1986; Cordner 1988; Taft 1986). Utilizing many of the problem-solving techniques dictated by Goldstein, the Baltimore County Police Department was able to show that the philosophy, when created into a program for implementation, was successful. However, the COPE program was not only problem oriented, but initiated some programs that fell into other categories such as strategic policing and neighborhood-oriented policing styles. It was not until 1986, when the National Institute of Justice studied the feasibility of a problem-oriented approach to policing in its chosen test site of Newport News, Virginia, that a study dedicated specifically to the problem-oriented approach would be conducted.

COP IN ACTION

POLICING IN TOUGH BUDGETARY TIMES

For eight years, Gaston County Police Department recruits have had to hold a four-year college degree. This requirement ensures that we have a group of officers who are thinkers. Problem-oriented policing (POP) encourages officers to think about solutions. Innovation is encouraged and participatory decision making is promoted through an advisory board, the use of a suggestion box, and ad hoc committees involving all levels of department personnel.

The preferred term in Gaston County, North Carolina is "problem-oriented policing" (POP). This approach encourages officers to identify problems and seek their resolution, rather than continuing to respond (again and again) to incidents. Thus officers are proactive.

In 1989, Gaston County made its first efforts to implement problem-oriented policing by introducing POP to the county manager and his staff, the district attorney's offices, the district court judges, and all county agency department heads. This session helped ensure cooperation across the board and removed some obstacles which may have arisen through ignorance. With these administrators "buying into POP," all departments became cooperative partners with the police department rather than competitive departments within county government.

A six-phase approach was adopted in order to implement the objectives of the Citizen-Oriented Police Enforcement Unit (COPE). Phase one, creation and training of the COPE Unit, was accomplished through attendance at national conferences on problem solving and a seminar by the Police Executive Research Forum on problem-oriented policing. Ongoing, department-wide in-service training and "hands on" learning through practical experience continue to increase officers' awareness and effectiveness of the problem-solving approach. To assure that problem solving does not become the activity of just the COPE Unit, the training seminar was attended by all first-line supervisors and field training officers.

Phase two was the development of a network of agencies and organizations to serve the members of this target community. Cooperation, started two years earlier, continued through correspondence between department heads and the COPE Unit, joint projects, media coverage of the COPE Unit, and in-person introductions made by COPE Unit members.

Phase three established a reliable method of collecting data used for crime analysis. Calls for service to mobile-home parks now include a special code allowing them to be collected and reviewed separate from all other calls for service. Computer access and availability, as well as additional programming, has put crime analysis within the reach of all department personnel.

Phase four set problem-solving strategies that focus on particular problems and their sources, rather than just responding to similar incidents again and again. COPE officers support these efforts through updates, follow-ups, and personnel when possible. Successful endeavors are shared with officers throughout the department.

Phase five measures effectiveness, evaluates efforts, and obtains feedback on the COPE Unit. This phase is being initiated through citizen-group meetings, public surveys, and a recent department survey. The results have been encouraging. The public is overwhelmingly in favor of this departmental effort. Statistical analysis shows some favorable figures, and department personnel express an increase in both knowledge and implementation of problem solving.

Phase six will access the yearly results through statistical analysis. Although this has yet to be done on a yearly basis, the quarterly reports have all been extremely favorable.

Problem-oriented policing demands that officers go beyond the police department in their quest for solutions. As problem solvers, members of the unit utilize resources from both the public and private sectors. Many times the concerns of citizens involve situations that impact the quality of life in their community. A traditional police response may have been no response at all, but as problem solvers, efforts are made to seek the appropriate resources, agencies, or persons to correct the situation.

New methods of evaluating the effectiveness of a department will also need to be developed. If a department is truly committed to problem-solving policing, it makes little sense to evaluate successes in terms of arrest rates or tickets written, etc. Far from being successes, they may well indicate the failure of problem-solving strategies, since if POP is effective we might expect to see a reduction in the number of arrests. Again, to measure efficiency in terms of an overall response time (another traditional measure of police effectiveness) is meaningless in the context of call prioritizing and the problem-solving police department.

In Gaston County, problem-oriented policing was adopted to make more effective and efficient use of police officers already employed. It is part of the solution of allocating scarce resources. It is not an additional service, but an alternate way to provide quality service given the current budgetary realities and low officer/population ratios.

Source: Adapted with permission from Farley, William J. "Policing in Tough Budgetary Times: Gaston County Finds New Methods Increase Service." *Law and Order*. August 1993, 53–57.

According to John E. Eck and William Spelman (1987a, xvii), in their book reviewing the National Institute of Justice study in Newport News, five areas of police research contributed to the formulation and implementation of problem-oriented policing. These five areas include: 1) effectiveness, 2) community, 3) problem studies, 4) discretion, and 5) management (Eck and Spelman 1987a, xviii–xix). The effectiveness studies include those on preventive patrol, response time, and investigations revolving around the central question of how effective are the police (Eck and Spelman 1987a, xviii). Community studies were largely seen as a result of the policing styles and communication between both the police and community which sparked the implementation of police–community relations (Eck and Spelman 1987a, xviii). The problem studies Eck and Spelman discuss are predominantly in the area that Goldstein was studying during the 1970s in an attempt to discover how police handle the types of calls they received (Eck and Spelman 1987a, xviii). The issue of police discretion has also sparked a complete area of research on its own that attempts to analyze how police officers utilize the wide amount of discretion they have available when handling various complaints and problems (Eck and Spelman 1987a, xviii). And finally, they detail the study of police management as it has changed over the past several decades as a growing impetus for the development of problem-oriented policing (Eck and Spelman 1987a, xix). These five reasons, according to Eck and Spelman, were why problem-oriented policing evolved in the manner it did, and why it was important to study the potential of this new program.

The National Institute of Justice chose the Police Executive Research Forum to conduct this study in Newport News and Eck and Spelman became the key authors and proponents of this system (See Eck and Spelman 1987a; Eck and Spelman 1987b; Spelman and Eck 1987a; Spelman and Eck 1987b). The Police Executive Research Forum essentially developed their own method of problem-solving policing which allowed them to implement the program on the street. The program's success was lauded, but not without some implementation problems (Eck and Spelman 1987a, 97).

Eventually, many problem-oriented policing programs were implemented across the United States largely based on three methods and philosophies of implementation: Goldstein's model of problem-oriented policing, the Citizen-Oriented Police Enforcement (COPE) programs, and the methodology dictated by Spelman and Eck known as the SARA model, which will be detailed later in this chapter. Police departments, such as the San Diego Police Department with the assistance of the Bureau of Justice Assistance (BJA) and the Police Executive Research Forum (PERF), implemented a problem-oriented policing approach to their drug problems with some success (Capowich and Roehl 1994). In 1986, the New York City Police Department began preparation to implement the Community Patrol Officer Program (CPOP); data collected on problem-oriented policing from December 1986 through February 1988 showed favorable results (McElroy, Cosgrove, and Sadd 1993). In 1990, in Lawrence, Massachusetts, the Lawrence Police Department implemented a problem-solving method of policing that was perceived as a successful program (Cole and Kelly 1993). A Community-Based, Problem-Oriented Policing Program (CBPOP) directed largely at the local drug problem was implemented in Arlington County, Virginia in 1992 with anecdotal success. And in the Fresno Police Department in Fresno, California, the problem-oriented approach to policing was implemented over a twelve-month period utilizing a problem-oriented policing (POP) team with much success (West 1995).

Many more police departments across the United States are implementing problem-oriented policing. The majority of police departments are not conducting full-scale data collection and analyzing the data in any format to determine the successes or failures of their programs. Most rely on either police-collected data, which poses many problems of validity and reliability, and anecdotal evidence, which in and of itself must only be accepted at face value. However, most police departments that have implemented problem-oriented policing or problem-oriented programs have done so based on the formulas created by Goldstein, and more likely on the simplistic formula utilized in Newport News, based on the studies of Eck and Spelman. These two methodologies are perhaps the two most common forms of implementing problem-oriented policing and will therefore be described in detail.

COP IN ACTION

REPEAT CALLS AT FIRST AND THIRD AVENUES

Scanning

The intersection of First and Third Avenues was considered one of the busiest in southeastern San Diego. The only gas station and convenience store in the area occupied two corners of the intersection. In 1988, radio calls concerning belligerent panhandlers and drug-related activity at this corner increased dramatically.

Analysis

The gas station was the site of heavy pedestrian and vehicular traffic, and the liquor store across the street attracted gang members and panhandlers. Initially, patrol officers believed that the numerous radio calls resulted from traffic in and around the gas station.

Officer A., a veteran of the area, had responded to many calls for service from the gas station, but had seldom observed evidence of illegal activity. Other officers responding to identical calls at the station confirmed her observations.

A call to the crime analysis unit for a breakdown of the area's calls for service revealed that more than 100 radio calls had been dispatched to the gas station location in the previous month, yet no arrests had been made. Officer A. became suspicious and decided to investigate more closely.

Response

While on patrol a short time later, Officer A. responded to a radio call that reported panhandlers harassing customers at the gas station. When she arrived, however, the station clerk told her the panhandlers had just left the parking lot. The officer then drove across the street to observe the store while writing her report.

While Officer A. observed the activity around the gas station, a second radio call was dispatched that again reported panhandlers harassing customers. When she saw no panhandlers, however, she drove across the street to speak with the manager. She learned from their discussion that the station's clerks were afraid of its clientele and thought that if the police were called on a regular basis (whether needed or not), the station's owner might be compelled to hire full-time security guards.

Officer A. explained that initiating false calls was illegal and that police would not participate in any scheme to manipulate the station's owner. She encouraged the clerks to discuss their fears with the owner, and she stressed that they must not call for police assistance unless it was really needed.

Assessment

The radio calls to the property decreased to only a few per week. When she was in the vicinity, Officer A. occasionally stopped by the store to check on the clerks.

Source: Bureau of Justice Assistance, *Problem-Oriented Drug Enforcement: A Community-Based Approach for Effective Policing*, Washington D.C.: Bureau of Justice Assistance, October 1993.

IMPLEMENTATION

Herman Goldstein, as previously discussed, articulated the concept of Problem-Oriented Policing first in his 1979 article, and then he expounded upon it in his 1990 book. The book details the concept of problem-oriented policing, but more importantly, it provides the framework for a police department to be able to implement the program. Goldstein (1990) carries the progression of steps from identifying the problem to evaluating the problem in a logical and concise order. This process is critical to understanding problem-oriented policing and how it integrates with community-oriented policing.

Goldstein commences his method with the identification of a problem (Goldstein 1990, 65). Goldstein identifies a problem as consisting of three components for the purposes of problem-oriented policing:

1) A cluster of similar, related, or recurring incidents rather than a single incident;

2) A substantive community concern; and

3) A unit of police business (Goldstein 1990, 66).

He specifically states that in identifying a problem, it is important to select those clustered recurring problems and identify the sole problem involved (Goldstein 1990, 32–33). It is often the case that a police officer will respond to a variety of calls at a particular location and although each call may be uniquely different, they can be grouped together as a problem focusing on that particular address, as opposed to any one situational "problem."

Goldstein (1990, 70) also discusses a central theme to community-oriented policing, and that is who identifies what is considered a problem. He recognizes that the community should be largely concerned with identifying those things they perceive as problems because under his definition of problem, it must be of a "substantive community concern" which in reality can only be

Officer Cliff Jewell of the Phoenix Police Department,
Phoenix, Arizona, speaking with local parents about
child safety on the playground. (Courtesy of Phoenix
Police Dept., Phoenix, Arizona, and Mr. Bob Rink.)

recognized by members of the community (Goldstein 1990, 70). Police management should also have a large role in identifying problems, because they
should be communicating with the community in various settings and be
acutely aware of those criminal problems that are ongoing in a particular
neighborhood (Goldstein 1990, 72). And finally, Goldstein (1990, 73) recognizes the contribution of rank-and-file officers who can identify problems from
their perspective as police officers on the street.

One concern shared by the community, police managers, and rank-and-
file officers identifying various problems within the community is the resources
available to address every problem. Goldstein (1990, 77) articulates that not
every problem can be addressed and therefore they must be prioritized
through some form of consensus. The decision-making process for determining how the problems should be prioritized is based on a multitude of factors
and cannot be reached by one individual or one simple formula. Many things
must be considered and among them Goldstein elaborates on the following:

- The impact of the problem on the community—its size and costs
- The presence of any life-threatening conditions
- Community interest and the degree of support likely to exist for both the inquiry and subsequent recommendations
- The potential threat to Constitutional rights—as may occur, for example, when citizens take steps to limit the use of the public way, limit access to public facilities, or curtail freedom of speech and assembly
- The degree to which the problem adversely affects relationships between the police and the community
- The interest of rank-and-file officers in the problem and the degree of support for addressing it
- The concreteness of the problem, given the frustration associated with exploring vague, amorphous complaints
- The potential that exploration is likely to lead to some progress in dealing with the problem (Goldstein 1990, 77–78).

Once the prioritizing decision has been made, the list must also be fluid, subject to change and re-ranking of those issues, based on the analysis of new information. New concerns should be added to the list and old concerns either removed from the list or moved up and down based on the current status and the above and other factors. From this living and breathing list of problems, those at the top, those that are of the greatest concern to the public, can be addressed.

It is important to remember, as Goldstein (1990, 34) explains, that the substantive problem must be addressed rather than those that are ancillary to the issue. Again, the root of the problem must be addressed—the actual illness, rather than the symptoms. Once this is completed, whether through discussions with the community, surveying the officers working the area to be targeted, or through research of the problem, then, and only then, can a systematic inquiry take place. Otherwise the capability of problem-oriented policing is degraded and only an effect of the problem is addressed, rather than the cause.

The systematic inquiry entails a "systematic collection and analysis of information" regarding the problem (Goldstein 1990, 36). An in-depth probe of the problem must be accomplished by gathering as much information, from as many varying sources as possible, in order to acquire the knowledge necessary for determining a course of action to address the problem of concern (Goldstein 1990, 84). Some of this key information should come from police files, rank-and-file police officers, victims, the larger community, direct inquiries of those causing the problems, other agencies in the community, other communities in the area, and possibly department archives (Goldstein 1990, 85–88). To borrow on an old cliché, no stone should be left unturned. Every piece of evidence or fact must be found and reviewed as if it were a homicide investigation. Albeit this is time consuming and requires abundant resources; however, if performed in accordance with all of the tenets of problem-oriented policing, the benefit of this research will be the abolition of the problem.

COP IN ACTION

HAWAII INNOVATIONS

Hawaii has an unusual problem. The islands' near-perfect climate allows homeless people to stay outdoors almost indefinitely. Skyrocketing housing prices, especially on the island of Oahu, have forced some low-wage job-holders into homelessness. Many were forced to camp out in the state parks; their makeshift shelters ranged from primitive tents to automobiles. Some state parks away from the popular tourist areas became small villages for the homeless. As the number of homeless individuals increased, the associated impact on the residents and tourists dictated that something be done. The City & County of Honolulu Police Department (CCHPD), which covers the island of Oahu, decided that an aggressive, proactive program was needed.

In 1992 the CCHPD started a pilot program called Project Outreach, designed to assist law enforcement personnel and the community in dealing with their area's homeless and mentally challenged. To implement this project, a social worker was hired to be "on call" twenty-four-hours per day and was provided with an unmarked vehicle, portable radio, page cellular phone, and office space. The plan was that the first officer responding to a scene would assess the individuals involved, and if it was determined that they would benefit from the outreach program, the social worker would usually take over and the officer was free to return to his or her duties. This non-traditional approach to the homeless population proved to be effective in channeling those in need into the appropriate agencies for help before they became entangled in the criminal justice system.

In another area of police duties, in an attempt to reduce the level of domestic violence, a law in Hawaii requires the surrender of all personally owned weapons to the police whenever a person is charged with a violent crime or has a restraining order issued against him or her. The CCHPD has had a high level of voluntary compliance with the law: in the period from August 1993 to January 1994, more than fifty weapons were turned in.

The Hawaii County Police Department, which covers the island of Hawaii ("The Big Island"), instituted a separate Word Processing Center (WPC) in 1980. They were the only one of the four departments on the islands to use such a system, until recently when Maui instituted a similar system. A separately staffed word processing center allows officers to dictate their reports and receive polished, printed copies in a short period of time. This innovation has paid off for the small department with a dramatic improvement in officer productivity, substantially increased time available for patrol, and cost savings. The WPC is a centrally located operation that allows officers to dictate their daily reports to a voice management system. The WPC replaced the practice of the officers manually drafting their own reports during duty time.

Typically, an officer dictates a report after completing a call. During the initial dictation, the officer can edit the report by simply pressing certain buttons on the touchtone phone that connects to the WPC. The report is then transcribed by a member of the stenography pool, and the officer receives a hard copy. After making any needed changes, a final copy is produced, signed by the officer, and entered into the department's permanent files. The average time spent by an officer preparing a typical report dropped from one hour using the old manual system to ten minutes for the same report using WPC.

Source: Adapted with permission from O'Shaughnessy, Leslie. "Hawaii Innovations." *Law and Order*, September 1994, 50–52.

At this point in the process, Goldstein (1990, 40) interjects the issue of analyzing multiple interests. This may reveal a vast amount of beneficial information and should be addressed during the systematic inquiry. A simple crime such as prostitution, that Goldstein (1990, 40–41) refers to in his book, may have a compounding effect on the community as a result of its presence. Perhaps the best example of this returns us to the "Broken Windows" theory as articulated by Wilson and Kelling (1982). Once an abandoned building has one window broken, if the window is not repaired, it leads the way to additional broken windows in the building. This may then lead to graffiti painted on the building and the smashing of windshields on cars parked nearby. Eventually the area decays by the community's allowance of one broken window.

Goldstein (1990, 41) articulates that all of these multiple interests should be identified and addressed by the community. At the same time the current police response to the problem must be identified and critiqued, whether it is in the form of a program, a proactive patrol, or merely a reactive patrol (Goldstein 1990, 42). This is essentially the final stage of the systematic inquiry, as all of the possible research and knowledge has been compiled on the problem and all of the different factors of the problem have been addressed. It is then that the police and the community must work together to create a course of action in order to address the problem.

The police should work with the community when creating responses to the problem in order to create solutions that are acceptable to both. The solutions should also be tailor-made responses for the problem at hand and not a blanket response as is so often the case in police work (Goldstein 1990, 43). At the same time this community-police coalition is forming a response, they should also be developing alternative solutions to the problem (Goldstein 1990, 102). The possible alternative solutions may become the key alternatives to the problem or may be implemented later if the first solution fails (Goldstein 1990, 103). It is here that the police and community must have free reign to brainstorm various solutions that have no limiting criteria placed on them.

Once a list of possible solutions has been created, the police and community coalition must choose among the possible alternatives (Goldstein 1990, 141). As Goldstein (1990, 141) states, "any single tailor-made response to a problem is likely to consist of a blend of alternatives." Although a single choice may be selected, the integration of various aspects from various alternatives is acceptable. Reaching this decision, however, will often prove difficult and the choice should be made based on a host of varying considerations. These, according to Goldstein, include:

- The potential that the response has to reduce the problem;
- The specific impact that the response will have on the most serious aspect of the problem (or those social interests deemed most important);
- The extent to which the response is preventive in nature, thereby reducing recurrence or more acute consequences that are more difficult to handle;
- The degree to which the response intrudes into the lives of individuals and depends on legal sanctions and the potential use of force;
- The attitude of the different communities most likely to be affected by adoption;
- The financial costs;
- The availability of police authority and resources;
- The legality and civility of the response, and the way in which it is likely to affect overall relationships with the police; and
- The ease with which the response can be implemented. (Goldstein 1990, 143)

Once the choice has been made, it is important to implement the solution in a timely manner, and to not make excessive alterations to the plan because initially people believe it might not work. Instead, the program that is implemented must be evaluated to determine the success or failure, as well as the possible need for one of the alternative responses (Goldstein 1990, 49). The type of evaluation is also left to the devices of the police and community coalition as well. Each tailor-made response will most likely necessitate a tailor-made evaluation. The evaluation, whether a pre/post analysis, a survey, or a police data analysis, must be done in a fair and unbiased manner to truly assess the viability of the program.

This process, from identifying the problem to evaluating the tailor-made response to the problem, is the concept of problem-oriented policing as articulated by Herman Goldstein. The steps in the process are similar to those articulated by Eck and Spelman in their SARA model which was utilized in Newport News, Virginia. However, the SARA model, despite largely being a derivative of the problem-oriented policing model just reviewed, has a simplistic method for easy application and has been tested in a variety of jurisdictions, allowing it to become a widely accepted model for problem solving.

COP IN ACTION

SOLUTION-DRIVEN PARTNERSHIPS: JUST SIX STEPS AWAY

Partnerships, partnerships, partnerships. Everywhere we go we hear about partnerships. You know how difficult partnerships are. Give and take. Compromise. Win-win. Build consensus. Share information. Nurture relationships. Nurture relationships? Did I hear you right? This is police agency for Pete's sake! Our job is to enforce the law and solve crime problems, not nurture relationships!

It is true. Partnerships are difficult. It takes time to build relationships, to learn to trust each other, to find mutual interests and concerns, and to learn a common language that results in problems being solved. But what we're learning from officers all over the country is that long-term solutions to problems require partnerships.

A partnership is "a relationship involving close cooperation between parties having specified and joint rights and responsibilities" (Webster). The community is not our only potential partner. Potential partners include other agencies; social, religious, business, and educational institutions; and individuals. And in the context of community policing, partnerships make sense when they're formed to solve problems. If we're teaching our officers to solve problems anyway, let's teach them how to form partnerships using the same problem-solving model.

Picture this scenario. A sergeant instructs patrol officers to go to a neighborhood meeting. Residents have complained of prostitution and drug dealing and want to form a partnership with the police. The officers walk in. The residents are glad to see the officers but are angry because they feel helpless and afraid of what is happening in their neighborhood. The officers invite their angry audience to "share their concerns." The floodgates open, and for the next two hours every "concern" is heard. The officers hear about the prostitution and drug dealing in the neighborhood. Then they hear about the poor response time to calls for service, the lack of sensitivity on the part of officers in dealing with residents, and the failure of police to take action on a crime that was committed five years ago. The officers defend the police response. Community members get more frustrated. Now the officers say, "Thanks for sharing your concerns. We'll handle it from here."

We've all been to meetings like this. At the end of the evening, are those officers praising the virtues of partnerships? Are they creatively thinking about how to solve the problems of that community? They're thinking creatively, all right. They're thinking creatively about how to avoid ever going to another community meeting. Using a problem-solving approach, let's revisit this scenario. You are one of the officers.

STEP 1: Build a Relationship

"You can either be right or you can be in a relationship." Wise words spoken by a father to his son before the son's wedding. A relationship requires trust and understanding. Trust and understanding result when one can listen to someone else's concerns in an open, nonjudgmental way. When frustration, fear, tension, and anger are present in a community, creating a safe environment where people can vent is important. You open the meeting by explaining that you are there to listen and to try to understand the problems from the community's perspective. To demonstrate that you have heard every voice, record each problem on a large sheet of paper that is visible to everyone in the room

Once the problems have been listed, ask the group if people are willing to work with you to solve the problems. If people are willing to work together, move on. If not, restate your willingness to try to understand more about the community's perspective. Also, state clearly that the police will do whatever they can to help, but you can't solve these problems without help from the community.

STEP 2: Defining the Problem

The next step borrows from Stephen Covey's work on "Principle Centered Leadership." Covey suggests that all problems fall into one of two circles. The Circle of Concern contains everything that worries or concerns us. We have little control over these problems. The Circle of Influence contains everything we can control or influence in some way.

Explain the circles to the group. Then go through the list of problems with the community, one by one, identifying whether the problem falls under the Circle of Concern or the Circle of Influence. Discuss the Circle of Concern problems to determine what other agency or group may be able to influence or control the problem. Later, the group can return to the Circle of Concern list to determine if they want to meet with the other agencies or groups.

Ask the community to focus on and prioritize the problems identified on the Circle of Influence list. The problem identified as the number-one priority is the starting point for the group's problem-solving efforts.

STEP 3: Ask questions about the problem

Analyzing the problem starts with asking "Who is affected by the problem?" Brainstorm to create a list of everyone who is affected. In the scenario presented earlier, the list may include children, families, police, prostitutes, drug dealers, social service agencies, probation and parole officers, prosecutors, etc. From this list, have the group decide who should be included in the problem-solving effort. Make sure that someone takes responsibility for inviting the appropriate people to future meetings. Identifying people who are affected by the problem ensures that the quiet, unrepresented voices in our communities that are seldom, if ever, heard are included in the problem-solving process.

The next question is, "What do we want to know about this problem?" List everything that the group can think of that they want to know. Then go back to the list and ask, "Where do we go to get the information?" Once you identify the source of the information, people can volunteer to get the answers to the questions. Delegate the responsibility for finding information to a number of people. Relationships can be enhanced even further if a lot of people take ownership in the process. Set the date and time for the next meeting so folks know you're committed to the process.

When most questions have been answered, redefine the problem based on the information gathered. Is the group clear about the specific problem (e.g., drug dealing at the corner of First and Imperial, or prostitution activity on Aurora Avenue the first and third weekends of each month)? If the problem is defined too broadly (e.g., prostitution in the city), ask the group to reexamine it in light of the Circle of Concern and Circle of Influence. Once the problem is defined so that it falls within the group's influence, it's time to set goals.

STEP 4: Set Short-Term and Long-Term Goals

Aim for small wins initially. What short-term goal can the group reach that will create hope and enthusiasm to keep people involved and optimistic? Ask the group to identify some small wins.

Then look at the big picture. What underlying condition or root causes of the problem need to be addressed? Is it possible to eliminate the problem? A problem-oriented approach, according to Herman Goldstein, has five possible solutions. Eliminating the problem is one. Other alternatives include reducing the problem, reducing the harms created by the problem, managing the problem better, and removing the problem from police consideration. Again, consider the Circles of Concern and Influence. Is it realistic to set a goal of eliminating prostitution, for example? Only the group can decide. But keeping alternatives within the Circle of Influence will help maintain trust and credibility in the budding relationship.

The community knows what the problem looks like now. What will the problem look like after the goals have been reached? Once goals have been established, take time to decide how the group will know that the problem has been solved.

STEP 5: Take Action

It's amazing how little time it takes to develop responses to meet the goals. If the right questions have been asked and the group understands what it can influence, responses to problems become clear. If one short-term goal is to get used condoms and syringes out of the neighborhood, whose responsibility is it to take care of this? Who is responsible for doing more enforcement on the first and third weekends of the month? Who should clean up the overgrown shrubs and bushes that hide illegal activity on the street?

Get the action rolling and report back regularly. Ongoing communications are critical to keep the collaboration healthy and alive.

STEP 6: Assess Effectiveness

Was the problem solved? If more work needs to be done, do you need to start with Step One or can you reenter the problem-solving process at another step along the way? How do people feel about the process? The most important question at this point is, "Where does the group want to go from here?" If the problem is solved, the group may want to stay in place to monitor the situation and begin work on another problem. Maybe the group is ready to organize formally. Perhaps it wants to plan a community-education campaign or social events. It is the responsibility of the group, not the officers, to decide what the future holds. Our job is to reaffirm our commitment to working with the group to solve problems and to maintain the relationship through continued communication.

What Are the Barriers to This Approach?

"We have seen the enemy, and it is us." We create a formula for frustration and ineffectiveness when

- we don't take time to listen
- we don't take time to understand and respect different perspectives and the helplessness that crime victims feel
- we think partnerships are programs designed to make the community feel good about us
- we refuse to learn and practice a step-by-step process for joint problem solving that includes mutual rights and responsibilities
- we think "nurturing relationships" are only for moms and social workers

Problem solving is a process, not an event. It starts with building a relationship and follows a systematic, step-by-step process that leads to reducing or solving crime and community problems. Police chiefs and sheriffs who commit to the process support their officers by teaching them skills to facilitate effective problem solving. Their officers won't be leaving community meetings frazzled, disgusted, and feeling unappreciated. They can say "good night" to their community partners with a sense of satisfaction and pride in knowing that they've made a difference in the lives of people who matter to them.

Source: Adapted with permission from McPherson, Nancy. "Solution-Driven Partnerships: Just Six Steps Away." *Community Policing Exchange.* Washington, D.C.: The Community Policing Consortium, September/October 1995.

The National Institute of Justice chose Newport News, Virginia as its test site for several reasons. The three chief reasons were 1) the police department consisted of 280 employees and was therefore a manageable size, 2) it was close to Washington, D.C., and 3) the police chief was already familiar with the background of problem-oriented policing and was committed to the program from the beginning (Eck and Spelman 1987a, 5). The initial stages of the study began with the creation of a task force in 1985.

The task force had to determine if the problem-solving techniques would work in a police department without altering the organization and if these techniques would be effective (Eck and Spelman 1987a, 5). Perhaps the most difficult step in the process, however, was "the theory of problem-oriented policing had to be translated into a practice of problem-oriented policing" (Eck and Spelman 1987a, 6). The task force accomplished this by not only developing practical methods on their own, but by soliciting outside counsel, including Herman Goldstein (Eck and Spelman 1987a, 7). The model they developed became known as the SARA model.

SARA is an acronym for the problem-solving process consisting of four stages: 1) scanning, 2) analysis, 3) response, and 4) assessment (Eck and Spelman 1987a, 42). These four stages became the ongoing process for problem-oriented policing during the study at Newport News, Virginia, and later at other police departments adopting the program.

The scanning stage of the SARA model consists of reviewing the various calls and complaints in a neighborhood and attempting to identify a problem (Eck and Spelman 1987a, 43). It was not the mission of a small group of selected officers to identify these problems, but rather the responsibility of every member of the department (Eck and Spelman 1987a, 44). It was also the responsibility of the police officers to utilize every potential source of information to assist them in identifying the problems, ranging from seeking assistance from members of the department such as vice and the crimes analysis unit, to seeking information from the community such as the local schools and neighborhood watch groups (Eck and Spelman 1987a, 46). However, the problems had to be identified as legitimate problems with a root cause, and not individual incidents

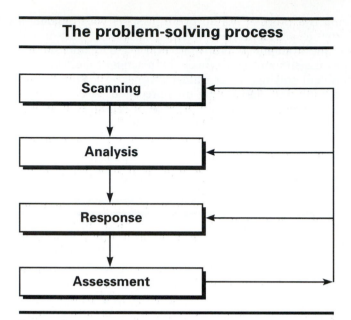

The problem-solving process

FIGURE 5.2   *Source:* William Spelman and John E. Eck. "Problem-Oriented Policing. *"National Institute of Justice: Research in Brief.*" January 1987.

with no connection in the same manner as Goldstein described in his identification phase. The officers were to then list those problems discovered, conduct a limited investigation to verify their legitimacy, and establish a prioritized list of those problems needing further analysis (Eck and Spelman 1987a, 44). Once this was accomplished, then a particular problem or in some cases, multiple problems, would be carried into the next stage of the SARA model.

The second stage of the SARA model is the analysis stage. This stage has two objectives that the officer should accomplish before moving on to the third stage of the model. The first objective is to obtain as much information as possible on the problem and develop a full understanding of the problem (Eck and Spelman 1987a, 47), A checklist is utilized by the officer in this stage which allows him or her to gather information in a methodical manner by addressing "three categories of problem characteristics: actors (victims, offenders, and third parties); incidents (physical setting, social context, sequence of events); and responses (by the community and its institutions)" (Eck and Spelman 1987a, 47). Once this review of the information on the checklist is completed to the best of the officer's ability, then he or she moves on to the second part of the analysis stage—developing the response.

In developing a set of responses to the problem, the options the officer creates must remain consistent with the problem as identified in the information-gathering process (Eck and Spelman 1987a, 47). A variety of responses should be considered for implementation and they should not be immediately dismissed as impossible or foolish to implement. The solutions to the problem

FIGURE 5.3   The Problem Analysis Model

Actors
Victims
Lifestyle
Security measures taken
Victimization history
Offenders
Identity and physical description
Lifestyle, education, employment history
Criminal history
Third parties
Personal data
Connection to victimization

Incidents
Sequence of events
Events preceeding act
Event itself
Events following criminal act
Physical contact
Time
Location
Access control and surveillance
Social context
Likelihood and probable actions of
witnesses
Apparent attitude of residents toward
neighborhood

Responses
Community
Neighborhood affected by problem
City as a whole
People outside the city
Institutional
Criminal justice agencies
Other public agencies
Mass media
Business sector

Source: Spelman, William and John E. Eck. "Problem-Oriented
Policing." *National Institute of Justice: Research in Brief*, January 1987.

can be derived from the officer, assistance on the part of the community, or
through contact with other members of the police department. Regardless of
how the list is created, there should be a variety of possible responses created
in order for the officer to move into the third stage of the SARA model.

Community services council meeting organized under the auspices of Ft. Wayne, Indiana's "Community-Oriented Government." Featured at the council meeting are council facilitator Dr. Ron Powell (at the lectern) and the Alcoholic Beverage Commission, handicapped community, Juvenile probation, Ft. Wayne community schools, local neighborhoods, the media and the Ft. Wayne Police Department. (Courtesy of the Ft. Wayne Police Dept., Fort Wayne, Indiana.)

The third stage of the SARA model is the response stage and it is here the officer must meet two objectives: "Select a solution and implement it" (Eck and Spelman 1987a, 48). The necessity of developing multiple responses then becomes clear in this stage, for without a variety of choices, the police officer would be forced to implement only one or two courses of action which may not be beneficial to solving the problem. It also assists in the final stage of the SARA model in the event the solution selected does not pan out as a viable solution—an alternative from the list can then be selected.

In selecting the particular response to be utilized, the officer must consider many of the same things Goldstein articulated in his model of problem-oriented policing such as financial costs and the overall effect on the community. However, once a response has been selected, it must be implemented without reservation and allowed to reach the final stage of the SARA model.

Eck and Spelman (1987a, 49) discuss one additional item in the response stage of the SARA model and that is categorizing the solution selected into one of five groups in order to assist in not only the overall understanding of what the response is attempting to accomplish, but how it will be reviewed in the final stage of the SARA model. Accordingly, each response should fit into one of five groups:

1. Solutions designed to totally eliminate a problem;
2. Solutions designed to substantially reduce a problem;
3. Solutions designed to reduce the harm created by the problem;
4. Solutions designed to deal with a problem better (treat people more humanely, reduce costs, or increase effectiveness); and
5. Solutions designed to remove the problem from police consideration. (Eck and Spelman 1987a, 49).

In order to understand the types of problems that fit into these categories, Eck and Spelman (1987a, 49—50) detail that "group one solutions probably will be most often applied to small, simple problems—problems affecting a small number of people and problems that have only recently arisen" while "group two solutions will be applied most often to neighborhood crime and disorder problems." Group three solutions would "be applied most often to problems where it is almost impossible to reduce the number of incidents that they create, but it is possible to alter the characteristics of these incidents" and the fourth group of solutions would only "be applied to problems that are jurisdiction-wide and involve larger social concerns" (Eck and Spelman 1987a, 50). The final group, group five, would essentially be applied to those problems that are created by specific businesses or groups and are the result of the way they do business or those problems that cannot be handled by the police (Eck and Spelman 1987a, 50). These categories of solutions essentially provide the goal of the response selected and in the final stage of the SARA model will "affect how its effectiveness should be judged" (Eck and Spelman 1987a, 50). Which brings us to the final stage of the SARA model—the assessment stage.

In the assessment stage, the type of problem and the group of solutions it falls into will depend upon how it is evaluated (Eck and Spelman 1987a, 50). The type of problem and the type of solution also provide some insight into the type of assessment tool utilized. Every problem is different, and this necessitates different styles of evaluation. The goal or objective in the assessment stage is essentially to provide feedback to the police department, and it allows the officer to determine if the response selected is working and whether or not an alternative response should be implemented (Eck and Spelman 1987a, 50).

The success of the SARA model with Newport News and other police departments that have implemented the problem-solving process is perhaps best assessed by the four basic principles of the program that the police chief of Newport News and the National Institute of Justice insisted on for the program (Spelman and Eck 1987b). It was determined that the design for the practical model would allow for total participation by everyone in the police department, use a wide range of information available to the police, encourage a variety of responses not limited to typical police response, and perhaps most important, ensure that the program is reproducible in any police department, regardless of size (Spelman and Eck 1987b, 4). The SARA model was able to accomplish all four principles and has become a successful model in the practical implementation of problem-oriented policing.

Cop in Action

The "Pipe House" at 940 Dove street

Scanning

Located within Queen Village, the 900 block of Dove Street was a residential street with twenty-two homes. The street was one of the most recent blocks in the neighborhood to undergo gentrification. Many of its 18th-century homes were purchased and renovated either by developers or young married professionals, and subsequently sold for up to $400,000.

Analysis

Homes on Dove Street were either occupied or undergoing renovation, with the exception of 940 Dove Street, which was vacant. Unsecured, the house became a crack den or "pipe house." Between January and March 1989, the police department received thirty-seven 911 complaints from area residents about sanitation problems, abandoned vehicles, narcotics use, and disturbingly loud noises during the night. Residents expressed concern that the crack smoking might be a fire hazard and they feared for their personal safety. Many reported that they were afraid to leave their homes because of the drug users at 940 Dove. Area businesses suffered from the reputation of the pipe house as well. One restaurant, located on the corner of Dove Street, experienced a sharp decline in patronage, which the owner attributed to residents being afraid to leave their homes and dine at his restaurant.

Response

Sergeant C. Of the 3rd Police District investigated the problem in February 1989. He immediately arrested two area drug dealers, but this had little impact on the problem. Sergeant C. soon turned his attention to the vacant house and discovered that its owner had recently died and left the house to family members. Further inquiries revealed that the decedent's daughter was anxious to cooperate with police to solve the pipe house problem. She had been trying to sell the house, but two local real estate firms had dropped their listings because their agents were afraid to go onto the property to show the house to prospective buyers.

The daughter agreed to have the property secured, although she had done this twice before. With Sergeant C. present for protection, a construction crew secured the vacant house. The officer, along with block residents, contacted a realtor. Sergeant C. provided increased patrolling to the area, and area residents vigilantly monitored the boarded-up property.

Assessment

The house was listed for sale by a realtor, and its sales potential greatly increased. Dove Street residents were no longer afraid to leave their homes, and many said that the quality of life on their street had dramatically improved.

Source: Bureau of Justice Assistance. *Problem-Oriented Drug Enforcement: A Community-Based Approach for Effective Policing*, Washington, D.C.: Bureau of Justice Assistance, October 1993.

CONCLUSION

Problem-oriented policing, although created separately from community-oriented policing, is the third and final component of the community policing model. Problem-oriented policing is capable of functioning within a police department based on its own merits and is not synonymous with community-oriented policing; however, it is important to remember that community-oriented policing is synonymous with problem-oriented policing. Without the problem-oriented component, community-oriented policing cannot be fully implemented.

The creation of problem-oriented policing is accredited to Herman Goldstein, who has written in detail about the philosophy and concepts surrounding this program. A clear and detailed method of implementing problem-oriented policing can be abstracted from these details; however, it is the SARA model that is most often utilized when a police department uses the concept in a practical setting. The clarity and reproducibility of the SARA model—scanning, analysis, response, and assessment—allows for any police department across the nation to easily implement all of the tenets of problem-oriented policing, and in turn the overall concept of community-oriented policing.

COP IN ACTION

POLICE AND PRIVATE SECURITY

Street prostitutes have long been a problem in Fresno. According to police estimates, nearly 800 prostitutes frequent Fresno annually from all regions of the United States. In 1993, the prostitution problem along Blackstone Avenue had become so chronic that business owners, their patrons, homeowners, and residents demanded that police take action.

Responsibility for addressing the problem was relegated to the already overburdened and understaffed patrol division. Patrol officers were instructed to periodically cruise Blackstone Avenue, identify suspected prostitutes, and check them for outstanding warrants. Realizing the problem could not be resolved in this manner, members of the police department, the Fresno County District Attorney's Officer, local merchants, and those residents most affected by the problem met to seek alternative solutions. One idea that emerged was the possibility of using private security patrols to augment regular police operations targeting prostitution.

A local security firm agreed to place eight security officers along Blackstone Avenue free of charge. Four of the eight security officers were assigned to patrol business frontage areas along Blackstone Avenue on foot. They were given instructions to discourage prostitutes from loitering, confronting potential customers on business storefronts, and disrupting residential neighborhoods and normal business activities. The remaining four security officers patrolled along Blackstone in distinctly marked cars. All eight officers wore security uniforms which proved to be an added deterrent to loitering, drug dealing, and other associated problems. Two uniformed Fresno police officers were also assigned to patrol exclusively along Blackstone and to work in conjunction with security personnel.

Within two weeks of the operation, local merchants and residents noticed a dramatic decrease in the number of prostitutes. The increased uniform presence created less opportunity for passersby to patronize the prostitutes who frequented the area. There was also less traffic congestion caused by those stopping along the side of the road to engage prostitutes. The operation demonstrated that police-private security partnerships can effectively address chronic community problems, especially in an era of tight budget constraints and diminished resources.

Source: Adapted with permission from West, Marty L. "Police and Private Security." *Law and Order.* July 1994, 86–88.

REFERENCES

Capowich, George E. and Janice A. Roehl. "Problem-Oriented Policing: Actions and Effectiveness in San Diego." In *The Challenge of Community Policing: Testing the Promises.* ed. Dennis P. Rosenbaum. Thousand Oaks, CA.: SAGE Publications Inc., 1994.

Cole, Allen W. and David Kelley. "Non Traditional Problem Solving: Barricades Eliminate Drug Dealing, Restore Neighborhood." *Law & Order,* August 1993, 59–64.

————. *The Baltimore County Citizen Oriented Police Enforcement (COPE) Project: Final Evaluation.* New York: Florence V. Burden Foundation, 1985.

————. "Fear of Crime and the Police: An Evaluation of a Fear-Reduction Strategy." *Journal of Police Science and Administration* 14, no. 3: 223–233.

Cordner, Gary W. "A Problem-Oriented Approach to Community-Oriented Policing." In *Community Policing: Rhetoric or Reality.* ed. Jack R. Greene and Stephen D. Mastrofski. New York: Praegar Publishers, 1988.

Eck, John E. and William Spelman. *Problem Solving: Problem- Oriented Policing in Newport News.* Washington D.C.: Police Executive Research Forum, 1987a.

————. "Who Ya Gonna Call? The Police as Problem-Busters." *Crime & Delinquency* 33, no. 1 (January 1987b): 31–52.

Farley, William J. "Policing in Tough Budgetary Times: Gaston County Finds New Methods Increase Service." *Law & Order,* August 1993: 53–57.

Goldstein, Herman. "Police Policy Formulation: A Proposal for Improving Police Performance." *Michigan Law Review* 1967 65: 1123–1146.

————. "Improving Policing: A Problem-Oriented Approach." *Crime & Delinquency* 25, no. 2 (1979): 236–258.

————. "Toward Community-Oriented Policing: Potential, Basic Requirements, and Threshold Questions." *Crime & Delinquency* 33, no. 1 (January 1987): 6–30.

————.*Problem-Oriented Policing.* New York: McGraw Hill Publishing Co., 1990.

Lurigio, Arthur J. and Dennis P. Rosenbaum. "The Impact of Community Policing on Police Personnel." In *The Challenge of Community Policing: Testing the Promises.* ed. Dennis P. Rosenbaum. Thousand Oaks, CA.: SAGE Publications Inc., 1994.

Spelman, William and John E. Eck. "Newport News Tests Problem-Oriented Policing." *National Institute of Justice: Research in Action.* Washington, D.C.: National Institute of Justice, January/February 1987a.

————. "Problem-Oriented Policing." *National Institute of Justice: Research in Brief.* Washington, D.C.: National Institute of Justice, January 1987b.

Trojanowicz, Robert C. and Bonnie Bucqueroux. *Community Policing: A Contemporary Perspective.* Cincinnati: Anderson Publishing, 1989.

Wilson, James Q. and George L. Kelling. "Broken Windows: The Police and Neighborhood Safety." *The Atlantic Monthly,* March 1982, 29–38.

————. "Making Neighborhoods Safe." *The Atlantic Monthly,* February 1989, 46–52.

CHAPTER 6

Integration

Justice begins with the recognition of the necessity of sharing. The oldest law is that which regulates it, and this is still the most important law today and, has remained the basic concern of all movements which have at heart the community of human activities and of human existence in general.

-Elias Canetti-

Community-oriented policing, as previously described, consists of three integral parts: strategic-oriented policing, neighborhood-oriented policing, and problem-oriented policing. These three components when utilized together in a system to address criminal problems and order maintenance issues are not only the conceptual framework of community-oriented policing, but the practical framework as well. In order to implement this framework, all three components must be integrated into a continual process that operates on the foundation of mutual dependence. This style of policing does not work in a consecutive manner, nor does it work in a cyclical manner, but rather it is a web of interdependence where each component complements the others. From the initial establishment of the program within a community to the continual process of planning and evaluating, the three components must work in concert to accomplish the goals of reducing fear, alleviating criminal problems indigenous to a community, and addressing the order maintenance issues that affect the sense of "community" in a specific geographical setting. The integration of these programs is critical to undertaking the community-oriented approach to policing. If one component is not implemented with the concept of community-oriented policing, then the failure of the program is predetermined. Understanding this concept is the key to this chapter.

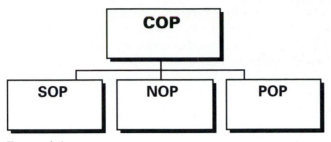

FIGURE 6.1

Although the chapter will allude to methods of implementing community-oriented policing, the primary focus will be on how the three components work together and how they should be managed for maximum potential. A discussion of who becomes the catalyst for community-oriented policing and who should actually oversee the implementation of the three components becomes critically important for enabling the three components to be addressed in a variety of manners. This will be discussed through a review of the key players in community-oriented policing and how they are involved in the program. In order to illustrate the concept in a broad manner, three current case studies exploring community-oriented policing across space, time, and through various endogenous programs will be reviewed to articulate how certain police departments and communities have implemented each of the three components and how they operate in concert.

"CRIME FILES"

FOOT PATROL—PART 27

This edition of the "Crime Files," hosted by James Q. Wilson, features Hubert Williams, Newark Police Director; Dr. George L. Kelling, Harvard University; and Crisley Wood, Director, Justice Research Institute, Neighborhood Crime Prevention Network. The discussion revolves around the effects of deploying police officers on foot into the local neighborhoods in order to reduce crime and fear. The focus is on foot patrol programs in Newark, New Jersey, and Boston.

WHO INITIATES?

Who initiates community-oriented policing is a question that is often pondered by academics when discussing the conceptual feasibility of the program. Inherent within the title, one would assume that the initiating party of community-oriented policing should be the community itself. However, realizing the current status of life in the United States, the community that we look for to implement programs along these lines is often broken, transient, or non-existent in the sense that members of the "community" desire to remain anonymous and "don't want to get involved." Without the sense of community or any established methods of communicating between neighbors, there is little likelihood that the community-at-large is suddenly going to sign on to a program that brings them together, along with the police and local government, in order to "clean-up" the neighborhood and solve all of their problems. Living in a high-rise building in the center of a city, despite the close proximity, does not create a better sense of community than living in a pre-planned community of single-family dwellings. Realizing the lack of community in a society that tends to migrate toward populations where they are closer to their fellow man or woman poses problems on many varying levels.

Extensive research in the field explores the type of people that participates in voluntary organizations and those that do not. The primary group of people who do participate in these types of community programs are generally those of the middle-class with a middle-class income and who are well educated, married with children, and homeowners (Skogan and Maxfield 1981). Although community-oriented policing is directed at those individuals fitting these characteristics, it is also aimed at every type of community with every type of people and all their varying characteristics.

There has always been and will always be the issue of directing the efforts of community-oriented policing toward those communities suffering from crime and disorder. This is not to say that those fitting the characteristics described above do not have their own set of unique problems or that they should not have their needs addressed, but rather the severity is generally not

A Dallas police officer from the Dallas Police Department works with local youth. (Courtesy of the Dallas Police Dept., Dallas, Texas.)

as critical an issue in these types of neighborhoods. Therefore, it is probably safe to conclude that those neighborhoods where organized communities exist may more readily initiate a form of community-oriented policing, and those communities that are disorganized and need the assistance and implementation of this style of policing will most likely not initiate the systemic approach. In sum, those communities that are in the greatest need of community-oriented policing will, in most cases, not initiate the philosophy.

Recognizing the problems when determining who initiates community-oriented policing, the focus must then shift to one of understanding not necessarily "who should implement" but who are the actors involved. The key actors in community-oriented policing are namely the police and the community. The broad definitions of each must be relegated to all-inclusive terms in order to suffice the current explanation. The police or the community may be the initiators of community-oriented policing and either the police or the community may respond to the implementation of community-oriented policing. Utilizing a simple box chart (see Figure 6.2), we can see that the police can initiate and respond (I), the police can initiate and the community respond (II), the community can initiate and the police respond (III), the community can initiate and the community respond (IV), or ideally, the police and community initiate and the police and community both respond (V). Each of the first four scenarios presents many considerations that weigh upon the future success of the systemic approach to policing, while the fifth scenario is presented as "ideal community-oriented policing."

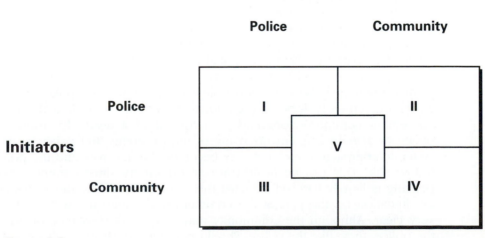

FIGURE 6.2

It is more likely that in order for community-oriented policing to be initiated, it must be done on the part of the police. The majority of police departments in the United States that have initiated the systemic approach have had to do so with the police department acting as the catalyst. However, it is what happens after the department has created and implemented the systemic approach that can affect the outcome. In some cases the police department may have created the program with the intent of including the community, but as a result of community apathy and perhaps as a result of some initial success without the community, the police may find it easier to exclude the community from any future participation in the systemic approach (See Figure 6.2 part I). A second potential drawback is if the police initiate and the community comes to recognize the increased benefits that do not require their assistance, the community may resign themselves to a form of learned helplessness. The community may become so dependent upon the police that they abdicate any and all responsibility and authority to the police rather than attempting to achieve a beneficial relationship based on a mutual understanding. A third drawback is the possibility that as the police are attempting to draw the community into the systemic approach, the community may become suspicious, reluctant, and in extreme cases, militant toward the concept.

It is important to remember, however, that the function of community-oriented policing is the involvement of the community in both crime fighting and addressing order maintenance issues. Therefore, it would be inappropriate and unhealthy for the program if the police implement the concept and ignore the community. Community-oriented policing is not a "police-only" program. The police department must attempt to integrate the community with the police in the very rudimentary stages of creating community-oriented policing. However, recognizing that community members will often be reticent about working with the police, the police will often have to "sell" the concept to an unwilling public, but they should never stop trying to include the public in every possible way (see Figure 6.2, part II).

In rare situations, strong community ties and frustration with either criminal problems, order maintenance issues, or both, will lead the community to initiate community-oriented policing and to attempt to draw in the police (see Figure 6.2, part III). This is essentially the reverse of scenario II, where the police attempt to "sell" the systemic approach to the community; here the community tries to "sell" the new policing approach to the police. Whether the community merely lobbies their local politicians or police department to implement community-oriented policing out of a desire for more effective police or actually implements many of the programs and concepts under the systemic approach, the community becomes the initiators and the police must follow suit. This can be healthy for a community since community-oriented policing is largely focused on what the community needs and wants and with the initiation on the part of the community, the message will most likely be very clear. Although the community may also meet resistance on the part of the police, they, like the police, should not give up easily.

However, in some cases the police may be so well entrenched into a method and way of conducting their business that the resistance to changing the way they police may be difficult to overcome. The community attempting to initiate community-oriented policing may find themselves failing to include the police in their decisions and may venture down the road of "taking things into their own hands" (see Figure 6.2, part IV). This can be beneficial if the community's actions do not overstep the boundaries of the police. If in the event the community does begin to encroach on what are considered by the local police to be "police duties", conflicts can arise. And in the worst case scenario, the community may either be seen as, or actually begin conducting, vigilante acts.

Obviously, the fifth alternative of creating the systemic approach through a concerted effort on the part of both the police and the community, with both the police and the community responding to the implementation, would be ideal. This concept of "ideal community-oriented policing" would then see both of the actors involved in initiating and responding to the systemic approach to policing through planning, creating, implementing, and evaluating the concept. The ideal would see the concept revolve around all three components: strategic-oriented policing, neighborhood-oriented policing, and problem-oriented policing, and eventually the integration of all three. Additionally, both of the actors would fill certain roles within the larger concept in order to achieve the desired outcomes of community-oriented policing, namely a safer community. These roles on the part of the police consist of changes to organization and management (Chapter 7) and to the overall role of the police (Chapter 8); while the overall role of the community in addressing criminal and order maintenance problems must change as well (Chapter 9). The link, however, between the police and the community should start with the police chief, who also plays a pivotal role in the systemic approach (Chapter 10). For now, let it suffice to detail specifically how the three components become integrated in the systemic approach.

COP IN ACTION

A DEPARTMENT'S ROLE AS A SOCIAL ACTIVIST

The City of Monrovia, California, a city of approximately 37,000 people encompassing about thirteen square miles, recognized that safe, well-kept neighborhoods are the responsibility of every employee in the city's work force. Conversely, the city realized that crime and poor living conditions impose a heavy cost not only on the neighborhood but on every department in the city's work force.

As a result, Monrovia established the Community Activist Policing (CAP) strategy to draw upon every resource, from the mayor and council members through every city department and community resource needed to solve the community's problems. The task force is chaired by a police officer who coordinates the activities of the group and cuts through government red tape.

Other members include the chief of police, two police captains, a detective lieutenant, a special enforcement team sergeant, a crime prevention officer, community development director, community services director, fire chief, fire inspector, code enforcement officer, building inspector, and community services manager. For this strategy to be effective, the task force calls on community groups, social service agencies, and mental health providers, and seeks the help of businesses or volunteers and church groups to solve problems.

The chairperson is empowered to get problems solved. He or she accomplishes this by:

- Organizing neighborhood groups to become activists with city officials to deter criminal activity.
- Working with code enforcement officers and building inspectors to identify dilapidated, roach-infested, and poorly-maintained properties that are the center of criminal activity.
- Documenting poorly maintained properties by videotaping their condition.
- Encouraging the cooperation of landlords in rehabilitation and management of their properties.
- Enforcing all applicable city, county, state, and federal laws required to resolve problems.
- Determining after an evaluation period if special enforcement operations are needed by the police department patrol division and/or special enforcement team.

This concept emphasizes analysis of incidents by the task force to determine if the incidents are related. The solutions proposed by the task force vary depending on the neighborhood and the problems being addressed. Every resource of the police department is committed to the CAP program. Ongoing communication with residents and businesses in the community is stressed.

- The task force sponsors block parties, in the middle of the street in the target areas to announce the beginning of C.A.P. task force activities.
- The police department created a bicycle patrol program to go hand-in-hand with CAP. Bicycle officers enhance community support and confidence in the police while addressing drug and alcohol violations, gang-related and other serious crime.
- The task force investigates locations where drugs are being used or sold. The landlords of the residences are contacted and advised of the activity. They are encouraged to evict tenants identified as being involved and to make any necessary property repairs.
- Letters are delivered to the owner and/or person in control of any property where search warrants for drugs have been served.
- One-on-one counseling sessions on the proper procedures of tenant selection and evaluation are given to landlords.
- The CAP task force initiated a cul-de-sac program. One popular drug street in the city was blocked off to create a cul-de-sac to deter drive-thru drug and gang activity. The cul-de-sacs also offer a more well-defined "neighborhood" and create a safer environment for children to play.

- The Community Services Department established a program that provides graffiti removal services within twenty-four hours after the graffiti is reported.
- The task force has been responsible for declaring nuisance properties substandard and tearing them down at the owner's expense. At the same time, the task force helps innocent residents find new housing, again, at the landlord's expense.
- The task force and Community Services Department implemented a neighborhood recreation program in the CAP areas to reach out to youngsters who find gang membership appealing.

The CAP strategy is now a routine part of daily activities, and the city has solved long-festering problems. CAP is as much a philosophy of policing as it is a set of techniques and procedures that help bridge nontraditional departmental lines and build good management, a caring outlook towards solving community problems, and a commitment to doing something about them. CAP works because everyone works together.

Source: Adapted with permission from Santoro, Joseph A. "A Department's Role As A social Activist." *Law and Order*, May 1993, 63–66.

THE THREE COMPONENTS

The ideal initial step in community-oriented policing is to form a coalition that would include a cross-section of the community, both residential and business, as well as a cross-section of the police department. This group would then be responsible for the initial planning of community-oriented policing and would be responsible for directing where the police will establish the first component, strategic-oriented policing, and the types of methods they will utilize. As is often the case, this may be the first step in implementing community-oriented policing where the police enact the program without any assistance from the community. The police are fully capable of determining which areas need to be targeted and the type of strategic-oriented policing methods that should be utilized, due in large part to the fact that these steps are essentially enhanced traditional police tactics. While it should be recognized that the police will base their selection of areas on objective criteria such as crime statistics and that this method is readily acceptable for addressing criminal issues, it may leave out many unknown variables regarding crime of which the police may not be aware and it may almost completely ignore the issues of social disorder.

Whether it is the community and the police working in concert together, or solely the police, the first step in the implementation of community-oriented policing should be strategic-oriented policing. The initial decision, regardless of the methodology utilized, must be the selection of a target or multiple targets to determine what area, crime, or order maintenance issue is to be addressed and then the type of strategic policing tactic to be used. If it is the police working with a previously established community group, then some things to consider in the selection of the target would be the consensus of the coalition, anecdotal evidence, or any data the community can provide. In the event there are no community groups previously formed, the police must work to not only create a community coalition, but they must determine what problems or areas to initially target based on police-gathered data, officer experience with the problem or area, and any additional data from other sources such as the fire department, public works, or the local government board.

Again the target can be selected based on a single problem such as prostitution, an area or localized problem such as a crack house, or an order maintenance issue such as a city park that is home to the homeless, drug addicts, and is in a state of constant disrepair. All of these are common examples of targets that could be addressed through a community-oriented policing approach and could start with the strategic-oriented policing methods. Once the target or targets are selected, the next step is to determine what type of strategic-oriented policing method should be utilized.

As described in Chapter 3, the possibilities are endless but generally revolve around various forms of directed patrols, aggressive patrols, or saturation patrols. The police or coalition should determine which type of patrol to utilize based on what they think will have the most impact on the identified target. While the saturation patrol may work well in the city park, it may be more beneficial to utilize various aggressive patrol tactics on the prostitutes and johns that enter the targeted area, such as a street corner, a particular motel, or a neighborhood residence. The selection should be made on a multitude of criteria ranging from geographical area, police resources, and criminal element, to the time available to address the issue.

The goal of implementing the strategic-oriented policing component first is to physically drive out the criminal or order maintenance element, or at a minimum, drive it underground and behind closed doors. Once this element has been removed from the area and once the police vacate the location, the criminal element will return. This is no different from squeezing a water balloon on one end. All one accomplishes is the displacement of water. Once we let go, the water refills the area we were squeezing. Similarly, once we remove the police from their strategic-oriented policing assignments, the elements we removed from the neighborhood will return. The police cannot stay in one place forever, although it would perhaps be comforting to have a police officer on every corner, it is just not feasible based on resources available. So, once the element is removed from a neighborhood and the police begin to extricate themselves, something must be put in place of the police. This is where neighborhood-oriented policing comes into play.

COP IN ACTION

"BROKEN WINDOW" STOPS DRUG SALES

The Wilson Police Department, North Carolina, began exploring new ways to attack the drug problem in Wilson, and "Operation Broken Window" was born. The name came from the old theory that once a window is broken in a car or a building, individuals will begin to break other windows because of the open invitation offered by that first broken window.

The operation had four main objectives:

- Force drug users to look elsewhere for drugs;
- Force drug dealers to move or change their method of operation;
- Attack social conditions feeding the drug problem and;
- Make the area safer for residents and businesses.

Prior to the start of the operation, community meetings were held to determine the level of support the department had for such an operation, and to receive feedback from the community concerning their feelings toward how the police should attack the growing problem. A meeting held at a church in the heart of the operational area was attended by approximately 100 businessmen and residents. Support was overwhelming and was vital to the success of the operation. Planning of Operation Broken Window involved the city council, all city departments, and virtually every member of the police department. The final operation was divided into four areas.

In this phase, undercover officers were borrowed from nearby police agencies through a mutual aid agreement to conduct buys. As another part of the operation, a number of uniformed officers moved into the target area to establish control over the movement of people and vehicles.

During the first two weeks, twenty-one uniformed officers were on duty twenty-four hours per day. Officers were directed to make contact with individuals for any violation that occurred in their presence. The major portion of the phase was funded by the use of overtime monies. Also as part of the operation, two K-9 units were assigned to drug interdiction at the local bus station. Prior to this assignment, these officers received special training by the North Carolina State Bureau of Investigation in conducting constitutional stop and talk operations.

In an important part of the operation, social conditions that facilitated the drug sales in the target area were identified. Grass was cut, trash was removed. Street lights were installed, repaired or replaced. Buildings were inspected for code violations, and owners were notified to correct the problems.

In addition to the community meetings held prior to the beginning of the project to solidify community support, a meeting was held afterwards to determine the level of satisfaction in the community and to receive their input on how the continuing drug problem might best be attacked.

From a law enforcement perspective, the operation was a success. A number of dealers were arrested, sales transactions were interrupted, and information from informants indicated that the operation had an impact on drug sales in the city as a whole. Additionally, crime decreased substantially in the target area and remains down.

An important by-product of the operation was a fundamental change in the attitudes of officers within the department concerning the target area. As a result of the long hours that many invested in the area, their attitude is now one of partnership and ownership, and a resolve not to allow the dealers back in.

However, the yardstick by which we must measure the success of this type of operation is how the people in the area feel. In a local newspaper article praising the actions of the city in returning the streets to the people, residents reported that they were able to walk the streets again and sit on their front porches.

The process started with Operation Broken Window continues today and is an integral part of how the Wilson Police Department attempts to solve problems within the community. Several smaller projects have been initiated since the conclusion of Operation Broken Window, and the department has expanded its use of problem-oriented policing and involving the community in its efforts to abate crime.

Source: Adapted with permission from Younce, Thomas. "'Broken Window' Stops Drug Sales." *Law and Order*. April 1992, 67–70.

The removal of the crime and disorder from a specific area, by means of strategic-oriented policing, allows the community a respite from this element and thereby reduces the fear the community has suffered. It also allows time to implement neighborhood-oriented policing programs without the concerns of the element that may have prevented or inhibited the implementation of similar programs earlier. It then provides the time necessary for the program to take hold, allowing it to grow stronger and influence more and more people in the neighborhood. As more people become involved, the police can then remove themselves from the neighborhood, leaving a smaller presence behind, ideally a community-oriented police officer, and redirect their resources elsewhere.

The type of neighborhood-oriented policing program that should be implemented in the community should also result from the cooperation of the police and the community. The selection of the various types of programs such as community patrols, community crime prevention, communication programs, and community social-control programs, should all be considered. Some cases may call for an officer to walk a foot patrol of the area or, if too large an area for this, bike patrols may be necessary. In other cases, the community may get involved by creating a Neighborhood Watch Program and implementing citizen patrols, either by foot, bike, or automobile. Other possibilities include organized clean-up days, neighborhood block parties with the police, or establishing citizen academies and ride-along programs. Implementing one or several of the community communication programs would help open the lines of communications and may allow for some understanding or revelations of what the community perceives as a problem. All of these should be considered and implemented based on the needs of the community.

In some cases, the neighborhood-oriented policing programs implemented may have no effect on keeping the criminal element from returning to the area. In this event, the police may have to return to the strategies underlined in the strategic-oriented policing component, or utilize some of the methods detailed in the third component, problem-oriented policing. Regardless, the police and community must continue to address these issues and reallocate resources to best suit the needs of the community.

The third component of community-oriented policing, problem-oriented policing, plays a major role in the overall implementation of the concept and

Officer V.G. Cowan (l) and Officer D.E. Boone (r) of the
Parkersburg Police Department, Parkersburg, West Virginia,
working in the local neighborhood on the "Walk and Talk" patrol.
(Courtesy of the Parkersburg Police Dept., Parkersburg, West
Virginia.)

is a continual process that should also be conducted on the part of both the
police and the community. Problem-oriented policing should commence at the
same time as strategic-oriented policing strategies are implemented and should
never stop. In some cases, the methods utilized to address a perceived problem may assist in the identification of those targets for strategic-oriented policing. In other cases, the techniques may be utilized to determine the root of the
problem in a particular neighborhood and develop various alternatives that
can be implemented under the multiple programs of neighborhood-oriented
policing. And in other situations, the concept of problem-oriented policing
may be conducted entirely separate from the first two components and later
integrated if there exists some connection in the problems discovered and the
alternatives selected to address these issues.

This connection is the key revolving around the web effect created from
the three components. Each of the components does not operate independently,
nor are they mutually exclusive. That is not to say that at times they will not
operate without any influence from the other two components, but eventually,
everything that results from one component will have a direct bearing on the
other two. The response that may be derived from a particular method of strategic-oriented policing may dictate what type of neighborhood-oriented policing
program is implemented. During this time, a study may be conducted from the
problem-oriented policing component, and what is actually causing the problem
may be different from what was originally considered. There is then the chance
that the alternative selected from the problem-solving process may be a different form of strategic policing, which may then impact the programs under

neighborhood-oriented policing. A continual evaluation of the methods utilized, followed by a reassessment of what may or may not work, and then augmented by a change in the methods utilized, will all impact and create a web between the three components of community-oriented policing.

COP IN ACTION

CRIME SUPPRESSION: A MULTI-AGENCY APPROACH

Butte County (in rural Northern California) has experienced an escalation in crime, particularly narcotics and/or violence. The routine law enforcement approach, such as proactive patrol efforts, an interagency narcotics task force, and similar approaches, resulted in arrests and investigations but actual impact was sporadic and difficult to measure. After a driveby shooting of the district attorney's residence, it was clear that additional approaches were required.

Due in part to limited resources, a new multiagency approach was developed with the focus on a proactive, crime-prevention format. Dubbed "Operation Clean Sweep," this program does not necessarily rely on traditional narcotics operations, "stings," or similar approaches. It is based instead on high-profile contact with the most likely offenders; those already convicted of crimes and on searchable probation or parole. Butte County law enforcement agencies take turns organizing the operations, which usually involve several of the participating agencies. The agencies include a variety of police departments, the sheriff's department, the district attorney's office, and an assortment of associated agencies such as probation and parole agencies, Child Protective Services and Welfare Fraud. The program moves through the various communities on an unpredictable basis. In that manner, especially for those on probation or parole, a clear signal is sent that law enforcement contact can occur at any time.

The combined resources of both personnel and equipment of each agency is based on their ability to contribute. Cellular phones, pagers, drug-detecting dogs, vehicles, and unique services are shared in a manner which allows an agency to monitor its contributed resources. Personnel are assigned to functions and operational units based on expertise and/or other needs.

An operation might occur as follows: A team leader receives a series of "packets" (previously submitted by participating agencies) containing information on searchable probationers. He reviews the packets and determines likely candidates for search by consulting with the team probation officer. The full team, utilizing appropriate officer-safety techniques, makes contact at the probationer's residence utilizing the packets and advising their group coordinator of their change in status. The operations commander then has the ability to monitor the location, progress, and concerns of all teams, groups, and resources under his command.

Butte County law enforcement has conducted three major operations utilizing up to seventy-five officers. Numerous felony and misdemeanor arrests have been made, assets seized, drugs confiscated, and probationers/parolees found in violation of the conditions of their probation or parole. Forty percent of the individuals contacted are arrested on a fresh charge and/or found in violation of their probation or parole.

Source: Adapted with permission from Aeilts, Tony. "Crime Suppression: A Multi-Agency Approach." *Law and Order*. September 1993, 121–122.

This then becomes the key to community-oriented policing. All three components must be present in order for the concept to work in a practical application. The police and community must work in concert and apply all three components to the criminal and order maintenance problems that are both real and perceived. Then and only then can we truly evaluate the community-oriented policing method for what it is, an entirely new and systemic approach to policing.

One final aspect of the integration of the three components under community-oriented policing is the possibility of not only integrating, but diffusing the three components. The diffusion of components is when strategic-oriented policing, neighborhood-oriented policing, and problem-oriented policing begin to occur simultaneously, by the same community group and police officers in the neighborhoods. In many cases, the problem-oriented team may be deciding what strategic-oriented policing tactics to utilize and how they can be replaced with neighborhood-oriented policing programs. What happens to the three components is a blurring of lines and a loss of clear focus on any of the three distinct components.

Diffusion can occur at any time during the implementation process, but earlier in the process will most likely be detrimental to the implementation process. In the later stages of implementation, diffusion may prove beneficial. The reason is simply that the police and the community must understand all the components, their foundations, how they operate individually, and subsequently how they operate together. All of this should be clear and simplified before they are diffused into one system under community-oriented policing. If, in fact, they are diffused in the later stages, it can be beneficial to the systemic approach, because it can clearly signify that cooperation between the community and the police is occurring and that all three components are being utilized to implement community-oriented policing.

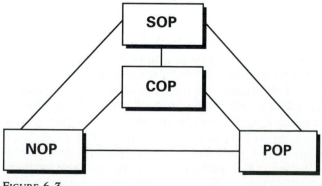

FIGURE 6.3

CASE STUDIES

In order to fully understand how the three components of community-oriented policing work together and become diffused, it is important to review several police departments in the United States that have implemented the systemic approach. Although the majority of police departments across the nation are still initiating or developing their programs, there are many police departments that have been through the trial and tribulations of implementation. The cases to be analyzed will reflect as wide a range of circumstances as possible. They will examine police departments through the understanding of space, time, and the endogenous programs implemented that embody the community-oriented policing philosophy. In order to accomplish this within the confines of three case studies, the issue of space will include the largest police department in the nation, a medium-size police department, and a small police department; the issue of time will include a department that commenced implementation in the early 1980s, one in the late 1980s, and one in the mid-1990s; and the issue of endogenous programs will be analyzed on the basis of various programs under the three integral components. The three police departments focused on in the case studies exploring these three issues will be New York City Police Department, Spokane Police Department, Spokane, Washington; and Parkersburg Police Department, Parkersburg, West Virginia.

There is a distinct advantage to analyzing community-oriented policing in New York City because they began their program over a decade ago, it has seen various interpretations, and it is the largest police department in the United States, making it the ultimate testing grounds for the systemic approach. The current status of Spokane Police Department, a medium-size department, provides an excellent example of the three components working together in a variety of ways and means to actualize that which is truly community-oriented policing. And finally, it is important to look at a police department that is in its infancy stages of community-oriented policing, is a small police department serving a small community, and is one that to some degree has implemented community-oriented policing long before the name was ever applied to the behaviors that have come to entail the systemic approach.

New York City, New York

New York City, New York, the largest city in the United States, with the largest police department (38,000 officers) serving a population of over 7 million people, is essentially the largest testing grounds for community-oriented policing. The New York City Police Department has seen various interpretations of the community-oriented policing philosophy since it was first introduced there in 1984, and the philosophy's application in the department has received much attention in the media, as well as in the research (Farrell 1988; Lacayo 1996; McElroy, Cosgrove, and Sadd 1993; Pooley 1996; Roberg 1994; Weisburd and McElroy 1988). Regardless of the interpretation over the span of twelve years, the New York City Police Department has been very successful with its implementation of community-oriented policing and as it has incrementally changed and advanced with new programs and ideas, it has proven that the systemic approach can work on such a grand scale.

In the mid-1970s, like so many other police departments across the nation, the number of officers was dramatically reduced, while the number of calls for service dramatically increased. In attempting to address many of the growing criminal and order maintenance issues in New York City, a proposal for designing a new method for delivering police services that would address many of the neighborhood quality-of-life issues was designed in 1983. In July of 1984, with the arrival of a new police commissioner, Benjamin Ward, a pilot community-oriented policing program was implemented in Brooklyn's 72nd Precinct and it was dubbed CPOP for the "Community Patrol Officer Program." The concept was to integrate permanently assigned police officers into the community and allow them to assume many nontraditional tasks, such as holding community meetings and developing strategies to address crime and disorder. The Vera Institute of Justice assisted in the early implementation of this test-pilot program through planning, implementation, and evaluation; and eventually assisted in the full implementation of community-oriented policing on a department-wide basis (McElroy, Cosgrove, and Sadd 1993).

The pilot was received so well by the citizens it was directed toward, and by the police officers implementing the program and the police officials responsible for it, that the move was made to go department wide. From January 1985 through September of 1988, all seventy-five of New York City's police precincts made the move to community-oriented policing and all with successful results. As the program was continually evaluated and implemented in the various precincts, with the assistance of the Vera Institute of Justice, the police department created a conceptual framework that embodied many of the tenets of community-oriented policing. It became the philosophy of the department that the CPO (Community Patrol Officer) had the following four key functions: 1) Planner, "to identify the principal crime and order maintenance problems confronting the people within each beat area"; 2) Problem Solver, "to see themselves as problem solvers for the community"; 3) Community Organizer, "increasing the consciousness of the community about its problems, involving community people and organizations in developing strategies to address the problems, motivating the people to help implement the strategies, and coordinating their actions so that they may contribute maximally to the solution"; and 4) Information Exchange Link, where "through his or her links to the community, the CPO would be in a position to provide the department with information about problem conditions and locations, active criminals, developing gangs, illicit networks for trafficking in drugs and stolen property, information about citizens' fears, and insights into their perceptions of police tactics" and "in turn, the CPO could provide citizens with information pertinent to their fears and problems, technical information and advice for preventing crimes and reducing the vulnerability of particular groups of citizens, information about the police view of conditions in the neighborhood and strategies for addressing them, and information about police operations in the community"

(Farrell 1988, 78–79). These four components guided the police department toward full implementation of community-oriented policing.

In mid-1989, Police Commissioner Benjamin Ward left the New York City Police Department and a search was made for a replacement who would continue the implementation of community-oriented policing. The choice was Lee Brown who was already an advocate of the systemic approach to policing and had previously implemented the philosophy in Houston, where he had served as the police chief. Commissioner Brown began his tenure with the development of a strategic plan that would guide the police department toward a more integrated, and hence a more systemic, approach to the community-oriented policing philosophy. His report was released in 1991 and called for a variety of guiding principles to be implemented (Brown 1991). The principles translated into various methods of implementation and included: increase the number of officers on patrol and assign them permanent beats, allow the officers greater flexibility to develop ties to the community and to problem solve by freeing them from the constraints of reactive policing, provide additional training to all members of the department on the mission, values, and operations of community-oriented policing, move the management philosophy toward one that was conducive to the systemic approach, and develop committees in each precinct that incorporate management, line officers, and local citizens for identifying problems, prioritizing these problems, and developing plausible solutions (Brown 1991). The New York City Police Department was able to implement many of these principles, programs, and ideas, despite the fact that Commissioner Brown's tenure was cut short in 1992 by personal reasons.

In 1993 and 1994, Rudolph Giuliani ran for mayor of New York City, basing his campaign on improving the quality of life in the city of which one key element was to reduce the amount of crime. Community-oriented policing strategies that had previously been implemented were making some headway in both the rate of crime and quality of life, but the campaign called to intensify the movement. Once elected, Mayor Rudolph Giuliani appointed William Bratton as the police commissioner to carry out this movement. Bratton came from the Boston Police Department where he served as the police chief. However, prior to the move to Boston he had held the position of police chief of the New York Transit Authority, during which an increase in officers working on the subways was implemented. Subsequently, the number of monthly ejections from the subway increased from 2,000 to 16,000, the number of "fare-jumpers" reduced, and the number of felonies fell by 30 percent (Eggers and O'Leary 1995, 9). Commissioner Bratton immediately began implementing his same interpretations of community-oriented policing with the New York City Police Department.

In order to communicate with all seventy-six precinct commanders and hold them liable for the implementation of community-oriented policing, he established a program known as "Comstat" which stands for "Computer Statistics" (Pooley 1996, p. 54). The Comstat meetings were designed to update Bratton on the success or failure of each precinct, to determine what efforts they had made and what programs had been implemented. However, Bratton matched this with an immediate demand to reduce crime by 10 percent (Pooley 1996, 55). Although this style of demanding results by setting objectives was met with much resistance, necessitating that many precinct commanders be removed from their posts, in 1994 the reduction of crime was at 12 percent (Pooley 1996, 55). Commissioner Bratton then demanded a 15 percent reduction for 1995 and obtained a 17 percent reduction, and he has since demanded a 1996 reduction of 10 percent (Pooley 1996, 55).

All of this has been dramatically implemented through various types of crackdowns on public nuisances such as public drinking, graffiti, vandalism, panhandlers, and other types of order maintenance issues (Dilulio 1995). Various programs began directing their efforts toward addressing street gangs, drug traffickers, and habitual offenders. And various programs were incorporated that are oriented toward at-risk members of the community such as the local youth, including New York Police Department-sponsored youth academies, an increased number of Law Enforcement Explorers, and an expanded cadet program to provide the children of today the chance to be the police officers of tomorrow (Bratton 1996, 26–27). And, one final move being implemented is the raising of qualifications to be a New York City police officer by requiring candidates to have sixty college credits and to have reached the age of 22, thus securing more officers suitable for enacting many of the roles of a community-oriented police officer (Bratton 1996, 26–27). In the end, community-oriented policing has reduced violent crimes in New York City (Pooley 1996). It has made the precinct commanders more accountable to the public through demands for the reduction in crime and order maintenance problems (Dilulio, 1995) and it has incorporated the community into many of its decisions.

In understanding community-oriented policing as consisting of the three components of strategic-oriented policing, neighborhood-oriented policing, and problem-oriented policing, when applied to the New York City Police Department's methods of implementation since 1984, it provides a colorful scenario of the incremental implementation of the systemic approach. The early pilot program of community-oriented policing in New York City was focused predominantly on the implementation of neighborhood-oriented policing programs by establishing community patrols, developing community crime prevention programs, opening up the lines of communication with the public, and to some degree establishing community social control programs. Once the pilot program was implemented department wide in all seventy-six precincts, the neighborhood-oriented policing strategies were implemented through the principle of the community patrol officer (CPO) becoming both a "community organizer" and an "information exchange link" to the public. However, they incorporated the idea of "problem-solver" into the expanded community patrol officer program (CPOP) and essentially implemented the third component of problem-oriented policing. It was not until the hiring of former Police Commissioner William Bratton that the police department began utilizing the methods found within strategic-oriented policing. To date then, the New York City Police Department has implemented all three components of community-oriented policing and continues to move toward a full implementation of the systemic approach to policing.

Although it has taken New York City Police Department over twelve years to implement community-oriented policing, it has done so incrementally which is in line with the systemic philosophy. At each stage of implementation, the police department has had both successes and failures and many of the programs that have moved the philosophy to the practical have either been abandoned or expanded. As New York City remains the ultimate testing grounds for community-oriented policing, it is important to continue to monitor both their successes and failures to understand how the systemic approach to policing works, to recognize its advantages, to document its shortcomings, and to see the future of community-oriented policing unfold.

Spokane, Washington

Spokane, Washington, is a relatively large and urban city with a population of 185,000, which is settled in the center of the Spokane–Coeur d'Alene area and has a combined population of over 450,000 residents. A large proportion of these area residents work in Spokane, increasing the day population by a factor of two. The demands on local government services by the local population is great; however, as a result of the daytime population increase, there exists an almost equal demand by nonresidents of Spokane. The demands on the police department itself, like so many other cities in the early 1980s, was rising dramatically while the number of both sworn and non-sworn personnel remained fairly stable. Additionally, the resources available to the police seemed to be decreasing in the wake of the increase in violent crimes, drug-related crimes, and many quality-of-life issues that the police did not have time to address. The police department was reactive in nature, incident driven, and the problems with officer satisfaction on the job was causing excessive amounts of lost time due to leave, sick-leave, and stress-related illnesses. The city of Spokane realized it needed to address many of these growing concerns and elected to implement change within the police department.

The first step toward this change can be traced to the hiring of Police Chief Terence J. Mangan in 1987, who had previously served in Bellingham, Washington, as the police chief for approximately eleven years. His unusual background provided the impetus for much of the change, as Chief Mangan was both a counselor and clergyman in the 1960s when he began working as a reserve officer with the Seaside Police Department in Seaside, California, where he eventually became a full-time police officer. His work in law enforcement during the 1970s, through much of the Law Enforcement Assistance Administration's movement to improve policing, and his eventual move to Bellingham as the police chief provided the necessary background to understand what had both worked and failed in policing throughout the 1970s and 1980s. Moving into Spokane, with a fresh start and an open call for change, provided Chief Mangan the chance to implement a community-oriented style of policing.

Chief Mangan made his first change with a call to update the mission statement of the Spokane Police Department by putting the values and mission statement together that would represent the police department. In doing this he decided to focus on the future by incorporating the values and mission statement into a vision for where the police department should be by the year 2000. In keeping with the community orientation which includes input from all employees, the draft was circulated throughout the department for discussion, revision, and final approval by all members of the police department. After a two-year period of discussion, the new orientation, values, and mission were implemented in "Vision 2000" and "Community Policing" both of which follow:

> Vision 2000 - In the year 2000, the Spokane Police Department will be a culturally diverse, highly motivated, professional law enforcement organization representative of and respected by the community it serves.

> Community Policing - We are dedicated to a philosophy of policing which commits us to a working partnership in our community, and to proactively address those issues which can enhance its quality of life.

The values of the police department were laid out with the acronym SPD, standing for not only Spokane Police Department, but for Service, Pride, and Dedication. The Police Department adopted these three values to guide itself toward Vision 2000 and the adoption of Community Policing.

The cover of the Spokane Police Department's (Spokane, Washington) "Community Oriented Policing Programs" guide published for the local community by the Spokane Police Department. (Reprinted with permission from the Spokane Police Dept., Spokane, Washington.)

Recognizing that community-oriented policing is a philosophy and not a program, the police department adopted the philosophy department wide. As Chief Mangan himself has articulated, "We don't just have some people doing community policing; the whole agency is doing community policing. And it's a real relationship [between the police and the citizens]. It's not just pieces of the community working with pieces of the department" (Painter 1995a, 5). Chief Mangan also recognized that the systemic approach to policing could not be implemented overnight and that "community policing has to happen slowly, it has to happen from the bottom up, and it has to allow for adjustments" based on community needs (Painter 1995a, 5). Therefore, the chief allowed the line police officers and members of the community to begin implementing the systemic approach based on mutually identified needs.

A strategic planning committee was created in 1991 to assist in identifying the various problems in Spokane, both criminal and order maintenance, and to determine various methods of how these problems could be addressed. To assist in the communication of the work conducted by the committee, a monthly newsletter was created. Additional subcommittees were formed to address specific areas, such as the West Central citizens' subcommittee which was formed in 1991 and called for "more police presence" (Painter, 1995b, p. 5). Additionally, the Washington State Institute for community-oriented policing (WSICOP) was solicited to help the Spokane Police Department develop evaluation tools to determine what type of assistance was needed and to determine the success of the programs implemented under community-oriented policing.

Since 1992, and through 1996, multiple programs have been implemented that identify with the philosophy of community-oriented policing. As it is necessary to translate the philosophy of the systemic approach into practical application, the Spokane Police Department has done an excellent job in achieving this end. The majority of programs can be divided up into community-oriented policing programs geared toward the youth of Spokane, those aimed at all of the citizens of Spokane, and those programs that create a working relationship between the public and the police to address crime and social disorder issues. Finally, there are some additional programs that have been extremely beneficial to the Spokane Police Department, but one of the key ones is SHOCAP.

The programs implemented for Spokane's youth consist of many of the common programs found nationwide, including the DARE program, McGruff the Crime Dog, drug-free/gun-free school zones, and police trading cards. Additionally, the police department implemented a program known as "Every 15 minutes" that is a two-day program detailing what happens when people drink and drive, as well as a program known as SKID (Safe Kid Identification Disc) that is a child identification kit placed on a computer disc for future identification purposes.

Other youth programs that have been successful and continue to run are the COPS & KIDS program which brings together police officers and young people on a weekend night every August to demonstrate what the police do, and local businesses provide donated food, sodas, and prizes.

Another program known as LEAD (Leadership, Education, and Development Program) formed in 1994, takes eighth- and ninth-graders who have demonstrated leadership abilities through a one-week summer academy that teaches them management and leadership skills, all managed and taught by police officers. Another program that was developed through the innovative idea of one man in the local Spokane community, Don Gerling, pools the police, parents, and concerned neighbors together to walk children home from school to ensure their safety.

Perhaps one of the more renowned and innovative programs conducted by the Spokane Police Department is known as COPY Kids (Community Opportunities Program for Youth) which was started in 1992. The program takes eleven to fifteen-year old youths from disadvantaged neighborhoods, teaching them about community involvement through clean-ups, etc., and at the end of the week they receive a rewarding day of local tours, an afternoon lunch of free pizza, a visit to a local bank where they receive their own savings account of $40, and they "graduate" at the city hall in a ceremony where they are awarded a certificate and T-shirt. This program was evaluated during the 1992 implementation and published in 1993 with a positive response demonstrating the benefits on the part of the youths who participated, the satisfaction of the parents/guardians of the youth, and satisfaction on the part of the employees of the police department who participated (Thurman, Giacomazzi, and Bogen 1993).

The community-oriented policing programs implemented for the benefit of all the citizens of Spokane have also been very successful in their own right. One of the key programs started with the realization on the part of the West Central subcommittee that there were not enough police officers to enhance the full-time presence in their neighborhood, so they initiated the first community-oriented policing substation which opened on May 1, 1992. Since then, there have been nine additional substations opened and four more are in the planning stages. These substations are staffed by citizen volunteers who are trained by the Spokane Police Department and are assisted by the local police officers who work in the neighborhood, generally under another program known as "NRO" (Neighborhood Resource Officer). This program was created in 1992 as well, to match up police officers and residents in specific geographical areas to enhance the communication between both the police and the community. Additionally, a program known as NIRO (Neighborhood Investigative Resource Officer) was also implemented to match a police detective to the same specific geographical boundaries.

Programs implemented by members of the local community include a runaway poster program to help parents locate runaway children, a parents' coalition to help educate concerned parents on problems in the various neighborhoods, and a program known as NOP (Neighborhood Observation Patrol) where volunteers are trained by the Spokane Police Department and then work in the various neighborhoods to assist community members, contact the police in the event they are needed, and provide an extra set of eyes and ears for the police.

One additional program implemented in Spokane that has seen implementation in other community-oriented policing programs with much success, was a Citizens' Academy, where the citizens are provided a free ten-week program that exposes local citizens once a week to the role of the police. Spokane Police Department sponsors three academies a year and have graduated over 250 citizens each year. The benefits of educating and exposing citizens to the profession of policing have been demonstrated through the open communication between the police and the public.

The programs oriented on creating a more effective and efficient police department have consisted of various programs to enhance the police presence by working with community members to address their needs. Those programs implemented to increase the police presence have included an Explorer Scouts program for youths age fifteen to twenty-one, to work sixteen or more hours a month assisting the police and learning about the profession. A co-op program, which is currently being considered nationwide, allows for students working on law enforcement degrees at the local community college to work part-time to provide an experiential understanding of policing that they can bring back to the classroom and hopefully project into a future job with the police department. The co-op students attend a forty-hour academy and are then placed in particular assignments that give them additional hands-on experience because of this training. The co-op is different from the internship program established at the Spokane Police Department where local college students work in the police department for credits, but do not proceed through the miniacademy. A reserve officer program has also allowed police presence to be greatly enhanced as has the senior volunteer program, and the volunteer specialist program which has obtained the services of local citizens who have a special skill or knowledge that can be beneficial to the police department. Members of the community have contributed well over 100,000 hours of assistance per year to all these programs.

In addition, many programs have been established to obtain more information on the needs and wants of the community for addressing crime, disorder, and those items or programs that can increase the quality of life in the neighborhoods. Citizen surveys by the police department, with the assistance of Dr. McGarrel from Washington State University, have provided much in the way of feedback to the police department to understand the public concern about crime and their perceptions as to where additional resources should be allocated. Another method that has been employed to accomplish this form of communication is a monthly newsletter and a chaplaincy program that provides a unique form of communication with the public. And finally, and perhaps most important, is the establishment of the Spokane Police Advisory Committee and many of the subcommittees for particular neighborhoods. While the main advisory committee meets once a month to review community concerns, it also provides a review mechanism for police department policies, departmental hiring procedures, and the status of training and education of both officers and citizens. The subcommittees generally meet on a monthly basis and they provide input and feedback on the programs previously implemented in their neighborhoods, as well as planning for future programs and changes.

Although the Spokane Police Department has implemented many other programs under their community-oriented policing philosophy, one additional program that will be reviewed is one that has also seen implementation across the United States in various jurisdictions. Serious Habitual Offender Comprehensive Action Program (SHOCAP) focuses on juvenile repeat offenders to ensure that they serve time for multiple offenses and do not receive undue leniency. The premise of the program is that a small minority of juveniles commit the majority of juvenile-related crime and therefore they should be targeted through case studies. By recording all suspicious activities among juveniles, securing photos and personal information, as well as maintaining information on arrests, when a juvenile is actually convicted of a crime, their entire past history, including information through their schools such as attendance, crimes, and discipline problems, can be presented to the juvenile judge to allow for a more responsive decision.

As is apparent through the variety of programs provided by the Spokane Police Department and the many programs on the part of the community, Spokane has successfully implemented community-oriented policing. The response on the part of the community, the police, and the civilians who work for the Spokane Police Department has all been positive toward this paradigm in policing. As Spokane Police Department nears the year 2000 and the hopes of having realized their vision, additional programs and police–community cooperation can only enhance what they have all ready established to date.

In perspective of community-oriented policing consisting of the three integral components, it is also apparent that the Spokane Police Department has been successful in the full systemic approach. Although the majority of their programs are geared toward the neighborhood-oriented policing component of community-oriented policing, they have implemented the other two programs with equal success. The SHOCAP program is a strategic-oriented policing method that attempts to alleviate much of the criminal element from the community by targeting the habitual juvenile offender. As a large percentage of the criminal problems are usually committed by a small element of repeat offenders, removing these individuals from the neighborhoods provides immediate benefits to communities by allowing the neighborhood-oriented policing component to flourish. In Spokane, this task has definitely been accomplished and continues on.

The neighborhood-oriented policing programs in Spokane are numerous and they have been very successful because these programs have addressed various concerns: the youth of Spokane, the police and community relations of Spokane, and the lack of resources on the part of the police department. Through the implementation of these and many other types of programs, the police department has been able to provide police services to all the members of their community and live up to the values set forth in their acronym: Service, Pride, and Dedication.

And lastly, they have succeeded in implementing the final component of community-oriented policing, which is problem-oriented policing. Through the utilization of advisory committees, subcommittees, strategic planning committees, and citizen surveys, they have accomplished the key focus of this component, which is to include the concerns and perspectives of the public into their programs and policing practices. They have accomplished this by including input and feedback from the community, line officers, and civilians who work for the police department into most of the decisions that have affected the entire community. Therefore, with this accomplishment and the application of the other two components, Spokane Police Department can be said to have successfully implemented community-oriented policing. As Chief Mangan articulated, one of his main goals is to "structure the department so that interdependence and partnerships [becomes] so essential that we can't function without it" (Painter 1995a, 5).

Parkersburg, West Virginia

Parkersburg is a small city located on the Ohio River in Wood County, West Virginia. It has a population of 33,862 residents and has a unique mixture of industrial, agricultural, and modern technology businesses within its city limits. Parkersburg has traditionally maintained a very low crime rate and is often featured as one of the safest U.S. cities in which to live.

The police department in Parkersburg maintains sixty-five sworn police officers and has retained a strong working relationship with both residents and business owners in the community as a result of the "small-town" atmosphere. They have established many of the key programs associated with community-oriented policing, such as a street level drug unit to address the growing drug problems in the 1980s, the DARE program for the local school children, and the establishment of a policy providing each officer with a take-home cruiser, to be utilized both on and off duty, as a result of listening to the voice of the community, which desired additional police protection. Each of these programs, prior to the department's official adaptation of community-oriented policing, represents each of the three components and demonstrates that many smaller police departments have previously captured the tenets of the systemic approach. Parkersburg is one such police department.

However, in order to move closer to adopting the concept of community-oriented policing, the department implemented additional programs from 1992 to 1996, bringing it more in line with the systemic philosophy. In 1992, the department implemented several community patrol programs, including a Walk & Talk program which consisted of two police officers, permanently assigned, walking a beat in selected neighborhoods. In addition to the foot patrols, in those neighborhoods where walking is not environmentally feasible, the police department implemented a bicycle program.

The department also implemented various types of community crime-prevention programs including a video identification program for the children of Parkersburg and a safety talk program directed at various groups in the community for the prevention of criminal victimization. Additionally, the department implemented several communication programs that attempt to communicate to the public on a larger scale than one-on-one citizen–officer contacts through the use of events for both adults and children, such as the annual Fishing Derby which recently had an attendance of over 6,000 people and a Bike Rodeo that has had an equal response. In both instances the police officers, in uniform, work and play alongside the youth of Parkersburg, but at the same time they talk with the parents of the children. One additional communication program implemented in late 1995 is the "Parkersburg Police Department Speakers' Bureau, a program aimed at adults, where police officers utilize their special skills and knowledge to instruct any group or organization in the community on such topics as: drunk driving, drugs, business security, home safety, winter driving, travel/hotel safety, scams/confidence games, and a variety of additional topics.

In March of 1996, the Parkersburg Police Department moved into what it terms the "next phase of community policing for the department" as it implements the Community-Oriented Police Enforcement Program (COPE). This phase has made allowances for officers to not only develop additional forms

Officer N.E. Nelson (l) and Officer K.P. Blair (standing) of the Parkersburg Police Department, Parkersburg, West Virginia work with a local youth during the annual "Fishing Derby" when ponds are stocked for the event. (Courtesy of the Parkersburg Police Dept., Parkersburg, West Virginia.)

of neighborhood-oriented policing, but it has commenced with the implementation of the third component: problem-oriented policing. Through various changes in their organizational structure and management, the Parkersburg Police Department is providing their officers with the freedom to initiate new programs, to work with the community in addressing both criminal and order maintenance problems, and to reach a joint cooperation where both citizen and police officer will work toward common goals to address these problems.

Although the Parkersburg Police Department is still in what may be considered its infancy stage of community-oriented policing, many of the tenets of the systemic philosophy have long been adhered to by this police department. Formalizing the cooperation with the community under community-oriented policing, however, has allowed the police department to become more focused and goal oriented. The department, from the chief to the line officer, has demonstrated a sincere motivation to adopt the systemic approach, and despite the fact it is too early to truly evaluate the department's success, it appears that community-oriented policing will be successful in this small city along the Ohio River.

CONCLUSION

Community-oriented policing consists of three integral components: strategic-oriented policing, neighborhood-oriented policing, and problem-oriented policing. In order to fully embody the goals of community-oriented policing, all three components must be implemented, thus allowing for the larger concept to succeed. If one component fails to see implementation in cooperation with the other two, the systemic approach to policing is not complete and is therefore predestined to fail. Each component is reliant upon the other for the systemic approach to be actualized.

Strategic-oriented policing must be implemented immediately, whether with the involvement of local community groups or by the police department alone. The areas to be targeted must be determined and prioritized and the various tactics that would work best to address the criminal or order maintenance problem should be implemented. From there the community must be drawn into the program and planning for the neighborhood-oriented policing programs that would best suit the needs of the target area must be determined. As the sense of urgency of these programs is created and the criminal or order maintenance element is removed from the community temporarily, it allows the community to establish a sense of order and take back their corners, streets, and communities. A continual analysis of the problems must be conducted and new approaches to addressing these problems must be created. These programs must then be implemented and evaluated based on a variety of factors and a determination should be made for the program to be abolished, continued, or enhanced. And should the synthesis of the three components result in diffusion, this can only be considered beneficial to the interaction between the community and the police. Then, and only then, can community-oriented policing, a systemic approach to policing, be evaluated as the true paradigm of policing.

Recognizing the various scenarios for the implementation of community-oriented policing and how the three components become integrated under the systemic approach to policing, it is important to turn to the changes that should occur in order to provide an environment in which the framework of community-oriented policing can thrive. This must start with changes in the organization and management of the police (Chapter 7) as well as changes in the role of the police (Chapter 8). Additionally, changes on the part of the community must be observed (Chapter 9) as well as changes in the role of the police chief (Chapter 10). It is to these changes we must now turn.

REFERENCES

Bratton, William J. "William J. Bratton: Police Training for Youth." *Policy Review,* March/April 1996, 26–27.

Brown, Lee P. *Policing New York City in the 1990s: The Strategy for Community Policing.* New York: New York City Police Department, 1991.

Brown, Lee P. and Mary Ann Wycoff. "Policing Houston: Reducing Fear and Improving Service." *Crime & Delinquency* 33 no. 1 (January 1987): 71–89.

Dilulio, John J., Jr. "Arresting Ideas." *Policy Review.* no. 74 (Fall 1995): 12–16.

Eggers, William D. and John O'Leary. "The Beat Generation." *Policy Review* no. 74, (Fall 1995): 4–11.

Farrell, Michael J. "The Development of the Community Patrol Officer Program: Community-Oriented Policing in the New York City Police Department." In *Community Policing: Rhetoric or Reality.* ed. Jack R. Greene and Stephen D. Mastrofski. New York: Praeger Publishers, 1988.

Lacayo, Richard. "Law and Order." *Time,* January 15, 1996, 48–54.

McElroy, Jerome E., Colleen A. Cosgrove, and Susan Sadd. *Community Policing: The CPOP in New York.* Newbury Park, CA.: SAGE Publications Inc., 1993.

Painter, Ellen. "The Secrets of Their Success." *Community Policing Exchange.* Washington, D.C.: The Community Policing Consortium, May/June 1995a.

Painter, Ellen. "Tragedy Sparks Community Policing in Spokane, Washington." *Community Policing Exchange.* Washington, D.C.: The Community Policing Consortium, May/June 1995b.

Pooley, Eric. "One Good Apple." *Time,* January 15, 1996, 54–56.

Roberg, Roy. "Can Today's Police Organizations Effectively Implement Community Policing?" In *The Challenge of Community Policing: Testing the Promises.* ed. Dennis P. Rosenbaum. Thousand Oaks, CA.: SAGE Publications, Inc., 1994.

Skogan, Wesley G. and M.G. Maxfield. *Coping with Crime: Individual and Neighborhood Reactions.* Beverly Hills: SAGE Publications, Inc., 1981.

Thurman, Quint C., Andrew Giacomazzi, and Phil Bogen. "Research Note: Cops, Kids, and Community Policing—An Assessment of a Community Policing Demonstration Project." *Crime & Delinquency* 39, no. 4 (October 1993): 554–564.

Weisburd, David and Jerome E. McElroy. "Enacting the CPO Role: Findings from the New York City Pilot Program in Community Policing." In *Community Policing: Rhetoric or Reality.* ed. Jack R. Greene and Stephen D. Mastrofski. New York: Praeger Publishers, 1988.

CHAPTER 7

Organization and Management

Order or disorder depends on organization.

-Sun Tzu-

When a police department moves toward community-oriented policing, it should be understood that in order for the overall concept to be a viable program, the police department must implement all three components: strategic-oriented policing, neighborhood-oriented policing, and problem-oriented policing. However, the concept of community-oriented policing cannot stop there and have any hope of being successful. It must not only change the way the product of policing is delivered or what services are offered, but the entire organization and methods of management that provide and deliver these services must change as well. The police department must go far beyond the narrow confines of the three components and the current methods of policing. The police department cannot implement a few new programs, call it community policing, and hope it will become the panacea for all crime and disorder. This kind of thinking—that community-oriented policing is but one more short-term, fly-by-night program that the line officers will have to implement on a small scale until management realizes its ineffectiveness and allows the "program" to be folded and labeled a failure—must not be allowed to fester. This method of thought is too narrowly focused and does not comprehend the overall goal of community-oriented policing. Rather, community-oriented policing, should be seen as a long-term, systemic method of policing that must permeate the entire police department in order to achieve its goals. As Goldstein wrote, "Unlike many of the changes that have occurred in American policing over the years, community policing, if it is to realize its full potential, should not be viewed merely as a new project, method, or procedure that can simply be added, as an appendage of sorts, to an existing police organization. It can better be described as a way of thinking about policing—as an operating philosophy that, in order to succeed, must eventually have a pervasive influence on the operation of the entire agency" (Goldstein 1987, 10–11).

This change, beyond the three components of community-oriented policing, is then critical to its success.

"CRIME FILES"

STREET PEOPLE—PART 19

This edition of the "Crime Files," hosted by James Q. Wilson, features James Durkin, Philadelphia Police Department; Robert M. Hayes, National Coalition for the Homeless; and Gerald L. Lowry, Santa Barbara Police Department. The discussion revolves around how various police departments are taking a community-oriented policing approach to dealing with runaways, the mentally ill, temporarily homeless, alcoholics, etc.

In order to fully achieve the implementation of the systemic approach to policing, the organization and management structure must be changed. A police department that continues to utilize a traditional approach to policing but implements the components of community-oriented policing may realize some positive effects. Strategic-oriented policing, through the utilization of directed patrols, aggressive patrols, and saturation patrols, may indeed have some short-term success. However, without any programs to replace the police presence and an organizational structure to support such programs, strategic-oriented policing will fail. Neighborhood-oriented policing, without this structural change, will ultimately fail for lack of community support at the lowest level, and police officers will have no hope of successfully implementing the problem-oriented policing approach to dealing with crime and order maintenance issues. The current organizational structure and styles of management in policing will not allow this systemic approach to grow, and the same people who would give birth to this new idea would also in turn kill the idea through either ignorance, misunderstanding, or an unwillingness to change.

Ignorance of the program can be excused. In a time when such a vast number of people are attempting to learn about this new systemic approach to policing, an abundance of ignorance exists on everyone's part. Misunderstanding and disagreements are also very common in the area of community-oriented policing, for the literature is sketchy at best in the conceptual arena and generally lacking in the considerations for application. However, the unwillingness to change must be overcome, something that police have traditionally been slow to

Members of the Neighborhood Crime Watch Community
Resource Unit celebrate the "National Nite Out" with a sheet cake.
St. Petersburg, Florida.(Courtesy of St. Petersburg Police Dept.,
St. Petersburg, Florida.)

allow. This has been a major obstacle of policing throughout the twentieth century and will be no different with the advent of community-oriented policing.
Understanding the problems that cause this unwillingness to change can assist
us when implementing the systemic approach to policing, which will be
addressed in a later chapter. For now, it is important to understand the type of
organizational and management changes that must be made and how they
should progress.

This chapter will discuss the process of changing the organization and
management structure of a traditional police department to a community-oriented policing police department. It will first deal with the police department's
ability to communicate the values and goals of community-oriented policing to
both the members of the police department and the members of the community. This communication must be accomplished through the creation of a new
mission statement for the police department. Once this reorientation of the
mission of the police is complete, then the police department must move
toward establishing a decentralized organization, which includes decentralizing
by geography, personnel, and structure. Finally, the methods of managing the
police department must be altered, utilizing Total Quality Management (TQM),
to not only accommodate, but complement the overall process.

VALUES AND GOALS

As a police department begins implementing the three components, it must also
begin changing the organizational and management structure that will allow for

achieving the maximum potential under this concept. Making changes to the way police perform their duties is often difficult, but perhaps the greatest hurdle is changing the way officers think. As community-oriented policing is concerned with changing the values and goals of a police department in order to focus on the community, a clear statement about these values and goals can be beneficial to changing the way police officers think (Bureau of Justice Assistance 1994; Wasserman and Moore 1988). By expressing these values, the police department can put forth the beliefs of the organization, the standards that are to be maintained by its members, and the broader mission to be achieved through their activities (Kelling, Wasserman, and Williams 1988, 3). The vehicle for this value statement is the police department's mission statement.

COP IN ACTION

DENTON POLICE DEPARTMENT: THE MISSION

The mission of the Denton Police Department is to positively impact the quality of life throughout the community. To achieve these ends, the department is committed to forming practical partnerships with the citizenry, which includes a mutual goal-setting process aimed at resolving problems, reducing fear, preserving the peace, and enforcing the law; thereby providing a safe environment for all citizens.

Source: Denton Police Department. *Community-Oriented Policing: A Strategy.* Denton, TX.: Denton Police Department, 1995.

In order to create a new mission statement, the police department must first reorient the direction of the police department by focusing on the value and goals of community-oriented policing. It must determine those key aspects of policing that are most important to the community. The best way to do this is by soliciting the assistance of the community to determine what, overall, is most important to them. This should then be reflected within the police department by making the necessary changes to the mission statement.

COP IN ACTION

DENTON POLICE DEPARTMENT: THE VISION

The Denton Police Department's goal is to provide a system of delivering police services to neighborhoods based on three basic elements:

- Consultation
- Adaptation
- Mobilization

This system of service is termed Community-Oriented Policing Services (COPS). This system is one where every member of the department takes personal pride and ownership in the mission of the department. Members of the department should collectively internalize and rationalize the mission statement.

We see an organization that projects a positive attitude. We strive to achieve a reputation as a progressive and innovative organization. We want our COPS to be a model for any other organizations that wish to adopt its philosophies and strategies.

COPS must structure service delivery in a way that reinforces the strengths of the city's neighborhoods. COPS involves the community in all policing activities that directly impact the quality of community life. In order to accomplish this, we must develop a positive relationship between citizens and police that promotes ownership of neighborhoods.

In our COPS, line officers are the link between citizens and the management of the organization. Line officers create opportunities and situations to talk to average law-abiding citizens who are neither victims nor perpetrators. Through these activities, line officers collect information about what the citizens want in the way of police service in their respective neighborhoods. We must integrate all line officers into the consultation process because they routinely communicate with citizens regardless of their division assignment.

In days of shrinking budgets and financial crisis, we must manage resources in a careful and effective manner. As a progressive organization, we seek employee input into matters which impact job satisfaction and effectiveness.

Above all other things we are an organization committed to preserving and advancing constitutional values and rights of individuals. We shall endeavor to maintain the highest levels of integrity and professionalism in all actions.

Source: Denton Police Department. *Community-Oriented Policing: A Strategy.* Denton, TX.: Denton Police Department, 1995.

The mission statement should reflect the community's expectations of the police and should provide an orientation for every member of the department. It should articulate the values that are important to the community-oriented policing approach and it should state the overall goal of the police department. In turn, everything that the police department then does should reflect the new mission statement and should be conducted in such a manner that it supports these values and goals.

TABLE 7.1 THE ADVANTAGES OF MISSION-DRIVEN GOVERNMENT

- Mission-driven organizations are more efficient than rule-driven organizations.
- Mission-driven organizations are also more effective than rule-driven organizations: They produce better results.
- Mission-driven organizations are more innovative than rule-driven organizations.

- Mission-driven organizations are more flexible than rule-driven organizations.
- Mission-driven organizations have higher morale than rule-driven organizations.

Source: Adapted with permission from Osborne, David and Ted Gaebler. *Reinventing Government: How the Entrepreneurial Spirit is Transforming the Public Sector From Schoolhouse to Statehouse, City Hall to the Pentagon.* Reading, MA.: Addison-Wesley Publishing Company, Inc., 1992.

Additionally, when implementing a new mission statement, it should be short and simplistic in nature, and it should be published and readily available to all members of the community. An example of the perfect mission statement is the preamble to the Constitution of the United States which, in fifty-two words, is capable of orienting and focusing a nation of over 260 million citizens.

One example of a mission statement from a police department that shifted its style of policing to community policing in the latter part of 1992 is found in the Hercules Police Department, Hercules, California, in the San Francisco Bay area. The department shifted its focus and created the following mission statement to reflect such a change:

We, the members of the Hercules Police Department, are committed to the improvement of the quality of life for the citizens of Hercules by working in partnership with them. We will work to maintain safe and secure neighborhoods while treating everyone with respect and dignity. We will be open-minded and consistently improve ourselves professionally in order to serve the community. (Muehleisen 1995, 31).

TABLE 7.2   THE MOST IMPORTANT VALUES A POLICE DEPARTMENT CAN INCORPORATE

- Preserve and advance the principles of democracy.
- Place the highest value on preserving human life.
- Preventing crime as the number one operational priority.
- Involve the community in delivering police services.
- Believe in accountability to the community served.
- Commitment to professionalism in all aspects of operations.
- Maintain the highest standards of integrity.

Source: U.S. Department of Justice. *Community Relations Service.* Washington, D.C.: U.S. Department of Justice, 1987.

Another example of reorienting the police department can be found in the Madison, Wisconsin move to what it termed "quality policing" (Couper 1991; Wycoff and Skogan 1994). Between 1987 and 1990, the Police Foundation, through funding by the National Institute of Justice, studied the implementation of community-oriented policing in Madison, Wisconsin, and their orientation is quickly reflected in the police department's motto: "Closer to the People:

Quality from the Inside, out" (Muehleisen 1995, 77). However, the police department also created a form of a mission statement, their creation "Twelve Principles of Quality Leadership" (Muehleisen 1995, 76). By doing this, they provided an orientation for the entire police department, as well as simultaneously shifting the management philosophy, and in turn the organizational structure, through one "quasi" mission statement. In order to understand how this was achieved, it is important to review the twelve principles:

1. Believe in, foster, and support *teamwork*.
2. Be committed to the *problem-solving* process; use it and let *data*, not emotions, drive decisions.
3. Seek employees' *input* before you make decisions.
4. Believe that the best way to improve the quality of work or service is to *ask* and *listen* to employees who are doing work.
5. Strive to develop mutual *respect* and *trust* among employees.
6. Have a *customer* orientation and focus toward employees and citizens.
7. Manage the *behavior* of 95% of employees and not on that of the 5% who cause problems.
8. *Improve systems* and examine processes before blaming people.
9. Avoid "top down", *power-oriented* decision making whenever possible.
10. Encourage creativity through *risk-taking* and be tolerant of honest *mistakes*.
11. Be a *facilitator* and *coach*. Develop an *open* atmosphere that encourages providing and accepting *feedback*.
12. With teamwork, develop with employees agreed-upon *goals* and *a plan* to achieve them. (Wycoff and Skogan 1994, 76)

As in the case of the Hercules Police Department and the Madison Police Department, in order to change the organization and management structures from a traditional to community-oriented approach, the values and goals of the police department must be changed. This change should be reflected in the police department's mission statement and communicated to every member of the police force and the community as well. From this reorientation of values and goals, the police department can begin the overall organization and management changes to support and complement community-oriented policing. This is especially apparent when returning to the one key change the police department must undertake if community-oriented policing is to succeed—decentralization.

TABLE 7.3   NEWPORT NEWS POLICE DEPARTMENT STATEMENT OF VALUES

Value #1 - The Newport News Police Department is committed to protecting and preserving the rights of individuals as guaranteed by the Constitution.

Value #2 - While the Newport News Police Department believes the prevention of crime is its primary responsibility, it aggressively pursues those who commit serious offenses.

Value #3 - The Newport News Police Department believes that integrity and professionalism are the foundation for trust in the community.

Value #4 - The Newport News Police Department is committed to an open and honest relationship with the community.

Value #5 - The Newport News Police Department is committed to effectively managing its resources for optimal service delivery.

Value #6 - The Newport News Police Department is committed to participating in programs which incorporate the concept of shared responsibility with the community in the delivery of police services.

Value #7 - The Newport News Police Department actively solicits citizen participation in the development of police activities and programs which impact their neighborhood.

Value #8 - The Newport News Police Department believes it achieves its greatest potential through the active participation of its employees in the development and implementation of programs.

Value #9 - The Newport News Police Department recognizes and supports academic achievement of employees and promotes their pursuit of higher education.

ORGANIZATION THROUGH DECENTRALIZATION

The concept of decentralization is not new to police departments in the United States. One can trace back through the history of policing in America and find that the police were decentralized for all of the political era and to some degree the public relations era as described in Chapter 1. The variables of geography, poor administration, management, leadership, and the lack of communications and technology, all contributed to the fact that police departments were decentralized. Yet the single most important variable was the police departments' entrenchment in local politics. Most police departments consisted of specific ethnic groups that reflected the dominant ethnic group in the community, and they were so closely tied to the local politicians, that most, if not all of the police departments, during this era were considered corrupt (Fogelson 1977; Walker 1977). This prompted many reform-minded individuals such as August Vollmer and O. W. Wilson to move the police organization toward a strictly centralized organization utilizing key management concepts such as chain of command, unity of command, and span of control. The centralized organizational form presented itself as the best means for controlling the rampant corruption, political links, and deviant behavior among line officers. During the public relations era, centralization became the commonly accepted form of police management, and by the police–community relations era, it was an institutional norm.

This strict adherence to a centralized command and to standard operating procedures had an additional effect on policing that would not become evident until the late 1960s. The methods employed to prevent corruption involved strict centralized control, demanding scientific and impersonal methods for dealing with crime, and careful recording and documentation of any and all activity to demonstrate what officers were doing during their tours of duty. As Wilson points out, "this led police managers to treat their departments as if they were production agencies" and "in turn led the officers to emphasize those aspects of their job that were most easily standardized and recorded, that could be directed by radio transmission, and that generated statistics" (Wilson 1989, 170). The emphasis during the public relations era and into the police–community relations era was one of "law enforcement" because it was easier to document and generate arrest and traffic statistics then to describe how many personal interventions an officer made during a shift. As Wilson sums up, "one part of the police job, order maintenance, was sacrificed to another part, law enforcement" (Wilson 1989, 170). The public, dissatisfied with rampant disorder in their communities, called for government to address these growing problems; however, the centralized form of control was not a complementary method to address these types of problems.

Today, as police departments move toward a philosophy of responsiveness to community needs, there has been an overwhelming call for the decentralization of the police (Geller 1991; Goldstein 1990; Greene, Bergman, and McLaughlin 1994; Rosenbaum and Lurigio 1994; Skogan 1994; Wilkinson and Rosenbaum 1994). Despite the Byzantine effort to centralize the police throughout the twentieth century, the current undertaking across the nation is to decentralize the police. This has not been without good reason. Although there is little argument that a centralized police department can more effectively control the problems of corruption and misconduct, it does not allow the police to be responsive to the needs of the community. Additionally, in order for the three components of community-oriented policing to succeed, the organization and management of a police department must have decentralized authority. Community-oriented policing cannot thrive in a paramilitary, bureaucratic, authoritarian method of organization, but rather needs one that is democratic in nature and allows the line officers to participate in the management process. The implementation of neighborhood programs and problem solving must rest in the hands of the line police officer working in partnership with the community. Therefore, the decision-making process and operational methods must be pushed down the chain of command and into the hands of the line officer. All of this can be achieved primarily through the decentralization of the police.

The decentralization of the police department is in actuality a three-part process. There is the decentralization by geography, personnel, and by structure. The decentralization by geography, often called "physical decentralization" (Radelet and Carter 1994), is concerned with the geographical boundaries of communities within a police department's jurisdiction and how the police service these areas. The decentralization by personnel is concerned with the placement of the line officers within these geographical areas based on shifts, time, and location. And the decentralization by structure, often called "decentralization of authority" (Radelet and Carter 1994), is the process by which the police department decentralizes the structure of the department to include the areas of patrol, investigation, and administration. All three forms are extremely critical under community-oriented policing and the distinction is made for clarity, rather than for individual selection. All three must go hand-in-hand during the decentralization process in order for the overall concept of decentralization to be complete. Decentralization then becomes the glue to our community-oriented policing model.

TABLE 7.4 THE ADVANTAGES OF A DECENTRALIZED INSTITUTION

1) They are far more flexible than centralized institutions; they can respond quickly to changing circumstances and customer's needs.

2) Decentralized institutions are more effective than centralized institutions.

3) Decentralized institutions are far more innovative than centralized institutions.

4) Decentralized institutions generate higher morale, more commitment, and greater productivity.

Source: Adapted with permission from Osborne, David and Ted Gaebler. *Reinventing Government: How the Entrepreneurial Spirit is Transforming the Public Sector From Schoolhouse to Statehouse, City Hall to the Pentagon.* Reading, MA.: Addison-Wesley Publishing Company, Inc., 1992.

Police departments have traditionally organized their police officers along geographical boundaries. Police officers are usually assigned a specific area to patrol during their shift and these areas tend to rotate on a daily or weekly schedule. The geographical boundaries are often based on logical boundaries where main roads and the size of communities are the deciding factors in the parameters of a particular police beat. Other factors are generally not taken into consideration and the sole purpose of the boundaries is to tell the officer where he or she can and cannot patrol. Under community-oriented policing, this mentality must change, and the method is through a decentralization of area beats.

Police beats or posts are generally the smallest geographic areas that a police officer on duty is responsible for patrolling (Dempsey 1994, 60). A sector or zone is often the term utilized to distinguish several beats and posts as having a collective area for supervisory responsibility or to distinguish the outer limits of a patrol's responsibility (Dempsey 1994, 60). A precinct is generally the entire collection of beats and sectors established in a particular part of the city or county, such as a county with a north precinct and a south precinct (Dempsey 1994, 60–61). Although this division of the police department's jurisdiction is critical in traditional policing, it is also critical in community-oriented policing. However, the difference lies in how the pie is divided.

As previously stated, most jurisdictions will look to physical boundaries and size to determine beats, sectors, and precincts. Under community-oriented policing, the orientation of beats, sectors, and precincts is based on residential and commercial areas, as well as overall communities where the two are integrated. The police should recognize the various neighborhoods and create the beat around these collections of houses, townhomes, or apartments. Neighborhoods can be identified by various methods such as homeowner's associations, pre-planned community areas, and from the various government organizations that divide areas based on community names. In some cases the beats may be organized along the lines of commercial areas that form their own type of neighborhood, but are all a collection of similar businesses and stores. In other cases, the beats can become so small that they may fit the needs of a particular place that creates, in a sense, its own community, such as a school or park.

The larger concentration of beats, known as sectors or zones, should still be established, but they should be a collection of schools, churches, and commercial establishments that service a particular neighborhood, or several neighborhoods that are similar in nature. The supervisor can then remain in charge of this area, but must work with the community through his or her officers, as a quasi-police chief for the area. As the officers implement the three components in their particular beats, the supervisor becomes responsible for coordinating and distributing or redistributing resources among the various beats, tracking each officer's progress, and maintaining a larger perspective of how each beat or each problem affects the others identified by his or her officers.

The precincts only become necessary in the case of large jurisdictional areas where the collection of communities that congregate in the various areas are dissimilar in nature. A division by precinct may be made necessary if, for example, returning to the north and south division, one is middle class to upper class with low crime rates, while the other is predominantly lower class with high crime rates. The overall emphasis of community-oriented policing will take on different roles in both of these jurisdictional areas, and therefore may necessitate the use of precincts. Regardless, when utilizing beats, sectors, and precincts, they must be divided based on how the community sees their neighborhoods and commercial areas, rather than logical, visible, physical boundaries.

One method that may assist in the decentralization by geography is the establishment of neighborhood police stations, based on the community's neighborhoods and commercial areas. These are often called ministations, substations, or storefront stations (Bennett 1994; Kelling and Moore 1988; Klockars 1988; Skolnick and Bayley 1986). The police department can create a miniature police department within a particular community in a variety of ways. Establishing a storefront by renting a store or borrowing space within a store to establish a place that members of the community may go to speak with, report crime to, or discuss issues with the police is one possibility. Another possibility is reopening a closed precinct station located in an area accessible to a particular community or several communities whereby several beats may be able to utilize the space.

There is also the possibility that a police department may confiscate a condominium, townhome, or house through asset forfeiture related to drugs or by having one donated to the police department. This becomes an excellent substation because it is already established within the community and is readily accessible to all members of that neighborhood. The Manassas Police Department, Manassas, Virginia, did just that by establishing a substation in a

The Fall 1995 Berkeley Police Department, Berkeley California;
Youth Baseball League. A true example of Neighborhood-Oriented
Policing. (Courtesy of the Berkeley Police Dept., Berkeley, California.)

townhome in an area known for high crime rates and drug activity. This essentially allowed the police to have a foothold in the community and it afforded an opportunity by which the law-abiding members of the community could report criminal and order maintenance problems, as well as having a nearby shelter in the event it was needed.

Another possibility is the establishment of substations within the local school system. Every public school, from elementary to high schools, have their own unique problems, ones indigenous to that particular school. By having a police officer permanently assigned to the school as his or her beat, the benefits inherent in community-oriented policing are quickly realized. The Arlington County Police Department, in Arlington, Virginia, established this type of program in their county, and crime rates in the schools dropped, order maintenance problems were addressed, and the students and teachers had their own full-time police officer. Eventually, Arlington established a policy that when a student was picked up by another police officer, that student would be brought to his or her school's assigned police officer. Because that police officer was more familiar with the student's background, it provided additional methods of dealing with the youth, and it created a more personal relationship between the officer and the student as the student always had to deal with one particular officer.

There are generally mixed views on the benefits of police substations (Skolnick and Bayley 1986), however much of the discourse is a result of the failed "team policing" project in the early 1970s that utilized a storefront approach without any backing from their respective police departments (Sherman, Milton & Kelly 1973; Sherman 1975). The storefront or substation design can be of great benefit to the community-oriented policing approach as long as officers do not utilize the substation as a barrier to the public, but rather as one method of creating a bridge between the police and the public. These storefronts, substations, and ministations are important because, "the purpose behind all of them is to create the possibility of more intensive police–community interaction and heightened identification by police officers with particular areas" (Skolnick and Bayley 1986, 214). This concept can be extremely helpful in assisting police departments decentralize by geography.

In response to decentralizing by geography, there becomes an even greater need to decentralize by personnel. The decentralization of personnel is based on shifts, time, and location. As many police departments in the United States utilize rotating shifts, the officers are generally never in the same beat, during the same particular time, for any great length of time. Although this was desired during the reform era and was regarded as the standard in policing, it is no longer desirable. Over the past several decades there has been a move to establish fixed shifts in many police departments, where police officers work the same shift the same days of the week. However, in both the rotating and fixed shifts form of policing, the beat the officer is assigned to is generally not fixed. Beats will rotate from day to day and the officer is at a disadvantage when trying to learn what criminal or order maintenance problems exist in a neighborhood. And in the event they do ascertain the problems, they have no ties to the community and are not around enough to implement any type of program. Under a community-oriented policing approach, the officers must be decentralized to the degree that their shifts, times, and the location, or beat, they are responsible for, remains the same.

This form of decentralization would establish a police officer in a particular beat enabling him or her to come to know all of the citizens that live in the neighborhood and what they perceive as criminal and order maintenance problems. It "enables an officer to get to know the problems of a community, the strengths and weaknesses of existing systems of control, and the various resources that are useful in solving problems" (Goldstein 1990, 160). Even the difference between rotating the times, but not the beats, creates many difficulties for the officer, because those problems that need to be addressed during the night are different than those revealed during the day. Therefore, the police officer should be assigned permanently to a shift, time, and location for a period of several years.

Along with the decentralization of personnel, it is inherent within the establishment of a permanent assignment in a specific beat that the decentralization of decisionmaking and authority rest in the hands of the police officer. The police officer, by having the capabilities of working within the community on a regular basis, must have additional authority to work with the community members to establish the three components and have the freedom to implement those that the officer and the community believe would best work to meet the community's needs. The centralized method of authority, top-down management, cannot work in this setting, for the top level management will not have the vast amount of information and interaction that the community policing officer will have.

In accordance with this additional authority and decision-making ability, the police officer must become more involved in top level planning and implementation through an increase in the participatory style of management (Kelling and Moore 1988; Wilkinson and Rosenbaum 1994). Officers must be a part of the management process that creates, implements, and evaluates those programs under the three components. They must be involved in the coordinated efforts to respond to all criminal and order maintenance problems within their patrol area. And their contact with the community, their understanding of the real and perceived problems, must be heard and their decisions respected. However, in order to achieve these varied roles, tasks, and requirements of the police officer under community-oriented policing, it is imperative that under these personnel changes, the personnel position of police officer change as well.

Every aspect of the position of police officer will change as a result of the adoption of the systemic approach to policing. The adoption of the mission statement, values, and goals under the community-oriented policing philosophy should be the guiding principles for the department; however, police officers will find their own mission statement in terms of the job description which must be "comprehensive in terms of duties, responsibilities, working conditions, knowledge, skills, and abilities required for successful performance of the job, and it should indicate the relative importance of the various work behaviors so identified" (Geller 1991, 365–366). These duties will be drastically different from those of traditional policing, and they should be based on the new community-oriented mission statement, as well as a job analysis "which consists of describing and evaluating a job in terms of tasks performed, methods or tools used, services provided, and knowledge, skills, and abilities required to perform the tasks successfully" (Geller 1991, 365). These will include traditional aspects of the job, along with such things as public speaking, organizational skills, and problem-solving abilities. It is this job description of the community-oriented policing officer upon which all other personnel issues will be based.

COP IN ACTION

INVESTIGATION AT THE LOCAL LEVEL

The minds of investigators who implement the methodologies of community policing allow for citizens to be "customers" of the system. Decentralized investigative functions are customer-focused, proactive, autonomous, and accountable. Decentralization enables investigators to provide localized service, which is more effective against crime. In contrast, large, centralized police departments may consider citizens to be "complainants" who are easily lost in the sprawling bureaucracy.

An example of the success of investigative decentralization is found in the Philadelphia Police Department (PPD), where administrators as well as the rank-and-file employees personalize service and provide a localized link between the police and the people. Philadelphia is the fourth largest city in the United States (population 1.6 million) and the police department is one of the oldest in the nation. It deploys some 6,300 sworn police officers and 1,000 civilian employees responsible for public safety within 130 square miles. In 1990, a comprehensive plan was undertaken which delineated strategies for improving public safety and service.

The five-year plan is a new vision for the PPD, a guide to building a better department and a better city. In addition to implementing the decentralization process on a department-wide basis, the plan also included ideas for fostering continued efficiency and productivity in the investigative function. The plan was directed toward improved public safety and quality of life. The department took the first step toward achieving their goals by decentralizing the investigative and patrol functions. Detective headquarters was organizationally dismantled and responsibility was spread among seven field divisions headed by a department called "Command Inspection."

According to a study by the Citizens Crime Commission of the Delaware Valley, decentralization of the investigative function in Philadelphia is generally regarded as a positive achievement. By adopting community policing philosophies and strategies at the local level, both the department and the community realized the intended benefits of a better-integrated system. Officers and investigators are more directly involved and accountable to the communities they serve and communication, both internal and external, has improved. Investigators are encouraged to establish, build, and further develop positive working relationships with victim advocacy groups, civic organizations, police district advisory councils, and other stake-holders in the system.

Another result has been to speed up investigative response time. Decentralization advocates propose that community policing gives officers and investigators the chance to concentrate efforts locally and more easily track criminal patterns. But there were some doubts whether decentralized functions were as effective when confronted with crime patterns on a city-wide scale.

Decentralization is an evolutionary process, constantly changing as the social environment of American life changes. Community policing involves continual flexibility and adjusting to the needs of the communities. It is a new era for police work in this country: a time when public servants and citizens are true partners against crime.

Source: Adapted with permission from J. Smith, William "Investigation at the Local Level." *Law and Order*, September 1994, 63–65.

These additional personnel areas will include everything from recruiting, to training, to performance appraisals, to promotion of community-oriented policing officers. The criteria for hiring, from the written test to the interview, should see systemic changes that reflect a community-oriented policing approach, thereby giving the police department an excellent opportunity to hire based on its values and goals (Booth 1995). Once hired, the training of the new recruit will become a concern that must go far beyond the traditional police academy emphasis on law, rules, and procedures (Kelling, Wasserman, and Williams 1988, 5). Although these three areas of training are still critical to the police officer, additional areas must be emphasized such as community relations, the problem-solving process, and organizational skills for coordinating meetings, activities, and programs. Additionally, in-service training must be provided on these same skills for officers who worked for the police department prior to the adoption of community-oriented policing. A number of police departments that have implemented the systemic approach have had significant success training officers to identify, analyze, and implement various responses to community concerns (Goldstein 1990; Eck and Spelman 1987; Higdon and Hubert 1987).

Two additional police personnel issues that come into play include the method of evaluating the officer's performance as a community-oriented policing officer and, based upon this, the promotion process under the systemic approach. The system utilized for performance evaluations must be changed to reflect the goals of community-oriented policing, which, again, may include problem-solving capabilities, community interaction, and community mobilization capabilities (Bureau of Justice Assistance 1994, 37–38). These evaluations under the new job descriptions and mission statements will be the impetus for promotions. These promotions to the next higher rank or position should not be based upon traditional policing methods such as quota systems, but rather on many factors such as the number and effectiveness of neighborhood-oriented policing programs implemented and the abilities of the officer to solve problems under the problem-oriented policing approach. There must be some recognition for the community-oriented policing accomplishments that complement the promotion process (Booth 1995; Goldstein 1990), because there are fewer opportunities in a decentralized or "flattened pyramid" organization when it comes to promotions. This then leads to the issue that in order for the police officer to be able to perform and succeed under this added weight of authority and decision-making and reduced room for advancement, the organization itself, must be decentralized in such a manner that it will support and encourage the community-oriented policing officer.

The final form of decentralization is the decentralization by structure. Traditionally, police departments have organized along the lines of a bureaucracy, as was previously discussed, and therefore established the hierarchy by function. Most police departments see the division along the lines of patrol, administrative, and support services. Within this structure of the police department there is a strict chain of command that all members of the department must adhere to and this generally promulgates multiple layers of mid-level and upper-level management. This standard structure of management and organization must change if community-oriented policing is to remain a viable program. The police department must decentralize the functions and the levels of command by flattening the organizational pyramid.

If we understand the police department as being a pyramid with all of the line officers at the bottom, the police chief at the top, and multiple layers of management in between, we then understand the structure of a typical police department. The goal of community-oriented policing is to flatten this hierarchical pyramid. We must realign the levels of management, integrating various levels of management, then pushing them outward, not upward. By

Figure 7.1

reducing the number of levels, as Kelling and Moore point out (1988, 20), it creates a paradox, because "while the number of managerial levels may decrease, the number of managers may increase." In other words, if we have a police department with the simple ranks of police officer, corporal, sergeant, lieutenant, captain, and chief, we will abolish the ranks of corporal and captain, but create additional sergeant slots and lieutenant slots. Although we are disrupting the rank structure, we succeed in abolishing two levels of management and we create more management responsibility and authority for those existing managers than they previously had under the centralized form of police organization (Kelling and Moore 1988, 20). One example commonly cited is the decentralization of the Roman Catholic Church which cut its multiple levels of management to five, and despite this major decentralization has managed to oversee and provide for over 1 billion people in the world.

Figure 7.2

Recognizing, however, that there are fewer opportunities in a decentralized organization when it comes to promotions, the community-oriented police department may want to consider alternatives. One possibility that police departments may consider is a reorientation of the rank structure that allows police officers room for advancement in both rank and pay, yet at the same time remains true to the concept of flattening the pyramid or hierarchical structure of the police department. The police department could establish some other form of promoting police officers into higher ranks, without necessarily placing them into management positions. This could be accomplished through the creation of two separate tracks, one for management and one for line officers, where certain ranks or grade levels can denote level of authority, expertise, or experience.

The areas of function within a police department, specifically the administrative and service operations, must also be decentralized as well to assist the line officers on the street. This includes the entire work force, both sworn and non-sworn personnel, working within the police department. The structure then focuses on the most important asset the police department has in its community relations—the police officer—or, for clarity in relation to the new form of policing, the community-oriented policing officer. This is the ultimate goal for not only the decentralization by function, but by geography and personnel as well.

There are essentially five clear benefits to the decentralization of a police department. First and foremost is the fact that the overall decentralization supports community-oriented policing. Without the decentralized organization and management structure, police officers would not have the support, freedom, or authority to make the decisions and implement the programs at their level. The difficulty in a top-down approach lies in information that is not connected to the concerns of the public, but rather the concerns of management. If all of the decisions made on the street with citizen input were required to be processed up the chain of command for approval and then processed back to the line officer, this would make for a slow, burdensome, and often incompetent form of management. What is then needed is more authority vested in the line officers, the ones working with the citizens, to make the decisions at their level. The decentralized organization and management structure are both complementary to this style of management and allow for a method by which community-oriented policing can be supported for the long term.

The second benefit of decentralization are the fewer layers of management that the line officers must deal with; hence, less layers of management that decisions must be administered through before arriving at a resolution (Kelling and Moore 1988, 21). Through a reduction in the multiple echelons of management in the typical police department, the communication flow between line officer and the police chief can be greatly improved, the time in which a decision is to be made can be reduced, and many of the problems with the typical bureaucracy can be reduced if not alleviated altogether.

A third benefit is the opportunity afforded to upper level management to move away from concentrating on details, or dealing with the "small picture," and move toward the creation of strategies on a macro-level, or ones that deal with the "big picture" (Geller 1991, 43). Good leadership focuses on the goals and results of an organization, rather than the day-in and day-out operations. If high-level administrators and upper-level management must be involved in every decision, they will find themselves locked into micro-managing their organizations, constantly worrying about minor details, and losing sight of the overall systemic perspective. Upper-level management should concentrate more on assessing where the organization is and where it should be in the future, rather than focusing solely on the means to achieve these goals. Lower levels of management and line officers are then free to concentrate on the issues at hand and to deal with them without interference from managers far removed from life on the street.

A fourth benefit is the creation of better operational decisions, because those decisions are being made at the appropriate level (Geller 1991, 44; Wilson and Kelling 1989, 50). Situational imperatives can have a decisive impact on police officers and how they perform their job as they deal with a variety of people, events, and situations each shift. Police officers do not resort to "street justice" in these situations to the degree the media would have one believe, but often they resort to what one author calls "street-level bureaucracy" (Lipsky 1980). As an organization that deals with the lowest common denominator, the public, the police essentially deliver the end result of a bureaucracy, namely services. However, there are often constraints on the actions that officers take far beyond the reality of the street and they can be found in centralized decision making, politics, and policy, all of which can have an impact on the officer's ability to make decisions. Although officers should be constrained from misconduct and the excessive use of force, officers should not be constrained by bureaucratic supervision. At the street level, variables change from situation to situation and second-guessing one's actions based upon politics, bureaucracy, and decision-makers far removed from the street can be dangerous. Freeing officers from this burden, allowing them to make decisions at street level, places the decision-making process at the appropriate level.

And finally it allows the police department to utilize the full potential of each individual officer, generally creating an atmosphere that fosters higher job satisfaction and allows the individual to grow, where standard management practices do not accommodate this (Denhardt 1993, 114; Geller 1991, 44). Decentralizing the police department and placing the decision-making authority in the hands of the police allows the individual police officer the opportunity to utilize more than a simple ability to apply policies and procedures to life on the street. Community-oriented policing, through the decentralization process, allows each individual police officer to utilize a variety of skills and knowledge that he or she may already have and to learn and develop new ones. It promotes innovative thinking, analytical thought, and the creation of solutions for problems plaguing the community. This demand on the officers in turn allows for continual growth on the part of the employees and the department, prevents boredom in a job that can become very routine, and

A Dallas Police Officer of the Dallas, Texas Police Department,
gives a tour to students in the mobile Community-Oriented
Policing van. (Courtesy of the Dallas Police Dept., Dallas, Texas.)

allows for a personal connection to specific problems in "their" neighborhood.
The adherence to doctrine and standardized procedures, under traditional
police organization and management, does not allow any room for individual
officer growth.

The overall decentralization of the police department is critically important to the success of community-oriented policing. This structure essentially
requires that supervisors give officers more autonomy, in allowing them to
handle problems on their level and supporting them in their operations
(Wilson and Kelling 1989, 50). It must decentralize along geographical, personnel, and structural lines, pushing the responsibility and decision-making
process down into the hands of the line officer and providing the organizational structure support. Through the combination of decentralization by geography, personnel, and structure, the police department will accomplish the
overall concept central to the success of community-oriented policing—decentralized authority. This element, along with the synthesis of the three components, becomes the fundamental basis for community-oriented policing. It
becomes the system.

MANAGEMENT THROUGH "TOTAL QUALITY MANAGEMENT"

In order to guide a change from the traditional police department to one that
adopts the systemic approach to policing, not only must the mission statement and organizational structure change, but so too must the management
style be utilized. Although there are multiple methods and philosophies on how

to manage organizations found in the vast amounts of literature surrounding both public and business administration, managing a police department and police officers is particularly unique, and managing them under community-oriented policing is exceptionally unique. There must be a management style that complements not only the change to decentralization and community orientation, but the police professional as well. The management style of Total Quality Management (TQM), created by W. Edwards Deming, rises to this challenge.

COP IN ACTION

SOLVING PROBLEMS THROUGH TEAMWORK

The success of any organization, public or private, depends on a positive labor/management relationship. If developed around a true partnership in the pursuit of common goals, such a relationship will employ the concept of cooperative problem solving.

The Burlington Township, New Jersey, Police Department established a joint labor/management cooperative problem-solving mechanism to assist in the quality of performance as well as reduce labor grievances. "Partners in Problem Solving" is an adaptation of Deming's Total Quality Control Management model with modifications to make the model compatible to the idiosyncrasies of a police department. This model is a prototype that can assist other departments in developing a true team concept.

The initial phase in implementing a Quality Through Partnership (QTP) program is to establish a management/labor relationship which mutually accepts that the traditional adversarial relationship is not the only option available to running the organization. Both parties must be willing to implement an additional option to dispute resolution and problem solving. Once this relationship had been established, a document needs to be jointly written to establish the ground rules in which the QTP process will exist. This second phase of the process requires an order outlining QTP operation procedures. These procedures cover the establishment of partnership committees, membership on the committees, meetings, governing rules, problem identification, and documentation procedures.

Training, of all team members, consists of labor/management relations, rights and responsibilities, brainstorming and facilitation techniques. Finally, a cause–effect analysis of the entire QTP process is afforded all participants. This training brings together the management team with representatives from labor, allowing them to join together as partners in problem solving.

Only after this training is completed can the actual team meetings take place. Advising all employees that the QTP process is beginning through a clearly written and concise outline of the process completes the final phase in implementation. The rationale for this process includes the following statements of values or beliefs:

- Employees are a department's most valuable resource and should have opportunities to provide input to operational decisions.

- Employees should have opportunities to develop interpersonal communication skills, be allowed to be active participants in problem identification, demonstrate analysis and problem-solving skills, and to develop personally and professionally in the work environment.

- Operational decisions should be handled at the lowest appropriate level, involving those most directly concerned with decision implementation in order to hasten an increased sense of responsibility and accountability for system operation and performance.

The relationship between management and labor should be a partnership that works to achieve mutually identified objectives while delivering the highest quality end product or service (public safety) to the general public. The QTP process is designed to implement these goals and values.

Source: Adapted with permission from Corter, Walter J., Richard Whelan, and James J. Lynch. "Solving Problems Through Teamwork." *Law and Order*. August 1993, 64–66.

In the early 1970s, W. Edwards Deming created TQM, what has become the paradigm for good management (Cohen and Brand 1993). Although the concept developed over the past three decades into a working management style, Deming's original concept was oriented toward private business. The ultimate question that has been wrestled with by a variety of authors, from a variety of disciplines, revolves around the issue of TQM's application to the public sector (Bassett 1995; Cole 1993; Osborne and Gaebler 1992; Simonsen and Arnold 1993; Swiss 1992). Can the public sector, with a basic orientation of serving the public, utilize a management style originally designed for the private sector, whose basic orientation is for profit? The answer in most of the literature has been in the affirmative, with some qualifications by the various authors exploring this possibility.

In order to understand the concept of TQM, one must understand the definition. However, this is difficult, because there is no strict definition (Bassett 1995). Some authors describe TQM as "a management process and set of disciplines that are coordinated to ensure that the organization consistently meets and exceeds customer requirements" (Capezio and Morehouse 1993, 1), Others describe it as "providing the customer with quality products at the right time and at the right place" (Pegels 1995, 5). Deming himself, however, has a different understanding that concentrates more on the quality of the worker, workplace, and product, rather then on product quality itself. In order to achieve this fundamental goal, Deming created "fourteen points" for TQM:

1. Create constancy of purpose for improvement of product and service.
2. Adopt the new philosophy.
3. Cease dependence on mass inspection.
4. End the practice of awarding business on the basis of price tag alone.
5. Improve constantly and forever the system of production and services.
6. Institute modern methods of training on the job.

7. Institute modern methods of supervision.
8. Drive fear from the workplace.
9. Break down barriers between staff areas.
10. Eliminate numerical goals for the work force.
11. Eliminate work standards and numerical quotas.
12. Remove barriers that rob people of pride of workmanship.
13. Institute a vigorous program of education and training.
14. Create a structure that will accomplish the transformation. (Deming 1986, 17).

Although it is clear that all of these points may not be directly applicable to the public sector, it is apparent that many of the points detail aspects of community-oriented policing in an overall sense. Former Chief of Police David Couper of the Madison Police Department, Madison, Wisconsin, saw the opportunities under Deming's approach to management and was able to successfully apply them to the department's adoption of community-oriented policing (Osborne and Gaebler 1992; Wycoff and Skogan 1994). Through the application of Deming's fourteen points, Chief Couper was able to create the police department's Twelve Principles of Quality Leadership, detailed earlier in this chapter, to develop a guiding philosophy. This philosophy not only allowed for the public to be seen as the "customer" under this approach, but the employees of the department were seen as "internal customers" who have their own problems in need of identification and resolution (Wycoff and Skogan 1994, 76). In this instance, TQM proved very successful and demonstrated that this approach to management was complementary to the systemic approach to policing.

TQM has more recently seen adaptation at the federal level. In Office of Management and Budget, Draft Circular A-132, 1990, the federal government stresses seven methods to integrating TQM:

1. Top management needs to give TQM its leadership and support.
2. Quality improvement should be included in the organization's strategic plan.
3. The main focus should be on the customer.
4. A true commitment to training and recognition must be made. Employees are motivated to achieve total quality through trust, respect, and recognition.
5. Employees need to be empowered and work in teams in addressing quality issues.
6. Techniques in measurement and analysis of process and outputs need to be implemented.
7. Quality assurance through meeting customers' needs, standardization and benchmarking will assure quality. (Denhardt 1995, 336–339).

Additionally, the U.S. Department of Justice and the Federal Bureau of Investigation have also drafted out their concept of TQM and have begun implementation to ensure quality and to incorporate the creativity and capabilities of every individual in their employment. In order to assist in this implementation, their concept provides an overview on "What Total Quality Management Is And Is Not" (U.S. Department of Justice 1990). TQM has truly become the paradigm of public management in the same manner that community-oriented policing has become the paradigm in policing. It is through the combination of these two paradigms that police management should focus their attention for the improvement of both the community and the police.

TABLE 7.5   WHAT TOTAL QUALITY MANAGEMENT IS AND IS NOT

IT IS	IT IS NOT
A structured approach to solving problems	"Fighting fires"
A systematic way to improve products and services	A new program
Long term	Short term
Conveyed by management's actions	Conveyed by slogans
Supported by statistical quality control	Driven by statistical quality control
Practiced by everyone	Delegated to subordinates

Source: Federal Bureau of Investigation, Administrative Services Division. *Total Quality Management*. Washington, D.C.: U.S. Department of Justice, October 1990.

In order to focus on the link between community-oriented policing and TQM there are essentially six areas of concentration that management must explore, the first of which has already been explored in-depth. These areas include: 1) decentralization, 2) customer orientation, 3) long-term commitment, 4) proactive management, 5) training and education, and 6) evaluation.

The first area is the decentralization of the organizational structure. Smaller workgroups of personnel, placing the line officers closer to the public geographically, and reducing the layers of management, all concepts of decentralization, are all tenants of TQM (Wycoff and Skogan 1994). The last of Deming's fourteen points brings this reality to fruition in the sense that the decentralized structure will accomplish the transformation of management from past practices to TQM. The creation of a new mission statement, values and goals, along with the decentralization of authority, allow for the paradigm of TQM to be implemented within the police department.

The second area of focus under both paradigms is the movement to a customer or community orientation. There is also a dual focus that should be maintained in that the customer should be seen as being both the employee of the police department and the public. If management is customer-oriented, and line officers are seen as customers, the department then has an obligation to listen to their concerns and determine how best to address them, in similar fashion to the problem-solving methods employed under problem-oriented policing. The officers should have input into management decisions, they should be responsible for their actions, and they should be afforded more responsibility in the performance of their jobs. Both management and the police officers then also have an obligation to view the public as the "customer" to the services that they provide and adopt this orientation, which again should be captured in the mission statement, values, and goals of the entire police department. The customer or public should also be afforded the same opportunity for input by incorporating them into the decision-making process.

The third area of focus is in understanding that both TQM and community-oriented policing are long-term concepts that cannot be implemented overnight and do not end within any certain time frame. Managers and leaders under TQM and community-oriented policing must look forward to the challenging task ahead, often by determining first what the organization wants to achieve and then working backwards to figure out how the organization will get there. As Deming himself stated in the opening of the Federal Bureau of Investigation's manual on TQM, "A big ship, traveling at full speed, requires distance and time to turn" (U.S. Department of Justice 1990, 1). A department's goals should have this long-term outlook, incorporated in a strategic plan and implemented in an incremental fashion.

The fourth area of management focus should be the movement away from mass inspections and the utilization of numerical quotas as they are poor management tools, ignore qualitative issues, and are reactive in nature. Rather, management should focus on methods of incorporating proactive methods of management that focus on outcomes and customer satisfaction. Even in the area of discipline, where there is much resistance to focusing on outcomes rather then means, there are proactive methods available to management. One such method is through the utilization of an early warning system that utilizes a proactive stance to assess employees performance and intervene before misconduct occurs (Moore and Wegener 1996; Oliver 1994). The early warning system has been described as part of the TQM commitment to personnel development within the police department (Alpert and Dunham 1992).

The fifth area of concentration under TQM should be the emphasis on education and training for all employees. This includes not only an emphasis

St. Petersburg Police Department (Florida) DARE vehicle obtained via a drug seizure. (Courtesy of St. Petersburg Police Dept., St. Petersburg, Florida.)

on training in the line officer's job position, but training line officers in TQM and community-oriented policing. Management cannot incorporate TQM and community-oriented policing into their management philosophy and style unless the line officers understand the process and methods utilized under both of the philosophies and practices. Employees must understand not only their role under TQM, but under their new job descriptions, and under the community-oriented policing department as well.

And finally, management must concentrate on utilizing a variety of methods in the evaluation process. As one of the principles of quality management in the Madison Police Department states, "Be committed to the problem-solving process; use it and let data, not emotions, drive decisions" (Wycoff and Skogan 1994, 58). It is important that management under both TQM and community-oriented policing be responsible for evaluating and assisting in the evaluation of various programs to determine if they are truly effective and should be continued, or are ineffective and should be abolished. These types of decisions must not be made under the pretenses of either personal influence, misguided perceptions, or political influence. These decisions must be based upon the quality of delivery and the honest satisfaction of the customer, namely the community. Evaluations are a daunting undertaking and one that will prove most difficult to police departments, but they must be considered central to the success of not only TQM, but to community-oriented policing as well. Evaluations are the guide to incremental changes in the implementation process, therefore they will be discussed in greater depth in a later chapter.

COP IN ACTION

NONTRADITIONAL PROBLEM SOLVING

Three years ago, the Lawrence, Massachusetts, Police Department realized that the traditional way of doing things was not always effective in resolving some crime issues. Nor were they dealing with the needs of many of their citizens. Lawrence is an urban city of 70,000 people in seven square miles, twenty-eight miles north of Boston. Its population is 50 percent white and 47 percent Hispanic. It was once a prosperous working class city, but the textile mills closed down and urban decay set in. Lawrence saw crime rates increase as drug use and sales grew, home ownership dropped drastically, and gang activities increased.

From our readings on community policing and talking with agencies that have implemented such programs, we decided three underlying principles would meet the needs of the city: 1) community policing is a philosophy that should be practiced by the whole department. It is not just a program that may be here today and gone tomorrow; 2) community policing uses problem-solving techniques to deal with neighborhood problems; 3) problem solving involves both line officers and the people living in a neighborhood.

Since we were going to make a fundamental change in our operations, we needed a management system that would not only help us implement the community policing philosophy, but also support it once it was in place. The Total Quality Management (TQM) philosophy is a structured system focusing on exceeding customer needs. It involves the whole organization in the planning and implementation of break-through operational processes and the continuous improvement of the daily operations of the organization. TQM uses many different management and planning tools and involves customers, managers, and employees in the development of a system that meets the needs of not only the external customers but also the internal customers of an organization. Law enforcement is a service industry, therefore the philosophy, tools, and methods of TQM can effectively focus law enforcement services on the customer (citizen) and involve everyone in the organization with the delivery of those customer-focused services.

TQM and community policing, therefore, have the same underlying concepts: customer focus, problem solving, total organization participation, customer focus. TQM is not only an excellent customer-focused management philosophy in its own right, but is also an excellent management system that will drive the community policing philosophy. The TQM process allowed the Lawrence Police Department to see that what our customers were really concerned with was "feeling safe" and having their neighborhoods free of "disorder problems."

Operating within the community policing and TQM philosophies, the department was able to work with people in the neighborhood and was willing to try nontraditional responses to resolve problems. One nontraditional solution involved the use of barricades and the monitoring of traffic in a neighborhood with an open drug market problem. This limited access to the neighborhood to one entrance, vehicle tag numbers of people cruising the neighborhood were recorded, and letters were sent advising vehicle owners that they were seen in the area.

Any time such an operation is planned, we first ensure that it is within our Value and Mission: (1) protecting individual rights; (2) involving the community in solving their own neighborhood problems; and (3) reducing fear of crime and improving the quality of life through the use of creative problem solving.

The Lawrence Police Department feels that it is important to have residents involved. Meetings are scheduled to address other neighborhood concerns, including poor street lighting, abandoned buildings, speeding cars, and litter-strewn vacant lots. We have assured residents that we will continue to work with them to resolve their problems. We told them that they need to organize and participate in controlling their neighborhood and together we will be able to have a positive impact in their neighborhood.

Source: Adapted with permission from Cole, Allen W. "Non Traditional Problem Solving." *Law and Order*. August 1993, 59–64.

As the concepts and philosophical underpinnings of community-oriented policing and TQM are similar in nature, it is only fitting that this style of management is the method of choice and most applicable to the systemic approach to policing. TQM is focused on the achievement of long-term goals and is complimentary to a decentralized organizational structure, clearly meeting all of the needs of the community-oriented policing department. Therefore, by adopting all three of the components of community-oriented policing, decentralizing the organizational structure, and adopting TQM as the guiding management style, a police department ensures its success in achieving the values and goals set forth in the mission statement which will foster a better working relation between the public and the police.

TABLE 7.6   SYSTEMIC CONSIDERATIONS

* Mission statement	* Job description
* Recruiting	* Hiring
* Performance evaluations	* Training
* Promotions	* Awards
* Rank	* Research
* Planning	* Technology
* Reserve officers	* Auxiliary officers
* Seasonal officers	* Volunteers
* Budget	* Media operations
* Criminal investigation	* Police detectives
* Organization	* Management
* Leadership	* Unions
* Police culture	* Dispatch
* 911 response	* Discipline
* Field training	* Counseling
* Accreditation	* Equipment
* Facilities	* Consultants
* Education	* Policy
* Procedures	* Regulations

CONCLUSION

In order to effectively restructure the organization and management of a traditional police department and move it toward a community-oriented policing police department, the police administration must first determine the values and goals of the police department. This should be based on the fundamental concepts of community-oriented policing and should receive some input from the members of the community and the police officers themselves. The police department must then create a new mission statement that will focus the department on the undertaking of this systemic approach to policing. This new mission statement should reflect the values and goals of the community-oriented policing police department and should be based on a new job analysis, the concepts of community-oriented policing, and the community's concept of the role of the police. This mission statement should be communicated to every member of the police department, both sworn and non-sworn personnel, as well as to every member of the community.

Based on the new mission statement, the process of decentralizing the police department and implementing the three components can commence. The foundation for the systemic approach to policing is a decentralized departmental organization, which can be achieved through decentralization by geography, personnel, and structure. Decentralization by geography consists of decentralizing the beats, sectors, and precincts based on neighborhoods, business districts, and the various communities found in the police department's jurisdiction. Decentralization of personnel should be based on shift, time, and location, to allow the police officers to work within a neighborhood beat, on a regular basis for a period of several years, and it should include a complete and systemic change in the position of police officer. The final form of decentralization is by the structure of the department which consists of removing multiple layers of mid-level management and "flattening the pyramid", and by incorporating these systemic changes into every facet of the police department. This enables the police department to deal more effectively with the community-oriented policing officer, it places management closer to the street level, and provides the authority and decision-making capabilities the officer will need to perform his or her duties.

In order to accomplish the implementation of community-oriented policing and the decentralization of organization, it also becomes necessary to change past practices of management. TQM, as applied to the public sector, becomes the management style of choice for its adaptability to the systemic approach to policing. In addition to the adoption of the three components, the decentralized of the organization, and the adoption of a new management style, the roles of three key players in community-oriented policing—the police officer, the community, and the police chief—must change. It is this triangle of players that will be discussed in-depth over the next three chapters.

REFERENCES

Alpert, Geoffrey P. and Roger G. Dunham. *Policing Urban America*. 2nd edition. Prospect Heights, IL: Waveland Press Inc., 1992.

Bassett, Nicholas. "Total Quality Management in the Public Sector." Unpublished Paper. June 1995.

Bennett, Trevor. "Community Policing on the Ground." In *Community Policing: Testing the Promises*. ed. Dennis P. Rosenbaum. Thousand Oaks, CA.: SAGE Publications, Inc., 1994.

Booth, Walter S. "Integrating COP into Selection and Promotional Systems." *The Police Chief,* March 1995, 19–24.

Bureau of Justice Assistance. *Understanding Community Policing: A Framework for Action*. Washington, D.C.: U.S. Department of Justice, 1994.

Cohen, Steven and Ronald Brand. *Total Quality Management in Government*. San Francisco: Jossey-Bass, 1993.

Cole, Allen W. "Better Customer Focus: TQM & Law Enforcement." *The Police Chief,* December 1993, 23–26.

Couper, David C. *Quality Policing: The Madison Experiment*. Washington, D.C.: Police Executive Research Forum, 1991.

Deming, W. Edwards. *Quality, Productivity, and Competitive Position*. Cambridge, MA.: Massachusetts Institute of Technology, Center for Advanced Engineering Study, 1982.

————. *Out of the Crisis*. Cambridge, MA.: MIT Press, 1986.

Dempsey, John S. *Policing: An Introduction to Law Enforcement*. St. Paul, Minn.: West Publishing Company, 1994.

Denhardt, Robert B. *Theories of Public Organization*. 2nd ed. Belmont, CA.: Wadsworth Publishing Company, 1993.

————. *Public Administration: An Action Orientation*. 2nd ed. Belmont, CA.: Wadsworth, 1995.

Eck, John E. and William Spelman. *Problem Solving: Problem- Oriented Policing in Newport News*. Washington, D.C.: Police Executive Research Forum, 1987.

Fogelson, Robert. *Big-City Police*. Cambridge, MA.: Harvard University Press, 1977.

Geller, William A. ed. *Police Leadership in America: Crisis and Opportunity*. New York: American Bar Foundation/Praegar Publishers, 1985.

————. *Local Government Police Management*. 3rd ed. Washington, D.C.: International City/County Management Association, 1991.

Goldstein, Herman. "Toward Community-Oriented Policing: Potential, Basic Requirements, and Threshold Questions." *Crime & Delinquency* 33, no. 1, (January 1987): 6–30.

————. *Problem-Oriented Policing*. New York: McGraw Hill Publishing Co., 1990.

Greene, Jack R., William T. Bergman, and Edward J. McLaughlin. "Implementing Community Policing." In *The Challenge of Community Policing: Testing the Promises,* ed. Dennis P. Rosenbaum. Thousand Oaks, CA.: SAGE Publications, Inc., 1994.

Higdon, Richard Kirk and Phillip G. Hubert. *How to Fight Fear: The Citizen-Oriented Police Enforcement Program Package*. Washington, D.C.: Police Executive Research Forum, 1987.

Kelling, George L. and Mark H. Moore. "From Political to Reform to Community: The Evolving Strategy of Police." In *Community Policing: Rhetoric or Reality,* ed. Jack R. Greene and Stephen D. Mastrofski. New York: Praegar Publishers, 1988.

Kelling, George, Robert Wasserman, and Hubert Williams. "Police Accountability and Community Policing." *Perspectives on Policing*. Washington, D.C.: National Institute of Justice and the John F. Kennedy School of Government, Harvard University, 1988.

Klockars, Carl B. "The Rhetoric of Community Policing." In *Community Policing: Rhetoric or Reality,* ed. Jack R. Greene and Stephen D. Mastrofski. New York: Praegar Publishers, 1988.

Lipsky, Michael. *Street-Level Bureaucracy*. New York: Russell Sage Foundation, 1980.

Moore, Harry W. and W. Fred Wegener. *Effective Police Supervision*. 2nd ed. Cincinnati: Anderson Publishing Company, 1996.

Muehleisen, Tom. "Community Problem Solving." *Law & Order,* June, 1995, 31–32.

Oliver, Will. "The Early Warning System." *Law and Order*, September 1994, 182–183.

Osborne, David and Ted Gaebler. *Reinventing Government: How the Entrepreneurial Spirit is Transforming the Public Sector*. Reading, MA.: Addison-Wesley, 1992.

Pegels, C. Carl. *Total Quality Management: A Survey of Its Important Aspects*. Danvers, MA.: Boyed and Fraser, 1995.

Radelet, Louis A. and David L. Carter. *The Police and the Community*. 5th ed. Englewood Cliffs, N.J.: MacMillian Publishing Company, 1994.

Rosenbaum, Dennis P. *The Challenge of Community Policing: Testing the Promises,* ed. Dennis P. Rosenbaum. Thousand Oaks, CA.: SAGE Publications, Inc., 1994.

Sherman, Lawrence W. "Middle Management and Democratization: A reply to John E. Angell." *Criminology* 12, no. 4 (1975): 363–377.

Sherman, Lawrence, W., Catherine H. Milton, and Thomas V. Kelly. *Team Policing: Seven Case Studies.* Washington, D.C.: Police Foundation, 1973.

Simonsen, Clifford and Douglas Arnold. "TQM: Is it Right for Law Enforcement?" *The Police Chief*, December 1993, 20–22.

Skogan, Wesley G. "The Impact of Community Policing on Neighborhood Residents." In *The Challenge of Community Policing: Testing the Promises,* ed. Dennis P. Rosenbaum. Thousand Oaks, CA: SAGE Publications, Inc., 1994.

Skolnick, Jerome H. and David H. Bayley. *The New Blue Line: Police Innovation in Six American Cities.* New York: The Free Press, 1986.

Swiss, James. "Adapting Total Quality Management (TQM) to Government." *Public Administration Review* 52 (1992): 356– 362.

U.S. Dept. of Justice, Federal Bureau of Investigation, *Total Quality Management,* Washington, D.C.: U. S. Dept. of Justice, 1990.

Walker, Samuel. *A Critical History of Police Reform: The Emergence of Professionalism.* Lexington, MA.: Lexington Books, 1977.

Wilkinson, Deanna L. and Dennis P. Rosenbaum. "The Effects of Organizational Structure on Community Policing." In *The Challenge of Community Policing: Testing the Promises,* ed. Dennis P. Rosenbaum. Thousand Oaks, CA.: SAGE Publications, Inc., 1994.

Wilson, James Q. *Bureaucracy.* New York: Basic Books, Inc., 1989.

Wilson, James Q. and George L. Kelling. "Making Neighborhoods Safe." *The Atlantic Monthly,* February 1989, 46–52.

Wycoff, Mary Ann and Wesley G. Skogan. "Community Policing in Madison: An Analysis of Implementation and Impact." In *The Challenge of Community Policing: Testing the Promises.* ed. Dennis P. Rosenbaum. Thousand Oaks, CA.: SAGE Publications, Inc., 1994.

CHAPTER 8

The Role of the Police

Every society gets the kind of criminal it deserves. What is equally true is that every community gets the kind of law enforcement it insists on.

-Robert Kennedy-

There is one ultimate determining factor regarding the viability of community-oriented policing and that is the police officer. The police officer is the foundation of community-oriented policing. Although a jurisdiction may have the support of the community, if the police are not responsive to the changes, community-oriented policing will fail. Equally, if the police chief attempts to force community-oriented policing on the police officers in a top-down approach, the police officers hold the key to success. If they do not support it, it will fail. If they are supportive of the concept, it will succeed. Therefore, if a police department attempts to move away from the traditional style of policing to a community-oriented policing department, the police officers are of critical importance to the overall plan.

It is important to look at the role the police have played under traditional forms of policing and how these roles have developed. It is only then that we can understand some of the differences in the role of the police officer under community-oriented policing. Defining that role is difficult at best; however, creating that role is perhaps the greatest challenge to the police management, the community, and the police themselves.

In order to understand the police officer's role in community-oriented policing, it is helpful to look at what bearing this systemic approach to policing will have on the police officer's perceptions of his or her job. Attempting to

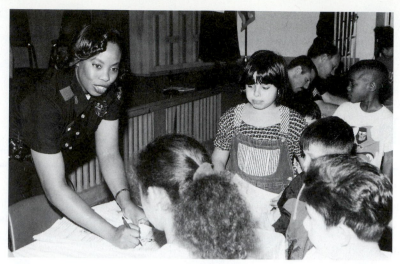

A Dallas Police Officer from the Dallas, Texas Police Department working with local elementary school students signing a safety pledge. (Courtesy of the Dallas Police Dept., Dallas, Texas.)

communicate the benefits of community-oriented policing to the line officer can be difficult, but gaining his or her support, as previously stated, is critical to the success of failure of this new method of doing business. It is also critical that the police be afforded the opportunity to develop new skills that will be necessary under community-oriented policing, prior to taking on the challenge, rather than beginning with no understanding of how they should perform their new mission.

"CRIME FILES"

DRUG EDUCATION—PART 11

This edition of the "Crime Files," hosted by James Q. Wilson, features Michael S. Goodstadt, Addiction Research Foundation, Toronto; Stephen Leinen, School Program to Educate and Control Drug Abuse; and Joyce Nalepka, National Federation of Parents for Drug-Free Youth. The discussion revolves around various drug education programs in which police officers work with elementary school children to help them "say no to drugs."

All of these issues, from understanding the role of the police officer to the attitudes exhibited toward community-oriented policing, and those skills necessary under this systemic approach to policing will be explored in this chapter. The traditional role of the police will be explored and the debate between the law enforcement role and order maintenance role, as has been previously referenced, will be discussed, followed by a review of the new role the police will assume under community-oriented policing. The attitudes that police officers have had toward community-oriented policing and variations on this theme will be analyzed through past research on officer's perceptions of the programs and their reports of job satisfaction. This chapter will also address all of those skills a community-oriented policing officer will need to be effective and successful in this new environment.

TABLE 8.1   REPORTED CONFIDENCE IN THE POLICE

Question: "I am going to read you a list of institutions in American society. Please tell me how much confidence you, yourself, have in each one—a great deal, quite a lot, some, or very little: the police?"

	Great deal/ quite a lot	Some	Very little	None
National	58%	30%	10%	1%
Sex				
Male	57%	28%	12%	2%
Female	58%	31%	9%	1%
Race				
White	63%	28%	8%	1%
Non-white	30%	40%	26%	3%
Black	26%	37%	32%	4%
Age				
18 to 29 years	50%	32%	16%	2%
30 to 49 years	58%	32%	9%	1%
50 to 64 years	57%	31%	10%	2%

Source: Maguire, Kathleen, and Ann. L. Pastore. *Bureau of Justice Statistics Sourcebook of Criminal Justice Statistics—1994*. Washington, D.C.: Bureau of Justice Statistics, 1995.

THE TRADITIONAL ROLE OF THE POLICE

In order to understand the importance of the police officer under community-oriented policing, it is imperative that there is an understanding of their role in society. For the greater part of the twentieth century the police, the communities, and academia have wrestled with the question: What is the role of the police? In order to define the role of the police, one cannot look to the individual police officer, but rather one must look to the system in which they work. In most cases the police style can be categorized into two distinct functions that reflect the overall role of the police. These functions are the enforcement of laws and maintaining order in society. Whether we utilize various terms such as crime fighters and order maintenance (Dempsey 1994), law officers and peace officers (Banton 1964), or the legalistic and watchman style (Wilson

1968), we are generally discussing the two key roles of the police. Some researchers have identified other roles of the police, such as the ambiguous role (Dempsey 1994) and the service role (Wilson 1968); however, these are ancillary to the greater debate about the traditional role of the police. Therefore, the two roles of the police, under the traditional role of the police, have been the law enforcement and order maintenance functions.

TABLE 8.2   RESPONDENTS' RATINGS OF THE HONESTY AND ETHICAL STANDARDS OF POLICE

Question: "Next, please tell me how you would rate the honesty and ethical standards of people in these different fields—very high, high, average, low, or very low: Police?"

	Very high	High	Average	Low	Very low
1977	8%	29%	50%	9%	3%
1981	8%	36%	41%	9%	4%
1983	7%	34%	45%	7%	4%
1985	10%	37%	41%	7%	3%
1988	10%	37%	39%	8%	3%
1990	9%	40%	41%	7%	2%
1991	7%	36%	42%	10%	3%
1992	8%	34%	42%	10%	4%
1993	10%	40%	39%	7%	3%
1994	9%	37%	41%	9%	3%

Source: Maguire, Kathleen and Ann L. Pastore. *Bureau of Justice Statistics Sourcebook of Criminal Justice Statistics—1994.* Washington, D.C.: Bureau of Justice Statistics, 1995.

Most people are familiar with the function of law enforcement. It is the image of the police that is most often portrayed in the media, and it is the one most recognizable by the public. It is the adherence to the strict letter of the law and subsequently the arrest of any violator of the law. The goal of the police in the law enforcement function is to make as many "good" arrests as possible and to see the successful prosecution of these criminals, whether adult or juvenile, felony or misdemeanor, or a criminal or traffic offense. The advantage to this crime-fighting function is that it allows for "real" police work to be conducted, evaluated, and quantified. It is a simple process with immediate identification of the value of the work, as well as the value of the officer's own self-worth. If the police officer goes to work and makes an arrest, it was a good day. If the police officer goes to work and cannot even issue a summons or find one good traffic offense in which to issue a summons, it was a bad day. The simplicity of quantifying this crime-fighting model allows supervisors to determine the value of the officer's work, the officer can determine his or her own worth, and the officer's peers can easily recognize whether or not that officer is a "good cop." Along with this, when an officer exhibits such behavior as handling himself or herself well in a high-speed pursuit, taking on a subject who resists arrest, or stopping the commission of a felony before it occurs, he or she is praised and admired by both management and peers.

TABLE 8.3   RESPONDENTS' RATINGS OF THE HONESTY AND ETHICAL STANDARDS OF POLICE FOR 1994

Question: "Next, please tell me how you would rate the honesty and ethical standards of people in these different fields—very high, high, average, low, or very low: Police?"

	Very high	high	Average	Low	Very low
National	9%	37%	41%	9%	3%
Sex					
Male	11%	40%	37%	8%	4%
Female	8%	34%	46%	9%	2%
Race					
White	10%	39%	41%	7%	2%
Non-white	4%	23%	44%	20%	9%
Black	4%	17%	43%	25%	11%
Age					
18 to 29 years	12%	33%	38%	12%	4%
30 to 49 years	8%	41%	42%	6%	3%
50 to 64 years	7%	36%	41%	13%	2%
65 yrs & older	10%	32%	45%	8%	3%

Source: Maguire, Kathleen and Ann L. Pastore. *Bureau of Justice Statistics Sourcebook of Criminal Justice Statistics—1994.* Washington, D.C.: Bureau of Justice Statistics, 1995.

The second function, order maintenance, is not interested in enforcing the law to such a strict standard or making multiple arrests. Rather, enforcing the law through an arrest is the last course of action to be taken, only after all other courses of action have been exhausted. The goal of the police under this function is to simply maintain social order within the community or at a minimum, the appearance of social order. The police utilize informal and formal intervention techniques and attempt to intimidate, persuade, and threaten people into compliance to achieve order. In looking at the police officer's function in order maintenance, we have a more difficult time recognizing good police work and often it is dismissed as nothing more than public relations. Police management has a difficult time recognizing and quantifying order maintenance, the officer does not receive the immediate gratification that is otherwise derived from the crime-fighting role, and the officer's peers criticize the officer for not doing "real" police work. Although an officer may implement a community action program under the order maintenance role, it may take several years for the program to become effective and deemed a success. In the meantime, the officer may be working hard in his or her role, but there is no recognition or feedback from either management or peers.

COP IN ACTION

A COPS SHOW OF YOUR OWN

The three most popular themes on television today are crime, crime, and more crime. Offerings include the likes of "Cops," "NYPD Blue," and "Unsolved Mysteries." The list goes on and on. Then there's the network and local news that drive their ratings up with a steady stream of mayhem, sensationalism, and celebrity murder trials. But police don't need to settle for thirty seconds on the nightly news to, or try to, explain the significance of the crime bill in twenty-five words or less. They can have a "cops show" of their own—and do it on a shoestring by utilizing government cable access television.

That's what the St. Petersburg, Florida, Police Department elected to do with a television program entitled "Police Report" that has attracted a respectable audience of regular viewers. "Police Report" succeeds by making real cops the stars, focusing cameras on the drama of the streets, and dealing head-on with issues that people care about.

"Never before has it been so crucial for police to communicate effectively with their community residents and to present the facts about crime and law enforcement," St. Petersburg Police Chief Darrell Stephens said. "Today you have to actively market crime awareness and tell your side of the story. That's what we're doing with 'Police Report.'"

Stephens was instrumental in expanding St. Petersburg's highly successful community-policing program. It was one of the first cities in the nation to go citywide with community policing, with officers working closely with community leaders and neighborhood organizations to set priorities and solve problems. "Police Report" is consistent with Stephens' belief that everybody has a stake in making law enforcement work.

"Police Report" is currently broadcast to 70,000 households in St. Petersburg (about 60 percent of its population) on government access cable. Cost to the police department is basically staff time. That's primarily the five days a month that is devoted to a sixty-minute program that is seen at least once a day, every day, during the month.

What's the best thing about St. Petersburg's cops show?

"'Police Report' lets us talk directly to the people we serve, and gives our officers exposure that's better than almost anything we've been able to do," Stephens said. "That's what I like. It's a chance to enhance our image by making our cops the stars of the show and demonstrate to the community that our officers care."

Source: Adapted with permission from Getz, Ronald J. "A COPS Show of Your Own." *Law and Order*. February 1995, 43–49.

In attempting to determine the role of the police in our society, it is important to look at the historical approach to policing in the United States. According to James Q. Wilson (1969), from the founding of the United States to the early part of the twentieth century, the police were largely concerned with order maintenance, rather than law enforcement. He describes the shift away from order maintenance to law enforcement as beginning with Prohibition and the Great Depression (Wilson 1969) and ending in the 1960s and 1970s as a response to the crime wave which began in the early part of the 1960s (Wilson and Kelling 1982). It is this shift that Wilson and Kelling found most disturbing and subsequently called for the return of order maintenance in their famous article and theory, "Broken Windows" which would become the impetus for community-oriented policing.

TABLE 8.4   HIGH SCHOOL SENIORS REPORTING POSITIVE ATTITUDES TOWARD THE PERFORMANCE OF THE POLICE AND OTHER LAW ENFORCEMENT AGENCIES, 1982–1994.

Question: "Now we'd like you to make some ratings of how good or bad a job you feel each of the following organizations is doing for the country as a whole...How good or bad a job is being done for the country as a whole by...the police and other law enforcement agencies?"

(Percentage responding "good" or "very good")

Class of:	Total:
1982	37.2%
1983	37.4%
1984	36.9%
1985	37.3%
1986	40.5%
1987	39.5%
1988	37.4%
1989	33.6%
1990	34.3%
1991	28.0%
1992	26.9%
1993	27.1%
1994	29.3%

Source: Maguire, Kathleen and Ann L. Pastore. *Bureau of Justice Statistics Sourcebook of Criminal Justice Statistics—1994.* Washington, D.C.: Bureau of Justice Statistics, 1995.

However, even a return to order maintenance is not necessarily the goal of community-oriented policing. Although there is no conceding that order maintenance is extremely important under the new approach to policing, it is important that the law enforcement function is not entirely dismissed. Rather, there must be a synthesis of these two traditional functions of the police as well as the addition of new functions. This is then the contextual setting for community-oriented policing.

TABLE 8.5   TRADITIONAL POLICE OFFICER VERSUS COMMUNITY-ORIENTED POLICE OFFICER

Police Personality	
Traditional	Community Oriented
Authoritarian	Democratic
Cynical	Hopeful
Hostile	Peaceful
Individualistic	Team player
Insecure	Secure
Efficient	Efficient
Secretive	Open
Prejudice	Unbiased
Honorable	Honorable

THE ROLE OF THE COMMUNITY-ORIENTED POLICE OFFICER

If a police department does in fact plan to move from the traditional style of policing to community-oriented policing, it must then answer the question: what is the role of the police in community-oriented policing? The role of the police under community-oriented policing becomes a synthesis of both the law enforcement and order maintenance roles found under the traditional form of policing. It also includes the service style that Wilson (1968) details as being the third style of policing, where the servicing of the community is the primary goal of the police. Community-oriented policing does not mean the police have to give up the nature of police work that they have been enamored with. In some cases, community-oriented policing may not mean the officers must arrest less, and in many situations it may entail more arrests. The deciding factor is the situation and, in a sense, the function of police, which under community-oriented policing could be called "situational policing," a form of situational leadership (Hersey and Blanchard 1993). In some cases, the law enforcement approach may be more productive in solving the problems of the community, than would the order maintenance or service style of policing. In other cases, the community may desire a service approach to certain problems within their neighborhoods, and this may be the applicable approach. Regardless, all three functions of policing play into the role of the community-oriented policing officer.

The role of the community-oriented police officer must also be one of leadership within the community he or she serves. The officer must, in many

The Cincinnati Police Division's District One Mountain Bike Patrol in Cincinnati, Ohio. (Courtesy of Concinnati Police Division, Cincinnati, Ohio.)

cases, become the *de facto* leader of the community, while in other cases the role may actually be that of advisor or even follower. It is in this sense that the police officer abides by the tenets of situational leadership, where depending upon the community and the various situations, the officer may have to be a autocratic, democratic, or laissez-faire leader (Hersey and Blanchard 1993; Holden 1986; Peak 1995). The officer must have the support of the police department to be this type of leader. The department must have a vested interest in what is accomplished through community-oriented policing.

This vested interest is often articulated in one area of community-oriented policing research where the police department is conceptualized as being a corporation, and corporate strategies are employed to "define for the organization how the organization will pursue value and what sort of organization it will be" (Moore and Trojanowicz 1988, 2). However, a more accurate representation would be the employee-owned corporation, often called a cooperative or simply an employee-owned business. Here the employees of a business are essentially all in business together, and if the business fails, they all fail. The community-oriented policing officer is then considered a "partner" in the police department and is no longer seen as being at the bottom of the hierarchy.

COP IN ACTION
TRADITIONAL OFFICERS VS. COMMUNITY-ORIENTED POLICING OFFICERS

"The difference between the CBPOP team and the regular officers was the fact that it was always the same four guys working the area and we would learn the names and faces of all the players in our community. We developed confidential informants and got to know the actual names of the dealers and the users. We didn't develop the use of community groups very well in my neighborhood, but one of the teams did a good job. This was mainly done though the supervisory role. We would tell them how to organize, but nothing happened. We didn't work with the community groups per se; we were actually more liaisons talking with the community, to help with things like trash removal by speeding up the bureaucratic process.

"Some of the friction between the regular patrols and the community-oriented policing patrols was caused because one, regular patrol was weakened as far as manpower. Two, they [community-oriented policing patrols] got the reputation as being lazy because we set our own hours, worked in plain-clothes, and we didn't take action type of calls. For instance, in Nauck, where I worked, we would set up drug surveillance. When a call would go out for a domestic, we wouldn't respond, because we had to stay on the surveillance. They didn't know we were out on a drug surveillance so they thought we weren't answering the radio because we were lazy. There's a lot of friction. It's just like in any police department with the different units, where you have a detective bureau and the regular patrol and everyone is complaining about the lack of communication and the problems that arise between units. Patrol always says that the detectives never tell them what is going on and the same has been occurring with the community-policing patrols. Another reason the community policing teams obtained a bad reputation was because these teams enlisted junior officers and it was actually considered a good assignment and a lot of officers put in for it, but the junior officers were selected over a lot of senior officers. Most of the junior officers were selected because of their ability with a second language, particularly Spanish and Vietnamese."

Source: Interview with Officer Jackson Hunter Miller of the Arlington County Police Department, Arlington County, Virginia, December 28, 1995.

The community-oriented policing officer should be given the authority to act independently when working with the community to plan and implement certain strategic-oriented policing tactics, to organize the community under various neighborhood-oriented policing programs, and to determine the problems within a community, develop alternatives to solving these problems, and implement and assess these solutions. Officers must be allowed to utilize all of their capabilities when performing their function within community-oriented policing, and must receive the assistance from the police department.

The community-oriented police officer, like the traditional police officer, must be "all things to all people," only in a different manner. Under community-oriented policing, the officer becomes a leader of the community as well as a follower of the community. He or she must be an ombudsman to the police department, as well as an ombudsmen and coordinator among varying community groups, business groups, and government institutions. The officer must listen to the community to determine those criminal and order maintenance issues that need to be addressed, he or she must address and inform the community of varying concerns, and the officer must motivate the community to action when necessary.

TABLE 8.6   COMMUNITY POLICE OFFICER'S DAY

In addition to traditional law enforcement activities, such as patrol and responding to calls for service, the day might include:

- Operating neighborhood substations
- Meeting with community groups.
- Analyzing and solving neighborhood problems.
- Working with citizens on crime prevention programs.
- Conducting door-to-door surveys of residents.
- Talking with students in school.
- Meeting with local merchants.
- Making security checks of businesses.
- Dealing with disorderly people.

Source: Mastrofski Stephen D. "What Does Community Policing Mean for Daily Police Work?" *National Institute of Justice Journal*, August 1992, 24.

Above all, however, in order for the community-oriented police officer to function, he or she must change the perception of the community toward the police. This is often one of the more difficult aspects of community-oriented policing. When the systemic approach is implemented, there is often a resistance to change and a negative perception on the part of the police. If the police themselves do not find satisfaction in their role as community-oriented policing officers, then they will not want a desire to fill this new role and may revert back to their old roles. This can be detrimental to the police department attempting to implement the change from traditional policing to community-oriented policing and necessitates a review of the literature based on police departments that have implemented programs in the community-oriented policing vein.

COP IN ACTION

COP CARDS

If you run into Police Chief James A. Cost on the streets of Campbell, California, he will hand you a cop card.

The chief decided to steal a play from baseball by printing up the trading cards in October 1991 as part of an effort to improve community relations in a neighborhood dominated by Southeast Asian immigrants.

Twenty police officers volunteered to have their photos taken and to hand out the cards. An initial order of 4,000 cards, 200 per officer, was placed. It turned out to be not nearly enough.

"The kids went crazy," the chief recalled. "Even adults started collecting them."

The department quickly reordered 40,000 cards. Half of this order was packaged and sold to adults for $10 a packet. The kids continued to get them for free from officers. Money received from the sale of the cards to collectors pays for the printing cost of the program—an unexpected windfall.

But the main benefit has come from the kids. "Officers used to drive by and the kids wouldn't make eye contact," Cost said. "Now, they flag down patrol cars and ask for a card. It's been good for the officers, particularly if they're reluctant about approaching a kid."

Cost, not one to let a public relations gesture slip by, sent a packet of the trading cards to President George Bush. Bush's response is framed in the hallway: "I appreciate...the outstanding job that you and your law enforcement community are doing. Keep it up."

After an appearance on CNN, the Campbell Police Department was besieged with calls from all over the country from police departments who wanted information on how to create their own cards. "For 30 days our life was trading cards," the chief said.

Source: Adapted with permission from Leal, Carolyn V. "Cop Cards." *Law and Order*. October 1992, 63–64.

POLICE ATTITUDES TOWARD COMMUNITY-ORIENTED POLICING

It is probably safe to say that the police are generally a very skeptical group of people. The reasons why may range from the theories of the police subculture to a simple reactionary method for dealing with life on the street. Regardless as to why police harbor such feelings, we must recognize the skepticism and look to the outcome for the line officer under community-oriented policing. Police officers, like everyone else, will often ask what is in it for them when a new program is implemented or management alters the way they perform their mission. Although it is more beneficial to provide an explanation of what they can expect under the new program, often we can only explain the concepts of what we believe will occur and why it is to their benefit, due to the lack of a knowledge base on the program.

The conceptual benefits such as more freedom to perform their job, a better commitment by management, and better working conditions may all sound pleasant, but in reality are hard to comprehend. The more simplistic benefits such as additional pay, better uniforms, and fewer hours are something anyone can quickly grasp and so usually create a more immediate desire within the worker. However, in the overall picture, these benefits are quick-fix solutions and do not solve many of the underlying problems that would better serve the officer over the span of his or her career. As Herman Goldstein pictures the conceptual benefits, he touches on one of the greatest benefits in the officer's career. Goldstein (1990, 28) states that there are two potential benefits, "the most important is the improvement that this could produce in the quality of the responses that the police make to oft-recurring community problems," and that "such a change would be directly responsive to some critical needs in the police organization—the need to treat rank-and-file police officers as mature men and women; to demonstrate more trust and confidence in them; to give them more responsibility and a stake in the outcome of their efforts; and to give them a greater sense of fulfillment and job satisfaction." It is job satisfaction that is of greatest concern to the line officer.

There is one thing that all workers, including police officers, desire in their job and that is greater job satisfaction (Hersey and Blanchard 1993; Peak 1995). This has been true through the ages and is readily apparent in various studies from the Hawthorne Plant studies, to Herzberg's Motivation-Hygiene theory, to the ultimate theory of human needs found in Maslow's Hierarchy of Needs (Hersey and Blanchard 1993; Peak 1995). If we look solely at this last familiar theory, we find that the top of Maslow's hierarchy, self-actualization, states that the job-related satisfiers include planning one's work, freedom to make decisions affecting work, creative work to perform, and opportunities for growth and development (Maslow 1970; Peak 1995). In other words, the ultimate goal is job satisfaction. If the change from a traditional police department to a community-oriented policing police department can improve police officer job satisfaction then this is inherently their greatest benefit for assisting in the successful implementation of this systemic approach to policing.

The ability to communicate whether or not this change will promote greater job satisfaction is difficult at best. However, through an analysis of those studies conducted on police programs that were implemented under the auspices of community-oriented policing, the potential for deriving at least an understanding of the effect these programs had on police officers' job satisfaction is great. With this understanding, the communication of job satisfaction can be greatly enhanced and allow for some of the police skepticism to be dispelled.

COP IN ACTION

OFFICERS 'LOVE OUR KIDS'

The Love Our Kids program, sponsored by the Coalition of Ministers Against Crime, pairs a mentor with a school child, chosen by the school, considered at risk for dropping out of school. The mentor works individually with the child several times a week. The police department even allows this time to be spent during working hours. The premise is that one person helping one child to build self-esteem and reinforce positive values, along with tutoring, will help them remain in school. It is estimated that up to 50 percent of the students in the area are at risk of dropping out of school by age sixteen. Students rarely drop out of school because of academic reasons, but rather because of overwhelming personal problems.

While the focus of the program is geared to expanding certain areas of a child's specific needs, it shows the pattern of a two-fold purpose. When many of today's youth show little or no respect for authority figures, these children learn that a police officer is truly a friend.

The Love Our Kids program is headed by Sgt. Dennis Carter in the Houston Police Department's Community Services Division. "We sent out the initial information shortly before the holiday season in December, and I didn't expect the response to be very good," he explained. Carter said thirty-one officers signed up immediately, often working with more than one child each. The program has evolved into five elementary campuses located throughout the inner city. "I did not expect such a response and was pleasantly surprised."

Officers receive training prior to their involvement with the children. They are taught how to tutor and about the rules and regulations necessitated by Texas state law and the Houston Independent School District. They learn about target schools, the neighborhoods, and typical family situations involving the children. Tutors sign a formal commitment with the intent to be involved in the program for at least one year, and make visits with the students from one to three times weekly. They also sign a confidentiality agreement protecting the children's rights.

"The goal of the program is to provide love and caring for the children, without expectations of anything in return," Carter explained. "We are told to never expect any thanks. However, my fellow officers who have been involved have seen the results and received many thank-you's from the children and their families."

Source: Adapted with permission from Worrell, Ann. "Officers 'Love Our Kids'." *Law and Order.* September 1993, 109–110.

One study, conducted by Lurigio and Rosenbaum (1994), recently reviewed the literature to determine the impact of community-policing on the police. Lurigio and Rosenbaum (1994) explored some programs from the 1970s that were more in line with the police–community relations movement of the time, but some rudimentary concepts of community-oriented policing can still be seen. The study, conducted in 1973 and 1974 in San Diego was known as Community Profile Development. It revealed that these officers were "more likely to report that their job was interesting and less likely to report that their job was frustrating" (Lurigio and Rosenbaum 1994, 149). In Cincinnati, Ohio, in the early 1970s, the police implemented a program known as Community Sector Team Policing (COMSEC), which reported little evidence that police officers' job satisfaction was enhanced (Lurigio and Rosenbaum 1994, 150). The studies of other team policing projects also seemed to report similar findings during the 1970s (Sherman 1975; Sherman, Milton, and Kelly 1973).

In reviewing those programs implemented in the 1980s there is generally a closer resemblance to the community-oriented policing programs found under the three components. In Flint, Michigan, in the early 1980s, a Neighborhood Foot Patrol Program (NFPP) was implemented and interviews with the foot-patrol officers compared with interviews of motor patrol officers proved quite revealing in the area of job satisfaction (Lurigio and Rosenbaum 1994, 151–152). The officers in the foot-patrol program had much higher job satisfaction than those riding in motor vehicle patrols, and the factors that enhanced job satisfaction consisted of the fact the "officers were more likely to perceive that they were doing an important job in the department and in their patrol areas, improving police–community relations, performing a job that the police department views as important, and working as part of a police team" (Lurigio and Rosenbaum 1994, 152.)

Another study in the early 1980s was the Baltimore County, Maryland, Citizen-Oriented Police Enforcement (COPE) project which was developed as a community policing initiative, but developed into a problem-oriented policing program, thereby utilizing two of the three components (Cordner 1988; Hayeslip and Cordner 1987; Lurigio and Rosenbaum 1994). It was found that "those officers who participated in COPE had higher levels of reported job satisfaction, more cooperative and service-oriented attitudes about the police role, more positive attitudes toward the community, and more positive evaluations of the COPE project's effects" (Hayeslip and Cordner 1987, 115).

Previously discussed programs such as the Police Foundation's Fear Reduction Study in Houston, Texas and Newark, New Jersey, utilized mainly neighborhood–oriented policing strategies in their programs' implementation (See Brown and Wycoff 1987; Lurigio and Rosenbaum 1994; Pate, Wycoff, Skogan, and Sherman 1986; Williams and Pate 1987; Wycoff 1988). The reports for the purposes of police officers' job satisfaction are anecdotal in nature in both studies, but they are revealing for the same high job satisfaction that is found in these studies are similar to those found in other studies (Wycoff 1988, 112).

In New York City, the Vera Institute implemented a study known as the Community Patrol Officer Program (CPOP) in the latter part of the 1980s which utilized neighborhood-oriented policing and problem–oriented policing components (Lurigio and Rosenbaum 1994; McElroy, Cosgrove, and Sadd 1993). Although the study revealed some anecdotal evidence as to an increase in job satisfaction, it collected data on those things which inferred job satisfaction with some mixed results (McElroy, Cosgrove, and Sadd 1993). The officers were skeptical at the outset of the program but eventually came to see the importance of the CPOP as revolving around such things as working as a unit, visibility, and addressing problems (McElroy, Cosgrove, and Sadd 1993, 44). And the attitudes of the officers changed to a more positive one toward the CPOP program, the community, and to some degree about being a police officer, but their attitudes grew more despondent over the functioning of the police department (McElroy, Cosgrove, and Sadd 1993, 45).

Additional studies conducted during the early 1990s almost uniformly reveal a skepticism on the part of the police officers before implementing community-oriented policing, but in post-tests, they find an increase in overall job satisfaction. In Madison, Wisconsin, a study on the Quality Policing program showed an increase in police officers' satisfaction with their jobs in a variety of areas to include greater working conditions, more participatory management, and greater community support (Lurigio and Rosenbaum 1994; Wycoff and Skogan 1994). In Joliet, Illinois, officers reported an increase in job satisfaction the first year for those in the Neighborhood-Oriented Policing (NOP) program, while in the second year officers both working in the program and outside of

A Community-Oriented Policing "Top Cop Charity Race" sponsored by Tampa Bay area police officers who race for different charities. (Courtesy of the St. Petersburg Police Dept., St. Petersburg, Florida.)

the program reported a more positive change in both the characteristics of their job and their level of satisfaction (Rosenbaum, Yeh, and Wilkinson 1994). Finally, in Louisville, Kentucky, officers reported higher job satisfaction and the researchers also found the results of this higher satisfaction were related to the level of support the officers received from the community, department, and other agencies (Wilson and Bennett 1994).

There are some reported studies, however, where community-oriented policing was not so successful. One study in Chicago, where the police department implemented the Chicago Alternative Policing Strategy (CAPS), a form of community-oriented policing, found that after implementation in the early 1990s the "officers were very ambivalent about community policing in Chicago" (Lurigio and Skogan 1994). While another study in Philadelphia, where another program known as Community-Oriented Police Education (COPE) was implemented in the 1980s found that officers, when questioned about job satisfaction, reported that they "were less satisfied with their police career and direct assignment, and were less likely to see their job as providing challenges and opportunities for self-initiative" (Lurigio and Rosenbaum 1994). These, however, seem to be the exception to the rule.

The overall analysis reveals that most of the police officers' responses to the implementation of community-oriented policing are somewhat skeptical at first. Once the officers are involved in the community-oriented policing programs, however, as long as the department offers the support necessary through the decentralization concept and implements a participatory style of management, the officers' attitudes become more positive and job satisfaction increases. The officers in most of the studies show signs that they are challenged more, have more input into their role as police officers, and feel they are truly helping the community deal with its criminal and order maintenance problems.

DEVELOPING THE COMMUNITY-ORIENTED POLICING OFFICER

Although community-oriented policing may create an atmosphere where a police officer is more challenged and achieves a higher level of job satisfaction, it is imperative that the police department assist the police officer in training to be a community-oriented policing officer. As Edwin Meese (1993, 5) wrote, "changes in titles and organization can provide the conditions for improved professionalism, but only human beings can fulfill the potential of the new strategies for police work." If a police chief changes the police department overnight from a traditional orientation to one of community-oriented policing, he or she cannot expect the police officers to adapt instantaneously. The police officers must be provided the conceptual aspects of the new philosophy as well as the understanding of the managerial changes that will complement this new approach to policing. Then the officer must be instructed in his or her role in community-oriented policing, provided the skills and training necessary to perform these duties, and given every opportunity to expand his or her potential.

COP IN ACTION

OFFICER EXCHANGE PROGRAM

In order to remain on the cutting edge of community-oriented policing, we must remain abreast of new developments and develop relationships with other professionals. An exchange program would allow our personnel to see what other agencies are doing as well as give us the opportunity to showcase our operation.

The program should be structured similarly to that of foreign exchange student programs and would not have to be limited to other police agencies. The benefits of such a program would include:

A. Improved morale

B. More knowledgeable personnel

C. Generation of new ideas

D. Improved professional relationships

E. Stress reduction for participants

Source: Denton Police Department. *Community-Oriented Policing: A Strategy*. Denton, Texas: Denton Police Department, 1995.

In a perfect world, it always seems easier to start from scratch when creating an entirely new program. It may seem easier to begin anew by hiring all new police officers hired specifically for community-oriented policing, training them in the academy and on the street for this new approach, and providing them additional training and opportunities to excel as community-oriented policing officers. This is not only an impossible idea, but it is not desirable either. The skills and understanding of the community that the police officers have gained under a traditional police department are still necessary and desirable to some degree under community-oriented policing. However, that is not to say that under this approach new officers being hired, trained, and placed into neighborhoods as community-oriented policing officers should not receive additional, and often very different, training than those under the traditional methods of police training.

The hiring of new police officers, based on the new job analysis and mission statement of the police department, should be specifically for community-oriented policing. The officers should already possess many of the skills and education necessary to perform the function and duties of this new style of policing. And when the officers are hired and entered into the police academy, their instruction should at a minimum be supplemented with some of the training necessary to create officers who can handle many of the new situations they will find themselves in, such as community leader, problem solver, and coordinator among various government agencies. Some possibilities have included creating an entirely new police academy for the community-oriented policing officers and sending them solely through this academy, or sending them through the community-oriented policing academy and then the traditional police academy. Other possibilities include expanding the length of time spent in the police academy to accommodate all of the additional training time necessary for the new curriculum. This would obviously be extremely cost prohibitive for most police departments and there is some doubt as to the potential benefit of this concept. Meese (1993, 7) suggested a split academy where the officers would obtain traditional police training, enter field training for a designated period of time, then return to the academy for enhanced community training. However it is conducted, the police officers must be indoctrinated into the role of the police under community-oriented policing to foster the perception and understanding of this new systemic approach to policing, allowing them to be successful in this new role.

In regard to officers who have previously been hired and have worked under the traditional form of policing, additional training must be provided to, first and foremost, alter any negative perceptions they may have of this systemic approach. Knowledge is the greatest combatant to fear of change and animosity and should be utilized to the greatest extent prior to the implementation of community-oriented policing. If possible, just simple training on the concept, understanding of the three components, and providing some of the literature on community-oriented policing can assist in breaking down some of the barriers and resistance to change that will no doubt be experienced. These familiarization briefings can go a long way in the preparation for actual training programs the officers will be required to attend to enhance the specific skills they will need under community-oriented policing.

The basic skills police officers will need under community-oriented policing will be reviewed; however, they are by no means all-inclusive as each police department, through specific needs dictated in large part by the community, will develop their own list of required training. The majority of skills necessary under community-oriented policing are communicative in nature. However, they will also include many basic skills critical in the officers' new role. The communications skills include enhanced listening skills, public speaking skills, preparation and delivery of communicative briefings, conflict resolution and mediation skills, the ability to organize and preside over formal meetings, and possibly instruction on the way other cultures communicate, and in some cases, language skills. The enhanced listening skills are extremely important because we have little to no training in listening, but utilize it more in the workplace than speaking, reading, and writing (Hersey and Blanchard 1993, 328). Learning the ability to listen to not only words, but such things as paralanguage, the rate of speech, diction, tone, rhythm, and volume; as well as various forms of nonverbal communication such as gestures, facial expressions, eye contact, body language, and positioning; can greatly assist the officer in various situations within the community (Hersey and Blanchard 1993, p. 328–329).

Public speaking skills are a must in community-oriented policing and a form of training most police officers do not receive (Meese 1993). As the community-oriented policing officer begins coordinating among various governmental agencies and creates, or help create, community groups for both neighborhood-oriented policing and problem-oriented policing, he or she

A Community-Oriented Policing School Resource Officer of the Berkeley Police Department, Berkeley, California, speaking with students from Berkeley High School. (Courtesy of the Berkeley Police Dept., Berkeley, California.)

will need the skills to communicate effectively to the various participants. As the majority of problems in the workplace arise out of miscommunications or the failure to communicate, the ability to speak in public, to address mass numbers of people at one time, is critical to all of the tenets of community-oriented policing.

The ability to speak in public also will assist the community-oriented policing officer in various forms of briefings. The officer may be called upon to brief various groups or people such as the police chief, the neighborhood supervisor, other officers, the community, or other government organizations on their actions or the actions of the community under community-oriented policing. These briefings may include simple informational briefings, or they may be as complex as a decision briefing where the officer must detail not only the situation or problem, but all of the alternatives to solving the problem, and the course of action that was taken or the one that is recommended. Again, these briefings provide a format for communication among the community, management, and the other line officers.

Police officers should also be provided conflict resolution and mediation skills. As the officer spends a majority of his or her time getting involved in disputes, there must be a move away from the traditional policing reaction of making an arrest or declaring "it's not a police problem." Community-oriented policing officers should be provided with those skills necessary to resolve these types of conflicts and to defuse their situations, rather than waiting to be called back to the scene. Also, when working with various segments of the community and deciding on tactics to utilize under the three components, the community-oriented policing officer will often find community members may disagree on what should be done about a particular problem or what the priority for addressing these problems should be. Here, the conflict resolution and mediation skills can provide the officer the tools to reach a valuable conclusion to the disagreement.

In holding these community meetings, the police officer will also find, at least initially, that the community members look to their authority and position as a simple declaration that they are in charge. Eventually, it is more desirable to have a community member preside over the meetings, but the officer should set the standard initially. Therefore, the officer must have some understanding of the various types of meetings and the various skills to effectively run a meeting. The meetings of the community should not be a "complaint" session directed toward the police or other members of the community, but rather it must be an open discussion to those things that affect the entire community.

In some cases, in some communities, various cultures will be represented. As every culture has different ways of communicating both verbally and nonverbally, it is important that the police officer has at least some familiarity with these differences prior to conducting these meetings. It can assist the officer in defusing some uncomfortable situations just through the education on various cultural attitudes, beliefs, and values. It may also be equally important for the police officer to learn at least some basics of the various languages spoken in the community, and the police officer should be provided every opportunity to learn a language both inside and outside the police department, with departmental assistance.

COP IN ACTION

SCHOOL RESOURCE OFFICERS: COMMUNITY OUTREACH BENEFITS EVERYBODY

Although crime rates in the United States have generally dropped in recent years, the rate of juvenile crime has risen rapidly. Also, a recent survey reported that one in every four students feels that violence has lessened the quality of education in his or her school. One program to combat the increase of juvenile crime is gaining popularity across the country. It involves a partnership between law enforcement and the schools known as the school resource officer.

This program assigns uniformed police officers to schools, usually junior and senior high schools, to perform a variety of functions. The fact that it is not a structured program is often a benefit in that the program can be tailored to the individual needs of the community. The cost of the officers is often split between the city government and the school district, since hopefully each benefits. School resources officer programs, in use since at least the 1970s, have grown rapidly across the country during the past decade as a result of increasing crime and violence problems in the public school systems.

Although the duties of school resource officers are different in every jurisdiction, most programs have set the following goals:

1. Safety and security on the campus.
2. Teach students, school staff, and parents about law enforcement.
3. Reduce truancy by enhancing the learning environment.
4. Create goodwill and increase understanding of law enforcement.
5. Strengthen student–police relationships.

School resource officers can benefit law enforcement, school districts and the community in general. By having the officers in the schools every day, they can open lines of communication between school officials and the law enforcement community. Many times officers and school officials work on the same problems and have to handle the same "bad" kids, but are not able to work closely together for various reasons. The school resource officers help break down these barriers.

A school resource officer program is good public relations for the police department and the school system. The public wants governmental agencies to work together to help solve community problems, and this program is a good example of it working. Although a school resource officer program may be of help to many, each jurisdiction must decide what will work best for them. Each community should take into consideration the extent of their juvenile problem, their population demographics, the potential for participation by school officials, and the community's budgetary concerns. What works well in one community may or may not work equally well in a different one.

Source: Adapted with permission from Michael K. Ahrens. "School Resource Officers." *Law and Order*, July 1995, 81–83.

The additional skills that police officers will need beyond the communication skills under community-oriented policing include decision-making and problem-solving skills, computer skills, and how to obtain information on a community from every aspect possible, beyond just crime information. Decision-making skills are some of the most critical skills necessary under community-oriented policing. The ability to address a problem, create alternatives for solving the problem, and select the alternative for implementation are skills that are an integral part of community-oriented policing. As this is the primary emphasis of the third component, problem-oriented policing, it is easy to demonstrate the need for this skill.

Additionally, it is important that police officers have both typing and computer skills as the use of computers in the criminal justice field is increasing. This is particularly true because many police cruisers are now equipped with mobile data terminals from which police officers can quickly obtain information (Meese 1993, 7). The ability to work with computers can increase the police officers' productivity immensely and provide a large source of information for the officer about his or her community. This, to a large degree, will be where the officers will obtain the majority of information on their prospective communities, both criminal and non-criminal related. However, in many cases information cannot be obtained through a computer and the community-oriented policing officers must be instructed on the varying locations from which they can obtain information on their communities. This information should not be limited by any means and could include items revealing social, economic, and demographic information. The officers should also have an understanding of what information other governmental agencies can provide, how they can be contacted, and what support they can offer.

The ability of the community-oriented policing officer to adapt to all of these skills will be critical in his or her new role and can mean the difference between success and failure. In order to safeguard the community-oriented policing concept when implemented, many believe that in order for it to be truly successful, the new officer should have a college degree as this provides a police officer with many of these skills already intact (Meese 1993). The reasoning is perhaps best articulated by Riechers and Roberg (1990, 111) when they explained that:

> In doing community- and problem-oriented policing, line officers are asked to attempt to alleviate specific problems, which they have helped to identify by orienting themselves to the needs of the community, with *creative* and *innovative* solutions in a fair, just, and legal manner. This requires certain skills, including problem conceptualization, synthesis and analysis of information, action plans, program evaluation, and

communication of evaluation results and policy implications. Numerous studies have indicated that skills such as these are enhanced by a college education … suffice it to say that the sensitivity and demands of the role of community policing require an individual with a high degree of intelligence, open-mindedness, and nonprejudicial attitudes.

However, in a survey of police departments in the United States, 97 percent of local police departments had a formal education requirement, but the typical minimum education requirement of 86 percent of the departments was the completion of high school (Chaiken 1995). In total, 12 percent of the local police departments surveyed required some college education while only 7 percent required a two-year college degree and 1 percent required a four-year college degree (Reichers and Roberg 1990, 111).

Police departments across the nation are slowly encouraging their officers to seek out additional college education, and as seen from the percentages above, police departments are also beginning to require some college prior to the hiring process. However, the debate over college education for police officers has existed for nearly three decades, originally pushed to the forefront by the Law Enforcement Assistance Administration in the late 1960s. This has since created a storm of debate in both police and academic circles. With strong proponents on either side of the issue, there is no simple answer.

The ultimate question for determining the necessity of higher education is, generally, does it make a better police officer (Radelet and Carter 1994, 153)? For our purposes here, the question should be phrased as: Does it make a better community-oriented policing officer? Radelet and Carter (1994, 156) answer their question with a qualified "maybe" as a result of the literature; however, factoring in community-oriented policing they believe it does make for a more effective officer. If we sidestep the larger debate and incorporate the idea that the skills necessary for the community-oriented policing officer can be obtained through higher education, the question then becomes: why does it make the officer more effective?

As we reviewed those skills necessary for the community-oriented policing officer, supported by Riechers and Roberg, many of those skills are learned in the higher education environment. Computer classes and public speaking classes are generally required general education classes in most colleges and universities, which immediately provides the college-educated officer with a slight edge. As we reach the end of the twentieth century, we have seen a dramatic increase in the number of colleges and universities with formal programs related to the study of crime, criminology, law enforcement, and the criminal justice system (Oliver 1995, 3). Many of these programs incorporate the utilization of computer skills and public speaking skills, as well as decision-making skills and the study of ethics in the criminal justice system, all of which enhance the community-oriented policing officer. Additionally, if the college or university offers a course on community-oriented policing or even police-community relations, it provides a fundamental background for the police officer when entering the community-oriented policing police department.

TABLE 8.7   HIGHER EDUCATION AND POLICING

Degrees:

- A.S. Associate of Science
- B.S. Bachelor of Science
- B.A. Bachelor of Arts
- M.S. Master of Science
- M.A. Master of Arts
- J.D. Juris Doctorate
- Ph.D. Doctorate of Philosophy

Majors:

- Criminal Justice
- Criminology
- Law Enforcement
- Criminal Law
- Sociology
- Political Science
- Law
- Social Work
- Psychology
- Public Administration

There are also certain studies that have determined that many benefits accrue to police officers obtaining a higher education degree which are not as quantifiable as those listed above, but are still of critical importance in regard to community-oriented policing. Some of these benefits include more experience and maturity, understanding of both the government and criminal justice systems, greater creativity and innovation, capability of seeing the "big picture," greater tolerance for other lifestyles and ideologies, more effective communications, better equipped to work on their own, more professional demeanor, and a developed ability to adapt (Carter and Sapp 1990, 41–42). Higher-educated officers also tended to be less authoritarian and cynical (Carter and Sapp 1990, 41–42) Some studies also found that police officers with a higher education degree were also more ethical, had fewer complaints filed against them, and fewer disciplinary problems (Oliver 1995, 3). Additionally, the police departments themselves benefit overall from having police officers with higher education degrees. As Patrick Murphy states in the foreword to *The State of Police Education: Policy Direction for the 21st Century:*

> In general, a police department that has had a four-year college degree as an entry requirement for ten years or more can be quite a different

organization from one requiring only a high school diploma. More responsibility can be placed on the officers, and a more collegial style of management can be utilized. The college-educated force sets higher professional standards and goals, which in turn, command public respect and help shape public opinion. Finally, a college-educated force has the potential to proactively, rather than just reactively, address the crime and drug problems that plague society today. (Murphy 1989, iv)

The benefits of police officers receiving higher education are demonstrated by the research and the majority of those benefits detailed are befitting a community-oriented policing officer. Therefore, it should be an integral part of the requirements for being a police officer under this new systemic approach to policing. This is but one more aspect of the systems approach. This is not to say, however, that all police departments under community-oriented policing should no longer hire those with only a high school diploma. Rather, the police department must set the hiring standard as it sees fit. However, the department must also encourage and provide not only the opportunity, but incentives to ensure their officers receive some higher education classes and potentially a baccalaureate, master's, or professional degree.

CONCLUSION

The role of the police officer is dramatically different under community-oriented policing than it was under the previous traditional approach. Although police officers will still retain many of the old functions of policing under community-oriented policing, officers will have to practice situational policing to determine which of the three functions, law enforcement, order maintenance, or service is appropriate under the new circumstances in which they find themselves. Officers will also have to practice situational leadership when working with the community to determine not only the style of leadership they should assume, authoritarian, democratic, or laissez-faire, but whether they should even have a leadership role, or assume the role of advisor or follower. Whether leader or follower, police officers must be an integral part of the community under their new role as a community-oriented policing officers.

The police are a critical asset under community-oriented policing and their importance must not be ignored. Their perceptions of community-oriented policing when implementing this new systemic approach can be the difference between success and failure. They must be informed of both the conceptual and practical aspects of the system and they should be afforded every opportunity to participate in the management process. The new officer should be hired and trained with the express purpose of filling the role of community-oriented policing officer, and the previously hired officer should be afforded every opportunity to learn and improve upon the skills necessary under this new approach.

The department implementing community-oriented policing may face many obstacles when it comes to officer-participation officers. Animosity toward the program must be overcome through education and revealing the findings of job satisfaction from other police departments that have implemented similar programs. The benefits to the police under community-oriented policing far outweigh any negative aspects they may face. Community-oriented policing is not only beneficial to the community and the police department, it is beneficial to the police officer

REFERENCES

Banton, Michael. *The Police in the Community*. New York: Basic Books, 1964.

Brown, Lee P. and Mary Ann Wycoff. "Policing Houston: Reducing Fear and Improving Service." *Crime & Delinquency*. 33 no. 1 (January 1987): 71–89.

Carter, David L. and Allen D. Sapp. "Making the Grade." *Police Technology and Management*. December 1990, 39–43.

Chaiken, Jan M. *Local Police Departments 1993*. Washington, D.C.: U.S. Department of Justice, April 1995.

Cole, George F. *The American System of Criminal Justice*. 7th ed. Belmont, CA.: Wadsworth Publishing Company, 1995.

Cordner, Gary W. "A Problem-Oriented Approach to Community- Oriented Policing." In *Community Policing: Rhetoric or Reality,* ed. Jack R. Greene and Stephen D. Mastrofski. New York: Praegar Publishers, 1988.

Dempsey, John S. *Policing: An Introduction to Law Enforcement*. St. Paul: West Publishing Company, 1994.

Goldstein, Herman. *Problem-Oriented Policing*. New York: McGraw-Hill Publishing Co., 1990.

Hayeslip, D. W., Jr. and Gary W. Cordner. "The Effects of Community-Oriented Patrol on Police Officer Attitudes." *American Journal of Police* 6 no. 1 (1987): 95–119.

Hersey, Paul and Kenneth H. Blanchard. *Management of Organizational Behavior*. 6th ed. Englewood Cliffs, N.J.: Prentice-Hall, Inc., 1993.

Holden, Richard N. *Modern Police Management*. Englewood Cliffs, N.J.: Prentice-Hall, Inc., 1986.

Lurigio, Arthur J. and Dennis P. Rosenbaum. "The Impact of Community Policing on Police Personnel: A Review of the Literature." In *The Challenge of Community Policing: Testing the Promises* ed. Dennis P. Rosenbaum. Thousand Oaks, CA.: SAGE Publications, Inc., 1994.

Lurigio, Arthur J. and Wesley G. Skogan. "Winning the Hearts and Minds of Police Officers: An Assessment of Staff Perceptions of Community Policing in Chicago." *Crime & Delinquency* 40, no. 3 (July 1994) 315–330.

Maslow, Abraham H. *Motivation and Personality*. 2nd ed. New York: Harper and Collins, 1970.

McElroy, Jerome E., Colleen A. Cosgrove, and Susan Sadd. *Community Policing: The CPOP in New York*. Newbury Park, CA.: SAGE Publications, Inc., 1993.

Meese, Edwin III. "Community Policing and the Police Officer." *Perspectives on Policing*. Washington, D.C.: National Institute of Justice and the John F. Kennedy School of Government, Harvard University, January 1993.

Moore, Mark H. and Robert C. Trojanowicz. "Corporate Strategies for Policing." *Perspectives on Policing*. Washington, D.C.: National Institute of Justice and the John F. Kennedy School of Government, Harvard University, November 1988.

Murphy, Patrick. "Foreword." In *The State of Police Education: Policy Directions for the 21st Century,* by Carter, David L. Allen D. Sapp, and Darrel W. Stephens. Washington, D.C.: Police Executive Research Forum, 1989.

Oliver, Will. "Higher Education and Discipline." *Police Department Disciplinary Bulletin.* Boston, MA.: Quinlan Publishing Company, May 1995.

Pate, Anthony, Mary Ann Wycoff, Wesley G. Skogan, and Lawrence W. Sherman. *Reducing Fear of Crime in Houston and Newark: A Summary Report.* Washington, D.C.: Police Foundation, 1986.

Peak, Kenneth. *Justice Administration: Police, Courts, and Corrections Management.* Englewood Cliffs, N.J.: Prentice-Hall, Inc., 1995.

Radelet, Louis A. and David L. Carter. *The Police and the Community.* 5th ed. Englewood Cliffs, N.J.: MacMillan Publishing Company, 1994.

Reichers, Lisa M. and Roy R. Roberg. "Community Policing: A Critical Review of Underlying Assumptions." *Journal of Police Science and Administration* 17, no. 2 (1990): 105–114.

Rosenbaum, Dennis P., Sandy Yeh, and Deanna L. Wilkinson. "Impact of Community Policing on Police Personnel: A Quasi-Experimental Test." *Crime & Delinquency* 40, no. 3 (July 1994): 331–353.

Sherman, Lawrence W. "Middle Management and Democratization: A reply to John E. Angell." *Criminology* 12, no. 4 (1975): 363–377.

Sherman, Lawrence W., Catherine H. Milton, and Thomas V. Kelly. *Team Policing: Seven Case Studies.* Washington, D.C.: Police Foundation, 1973.

Williams, Hubert and Antony M. Pate. "Returning to First Principles: Reducing the Fear of Crime in Newark." *Crime & Delinquency* 33, no. 1 (January 1987): 53–70.

Wilson, Deborah G. and Susan F. Bennett. "Officers' Response to Community Policing: Variations on a Theme." *Crime & Delinquency.* 40, no. 3 (July 1994): 354–370.

Wilson, James Q. *Varieties of Police Behavior: The Management of Law and Order in Eight Communities.* Cambridge, MA.: Harvard University Press, 1968.

————. "What Makes a Better Policeman?" *The Atlantic Monthly,* March 1969.

Wilson, James Q. and George L. Kelling. "Broken Windows." *Atlantic Monthly,* March 1982.

Wycoff, Mary Ann. "The Benefits of Community Policing: Evidence and Conjecture." In *Community Policing: Rhetoric or Reality,* ed. by Jack R. Greene and Stephen D. Mastrofski. New York: Praegar Publishers, 1988.

Wycoff, Mary Ann and Wesley G. Skogan. "The Effect of a Community Policing Management Style on Officers' Attitudes." *Crime & Delinquency* 40, no. 3 (July 1994): 371–383.

CHAPTER 9

The Role of the Community

*Nothing will ruin the country if the people themselves will undertake its safety;
and nothing can save it if they leave that safety in any hands but their own.*

-Daniel Webster-

Inherent within the name of community-oriented policing is a role and position for the community in the systemic approach. The role is defined by the position the community holds in our society today and by the relationship necessary to eradicate crime and order maintenance issues that plague our streets and neighborhoods. The role of the community must be a powerful one under community-oriented policing. The community cannot be relegated to the role of silent partner or advisory board, rather, it must, at a minimum, obtain equality with the police, and in the most desired goals of community-oriented policing the community must become the leaders of the police. This role of the community is perhaps one of the most difficult aspects of community-oriented policing to conceive, but at the same time it is one of the most critical for the systemic approach to be complete. The community must be an integral component of community-oriented policing in order for the concept to succeed.

Despite this important substantive role the community must have under community-oriented policing, there has been little discussion in the literature reviewing this critical role (Buerger 1994a; Grinc 1994). Even less time has been spent by proponents of community-oriented policing providing for an accurate definition of what is meant by community, raising much criticism of this "new" approach to policing (Buerger 1994b; Grinc 1994; Manning 1988; Murphy 1988). The majority of the literature exploring the role of the partici-

The Berkeley Police Department's Citizen's Academy graduating class of spring 1995. (Courtesy of the Berkeley Police Dept., Berkeley, California.)

pants in community-oriented policing is generally relegated to the police officer with little mention of the community, except in passage of the term describing this new era in policing. The necessity for discussing the role of the community goes far beyond an understanding of the three components of community-oriented policing and the role that the community must undertake in this new approach. It is the understanding of why the community is necessary in this new approach and it is this that must be first addressed.

"CRIME FILES"

RESTITUTION AND COMMUNITY SERVICE—PART 18

This edition of the "Crime Files," hosted by James Q. Wilson, features Judge Albert Kramer, Quincy District Court, Quincy, Massachusetts; Michael Smith, Executive Director of the Vera Institute of Justice; and Newman Flanagan, District Attorney, Suffolk County, Boston. The discussion revolves around two alternatives to traditional sanctions for offenders, by taking a community approach to dealing with offenders. The focus is on the Quincy, Massachusetts program.

According to Wilson and Kelling in the article "Broken Windows" and as was discussed in the last chapter, the police, throughout the early part of the twentieth century, were focused on the role of order maintenance for performing their duties (Wilson and Kelling, 1982). As the crime wave of the early 1960s began with the largest population explosion the United States has ever experienced, the police began to focus more on law enforcement than order maintenance. The introduction of the "baby-boomers" and their ascension into those crime-prone, teenage years, caused the police to rethink their role in society. The order maintenance concept was not working with this new population and a switch to the role of law enforcement was made. The goal for better policing was then focused on ways "the police could solve more crimes, make more arrests, and gather better evidence" (Wilson and Kelling 1982, 33). Crime fighting became the central focus for all policing and the social control mechanisms, largely influenced by the community and reinforced by the police, collapsed. Both the community and the police began to change.

The community which influenced its own sense of social control over the people began to disappear from the inner city neighborhoods, and eventually disappeared from many of the suburbs found in metropolitan areas. People became more engrossed in their work, our society became more mobile, age-old institutions of family, neighborhood, and community crumbled, and government attempted to fill the void. Our societal makeup has changed dramatically since the early 1960s and has not supported the establishment of cohesive neighborhoods which in turn would foster the "sense of community" people speak of so often. Citizens drew up within much smaller groups and decided they "did not want to get involved" or it was "not their problem." Society allowed social disorder to reign and turned any semblance of social control over to the police. Crime fighting and social disorder is "their job" because "that's what we pay them for." Although this evidence is somewhat factual, partly anecdotal, and largely ontological in nature, the changes demonstrated in the police are not.

The police have changed dramatically since the early 1960s and most of it for the better. Speaking first of that which is better on the part of the police is the move to become more "professional" in their work, better equipped, and better trained. However, what the police have given up in return has not been worth the price. The police have given up their order maintenance role, their relationship with the community, and they have collectively determined they can handle all criminal problems on their own, and the rest is not their concern. However, there is even doubt the police can handle the crime. As Walinsky (1995, 39) reports "in the 1960s the United States as a whole had 3.3 police officers for every violent crime reported per year. In 1993 it had 3.47 violent crimes reported for every police officer." Despite the greatest endeavors of the United States Congress to add 100,000 police officers on the street via Title I of the 1994 Crime Bill, according to Walinsky (1995, 40), to retain the position the United States had in 1960, "we would have to add not 100,000 new police officers but about five million." This is prominently impractical and nearly infeasible, therefore we must look to that which we currently must endure. The police are consistently a small group in any society, whether it is the five police officers in Glenville, West Virginia, policing a community of 4,000; Arlington County Police Department with 325 officers serving a 100,000 population; or New York City Police Department with 38,000 police officers serving 8 million citizens. These three police departments and all of the departments in the United States, however effective they are, cannot hope to truly fight all the crime on their own and deal effectively with the order maintenance issues. As Herman Goldstein (1990, 21) stated, "a community must police itself" and "the police can, at best, only assist in that task."

This, then, demonstrates the need for the community to be an integral part of community-oriented policing. The police need the community and the community needs the police. In order to continue effectively fighting crime, the police must elicit the help of the community. In order to reestablish order out of disorder and to maintain the community through order maintenance, the police and community must work together. In order to achieve this and to work effectively together, the police and community must implement community-oriented policing and address all of the problems together through the three components. And the desired goal of the concept is to have the community dictate the problems, prioritize their importance, determine means to effectively address them, then either implement or assist in the implementation of the various solutions. In effect, the community becomes the leaders of the police.

In order to understand this concept better, the term "community" must be effectively defined for the purposes of community-oriented policing. It is also important to analyze what role the community has developed in regards to police relations since the early 1960s and what their practical role would be under community-oriented policing. And finally, it is important to look to the development of community involvement in this systemic approach, as some communities will call for community-oriented policing on their own, while others will have no desire to even discuss their involvement in the police function.

COP IN ACTION

VOLUNTEER CORP

The Denton Police Department has utilized volunteers on a limited basis for several years. In addition to volunteers, we have participated with local universities in intern programs for Criminal Justice Majors. We also have participated in the Job Training Partnership Act (JTPA) providing employment and training for young citizens. As budgets shrink and resource management becomes increasingly more difficult, we must find staffing alternatives. A policy that builds on the current activities could provide staff for duties that we might not otherwise be able to provide. The Volunteer Corps policy would seek qualified individuals who are willing to volunteer their time to their community by working as unpaid employees. The corps could consist of part-time or full-time employees who would be fully trained and work regular schedules. Their duties could conceivably consist of any duty now performed by a civilian or that does not require enforcement authority. We would ask that a written commitment be made by the volunteer and that they pass all requirements for paid employees. In the same spirit, a structured learning program would be developed for the criminal justice majors and the JTPA employees that include specific duties as well as training. Volunteers working in the department would provide another avenue for consultation.

Source: Denton Police Department. *Community-Oriented Policing: A Strategy*. Denton, Texas: Denton Police Department, 1995.

COMMUNITY DEFINED

Defining the term "community" is difficult as there are multiple definitions exploring everything from the tangible, to the way people organize, to a spiritual sense of the word. Exploring the various dictionaries provides a collection of confusing and often conflicting definitions that serve little purpose under our larger definition of community-oriented policing (Buerger 1994b, 421–422). As this larger definition is more concerned with the social behavior and the human aspects of defining community, we must look to the sociological definitions of community for assistance.

Unfortunately, even the field of sociology falls prey to the multiple definitions of community, despite their central focus on human social behavior (Schwab 1992). However, looking to general definitions of "community" in the field we find one definition detailing "a spatial or territorial unit of social organization in which people have a sense of identity and a feeling of belonging" (Schaefer and Lamm 1992, 546). While another definition is more analytical in its categorization of community when it states "the term community refers to a group of people who share three things: They live in a geographically distinct area (such as a city or town); they share cultural characteristics, attitudes, and lifestyles; and they interact with one another on a sustained basis" (Farley 1994, 506). Although these sociological definitions are helpful in perceiving some of

Berkeley Police Department DARE officer instructing his elementary school class in the spring of 1995. (Courtesy of the Berkeley Police Dept., Berkeley, California.)

the elements present in some communities, they are not as helpful as we would like them to be when analyzing the street from a police officer's perspective.

Some communities may adhere to the concepts of geographical distinction, sharing of culture, and interaction on a regular basis, but then they are most likely communities with low priority for the police. This is not to say that they are not important and deserve no attention under community-oriented policing, but these types of communities will most likely have fewer criminal, order maintenance, and environmental problems than those communities lacking in some area of the sociological definition. Those areas that are ridden with crime, where there is no consensus of attitudes or beliefs, and where there is little to no interaction among the residents, are still communities for our purpose. These are the communities the police are most familiar with, and these are the communities we must not forget in community-oriented policing. For hiding behind the doors and windows, even in the worst of inner-city deprivation, are good, honest, hard-working citizens who are caught in a situation that they cannot escape, but have come to endure.

There is another segment of society that the police recognize as a community, which may or may not be inclusive within the sociological definition of community, and that is the criminal community. Whether we are discussing the community of crack houses and drug dealers, gangs, or prostitutes, there still exists a community with which the police must interact. As Herman Goldstein (1990, 26) stated, "from a practical standpoint, 'community' is not synonymous with 'law-abiding'." The relations with this community will be different than with the law-abiding community; however, many of the central tenets of community-oriented policing will be utilized to maintain order and address the worst of the criminal problems within this criminal element.

COP IN ACTION

A KIDS' INTERVIEW ROOM

Rather than inflict the institutional, and often intimidating, atmosphere of a police station on small children, police in Jupiter, Florida, decorated an interview room to make child victims of crime feel more at ease during questioning. The "kids' room" features bright colors, Sesame Street wall posters, child-sized furniture, stuffed animals, toys, books, and a TV\VCR for cartoons and movies.

The cost to the municipality was minimal because the department turned it into a community project. Local high school students, who are members of the service-oriented Interact Club, volunteered to paint and wallpaper the room with the assistance of Jupiter officers. Most of the expenses for furnishings were covered by donations from local community service organizations and anonymous donors.

Source: Adapted with permission from Byrt, Frank. "A Kids' Interview Room." *Law and Order*, October 1995, 100–101.

The ability to clearly define the term "community" is clearly impossible and perhaps a futile endeavor. The ability to look to one strict analysis and definition of community is of no benefit to community-oriented policing, for there are always communities within communities. As Goldstein (1990, 26) explains, "communities are shifting groups, defined differently depending on the problem that is addressed." We therefore must be content with looking to community as it is defined by multiple parties, including the police, the citizens, and the government. We can look to geography to help us form a conceptualization of community by analyzing the police department's geographical boundaries and the institutionalized conception of geography such as a city, neighborhood, or business district. However, within these confines we can only define community as consisting of a group of people who interact and have some shared attitudes and beliefs, whether they are criminal or law-abiding, residential or business-oriented, socially acceptable or not acceptable.

Community-oriented policing, then, perceives the community as whatever collective group it is dealing with to address a criminal or order maintenance issue. As Mastrofski points out, a minimum standard for community-oriented policing is the "basis for police action requires a demonstration that a group of people—say a neighborhood—shares a definition of what constitutes right order, threats to it, and appropriate methods for maintaining it" (Mastrofski 1988, 49). He further states that "to the extent that community implies a basis for citizens to work collectively with police to restore and preserve order, it also requires a sense of group identity or attachment—a 'we-ness' derived from shared experience and interaction" (Mastrofski 1988, 49). In a perfect setting this may already exist, but in a conceptual sense it may require the creation of community where none exists.

This definition of community, or lack thereof, is important when exploring the past role of the community in policing, but more importantly in conceptualizing and understanding community's role within community-oriented policing. Without the community's involvement, in this systemic approach to policing, it will cease to exist, and the police will be forced, by default, to return to the isolated form of traditional policing.

TABLE 9.1   WHO IS THE COMMUNITY?

The following is a list of community members who can provide resources, information, and assistance for strategic-oriented policing, can assist in creating various programs under neighborhood-oriented policing, and should be involved in neighborhood groups assembled to address local problems under problem-oriented policing:

- Families
- Children
- Senior citizens
- Single people
- Transients

- Business people
- Service people
- Homeless people
- Residences
    Single-Family Homeowners
    Apartment dwellers
    Condominium owners
    Townhome owners
    Public housing dwellers
    Temporary renters
- Churches
- Businesses
    Service
    Retail
    Industrial
- Government
    Schools
    Hospitals
    Libraries
    Parks
    Recreation centers
    Police department
    Fire Department
    Human services
    Sheriff's department
    Mayor/City manager
    City council
    Small business administration
    Public works
    Planning and zoning
    City prosecutor
    Courts
- Charities
    United Way
- Civic Organizations
    Profits
        Chamber of Commerce
        Business associations
        Real estate associations
    Nonprofit
        Fraternal lodges
        Veterans of Foreign Wars
        Big Brothers/Sisters
        Advocacy groups

     Boy/Girl Scouts
     Neighborhood associations
     Homeowners' associations
- Unions
- Crime Prevention
     Police Athletic Leagues
     Guardian Angels
     Neighborhood Watch
     Crime Stoppers
- Utility Companies
     Water
     Gas
     Electricity
     Cable
     Telephone
- Federal agencies
- Federal law enforcement
- Neighborhood residents

THE TRADITIONAL ROLE OF THE COMMUNITY

Despite the call for greater community integration into policing, and essentially the greater institution of government, under community-oriented policing, this concept is not new to America. From the founding of the United States to present -day America, citizen participation has been a strong underlying facet of our form of government. Citizen participation is safeguarded within the Constitution, and the United States has a longer history of cherishing this noble endeavor than it does in its dismissal. This reaction of citizen participation in government, and more importantly for our purposes, in policing, can be seen as a result of the centralization of local governments after World War II (Johnson, Misner, and Brown 1981, 276) causing them to become "increasingly remote from neighborhood concerns" (Wilson 1975, 40). As this was occurring, government had to determine a method by which the citizens could be drawn back into the participatory process that was once the foundation of American government.

   Johnson, Misner, and Brown (1981, 276) highlighted three distinct stages whereby the government, since World War II, has attempted to draw upon citizen participation. The first stage, from 1949 to 1963, emphasized the creation of carefully appointed committees to the government process "that were only advisory in nature" and "had little or no influence on the official policies that were made" (Johnson, Misner, and Brown 1981, 276). In the second stage, from 1964 to 1968, governments selected "indigenous citizens" to participate in the policy-making procedure (Johnson, Misner, and Brown 1981, p. 276). This largely consisted of citizens from the local communities, specifically oriented on obtaining a cross section by race, gender, and national origin. The third stage of citizen participation as articulated by Johnson, Misner, and Brown (1981, 276) was said to exist from 1969 to the time of their writing in 1981, and this stage emphasized planning and advisory councils in a regional decentralized manner.

However, a clear and distinct category of citizen participation has emerged since Johnson, Misner, and Brown's book and subsequently a fourth stage should be added. In this stage, running from the early 1980s to the present, citizen participation has consisted of the same decentralized manner as the third stage, but it has commanded more power, moving away from the advisory role to one of authoritative action. In the police field, despite an enormous amount of debate (see for example, Dudley 1991; Kerstetter 1985), this form of citizen participation has increased dramatically through the 1980s in the form of the civilian review board, which generally reviews police misconduct and deadly shooting encounters (see for example, Geller and Scott 1992; Radelet and Carter 1994).

As Johnson, Misner, and Brown (1981, 276) articulate in their book, the important aspect of this historical interpretation is to understand that citizen participation in the governmental process "has a long history in this country." The role of citizen participation within the role of the police is no different. This can be clearly seen when we look to the historical correlation between the two. The role of the police in our society shifted from order maintenance, largely citizen participatory, after World War II, and moved to that of law enforcement, which is highly centralized and is not citizen participatory. Despite the shift of the police, along with the rest of government, away from citizen participation, it is important to remember that the citizen still played some role, albeit a minor one at times.

The traditional roles of the community in relationship to the police function are perhaps best articulated by Buerger's categorization of four standard roles (Buerger 1994a; Buerger 1994b). Traditionally, the first and primary role the community has had is acting as the "eyes and ears of the police" (Buerger 1994a, 270). Providing the police information about crime, criminals, and suspicious activity via the phone, personal contact, or clandestine contact, such as informants, has been the key way for citizens to participate in the police function. In the second role of "cheerleader," citizens, in a collective sense, articulate their support for the police (Buerger 1994a, 270; Buerger 1994b, 416). The third role the community has is a supportive role, usually in the form of monetary assistance through tax levies aimed at increasing the funding for the police (Buerger 1994a, 270–271; Buerger 1994b, 416). The fourth role is that of "statement-making" where the community makes statements that are "symbolically confrontational" such as "the annual Take Back The Night rallies—or activities with more lasting effects, such as posting 'Drug-Free School Zone' or Neighborhood Watch signs" (Buerger 1994a, 271). All of these roles are indicative of the traditional role the community has had over the past several decades, and is still yet a part of community-oriented policing. However, the systemic approach to policing allows for a much larger role on the part of the community.

THE ROLE OF COMMUNITY IN COMMUNITY-ORIENTED POLICING

The community must take on a larger role under community-oriented policing in order for this new approach to be successful. The community, one of the most important factors in both law enforcement and order maintenance, can effectively deal with crime and greatly improve the environmental conditions in which its citizens live, if they take on a wider role in policing and are provided the opportunity for this role. The community must be allowed to share power with the police, allowed decision-making capabilities under all three of the components, and must effectively lead the police. In order to accomplish this goal, it is important to look at the community's expanded role and function under community-oriented policing.

Eck and Rosenbaum (1994) identified five ways in which the citizens of a community can effectively deal with the criminal and order maintenance issues that face their neighborhoods. Eck and Rosenbaum (1994, 14) identified the first and primary function, found in the traditional role of the community, which continues in the community-oriented policing role, and that is to be the "eyes and ears" of the community. The second function is for citizens to form patrols, confront criminal and disorderly individuals, and drive them from the community (Eck and Rosenbaum 1994, 14). Although this was generally discouraged under the traditional role of the community in policing (Buerger 1994a, 271), some police now encourage such action under community-oriented policing (Eck and Rosenbaum 1994, 14). The third function of the community is to reduce its citizens' chances of victimization, reduce the opportunity for crime, reduce the actual amount of crime, and reduce the fear of crime (Eck and Rosenbaum 1994, 14; Skogan 1987). The fourth function is for citizens to "put pressure on others to act" (Eck and Rosenbaum 1994, 14). As Eck and Rosenbaum (1994, 14–15) articulate:

> They can demand more police resources, they can pressure businesses to change their practices, they can lobby local government agencies to obtain services and get favorable rulings from regulators, and they can threaten property owners and organizations with civil suits to change behaviors and physical conditions.

And the fifth function they discuss is allowing "the police to act on their behalf" (Eck and Rosenbaum 1994, 15). The police, through meetings with the community, can gather the opinions of the community and authorization from them to extend their capabilities beyond the normal routines of policing. These enforcement capabilities in any other environment may not be acceptable (Eck 1993; Eck and Rosenbaum 1994; Weisburd, McElroy, and Hardyman 1988), but it is a return to pre-World War II America where "the police in this earlier period assisted in that reassertion of authority by acting, sometimes violently, on the behalf of the community" (Wilson and Kelling 1982, 33). Although this is not a call for the community to allow police brutality, it is a call for the police to have greater authorization and capabilities to deal effectively with criminal and order maintenance issues. For example, in a neighborhood with an open-air drug market, obtaining the authorization of all the residents to allow the police to stop any and all vehicles entering and leaving the neighborhood without a reasonable suspicion can be one way to effectively deal with the drug problems through citizen authorization.

COP IN ACTION

BEYOND NEIGHBORHOOD WATCH: THE ROLE OF THE COMMUNITY IN COMMUNITY POLICING.

The bulk of what has been written about implementing community policing addresses what can be done within police agencies to promote community policing initiatives. And although most agencies interested in modifying traditional methods of police service delivery are working hard to establish and extend partnerships with business owners, public and private service providers, community groups, and the media (see Trojanowicz and Bucqueroux 1994), they have given less attention to the specifics of what the average community member's role is, or can be, under a community policing model. It appears, however, that we are at the point in this evolutionary process to further explore the role of the community in community policing.

Citizens have typically assisted the police with the detection and reporting of possible criminal activity in their communities (Buerger 1994). Members of groups such as Neighborhood Watch or citizen patrols are often defined as "the eyes and ears of the police." Unfortunately, the success of programs such as Neighborhood Watch may contribute to the problems that many agencies experience as they try to get community members involved in more proactive efforts to increase neighborhood safety. Citizens often believe that they have fulfilled their civic duties when they call 911 to report troublesome activity to the police. It is possible that these early crime-prevention efforts have actually created more, not less, of a dependency on the police. It is now time to work toward making community residents more proactive and less dependent.

A variety of obstacles, however, must be overcome in order to make community crime-prevention efforts more proactive. One of the first steps should be to increase citizens' knowledge of police operations, particularly regarding the limited resources police have at their disposal. In most areas of this country, regardless of whether the jurisdiction is urban, suburban, or rural, it is often impossible for the police to address every instance of crime and disorder in a community. Some police fear that if the public gets more involved in crime prevention, they may develop unrealistic expectations of the amount of time that the police can spend attending to their specific concerns. Such unrealistic expectations may lead to decreased levels of citizen satisfaction with police services if those expectations are not met. Police must make concerned citizens aware of the constraints (realities) within which the police must operate, and help them understand exactly how these constraints affect police practices.

The second step is to give the public a multitude of very specific suggestions about how they can contribute to neighborhood safety. Community members, possibly organized in neighborhood associations, local schools, or worship groups, can play an important role in several areas including the following: 1) identifying problems (identifying conditions of crime and disorder that threaten citizen safety); 2) prioritizing these problems; 3) identifying potential solutions to these problems (focusing specifically on what community members themselves can do to solve problems); 4) designing, implementing, and evaluating crime-prevention initiatives; and 5) educating and mobilizing other community members, friends, and relatives.

Third, most community groups will probably need some hands-on assistance with initiating and sustaining community involvement in community policing. Given that most police resources are already stretched to capacity, or beyond, police administrators may need to look outside their own organizations for assistance. For example, faculty and students at local and regional colleges and universities may be willing to help inform community groups of the community-policing philosophy. They may also be willing to work with these groups to systematically identify problems that threaten citizen safety and help to develop potential solutions to these problems. In addition to the obvious benefits to the community and the police, this strategy could provide an excellent opportunity for students to acquire a more complete understanding of how problems are viewed and addressed by citizens and the police.

The time is right to seriously explore how concerned citizens can play more active roles in the promotion of public safety in their communities. By providing citizens with an abundance of specific activities in which they can engage, it may be possible to further develop the concept of "community" in community policing.

Source: Adapted with permission from Lee-Sammons, Lynette. "Beyond Neighborhood Watch: The Role of the Community In Community Policing." *Community Policing Exchange*. Washington, D.C.: The Community Policing Consortium, September/October 1995.

The authors, however, all leave out one important function of the community under community-oriented policing, and that is the leadership role the community must have in order for the concept to be fully implemented. The community, made up of indigenous citizens from the targeted neighborhood, must be given the authority to determine what the criminal and order maintenance problems are in their neighborhood, their priority, the type of programs that should be implemented, and how police resources should be allocated. They must be given a leadership role in taking back the control of their community. As Friedman (1994, 263) states, "The community must have a voice in the forums that define community policing itself, must be a ready and knowledgeable ally to the forces of reform, and, in the neighborhood, where the benefits are supposed to be delivered, must have a serious part in implementing solutions as well as nominating problems." In order to accomplish this, the community must have a shared form of leadership in both the policy-making and decision-making processes, and like the police, the community's citizens should be held accountable for their actions. When the community works with the police in this

Citizens learn the art of fingerprinting at a Civilian Academy sponsored by St. Petersburg Police Department, Florida. (Courtesy of St. Petersburg Police Dept., St. Petersburg, Florida.)

shared leadership role, the citizens not only have a vested interest in how the police perform their role, but they have a responsibility for their role that has not existed since the loss of the order maintenance role around the 1950s.

The one major obstacle to this process of fully implementing community-oriented policing is community involvement. The police must not rely solely on "government backed" citizens (citizens employed by the government) or citizens from pre-existing organizations (for example, members of the local lodges, Veterans of Foreign Wars, or the various social organizations), but rather they must tap the common citizen who is indigenous to the particular neighborhood, as he or she is fully qualified to determine what is wrong with the community. Although the ultimate role for the community under community-oriented policing is one of leadership, involving the community to reach this point is difficult. The ways to involve the citizens is then critical to our discussion of community-oriented policing.

Community Involvement

Getting the community involved in all three components to address the criminal and order maintenance problems that plague their neighborhoods is critical to the success of community-oriented policing. There are multiple ways in which to get the community involved in this new systemic approach, but we will break it down into three categories, from the most common to the least common. The three categories of community involvement under community-oriented policing are police initiated, police and community initiated, and community initiated.

The police-initiated community-oriented policing program is the most common of the three (see for example, Brown and Wycoff 1987; Cordner 1988; Farrell 1988; Kratcoski and Dukes 1995; Lasley, Vernon, and Dery 1995; Weisburd and McElroy 1988). Although the ultimate goal of community-oriented policing is to have the community lead the police, it is often the case that the police will first have to motivate the community to action and slowly allow them to acquire the leadership role. In some jurisdictions, the police will be at an advantage, as they will be able to tap into community organizations, both public and private, to assist them in gaining the community's support in the programs. In other jurisdictions, most likely as a result of those criminal and order maintenance issues that community-oriented policing is designed to address, there are no community support groups, either public or private. In these situations, the police will have to create a sense of community where none exists, develop ties within and among the community where none exists, and assist in the creation of public and private community organizations where none exist, before the community can take the leadership role. Through strategic-oriented policing, the police can create an environment conducive to this creation of community by allowing the community a respite from the problems that plague their neighborhood. However, the police must then work to create and foster that sense of community in a place where the police are most likely treated with suspicion. Although this is the most difficult of the police-initiated community-oriented policing programs, it can also be the most beneficial to the community at-large.

COP IN ACTION

THE DARE PROGRAM

The DARE program consists of seventeen sessions that demonstrate how the program is administered. Although created without the assistance of community-oriented policing, it has become an integral part of the systemic approach to policing. The following are brief summaries of each lesson:

1. **Practices for personal safety**. The DARE officer reviews common safety practices to protect students from harm at home, on the way to and from school, and in the neighborhood.
2. **Drug use and misuse**. Students learn the harmful effects of drugs if they are misused, as depicted in a film, "Drugs and Your Amazing Mind."
3. **Consequences.** The focus is on the consequences of using or choosing not to use alcohol, marijuana, and other drugs. If students are aware of those consequences, they can make better informed decisions regarding their own behavior.
4. **Resisting pressure to use drugs**. The DARE officer explains different types of pressures that friends and others exert on students to get them to try alcohol or drugs, ranging from friendly persuasion and teasing to threats.
5. **Resistance techniques: ways to say no**. Students rehearse the many ways of refusing offers to try alcohol or drugs—simply saying "no" and repeating it as

often as necessary; changing the subject; walking away or ignoring the person. They learn that they can avoid situations where they might be subjected to such pressure and can "hang around" with nonusers.

6. **Building self-esteem**. Poor self-esteem is one of the factors associated with drug misuse. How the students feel about themselves results from positive and negative feelings and experiences. They learn to see their own positive qualities and discover ways to compliment others.

7. **Assertiveness: a response style**. Students have certain rights—to be themselves, to say what they think, to say 'no' to offers of drugs. They must assert those rights confidently without also interfering with others' rights.

8. **Managing stress without taking drugs**. Students learn to recognize sources of stress in their lives and to develop techniques for avoiding or relieving it, including exercise, deep breathing, and talking to others. Using drugs or alcohol to relieve stress causes new problems.

9. **Media influences on drug use**. The DARE officer reviews strategies used in the media to encourage tobacco and alcohol use, including testimonials from celebrities and pressure to conform.

10. **Decisionmaking and risk taking**. Students learn the difference between bad risks and reasonable risks, how to recognize the choices they have, and how to make a decision that promotes their self-interest.

11. **Alternatives to drug abuse**. Drug and alcohol use are not the only way to have fun, to be accepted by peers, or to deal with feelings of anger or hurt.

12. **Alternatives activities**. Sports or other physical fitness activities are good alternatives. Exercise improves health and relieves emotional distress.

13. **Officer-planned lessons**. The class is spent on a special lesson devised by the DARE officer himself.

14. **Role Modeling**. A high school student selected by the DARE officer visits the class, providing students with a positive role model. Students learn that drug users are in the minority.

15. **Project DARE summary**. Students summarize and assess what they have learned.

16. **Taking a stand**. Students compose and read aloud essays on how they can respond when they are pressured to use drugs and alcohol. The essay represents each student's "DARE pledge."

17. **Assembly**. In a schoolwide assembly, planned in concert with school administrators, all students who participated in Project DARE receive certificates of achievement.

Source: DeJong, William. "Project DARE: Teaching Kids to Say 'no' to Drugs and alcohol." *National Institute of Justice: Research in Action*. March 1986.

The second category of community involvement under community-oriented policing is the police and community initiated (see for example, Greene and Decker 1989; Tien and Rich 1994; Williams and Pate 1987). This form of community involvement is perhaps the most healthy for the implementing of community-oriented policing because the police and the community bring their perspectives of addressing criminal and order maintenance together at first, then the community slowly takes the leadership role. Since the community will have organizations, both public and private, already pre-existing, the effort to mobilize other members of the community is that much easier. And at the same time it allows the police and community to work together, on the same level, easing some of the suspicions they may have of each other. The process of implementing the three components is usually faster under this form of community involvement and they are usually more successful. Also, at the first sign of any failure, there is little likelihood that the community and neighborhood coalitions will disband. Instead, they usually remain intact to work through the difficult beginnings.

COP IN ACTION

POLICE ACADEMIES FOR CITIZENS

The department began its CPA (Citizen's Police Academy) program about seven years ago at the suggestion of Richard Overman, now a chief in Delray Beach, Florida. He attended a bobby "night school" on a trip to England and returned with the idea of offering citizens an in-depth education in police procedure. Under then-Chief Danny Wilson, OPD's community relations unit organized the first class, which met at headquarters for three hours every Tuesday evening for ten weeks.

The CPA was an instant success. Word of mouth and referrals from alumni and officers on the street soon filled a second class. Today, there is a waiting list for its twice-a-year sessions. Interested residents fill out a one-page application with two personal references—a safety check for the department since CPA participants ride on patrol and wear photo IDs that give them access to headquarters.

CPA condenses the official Central Florida police academy (minus physical training) into a thirteen-week syllabus. It's a serious undertaking: OPD makes clear that it expects regular attendance, although no one assigns homework. Most presentations take place in a classroom with officers from every unit of the department taking turns to explain their mission and their day-to-day routines. Responding to student demand for more information, OPD expanded the program to thirteen weeks. Otherwise, format has changed little over the years.

The CPA tries to build each week on previous lessons. It covers the following topics:

Week 1: Introduction/selection and training-welcome by the chief and majors, recruiting goals and results, training procedures and evaluations.

Week 2: Laws of arrest, search and seizure, internal affairs, constitutional vs. criminal law, probable cause, the chain of response to complaints.

Week 3: Communications, statistics, planning and evaluation, tour of communications center, meaning of crime tabulations.

Week 4: Patrol operations/organization of patrol, demonstration of arrest, panel of beat officers.

Week 5: Special operations/traffic enforcement, canine demonstration, trip to mounted patrol barn.

Week 6: Violent crimes section/homicides, convenience-store robberies, career criminals.

Week 7: Property section and special investigations/car theft, counterfeiting, photo lineups, child abuse, rape.

Week 8: Special investigations, technical services/polygraph tests, crime-scene protocol.

Week 9: Undercover narcotic operations, vice crimes, uniformed vs. masked enforcement, interagency drug stings.

Week 10: Special Teams/SWAT, crisis negotiation.

Week 11: Youth section, community involvement section/officers in the school, DARE, Neighborhood Watch.

Week 12: Special Problems in Law Enforcement, use of force—liability, hot pursuits, "Shoot! Don't Shoot!"

Week 13: Graduation-diplomas, speeches, photographs, cake.

Although optional, field trips always draw a large crowd. Students tour Orange County jail with a deputy, and at the range learn to fire the standard-issue 9mm semi-automatic pistol. Students may also ride for an evening on patrol.

By encouraging officers and students to speak freely and frankly, OPD fosters camaraderie between public and police that extends beyond the classroom. Some graduates join the CPA alumni association, which now numbers about seventy-five active members, according to Edwards. Every year the group cooks a Christmas breakfast for officers on duty, and volunteers answer phones, staff booths, and handle paperwork when needed. Recently, the association also chipped in to buy a horse for the mounted patrol.

The CPA alumni association is not the only measure of the program's success. Just as importantly, OPD has seeded the community with people who have walked in the shoes of a cop, if only for three months. When officers look into a crowd, they often see familiar, friendly faces.

Source: Adapted with permission from Whitman, Sylvia. "Police Academies for Citizens." *Law and Order.* June 1993, 66–71.

The third form of community, and the most rare, is where the community wants to implement community-oriented policing, and through their community groups, both public and private, they exert political pressure on the local government and police department to enact this program (see for example Friedman 1994). This obviously creates a situation where from the very ruminations of community-oriented policing, the community commands the leadership role. Although this may be beneficial to the overall implementation of the systemic approach to policing, it can cause animosity on the part of the police, and the community may expect the program to be a quick-fix to their ailments. Working through police animosity, although difficult, is feasible. Convincing the community that the program they desire is not a short-term fix, but a long-term solution can prove more difficult. However, under this form of community involvement, the public is serious about the concept and the police will have their full backing, which can mean that in the event some programs or solutions fail, the community groups will remain intact and will not abandon the program at the first signs of trouble.

The concept of community involvement will no doubt meet many obstacles along the way in any of the three forms. Although there may be fewer obstacles when the community initiates the movement from traditional policing to community-oriented policing, there may be some reservations by some committee members and there may be problems when attempting to draw the common citizen into the planning and decision-making process. The police will no doubt experience multiple problems when attempting to get the community involved, but the three most common responses will be mistrust, apathy, and no response.

The police, especially under the traditional forms of policing, are often viewed with a sense of mistrust on the part of the community (Grinc 1994; Sadd and Grinc 1994). Although they desire the presence of the police in an emergency, they feel the police serve no other function in their daily lives. Because the precepts of community-oriented policing call for the police and community to work together, the police must dismiss the "us versus them" mentality, while the community must do away with their mistrust of the police. Communication is generally the key, for a lack of information on anything tends to trigger a sense of mistrust, and community-oriented policing is no different.

In other cases the community will respond to community-oriented policing with a sense of apathy or lack of interest in the program (Grinc 1994; Sadd and Grinc 1994). This apathy is most likely in response to the centralized government where control of multiple life issues rests in the hands of the local government, and therefore getting involved in policing is seen as not part of the community's responsibilities. People often like the ideas and are very supportive of the issue, but lack the desire to get involved or perform any action to support the idea. This form of apathy is prevalent in the United States, and is perhaps best represented by the lack of voter turnout on any election day. However, the lack of interest is only an obstacle to community involvement and the education of the police role, police resources, and police programs under the three components will most likely alleviate some apathy. On the other hand, the police will have to learn that some people will not lift a finger to assist in the abolition of crime or order maintenance problems.

The third response of community involvement in community-oriented policing is no response at all. It is often the case that when implementing any program, there may be no response from anyone to participate. This does not necessarily mean there is no interest or that the program is not a viable program. It may only mean that people do not understand their role in the overall concept or they have received no information on the program. In most cases, all three of these responses can be rectified with various forms of communication with the public, explaining what is proposed under community-oriented policing and what role they must take as well as what role the police will take under this new form of policing.

The media can offer assistance in this area by publishing and updating the movement of a police department from traditional policing to community-oriented policing. Other methods may include meeting with established public organizations (Williams and Pate 1987) and private organizations ranging from social groups to neighborhood associations (Fleissner et al. 1992). In some cases, the police may have to go door to door to announce their campaign (Wycoff and Skogan 1994) or distribute a newsletter (Brown and Wycoff 1987) to keep citizens informed of police and community actions under community-oriented policing. And one very innovative way of educating the community on both their role in community-oriented policing, and the police role as well, is through the use of citizen police academies (Enns 1995; Radelet and Carter 1994). It is here the citizen can learn about community-oriented policing (i.e., the three components), various aspects of policing (i.e., legal, use of force, court procedures), the technical aspects of policing (i.e., evidence collection, firearms training), and they can participate in a hands-on sense (i.e., shoot/don't shoot scenarios, firearms, ride-alongs). All of these methods and numerous others will have to be utilized to reach every member of the community and to solicit their help and cooperation under community-oriented policing.

Members of VFW Post 2018 show off their latest contribution to the Pomona Police Department, Pomona, California, four K-9 officers, which demonstrates their commitment to police and community relations. Shown left to right are Officer Ceasar Rivera and his dog Rudy; Mike Vitelli with Ricky; Mark Shannon with Marko; Doug Wagman with Roy; VFW Post Commander Don Stockwell; Dick Mazzarella; Jerry Lamb; Dave Densmore; Richard Callipi; Bill Portee; Tom Jones; and Henry Alt. (Reprinted with permission from the March 1996 issue of VFW Magazine, Photograph by Jeff Dye.)

COP IN ACTION

K-9 CONTRIBUTORS

If a dog is a man's best friend, what is an expertly trained Belgian Malinois of the highest breeding? Well, that is a policeman's best friend, and something Post 2018 in Pomona, California, knows all about.

Over the past two years, this dedicated Post has donated four of the expensive canines, about $5,000 apiece, to the Pomona Police Department. And the dogs have already justified their hefty price tags.

"They've been responsible for the apprehension of hundreds of violent criminals," said Capt. Joe Romero, Jr. of the departments' Patrol Services Division. "Each K-9 team saves us time and man-power on area and building searches. More important, though, is the increased safety gained by the use of the dogs."

Post 2018 has also outfitted four police-mounted bikes for the department's Bicycle Patrol Unit. But these generous gifts are just the latest in a long history of community activism by the service-minded Post.

"During the last four years, our Post has donated approximately $40,000 every year toward our community, our local veterans and the VA hospital in Long Beach," said Post Commander Don Stockwell.

Last September, the Post donated POW/MIA flags to people and businesses to commemorate National POW/MIA Day. For Thanksgiving, it purchased 5,000 pounds of food for the Salvation Army and fed 500 people at a local church. Post 2018 also works closely with the Pomona Fire Department, recently contributing $5,500 for a defibrillator unit.

The police department hosted a luncheon last summer to honor local groups that contributed to the department's Community-Oriented Policing program. Post 2018 received special recognition.

"It is particularly gratifying to know that the members of Post 2018 stand shoulder-to-shoulder with law enforcement and are committed to making a difference in our community," Romero said.

Source: Reprinted with permission from *the March 1996 issue of VFW Magazine*. Tim Dyhouse, "K-9 Contributors" *VFW Magazine*, March 1996.

CONCLUSION

The role of the community in community-oriented policing is critical to the overall implementation of this systemic approach to policing. Although "community" is often difficult to define, and we must rely on a variety of factors such as geography, similar characteristics, and both the public and police perceptions of community; this does not detract from the understanding that the community, in whatever shape or form, must be an integral part of the overall concept. The community must take back its streets, corners, and neighborhoods, by working with the police to determine the type of programs they believe would be beneficial to their community, what problems ail their community, and they must develop policy, procedures, and programs to address these problems. The implementation of community-oriented policing must strive to make these community groups and coalitions the true leaders of the police.

Community involvement is then critical to this participatory form of policing and regardless of whether it is implemented via a police-initiated, police- and community-initiated, or community-initiated style, it must be allowed to exist in the overall plan and be allowed to grow. Despite things such as mistrust, apathy, and no response on the part of the community, the role of the community must become a mainstay of community-oriented policing.

In order to understand the movement from a traditional police department to a community-oriented policing department in relation to the community's role, we can look to the common stages that communities go through on their way to full implementation. Based on a study in Seattle, Washington, and as demonstrated in many other jurisdictions, the four stages are, 1) challenging and venting; 2) organizational; 3) success; and 4) long-term stability (Fleissner et al 1992, 8–9). The first stage, the challenge and venting stage, is where the police will meet the mistrust, apathy, and lack of response on the part of the police. This is also "when citizens vociferously criticize police methods and instances of abuse of power or fault the police for doing 'too little, too late'" (Fleissner et al. 1992, p. 9). The second stage is the organizational stage, and this is where the community participants agree to attend the meetings and work to address the specific issues (Fleissner et al. 1992, 9). Although the community may remain somewhat mistrustful or apathetic, they will give the program a chance and work toward the common goal of addressing the criminal and order maintenance problems. The third stage is the success stage where programs are implemented, a trusting relationship develops, and "the group is even secure enough to weather turnover and changes in leadership," moving from either the police or the police/community maintaining the leadership role, to the community taking over the leadership (Fleissner et al. 1992, 9). And finally the evolution of community-oriented policing achieves the ultimate goal of stage four, which consists of long-term stability of the systemic approach to policing and it is a stage where "the group can mount continuous efforts to resolve problems as well as recruit wider community representation" (Fleissner et al. 1992, 9).

The progression of community involvement from stage one to stage four is the overall goal of the role of the community in community-oriented policing. Although the issue of community involvement may be difficult at first, as the program is communicated to the public and more citizens participate, the return to the social order of pre-World War II can be achieved. The police and community will be able to, through a cooperative method, take back the streets and neighborhoods, drive out some of the criminal problems and suppress much of the disorder found in so many communities today.

REFERENCES

Brown, Lee P. and Mary Ann Wycoff. "Policing Houston: Reducing Fear and Improving Service." *Crime & Delinquency* 33, no. 1 (January 1987): 71–89.

Buerger, Michael E. "The Limits of Community." In *Community Policing: Testing the Promises*. ed. Dennis P. Rosenbaum. Thousand Oaks, CA.: SAGE Publications, Inc., 1994a.

————. "A Tale of Two Targets: Limitations of Community Anticrime Actions." *Crime & Delinquency* 40 no. 3 (July 1994b): 411–436.

Cordner, Gary W. "A Problem-Oriented Approach to Community-Oriented Policing." In *Community Policing: Rhetoric or Reality?,* ed. Jack R. Greene and Stephen D. Mastrofski. New York: Praegar Publishers, 1988.

Dudley, William. ed. *Police Brutality*. San Diego: Greenhaven Press, Inc., 1991.

Eck, John E. "Alternative Futures for Policing." *Police Innovation and Control of the Police,* ed. David Weisburd and C. Uchida. New York: Springer, 1993.

Eck, John E. and Dennis P. Rosenbaum. "The New Police Order: Effectiveness, Equity, and Efficiency in Community Policing." In *The Challenge of Community Policing: Testing the Promises,* ed. Dennis P. Rosenbaum. Thousand Oaks, CA.: SAGE Publications, Inc., 1994.

Enns, Tracy. "Citizens' Police Academies: The Farmington Experience." *The Police Chief,* April 1995, 133–135.

Farley, John E. *Sociology*. 3rd ed. Englewood Cliffs, N.J.: Prentice-Hall, Inc., 1994.

Farrell, Michael J. "The Development of the Community Patrol Officer Program: Community-Oriented Policing in the New York City Police Department." In *Community Policing: Rhetoric or Reality?,* ed. Jack R. Greene and Stephen D. Mastrofski. New York: Praeger Publishers, 1988.

Fleissner, Dan, Nicholas Fedan, David Klinger, and Ezra Stotland. "Community Policing in Seattle: A Model Partnership Between Citizens and Police." *National Institute of Justice/Research in Brief.* Washington, D.C.: National Institute of Justice, August 1992.

Friedman, Warren. "The Community Role in Community Policing." In *The Challenge of Community Policing: Testing the Promises,* ed. Dennis P. Rosenbaum. Thousand Oaks, CA.: SAGE Publications, Inc., 1994.

Geller, William A. and Michael S. Scott. *Deadly Force: What We Know*. Washington, D.C.: Police Executive Research Forum, 1992.

Goldstein, Herman. *Problem-Oriented Policing*. New York: McGraw-Hill Publishing Co., 1990.

Greene, Jack R. and S.H. Decker "Police and Community Perception of the Community Role in Policing: The Philadelphia Perspective." *The Howard Journal* (28) 1989: 105–123.

Grinc, Randolph M. "'Angels in Marble': Problems in Stimulating Community Involvement in Community Policing." *Crime & Delinquency* 40 no. 3 (July 1994): 437–468.

Johnson, Thomas A., Gordon E. Misner, and Lee P. Brown. *The Police and Society: An Environment for Collaboration and Confrontation*. Englewood Cliffs, N.J.: Prentice-Hall, Inc., 1981.

Kerstetter, Wayne A. "Who Disciplines the Police? Who Should?" *Police Leadership in America: Crisis and Opportunity,* ed. William A. Geller. New York: American Bar Foundation, 1985.

Kratcoski, Peter C. and Duane Dukes. "Perspectives on Community Policing." In *Issues in Community Policing,* ed. Peter C. Kratcoski and Duane Dukes. Cincinnati,: Academy of Criminal Justice Sciences and Anderson Publishing Company, 1995.

Lasley, James R., Robert L. Vernon, and George M. Dery III. "Operation Cul-De-Sac: LAPD's 'Total Community' Policing Program." In *Issues in Community Policing,* ed. Peter C. Kratcoski and Duane Dukes. Cincinnati: Anderson Publishing Company, 1995.

Manning, Peter K. "Community Policing as a Drama of Control." In *Community Policing: Rhetoric or Reality?,* ed. Jack R. Greene and Stephen D. Mastrofski. New York: Praeger Publishers, 1988.

Mastrofski, Stephen D. "Community Policing as Reform: A Cautionary Tale," In *Community Policing: Rhetoric or Reality?,* ed. Jack R. Greene and Stephen D. Mastrofski. New York: Praeger Publishers, 1988.

Murphy, Christopher. "Community Problems, Problem Communities, and Community Policing in Toronto." *Journal of Research in Crime and Delinquency* 25 (1988): 392–410.

Radelet, Louis A. and David L. Carter. *The Police and the Community.* 5th ed. Englewood Cliffs, N.J.: Prentice-Hall, Inc., 1994.

Sadd, Susan and Randolph Grinc. "Innovative Neighborhood-Oriented Policing." In *The Challenge of Community Policing: Testing the Promises,* ed. Dennis P. Rosenbaum. Thousand Oaks, CA.: SAGE Publications, Inc., 1994.

Schaefer, Richard T. and Robert P. Lamm. *Sociology.* 4th ed. New York: McGraw-Hill, Inc., 1992.

Schwab, William A. *The Sociology of Cities.* Englewood Cliffs, N.J.: Prentice-Hall, Inc., 1992.

Skogan, Wesley G. "The Impact of Victimization on Fear." *Crime & Delinquency* 33, no. 1 (January 1987): 135–154.

Tien, James M. and Thomas F. Rich. "The Hartford COMPASS Program Experiences with A Weed and Seed-Related Program." In *The Challenge of Community Policing: Testing the Promises,* ed. Dennis P. Rosenbaum. Thousand Oaks, CA.: SAGE Publications, Inc., 1994.

Walinsky, Adam. "The Crisis of Public Order." *The Atlantic Monthly,* July 1995, 39–54.

Weisburd, David and Jerome E. McElroy. "Enacting the CPO Role: Findings from the New York City Pilot Program in Community Policing." In *Community Policing: Rhetoric or Reality,* ed. Jack R. Greene and Stephen D. Mastrofski. New York: Praeger Publishers, 1988.

Weisburd, David, Jerome E. McElroy, and Patricia Hardyman. "Challenges to Supervision in Community Policing: Observations on a Pilot Project." *American Journal of Police* 7, no. 2 (1988): 29–50.

Williams, Hubert and Antony M. Pate. "Returning to First Principles: Reducing the Fear of Crime in Newark." *Crime & Delinquency* 33, no. 1 (January 1987): 53–70.

Wilson, James Q. *Thinking About Crime.* New York: Vintage Books, 1975.

Wilson, James Q. and George L. Kelling. "Broken Windows: The Police and Neighborhood Safety." *Atlantic Monthly,* March 1982, 29–38.

Wycoff, Mary Ann. "Community Policing in Madison." In *The Challenges of Community Policing: Testing the Promises,* ed. Dennis P. Rosenbaum. Thousand Oaks, CA.: SAGE Publications, 1994.

Wycoff, Mary Ann and Wesley G. Skogan. "Community Policing in Madison: an Analysis of Implementation and Impact." In *The Challenge of Community Policing: Testing the Promises,* ed. Dennis P. Rosenbaum. Thousand Oaks, CA: SAGE Publications, Inc., 1994.

CHAPTER 10

The Role of the Chief

A great leader never sets himself above his followers
—except in carrying responsibility.

-Jules Ormond-

The role of the police chief in today's society is dramatically different from the police leadership of the last generation. This shift is due in large part to an ever-changing America, the advancement in all areas of knowledge, especially in the field of management, and the increase in technology. Police chiefs are required to be more educated, more skilled, better adept at management, decision-making, and the disciplinary process. They are much more visible today through advancements in technology and multimedia capabilities and as a result they are held more accountable for their actions and particularly the actions of their officers, than they were just a generation ago. They are the pivotal figure of the community in good times, and often the easiest to blame in bad times. And amidst all of these responsibilities, trials, and tribulations, the police chiefs of today are being asked to advance their police departments with all the propositions of community-oriented policing.

In light of the national movement toward community-oriented policing, it is readily apparent that the police chiefs of today are being called upon to implement a style of policing that they know very little about. It is often assumed that since they are police chiefs, they will have a complete and total understanding of the concept. It is often believed by the public that all the chief has to do is "implement" community-oriented policing overnight and it will be the panacea to all crime and social disorder. The chiefs know that this is not possible and generally,

Police Chief Darrel Stephens of the St. Petersburg Police Department and McGruff the Crime Dog at a crime watch "National Nite Out" event. (Courtesy of St. Petersburg Police Dept., St. Petersburg, Florida.)

through a misunderstanding of the concept, they are hesitant to truly implement it. At the same time, many abide by the public's request and "implement" community-oriented policing by utilizing the moniker and driving on with "business as usual." This is detrimental to not only the concept of community-oriented policing, but it is detrimental to the police department and communities that must bear this new program that understandably is predestined to fail. However, this is not to say that the reasoning behind this decision for failure is beyond comprehension.

"CRIME FILES"

DRUG TRAFFICKING—PART 13

This edition of the "Crime Files," hosted by James Q. Wilson, features Mark Kleiman, Harvard University; The Honorable John Lawn, Drug Enforcement Administration; and Mark Moore, Harvard University. The discussion revolves around the issue of drug trafficking, but focuses on community-oriented policing methods, specifically strategic-oriented policing tactics, for successful targeting of resources on arrests of street-level dealers.

Police chiefs in the past generation, many of whom remain in office or whose legacy remains entrenched in the community today, were constantly dealing with the so-called rhetoric of police and community relations. The implementation of this policy was through the police-community relations model which usually consisted of an organizational addition that was touted as the panacea to the poor relationship the police had with the community during the turbulent 1960s. The programs were generally established as a separate unit, usually understaffed, underbudgeted, and largely ignored by the administration. The programs most often failed to please a large segment of the community and were in many cases not even known to exist. The hands-off attitude by the police chief relegated the program to obscurity in most jurisdictions, keeping the unit and its budget small.

Today, police chiefs are expected to "buy into" the latest form of police and community relations known as community-oriented policing, and they are skeptical. However, against the backdrop of Rodney King and the Los Angeles riots, faith in the police has waned, and community-oriented policing is often touted as the new panacea for improved relations with the public. This has chartered a difficult course for the police chiefs of today, for they are skeptical of the community-oriented policing philosophy as being another failed program that they will have to implement to appease the local government and the community and they are receiving little information on the concept. It is for these reasons that community-oriented policing is at a critical juncture as we approach the twenty-first century. The police chiefs of today are the central force in deciding the success or failure of community-oriented policing simply for the position they now hold.

The police chief has a pivotal role in community-oriented policing. If the chief implements community-oriented policing as a front for community appeasement, it will fail. If the chief implements it without seeing to its direction, the mid-level management and line officers will clearly see this and let the program fade away as a failure. If the mayor or city council desire the new style of policing, but the chief resists, it will fail. And without the support of the chief, even in a department where the line officers desire the change in policing and the community supports it, community-oriented policing will still die a certain death. This should not be a call for chiefs to let the new style of policing die so they can move on to "real police work." Rather it should be a call to every police department, local government, and community that without the support of the police chief, community-oriented policing will not succeed. The future of community-oriented policing looks promising and it is the dedication and commitment of the police chiefs that can be a crucial factor in this future.

In order to understand the role of the police chief, it is important to understand the past role of the police executive and how it has changed and evolved in the twentieth century. It is then equally important to understand the current role the police chief plays in the systemic approach in modern-day America. And finally, the key responsibilities of the police chief under community-oriented policing will be explored to assist in defining the role they will play now and in the future in this systemic approach to policing.

THE TRADITIONAL ROLE OF THE POLICE CHIEF

If we return to the simplistic division of traditional policing and community-oriented policing for the analysis of police leadership in America, there is an interesting evolution of change clearly demonstrated in the people, organization, and management styles of the police. The evolution from the political era of policing to the public relations was clearly a slow process taking well over a century to change. However, even the evolution within what we conceived of as traditional policing, the move from the 1930s to the era of community-oriented policing, was slow to change as well.

The traditional form of leadership during the traditional era can be "defined in neutral terms as an efficient, honest, apolitical manager, equipped to implement the professional model of policing" (Goldstein 1990, 152). It is this detachment from the community that so marked much of the change in policing since the 1930s and continues to mark the current evolution seen today, although in a different direction.

The police chiefs that were instrumental in moving the police from the political era into what we consider the traditional era of policing were August Vollmer and O. W. Wilson (Dempsey 1994; Geller 1991; Peak 1995). These two men were considered pioneers in the field of policing for both their foresight and their ability to reform.

August Vollmer was the chief of police in Berkeley, California, from 1905 to 1932, and it was Vollmer who was largely responsible for professionalizing the police and launching them into the traditional era (Dempsey 1994, 14). He was quick to call for the expansion of the police department to patrol both day and night, he applied the techniques of *modus operandi* to criminal investigation, and with the assistance of a biologist at the University of California he was able to apply the sciences as well (Douthit 1991). In 1908, he created the first police academy, he advanced police patrols with bicycles and motor vehicles, and he introduced the polygraph to policing (Douthit, 1991). In 1931, he became the first professor of police administration at the University of California and that same year he wrote the volume entitled "The Police" included in the Wickersham Report (Douthit). Despite all of these technical advancements, the importance of the police officer was not lost on Vollmer, as he wrote in 1931, "After spending nearly a quarter of a century instructing policemen I have come to the conclusion that the mechanics of the profession are of less importance than a knowledge of human beings" (Douthit 1991, 109). The key to Vollmer's success however was not so much his modernization of the police department, but his application of the management principles of his time to the police.

The movement in management at the turn of the century was toward scientific management (Hersey and Blanchard 1993, 96). Through the development of technology and the application of various methods to increase productivity in the workplace, science was applied to management, and the result was the Scientific Management Movement (Hersey and Blanchard 1993, 96). The use of such things as time-motion studies, organizing for optimum productivity, and making administration more efficient was the emphasis of this new movement that shaped both the organization and the methods of management. Although the founding theorist of the scientific application in management was Frederick Winslow Taylor, it was August Vollmer who first applied these techniques to the police.

A disciple of August Vollmer's, O. W. Wilson was the second police chief to greatly advance the police during the traditional era of policing. Wilson became the police chief of the Wichita, Kansas Police Department in 1928 and through the use of simple management tools he greatly advanced police organization and management (Dempsey 1994, 14). Wilson organized the police department in a very centralized manner with a strict chain of command and he applied such principles as communication, span of control, delegation, and accountability (Peak 1995, 59–60). He later authored two highly acclaimed books that are still the basis for many textbooks today: *Municipal Police Administration* and the International City Management Association's *Police Administration* which became affectionately known as the "green monster" by later police administrators, as it was often the study guide for promotions (Wilson 1941; Wilson 1950). These two books simply articulated basic scientific management techniques, applied them to the police, and presented them in a clear and concise manner.

In the early 1930s, studies revolving around the scientific management approach realized that there was another variable involved in successful management, namely the employee. In the famous Hawthorne Study at the Hawthorne plant of the Western Electric Company where researchers attempted to manipulate the environment of the workers, they found that whether they made the conditions better or worse, productivity continued to rise. The independent variable for the increase in output was a result of the human interaction between the researchers and the employees. Thus was born the Human Relations Management approach (Hersey and Blanchard 1993, 56–58). This same similar realization in police management did not take hold until the 1940s and 1950s when "the management structure began to shift toward the more democratic or participatory management that is familiar in law enforcement today" (Lynch 1995, 6). However, it is important to make note that the change to both scientific and human relations management was not immediate in either space or time, but varied in application from jurisdiction to jurisdiction and across time.

COP IN ACTION

OPERATION BOOTSTRAP: OPENING CORPORATE

CLASSROOMS TO POLICE MANAGERS

U.S. businesses spend over $30 billion a year to provide about 17 million formal training and career advancement courses for their employees according to recent estimates. This investment demonstrates the belief that what is taught in corporate classrooms can sharpen management skills and thus increase a company's competitive edge.

This same investment can also be a resource for the public sector. An infusion of high-quality corporate training into law enforcement agencies, for example, could help those agencies upgrade management skills to better address the increasingly complex and ever-changing demands society places on public safety professionals.

In fact, such a program already exists. Operation Bootstrap, begun in 1985, is an educational clearinghouse that provides tuition-free corporate management training programs to a cross-section of police administrators and officers across the country.

Launched as a pilot program of the International Association of Chiefs of Police (IACP), Operation Bootstrap now reaches into forty states with support from private foundations and the National Institute of Justice. It offers state-of-the-art management training and self-help programs that range in length from one day to one week and cover subjects such as effective supervision, conflict resolution, group problem solving, and stress management.

What law enforcement gains from the corporate classroom

1. While these outside training programs are designed for corporate managers and their role in the corporate environment, nearly every law enforcement attendee has cited the usefulness and relevance of the course instruction.

2. Operation Bootstrap offers a smorgasbord of courses, some of which might appear to be of limited value to the law enforcement profession, until the breadth of responsibilities faced by these managers and supervisors are taken into account.

3. Also important are the insights law enforcement officials gain from their brief but intense encounter with the corporate world. Cornelius Behan, chief of the Baltimore County Police Department, noted that "Training such as this enables us to have supervisors who are not only more thoroughly prepared for management roles, but also have a better understanding of the private sector."

How the community benefits

Bootstrap participants help combat any negative police stereotypes through their interaction in the classroom with business executives. "Corporate people realize we police officers are people too," commented one Connecticut commander. He added, "They discover we have the same management problems as they have." Moreover, business leaders appear gratified to find so many law enforcement personnel who are interested in learning modern management techniques. Meanwhile, America's future police leaders are gaining a better understanding of the business community and its concern about crime.

Ultimately, of course, society benefits as law enforcement executives improve their own agencies by adapting some of the techniques used successfully by business executives in reaching corporate decisions, managing personnel, and performing their own individual jobs.

Source: Bruns, Bill. "Operation Bootstrap: Opening Corporate Classrooms to Police Managers." *National Institute of Justice: Research in Action.* August 1989.

As policing moved into the 1960s, the current trend was toward police-community relations, and many police departments were still applying scientific management principles to this new philosophy of policing. The police administration treated police-community relations as the need for more specialization within the centralized structure. The police could not alter the entire organization and management structure that they had spent decades evolving, but rather they created a specialized unit in order to provide the service, but retain the centralized control. This technique and others such as quota systems or point systems, continued into the 1980s as a method of greater control and greater accountability on the part of the police officer. This then led to a greater detachment from the community and led to the infamous attitude of "us versus them." Under community-oriented policing, it is not just one specialized unit that must be created, but rather the entire police department must change and police organization and management must change as well. And most importantly, so must the chief.

As society evolves and people evolve, so too must management. The organizational structure and the style of management is not an entity etched in stone once the system is said to work. Rather it is a living and breathing concept that must grow, adapt, and evolve. The realization of this concept was captured in the management field under the auspices of systems management which "fused the individual and the organization" and was "designed to help managers use their employees in the most effective way while reaching the desired production goals" (Lynch 1995, 6). Since the incorporation of systems management in the mid-1960s some of the police chiefs were able to recognize this assertion, and many of the chiefs today recognize the need under the auspices of community-oriented policing. The next evolution in policing is to the systemic system of community-oriented policing, and it is the police chiefs of today who will carry us well into a successful future.

THE COMMUNITY-ORIENTED POLICING ROLE
OF THE POLICE CHIEF

As we move into the community-oriented policing era an interesting evolution of change already exists that, like the traditional era, is clearly demonstrated in the people, organization, and management style of policing. The key people in community-oriented policing are too numerous to mention, but many of the names have already been shared. Like the traditional era, the community-oriented policing era has its share of police chiefs and scholars. Many of the police chiefs include such names as Lee Brown (Houston Police Department and New York City Police Department), Willie Williams (Los Angeles Police Department), Reuben Greenburg (Charleston Police Department, South Carolina), Elizabeth Watson (Houston Police Department and Austin Police Department), Jerry Sanders (San Diego Police Department), Charles Moose (Portland Bureau of Police), Harry Dolan (Lumberton Police Department, North Carolina), and Darrel W. Stephens (St. Petersburg Police Department, Florida). All of these chiefs have greatly helped advance community-oriented policing and represent what is clearly a new breed of police leadership. As George Kelling so bluntly states, "Unlike the tendency in the past for chiefs to be local and inbred, chiefs of this generation are urbane and cosmopolitan" (Kelling 1988, 5). He goes on to say that "members of this generation of police leadership are well educated and of diverse backgrounds" and "have sponsored research and experimentation to improve policing" (Kelling 1988, 5). There are many more who are advancing the research and experimentation in policing and in the academic field, and in many instances both, to provide the latest advancements and innovations that will move the systemic approach well into the twenty-first century.

TABLE 10.1   POLICE CHIEFS' AND COUNTY SHERIFFS' ATTITUDES
TOWARD EFFORTS TO REDUCE VIOLENT CRIME, 1995.

Question: "If you had to choose just one of the following seven areas as a primary focus of efforts to reduce *violent* crime in your jurisdiction, which *one* area would you choose?"

Area of focus	Percent
Reducing drug abuse	31%
Better economy and more jobs	17%
Court rules with fewer technical barriers to prosecution	16%
Longer prison sentences for criminals	15%
More police officers on the streets	10%
Reducing the number of guns on the street	3%
Expanded use of the death penalty	1%

Source: Maguire, Kathleen and Ann L. Pastore. *Bureau of Justice Statistics Sourcebook of Criminal Justice Statistics—1994.* Washington, D.C.: Bureau of Justice Statistics, 1995.

As the decentralized organizational structure under community-oriented policing was previously discussed in chapter 7, it is important to focus solely on the style of policing that the chiefs will have to abide by under this systemic approach. The police chiefs of today do not have the luxury of simply managing from atop the centralized administration as their predecessors had. Today's generation of police leadership must focus on numerous roles and responsibilities that are inherent within their position. There is no greater truth in this than the fact that "today a chief is often the agency's major policy maker, a leader of the community, liaison to the media, negotiator with the unions, disciplinarian, public speaker, quasi-lawyer, quasi-accountant, administrator, and agency leader" (Oliver 1993, 85). The role of police chief is extremely demanding, and under community-oriented policing it will be even more so. In some cases, it can prove rather costly as has been demonstrated on numerous cases.

In one cited year, from mid-1991 to mid-1992, eight of the fifteen largest police departments had undergone a change in or were undergoing a change in the police chief position (Witkin 1992, 33). Expanding that time frame to

1991 through 1993, twelve out of the fifteen largest police departments experienced a turnover. The tenure of the average metropolitan police chief has gone from 5 1/2 years to between 3 1/2 to 4 1/2 years (Witkin, 1992). The police chiefs of today are under greater public scrutiny than any other time in our history and it must be recognized that in many cases, particularly under community-oriented policing, they are not directly to blame for their removal. The police chief is held in check by crime rates, officer misconduct and brutality, unions, the mayor or city manager, governmental policies, political considerations, and a host of additional variables that may prevent him or her from enacting many of the tenets of community-oriented policing. All of these stand as potential roadblocks to enacting the components of the systemic approach, decentralizing the police department by personnel, geography, and structure, or merely organizing the community for their input into both criminal and order maintenance concerns from their perspective. This can bring on adversity, it can realistically damage the chief's professional image, and it can also have the highest price—as was demonstrated in the one-year period cited—removal from office.

POLICE CHIEFS AND SHERIFFS SUPPORT COMMUNITY-ORIENTED POLICING!

Community Policing

Police chiefs and sheriffs were asked if they had community policing in their departments. Because community policing is a broad category, the survey did not attempt to determine the specific activities that comprised a department's community policing approach. (Indeed, community policing could be the subject of another survey of these agencies.) The survey results show that police chiefs and sheriffs strongly supported community policing. Several offered comments on why their departments decided to embrace community policing and the steps needed to continue it.

Broad Interest in Community Policing

Interest in community policing cut across the entire country in small, medium, and large agencies. Of the 337 responding police chiefs, 278 (82 percent) indicated that they had active community policing in their departments, and virtually all the remaining departments indicated that they wanted community policing. Sheriffs provided a similar result with 172 (65 percent) of the 265 responding sheriffs stating that they had community policing and 61 (25 percent) indicating that they wanted community policing in their departments.

It should be noted, however, that comments from the police chiefs and sheriffs clearly indicated that most community policing efforts were just developing and were confined to a few designated neighborhoods. Most comments mentioned foot beats, special units, and neighborhood substations as primary activities comprising their community policing efforts.

Some of the most interesting comments regarding community policing explained why the departments were interested in changing from a traditional/ professional model of policing to community policing. The primary reasons given were to improve quality of life in the neighborhoods, to involve citizens in crime fighting activities (especially against drug problems), and to have a more concerted effort towards crime prevention. With regard to quality of life, one police chief wrote,

> The workload increase for this department stems from neighborhood problems and quality of life issues rather than major crimes. We are adopting community policing in an effort to address these quality of life issues.

Other chiefs wrote comments on using community policing to address drug problems: "We have invested in community policing to better involve the public in solutions to our crack cocaine problems," and "We have been attempting to convince the community that drug problems are a community problem, not just a police problem."

Two chiefs cited broader problems as their reasons for introducing community policing:

> The contributing factors to our workload have been greater availability of guns for juveniles; more sophisticated firearms in possession of criminals; decline in family cohesiveness in inner-city neighborhoods; availability of illegal drugs; and inadequate prison space. We are responding by shifting resources from traditional vehicle patrol to community policing.

> During the past three years, we have experienced a dramatic surge in violent crimes, especially those committed by juveniles. Property crimes have increased as our local drug problem has come to the forefront as our major contributing factor to criminal activity. Subsequently, our caseload has dramatically increased. We are not implementing various forms of community-oriented policing strategies in our neighborhoods deemed "high crime" in an effort to decrease these problems.

Ironically, some police chiefs and sheriffs stated that community policing had increased, rather than decreased, their departments' workloads. One police chief wrote, "The move to community policing and problem solving has also increased workload. As we become more responsive and credibility increases, we achieve more neighborhood involvement and workload increases."

Training and Personnel Needs

A total of 293 police chiefs stated their departments had training programs for community policing, but 83 percent of these chiefs indicated that the training needed improvement. For sheriffs, 189 stated they had training, with 83 percent indicating that the training needed improvement. A total of 39 police chiefs and 44 sheriffs without community policing training would like to see the training develop in their agencies.

Several problems were indicated by the respondents in regard to their training efforts. One problem was simply making time available for the training sessions. Some respondents commented on mandated state and federal training requirements that take precedence over topics such as community policing. Other police chiefs were concerned about "selling" community policing to officers: "Currently, the department is making a transition to community policing. The training challenge is to train and involve sworn members in the understanding and implementation of this process in such a way as to make community policing eagerly embraced." "Problem solving is addressed in our community-oriented policing, and we are striving to get officers to think of themselves as problem solvers."

Police chiefs and sheriffs also commented on the need to have more officers in order to expand their community policing efforts. Typical comments follow:

> An effort was made to implement community policing; however, due to manpower shortages, we were unable to continue. (sheriff)

> Community policing is being vigorously looked into for further deployment, but due to manpower it is being postponed. (police chief)

> We currently have one community-based, problem-oriented police team. We wish to replicate this team's efforts in other neighborhoods because it has been effective in reducing drug crimes, has reduced overall calls for police service, improved citizen perceptions of safety, and has been effective in providing role models for adolescents. If resources become available, we would expand into neighborhoods where there is a large culturally diverse population. (sheriff)

> Our citizens are concerned with community policing and seeing officers walking in their neighborhoods. However, our department now has 828 officers, as opposed to 975 officers four years ago. This reduction, coupled with an increase in calls for service, makes it difficult. (police chief)

In summary, police chiefs and sheriffs have been implementing community policing in their agencies and appear to be enthusiastic about its future. The two primary obstacles to expansion have been the need for better training on community policing and for increases in the number of officers to perform community policing activities.

Source: McEwen, Tom. *National Assessment Program: 1994 Survey Results*. Washington, D.C.: National Institute of Justice, June 1995.

There are many examples where police chiefs have endured all of these for the sake of community-oriented policing. In Houston, Texas. Police Chief Lee Brown and his successor Police Chief Elizabeth Watson implemented neighborhood-oriented policing (NOP) as a pilot program in 1983 and citywide in 1987, when crime rates began to rise in the mid- to late-1980s (Witkin and McGraw 1993). Budget cutbacks added to these concerns by reducing the force by 655 police officers during this same period (Witkin and McGraw 1993). The mid-level managers relinquished little authority to the line officers, and morale for the program on the part of the police was diminished (Witkin and McGraw 1993). The public also became disenchanted with the program and eventually it came to be known as "NOP: Nobody on Patrol" (Witkin and McGraw 1993). Police Chief Brown had since moved on to New York City to serve as their police commissioner and Elizabeth Watson was replaced in 1992. Although Watson has since moved on to the Austin, Texas Police Department and has implemented community-oriented policing with great success, her commitment to the concept of community-oriented policing in Houston essentially caused her to lose her job. So, why should chiefs take the risk?

There should be little doubt that engaging in anything other than the status quo in a police department can have tragic results, but changing, advancing, and integrating the police with the community can also have a significant impact. If the performance and satisfaction of officers increase under community-

Officer K. Yourick (l) with a few participants of the "Kids with Cops" program sponsored by the Montgomery County Police Department, Montgomery County, Maryland. (Courtesy of Montgomery County Dept. of Police, Montgomery County, Maryland.)

oriented policing and, when implemented with sincerity, public satisfaction increases as well, taking the risks of implementing change should prove well worth the effort. It is important to also note that, "experience has shown that when decisions are based on the principles of whether the decision is right, moral, ethical, legal, and in the best interest of the community, and not on what is politically expedient, the chief has little to worry about. Those programs, those requests, and those decisions that do not meet these criteria present predictable sorts of problems for the chief" (Brown 1985, 83). There should be little doubt that community-oriented policing is premised on what is right, moral, ethical, legal, and in the best interests of the community. It meets the criteria, it has and will continue to be successful, but it is dependent upon police chiefs who are willing to take the risk, are forward thinkers, and who are dynamic leaders.

TEN PRINCIPLES FOR POLICE CHIEFS

Although many of the principles of management under community-oriented policing are being practiced by police chiefs today, many of the principles are new or have a different focus than they have had in previous years, by virtue of the organizational changes and tenets under the systemic approach. There are essentially ten principles that can be extracted from police chiefs, such as those previously mentioned, who have implemented community-oriented policing with great success in their communities. The ten principles community-oriented policing chiefs follow to manage community-oriented police departments consist of: (1) leadership, (2) ombudsmen, (3) policymaker, (4) commitment, (5) style, (6) change, (7) role sharing, (8) educator, motivator, trainer, (9) role model, and (10) disciplinarian. Each of these ten principles will be discussed in relation to their application under community-oriented policing.

Leadership is the most important skill a police chief must adopt in order to be successful under community-oriented policing. Although some may argue that leadership is an innate trait, others argue it is something that can be cultivated and expanded. There are many success stories of people who were considered "born leaders," but an equal amount of literature describes those individuals who were found to be great leaders as more of a result of their environment and situation than any innate skills. Some examples include Abraham Lincoln who was a mediocre senator, yet excelled in the role of the presidency, and Dwight D. Eisenhower who was a great military leader, but only functioned as a mediocre president. We must then bypass the argument of nurture versus nature and deal with the relevant fact that leadership is extremely important in any institution, as well as any police department, but it is especially important under community-oriented policing.

It is also important to understand that leadership does not necessarily equate with good management (see Goldstein 1977, 225–231). An individual could be an excellent administrator and run an efficient and effective centralized police department. However, under the community-oriented policing approach, good administration will prove inadequate for the success of the program. Community-oriented policing needs dynamic leadership that can motivate the mid-level management, detectives, unions, and line officers to reevaluate the way they have been policing for so many years. Good administration will assist in the transition from a centralized police department to a decentralized structure, but it will not motivate the department to accomplish this task. Good administration may be able to implement the three components, but it may not succeed in leading the community to action. As Lawrence Sherman (1985, 466) stated "without...leadership, it is unlikely that policing can be substantially improved."

The leadership however, must also transcend the current expectations of leadership from a police chief. The limitations of the office of the chief, the avoidance of entering into politics, and the watchful eye of the community and media can create a chief who is more interested in maintaining the status quo then venturing into experimentation and possible failures. However, under community-oriented policing, this must not be the case. The police chief "must be dynamic and forceful in taking the community and police force toward a goal of community values and community standards" (Oliver 1993, 86). The chief must be able to articulate where the community truthfully is, where it needs to go, and why the components and structural reorganization of community-oriented policing is the proper approach to achieve these goals. This is why the police chief must be more than a good manager, more than a good law enforcer, and more than an assistant to the mayor in the same vein as the director of public works or parks and recreation. Community-oriented policing calls for a police chief who can not only be a dynamic leader, but a "statesman."

Lawrence Sherman (1985, 462) argued that the police chief must be a "statesman," which he defined as a "leader of a democracy, someone who can transcend the current values of the day and lead both police and the public into accepting a better set of values and strategies for policing." Although many may argue this either falls beyond the parameters of the office of the chief or it is part of the mayor's responsibilities, under the systemic approach to policing, this can no longer be the case. The chief must be a leader of not only the police, but the community as well, when it comes to the issues of crime, safety, and order maintenance. These are the chiefs obligations and liabilities and they should not be relegated, nor delegated, to anyone except the chief. Despite the fact this will most likely place the chief in a highly visible and focal point within the community, this is necessary to drive the values and goals of community-oriented policing. The allegations of politics and interfering with the mayor's responsibilities will be a rallying cry from the pundits; however, in order for a chief to affect change they must be endured.

One question arises in relation to the principle of dynamic leadership and that is: Where do we find such dynamic leaders? Police chiefs, until the latter half of the twentieth century, were largely a product of the police department's hierarchy where they were cultivated up through the ranks. In the 1970s and 1980s there was a move to hire police chiefs from outside the police department and this has continued to generate a high degree of controversy. The "up-through-the-ranks" chief is better equipped to deal with both the informal and formal structure because he has personal knowledge via his longevity with the department. The outsider, a police chief hired from another police department, may only be familiar with the formal structure, but not the informal structure of the police department. The insider is at a disadvantage when it comes to change because of the ties to the informal structure and the outsider is at a disadvantage because of the lack of ties and information. However, to effect change, there must be a police chief who is willing to promulgate change, and this in most instances can only be done by an outsider. When large business corporations look for their chief executive officers, they generally do not look from within, but look for an effective leader from outside the corporation. In some cases they not only look for an outsider, but they look for a leader who has no background in what the corporation specifically does; instead seeking a candidate who simply has strong leadership qualities. Despite the many arguments about the uniqueness of being a police officer, the hiring of a police chief from outside the policing profession is but one additional possibility for implementing the systemic approach to policing. However, community-oriented policing to date, by and large, has had more success with the police chief being an outsider yet still from the policing profession.

Closely tied in with the leadership role the chief must accept is also the role of ombudsmen. In the community-oriented policing model, the chief is required to work with multiple agencies, community groups, and organizations that the police have to deal with during the planning, implementation, and maintenance of a community-oriented approach to policing. The greater the ability of the chief to act as the ombudsmen, the greater success the programs will have when they are implemented. This is readily apparent when dealing with organizations within the police department, such as unions, fraternal organizations, or spousal associations; dealing with organizations outside of the police department, such as the chamber of commerce, local fraternal organizations, and community associations; dealing with other police agencies, such as local college campus police, the sheriff's department, or state narcotic's units; dealing with other government agencies such as public works, engineering, and planning and zoning committees; and finally, dealing with the committees specifically established for the purposes of community-oriented policing, such as community groups assisting in the implementation of strategic-oriented policing, committees established to determine what neighborhood-oriented policing programs to implement, and problem-oriented policing committees designed to solve problems indigenous to their neighborhoods. All of these committees are important to the success of community-oriented policing and the office of the chief will become even more important as it becomes the focal contact point for all of these groups when they need to coordinate their activities among multiple groups.

COP IN ACTION

CHARLESTON TRIES VOLUNTARY PROGRAM

Chief Reuben M. Greenberg can be heard on the police radio day and night responding to calls. The chief also makes sure he is accessible to Charleston's citizens, and often acts as a sounding board. Two years ago, citizens asked Chief Greenberg to help parents keep their kids off the streets late at night.

Greenberg decided that a plan similar to an antitruancy program that he started in April 1991 could possibly help alleviate parents' concerns. The truancy program assists education administrators by picking up unsupervised kids in public areas and returning them to school.

In August 1993, Operation Midnight, a voluntary curfew program, went into effect. Under Operation Midnight, officers pick up juveniles on the streets between midnight and 6 A.M. and return them to their homes. Concerned parents and guardians fill out an Operation Midnight form and mail it to the Charleston Police Department to make their kids eligible. A complete list of registered youths, stored in a centralized database, is available for officers' reference.

The program applies to youths up to age 17 who are traveling by foot or vehicle. "By 12 A.M., kids who have gone out to a ball game or a movie should be back at home," says Greenberg. "A lot of parents have told us that they want their kids home by midnight. We're doing our best to ensure they are."

"Operation Midnight is not a mandatory curfew program and it does not require violators to appear in court," comments Greenberg. "It is totally voluntary, and the only way it works is if the parents want it to work." A voluntary program eliminates having to process youths at the station before they go home. "You're not going to lock kids up for being out too late at night, so why not just take them straight home. Also, a mandatory curfew presents problems for youths who work late or whose parents have no objection to them being out late," says Greenberg. "My officers are familiar with the kids working newspaper routes and others who have legitimate reasons for being out between midnight and 6 A.M."

Youths not registered with the program are not taken home if found on the street after midnight. However, the department does not tolerate parents who allow very young children to be out in the early morning hours. "Parents who think it's okay for kids aged eight, nine, and ten to be out late at night are referred to the juvenile courts. We don't see these parents as being responsible, nor do the judges," states Greenberg.

Parents' reactions to Operation Midnight have been overwhelmingly positive. In two years, parents have signed up 650 kids and to date, 150 have been picked up and returned home. "We've had numerous calls from parents voicing their approval of Operation Midnight," says Chief Greenberg. "So far, our only critic has been a teenager."

Chief Greenberg makes it clear that Operation Midnight is a partnership between parents and the police department. "We need the parents' support to make it work. For our part, if we see kids out on the street, we will stop them. We want to protect our youths from ending up as possible driveby shooting victims. Conversely, we want to ensure that kids aren't out at night committing crimes. Either way you look at it, Operation Midnight is a crime prevention program."

Source: Adapted with permission from Francis, Charles E.. "Charleston Tries Voluntary Program." *Community Policing Exchange.* January/February 1996.

A third principle the chief must adhere to, which is also closely related to the role of leader and ombudsmen, is the role of policymaker. Although the chief is the key policymaker for the police department, under community-oriented policing, this role must expand and grow beyond the confines of the police force. The police chief will no longer serve to dominate the actions of the police officers, but will serve to guide the police officers functioning under this systemic approach (Bureau of Justice Assistance 1994, 23). The police chief will then have to create a strong vision of the values, goals, and strategies of community-oriented policing in order for the policy to serve as a clear mandate for action. Those jurisdictions that have demonstrated this strong vision in their policy, have been successful in their implementation of community-oriented policing (Kelling and Bratton 1993, 10). Although there is little debate over the fact the chief is the key policymaker within the police department, there has been extensive debate on whether or not the police chief should be a major municipal policymaker (see Geller 1985, part 1).

Although this debate is clearly important for any police chief, police department, and community, it is even more important when introducing community-oriented policing. There should be left no doubt that the police chief will be a major policymaker in his or her community under this systemic approach. As Richard Brzeczek (1985, 53) articulated, the police chief is a policy initiator and the role of the chief should not be subordinate to the mayor, but rather supportive of the mayor and in our case supportive of the tenets of community-oriented policing. Another police chief expressed that the chief is a policymaker for three key reasons: "first, the chief is responsible for controlling the great discretionary power that police exert over the lives of individuals and groups" and "second, the chief's importance as a community leader stems from the extraordinarily important but rarely discussed role the police play in resolving conflict before the need to suppress it develops" and "third, the chief inevitably attains community prominence by virtue of the fact that the police touch the lives of an extraordinary number of citizens, exerting many different (often unpleasant) influences" (Andrews 1985, 11–12). This is why Andrews (1985, 17) concludes that under community-oriented policing "clearly, the community leadership style this calls for is not that of an administrative minion but that of an effective, innovative, and pioneering community leader." The chief must be a policymaker in the area of crime and social order within the police department and the community. The type of policymaker under the systemic approach, however, is just as important.

Officer James J. Stapleton III of the Lynchburg Police Department, Lynchburg, Virginia, oversees students from a local school working to remove graffiti. (Courtesy of the City of Lynchburg Police Dept., Lynchburg, Virginia.)

As James Q. Wilson (1968, 279) explained, policies do have an effect on police behavior; however, most policies have focused on the negative, or rather on what *not* to do rather than on what officers *should*. Under community-oriented policing, the focus of policy should be on the positive, by telling officers what they should be doing. This style of leadership in policymaking is more akin to the style of leadership, decentralization, and management necessary under the systemic approach. It takes into consideration that the workers are individuals who can perform their duties in a professional manner, and this style values workers' contributions to the organization and the community, rather then treating them as poor ineffectual workers who need constant negative reinforcement.

Another key aspect of the role of the police chief under community-oriented policing is a commitment to the systemic approach. Commitment is clearly an important aspect of the police chief's role in community-oriented policing (Goldstein 1990; Kelling and Bratton 1993; Reiss 1985; Skolnick and Bayley 1986). Police chiefs today, as previously discussed, often endure short tenures and move from police department to police department. Herein lies the importance of commitment to not only the position of chief, the community, and the mayor, but to community-oriented policing. There must be the understanding that community-oriented policing is a long-term solution to the problem of crime and social disorder. It is not a quick fix for what ails a community. Therefore, it cannot be implemented as a quick successful program that will "turn around" the police department and earn the chief high recognition. Under community-oriented policing, the recognition may be slow in coming. If the chief's tenure is short, the full implementation of community-oriented policing may not be revealed prior to a chief's vacating of the position. This is why police chiefs must remain committed to the program.

This commitment must also transcend to another level. Not only must the chiefs demonstrate their commitment to community-oriented policing through the sincere implementation of the system, but they must demonstrate this through personal action. In some cases, such as Chief Charles A. Moose in Portland, Oregon, the chief provides a forum for both police and citizens to discuss their concerns and he is directly involved. Another chief puts on a uniform once a week and works alongside the officers in the implementation of foot patrols, community meetings, and operating storefront posts, placing himself or herself not only closer to the community and the police, but truly demonstrating commitment to the success of community-oriented policing. This not only sends a strong message to the public, but perhaps an even stronger one to the line officers of the police department.

Another principle adhered to by the community-oriented police chief is the style of leadership and police management. This is a very broad category to analyze for there are multiple "styles" of both policing and management, but it is important that they are "characterized by receptivity to community involvement" (Reiss 1985, 64). This essentially means that the old autocratic and centralized style of policing and management must be replaced by a more conducive style to the values and goals of community-oriented policing. The

Situational Leadership

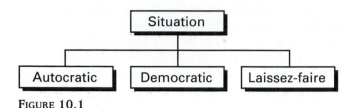

FIGURE 10.1

two most important styles that can and have been utilized are situational leadership and, as previously discussed in Chapter 7, Total Quality Management (TQM). Both of these align themselves quite well under the community-oriented approach to policing.

Situational leadership is focused on the environment and the situations that leaders encounter. By virtue of this, as Hersey and Blanchard (1993, 116) explain, "the emphasis is on the behavior of leaders and their group members (followers) and various situations. With this emphasis on behavior and environment, more encouragement is given to the possibility of training individuals in adapting styles of leader behavior to varying situations. Therefore, it is believed that most people can increase their effectiveness in leadership roles through education, training, and development." Although style theory states that most individuals will adopt one style, either autocratic, democratic, or laissez-faire, situational leadership follows the doctrine that the style utilized is based largely upon the situation (Peak 1995, 37). Under community-oriented policing, police chiefs will find themselves in a variety of settings where one style of management will not lend itself to every situation. Rather, depending upon the environment they find themselves in, such as a community focus group versus the overseeing a strategic-oriented policing program, the style of policing will have to shift. The tenets of situational leadership then lend themselves well to the precepts of community-oriented policing.

The style of management that lends itself well to the values and goals found in community-oriented policing is TQM. This style of management was first articulated by W. Edwards Deming in the 1950s with the five principles of focusing on results, customers, decentralization, prevention, and a systems approach (Peak 1995, 448). However, David Osborne and Ted Gaebler have advanced the propositions that Deming had articulated and found:

> ...most entrepreneurial governments focused on promoting competition between service providers. They empower citizens by pushing control out of the bureaucracy, into the community. They measure the performance of their agencies, focusing not on inputs but on outcomes. They are driven by their goals—their missions—not by their rules and regulations. They redefine their clients as customers and offer them choices...They prevent problems before they emerge, rather than simply

offering services afterward...They decentralize authority, embracing participatory management. They prefer market mechanisms to bureaucratic mechanisms. And they focus not simply on providing public services, but on catalyzing all sectors—public, private, and voluntary—into action to solve their community's problems. (Osborne and Gaebler 1992, 19–20).

It is easy to see how the precepts of TQM complement the precepts of community-oriented policing. Since TQM is focused on the customer, which in the case of the police is the citizen, this style of management should find successful implementation as a style of policing under community-oriented policing. Indeed it already has at least one success story in Madison, Wisconsin, where Police Chief David Couper implemented what he defined as "Quality Policing" (Couper and Lobitz 1991; Wycoff and Skogan 1993; Wycoff and Skogan 1994). Couper was able to create a set of twelve principles directly aimed at the police, which applied TQM to police management, and he was able to provide a guide to the police department for the style of police management and services, under the auspices of community-oriented policing (See Chapter 7 and Wycoff and Skogan 1994, 76–77). Similar success was achieved in the Lawrence Police Department, Lawrence, Massachusetts, when they applied TQM methods to policing (Cole 1993). Although situational leadership and TQM are not the only leadership and management styles of policing under community-oriented policing, the two are conducive to all of the underpinnings of the systemic approach.

Inherent within the entire philosophy of community-oriented policing is the principle that the police chief will have to abide by, that of remaining open to change. A police chief cannot hope to implement the true system of community-oriented policing if he or she is unwilling to change from the traditional methods of policing. As Reiss (1985, 64) explains, there can be no fixed solutions and the change must come "at all levels of function—from training to operations—and at all levels of staff and command." At the same time there is a willingness to change, there must also be a willingness to fail. The freedom to experiment and fail is all part of the advancement to providing better police services. Although it is understandable that at no time would we want our experiments to jeopardize the safety of the public, we must be willing to attempt new methods of service delivery, whether they are under the strategic-oriented or neighborhood-oriented components.

Perhaps the best example of not only commitment, but the concept of remaining open to change can be found in Newark, New Jersey. As Skolnick and Bayley (1986, 220–224) describe, no city in our country has experienced more racial tension, government corruption, less economic strength and higher crime rates than Newark, New Jersey. Yet, despite these odds the police department remained committed to change and allowed experimentation with new methods of providing police services to create a more effective police department. They were able to successfully address corruption, ease racial tensions, conduct strategic-oriented policing tactics such as street sweeps for loitering, public drinking, drug sales, purse snatching, and street harassment by local groups, establish neighborhood-oriented policing programs such as sub-stations, home visits, newsletters, and clean-up programs, and they were able to address local problems through the adoption of problem-oriented policing (Skogan 1990; Skogan 1994; Skolnick and Bayley 1986; Williams and Pate 1987). There are numerous examples of police departments that have success-fully implemented change through innovation and experimentation, but one key ingredient in each of their success stories has been the willingness to change on the part of the chief.

COP IN ACTION

PEDALING NOT HARD TO PEDDLE

Some ideas about new police techniques are hard to peddle to law enforcement traditionalists. One exception is the bicycle patrol. Large num-bers of police officers are pedaling bicycles today—and more agencies are introducing or expanding bicycle patrols. The most significant reason is the belief among police administrators that bicycle patrols are both an effective approach to law enforcement and a logical component of community polic-ing. Administrators rattle off a litany of bicycle patrol benefits. The largest is closer community contact. That is followed closely, in order of importance, by high visibility, a quiet approach, low cost, and the amount and diversity of territory bicycles can cover. There are other benefits, too. For example, bicycle patrols contribute to increased physical endurance of officers and greater officer accountability toward routine patrol duties.

The Bowling Green, Kentucky, Police Department is typical of depart-ments planning to expand their bicycle patrols. Chief Gary A. Raymer of Bowling Green said, "We have had a bicycle patrol during the past three years in one of our housing areas. We will add three bicycle units in 1995." That is another advantage to bicycle patrols. Departments can implement, expand, and fine-tune them incrementally as conditions allow.

Bicycle patrols are rapidly becoming an integral part of police work. The solid growth in the number of agencies adopting their own patrols is proof that they are here to stay. Bicycle patrols have proven to be effective in their short history. The use of bicycles is an idea whose time has come—and will no doubt be around for a long while.

Source: Adapted with permission from Sharp, Arthur. "Pedaling Not Hard To Peddle." *Law and Order*, July 1995, 35–40.

The next principle of the police chief's role in community-oriented policing is the requirement that police chiefs share their power with the community. Originally articulated by Police Chief Lee Brown (1985, 81), "the concept of power sharing is premised on the assumption that it is difficult for one person to serve another when the 'servant' possesses all the power, which is exactly the case in traditional police work: An inverse power relationship exists between the servants and those served." Although Brown was not calling for the abdication of power on the part of the police chief, as the chief is and always will be the final decision-maker and authority, he was calling for a larger role for the community.

As stated earlier, the best example is the relationship of the power sharing in the instrumental and expressive leader relationship. The community must take on the role of the instrumental leader by determining what the job, roles, and responsibilities of the police should be and to determine how they could best do their job. This is essentially a shared role within the police chief's policymaking role. The chief will not abdicate this role, but through a collaborative effort the chief will enhance not only his or her role, but the role of the community. The chief essentially becomes the expressive leader who is responsible for the police officers' welfare and instilling a sense of unit cohesion to create a police force that will carry out the goals and values that are part of community-oriented policing. Currently, under community-oriented policing, there are numerous examples of police-community power sharing, whether it is through the use of a forum with the public, such as the one found in the Portland, Oregon Police Bureau, through Neighborhood Advisory Committees and one city-wide advisory committee in the Spokane Police Department, Spokane, Washington, or through the implementation of Community Services Council Meetings in Ft. Wayne, Indiana, under their total concept of "community-oriented government."

The police chief, under the systemic approach to policing, also finds himself or herself as the key educator, motivator, and trainer on every facet of this approach to policing. If the police chief fully supports the concepts of community-oriented policing, it will show through these three principles that are distinctly different, while at the same time being quite similar. The chief must educate not only the police department on the concepts of community-oriented policing, but the mayor, community, and various groups and organizations as well. The police chief must continue to motivate the police officers to maintain a high level of community interaction, and the police chief must be the primary trainer of his or her police officers in community-oriented policing, as well as actively participating in the training. This training should also be provided to the public, the community groups, the mayor, other government officials and agencies, and to some extent it should be provided personally by the police chief.

The ninth principle in the role of the chief is that he or she must, at all times, be the role model for both the police department and the community. The police chief has always been the police department's main role model under the traditional form of policing, and this is strikingly more important under community-oriented policing. The values and goals espoused within the tenets of community-oriented policing must be the guiding philosophy of the chief both on and off duty, inside and outside the public purview, and both from the chief's office and amongst the line officers. At the same time, under the leadership principle of not only providing leadership to the police department, but to the community as well, the chief must be the role model for

Police Chief Michael C. Snowden of the Cincinnati Police
Department addresses youths participating in the "Police-Youth
Live-In." (Courtesy of Cincinnati Police Division, Cincinnati, Ohio.)

every facet of the community he or she serves. The police chief should reflect
the values and goals inherent within community-oriented policing and must
never forget that he or she not only represents the police department, but the
government and community policing philosophy as well.

The final principle is the role of the disciplinarian as it applies to police
accountability. Although there have been numerous instances of police misconduct and police brutality that have so marked the public eye and have damaged
the reputation of individual police departments, not to mention the reputation of
all police departments nationwide, any such conduct under the community-oriented policing philosophy cannot only damage the reputation, but destroy the
community's faith in the systemic approach. The community will easily raise the
banner of the police department having failed the community while pretending
to be more community oriented. This can have a detrimental effect on the new
approach to policing and it is, therefore, even more important that the police
maintain the public trust, become more accountable to the local populace, and
administer discipline under circumstances requiring such action. A disciplinary
program, in whatever form or shape it takes, must be open to the public, and not
secreted within the police department under the community-oriented policing
philosophy. However, an important note to make is the fact that the openness of
the disciplinary process may be in confrontation with due process procedures,

departmental policy, governmental policy, police unions, civil service, bargaining units, and a host of other variables that exist to protect the rights of the employees, perhaps at the expense of police–community relations. Every effort should be made to factor in the community and the impact the misconduct may have had on the community.

In attempting to achieve a disciplinary program under the community-oriented policing approach, Chief Stephens of St. Petersburg, Florida, has implemented a disciplinary process in which all the employees are actively involved (Quoted in Kappeler, Sluder, and Alpert 1994, 249–252). Although every disciplinary program should be consistent and fair, "for the St. Petersburg Police Department consistency is defined as holding everyone equally accountable for unacceptable behavior and fairness is understanding the circumstances that contributed to the behavior while applying the consequences in a way that reflects this understanding" (Kappeler, Sluder, and Alpert 1994, 250). In order to abide by this understanding, the police department looks at multiple factors in each incident, which include employee motivation, the degree of harm, employee experience, intentional/unintentional errors, and the employee's past record (Kappeler, Sluder, and Alpert 1994, 250–252).

CONCLUSION

The role of the chief is dramatically different under community-oriented policing than it was under the traditional approach to policing. The chief must become the central figure in this systemic approach to policing as he or she is the key to successful implementation of the concept. It is imperative that the chief abide by the ten principles in order to fulfill his or her role within community-oriented policing. The chief must be the key leader and policymaker within not only the police department, but the community as well. Although all of these principles are important, none can be listed as being more important than the principle of leadership. The community-oriented police chief must be a dynamic leader who is skilled at functioning on multiple levels, able to handle a variety of situations, and demonstrate the ability to instill the values and goals of community-oriented policing upon his or her police department, and direct it toward a goal of sustainment for the systemic approach to policing.

TABLE 10.2   TEN PRINCIPLES OF THE COP CHIEF

1) Leadership
2) Ombudsmen
3) Policymaker
4) Commitment
5) Style
6) Change
7) Role Sharing

8) Educator, Motivator, Trainer

9) Role Model

10) Disciplinarian

The advancement of the police, such as the advancement from the political era to the traditional era of policing, cannot be carried out without the tenacity of the police chief. The police chiefs of today must recognize community-oriented policing as being the next step in the evolution of the police much in the manner as August Vollmer saw the evolution from politics to strategic management. The chiefs of today must be willing to implement all of the tenets and all three components of community-oriented policing, and they must face the inquisition of the program by many pundits, from many fields. However, the rewards of successful implementation of the program will not be lost on the people who truly count, those members of the community who are tired of the high crime rates and the lack of social order. It is these citizens who will be indebted to the police chief for leading the community to a better life, marked by less crime and social order, and it is these citizens who will recognize the chief as a member and leader of the community.

REFERENCES

Andrews, Allen H. Jr. "Structuring the Political Independence of the Police Chief." In *Police Leadership in America*. ed. William A. Geller. New York: American Bar Foundation, Praeger Publishers, 1985.

Brown, Lee P. "Police-Community Power Sharing." In *Police Leadership in America*. ed. William A. Geller. New York: American Bar Foundation, Praeger Publishers, 1985.

Brzeczek, Richard J. "Chief-Mayor Relations: The View from the Chief's Chair." In *Police Leadership in America*. ed. William A. Geller. New York: American Bar Foundation, Praeger Publishers, 1985.

Bureau of Justice Assistance. *Understanding Community Policing:* Washington, D.C.: Bureau of Justice Assistance U.S. Department of Justice, August 1994.

Cole, Allen W. "Better Customer Focus: TQM & Law Enforcement." *The Police Chief,* December 1993, 23–26.

Couper, David C. and Sabine H. Lobitz. *Quality Policing: The Madison Experience.* Washington, D.C.: Police Executive Research Forum, 1991.

Dempsey, John S. *Policing: An Introduction to Law Enforcement*. St. Paul: West Publishing Company, 1994.

Douthit, Nathan. "August Vollmer." *Thinking about Police: Contemporary Readings*. 2nd ed. ed. Carl B. Klockars and Stephen D. Mastrofski. New York: McGraw-Hill, Inc., 1991.

Geller, William A. ed. *Local Government Police Management*. 3rd ed. Washington, D.C.: International City/County Management Association, 1991.

————. ed. *Police Leadership in America*. New York,: American Bar Foundation/Praeger Publishers, 1985.

Goldstein, Herman. *Policing a Free Society*. Cambridge, MA: Ballinger, 1977.

————. *Problem-Oriented Policing*. New York: McGraw-Hill Publishing Co., 1990.

Hersey, Paul and Kenneth H. Blanchard. *Management of Organizational Behavior*. 6th ed. Englewood Cliffs, N.J.: Prentice-Hall, Inc., 1993.

Kappeler, Victor E., Richard D. Sluder, and Geoffrey P. Alpert. *Forces of Deviance*. Prospect Heights, IL.: Waveland Press, 1994.

Kelling, George L. "Police and Communities: The Quiet Revolution." *Perspectives on Policing*. Washington, D.C.: U.S. Department of Justice and The Program in Criminal Justice Policy and Management, John F. Kennedy School of Government, Harvard University, June 1988.

Kelling, George L. and William J. Bratton. "Implementing Community Policing: The Administrative Problem." *Perspectives on Policing*. Washington, D.C.: U.S. Department of Justice and the Program in Criminal Justice Policy and Management, John F. Kennedy School of Government, Harvard University, July 1993.

Lynch, Ronald G. *The Police Manager*. 4th ed. Cincinnati, Anderson Publishing Company, 1995.

Oliver, Will. "The Changing Role of the Police Chief in Community Policing." *Law & Order,* March 1993, 85–86.

Osborne, David and Ted Gaebler. *Reinventing Government: How the Entrepreneurial Spirit is Transforming the Public Sector*. Reading, MA: Addison-Wesley, 1992.

Peak, Kenneth J. *Justice Administration: Police, Courts, and Corrections Management*. Englewood Cliffs, N.J.: Prentice-Hall, Inc., 1995.

Reiss, Albert J. Jr. "Shaping and Serving the Community: The Role of the Police Chief Executive." *Police Leadership in America*. New York: American Bar Foundation, Praeger Publishers, 1985.

Sherman, Lawrence. "The Police Executive as Statesman." In *Police Leadership in America,* ed. William A. Geller. New York: American Bar Foundation, Praeger Publishers, 1985, 459–466.

Skogan, Wesley G. *Disorder and Community Decline: Crime and the Spiral Decay in American Neighborhoods*. New York: The Free Press, 1990.

————. "The Impact of Community Policing on Neighborhood Residents: A Cross-Site Analysis" In *The Challenge of Community Policing: Testing the Promises,* ed. Dennis P. Rosenbaum. Thousand Oaks, CA: SAGE Publications, Inc., 1994.

Skolnick, Jerome H. and David H. Bayley. *The New Blue Line: Police Innovation in Six American Cities*. New York: The Free Press, 1986.

Smith, Bruce. *Police Systems in the United States*. New York: Harper and Brothers, 1960.

Vollmer, August. "Police Progress in the Past Twenty-Five Years." *Journal of Criminal Law and Criminology* 24 no. 1 (1933): 161–175.

Williams, Hubert and Antony M. Pate. "Returning to First Principles: Reducing the Fear of Crime in Newark." *Crime & Delinquency* 33, no. 1 (January 1987): 53–70.

Wilson, James Q. Varieties of police Behavior: The Management of Law and Order in Eight Communities. Cambridge, MA.: University Press, 1968.

Wilson, O. W. *Municipal Police Administration*. Washington, D.C.: International City Management Association, 1941.

————. *Police Administration*. New York: McGraw-Hill, 1950.

Witkin, Gordon. "Police Chiefs at War." *U.S. News and World Report,* June 8, 1992, 24–32.

Witkin, Gordon and Dan McGraw. "Beyond 'Just the Facts, Ma'am'." *U.S. News and World Report,* August 2, 1993, 28–30.

Wycoff, Mary Ann and Wesley G. Skogan. "Community Policing in Madison: An Analysis of Implementation and Impact." In *The Challenge of Community Policing: Testing the Promises*. ed. Dennis P. Rosenbaum. Thousand Oaks, CA: SAGE Publications, Inc., 1994.

————. *Community Policing in Madison: Quality from the Inside Out*. An Evaluation of Implementation and Impact. Washington, D.C.: Police Foundation, 1993.

CHAPTER 11

Implementing Community-Oriented Policing

The art of progress is to preserve order amid change
and to preserve change amid order.
-Alfred North Whitehead-

The most difficult aspect of community-oriented policing is transforming policy into action. The scholars can delineate and debate the subject from the armchair, while it is the police chief and mid-level management that must actually implement the policy into some type of executable program. This implementation process requires extensive research and planning on the part of the police department, whereas without it, the program will see poor implementation and little hope for institutionalization. Implementation then becomes the most critical aspect of community-oriented policing.

Police administrators must be aware of all the obstacles involving the implementation of community-oriented policing. The new policy and programs will have an effect on the line officers and this can add or detract from the implementation process. The environment of the police department and the attitudes of individual officers responsible for implementing and carrying the programs to fruition can impact on the success of the policy. As this will vary from police department to police department, it is important that the climate of the police department is taken into consideration during the planning stages to maximize the potential for success.

The climate of the police department consists of a wide variety of variables that should be analyzed to assess the current status of the police department. One author describes this as being the organizational maturity of the police department (Gaines 1994, 26). These variables consist of two predominant factors: management and the organizational structure. If management currently has a good working relationship between management and officers, and they provide leadership, discipline, and control, then the potential for moving the police department to community-oriented policing increases. Equally important is the organizational structure of the police department, for if they have a clear chain of command, strong division of labor, unity of command, and a reasonable span of control, the potential for implementing community-oriented policing is once again increased. Therefore, the climate of the police department, or its organizational maturity, must be assessed to determine if the police department has the capability of moving toward community-oriented policing, or if some areas of the police department need to be addressed prior to implementing the systemic approach.

"CRIME FILES"

JUVENILE OFFENDERS—PART 23

This edition of the "Crime Files," hosted by James Q. Wilson, features Barry Feld, University of Minnesota Law School; Peter Greenwood, Rand Corporation; and Gladys Kessler, D.C. Superior Court Judge. The discussion revolves around the evolution and current changes in the juvenile justice system and offers up various reforms to include the waiver of juveniles to adult courts. Discussion includes the impact of the rising juvenile crime rates on the police and how, through an understanding of juvenile offenders, the police can implement various community-oriented policing methods to address this group of offenders.

The ability to move community-oriented policing from policy, to program, to institutionalization, is based in large part on the management's ability to implement change. Any organization will resist change; however, within a police department, that resistance can be a little more stubborn. Effectively changing a police department is essentially changing a subculture and a bureaucracy, two of the most difficult things for even the best of managers to change. In order to implement change within these institutions there must be extensive and continual planning as well as goal setting in a long-term scenario, which must factor in institutionalization of community-oriented policing as the ultimate goal.

The management technique of incrementalism is the key to full implementation over the long term, as it will assist management in institutionalizing community-oriented policing without being excessively intrusive into the operations of the police and it allows for experimentation and alterations to the implementation process along the way. Although every police department will implement in a variety of ways, most, especially under the incremental

The Dallas Police Department, Dallas, Texas, mobile community-oriented policing van. (Courtesy of the Dallas Police Dept., Dallas, Texas.)

method, will implement in stages. Five stages for the implementation of community-oriented policing can be identified, commencing with the planning stage and moving through the micro community-oriented policing, transitional, and macro community-oriented policing stages, and culminating in the final stage, the institutionalization of the original policy. Through an understanding of change, incrementalism, and the various stages of implementation, community-oriented policing should find a place in every police department across the nation.

INCREMENTALISM

In 1959, Charles E. Lindbloom wrote an article entitled "The Science of Muddling Through," wherein he described how a manager "would settle on a limited objective to be achieved by the policy, outline the few options that were immediately available, and make a choice that combined into one 'the choice among values and the choice among instruments for reaching values'" (Denhardt 1993, 95). The incremental method of change is a slow-moving process that allows the manager to implement change on an acceptable level. The overall task of change is brought down to a realistic and operational level by selecting a small area of policy to change. By utilizing only the options that are readily available or easily obtainable, there is not a dramatic change in demands from the department. Personnel adapt more easily to a slow change than to any abrupt changes in policy, which in turn avoids both anarchy and apathy.

Although the incremental method of change seems fairly basic in premise, its simplicity brings with it many safeguards for the manager in implementing policy change. As Charles Lindbloom stated:

> In the first place, past sequences of policy steps have given him knowledge about the probable consequences of further similar steps. Second, he need not attempt big jumps toward his goals that would require predictions beyond his or anyone else's knowledge, because he never expects his policy to be a final resolution of a problem. His decision is only one step....Third, he is in effect able to test his previous predictions as he moves on to each further step. Lastly, he often can remedy a past error fairly quickly—more quickly than if policy proceeded through more distinct steps widely spaced in time (Lindbloom 1959, 86).

The advantages to Lindbloom's presentation of the incremental model are that it exists as an operational method of implementing policy and it easily adapts to the bureaucratic nature of a police department. The disadvantages to Lindbloom's presentation are that, in large part, "policy makers generally accept the legitimacy of established programs and tacitly agree to continue previous policies" (Dye 1987, 36). This could be of great concern to the policy maker, or police chief, entering a police department that is wrought by corruption or one where the establishment of past policies has caused irreparable harm to the police department's functioning.

As much of the literature on community-oriented policing has shifted to analyzing the application of business management and strategies to the police organization (see Moore and Trojanowicz, 1988), it seems only fitting to advance to a more recent study where incrementalism was utilized as a method of change in several large business organizations to affect this change (Quinn 1980; Quinn 1985). The theory of incrementalism was advanced by James Brian Quinn (1980), in a study of management that analyzed several large organizations attempting to implement change, and then subsequently created a method that would not only allow for the implementation process to be achieved, but the acceptance of the implementation as well. The theory became known as "logical incrementalism" which essentially "describes the process and focuses on the evolution of change as broad goals are more narrowly defined and adapted" (Hersey and Blanchard 1993, 370). The five stages of logical incrementalism are:

1. General Concerns: a vaguely felt awareness of an issue or opportunity.
2. Broadcasting of a general idea without details: the idea is floated for reactions pro and con, and for refinements.
3. Formal development of a change plan.
4. Use of a crisis or opportunity to stimulate implementation of the change plan—retirement of a senior manager or a sudden loss of market shares can facilitate rapid acceptance and implementation of the change.
5. Adaptation of the plan as implementation progresses. (Hersey and Blanchard 1993, 370)

These five stages of logical incrementalism complement the process of implementing community-oriented policing in a traditional police department. Any police chief today can say that with the current status of criminal activity, violence, and public outcry, a growing concern about crime exists. Community-oriented policing has been the essential buzzword in response to this growing concern and with 70 percent of police departments serving over 50,000 people having implemented the concept and with that number continuing to grow (Witkin and McGraw 1993, 28), little doubt exists that the opportunity has arrived.

Although the media has projected community-oriented policing into the mainstream, detailing all of the promises and all of the success stories, police departments still need to follow the second stage of logical incrementalism and "float" the idea to the police department. This not only allows the line officer to become familiar with the concept, but it also allows for some analysis of what will be seen as positive from this systemic approach and what will be portrayed as negative. This then allows the police chief and/or committee tasked with the job of implementing community-oriented policing to make some adjustments to the method of implementation, and provides advanced warning on the possible resistance that may be faced. This, then, allows the planning committee to enter the third stage.

A formal plan must be developed that will inaugurate the change from traditional policing to community-oriented policing. The plan should deal with

The winners of the Oceanside, California, Police Athletic League's annual surfing contest, pictured with the police officers who work with the youth. (Courtesy of Oceanside Police Dept., Oceanside, California.)

change from a systemic approach, by attempting to implement the change on multiple levels. Again, not everything can be changed at once, nor can it ever be changed overnight. Rather, the goal is to implement small amounts of change within the police department at various levels, through various departments, and with a variety of tactics. The plan should also incorporate all three components of community-oriented policing and it should begin the movement from a centralized to a decentralized structure. Once the initial plan is created, then the next increment is that of actual implementation.

Although Quinn speaks from a business perspective in the fourth stage, there exists a definite application in the policing field. Today, in many cases, community-oriented policing is actually implemented with the hiring of a new police chief expressly for the purpose of implementing this new systemic approach. Although this is an obviously fitting time to implement change, it is not necessarily the only time. Because the media has made the public aware of community-oriented policing, it stands to reason that any time is a good time to implement this system. However, in some jurisdictions the police may wait for some set date such as the police department's anniversary, the commencement of the new year, or with the election of a new mayor, rather than a new police chief. In other cases, the inauguration date of the systemic approach to policing may actually be as a result of a citizen call for the program and therefore can be implemented with the completion of the "change plan."

The final stage is then the most crucial within logical incrementalism, for it is here that adjustments can be made before the policy advances and grows too far beyond the reach of a simple alteration or two. Community-oriented policing provides the long-term values and goals that need to be obtained to achieve the institutionalization of the concept, and incrementalism insures the success of the program by implementing in small increments, thus avoiding confusion of an overly extensive policy, thereby reducing conflicts and maintaining stability and order in the face of change (Dye 1987; Hersey and Blanchard 1993; Quinn 1980). Through the continual focus on the values and goals inherent within community-oriented policing, the use of logical incrementalism will greatly assist the police department and community in achieving this institutionalization. Some additional leadership actions, on both the part of the police and the community, can also facilitate the implementation of the systemic approach and they include the following:

1. Use multiple information sources to refine and develop broad goals into specific objectives.
2. Build organizational awareness of the change.
3. Create credibility for the change.
4. Legitimize new viewpoints.
5. Use tactical shifts and partial solutions in refining the general ideas.
6. Establish political support and overcome opposition.
7. Maintain flexibility.
8. Use trial balloons and systematic waiting.

9. Create pockets of commitment.

10. Crystallize organizational focus on the changes at the right time.

11. Formalize commitments made to adopt the change.

(Hersey and Blanchard 1993, 370—371)

Through the integration of the five stages, the eleven leadership actions, and the adherence to the values and goals of community-oriented policing, the institutionalization of the system can be achieved in the long term. However, if one focuses on the long term, the plan of incrementalism can itself be broken down into stages, allowing for incremental goals in the short term. While the full institutionalization of community-oriented policing may be set for say, ten years, the short-term goals could be set for every two years, providing a clearer representation of where the organization currently is, where it needs to be in the two years, and what it should achieve along the way. Although the long-term goal may change with each increment obtained in the short term, the initial representation of the long-term goal still provides a source of direction.

An example of this type of short-term and long-term goal setting can be represented by the scenario of a traditional police department projecting to be fully in line with all the tenets of community-oriented policing in ten years, with five short-term stages, spaced at increments of two years, creating a total of five stages. Although this is not to be interpreted as a steadfast method of implementing community-oriented policing, for every police department will find itself with varying situations, goals, and values; it can serve as a guideline for the establishment of both short-term and long-term plans.

COP IN ACTION

HOW TO PLAN STRATEGICALLY FOR YOUR COMMUNITY

By Tom Potter and John Campbell

Yogi Berrra once said, "When you come to a fork in the road, take it." His mangled advice could describe how we often plan for the future. Most police chiefs and sheriffs were promoted through the ranks of their organization and still carry with them the old habits that made them good street cops—the ability to size up a situation, act quickly, and resolve the problem. But complex crime problems require police leaders to take a planned, community-based, long-term approach.

Many communities have developed strategic plans and know the problems and benefits associated with that process. Strategic planning can be done in any size agency. While the level of complexity will vary widely with the size and characteristics of each community, the fundamentals that lead to an effective plan are the same. By using some basic planning steps, communities and police organizations can avoid common mistakes and accelerate the benefits of community policing.

What is Strategic Planning?

A strategic plan is both a document and a process. The document is the map that helps keep both the community and police on track. It is the standard against which budgeting, workplans, hiring, promotion, deployment, organizational structure, and all other implementation elements are tested. The process strengthens the relationship between the community and police, while developing consensus and long-term political support for changes made as a result of strategic planning.

For strategic planning to achieve its potential, the police and community must jointly develop long-term solutions. This requires patience, understanding, and commitment to hearing the various involved groups and individuals, so the plan truly incorporates community ideas.

Making it Happen

The basics of good planning are simple: listen, plan, act, evaluate, then repeat. The challenge comes in listening well, planning appropriately, acting effectively, and evaluating with accuracy.

Key partners in the process include the following participants:

- Chiefs, sheriffs, and elected officials.
  In the hands of a good leader, a strategic plan is a tool for improving the organization. If the leadership doesn't support the plan, it will fail.
- Department personnel.
  The people who will be most responsible for implementation—supervisors, officers, and non-sworn personnel must be involved.
- Community leaders.
  The process should model the partnerships that are integral to community policing. It is crucial for developing the ongoing support of the community.
- Interagency partners.
  Involve other agencies and keep them informed.

The following pieces are key ingredients of an effective plan:

- Mission and values.
  These elements should be as constant as the northern star. Also, without a strong, guiding mission, an organization will be unable to adjust to change.
- Short-term strategies.
  While the document has a long-term vision, it must also define short-term steps. Personnel must clearly see how the mission is translated into action.
- A distinction between goal and process.
  The goal is to reduce crime, fear, and disorder. Don't confuse that with the process; partnership, problem solving, arrest, and investigation are processed that help achieve the goal.
- Required action by units.
  Units should create workplans that address how strategies will be implemented day-to-day. This is crucial for establishing internal ownership of the plan.
- Budget connection.
  Unless the plan is used to drive the budget process, it will remain a wish list. Work with the political leaders to develop multiyear budget projections.

Sustaining the Change

Making deep, institutional changes requires a long period of time. The following steps will help to ensure that the plan becomes a reality:

- Don't divide the mission.
  Some departments have described the "new" elements (partnerships and problem solving) in ways that suggest the "old" (call response, investigation, arrest) elements are obsolete. Community policing does not throw out existing tools. It adds to them by developing new ways to solve long-standing problems.

- Define new roles for everyone.
  It is essential to define new roles for patrol officers. But without specific roles for supervisors and managers, little can be accomplished. When an officer is given more discretion, the sergeant's role also changes. Each person in the organization must know that his/her role will change. People in the community should also work jointly with police to redefine citizens' roles in community safety.

- Institutionalize.
  To sustain community policing over the long term, each element of the organization and community must incorporate community policing into its behavior. Good ideas falter when they never become part of the daily life of officers, supervisors, or managers. Job descriptions, recruiting and hiring, training, rewards and discipline, promotions and management practices must all change. Community members must also change from being passive recipients of services to active participants in making neighborhoods safer.

- Focus on organizational culture.
  Sergeants and field training officers, in particular, must be involved. When these "keepers of the culture" adopt the approach, profound change will follow.

- Renew the plan.
  New strategies should be developed to ensure the plan remains pertinent and up-to-date for each new budget cycle.

- Maintain flexibility.
  The mission and values are constant. Goals and objectives are stable for five, or even ten years. But strategies evolve and timelines become obsolete. Plans that identify actions by the month for the next five years are unrealistic. Require that unit workplans fill in the short-term detail.

- Disseminate plan.
  After the plan is complete, distribute it. Make sure community and agency leaders who participated in developing the plan receive a copy. Make familiarity with the plan part of employee evaluations and promotions.

- Don't wait to implement.
  The transition is necessarily incremental—an agency that works 24 hours, every day, cannot stop to retool. Some strategies should begin right away.

Policing in America is at a fork in the road. One path leads to business as usual—reacting to individual crimes, but not focusing on solving problems that lead to crime, fear, and disorder. The other path leads to solving chronic problems and uses the resources of whole communities, not just "the thin blue line."

Transforming organizations and creating new community roles require planning, commitment, involvement, patience, and hard work. While community policing is not a panacea, it is an opportunity to make a difference. That's why we got involved. That's why an effective strategic plan matters.

Source: Adapted with permission from Potter, Tom and John Campbell. "How to Plan Strategically for Your Community." *Community Policing Exchange*. Washington, D.C.: The Community Policing Consortium, November/December, 1995.

STAGES

One of the difficulties of not only defining community-oriented policing, but understanding the concept, is the fact that the systemic approach to policing is not a predetermined program. No implementation plan exists that police chiefs can follow step-by-step in order to successfully implement the concept. Community-oriented policing comes in a variety of shapes and forms that are revealed through the changes in the police department, the community, and specifically in those things that change both of these entities in tandem. A wide variety of variables will have either negative or positive impact on the implementation process and in either case may change the basic makeup of the systemic approach.

The variables that cause community-oriented policing to vary from jurisdiction to jurisdiction consist of factors ranging from the macro to the micro, such as the environment of the community, organizational factors of the police department, the various players in the systemic approach, as well as individuals. The environment of the community will be based on such factors as the political, social, economic, and geographic dynamics, any one of which could dramatically alter the makeup of community-oriented policing. Organizational factors may consist of the differences in organizational maturity, leadership, management, and such things as the attitude of the line officers and non-sworn employees. The various players under community-oriented policing will also have a dramatic impact on its implementation and hence its makeup once implemented. These key players include the police, the community, and the police chief, but also mid-level management, social services, and other governmental service providers. And finally, the resistance or support on the part of one individual can play a major impact on the outcome of community-oriented policing, in that one citizen or one police officer can effectively block, enhance, or simply alter the final outcome during the implementation of the systemic approach.

Understanding that community-oriented policing will vary from jurisdiction to jurisdiction because the police and the community are different from jurisdiction to jurisdiction is important; however, some consistencies must exist among the wide variety of jurisdictions that have to date implemented community-oriented policing. The majority of police departments that began implementing in the 1980s and early 1990s have all focused on similar policies, methods, and tactics. In the same way that community-oriented policing has been defined in this book, through consensus, so too can we then identify a process of implementation that provides a rough outline. Through an analysis of many police departments working under a title of community-oriented policing, varying from small to large police departments, urban to rural, and sheriff's departments to police departments, five readily identifiable stages are apparent. The five stages under the concept of community-oriented policing are: 1) planning; 2) micro community-oriented policing; 3) transition; 4) macro community-oriented policing; and 5) community-oriented policing.

The establishment of a flexible outline and description of each stage for the demonstration of incremental steps in community-oriented policing is then the goal of the rest of this chapter. The concept of creating or reviewing certain stages of implementation is by no means new to the literature (Brown 1989; Bureau of Justice Assistance Sept. 1993; Fleissner et al. 1992; Gaines 1994; Pate and Shtull, 1994; U.S. Department of Justice 1992). However, by providing this workable framework for implementation, based on a review of community-oriented police departments to date, police chiefs, administrators, managers, and officers, as well as those involved in the study of this evolution of policing will have a better idea of how one turns a traditional police department into a community-oriented policing department.

TABLE 11.1 IMPLEMENTATION STAGES OF COMMUNITY-ORIENTED POLICING

Stage		Est. Timetable
I	Planning	6 months – 2 years
II	Micro community-oriented policing	1 ½ – 4 years
III	Transitional	2 ½ – 7 years
IV	Macro community-oriented policing	4 ½ – 10 years
V	Community-oriented policing	6 ½ – 14 years

Stage I

The first stage is the planning stage. Here, the police department and community should have an established plan for what the long-term goals of community-oriented policing will be, what the short-term goals will be, and how they will begin implementation. It is essentially the policy formation stage with the end result being a police department and community prepared to commence the incremental changes that will carry it through the second stage of micro community-oriented policing. This stage, as detailed before, must begin with an assessment of the current relations, foundation, and perceptions of crime between the local police department and the community.

Community-oriented policing must result in a strong collaborative effort between the police and the community, with the community assuming a larger and more powerful role. However, in most instances this is part of the long-term plan, rather than the short-term or immediate goals of community-oriented policing. This is generally the case, because in most jurisdictions community-oriented policing is planned and implemented without the community's support. In most cases, the police must seek out the community's assistance in order to move forward with community-oriented policing. In some cases, cooperation with some of the community already exists and the community can be drawn into stage I, while in a very few cases it is actually the reverse, where the community must draw the police into the action. Regardless of the situation, both parties must eventually be drawn into the concept and their inclusion in the planning stage must be actively sought. In the event of no initial response, they must still be factored into the planning stages despite their absence.

COP IN ACTION

COMMUNITY PROBLEM SOLVING

The Hercules Police Department serves a multi-ethnic community of approximately 20,000 in the San Francisco Bay area. The department and the city of Hercules made the philosophical shift to Community Problem Solving (CPS) in the latter part of 1992. One of our first goals, to establish a Mission Statement, resulted in the following:

"We, the members of the Hercules Police Department, are committed to the improvement of the quality of life for the citizens of Hercules by working in partnership with them. We will work to maintain safe and secure neighborhoods while treating everyone with respect and dignity. We will be open-minded and consistently improve ourselves professionally in order to serve the community."

With this statement in hand, we got the officers to commit to it. We encouraged them to spend more time out of their cars in order to identify and solve problems relative to the Mission Statement (quality of life issues).

Source: Adapted with permission from Muehleisen, Tom. "Community Problem Solving." *Law and Order*, June 1995, 31–32.

Once the climate of the police and community relationship is assessed, it is then important to begin moving toward the identification of both police personnel and community participants to begin the planning process. A team or panel of participants should be identified to review the literature, concepts, and practices of community-oriented policing to provide some foundation and mutual understanding. From there, the team or teams can begin working on the overall policy formulation for community-oriented policing.

The policy factors may include the long-term and short-term goals of the systemic approach, as well as defining some of the overall objectives. The mission statement of the police department should be reviewed, as well as the overall values and goals associated with the concept. One publication by the Bureau of Justice (1994a) includes a list of elements for consideration and they include the goals, objectives, strategies, activities, roles and responsibilities, resources, and potential problems, as well as proposed solutions. All of these are brought to bear on the overall necessity of the planning stage. The more planning accomplished in the first stage will result in the greater chance for successfully implementing in the later stages.

Further inclusion of members of the community should also be considered, to include not only community leaders, but the average citizen as well. Also, the further inclusion of the police must be factored in as well, since they will be an integral part of the overall concept. It is here that the first steps of incrementalism can be utilized, by essentially "floating" the idea of community-oriented policing. A later assessment of the line officers' reactions, perceptions, and concerns can than be addressed prior to actually implementing any change in police policy, practice, and procedures.

As the planning progresses, other planning concepts need to be addressed such as selecting targets for stage II, and perhaps immediately within this implementation, identifying targets for strategic-oriented policing. Education and training of community and police leaders should be factored in and the implementation plan for education and training of line officers and community members should also be determined. In many regards, the planning stage may actually create a marketing plan to "sell" the police and the community on the concept of community-oriented policing, as well as the programs and policies that will follow.

Depending upon the foundation of the police and community relationship, this will most likely determine the length of time it takes to achieve the end result of this first stage. Although there must always be a sense of urgency for implementing community-oriented policing, introducing the concept, developing these concepts to reflect the local community, and developing an implementation plan could conceivably take all of two years, as was projected in this framework. Police chiefs must be sensitive to time. Too little time may result in inadequate planning, while too much time may result in a lack of interest.

The end result of the first stage should be the establishment of a new mission statement with values and goals that project the community-oriented approach to policing. The long-term goal should be established and the short-term goals should be identified. Potential targets should also be identified and methods for implementing the three components to address these targets should also be established. The police department, as well as the community, should have some idea of the concepts of community-oriented policing and the proposals to move away from the traditional style of policing toward that of the systemic approach. The community and the police department should then be prepared to begin the practical application of the philosophy, concepts, policies, mission statement, values, and goals of community-oriented policing.

TEXAS POLICE DEPARTMENT, AUSTIN

Mission Statement

The Austin Police Department shall strive to improve the quality of life in Austin and promote the safety and security of the community. In the interest of community welfare, we will work in partnership with the neighborhoods. Our neighborhoods. Our efforts will be directed towards addressing community problems and enhancing customer service by utilizing all available resources and implementing creative techniques.

Vision Statement

The Austin Police Department is committed to providing outstanding service with fairness, justice, and equality for all. To this end, we will interact with our customers through a community policing approach to solve the problems of crime, safety, and the fear of crime in our community.

Goals

- Partnership
- Accountability
- Customer service
- Problem solving

The majority of police departments that have successfully implemented community-oriented policing to date have taken the time to implement stage I as a method of preparing the department and educating the community on this concept. Spokane Police Department, Spokane, Washington, went so far as to develop a mission statement and value statement by soliciting the input of every officer in the police department. In Portland, Oregon, the police bureau saw the community actually drive the move toward community-oriented policing and with the cooperation of many community members, the police bureau, and the local government, a community policing transition plan was put into effect, along with a mission and value statement for the police department to guide them in their implementation efforts. In Lumberton, North Carolina, the police chief implemented community-oriented policing by quickly adopting many of the strategic-oriented policing and neighborhood-oriented policing methods while simultaneously adopting and advancing the strategic plan, mission, and value statements of the police department with police and community input (Communicare, Lumberton, North Carolina Police Department, 1995). Whether the catalyst has been the police or the community and whether or not the police department has planned then implemented, implemented then planned, or conducted both simultaneously, police departments across the United States that have moved to the systemic approach have placed a large emphasis on the factors in stage I.

Stage II

The second stage of the five-stage process is micro community-oriented policing. Here the police department begins testing some of the concepts, programs, and the synthesis of the three components, without making major changes to the police department and community. Micro community-oriented policing establishes a test site to determine the potential of the overall systemic approach, to analyze the results, and to determine what to implement on a large scale (in other words, throughout the community) and what not to implement.

The most common form of micro community-oriented policing is the development of a team or special unit, specifically dedicated full time to implementing community-oriented policing on a selected target for a set period of time. One such experimentation project, detailed by Pate and Shtull (1984), is New York City Police Department's Community Patrol Officer Program (CPOP) in 1984, in the 72nd Precinct located in Brooklyn. The implementation and results of this "model precinct" allowed the New York City Police Department to assess the positives and negatives of the concept before implementing the concept department wide and throughout the city, as they did in 1990 (Pate and Shtull 1984)). This form of testing allows for an incremental change in the way policing is conducted on a small scale, and the incremental changes made to micro community-oriented policing can have a fundamental impact on the later stages of implementation.

A target should be selected from those generated in stage I, and the implementation of micro community-oriented policing should commence with strategic-oriented policing. If, for example, the selected target was a low-income housing/high-drug area, then the strategic-oriented policing would target the drug dealing. In the summer of 1991, the Arlington County Police Department did this with the launching of the Community Based Problem Oriented Policing (CBPOP) team which was directed at Arna Valley, a low-income housing area with an open-air drug market. The CBPOP team was formed with five officers who directed their efforts at aggressive policing tactics to remove the key drug dealers from the community, then high-visibility patrols drove the drug dealing underground, and finally directed patrols were aimed at specific areas known for a high incidence of drug and drug-related problems such as the local crack-houses.

COP IN ACTION

INTERVIEW: CBPOP: AN EXAMPLE OF MICRO COP

"In Arlington County there are three neighborhoods that have obtained grants to set up community-oriented policing. In Arlington the teams are known as Community Based Problem oriented Policing (CBPOP) teams. We responded to some calls in our neighborhood, but we mainly dealt with the drug and gang problems. The three neighborhoods are Nauck, Arna Valley, and Buckingham which just recently started up. Nauck is the oldest, and is subsidized by the county, although it started as a state grant. When the state grant ran out after two years, the team was doing so well that the county picked up the tab. Then came Arna Valley and Buckingham which were subsidized though a federal grant. These two started in the early 1990s and Buckingham was started in late 1995. There are twelve CBPOP officers, four on each team, with a lieutenant in charge. However, this was actually supposed to go throughout the entire county, where everyone tried to get rid of the bureaucratic red tape and help the community with their problems. But there seems to be no interest in expanding the police role of CBPOP unless more grants are received.

"The upstanding citizens in the community love the program. The brass loves the program as well. They loved it because it reduced the calls for service, because statistically it was to their advantage. Instead of calling the police, the community started calling for the CBPOP team, so a call wasn't actually logged with the dispatch, so the numbers dropped. It also dropped because we were down there on a regular basis.

"The programs that we implemented were a good idea, they developed a relationship between the community and the police department, but traditionally this isn't what police do. You may as well get rid of the police and just have the social workers in the county government take over the role of the police. We did good things, such as coaching little league team, we had an apartment complex under renovation in crystal city where a ton of bicycles were left behind, so we tried to identify the owners, and if that didn't work, we repaired them and gave them to the kids in the community that were indigent. In some cases we would set up a table at the local fairs to hand out literature on how to prevent crime. Some of the officers provided tutoring to problem kids, while they were on the payroll. But that's not police work, that's social work. It's like a big brother coaching little league or helping out, but it's social work not police work. I'm not saying it's bad, but the regular patrol guys see you doing this and they think you're lazy and you're not a real cop. You don't become a cop to go around giving hugs and kisses, you become a cop to lock up criminals."

Source: Interview with Officer Jackson Hunter Miller of the Arlington County Police Department, Arlington County, Virginia, December 28, 1995.

Once the strategic-oriented policing tactics begin to show results, the next step is implementing the neighborhood-oriented policing strategies by developing various programs that can assist the local community and mobilize community support for resisting the return and proliferation of the problem once the police are removed. This was accomplished in New York through the implementation of foot patrols, anti-crime operations, crime prevention programs, and the response to special functions (Pate and Shtull 1994). In Arlington County, this was accomplished by working with community patrols, and working with the local youth in various capacities, such as coaching a local softball team and sponsoring community activities. Community meetings continued to facilitate many of the programs implemented and became the foundation for problem solving at various stages.

The development of community support and understanding of community-oriented policing is important, as well as education on the concepts for both the community and the police. Those officers involved in micro community-oriented policing can not only provide training and education to the citizens in the target area, but as they come away with experience of the advantages and disadvantages of community-oriented policing, they can educate the management and line officers of the entire police department, as well as members of the local government, local leadership, and citizens in other parts of the community. The collection of data can also be utilized to show what some of these advantages and disadvantages are, as there may be differences between the police officer's perception and what actually occurred.

One critical concern with the second stage toward full community-oriented policing returns to the issue of time. The implementation of micro community-oriented policing must be established as a short-term goal for a certain period of time. If not enough time is allowed for this testing of the larger concept on a small scale, inadequate citizen response, police response, and data collection will create a lack of information available for implementing the next incremental stage. If too much time is allowed for the second stage, the special unit will become stagnant and will come under an excessive amount of scrutiny and criticism from other parts of the police department. Micro community-oriented policing is not an end to community-oriented policing, but only a means to the end. It must not be allowed to become the end result, for this will result in a false perception of community-oriented policing, as the complete systemic approach would never be able to grow and expand under the microscopic confines of the test site. Therefore, there is a danger if the police department or the community fails to declare the short-term goal of micro community-oriented policing accomplished and moves on to the next stage.

Moore (1992, 135) also recognizes four additional adverse effects if a police department fails to move beyond micro community-oriented policing: 1) "by isolating the function in a specialized unit, it becomes vulnerable to organizational ridicule," 2) "once a special squad is formed, everyone else in the department is seemingly relieved of responsibility for enhancing the quality of community relations," 3) "if the community relations unit should obtain important information about community concerns or ways in which the community might be able to help the department, it is difficult to make those observations heard inside the police department—particularly if what they have to report is bad news or imposes unwelcome demands on the rest of the organization," and 4) "the organization no longer looks for other ways to improve community relations." All four of these can be detrimental to community-oriented policing if the police department fails to move forward to stage III after the necessary evaluations have been obtained from the trial run implemented in stage II.

There is value, however, in implementing stage II, and the majority of police departments in the United States that have moved to community-oriented policing have invested much of their time and resources into micro-community-oriented policing, often called demonstration projects or test sites. In the late 1980s, Lt. Charles Moose of the Portland, Oregon Police Bureau, who later became the police chief, participated in a demonstration project known as the "IRIS Court Project." This project took a low-income neighborhood riddled with drugs, gangs, and prostitution, and through the three components of community-oriented policing reduced crime and problems in the neighborhood, and this success became the model for city-wide implementation (Communicare, Portland, Oregon Police Bureau, 1995).

COMMUNITY POLICING VIDEO SITE VISIT SERIES

FROM COMMUNICARE EDUCATIONAL VIDEO PRODUCTIONS

This video series is a comprehensive documentation of Community-Oriented Policing as implemented in nine cities across the United States, which include:

Austin, Texas	Portland, Oregon (in 2 videos)
Boca Raton, Florida	San Diego, California (in 2 videos)
Fort Worth, Texas	Sedgwick County, Kansas
Lansing, Michigan	St. Petersburg, Florida (in 2 videos)
Lumberton, North Carolina	

The video series features police chiefs, mayors, city council members, police mid-level management, and the heart of Community-Oriented Policing, citizens and police officers, discussing the various methods of implementing the systemic approach to policing and describing what has worked well and what has not. This 12 series tape is beneficial for any program in Community-Oriented Policing and for understanding the practical application of theory.

The video series can be ordered through Communicare Educational Video Productions by calling (614) 882-2228 or writing to 665 Cooper Road, Westerville, Ohio 43081-8962

Two police departments that are very dissimilar in nature, currently find themselves involved in stage II of community-oriented policing: the Boca Raton Police Department, Boca Raton, Florida, population 61,000 and the Sedgwick County Sheriff's Department, Sedgwick County, Kansas, population 400,000 (Communicare, Boca Raton, Florida Police Department 1995; Communicare, Sedgwick County, Kansas Sheriff's Department 1995). The Boca Raton Police Department created a community-policing unit that has the primary function of engaging the community and solving problems. They began their micro community-oriented policing project in a public housing area by permanently assigning a police officer to the community and establishing an office at the local community center. The officer has assisted in cleaning up the neighborhood, creating a new playground for the children, providing services as a liaison between the community and other government services, and, with the assistance of HUD, has purchased an apartment to become a study center for the local youth with tutors, a library, and computer equipment donated by IBM. Crime rates have dropped dramatically, the community has a sense of pride it previously lacked, and the relationship between the police and the community is at an all-time high.

The Sedgwick County Sheriff's Department has established a community-oriented policing section that consists of seven sheriff's deputies. The department has established a neighborhood storefront office in a problem area and through this office has begun implementing the three components of community-oriented policing. The sheriff's department has seen a very successful implementation on a small scale and has managed to incorporate the community, various institutions, businesses, other government agencies, and other law enforcement agencies into the overall concept. All of this has been successful despite the geographical make-up of the county where citizens are not densely located in one area. The micro community-oriented policing initiative has made an impact on not only the police officers involved and the community serviced, but the larger community as well.

Stage III

The third stage of implementing community-oriented policing is the transition stage. In this stage, the police department must begin applying the systemic approach to policing. The transitional stage should commence with all officers in the police department having some knowledge of the community-oriented policing concept: The micro community-oriented policing stage should have provided feedback on the long-term goal, and the department should now begin addressing the full implementation of community-oriented policing on all fronts. The transitional stage should conclude with every facet of the police department implementing some measure of incremental movement toward the full implementation of community-oriented policing.

COP IN ACTION

COMMUNITY POLICING: DEPARTMENT-WIDE 'TASK FORCE' IMPLEMENTATION

A prelude to disaster occurs when a police organization adopts a specialized unit approach to community policing as a department-wide philosophy. Regardless of the size of the task force (1, 10, or 100 people), when officers are singled out to conduct community policing activities with duties and responsibilities that are different from the rest of the organization, that agency has diminished its chances for total philosophical integration and success.

When an organization divides itself into "those who serve the public" and "those who do real police work," barriers of animosity are created. The department will find it difficult, if not impossible, to overcome this rift if the two factions do not believe they share a common goal.

Because police agencies are systemic organizations with each segment relying upon the interaction of the others to achieve common goals, such as the reduction of crime or improvement of quality of life, the entity must work together under one primary philosophy. When community policing is not adopted by the entire organization it becomes just another program implemented by just another specialized and often resented unit.

To instill a community policing philosophy department-wide, an agency must implement the approach simultaneously throughout the entire department. Each officer must be responsible for engaging in problem-solving activities with the community in his or her area of assignment in addition to normal patrol responsibilities. Small- to medium-size departments will find this easier to accomplish, but it may be logistically difficult for large agencies to implement. The key is that no segment of the organization is excluded from this indoctrination, and that everyone feels as if they are an integral part of the transition.

Source: Adapted with permission from Matthews, John. "Community Policing: Department-wide Versus 'Task Force" Implementation." *Law and Order*, December, 1995, 34–37.

It is not possible to detail every facet of the police department that should reveal some change in the transitional stage, for every police department is different and some are so large that to detail the changes would require its own book. However, it is possible to detail those central changes that will have an effect on the rest of the police department and subsequently cause some of the transitional change. These changes may include the reorganization of the shift, structure, and beat alignment to allow decentralization of police services. As shifts are redesigned based on consistent time and beat structures for police officers to begin working in "their" community, along with the beat realignment to coincide with the various communities, both residential and business, rather than with some geographical street system, there will then come some distinct changes as a result of this structural change. Ties with the community and community committees for these realigned beats will increase. The potential for altered patrol methods may result. For example, a new beat may exist with a smaller geographical area, such as a business district in a downtown area with only ten blocks to patrol, creating the need and adaptability of foot patrols. And this realignment also may allow for greater adaptability and implementation of the three components.

In other areas of the department, there should be similar transitional changes to community-oriented policing. The hiring process can begin implementing changes to the hiring of police officers by drafting, publishing, and hiring under a new job description that complements the new duties of the community-oriented policing officer. The training division can begin department-wide training on the philosophy, three components, and the relationship with the community under community-oriented policing. Management can reassess police officer evaluations under the systemic approach and begin the process of implementing them into the system. Coordination should be made with outside agencies to train them on community-oriented policing, garner their support, and explain their role under the new systemic approach. And the foundation of community-oriented policing, namely the community, should also be largely incorporated into all training, programs and the three components.

Once again, there should be a time constraint for this stage, which in our model was two years. In some police departments, such as the New York City

Police Department, the ability to implement on such a wide scale in two years may be impracticable, while implementing the concept in the Wildwood Police Department, Wildwood, New Jersey, may not need the full two years. In either case, the timeframe must be balanced with the sense of urgency for understanding the concepts, implementing the changes, and moving forward with the process. The implementation of community-oriented policing must never be allowed to stagnate. As problems arise, changes should be quickly made to the short-term goals and then the police department should continue moving forward to the long-term goals.

COP IN ACTION

CHARACTERISTICS OF DEPARTMENT-WIDE VERSUS TASK FORCE IMPLEMENTATION OF COMMUNITY POLICING

Department-Wide Implementation

- The philosophy is embraced by the entire department.
- There is not animosity based on job descriptions; everyone performs community policing initiatives.
- All officers are trained in community policing and problem solving.
- There is a single agenda; to resolve community concerns about crime and disorder by responding to calls for service, mobilizing the community and building partnerships.
- All officers are responsible for taking action and empowered with authority to make decisions.
- Entrepreneurial problem solving with action and creativity is encouraged.
- Pooling of common resources is encouraged, making them accessible to everyone.
- Community police officers are integrated throughout the organization.
- Officers work on all types and sizes of problems.
- The documentation is shared, department-wide.

Task Force Implementation Problems

- Acceptance of the philosophy is isolated to individuals in the community policing unit.
- Employee resentment exists because of job description, "real police" vs. "social worker" mentality.
- Only selected officers are trained in concept.
- The dual/competing agenda: primary responsibility results in calls for service and other police activities to be neglected.
- Officers are responsible for taking action, but decision-making authority resides with management.
- Bureaucratic entanglements occur due to agency restrictions.
- Specialized resources are permitted strictly for community policing unit.

- Community-based officers are segregated from others.
- Specific problems are targeted.
- Documentation is limited to isolated, special projects.

Source: Adapted with permission from Matthews, John. "Community Policing: Department-Wide versus 'Task Force' Implementation." *Law and Order*, December, 1995, 37.

Two police departments that currently find themselves in stage III of community-oriented policing are Fort Worth Police Department, Fort Worth, Texas, population 447,000 and Lumberton Police Department, Lumberton, North Carolina, population 18,000 (Communicare, Fort Worth, Texas Police Department 1995; Communicare, Lumberton, North Carolina Police Department 1995). The Fort Worth Police Department, through the cooperation of both the police chief and city mayor, has successfully moved the police department from stage I, which was conducted in the early 1990s, through stage II in 1992, to its current place in stage III. The police department implemented the concept of Neighborhood Police Officers (NPO) teams in early 1992 by creating a store-front office, creating a working relationship with the community and problem solving in specific areas. While the NPO teams were successful, the police department met resistance from older officers and officers not involved in the implementation of community-oriented policing. In 1994 and 1995, the Fort Worth Police Department brought the entire police department on line with the concept and it is now established city-wide through storefront offices, a mobile office that moves from neighborhood to neighborhood on a monthly basis, and by working with the community through organizations and volunteers. As a result of the department-wide implementation, the Fort Worth Police Department overcame the resistance on the part of the police and has created advocates out of those who were once detractors. The police department has successfully begun the transition to macro community-oriented policing by utilizing all three components of community-oriented policing, decentralizing by personnel, structure, and geography through a specific focus on the various communities in the city, and utilizing the storefronts as a focal point for working with the community.

The Lumberton Police Department under Chief Harry Dolan began implementing stage I and stage II of community-oriented policing in 1992 and has successfully moved into stage III at the present time. Through the cooperation of the elected officials, business community, media, service agencies, the community, and all the members of the police department, the Lumberton Police Department moved from testing a substation in South Lumberton in 1992 as a micro community-oriented policing project to having a substation in each quadrant of the city at present time. Although each substation is in various stages of development, the decentralization of the police department through geography, personnel, and structure has begun to take hold department wide. The department has also permanently assigned management, detectives, and line officers to permanent quadrants, thus creating "mini police departments."

Officer James J. Stapleton III of the Lynchburg Police Department, Lynchburg, Virginia, working with a local teacher and students to clean up the area around the school. (Courtesy of the City of Lynchburg Police Dept., Lynchburg, Virginia.)

The methods employed have included first moving into the area utilizing strategic-oriented policing methods, such as increased patrols in order to drive the criminal element out of the community. They then have successfully established neighborhood-oriented policing tactics such as foot patrols, bike patrols, school resource officer programs, and such programs as DARE and a DARE Band made up of police officers to establish ties with the community. Finally, through contact with the community members, they have worked with the community to address what their local problems are and how to solve them through problem-oriented policing. By combining stages I and II, Chief Dolan was able to implement with a sense of urgency and utilize the success and failures, as well as police and community input, to develop a strategic plan for how the police department should continue to move forward with community-oriented policing at a slightly faster rate of implementation.

Stage IV

The fourth stage of the implementation process is macro community-oriented policing. The beginning of this fourth stage should be at the point where the entire police department has seen some implementation of the systemic approach and the end should arrive with the full implementation of community-oriented policing. As opposed to its antithesis, micro community-oriented policing, macro community-oriented policing should see department-wide implementation. It should no longer apply to one or more target areas, but rather it should find its way into every facet of the department, every community, and every target to some degree. Again, as every police department is different, the short-term goals in this stage will be different. However, there do exist some commonalities regardless of size or location.

The complete decentralization of the police department should be apparent in this stage. Although some departments may still exist where the office of the chief may still feel uncomfortable decentralizing, such as homicide or robbery units, by and large the department should see a flattening of the pyramid. Permanent shifts and permanent beats should be the norm, with little rotation in and out. Training on all aspects of community-oriented policing should be a standard for in-service training, as well as for all members of the community, both government workers and the average citizen. The three components should be operating on a consistent basis with the support of the community and the community groups. strategic-oriented policing targets should be designated by the community, for their concerns both real and perceived. Neighborhood-oriented policing programs should be operating, evaluated and discussed among community committees. Finally, identifying problems, developing responses, implementing a response in concert, and evaluating the success or failure should be a common occurrence between the police and the community.

Although it would seem that all of the tenets of community-oriented policing would be satisfied during the macro community-oriented policing stage, this will most likely not be the case. As the police department begins to see the full implementation, the issues that the police chief, and the police department as a whole will face, will be larger in breadth and depth. The example drawn from above is the complete decentralization of the police department. This entails decentralizing all investigations as well, transforming "specialists" into "generalists." The police department cannot just decentralize the police on the beat and expect to see the complete application of community-oriented policing; they must decentralize the special units as well. It may prove difficult for a police chief to decentralize the homicide investigation unit in the face of perhaps several critical unsolved cases. The decentralization of the homicide unit at this point may not be feasible and may have to be delayed until the timing is right. Even without several high-publicity unsolved cases, it may still prove difficult to decentralize this unit. This is not to say that community-oriented policing has not been implemented, but rather, it has not yet been implemented at a macro level.

Two current examples of police departments that have successfully reached stage IV of implementation include the St. Petersburg Police Department, St. Petersburg, Florida, population 240,000, under Police Chief Darrell Stephens and the Austin Police Department, Austin, Texas, population 447,000, under Police Chief Elizabeth Watson (Communicare, St. Petersburg, Florida Police Department 1995; Communicare, Austin, Texas Police Department 1995). The success of the Saint Petersburg Police Department has been through a very positive response on the part of the police chief, citizens, elected officials, business community, and the line officers. The police department has been able to move quickly and methodically through the first three stages by soliciting input from all of the members mentioned and receiving their cooperation to move forward with the planning, testing, and transition stages to macro community-oriented policing.

The St. Petersburg Police Department has decentralized through a reassessment of where community boundaries lie and establishing permanently assigned officers to these areas. The police department then eliminated working based on rotating shifts, instead focusing on geographical areas and having the responsibility for covering those areas twenty-four hours a day. The police officers have more input as to when they work and what they do to address criminal and order maintenance issues during their shifts. Mid-level management has also decentralized into geographical areas and is now accountable for everything that occurs in their collection of beat areas. And to complement this decentralization by geography, personnel, and structure, both detectives and non-sworn personnel have also been assigned alongside the mid-level management and are accountable for these geographical areas as well.

The police department has also been heavily engaged in all three components of community-oriented policing. They have utilized strategic policing methods to remove drug and prostitution activity from various neighborhoods to allow for neighborhood-oriented policing methods to be employed. St. Petersburg has utilized a wide range of methods in this second component, such as bike and golf-cart patrols, community events, and creating community resource centers staffed by citizens who can assist the police and the public at large. Finally, through these specific neighborhoods they have been able to solicit the input of the community to determine where problems lie, develop ideas on how to address these problems, and implement and evaluate their actions.

The Austin, Texas Police Department has also managed to achieve stage IV of the implementation process through similar actions. Although the police department began implementing community-oriented policing in 1989, it suffered under many of the problems facing a department in stage II by not fully advancing to stage III. When Police Chief Elizabeth Watson was hired in 1992, coming from Houston Police Department, Houston, Texas, she immediately began to move the police department into stage III to reduce the resistance of traditional officers and the conflicts arising between "traditional officers" and "community-oriented police officers." The police department immediately reassessed its number of personnel and quickly reduced the layers of bureaucracy in mid-level management, and at the same time reduced the span of control of sergeants from fifteen-plus officers to an average of six. Once this personnel decentralization was complete and a geographical decentralization was conducted assigning officers for time periods of one to three years to a given beat, they moved to decentralization by structure. They accomplished this by assigning two lieutenants to a specific geographical area for accountability, selecting one to cover patrol and the other to cover community-oriented policing. However, in order to prevent conflicts between the two sets of officers, all were provided training on community-oriented policing and were detailed to work together. Although patrol had the responsibility for responding to calls for service, they were still required to work with the community-oriented police officer on their beat to coordinate many of the projects. Despite the split, this has worked extremely well for the Austin, Texas Police Department.

The department also increased the use of the three components of community-oriented policing by creating Crime Net teams to handle and conduct various methods of strategic-oriented policing. These teams are made up of officers who move into a pre-selected area and stay for a length of time to move the criminal element from the area. One additional tactic has been the use of a mobile substation that pulls into a high-crime area for approximately one month and becomes a substation for officers to work from to move the criminal element out of the neighborhood. Neighborhood-oriented policing methods have been utilized by working through neighborhood centers, advisory boards, and working hand-in-hand with "Citizens on Patrol." They have effectively used such programs as Neighborhood Watch based on the neighborhood centers and advisory boards, graffiti clean-up days, and education programs such as one to educate the community on the use of 911. Additional tactics such as bike patrols, creating youth centers for mentoring, and a job fair that managed to solicit over a hundred businesses to attend and secured over a hundred jobs in one day, have been very well thought of by the community. Finally, the police department entrenched the concept of problem-oriented policing into the daily workings of the police and community with much success. One such story is of a vacant lot where trash and abandoned cars were dumped, causing it to become a haven for drug dealers. It was cleaned up by the police and the community, effectively driving out the dealers from that area.

Stage V

The final stage is community-oriented policing itself or, in other terms, the institutionalization of community-oriented policing. The premise for naming it community-oriented policing is that once the entire police department has achieved this decentralization, has implemented the three components, and has shifted much of the power to the community, then and only then can a police department truly call itself a community-oriented policing department. Currently, there are only a few police departments in the United States that have reached this goal. Most police departments are generally in the micro stage or transition stage, while very few have made it to the macro stage. This is not to say that the fifth stage is unobtainable, but rather the movement toward community-oriented policing has just begun and it will take the dedication of many forward-thinking police chiefs, motivated line officers, and cooperative community members before the concept will achieve this end.

Two police departments that have realized the institutionalization of community-oriented policing include the San Diego Police Department, San Diego, California, population 1,110,000 under Police Chief Jerry Sanders, and the Portland Police Bureau, Portland, Oregon, population 438,000 under Police Chief Charles Moose (Communicare, San Diego, California Police Department 1995; Communicare, Portland, Oregon Police Bureau 1995). The San Diego Police Department began implementing community-oriented policing in 1988 utilizing mainly the problem-oriented policing methods under the SARA (Scanning, Analysis, Response, Assessment) model and has since moved through all four stages to reach, what is in effect, the institutionalization of community-oriented policing. The police department has effectively decentralized by geography, personnel, and structure and has found that as the sixth-largest city in the United States, they have a wide variety of differences in their communities. These differences consist of such variables as race, ethnicity, economics, and social and political differences, and the police department realized they had a number of varying communities needing a variety of varying services. Based on this realization, the decentralization of the police department became driven by these communities and essentially a number of mini-police departments were created, backed by neighborhood-oriented policing teams, management, detectives, and non-sworn personnel.

The community was brought into the concept through the implementation of problem-oriented policing in 1988, and through this pilot program the department realized the value of citizens assisting the police. Since that time, the police department, with the community's help, has established numerous storefront offices, obtained the help of over 600 volunteers to assist in this endeavor, created a Citizens on Patrol program with an additional 2,500 volunteers, established an eighty-hour academy to provide them training, and has established a program known as RSVP (Retired Seniors Volunteer Patrol) where senior citizens ride in patrol cars in teams of two to assist in traffic accidents, identifying problems in the neighborhoods, and taking police reports for minor incidents.

The police department has also institutionalized the concepts of strategic-oriented policing, neighborhood-oriented policing, and problem-oriented policing throughout the entire city. One example of this can be seen in the methods employed in a drug-house area. The police department utilizes a Drug Abatement Response Team (DART) as well as increased patrols to drive the criminal element out of a high drug-activity area. They then work with the community to get them involved in keeping the criminal element from returning once it is driven from the neighborhood by working with community groups, businesses, and individual citizens. Once established, or through the use of pre-established community groups, they then begin the process of problem-oriented policing to determine what other solutions are available to keep the drug activity from returning.

The catalyst for community-oriented policing in Portland, Oregon was as a direct result of the rise in crack cocaine and the gang activity associated with its sales. The police department under Chief Tom Potter, driven largely by the community, began the process of determining what methods could be utilized to address the many problems associated with the drug crisis. While a demonstration project was implemented during this timeframe to determine the success of community-oriented policing, the citizens of Portland, Oregon began pushing for a change in policing methods. Through a consensus on the part of the police, the community, and the local government, they defined community-oriented policing, defined the mission of the police, and created a Community Policing Transition Plan, published in 1990, that became the police bureau's guideline for implementing the systemic approach. Despite a change in police chiefs, when Chief Charles Moose was elevated to the position, the movement toward institutionalizing community-oriented policing continued.

PORTLAND, OREGON POLICE BUREAU
COMMUNITY POLICING TRANSITION PLAN

Statement of Purpose

The Portland Police Bureau will transition to a community-based philosophy of policing that encourages more citizen participation in crime reduction and allows greater coordination with other city bureaus and social agencies to address crime-related problems. Police officers will be catalysts who bring the necessary resources to bear on specific community safety problems throughout Portland.

Community Policing is a strengthening of the partnership among citizens, and public and private agencies. All are joint stakeholders in the vitality and livability of Portland's neighborhoods and business districts. Community policing expects a reduction in the fear of, and occurrence of, crime through cooperative resolution of immediate community safety problems and identification of root causes and remedies for crime and disorder.

Citizens and police officers will mutually participate in, and be responsible for, strategy design and problem solving that emphasizes comprehensive responses to criminal incidents. The key to problem solving is joint empowerment of police officers and citizens to allocate public and private resources as dictated by the uniqueness of the problem and its most effective and efficient resolution. Essential to this process are flexible police officers with good interpersonal communication skills who take a vested interest in, and are sensitive to, the cultural and ethnic diversity of the areas they serve.

The police bureau is committed to fostering a proactive origination climate that rewards its employees for initiative, innovation, citizen involvement, and consensus building in problem resolution. The bureau encourages decentralization of bureau resources and delegation of decisionmaking to those persons or units most impacted by the identified community safety problems.

The police bureau has designed this five-year incremental plan to gradually transition into community policing. This is a process of organization development which will examine, evaluate, and restructure, as necessary, bureau resources, policies, and practices. This transition plan is a guide to facilitate an orderly transition and to ensure the continuation of community policing as the basic mission and operational philosophy of the bureau.

Mission Statement

Old: The Bureau of Police is responsible for the preservation of the public peace, protection of the rights of persons and property, the prevention of crime, and enforcement of all Federal laws, Oregon State statutes, and city ordinances within the boundaries of the City of Portland.

New: The mission of the Portland Police Bureau is to work with all citizens to preserve life, maintain human rights, protect property, and promote individual responsibility and community involvement.

Goals

1. **Partnerships**—Develop a partnership with the community, city council, other bureaus, service agencies, and the criminal justice.

2. **Empowerment**—Develop an organization structure and environment that reflects community values and facilitates joint citizen and employee empowerment.

3. **Problem Solving**—Enhance community livability through use of proactive, problem-solving approaches for reduction of incidence and fear of crime.

4. **Accountability**—Foster mutual accountability for public safety resources and strategies among bureau management and employees, the community, and the city council.

5. **Service Orientation**—Develop a customer orientation in our service to citizens and our bureau members.

6. **Project Management and Direction**—Develop a process for overall management and direction of the community policing transition.

A Call to Action

Community policing requires the best of everyone. Whether it is citizens improving the safety of their local communities, officers directing resources to the root problems in their districts, or agency heads and council members pursuing more effective solutions, each individual must feel as if the problem was his or her own, and they must push themselves, and work with others, to solve them.

Community policing will work to the degree that we, as a community, can assume individual responsibility for making our city work, and to the degree that we, as a community, fulfill our role in helping to make that happen.

The task ahead is a large one and changes are required. Community policing will require new resources and new attitudes—one without the other will make little difference. The combination will be powerful.

No one of us should wait for community policing to come to our doorstep, or find its way onto our desk. Rather, we must go out and get started.

The men and women of the Portland Police Bureau: We ask that you be open-minded, yet impatient. Success will require your openness to new approaches and your willingness to give those approaches the very best chance to work. But it will also require that you not wait for innovations, but instead pursue them. Look for new ways, large and small, that can help address crime and its root causes in the city. Search for ways to build a more effective partnership with the citizens we serve. And when you find solutions, share them.

Those who are in a position to influence policy and allocate resources: We ask that you maintain the courage of your commitment to a fully implemented community policing—providing resources equal to the job and support for a more active, empowered citizenry. We ask you to challenge us—to use our resources wisely so we can realize community policing's full potential and restore Portland as one of America's premier cities.

The citizens of Portland: If you haven't already, get involved! Whether it is through the police bureau, the office of Neighborhood Associations, some other agency, or on your own, learn what you can do to strengthen the safety of your own block, your own community. Once you have begun that, look around to see if you can help someone with their problem. Think of our city as our family. As neighborhood organizers have pointed out, "living in a decent neighborhood is both a right and a responsibility." Without your help, we can't succeed. The success of community policing depends on the willingness of each of us to get involved.

Much has been done. Much remains to be done. Make it happen today.

Source: Portland Police Bureau. *Community Policing Transition Plan*. Portland, Oregon: Portland Police Bureau, 1990.

The police department, like San Diego, decentralized by geography, personnel, and structure and effectively implemented all three components of community-oriented policing. Dividing the police department into precincts allowed management to be held accountable for what occurred in their area and in turn the Neighborhood Liaison Officer Teams were held accountable for what occurred in their specific neighborhoods. All of this was backed by detectives, non-sworn personnel, the district attorney's office, community associations, coalitions, and contact offices, as well as by the local police union. The success of the Portland, Oregon Police Bureau continues today and with the institutionalization of community-oriented policing will continue well into the twenty-first century.

Although it is apparent that both San Diego Police Department and the Portland Police Bureau have obtained the final stage, the institutionalization of community-oriented policing, this achievement is not an end to itself, but the creation of a whole new beginning for the advancement of the systemic approach. The move beyond the fifth stage of community-oriented policing in programs that have seen implementation to date, is only limited by the creation of new theory, policy, practice, and programs that can be created under this concept. Community-oriented policing could potentially be the foundation for another generation of policing, a link in the evolution process, in similar form and fashion in the way police–community relations was a stepping stone to community-oriented policing. However, for now, the goal for the police department moving toward the systemic approach, should be this "final" stage.

TABLE 11.2   COMMUNITY-ORIENTED POLICING COMMUNITY STAGES

Four Stage Process:

Stage 1:	Challenging/Venting Stage
	When citizens vociferously criticize police methods and instances of abuse of power or fault the police for doing "too little too late." The police, put on the defense, can do little but explain their lack of resources and power. Many of their accusers may abandon the fray once they have vented their anger.

Stage 2:   Organizational Stage

Participants agree to "play ball." Community members start to attend meetings regularly, ready to work on specific issues. A stable relationship is developed within which police and community can hammer out a mutual agenda.

Stage 3:   Success Stage

Actions are accomplished. Success breeds not only more success but also a trusting relationship. The group is even secure enough to weather turnover and changes in leadership.

Stage 4:   Long-term Stability Stage

The group can mount continuous efforts to resolve problems as well as recruit wider community representation.

Source: Fleissner, Dan, Nicholas Fedan, David Klinger, and Ezra Stotland. "Community Policing in Seattle: A Model Partnership Between Citizens and Police." *National Institute of Justice: Research in Brief,* August 1992, 8–9.

COMMUNICATION AND TRAINING

Two central themes running through the implementation process are the key topics of communication and training. These two topics must be factored into every facet of community-oriented policing and must be included at every stage of the implementation process. Each one becomes a determinant factor in the success of achieving the next stage and implementing all of the policies and programs under community-oriented policing.

Communication is a key ingredient for any successful organization and this is no different in the traditional police department versus the community-oriented police department. However, as the concepts of community-oriented policing are implemented and the number of people involved in criminal and order maintenance issues grow, there will be a distinct need for better communication. Open lines of communication must be maintained between not only management and line officers, but with the local government, private organizations, businesses, community groups, and those community committees formed under neighborhood-oriented policing and problem-oriented policing. The decentralization of the police also creates a need for greater communication among every member of the police department, as well as every member of the community. Written communication should be generated to keep everyone informed at both the community level and at the government level. This can be accomplished through such things as the local newspapers, newsletters for individual communities, the police, and the local government, and special publications on the mission, goals, programs, and successes/failures of the implementation process (Bureau of Justice Assistance, 1994a, 54). Oral communication must also find its way into the homes of the community and at the highest levels of community leadership under community-oriented policing. This may include the use of radio stations, various group meetings, a mass community meeting, cable television, local news, in-service training, and various community events to name a few (Bureau of Justice Assistance 1994a, 54). Informing the community about all of the programs and methods of policing utilized under community-oriented policing not only keeps the public informed and educated, but it breaks down many of the barriers between the police and the community.

One additional form of communication that is extremely important under community-oriented policing and throughout the implementation process is feedback from all of the new programs on their successes and failures. This feedback should come from not only the factual data generated through statistical studies of the crime rates, but from the perceptions of crime and order maintenance issues on the part of the police and the community. This feedback becomes critical to the incremental process of implementation for it provides the input for making corrections along the way to implementing new policy and new procedures. This is then the sole focus of the next chapter discussing the evaluation and assessment of community-oriented policing.

TABLE 11.3   COMMUNITY-ORIENTED POLICING TRAINING MODULES
SAVANNAH POLICE DEPARTMENT, SAVANNAH, GEORGIA

Module I	-	Participatory Decisionmaking and Leadership Techniques for Management, Supervision, and Street Officers • Reviews COP for administrators and managers • Reviews overview of all seven modules
Module II	-	Community-Oriented Policing • Review of the principles and elements of COP • Reviews "Broken Windows" theory
Module III	-	Problem-Oriented Policing • Review of problem-solving methods • Reviews problem-oriented policing method (SARA model)
Module IV	-	Referral System, Materials, City Ordinances • Reviews resources outside of the police department • Reviews the utilization of city ordinances
Module V	-	Developing Sources of Human Information • Reviews listening and communication techniques • Reviews various types of police—citizen contacts
Module VI	-	Neighborhood Meetings, Survey of Citizen Needs, Tactical Crime Analysis • Reviews methods of soliciting citizen input • Reviews methods of crime analysis
Module VII	-	Crime Prevention Home and Business Surveys • Reviews methods of crime prevention • Summarizes and integrates concepts from all seven modules

The other key factor in the successful implementation of community-oriented policing is training. Training must be provided to every member of the police department, both line officers and management, as well as to the local government, businesses, and members of the community. Training should not be solely directed toward the police officer on the street, leaving everyone else out of the loop. Management must receive the same training as well as additional training on their role and function under the systemic approach. At the same time members of the community outside of the police department must also be trained by offering community seminars, training for other government agencies, and business seminars. Much of the same training should be applied to all of these groups and individuals, but additional, tailor-made training, should also be applied.

The type of training offered should also be created along the incremental process, by providing training on all of the different aspects of community-oriented policing. One such police department, Savannah Police Department, in Savannah, Georgia, was able to accomplish this with their implementation of community-oriented policing and the use of seven training modules to train not only their line officers, but their management and local government members as well (Donahue 1993; McLaughlin and Donahue 1995). The seven training modules included training on various aspects of community-oriented policing and integrated much of the literature on community-oriented policing into their training such as the "Broken Windows" article by James Q. Wilson and George L. Kelling and *Problem-Oriented Policing* by William Spelman and John E. Eck. The modules included one on "community-oriented policing" as an overview, one on "Problem-Oriented Policing," and one on "Participatory Decisionmaking and Leadership Techniques for Management, Supervision, and Street Officers" (McLaughlin and Donahue 1995, 128–132). This approach to training was found to be the most complementary method of training in the Savannah Police Department and would complement most police departments implementing community-oriented policing because of its ability to train both the police, local government and members of the local community with ease (McLaughlin and Donahue 1995, 138). As the members of a traditional police department move forward with the implementation process of community-oriented policing, a good guideline for training would be to emulate the Savannah Police Department method or to utilize the sequence of chapters in this book as a education guide for community-oriented policing, moving from its historical evolution, through the basic concepts, the three components, departmental restructuring, to implementing and assessing the systemic approach to policing.

TABLE 11.4   COMMUNITY-ORIENTED POLICING TRAINING SESSIONS

Session 1	-	Evolution of community-oriented policing
Session 2	-	Community-oriented policing
Session 3	-	Strategic-oriented policing

Session 4   -   Neighborhood-Oriented policing

Session 5   -   Problem-Oriented Policing

Session 6   -   Integration of the three components and implementation

Session 7   -   Systemic decentralization

Session 8   -   Police role

Session 9   -   Community's role

Session 10 -   Chief's role (management/administration's role)

Session 11 -   Assessing community-oriented policing

Session 12 -   Summary of COP and review of potential problems

CONCLUSION

The implementation of community-oriented policing is the most difficult aspect of the systemic approach. The application of policy to the practical world is always difficult, and in policing, with many compounding problems, it can prove to be even more difficult. The implementation of this new approach to policing is largely predicated on policy and the success of implementation is based on the ability of the police chief and police administration to implement change. This is no easy task, for the obstacles one faces is a natural resistance to change, the police subculture, and the police bureaucracy. Each difficult to change in its own right, but added together create a monumental task.

In order to accomplish this task, police chiefs, with the assistance of their staff, line officers, and the community, should define the long-term goals for achieving community-oriented policing, and then define short-term goals that will assist in moving the police department toward this end. By utilizing an incremental method of change, the police department can commence the implementation process in a slow and methodical manner, addressing concerns and dealing with minor issues along the way. This will then create a realistic workload for both management and the line officers, and it will reduce the resistance to change, because change will come at a quantity that is acceptable.

A plan for accomplishing this task is drawn from the literature and worked into five stages that create short-term goals for the police department and allow for incremental changes to be made in the process of proceeding from one stage to the next. The first stage is the planning stage, when the ideas and concepts of community-oriented policing are floated throughout the police department and community. Preparations are then made for a departmental-wide implementation. As the police department moves toward this short-term goal, an interim goal, the second stage, is the implementation of micro community-oriented policing. By implementing the concept on a small scale, the reaction of the police, community, and other factors can be evaluated and changes can then be made to the departmental plan allowing for the correction of what could be bad policy or procedure within a particular police department. Once this reassessment has been made, the police department can enter the third stage which is the transition stage. It is here that the police department utilizes the systemic approach by implementing at all levels and in all departments within the police department to achieve the next stage of macro community-oriented policing. It is in this fourth stage that the majority of the police department should see full implementation and the police department should move toward full institutionalization of the concept by achieving the fifth and final stage of community-oriented policing.

REFERENCES

Brown, Lee P. "Community Policing: A Practical Guide for Police Officials." *Perspectives on Policing*. Washington, D.C.: National Institute of Justice and the Program in Criminal Justice Policy and Management, September 1989.

Bureau of Justice Assistance. *Neighborhood-Oriented Policing in Rural Communities: A Program Planning Guide*. Washington, D.C.: Bureau of Justice Assistance, U.S. Department of Justice, 1994a.

Bureau of Justice Assistance. "The Systems Approach to Crime and Drug Prevention: A Path to Community Policing." *Bulletin: Bureau of Justice Assistance*. Washington, D.C.: Bureau of Justice Assistance, U.S. Department of Justice, September 1993.

Bureau of Justice Assistance. *Understanding Community Policing*. Washington, D.C.: Bureau of Justice Assistance, U.S. Department of Justice, August 1994b.

Communicare. *Community Policing Video Site Visit Series*. Austin, Texas Police Department. Westerville, Ohio: Communicare Educational Video Productions, 1995.

Communicare. *Community Policing Video Site Visit Series*. Boca Raton, Florida Police Department. Westerville, Ohio: Communicare Educational Video Productions, 1995.

Communicare. *Community Policing Video Site Visit Series*. Fort Worth, Texas Police Department. Westerville, Ohio: Communicare Educational Video Productions, 1995.

Communicare. *Community Policing Video Site Visit Series*. Lumberton, North Carolina Police Department. Westerville, Ohio: Communicare Educational Video Productions, 1995.

Communicare. *Community Policing Video Site Visit Series*. Portland, Oregon Police Bureau. Parts I and II. Westerville, Ohio: Communicare Educational Video Productions, 1995.

Communicare. *Community Policing Video Site Visit Series*. St. Petersburg, Florida Police Department. Parts I and II. Westerville, Ohio: Communicare Educational Video Productions, 1995.

Communicare. *Community Policing Video Site Visit Series*. San Diego, California Police Department. Parts I and II. Westerville, Ohio: Communicare Educational Video Productions, 1995.

Communicare. *Community Policing Video Site Visit Series*. Sedgwick County, Kansas Sheriff's Department. Westerville, Ohio: Communicare Educational Video Productions, 1995.

Denhardt, Robert B. *Theories of Public Organization*. 2nd ed. Belmont, CA: Wadsworth Publishing Company, 1993.

Donahue, Michael E. "A Comprehensive Program to Combat Violent Crime: The Savannah Experience." *The Police Chief,* September 1993, 12–22.

Dye, Thomas R. *Understanding Public Policy*. 6th ed. Englewood Cliffs, N.J.: Prentice-Hall, Inc., 1987.

Fleissner, Dan, and Nicholas Fedan, David Klinger, and Ezra Stotland. "Community Policing in Seattle: A Model Partnership Between Citizens and Police." *National Institute of Justice: Research in Brief.* Washington, D.C.: U.S. Department of Justice, August 1992.

Gaines, Larry. "Community-Oriented Policing: Management Issues, Concerns, and Problems." *Journal of Contemporary Criminal Justice* 10, no. 1 (March 1994): 17–35.

Hersey, Paul and Kenneth H. Blanchard. *Management of Organizational Behavior.* 6th ed. Englewood Cliffs, N.J.: Prentice-Hall, Inc., 1993.

Lindbloom, Charles E. "The Science of Muddling Through." *Public Administration Review,* no. 19 (Spring 1959): 79–88.

McLaughlin, Vance and Michael E. Donahue. "Training for Community-Oriented Policing." In *Issues in Community Policing,* ed. Peter C. Kratcoski and Duane Dukes. Cincinnati: Academy of Criminal Justice Sciences, Anderson Publishing Co., 1995.

Moore, Mark Harrison. "Problem-Solving and Community Policing." In *Criminal Justice: A Biannual Review of Research,* vol. 15, ed. Michael Tonry and Norval Morris. Chicago, IL.: The University of Chicago, 1992.

Moore, Mark H. and Robert C. Trojanowicz. "Corporate Strategies for Policing." *Perspectives on Policing.* Washington, D.C.: National Institute of Justice and the Program in Criminal Justice Policy and Management, November 1988.

Pate, Antony M. and Penny Shtull. "Community Policing Grows in Brooklyn: An Inside View of the New York City Police Department's Model Precinct." *Crime & Delinquency* 40, no. 3 (July 1994): 384–410.

Quinn, James Brian. *Strategies for Change: Logical Incrementalism.* Homewood, IL: Irwin, 1980.

————. "Managing Innovation: Controlled Chaos." *Harvard Business Review,* no. 3 (May–June 1985): 73–84.

U.S. Department of Justice. *Operation Weed and Seed Implementation Manual.* Washington, D.C.: U.S. Department of Justice, 1992.

Witkin, Gordon and Dan McGraw. "Beyond 'Just the Facts, Ma'am'." *U.S. News and World Report,* August 2, 1993, 28–30.

CHAPTER 12

Evaluation

That evil is half-cured whose cause we know.

-Shakespeare-

As police departments across the nation begin moving through the various stages of community-oriented policing, from strategic planning to institutionalization, one necessary tool for success are evaluations. As the police begin testing the waters with a host of programs, tactics, and methods under the three components, they must be able to adequately assess whether or not those practices employed are beneficial to both the community and the police. As community-oriented policing must be tailored to the community the police serve, a sound program in one community may prove to be a failure in another. Therefore, it is of utmost importance that each police department institute its own evaluation process for implementation of community-oriented policing.

The practice of conducting evaluations in a community-oriented police department is a key aspect of the systemic approach which complements not only the preferred style of management, Total Quality Management (TQM), but it complements the concept of incrementalism as well. As TQM is premised on improving the system of production and services and ensuring customer satisfaction, evaluations are a tool to determining if the delivery of police services are the best they can be and if the citizens are satisfied with their police. In the case of incrementalism, evaluations are the necessary tool to determining if programs or certain practices are beneficial to the implementation of community-oriented policing and if adjustments need to be made mid-stream. This

Officer Dennis of the Dallas Police Department, Dallas, Texas,
working with local youth at a community fair. (Courtesy of the
Dallas Police Dept., Dallas, Texas.)

allows the police department to make changes while the programs develop,
rather than allowing the development of a lasting mistake. Combining the
need for the evaluation process under both TQM and incrementalism solidifies
the need for evaluations under the systemic approach.

Recognizing a need for police departments to utilize evaluations as
another tool in their implementation of community-oriented policing is important, but some would argue that police have always utilized various evaluation
methods. As in the evolution of police–community relations, we have also
seen an evolution in how police utilize evaluations. In the past, the police utilized evaluations to assess how well their officers were doing, rather than
assessing how well they were delivering their services. It was assumed that if
the number of arrests, tickets, and calls for service were high and the response
time was low, the police officer was performing well. The central question
police management asked was, "How many?" Under the systemic approach,
police management must ask the question, "How well?" It is no longer adequate to analyze the success of the police based on quantitative and objective
criteria, but rather an assessment must be based on qualitative and subjective
criteria as well. In doing this, as described under the precepts of TQM, the
focus must not be on the individual police officer, but rather the system for
delivering services and customer satisfaction. Evaluations must be utilized to
assess programs, environment, and citizen satisfaction under community-oriented policing and not the number of parking tickets a police officer can write
during a given shift.

"CRIME FILES"

DOMESTIC VIOLENCE—PART 24

This edition of the "Crime Files," hosted by James Q. Wilson, features Barbara Hart, National Coalition Against Domestic Violence; George Napper, Public Safety Commissioner, Atlanta; and Lawrence Sherman, University of Maryland. The discussion revolves around various aspects of the police response to domestic violence and focuses on the Minneapolis police experiment that evaluated the effect of arresting violent spouses.

This chapter will look to the three eras of police evaluations—the traditional, the transitional, and the community-oriented—to determine how police departments have utilized evaluation methods over time and to detail past criticisms of both the use and methods employed. This chapter will look to the traditional methods of evaluating police and how the overall effectiveness of traditional policing has been considered to have limiting effects on crime. We will then analyze the evaluations utilized during the transitional period, moving evaluations from the traditional to the community-oriented. As the focus for evaluations has changed under the community-oriented policing approach, those key criteria for evaluating the systemic approach will be then be detailed. The actual methods that have been utilized for assessing community-oriented policing will then be described and reviewed for how evaluations should be conducted and utilized by police practitioners during the implementation process of the systemic approach to policing.

EVALUATION OF TRADITIONAL POLICING

In most police departments, specifically under the traditional style of policing, the bottom-line assessment for determining the overall capabilities of the police has been through the use of crime statistics. The Uniform Crime Reports, started in 1930 by the Federal Bureau of Investigation, requested city, county, and state law enforcement agencies to voluntarily submit their jurisdictions' crime statistics for specific crimes (Dempsey 1994, 37). This became the main emphasis for evaluating the effectiveness and efficiency of individual police departments throughout much of the twentieth century. If crime rates went up, the police were failing in their mission; if crime rates went down, the police were said to be doing their job. Even Sir Robert Peel, in 1829, believed this was the case when, in the publication of Peel's Principles, he stated, "the absence of crime will best prove the efficiency of police" (Sullivan 1977, 11). However, realizing that law enforcement is only one aspect of policing, factoring order maintenance into the equation for the effectiveness of the police, crime rates may reveal very little about the police officer's ability to handle and suppress these types of issues.

Another method of determining the effectiveness of the police in many traditional police departments has been through the use of quotas. Although most police departments will deny the utilization of quotas for their police officers and call them various names such as "work load evaluations" or "daily activity reports," they are still a collection of the number of arrests made, calls for service taken, and number of citations issued. Although they speak dramatically about what type of "police" work officers are performing during their shift, it speaks little to the interaction with the public, how officers deal with order maintenance issues, and the overall effectiveness of the officers in delivering police services. Additional indicators that have traditionally been utilized by police departments are "time spent at work," "percentage of arrests that lead to convictions," and "citizen complaints against officers" (Peak, 1995 151). Although these indicators may represent individual officer performance, they show very little correlation to the effectiveness of the police in dealing with the underlying causes of crime, disorder, and essential quality-of-life issues within the communities they police.

The drawback to evaluating the police in any of these manners is they only make statements about local crime statistics or about the police themselves. They do very little to address the true problems in a neighborhood and do even less to show causation. A correlation does not necessarily equal a causation. If the number of police arrests drop and the number of crimes reported rise, the independent variable of arrest rates does not necessarily correlate to the dependent variable of crimes reported, the independent variable being the cause and the dependent variables being the various effects. It is equally possible that multiple independent variables are influencing the dependent variable, such as an increase in the teenage population, the prevalence of drug dealing and prostitution, or environmental factors such as poor street lighting, the presence of graffiti, and "broken windows" in a neighborhood. In sum, it is possible that no matter how hard the police work under the traditional methods, crime rates may continue to rise.

The first true evaluation, and in this case a quasi-experiment, of police practices was in Kansas City in the early 1970s. The experiment was known as the Kansas City Preventive Patrol Experiment and it set out to evaluate the effectiveness of the preventive patrol methods. It was conducted by designating that certain areas of Kansas City were to have no proactive patrols with police responding only when summoned; others were to have enhanced proactive patrols by doubling or tripling police presence; and, finally, certain areas were designated as control areas, where traditional police practices remained unchanged (Kelling et al. 1974; Kelling et al. 1975). The researchers evaluated in a pre-test/post-test method with a time lapse of one year, by collecting data on the number of crimes reported, arrest rates, traffic accident rates, police response time, and both citizen attitudes and victimization rates (Kelling et al. 1974; Kelling et al. 1975). The evaluation findings revealed that preventive patrols were not effective in altering crime, citizen fear of crime, community attitudes toward the police, police response time, or traffic accidents (Kelling et al. 1974, 16). The Kansas City Preventive Patrol Experiment, with the release of these results, received a vast amount of criticism because it negated basic assumptions about police work. In many cases, the results of the experiment necessitated words of caution (Wilson 1975, 99) while in other cases, critics challenged the experimental design itself, stating that the methods utilized were flawed (Larson, 1975). It also created a profusion of similar studies in various jurisdictions across the country with largely similar results (see Lewis, Greene, and Edwards 1977; Schnelle et al. 1975; Wagner 1978). As a result of the Kansas City Experiment, past practices and assumptions about evaluating the police changed dramatically.

Transitional Evaluations

The Kansas City Preventive Patrol Experiment eventually led to multiple evaluations of police departments and their standard-held beliefs and practices, to determine if traditional policing tactics were in fact viable methods of policing. The research from the 1970s and into the 1980s revealed significant limitations in traditional police practices and procedures. Kansas City returned to the specific issue of rapid police response and its effectiveness in dealing with crime (Kansas City Police Department 1980) and this too was followed by multiple evaluations (Scott 1981; Spelman and Brown 1984), demonstrating little effectiveness on faster police responses. Additional studies in the area of criminal investigations also revealed little effectiveness, regardless of the traditional methods utilized (Eck 1982; Greenwood and Petersilia 1975; Greenwood, Petersilia, and Chaiken 1977). As Dennis P. Rosenbaum (1988, 371) concluded, "considerable time and effort have been expended to improve police management and efficiency, but the fundamental approach to policing has remained the same: namely, responding to and investigating individual citizen calls for service in a reactive fashion (rather than seeking to identify and address community problems) and treating local citizens as passive recipients of police services (rather than as co-producers of public safety)." As the evolution of policing moved from police-community relations to community-oriented policing, so too would the use of evaluation methods.

As community-oriented policing was born in the early 1980s and implemented in a wide variety of formats during most of the 1980s, evaluations were adopted by many police departments to assess the viability and capabilities of this new concept. The majority of evaluations conducted during this time frame were as a result of various grants from research institutions such as the National Institute of Justice, the Police Executive Research Forum, the Vera Institute of Justice, and the Police Foundation. These evaluations provided a vast amount of literature on the up-and-coming concept of community-oriented policing and presented many of the advantages and disadvantages of programs, methods, and practices under this new umbrella term.

In 1988, Jack Greene and Ralph Taylor (1988) presented a review of the key studies that had been conducted to that date, including those in Flint, Michigan; Newark, New Jersey; Oakland, California; San Diego, California; Houston, Texas; Boston, Massachusetts; and Baltimore, Maryland. Their findings

The Oceanside Police Department, Oceanside, California, annual
Community Relations Fair to bring the community and police
closer together. (Courtesy of Oceanside Police Dept., Oceanside,
California.)

presented a list of salient shortcomings with the evaluations that are still key
concerns today for improving the evaluation process. The first issue raised
was the "inadequate operationalization of 'community'" which was discussed
in this book in chapter 9 (Greene and Taylor 1988, 216). In every study the
term "community" is never defined with any clarity, nor any "attempt to use
ecologically valid neighborhood units" (Greene and Taylor 1988, 217) despite
all of the researchers utilizing the term to definitively describe what impact
the programs had on the "community" and how the "community" responded
in kind.

　　A second shortcoming, largely a result of the first shortcoming, consisted
of "confusion about the appropriate level of analysis" (Greene and Taylor
1988, 217). When attempting to evaluate community-oriented policing, the
focus has been placed on the community and how the community, as the customer, has responded to the change in police services. The authors criticize
the evaluations conducted during this transitional period for not evaluating
that which they set out to evaluate. In many cases, researchers analyzed and
interpreted at the community level, but surveyed individuals. The satisfaction
on the part of individuals versus the community as a whole can present two
varying viewpoints. It is then important for researchers to analyze at the level
they are evaluating and interpret their findings as such.

　　The third shortcoming the authors described revolved around poor evaluation design, specifically in the area of weak, quasi-experimental designs and
the lack of control groups (Greene and Taylor 1988, 217–218). The use of

quasi-experiments and the methods employed will be detailed later in this chapter; however, the authors distinctly point out the lack of control groups in many of the experiments. In many cases, during the initial stages of implementation, control groups can be designated in neighborhoods that have not been integrated into the community-oriented policing concept. However, once the systemic approach begins to see full implementation city-wide, the control groups will have to be redefined based on types of services, programs, or methods employed.

The fourth shortcoming the authors found at the time was a problem with the implementation of community-oriented policing (Greene and Taylor 1988, 218). The authors found that in many cases either very few officers or very few citizens were actually involved in the systemic approach, and so contact between the police and community was minimal. This caused difficulties in assessing the success or failure of community-oriented policing because so few people had been exposed to the programs and services. This necessitates the importance of effective implementation strategies as described in Chapter 11, prior to the police department moving to evaluate.

A fifth shortcoming the authors cited was "defining the treatment" or determining exactly what actions the police were taking that should be evaluated as being community-oriented policing (Greene and Taylor 1988, 218). In many cases, multiple programs and methods of delivering police services were being evaluated while in other cases it was unclear as to what policing services were actually being performed under the guise of community-oriented policing. It is important that the services or programs the police are providing are identified and specifically evaluated for their individual merit, rather than evaluating a host of services, otherwise the evaluation results will be unclear as to what can be deemed successful and what can be considered a failure.

The final shortcoming delineated by the authors consisted of "outcome specification" or understanding what the desired outcome under community-oriented policing should be and how it should be measured (Greene and Taylor 1988, 218). Although it may be a long-term goal to reduce crime under community-oriented policing as a result of community involvement, initially crime rates may not decrease. If the intent of community-oriented policing is to increase the quality of life in a community, evaluating whether or not crime rates rise or fall is an inadequate method of measuring this outcome. Therefore, consideration must be made on what the desired outcome is from the implementation of a program, how it will be measured, and how it will be interpreted to be a success or a failure. If the program is oriented on enhancing the relationship between the police and the public, then the outcome specification should focus on citizen satisfaction with the police and police satisfaction with the community, not the rise and fall of crime rates.

Two additional shortcomings consist of one the authors touched on, the specific target of the evaluation, and one they did not address, the need for long-term studies. The specific need to determine what the evaluation will target is important in two distinct ways. First, the evaluation must identify which program or service is being targeted, and second one must determine who is being targeted for study. In many cases, community-oriented policing is a packaged program that may consist of multiple methods to address a community's concern, for it is after all a systemic approach. The police may utilize all three components at the same time, thus creating a blend of programs and services. When it comes time to evaluate the benefit of those things implemented, it is important that the evaluation process be tailored specifically to what is being targeted. If it is the benefit of foot patrols in a community, the evaluation must be careful to avoid the influence of a police substation or saturation patrol in the process. It is equally important that the target of the evaluation be identified and the evaluation directed toward these individuals. In a police department engaged in micro community-oriented policing, unless divided into an experimental group and control group, it makes little sense to evaluate all officers in the department on community-oriented policing since only a limited number are actually participating in the program.

The second shortcoming is the lack of long-term studies. Although the systemic approach to policing is relatively new, the possibility still exists for long-term studies to be conducted for evaluation purposes. The majority of studies are solely focused on short periods of time, ranging from several months to as much as a year. However, as community-oriented policing and its implementation is a long-term process, the evaluation process should also be a long-term process. Studies are needed that evaluate the systemic approach for multiple years rather than multiple months. In a similar vein, it is also critical that the evaluation process remain a long-term and ongoing process. Too many police departments evaluate at the micro community-oriented policing stage, make adjustments, and move forward without any additional evaluations. This does not provide for current and up-to-date information, nor does it allow for any incremental changes to be made based on these assessments. The evaluation process must be part of an ongoing process to assess the current status of police services, customer satisfaction, and the advantages and disadvantages of community-oriented policing.

As the evaluation process moved into the community-oriented policing stage, many police departments recognize the importance of the evaluation process and have begun utilizing it as a tool to ensure quality policing. In wake of many of the shortcomings during the 1980s, there has been a movement to adopt certain criteria for articulating the basis of evaluation under the systemic approach. The criteria necessary for this basis has had to not only allow for the qualitative and subjective standards that are desired, but for a revision of the quantitative and objective standards necessary to assess the success of community-oriented policing. A positive stance has been taken to ensure that the criteria reflect all of the values and goals inherent under this approach, and the literature is replete with the description of effectiveness, efficiency, and equity as being the primary foundation (Bureau of Justice Assistance 1994a; Bureau of Justice Assistance 1994b; Eck and Rosenbaum 1994; Goldstein 1990; Miller and Hess 1994; Skogan 1994). However, equally important are two additional criteria that make up this foundation: accountability and authority.

COP IN ACTION

CITIZEN FEEDBACK LINE

Citizens in Clearwater, Florida are considered "customers" of the police department. And, as any well-run organization knows, what your customers think of your business is important. With this business-world edict in mind, the police department developed a "customer satisfaction" survey three years ago to better serve the needs of the citizenry.

Clearwater is a city of 100,000 permanent residents with an additional influx of about 30,000 seasonally. Located on the west central coast of Florida, Clearwater is about thirty-five square miles, bounded on the west by the Gulf of Mexico and on the east by Tampa Bay.

In 1990 the Clearwater Police Department and the Clearwater City Managers' Office developed an eleven-page survey with thirty-two questions. The questions were designed to obtain feedback in two main areas: (1) the feelings and concerns of the respondents about their neighborhoods; and, (2) the respondents' feelings about the performance of the police department and its employees. Throughout the process, the intent was to gather information from the public that would be useful in evaluating the performance from the public that would be useful in evaluating the performance of the police department and in planning future programs and strategies.

The survey instrument was printed on 5" x 8" paper with the police department's emblem and city seal on the cover. Inside the front cover is a letter from Police Chief Sid Klein and City Manager Michael Wright.

The first section asks nine specific questions about the respondent's neighborhood and provides space for respondents to write what they believe are the most significant police-related problems in their neighborhoods.

The second section is for respondents who have had contact with a police department employee. The survey asks the nature of the contact, how many times they had contact, and with which police department employee they have had the most recent contact. Then they are asked to rate the appearance, courtesy, helpfulness, and overall competence of the employee. Citizens are also asked two questions concerning their overall satisfaction/dissatisfaction with the encounter. The respondents are asked to detail what specifically dissatisfied them about their encounters with police department employees.

The third section is for all respondents, regardless of whether they had personal contact with the police department. They are asked to rate the appearance, courtesy, helpfulness, and overall competence of the department as a whole and to explain how they formed the impression. This is followed by three questions about the police department and the city of Clearwater:

- The members of the Clearwater Police Department respond in a fair and impartial manner when dealing with the racial, religious, and ethnic communities of Clearwater.
- I would feel comfortable calling the Clearwater Police Department for assistance.
- Overall, I feel that the city of Clearwater is a safe place in which to travel, live, work, and conduct business.

A write-in section follows the above questions for suggestions on how to make the department better.

The fourth section covers demographics. Respondents are asked for their zip code so the responses can be categorized, and requests the residents' marital status, age, education level, race/ethnic background, children, income, and sex. Finally, there is one page for the respondents to write any comments they feel necessary.

The city is divided into three patrol districts, Beach, West and East. Population is broken down by patrol districts, and proportional number of surveys is sent to each district. Survey recipients are selected randomly from the Clearwater Utility billing list, the most accurate and up-to-date information available. An inherent problem is that the utility department serves some homes outside Clearwater city limits. We targeted approximately 2,500 people, or about 2 percent of the city's population. Two weeks before the survey is mailed, an introductory letter signed by Chief Klein and the city manager is sent to the citizens selected. The letter explains the intent of the soon-to-be-delivered survey and asks them to take some time to fill it out. The survey is then sent with a letter, thanking the respondent in advance for filling out and returning the survey. There is no cost to the respondent to mail the survey; all returns are business reply by mail. All costs of the survey are budgeted annually by the police department. Survey results are tabulated in a database computer program designed specifically for the project. In the three years the survey has been in use, the average return rate is well over 40 percent, a rate considered exceptional.

Police management uses the survey to get feedback on public concerns and opinions of the department in general. It also enables the public to grade the department on the way it looks and the efficiency of its operations. The survey has opened avenues of communication that have traditionally been closed and is certainly an asset to the department

Source: Adapted with permission from Griffith, Douglas L. "Citizen Feedback Line." *Law and Order*, December 1993, 37–40.

EVALUATION CRITERIA

The term "effectiveness," up to this point, has been utilized to discuss past quantitative and objective criteria that the police utilized through various arrest statistics and quotas. The emphasis on "effectiveness" under the systemic approach is different from that of traditional policing. An effective implementation of community-oriented policing will not increase the number of arrest statistics for an officer or satisfy the quotas of the police department, but will reduce crime in the community through a variety of means beyond arrests. It will also reduce the community's fear of crime, and it will enhance the overall quality of life. As the true mark of effectiveness will concentrate on the delivery of police services and customer satisfaction, those measures of this effectiveness should concentrate on solving community problems, how well the community and police work in partnerships, and the level of customers' satisfaction with their police. These are the methods of determining the true effectiveness of the police.

If a community-oriented policing program is implemented and it does not reduce the number of crimes or the number of calls for service, it cannot be called a failure, where under the traditional style of policing that may have been the case. Eck and Spelman (1987), under their development of a problem-oriented policing program for Newport News Police Department in 1987, also defined "effectiveness." They established five methods of determining if a problem-solving effort was effective and we can utilize the same five methods under the larger concept of community-oriented policing (Eck and Spelman 1987). The five ways are 1) a problem can be solved by totally eliminating it; 2) reducing the number of incidents it creates; 3) reducing the seriousness of the incidents it creates; 4) designing methods for better handling the incidents; and 5) removing it from police consideration (Eck and Spelman 1987, 5–6).

The ability to totally eliminate a problem via strategic-oriented policing, neighborhood-oriented policing, or problem-oriented policing, would certainly be the ultimate goal, but despite all hopes for full elimination, the reality of the matter is very few criminal or order maintenance issues will ever fully disappear. However, the second method of solving the problem is reasonable, and more likely to occur. An example may be the use of strategic-oriented policing tactics to drive out the criminal element, or at least drive it underground. In either case, the problem will be reduced. The third possibility can also be called effective, especially if we can isolate the problem, and make it less of a threat to the general public. An example may be isolating the areas frequented by drug users and keeping the drugs away from the children and the abandoned needles away from the playgrounds. The fourth method may make better sense in evaluating many of the programs under community-oriented policing because the police and community may not be able to change or alter the make-up of the problem, but they can deal more effectively in the delivery of services, referrals, and costs. Finally, the removal of a problem from police consideration details that the police may not be the best organization to provide the solution or effectively deal with the problem. Another agency may be able to deal more effectively with the problem and hence resolve it in one of the above four manners, freeing the police to deal with those problems they are equipped to handle. However, under community-oriented policing, this should not equate to pawning the problem off on someone else. The police must continue to monitor the problem, follow its own success or failure, and determine if it may eventually have to be returned to police consideration.

Therefore, to accurately gauge the effectiveness of the police, the goals of the community-oriented policing program should be addressed, and what is considered an acceptable measure of effectiveness should be determined prior to the implementation process. This is essentially addressing what has been identified as a past shortcoming of outcome specification. Once these issues are resolved then the method for gauging effectiveness should be introduced. This may consist of numerous evaluation methods ranging from assessing citizens' fear of crime, the number of citizens active in addressing problems in their community, the number of citizens serving on community-oriented policing committees, citizens' assessment of their quality of life, and perhaps a decrease in the calls for criminal activity and an increase in calls for service.

A second criterion for evaluating community-oriented policing is through an assessment of the efficiency of the police department. As community-oriented policing entails a decentralization of the organizational structure and the utilization of police resources in a more efficient manner, the ability to gauge this efficiency should be a key method of gauging the success or failure of the systemic approach during the implementation process. The goals of becoming more efficient are closely related to exercising a greater use of the resources the police already have on hand and utilizing the relationship with the community to push for even greater efficiency by garnering community support and assistance.

COP IN ACTION

HOW TO SAVE MONEY

An unreliable survey isn't worth the paper on which the questionnaire is printed. But most police departments don't have $30,000 to hire a professional surveying firm. How can they get affordable yet reliable results?

One way to do it is with some advice from a professional and help from volunteers. Using volunteers can cut a survey's cost in half. Both the San José Police and Sacramento County Sheriff's departments used volunteers to do telephone interviews for their surveys.

Departments can recruit volunteers through the media or by contacting civic organizations. Aim for a large number because some will drop out, especially toward the end of the survey. Sacramento County relied on a pool of 200 volunteers. But the telephone polling took a week longer than expected, and turnout dwindled the last few nights. Polling is a slow process. Sacramento County volunteers completed about two telephone surveys an hour per volunteer. Sacramento County Deputy Sheriff Anthony Taylor, survey coordinator, said the next time he would conduct polling on weeknights only. Productivity on Saturdays dropped by half because it was harder to reach people.

There's more to a survey than interviewing. There's deciding the focus, picking the sample, writing the questionnaire, tabulating the results and analyzing the data. You can't get volunteers to do these jobs, you must assign them in-house; remember you're spending your employees' time. It's not free.

Hiring a professional has advantages. Most have computer programs to tabulate results, and they have experience in gleaning insight from the data. Most data-based programs aren't designed to handle survey results. In addition, professionals have no axes to grind and can analyze the numbers from an unbiased standpoint.

Source: Adapted with permission from Marquand, Barbara. "How to Save Money." *Law and Order.* December 1994, 44.

It has largely been the case that the government agencies have not been the most efficient because of a number of factors. The police are essentially no different. James Q. Wilson (1989, 349–353) points out three key reasons why this is the case. The first is that "government executives are less able than their private counterparts to define an efficient course of action" (Wilson 1989, 349–353). The variety of goals found in policing have prevented the police department from concentrating on specific methods to work more efficiently and the department has thus been allowed to ignore any defining course of action. A second problem has been that "public executives have weaker incentives than do private executives to find an efficient course of action" (Wilson 1989, 349–353). The police department has generally had little incentive to make the delivery of its police services more efficient in the past and therefore little concern has been placed on this initiative. And finally, "public executives have less authority than private ones to impose an efficient course of action" (Wilson 1989, 349–353). Police departments, from chiefs to the line officers, in the past, had little authority to even attempt making the delivery of police resources more efficient, and this has created a high degree of wasteful spending of resources, time, and money.

Under the systemic approach to policing, these three shortcomings will be addressed in a variety of ways. The police chief and management should not only be required to make the police department more efficient, but they should also have the authority to impose an efficient course of action, derived from community support. The incentives to make the police department a more efficient one under the systemic approach should be derived from the mission, values, and goals inherent within community-oriented policing. In addition, this efficiency can be obtained from the decentralization process, by reducing the layers of bureaucracy, as well as moving the authority further down the chain.

Efficiency is then closely tied with moving the responsibility of policing down to the individual police officer, forming closer ties with the community, and obtaining their support, and through the decentralization process, ridding the department of the bureaucracy that is inherent within any traditional police department (Eck and Rosenbaum 1994, 17). If line police officers can implement methods that are more cost-effective, working smarter, not harder, then valuable resources, time, and money can be saved. If close ties to the community can solicit the assistance of volunteers for those functions that were once relegated to the police officer or equipment and services can be obtained through a cooperative effort with the business community, again, valuable resources, time, and money can be saved. And if reducing the layers of bureaucracy in a police department can be reduced, the police department can be more efficient in its delivery of services. Therefore, an assessment over time, as the incremental implementation of community-oriented policing goes into effect, can assist in the evaluation of determining the efficiency of the community-oriented police department.

Another criterion, which some believe has the greatest impact on community-oriented policing, is equity (Bureau of Justice Assistance 1994a; Bureau of Justice Assistance 1994b). Equity is essentially the belief that all citizens should have a say in how they are governed and specifically in how they are policed. It is a central belief of the American people, held definitively in our Constitution, and is that to which police officers are sworn to enforce. The delivery of services to the people must allow for equal access, it must provide equal treatment and be distributed in a fair and nondiscriminatory manner.

The equal access to police services is an extremely important criteria for the implementation of community-oriented policing. Under traditional policing, police officers generally spend 90 percent of their time with 10 percent of the community, often ignoring the 90 percent of law-abiding citizens. The reasoning usually lies in the fact that those citizens are not breaking the law and therefore "their" neighborhoods are not important. This, under community-oriented policing, must never be the case. Those neighborhoods with low crime rates do in fact have their own particular problems. Albeit their crimes may not be as serious, but that does not negate their importance. They are as deserving of a police response to their problems as those who live in high-crime areas. At the same time, it is often certain homogenous groups, such as recent immigrants who may speak little to no English, that are often not provided equal police service because of language and cultural barriers. These groups are equally deserving of a police response and must be factored into the programs of community-oriented policing. All of this is largely the premise of the United States Constitution and the equal treatment under the law clause, which should be the foundation of any community-oriented policing program.

Therefore, the method of measuring equity under community-oriented policing is vastly different from any form of measurement under traditional approaches to policing. As Eck and Rosenbaum (1994, 12) stated, "the most relevant measures are the perceptions of the various publics served by the police…both the quantity and quality of police–citizen contacts are considered important measures of police performance under many community-policing programs." Through the use of interviews and surveys, the police will be able to gauge the equity of the police under community-oriented policing.

Another key criterion for assessing the success of community-oriented policing is the critical aspect of accountability. The police must be held accountable to the community rather than only being accountable to themselves. The key distinction revolving around accountability is that centralized control may be an easier method of managing and overseeing the police organization, but it removes the authority from the line officer who deals with the community on a daily basis. While community-oriented policing decentralizes the structure, hence giving the line officer more authority, it also decentralizes by personnel and geography, thus placing a particular officer, in a particular neighborhood, for a particular length of time. This in turn makes that officer more accountable to the citizens of that neighborhood, for they should recognize that officer as "their officer" and it allows management to hold that officer more accountable for what occurs on his or her beat. This can also work with management, by placing mid-level managers in charge of specific geographical areas rather than based on specific times of the day, thus making them more accountable for what occurs in their geographical area.

The final criterion that must be the basis for evaluating community-oriented policing is authority. The authority of the police under traditional concepts has largely focused on the authority of the position of police officer or on a specialization such as SWAT teams or homicide investigators. The concept of authority was then as a result of one's position or specialization, enhanced or reduced through policy, procedures, rules, regulations, or directives on the part of management. The majority of these generally limited the amount of authority, such as the restriction on the use of force, policies on the use of deadly force, or policies detailing when officers are authorized to pursue. Authority for policing was only created by the public through pressure on the local government and police department, and then it was driven again through these same procedures.

Under community-oriented policing, authority is derived from the community. Although some authority is still derived from traditional means, the customers of policing services must determine what authority they wish to delegate to their police officers. Community groups, problem-solving groups, and community-oriented policing coalitions in a particular community will become the authority-granting institution that determines what they will allow their police to do and not to do. For example, although they cannot override officers'

From Left to right: Asst. Chief Brian Reuther, Councilwoman Maryann Cernuto, Police Chief C.L. "Chuck" Reynolds, Mayor Robert Minsky, and Councilwoman Paula Lewis of the City of Port St. Lucie, Florida, inaugurating a neighborhood policing office in District II. (Courtesy of City of Port St. Lucie Police Dept., Port St. Lucie, Florida.)

authority to write speeding tickets, this is a reasonable action to protect the majority of citizens by enforcing speed zone regulations. However, the community can provide additional authority to the police by granting access to information and property that they may not have had otherwise or the community can remove the authority of the police if they disagree with methods employed by the police, say under problem-solving techniques, by refusal or action. As community-oriented policing is implemented, the further along the systemic process moves toward institutionalization, the more authority the community will have and hence the more authority they will have over policing. In order to control policing, to make the police more effective and accountable, increased authority in the hands of the community through empowerment will be healthy for the sake of community.

Recognizing these five key terms can assist police departments in determining how to evaluate their implementation of community-oriented policing. By utilizing the tenets of Effectiveness, Efficiency, Equity, Accountability and Authority when implementing the various programs under the systemic approach to policing, a variety of evaluation measurements can be developed for a clearer understanding of gauging success and failure. As the incremental implementation process continues, these assessments can assist both the police and community in focusing on the goals and objectives of community-oriented policing and can help determine what changes must occur throughout the process.

COP IN ACTION

HOW ARE WE DOING?

When residents called the Sacramento County, California, Sheriff's Department to make routine reports, they seldom ever heard what happened afterward. Now volunteers make follow-up calls to advise residents the outcome of the cases—an improvement made because a survey showed there was a problem.

As law enforcement agencies strive to become better partners with their communities, some have found surveys to be a key in establishing communication. After all, survey advocates ask, how can departments be community-oriented if they don't know what the community thinks?

Surveys provide several benefits. They can spark positive media attention by showing that police are concerned about the community's needs. They can help assess the community's concerns and expectations. They also help law enforcement officials set priorities—a crucial task as government resources dwindle.

The San José Police Department, with 1,300 sworn officers, conducted surveys in August 1992 and 1994 as part of its commitment toward community-oriented policing. "Cops are real good at telling people what they need," San José Capt. Stephen D'Arcy, who coordinated the surveys, said. "But it's important to be a good listener, for an organization as well as an individual." D'Arcy said some of the 1992 results surprised officials. Predictably, violent crime and gangs were a big concern among residents. But when it came to their own neighborhoods—even those considered gang infested—the top concerns were basic quality-of-life issues such as graffiti and abandoned cars.

The same was true in Sacramento County. Also surprising in Sacramento County was the gap between the public's perception and reality. The survey showed, for example, residents thought the department's emergency response time should be 8 minutes or less, the same as the county ambulance service. But the actual response time is 15.8 minutes, Taylor said. The department either needs to improve performance or educate the public about what it can realistically expect, given constrained resources, he said.

Subsequent surveys can measure changes in public perception. How long a department waits before it does another survey is a judgment call. But it should wait long enough to give the public a chance to recognize any changes made since the last survey.

Source: Adapted with permission from Marquand, Barbara. "How Are We Doing?" *Law and Order*. December 1994, 41–943.

EVALUATION RESEARCH

In order to accurately assess the success and failure of various applications of community-oriented policing, it is important that the police department conduct evaluation research. The evaluation research should not be limited to a particular time of studying, such as during micro community-oriented policing, but should be utilized at all stages of implementation. It should also attempt to incorporate not only evaluations of various programs themselves, but also evaluation of police and community response to these programs. As the majority of community-oriented policing action will come in the form of programs, the purpose of the research should then fall under the broad category of program evaluation.

Program evaluation is not necessarily a type of research, but instead is a focus on the purpose of certain research. As programs are implemented, such as foot patrols or community substations, it is important to assess how well these programs have been implemented and the impact they have had on their intended target. Program evaluations are therefore focused on answering two questions: "1) Are policies being implemented as planned?" and "2) Are policies achieving their intended goals?" (Maxfield and Babbie 1995, 304). In order to answer these two questions, there are two types of corresponding program evaluations: process evaluation and impact assessment (Maxfield and Babbie 1995). Process evaluation is a method that seeks to determine if the original policy was implemented in accordance with the original plan. In the case of community-oriented policing, this may consist of the strategic plan or a plan of action determined by the community to address a local problem. The focus of the study is generally on program outputs and the methods utilized in the implementation. If the police and community have implemented a plan of foot patrols to reduce the prevalence of drug-dealing in their neighborhood, the process evaluation will focus on the number of officer hours on foot patrol in that area as well as analyzing what the officers spent the majority of their time doing during these foot patrols. If officers spend the majority of their time interacting with the community and dealing with the problem, the process evaluation would state the plan was implemented accordingly. If the number of hours on foot patrol has not increased or the officers' time is not spent communicating with the community and addressing the problem, the process evaluation would conclude the implementation of the plan was poor.

TABLE 12.1   WHAT TO MEASURE?

Method	General Definition	i.e. Foot Patrol
Output (or process)	Volume of units produced	Number of officers
Outcome (or results)	Quality/effectiveness of production: degree to which it creates desired outcomes	Increase/decrease of crime and fear of crime
Program outcome	Effectiveness of specific program in achieving desired outcomes	Increase/decrease in crime rates, number of citizen contacts, number of self-initiated arrests, over six months
Policy outcomes	Effectiveness of broader policies in achieving fundamental goals	Measures indicating how crime and disorder is perceived in the foot patrol area
Program efficiency	Cost per unit of output	Cost per foot patrol officer
Policy efficiency	Cost to achieve fundamental goals	Cost for X level of order and safety
Program effectiveness	Degree to which program yields desired outcomes	Level of citizen satisfaction with foot patrol officers
Policy effectiveness	Degree to which fundamental goals and citizens needs are met	Do citizens want to continue spending their money on foot patrols? Would they rather spend their money on motor patrols?

Source: Adapted with permission from Osborne, David and Ted Gaebler. *Reinventing Government: How the Entrepreneurial Spirit is Transforming the Public Sector From Schoolhouse to Statehouse, City Hall to the Pentagon.* Reading, MA.: Addison-Wesley Publishing Company, Inc., 1992.

Impact assessment is a program evaluation method that seeks to determine if the program implemented has had any impact on its intended target. If the program had a well-developed plan and it was implemented accordingly, then the researchers have the capability of determining what impact this action had on the intended target. In the case of the foot patrols in a high drug area, the impact assessment may look at the reduction of drug-dealers and drug arrests in the area, the impact on overall crime rates, or they may simply ask the community for their perception of how effective the foot patrols were.

The program evaluation methods of process evaluation and impact assessment are complementary to the systemic approach and should be utilized as the two key areas of evaluation research. However, in order to focus on these two areas and utilize the various methods of evaluation available, it is important to recognize many of the questions that must first be answered. The first question that must be answered is, "What is going to be studied?" The difficulty that lies with this question is revealed in the definition of community-oriented policing. If one were to attempt to evaluate community-oriented policing, one must first ask how one would operationalize the overall concept of strategic-oriented policing, neighborhood-oriented policing, problem-oriented policing, and decentralization into a workable form. This is equally true if the police department were to focus on their mission statement or values and goals under community-oriented policing. The problem lies in the fact that "Community policing expressed merely as a nice idea simply cannot be evaluated" (Hornick, Leighton, and Burrows 1993, 62). Therefore, in the same manner that community-oriented policing must be operationalized into various programs, so too must it be evaluated in this manner. Therefore, the question of "what is to be evaluated" must be answered with a specific program.

One alternative to evaluating a specific program is to evaluate the perceptions of the police and the community. Although this may be conducted as part of evaluating a specific program, such as the foot patrol scenario, it can also be conducted independently to determine the overall view of the public and the police. Evaluating the perceptions of the police can be beneficial to understanding what they like and don't like about the concept, and more importantly what they support and what they don't support. It can also be a yardstick for how their perceptions change over time as the concept is implemented to see what additional needs the officers may have. In the case of evaluating the perceptions of the community, it only makes sense to evaluate how the customer feels about the "product." Determining how the community feels about the systemic approach can provide feedback to the police department as to where they are, where they need to go, and how they can get to the point of truly being integrated with the community.

The second question that must be answered is "who is going to conduct the study?" This question, as a result of the community-oriented policing philosophy, can be answered in multiple ways. If the police department is fortunate enough to have a researcher or research unit within their police department, the answer may be readily apparent. If the police department does not have this asset available to them, they may find that they have the untapped asset already existing somewhere in their police department. As more and more police officers enter the field with a college degree or obtain one while working for the police department, they may have the capability to conduct evaluation research. This can be beneficial to both the department because of cost and to the officer because it maximizes their abilities. However, it can also be non-beneficial because the officer would not be a true "non-interested, third-party." This must be weighed before selecting someone internally.

If the department chooses to find someone outside of the police department, they may always hire a researcher, but this can become costly. If the police have established strong community ties, they may find someone in their own community who is capable of conducting such research for free or who may be able to obtain a grant to conduct such studies. If the community is also privy to a nearby university or college, they may be able to obtain the assistance of both college professors or students to perform the study. In any case, utilizing the resources available within the department and community is a primary focus of the community-oriented approach to policing.

Once the police department has determined what will be studied and who will conduct the study, the next thing the researcher or researchers must carefully review are the definition and goals of the program, as well as specifying the outcomes desired from its implementation. Every aspect of the process must be defined and the goals pre-determined and although predicting what will happen after the implementation of the program, the desired outcomes of the program should be clarified. In the foot patrol scenario, the researchers must define what is meant by "foot patrol" so the focus of their study is on this particular variable. Is foot patrol interpreted as officers getting out of their patrol vehicles on occasion and walking the neighborhood or is it the specific placement of two officers, walking a specific geographical area, for a specific number of hours? Once these operationalization questions are answered, then the question focuses on the desired outcome. Is the desired impact of the foot patrols to reduce crime, reduce public fear, to show a visible presence, or all of these?

Once the program, goals, and specific outcomes are defined, the key to program evaluation then comes into play. The researchers must determine whether the focus of the program evaluation will be on the process or impact of a program and specifically how these goals will be measured. If the focus is on evaluating the process then the methods utilized to implement the program and whether or not it was implemented as planned becomes the key goal. These goals may consist of determining the number and types of problems identified for resolution, how many programs are proposed under neighborhood-oriented policing versus how many are actually implemented, the level of community participation, the number of community participants, changes in the number of calls for service, or changes in the type of calls for service. If the focus is on evaluating the impact of the program then what the specific outcomes were will become the key goals to be analyzed. These goals may consist of reducing crime rates due to strategic-oriented policing tactics, citizen satisfaction with police services, job satisfaction on the part of the police, level of fear on the part of the citizens, or the reduction of specific crimes or neighborhood problems.

Once the type of program evaluation is determined and the specific goals determined, how the goals will be measured becomes an important aspect of the evaluation process. The goals must be transformed into specific variables that can be measured to determine whether or not a program is considered a success or failure. In the case of the foot patrols in a high-crime area, if the goal is to reduce public fear, then this must be operationalized to determine what fear is and how it will be measured. As this is largely a perception on the part of the community, rather than any fact-based data gathering, a method must be employed to assess the public's perception. This could be operationalized by simply asking the public what their level of fear is, or it could be operationalized by observing the number and type of foot traffic in a community after dark to determine if people are more willing to walk alone at night or even come out at all. The way that the researcher attempts to operationalize the goals to be studied, generally determine the methods that will be utilized in the study. However, prior to discussing the actual methods used, two other concerns must be addressed.

The first concern is the other variables that may influence or control the outcome. Although the program may be implemented and the specific outcomes previously identified achieved, it is possible that the outcomes were not a result of the program being implemented, but another variable. Therefore, it is important that the researchers spend some time considering other variables that may alter the outcomes. As previously discussed, the program may be the independent variable and the outcomes the dependent variable, but it may have been another variable that was introduced that actually produced the desired outcomes. In the foot patrol example, if the public's fear of crime was the gauge and it was operationalized by the number of neighborhood residents outside during a specific time in the evening, the program may be implemented and the number of residents outside may increase, but it may not be as a result of the foot patrols. A possible intervening variable may be daylight savings time which allows for more light during the specified evening hours, hence causing public fear during this time period to decrease. Although foot patrols were implemented and public fear was reduced, the foot patrols were not the cause. Therefore, it is important to consider all of the possible variables that may influence the evaluation in order to more accurately determine the effect of the program itself.

The second concern that must be addressed once the operationalization of the goals has been determined consists of analyzing both the population and the sample size to be utilized in the evaluation. The population in the evaluation consists of the total collection of individuals that could possibly be part of the study. In most cases, it is very difficult, time consuming, and expensive to study and evaluate each individual; therefore a group of individuals must be selected that represents the entire population and this is known as a sample. The most common method utilized is a random sample where a certain number of individuals will be selected and every individual in the population has an equal chance of being selected. If police officers wish to survey a neighborhood's perceptions of community-oriented policing, but there are over 20,000 residences in that neighborhood, they may obtain all of the addresses through the local government or through local utility services, randomly select 200 of these residences and send the survey to these randomly selected residences. The survey findings will then be representative of the larger population.

Once all of these steps, from determining what is to be evaluated to determining the population and sample of the study, have been pre-determined, then the actual evaluation methods must be selected. Program evaluation under community-oriented policing has generally focused on the use of surveys, but in some cases the use of case studies or multiple variables has also been utilized. This has been the case when researchers have analyzed specific programs, as well as when they have evaluated both the police and the community. The following will review the types of methods employed and will explore some of the more recent studies conducted on community-oriented policing programs, police perceptions, and community perceptions of the systemic approach.

METHODS

The primary methods of evaluating the police have been through the use of surveys. Surveys are a relatively easy method for gathering data from the police and community and have proven to be less time- and cost-consuming then other methods. Surveys gather information about the public's attitude toward the police and neighborhood problems, and they can be used to detect and analyze problems in neighborhoods or among special population groups, to evaluate problem-solving efforts and other programs, to control crime and reduce fear of crime (Bureau of Justice Assistance 1993), to assess the police attitude toward the public and neighborhood problems, as well as for a method to gauge the physical environment.

In order to understand specifically how surveys can be utilized, it is important to discuss the three types of questions they can answer. Surveys will generally assess attitudes and opinions, behavior and experience, and characteristics (Bureau of Justice Assistance 1993). The surveys that attempt to address attitudes and opinions are surveys that seek information on the mental state of individuals by asking about their feelings on a number of things, which may include attitudes toward police performance, fear of crime, future plans and intentions, concerns about specific problems, and possible suggestions for police actions. When gauging behavior and experience, these surveys gather data to determine those things that people have been exposed to in their neighborhoods. This may consist of certain behaviors they have seen or exhibited, or most likely it will consist of experiences they have had as a victim of a crime, with the police, with a specific problem, or as part of a specific program. The final question that may be answered through surveys consists of the characteristics of various groups of people found in a particular neighborhood or community. These characteristics may consist of the lifestyles of individuals, the personal history of offenders, the background of victims to crimes, or just simple census information that reveals various social factors.

In order to answer the questions focusing on the three areas of attitudes and opinions, behavior and experience, or characteristics, there are three types of basic survey data collection methods that can be utilized. These survey methods include mail surveys, telephone surveys, and personal interview surveys. The easiest method of data collection out of these is the delivery of a survey through the mail. It is less time- and cost-consuming than the other two methods and it is a method of reaching large sample sizes. However, on many occasions people do not return the surveys which can prove frustrating. Many police departments utilize this method with great success to assess all three of the questions above, while some have reported low response rates and have had to implement multiple follow-up survey mailings.

Telephone surveys are a good method for increasing the lack of response to mail surveys, but they can become more expensive as they generally take more time from repeated call backs and time on the phone to proceed through the questions. However, there are benefits because they promote more willingness on the part of the individual to answer questions because of the interpersonal effect. They can also ask for clarification of questions, and such barriers as illiteracy and not speaking the language can be overcome on the phone. Very few police departments themselves have utilized this method; however, external researchers for the community-oriented policing programs have used this with much success.

Officer K. Gunn passes out coloring books during an open house sponsored by the Montgomery County Police Department, Montgomery County, Maryland. (Courtesy of Montgomery County Dept. of Police. Montgomery County, Maryland.)

The final method of surveying is through the use of personal interviews. This method has the highest response rate because the interview is much more personable; however, it is the most time-consuming of the three methods. Police departments such as Baltimore, Maryland; Newport News, Virginia; Tampa, Florida; and Philadelphia, Pennsylvania have all utilized police officers to conduct these interviews with positive results. In some jurisdictions such as Tulsa, Oklahoma; Atlanta, Georgia; and Portland, Oregon, the use of non-sworn employees has been very successful as has the use of volunteers in police departments such as San Diego, California. One important aspect of utilizing uniformed police in the conduct of interviews has been that it provides the individuals being interviewed a chance to address their concerns and speak one-on-one with a police officer. This method has been found to reduce fear on the part of citizens and it can create or enhance a positive attitude toward the police (Pate 1986; Pate 1989; Pate et al. 1986; Uchida, Forst, and Annan 1992). This is a good example how, even in the use of an evaluation method, largely unintended positive results can be achieved through the process that were enhancing the benefits of the systemic approach.

TABLE 12.2   METHODS FOR LISTENING TO THE VOICE OF THE CUSTOMER

- Customer surveys
- Customer follow-ups
- Community surveys
- Customer contact
- Customer contact reports
- Customer councils
- Focus groups
- Customer interviews
- Electronic mail
- Customer service training
- Test marketing
- Quality guarantees
- Inspectors
- Ombudsmen
- Complaint tracking systems
- 800 numbers
- Suggestion boxes or forms

Source: Adapted with permission from Osborne, David and Ted Gaebler. *Reinventing Government: How the Entrepreneurial Spirit is Transforming the Public Sector From Schoolhouse to Statehouse, City Hall to the Pentagon.* Reading, MA.: Addison-Wesley Publishing Company, Inc., 1992.

Surveys

Surveys have effectively and efficiently been employed in numerous ways to assess both community-oriented policing programs and police and community perceptions of the systemic approach. One example of the use of surveys on a community-oriented policing program was in Delray, Florida, where their program commenced in the fall of 1990. The police department utilized a pre-test/ post-test survey design and showed that despite little to no change in public fear, police–community interactions increased, officer performance increased significantly, and the author concluded "that there has been a rather substantial change in the community behavior and attitudes, and in how the community functions as a result of the community policing program" (Wiatrowski 1995, 69–83).

The analysis of foot patrol programs, under the concept of community-oriented policing, has relied heavily on the use of surveys for its evaluation methods, which can reveal valuable information about this one kind of program under the systemic approach. The results of these studies generally find that citizens do recognize the increase of foot patrols in their neighborhood and, additionally, they distinctly notice the absence of foot patrols when they are removed from the neighborhood (Greene and Taylor 1988; Pate 1989). In some cases, foot patrol programs are reported to increase citizen satisfaction (Brown and Wycoff 1987; Oettmeier and Brown 1988; Williams and Pate 1987; Wycoff 1988), while in others no change occurs (Esbenson 1987; Pate 1989). Additionally, fear of crime (Brown and Wycoff 1987; Cordner 1994; Greene and Taylor 1988; Pate 1989; Williams and Pate 1987), effect on order maintenance (Cordner 1994; Greene and Taylor 1988; Pate 1989), effect on calls for service (Bowers and Hirsch 1987; McElroy, Cosgrove, and Sadd 1993; Pate 1989), and the effect on reported crime (Bowers and Hirsch 1987; McElroy, Cosgrove, and Sadd 1993; Pate 1989; Wilson 1975), have all been found to have either mixed results or results so statistically insignificant as to not be an indicator, either positive or negative. One additional foot patrol study, utilizing a pre- and post-survey design, conducted from January of 1991 to January of 1992 in a public housing area, found that the supplementary foot patrol program "succeeded in achieving greater police visibility in the public housing site, increased positive police contacts...and calls for service in the area declined during the project year, and crime victimization, as measured by global survey items, decreased" (Cordner and Jones 1995, 189–198). However, it is important to note that the study also found that "fear of crime" increased over the one-year study and that attitudes toward the police by the community showed both favorable and unfavorable results (Cordner and Jones 1995, 189–198).

The findings through program evaluation in regards to a variety of programs implemented under community-oriented policing have shown very mixed results. In some cases the level of fear was reduced, but satisfaction with police did not go up. In other cases, crime rates, local problems, and calls-for-service dropped, but citizen fear increased. Although this may not sound very promising to the future of the systemic approach, these studies reveal something that should be central to program evaluations, the truth. If the studies do not reveal honest attitudes and opinion, behavior and experiences, or characteristics, then the police do not know and will have no way of knowing what programs need to be altered, enhanced, or abolished. It is only with legitimate, reliable, and valid results through evaluation research that the police and community can address the success or failure of their programs.

The use of surveys to assess police officers' attitudes is also common among community-oriented police departments. Generally these departments utilize a one-time survey to assess police officers' attitudes at a certain point in the implementation process of community-oriented policing. It is important to note that a one-time survey is merely an assessment of perception at the time of the survey and cannot be utilized for broad interpretation. One study on officer perceptions of Chicago's Community Policing Program, known as CAPS, was conducted in 1993 and found "that police officers in Chicago are neither unanimously in favor of community policing nor are they equally disposed toward all elements of such programs" (Lurigio and Skogan 1994, 315–330). However, as a one-time study it was conducted prior to the implementation of the program by surveying officers at the beginning of the orientation sessions with no follow-up (Lurigio and Skogan 1994, 315–330). Therefore, this survey cannot be used to assess officers' attitudes of community-oriented policing after their exposure to the program, only prior to its implementation.

Another one-time survey evaluated two cities and looked at police officers' acceptance of community-oriented policing in Cleveland, Ohio, where a mini-station program was started in 1984, and in Cincinnati, Ohio, where community-oriented policing was started in 1991 with thirty-one officers assigned to eleven neighborhoods (Kratcoski and Noonan 1995, 169–185). The study found that officers' attitudes in both cities "considered community policing in a positive light." However; some misunderstanding existed on the role of the community-oriented policing programs by other rank-and-file officers who generally were not exposed to the program or educated on what the program entailed. This one-time survey was conducted shortly after the implementation process began and therefore can only be used to assess officers' attitudes, opinions, and concerns at that time.

A more accurate method of determining police officers' perceptions of community-oriented policing is through the use of surveys either in a pre-test/post-test design or by surveying multiple times throughout the implementation process in order to avoid just taking a snapshot of attitudes, and instead actually gauging changing perceptions over time. One study conducted in Joliet, Illinois examined a community policing demonstration project started in 1991. A two-year study of police personnel was conducted to gauge such things as job satisfaction, attitudes toward community policing, and whether or not management was successful at implementing change (Rosenbaum, Yeh, and Wilkinson 1994). This was accomplished through one pre-test prior to implementation, one mid-implementation test conducted ten months after implementation, and one post-test twenty-two months after implementation (Rosenbaum,

Yeh, and Wilkinson 1994). Those officers involved in the program reported "the most favorable changes in attitudes about community policing, perceived skillfulness in problem solving, and relevant street-level behavior" while those officers not participating in the program reported "change in areas related to the characteristics of their jobs, especially changes in the nature of their work…and their level of job satisfaction" (Rosenbaum, Yeh, and Wilkinson 1994, 349). However, the authors point out that at the end of the two-year study, "the fact remains that the absence of change was the norm rather than the exception" (Rosenbaum, Yeh, and Wilkinson 1994, 349).

These mixed results in studying officers' attitudes seem rather consistent in the literature (Wilson and Bennett 1994) and when looking at the effect management style has on the officers (Wycoff and Skogan 1994). However, it is generally the case that when tracking these studies over time, police attitudes and opinions toward community-oriented policing are generally very negative before any exposure to the program, mixed during the initial phases of the implementation process, and extremely positive once the program is in full implementation. Therefore, one key lesson that can be drawn from this fact is that it pays to educate all officers in a police department and solicit their input prior to implementation.

One additional area where surveys have been utilized is in gauging public attitudes and opinions of community-oriented policing. A review of the literature by Lurigio and Rosenbaum looked to the citizen's perspective in evaluating the success of community-oriented policing through the use of surveys. In their conclusions from the community's perspective, "officers engaging in community policing are rated as more visible, helpful, polite, and effective on a variety of job activities" (Lurigio and Rosenbaum, 1994, 160). Surveys of communities after community-oriented policing has been implemented have revealed generally very consistent findings. If community-oriented policing was actually implemented as a program and not merely in "name-only" the public attitudes and opinions, as well as their experiences with the systemic approach, have been largely positive.

The use of interviews has also been widely utilized as a survey method to assess the capabilities of the programs under community-oriented policing, as well as police and community perceptions. This methodology is generally utilized in concert with written forms of surveys to provide a stronger method of evaluation. The two studies of community-oriented policing, which have produced an enormous amount of research in this field, are the Newark, New Jersey and Houston, Texas projects (Brown and Wycoff 1987; Oettmeier and Brown 1988; Pate 1986; Pate et al. 1986; Williams and Pate 1987; Wycoff 1988). The use of both surveys and interviews found that the most successful programs were those that involved direct contact between the police and the community (Brown and Wycoff 1987). Problem-oriented policing study was conducted in Baltimore County, Maryland under the Police Department's Citizen-Oriented Police Enforcement program or COPE, which also utilized both surveys and interviews and found it not only useful for the evaluation of the program, but as an "integral part of the COPE strategy" (Cordner 1988,

222–223). The evaluation of the COPE program was found to be "at least moderately successful at reducing fear, satisfying citizens, and solving neighborhood problems, and may even succeed at displacing or deterring certain crimes" (Cordner 1988, 151; see also Cordner 1986). The evaluation methods of surveys and interviews to address attitudes and opinions, behavior and experiences, as well as characteristics have been extremely valuable to community-oriented policing. As articulated previously, even the evaluation methods of the programs have some usefulness in reducing fear of crime and improving the relations between the police and community as it opens up the lines of communication.

In the evaluation of police officers' and the community's attitudes and opinions toward the systemic approach, again surveys and interviews have also proven to be valuable tools. In one such study, the authors looked to a cross-site analysis where community-oriented policing was implemented in six cities (Baltimore, Maryland; Oakland, California; Birmingham, Alabama; Madison, Wisconsin; Houston, Texas; Newark, New Jersey), while other cities were designated as control cities where no community-oriented policing programs were implemented (Skogan 1994, 167–181). Through the use of survey/interviews in a pre-test/post-test study design, with a ten-month time lapse, the evaluation revealed mixed results, although fear of crime generally decreased and police service was considered to be increased overall (Skogan 1994, 167–181). Additionally, one study gauging citizens' responses to community-oriented policing utilized both surveys and interviews and was conducted in Cleveland, Ohio, which has utilized the police mini-station program as a vehicle for implementing community-oriented policing. Through a survey mailing, with follow-up interviews, they found "a great deal of support for the program, considerable satisfaction with the performance of the officers and a desire to have the program expanded" (Kratcoski, Dukes, and Gustavson 1995, 199–211). In general, both the police and the community have favorable responses to community-oriented policing, that tend to increase over the longevity of the programs.

Case Studies

One other research method that has been utilized to evaluate community-oriented policing programs, as well as police officer and citizen attitudes toward the systemic approach, has been the case study. Case studies are a method of research evaluation that tracks the implementation of a program of the response of people over time, by recording the events as they occur and looking for common denominators and indicators that indicate a program's success or failure, or in the case of people's perceptions, favorable or unfavorable attitudes. In one analysis of a problem-oriented policing program implemented in San Diego, California, which utilized the Eck and Spelman "SARA" model, they tracked sixteen problem-oriented policing cases over a six-month period (Capowich and Roehl 1994, 127–146). The study found that 69 percent of the cases (eleven out of sixteen) were deemed successful.

The case study format has also been utilized in evaluating police officers' perceptions of community-oriented policing as a policing strategy. One such case study attempted to determine whether or not community-oriented policing was "here to stay" or "on the way out" and was conducted in the following six cities: Santa Barbara, California; Las Vegas, Nevada; Savannah, Georgia; Newport News, Virginia; Edmonton, Canada; and Philadelphia, Pennsylvania (Weisel and Eck 1994, 53–72). The overall findings of the study, controlling for years of service, educational level, race, and sex, concluded that the majority of officers believed community-oriented policing was "here to stay" (Weisel and Eck 1994, 53–72). The advantage of case studies such as these is that they provide much more information than a survey or interview and they are qualitative in nature. A disadvantage to this type of research is often inconsistent findings due to a variety of perceptions on the part of the researchers.

COP IN ACTION

REQUIREMENTS FOR SUCCESSFUL EXPERIMENTATION

First, if experimentation is to be successful in a criminal justice agency, it must be the result of sincere collaboration between agency personnel and researchers. The conception, implementation, and conduct of an experiment is, most often, a time-consuming set of activities which departs from the routine business of an agency. Unless agency personnel are deeply committed to knowing what works, and aware that answering questions requires considerable effort on their behalf, experiments will collapse under the pressures of business as usual.

Second, subjects or areas involved in an experiment should be selected randomly. Random selection eliminates biases in the selection of samples of subjects or areas that may distort the findings of the experiment.

Third, the experimental group that receives the treatment should be compared with a randomly selected control group which does not receive the treatment. By comparing differences between the two groups at the end of the experimental period, researchers will be able to determine the effects of the treatment.

Fourth, relevant data testing the effect of the treatment should be collected immediately before the initiation of the experiment and immediately after its termination in the experimental and control groups. Collection of data in this way allows for comparison both within the groups and between the groups. Moreover, in social experiments it is generally required that careful observation be made of the program's operation over time. It is often the case that experimental programs either function differently than expected or less efficiently. Under such circumstances the meaning of differences, or lack of them, between experimental and control group may result from improper implementation of the new program rather than from the effects of the experiment.

Finally, evaluators should be independent of program managers. Program managers, often deeply committed to the success of programs, can unintentionally destroy the integrity of experiments. Moreover, the credibility of experiments is enhanced when evaluators are independent of program operations.

Police tactics are being revised on the basis of systematically asking and answering the question "What works?" Police are not alone in this. Experimentation is being used throughout the criminal justice system to improve the quality of criminal justice practice. It is a sign of the growing professionalization of the field.

Source: Kelling, George L. "What Works—Research and the Police." *National Institute of Justice: Crime File Study Guide*. Washington, D.C.: National Institute of Justice, 1988.

Various Methods

Expanding beyond just the use of surveys and case studies, many studies will utilize other methodologies, as well as multiple methodologies, to verify their findings. One community-oriented policing program known as Operation Cul-De-Sac under a Total Community Policing model in the Los Angeles area, which utilized barriers to create geographical communities, derived its findings from "a variety of official and unofficial data sources (i.e., Part I crime data), CRASH Unit (Community Resources Against Street Hoodlums) gang intelligence information, community surveys and police officer interviews" (Lasley, Vernon, and Dery 1995, 51–67). The study found "that imposed community boundaries can serve as a vital point of reference for effective police-community partnerships and the regeneration of lasting informal social control networks" (Lasley, Vernon, and Dery 1995, 51–67). Another community-oriented policing project known as "Community Opportunities Program for Youth (COPY Kids) was an attempt to reach out to local youths at risk of abusing alcohol or illegal drugs or of joining a criminal gang" in Spokane, Washington during the summer of 1992 (Thurman, Giacomazzi, and Bogen 1993, 554–564). The kids performed community work, visited various businesses, and spoke with the police officers on a variety of subjects. Through the use of direct observation, group interviews, and survey research, the study concluded that "program recipients...benefited from the community service they performed and did" and that "COPY Kids was held in high regards by the parents or guardians of participating youth," and "positive effects on COPY kids staff also were noted" (Thurman, Giacomazzi, and Bogen 1993).

In the evaluation of two additional cities, Aurora, Illinois and Joliet, Illinois, "several field methods were employed, including in-person interviews with key participants, focus group interviews, observations, and a comprehensive review of documents." The study concluded that a bureaucratic police department will have a difficult time with the implementation process, that it is important to emphasize a departmental-wide implementation, that participatory management can be successful, that the organization's commitment to bureaucracy is inversely related to the speed of implementing community-oriented policing, and that although there is no right or wrong way to implement community-oriented policing, a change in the style of management and decentralization must occur (Wilkinson and Rosenbaum, 1994, p.110-126).

TABLE 12.3   EVALUATING THE POLICE

Goals	Performance Indicators
Doing justice, or "treating citizens in an appropriate manner based upon their conduct."	Nature and type of patrolling strategy, number of traffic tickets issued, crimes cleared, analysis of who calls the police, quality of investigations, cases released because of police misconduct, citizen complaints, law suits filed, and results of dispositions, and officer-initiated encounters.
Promoting secure communities, or "enabling citizens to enjoy a life without fear of crime or victimization."	The existence of programs and resources allocated to crime prevention programs, time and money dedicated to problem-solving, rewards, monitoring of police, degree of public trust in the police, fear of crime, and home and business security checks by the police.
Restoring crime victims, by "restoring victims' lives and welfare as much as possible."	Number of contacts with victims after initial call for assistance, types of assistance provided to victims, including information, comfort, transportation, and referrals to other agencies.
Promoting noncriminal options, by "developing strong relationships with individuals in the community."	The existence of programs and resources allocated to strengthening relationships between the police and the community, including traditional community relations programs, school programs, storefront operations and officer contact with citizens.

Source: Alpert, Geoffrey and Mark H. Moore. "Measuring Police Performance in the New Paradigm of Policing." In *Performance Measures for the Criminal Justice System: Discussion Papers from the BJS-Princeton Project* ed. John J. Diluilo, Jr. et al. Washington, D.C.: Bureau of Justice Statistics, October 1993.

In sum, while surveys are the predominant method of choice, which includes mail surveys, telephone surveys, and interview surveys, followed by case studies, there are other evaluation methods to consider. Program evaluations can be conducted through the use of combining such methods as mail surveys and follow-up interview surveys or through such innovative techniques as group interviews or the direct observation of participants. The use of documents, both official and unofficial, can also enhance the evaluation process, as can surveys of the environment conducted by the police or community members. As there are multiple types of program evaluation methods available to researchers, it is important that a variety of these be explored. Police departments should seek out individuals who are adept at performing these types of evaluations and should consult a variety of publications concerned with the evaluation research methods.

CONCLUSION

The use of evaluative research is an integral part of community-oriented policing. As this systemic approach is largely about reassessing traditional police methods and looking to new and innovative methods of delivering police services, the use of evaluative research to determine what works and what does not should become a common occurrence within community-oriented police departments. As the implementation process for the systemic approach entails an incremental concept to ensure the long-term viability of the policy, this provides a complementary method for program evaluation findings to be integrated into the various programs. As community-oriented policing continues to evolve, program evaluations allow the police to learn from past successes and failures, of not only the programs implemented, but how well the community and line police officers have been involved in, and responses to, the systemic approach. In addition, continued program evaluation research also allows for past research mistakes to not be repeated and for successful research methods to be frequently utilized as part of a continual evaluation process.

All of the evaluation research should be based on the five key criteria that should be the fundamental roots of community-oriented policing: effectiveness, efficiency, equity, accountability, and authority. Community-oriented policing, in whatever form it takes through the various programs implemented in support of the systemic approach, should all be based on these five criteria and this in turn should be how they are evaluated. The programs must be effective in addressing crime and order maintenance problems. The programs must be efficient in their use of police resources. They must be equitable, delivered and available for the entire community and not for just a small homogenous group. They must hold management, line officers, and the community accountable for the programs that they implement. Finally, they must transfer authority into the hands of the proper people, whether this consists of line officers or the community, in order to accomplish the goals dictated under the systemic approach.

In assessing the success and failure of community-oriented policing programs, based on these five criteria, program evaluation research methods should be employed. Both process evaluations and impact assessments should be conducted on a continual basis for long periods of time in order to fully determine whether or not a program should be considered successful or a failure. These evaluations should attempt to assess not only attitudes and opinions, but behavior, experiences, and characteristics as well. Methods such as surveys, whether through the mail, by telephone, or through interviews, are helpful tools in making this determination. Additional methods that may be utilized include case studies, group interviews, and the use of official and unofficial documents. In addition, it is beneficial to utilize not just one, but multiple methods for a more accurate assessment. Police departments that plan to conduct evaluations should seek out assistance from both inside and outside the department. They should also review the wide variety of publications detailing program evaluation research prior to starting.

THE BILL OF RIGHTS

The first ten Amendments of the Constitution, known as the Bill of Rights, were ratified effective December 15, 1791.

Amendment I

Congress shall make no law respecting an establishment of religion, or prohibiting the free exercise thereof; or abridging the freedom of speech, or of the press, or the right of the people peaceably to assemble, and to petition the Government for a redress of grievances.

Amendment II

A well regulated Militia, being necessary to the security of a free State, the right of the people to keep and bear Arms, shall not be infringed.

Amendment III

No Soldier shall, in time of peace be quartered in any house, without the consent of the Owner, nor in time of war, but in a manner to be prescribed by law.

Amendment IV

The right of the people to be secure in their persons, houses, papers, and effects, against unreasonable searches and seizures, shall not be violated, and no Warrants shall issue, but upon probable cause, supported by Oath or affirmation, and particularly describing the place to be searched, and the persons or things to be seized.

Amendment V

No person shall be held to answer for a capital, or otherwise infamous crime, unless on a presentment or indictment of a Grand Jury, except in cases arising in the land or naval forces, or in the Militia, when in actual service in time of War or public danger; nor shall any person be subject for the same offense to be twice put in jeopardy of life or limb, nor shall be compelled in any criminal case to be a witness against himself, nor be deprived of life, liberty, or property, without due process of law; nor shall private property be taken for public use without just compensation.

Amendment VI

In all criminal prosecutions, the accused shall enjoy the right to a speedy and public trial, by an impartial jury of the State and district wherein the crime shall have been committed; which district shall have been previously ascertained by law, and to be informed of the nature and cause of the accusation; to be confronted with the witnesses against him; to have compulsory process for obtaining witnesses in his favor, and to have the assistance of counsel for his defense.

Amendment VII

In Suits at common law, where the value in controversy shall exceed twenty dollars, the right of trial by jury shall be preserved, and no fact tried by a jury shall be otherwise re-examined in any Court of the United States, than according to the rules of the common law.

Amendment VIII

Excessive bail shall not be required, nor excessive fines imposed, nor cruel and unusual punishment inflicted.

Amendment IX

The enumeration in the Constitution of certain rights shall not be construed to deny or disparage others retained by the people.

Amendment X

The powers not delegated to the United States by the Constitution, nor prohibited by it to the States, are reserved to the States respectively, or to the people.

Amendment XIV

The Fourteenth Amendment was ratified July 9, 1868.

Section 1. All persons born or naturalized in the United States and subject to the jurisdiction thereof, are citizens of the United States and of the State wherein they reside. No State shall make or enforce any law which shall abridge the privileges or immunities of citizens of the United States; nor shall any State deprive any person of life, liberty, or property, without due process of law; nor deny to any person within its jurisdiction the equal protection of the laws.

REFERENCES

Bowers, W. J. and J. H. Hirsch. "The Impact of Foot Patrol Staffing on Crime and Disorder in Boston: An Unmet Promise." *American Journal of Police* 6, no. 1 (1987): 17–44.

Brown, Lee P. and Mary Ann Wycoff. "Policing Houston: Reducing Fear and Improving Service." *Crime & Delinquency* 33, no. 1 (January 1987): 71–89.

Bureau of Justice Assistance. *A Police Guide to Surveying Citizens and Their Environment.* Washington, D.C.: Bureau of Justice Assistance, October 1993.

Bureau of Justice Assistance. *Neighborhood-Oriented Policing in Rural Communities: A Program Planning Guide.* Washington, D.C.: Bureau of Justice Assistance, August 1994a.

Bureau of Justice Assistance. *Understanding Community Policing: A Framework for Action.* Washington, D.C.: Bureau of Justice Assistance, August 1994b.

Capowich, George E. and Janice A. Roehl. "Problem-Oriented Policing: Actions and Effectiveness in San Diego." In *The Challenge of Community Policing: Testing the Promises,* ed. Dennis P. Rosenbaum. Thousand Oaks, CA.: SAGE Publications Inc., 1994.

Cordner, Gary W. "Fear of Crime and the Police: An Evaluation of a Fear-Reduction Strategy." *Journal of Police Science and Administration* 14, no. 3 (1988): 223–233.

———. "A Problem-Oriented Approach to Community-Oriented Policing." In *Community Policing: Rhetoric or Reality* ed. Jack R. Greene and Stephen D. Mastrofski. New York,: Praeger Publishers, 1988.

——————. "Foot Patrol Without Community Policing: Law and Order in Public Housing." *The Challenge of Community Policing: Testing the Promises,* ed. Dennis P. Rosenbaum. Thousand Oaks, CA.: SAGE Publications Inc., 1994.

Cordner, Gary W. and Michael A. Jones. "The Effects of Supplementary Foot Patrol on Fear of Crime and Attitudes Toward the Police." In *Issues in Community Policing,* ed. Peter C. Kratcoski and Duane Dukes. Cincinnati: Academy of Criminal Justice Sciences and Anderson Publishing Company, 1995.

Dempsey, John S. *Policing: An Introduction to Law Enforcement.* St. Paul, Minn.: West Publishing Company, 1994.

Eck, John E. *Solving Crimes: The Investigation of Burglary and Robbery.* Washington, D.C.: Police Executive Research Forum, 1982.

Eck, John E. and Dennis P. Rosenbaum. "The New Police Order: Effectiveness, Equity, and Efficiency in Community Policing." In *The Challenge of Community Policing: Testing the Promises.* ed. Dennis P. Rosenbaum. Thousand Oaks, CA.: SAGE Publications, Inc., 1994.

Eck, John E. and William Spelman. *Problem Solving: Problem-Oriented Policing in Newport News.* Washington, D.C.: Police Executive Research Forym, 1987.

Esbenson, F. "Foot Patrol: Of What Value?" *American Journal of Police.* vol. 6 no. 1 (1987): 45–66.

Goldstein, Herman. *Problem-Oriented Policing.* New York: McGraw Hill Publishing. Co., 1990.

Greene, Jack R. and Ralph B. Taylor. "Community-Based Policing and Foot Patrol: Issues of Theory and Evaluation." In *Community Policing: Rhetoric or Reality,* ed. Jack R. Greene and Stephen D. Mastrofski. New York: Praeger Publishers, 1988.

Greenwood, Peter W. and Joan Petersilia. *The Criminal Investigation Process—Volume I: Summary and Policy Implications.* Santa Monica, CA.: Rand Corporation, 1975.

Greenwood, Peter W., Joan Petersilia, and J. Chaiken. *The Criminal Investigation Process.* Lexington, MA: Heath Publishing, 1977.

Hornick, Joseph P., Barry N. Leighton, and Barbara A. Burrows. "Evaluating Community Policing: The Edmonton Project." In *Evaluating Justice: Canadian Policies and Programs,* ed. Julian V. Roberts and Joe Hudson. Toronto, Canada: Thompson Educational Publishing, Inc., 1993.

Kansas City Police Department. *Response Time Analysis: Volume II-Part I, Crime Analysis.* Washington, D.C.: U.S. Government Printing Office, 1980.

Kelling, George L., Tony Pate, Suzane Dieckman, and Charles E. Brown. *The Kansas City Preventive Patrol Experiment: A Summary Report.* Washington, D.C.: Police Foundation, 1974.

Kelling, George L., Tony Pate, Suzane Dieckman, and Charles E. Brown. *The Kansas City Preventive Patrol Experiment: A Technical Report.* Washington, D.C.: Police Foundation, 1975.

Kratcoski, Peter C., Duane Dukes, and Sandra Gustavson. "An Analysis of Citizens' Responses to Community Policing in a Large Midwestern City." In *Issues in Community Policing,* ed. Peter C. Kratcoski and Duane Dukes. Cincinnati: The Academy of Criminal Justice Sciences and Anderson Publishing Company, 1995.

Kratcoski, Peter C. and Susan B. Noonan. "An Assessment of Police Officer's Acceptance of Community Policing." In *Issues in Community Policing,* ed. Peter C. Kratcoski and Duane Dukes. Cincinnati: Academy of Criminal Justice Sciences, Anderson Publishing Company, 1995.

Larson, Richard C. "What Happened to Patrol Operations in Kansas City? A Review of the Kansas City Preventive Patrol Experiment." *Journal of Criminal Justice* 3, no. 4, (1975): 267–297.

Lasley, James R., Robert L. Vernon, and George M. Dery III. "Operation Cul-De-Sac: LAPD's "Total Community" Policing Program." In *Issues in Community Policing,* ed. Peter C. Kratcoski and Duane Dukes. Cincinnati: Academy of Criminal Justice Sciences and Anderson Publishing Company, 1995.

Lewis, R. G., Jack R. Greene, and Steven M. Edwards. *Special Police Units in Michigan: An Evaluation*. East Lansing, Mich.: Criminal Justice Systems Center, Michigan State University, 1977.

Lurigio, Arthur J. and Dennis P. Rosenbaum. "The Impact of Community Policing on Police Personnel: A Review of the Literature." In *The Challenge of Community Policing: Testing the Promises,* ed. Dennis P. Rosenbaum. Thousand Oaks, CA.: SAGE Publications Inc., 1994.

Lurigio, Arthur J. and Wesley G. Skogan. "Winning the Hearts and Minds of Police Officers: An Assessment of Staff Perceptions of Community Policing in Chicago." *Crime & Delinquency* 40, no. 3 (July 1994): 315–330.

Maxfield, Michael G. and Earl Babbie. *Research Methods for Criminal Justice and Criminology*. Belmont, CA.: Wadsworth Publishing Company, 1995.

McElroy, Jerome E., Colleen A. Cosgrove, and Susan Sadd. *Community Policing: The CPOP in New York*. Newbury Park, CA.: SAGE Publications, 1993.

Miller, Linda S. and Karen M. Hess. *Community Policing: Theory and Practice*. St. Paul, Minn.: West Publishing Company, 1994.

Oettmeier, Timothy and Lee P. Brown. "Developing a Neighborhood-Oriented Policing Style." In *Community Policing: Rhetoric or Reality?* ed. Jack R. Greene and Stephen D. Mastrofski. New York: Praeger Publishers, 1988.

Pate, Antony M. "Experimenting with Foot Patrol: the Newark Experience." In *Community Crime Prevention: Does it Work?* ed. Dennis P. Rosenbaum. Beverly Hills: SAGE Publications Inc., 1986.

————. "Community-Oriented Policing in Baltimore." *In Police and Policing: Contemporary Issues,* ed. D. J. Kenney. New York: Praeger Publishers, 1989.

Pate, Antony, Mary Ann Wycoff, Wesley G. Skogan, and Lawrence W. Sherman. *Reducing Fear of Crime in Houston and Newark: A Summary Report*. Washington, D.C.: Police Foundation, 1986.

Peak, Kenneth J. *Justice Administration: Police, Courts, and Corrections Management* Englewood Cliffs, N.J.: Prentice Hall, Inc., 1995.

Rosenbaum, Dennis P. "Community Crime Prevention: A Review and Synthesis of the Literature." *Justice Quarterly.* 5 no. 3 (September 1988): 323–395.

Rosenbaum, Dennis P., Sandy Yeh, and Deanna L. Wilkinson. "Impact of Community Policing on Police Personnel: A Quasi- Experimental Test." *Crime & Delinquency* 40, no. 3 (July 1994): 331–353.

Schnelle, John F., Robert E. Kirchner, Jr., J. R. Lawler, and M. Patrick McNees. "Social Evaluation Research: The Evaluation of Two Police Patrol Strategies." *Journal of Applied Behavioral Analysis,* no. 8 (1975): 232–240.

Scott, Eric J. *Calls or Service: Citizen Demand and Initial Police Response*. Washington, D.C.: U.S. Government Printing Office, 1981.

Skogan, Wesley G. "The Impact of Community Policing on Neighborhood Residents: A Cross-Site Analysis." In *The Challenges of Community Policing: Testing the Promises,* ed. Dennis P. Rosenbaum. Thousand Oaks, CA.: SAGE Publications, Inc., 1994.

Spelman, William and Dale K. Brown. *Calling the Police: Citizen Reporting of Serious Crime.* Washington, D.C.: U.S. Government Printing Office, 1984.

Sullivan, John L. *Introduction of Police Science.* 3rd ed. New York: McGraw-Hill, Inc., 1977.

Thurman, Quint C., Andrew Giacomazzi, and Phil Bogen. "Research Note: Cops, Kids, and Community Policing–An Assessment of a Community Policing Demonstration Project." *Crime & Delinquency* 39, no. 4 (October 1993): 554–564.

Uchida, Craig D., Brian Forst, and Sampson O. Annan. *Modern Policing and the Control of Illegal Drugs: Testing New Strategies in Two American Cities.* Washington, D.C.: National Institute of Justice/Police Foundation, 1992.

Wagner, W.F. *An Evaluation of a Police Patrol Experiment.* Pullman, Wash.: Washington State University, 1978.

Weisel, Deborah Lamm and John E. Eck. "Toward a Practical Approach to Organizational Change: Community Policing Initiatives in Six Cities." In *The Challenge of Community Policing: Testing the Promises,* ed. Dennis P. Rosenbaum. Thousand Oaks, CA.: SAGE Publications Inc., 1994.

Wiatrowski, Michael D. "Community Policing in Delray Beach." In *Issues in Community Policing,* ed. Peters C. Kratcoski and Duane Dukes. Cincinnati: Academy of Criminal Justice Sciences and Anderson Publishing Company, 1995.

Wilkinson, Deanna L. and Dennis P. Rosenbaum. "The Effects of Organizational Structure on Community Policing: A Comparison of Two Cities." In *The Challenge of Community Policing: Testing the Promises,* ed. Dennis P. Rosenbaum. Thousand Oaks, CA.: SAGE Publications Inc., 1994.

Williams, Hubert and Antony M. Pate. "Returning to First Principles: Reducing the Fear of Crime in Newark." *Crime & Delinquency* 33, no. 1 (January 1987): 53–70.

Wilson, Deborah G. and Susan F. Bennett. "Officers' Response to Community Policing: Variations on a Theme." *Crime & Delinquency* 40, no. 3 (July 1994): 354–370.

Wilson, James Q. *Thinking About Crime.* New York: Vintage Books, 1975.

————. *Bureaucracy.* New York: Basic Books, 1989.

Wycoff, Mary Ann. "The Benefits of Community Policing: Evidence and Conjecture." In *Community Policing: Rhetoric or Reality,* ed. Jack R. Greene and Stephen D. Mastrofski. New York: Praeger Publishers, 1988.

CHAPTER 13

Caveats

You must first enable the government to control the governed; and in the next place oblige it to control itself.

-James Madison-

It would be rather naive to believe that community-oriented policing, as policy, as philosophy, and in its programmatic format, will be implemented without any difficulty and in such a manner that every police department in the nation will immediately sign on. We live, rather, in a world full of uncertainties and no individual or group can adequately predict what problems will arise out of a new policy. As policy, community-oriented policing has been debated and discussed for over fifteen years and multiple scholars and practitioners have recognized a multitude of problems (see Bayley 1988; Brown 1989; Goldstein 1987; Joseph 1994; Riechers and Roberg 1990; Rush 1992; Skolnick and Bayley 1988). Some of these pre-designated problems have proven to be false rhetoric of institutions resisting change, while others have proven to be well-predicted problems that remain without solutions.

In addition to the predicted and deliberated problems revolving around community-oriented policing, there are also those problems arising out of new policy implementation. New policy creates problems. It is the hope that through reliable and valid evaluation research that these problems will be exposed, addressed, and dealt with in a manner tantamount with the original policy. However, as is often the case with public policy, new policy begets more policy. As we learn and identify that which was unrevealed to us, and that which could not or simply was not predicted, we must address these problems anew.

Police Officers from the Albany Police Department, Albany, New York, work with local youth to improve their basketball game and jump shots. (Courtesy of the Albany Police Dept., Albany, New York.)

This mere fact should not be a problem in and of itself, but the understanding that new policy will create new problems must be understood in order for the scholars to explore new areas in their research, but more importantly for the practitioner implementing community-oriented policing to effectively and efficiently deal with the new problems as they arise.

"CRIME FILES"

FAMILIES AND CRIME—PART 14

DRINKING AND CRIME—PART 25

JOBS AND CRIME—PART 32

These three editions of the "Crime Files," hosted by James Q. Wilson, provide an overview of three key causes and contributing factors to crime. Understanding how each of these impacts on crime can assist the police in developing community-oriented policing programs to assist in alleviating local crime in the local neighborhoods.

As it is most difficult to discuss problems that have not yet occurred, it is then the focus of this chapter to discuss and debate those problems which are currently known. The exposure of past problems with community-oriented policing are not revealed and detailed to place blame on past participants in the systemic approach, nor are they detailed to discourage current and future police departments from implementing community-oriented policing. Rather, they are detailed because they present a sort of "caveat emptor" to this new paradigm in policing. They are essentially details that articulate that the "buyers" of the systemic approach "beware" of what they are attempting to accomplish. Community-oriented policing is a method of policing that holds many benefits in its implementation, but also hides many dangers of false hope. Exposing past problems allows police practitioners to be aware of these false hopes and to deal with them effectively as they are exposed to them in a variety of situations.

Many of the key problems have been addressed throughout the previous chapters, but a recapitulation can do no harm to understand the problems that community-oriented policing will face during the implementation process. The main areas of focus that can be extracted thus far include the problem with defining what is meant by community-oriented policing, All of the problems are inherent within the changing role of the police, community, management, and organization, as well as many of the problems found within the methods and practices of evaluations. All of these issues should be of key concern for any police department moving toward the systemic approach because they all revolve around the implementation process. Each of these distinct categories lie at some point in the implementation process, and each of these categories can bring with it a host of problems as a result of moving a police department from the traditional to the community oriented.

A broader category of caveats that exist with community-oriented policing may be as a result of the implementation process either directly or indirectly, but can also occur ancillary to the systemic approach. The issues of concern fall into five distinct categories: 1) the limited resources and cost, 2) police corruption, 3) politics, 4) pseudo community-oriented policing programs, and

5) the paradox of the future. The larger discussion will concentrate on the first three categories, while the fourth will be debated between this chapter and the next, and the final category will be explored in the next chapter detailing the future.

IMPLEMENTATION CAVEATS

The process of implementing the systemic approach to policing has focused on many of the obstacles that practitioners will have to face and overcome in order to achieve the final stage and the ultimate goal: community-oriented policing. Prior to even beginning the process, one difficulty that continues to arise is the lack of a clear definition of community-oriented policing, describing what is meant in both philosophical and practical terms. An organization cannot avoid problems if the organization has no conceptual understanding of what is meant by the term community-oriented policing. Additionally, the organization will confront multiple problems if it does not take into account the changing role of the police officer and the new role the community must play in accomplishing all of the tenets of the systemic approach. It is also imperative that the style of management and the organization itself change to complement community-oriented policing, or the implementation process will bear witness to multiple problems that will not, and cannot, derive solutions without these critical changes. And finally, as previously explored, the use of evaluations must be integrated into the implementation process, to ensure the incremental process proceeds without continuing programs that fail to produce effective, efficient, and equitable results.

The first implementation caveat arises in the lack of a definitive definition. It should be a foregone conclusion that an organization cannot implement a policy without a clear understanding of what the policy entails. The first step in achieving this understanding is through a definition of the concept. In the case of community-oriented policing, despite many years of scholarly research and practical application, no consensus has been reached as to a standard definition (Bayley 1994; Goldstein 1990; Greene and Mastrofski 1988; Murphy 1988; Oliver 1992; Rosenbaum 1994; Rush 1992). It has been stated that community-oriented policing means many different things to many different people (Bayley 1994). Much evidence supports this which is revealed through the writings of the scholars in the criminal justice/criminology fields, as well as through the various methods police departments have utilized in implementing community-oriented policing. However, despite the vast differences articulated, there are in fact more similarities in both the academic and practical perspectives of community-oriented policing than there are differences. By analyzing the similarities, one can derive a consensus and hence a definition to articulate what is meant by the term community-oriented policing. Once this consensus is shared and is understood as defining the term, policy can be articulated and programs implemented with a clearer understanding and, hopefully, with fewer problems.

The second key area of concern when implementing community-oriented policing is the role of the police. It is recognized that the role the police have traditionally played in society is dramatically different under the systemic approach to policing. The change that is called for in community-oriented policing is not necessarily limited to changing the way police deliver their services, but is instead one of actually changing the police subculture (Goldstein 1990; Reuss-Iianni and Iianni 1983; Skolnick and Bayley 1988). The police will most likely demonstrate the typical reluctance that accompanies any change, but as a byproduct of the police subculture, it is widely believed that there will be an even stronger resistance to change (Anderson 1988; Brown 1989; Dolan 1994; Skolnick and Fyfe 1995; Sparrow 1988). While some of this resistance to change is thought to originate from the police officers themselves, some believe that there will be organized resistance by way of the police unions (Rush 1992; Skolnick and Bayley 1986; Skolnick and Bayley 1988). In either case, police management must take the police subculture and the possibility of a resistance to change into consideration when implementing community-oriented policing, in order to avoid many of the problems inherent with the implementation process.

Another caveat that exists when discussing the police role in community-oriented policing is the ability to fail. The traditional practice of policing leaves little room for the police to attempt new and innovative ideas because there is no freedom to fail. Under community-oriented policing, the police officers must be afforded the opportunity to try different approaches to policing and in the event the method does not prove effective, they must not be reprimanded or receive a negative evaluation for their failure. Rather, they must be encouraged to continue to address the problem, develop alternative solutions, and implement them until a problem is considered solved or alleviated. Essentially, the police must receive not only the resources, but the support, allowing them to accomplish the new objectives under a community-oriented approach to policing (Eck et al. 1987a; Eck and Spelman 1987b; Meese 1993; Rush 1992; Skolnick and Bayley 1986; Skolnick and Bayley 1988). Without this support from the organization and management, the problem that the systemic approach will face is ultimately total failure.

Finally, and critically important to the community-oriented policing implementation process are the changing qualifications for police officers. As the police department moves from a traditional style of policing to the community-oriented policing approach, the necessary skills for a police officer to function and perform his or her everyday duties changes. The ability to communicate in public, to organize meetings, to analyze problems and create alternative solutions, all become additions to the job requirements. It is therefore imperative that the police department considers a change in the job description for the position of "police officer" that closer reflects the community-oriented policing approach and then hires accordingly (Anderson 1988; Dolan 1994; Riechers and Roberg 1990; Roberg 1994). Additionally, the police department must also decide whether to make higher education a requirement for the job position (Carter, Sapp, and Stephens 1989; Meese 1993; Radelet and

Police officers from the Oceanside Police Department,
Oceanside, California, pictured at a local "Surf Event" in honor of
the community's youth. (Courtesy of Oceanside Police Dept.,
Oceanside, California.)

Carter 1994). It is critical that these decisions be addressed early on in the
planning stages of community-oriented policing, in order to avoid problems
further down the road.

As with the police and their changing role, there is also a changing role in
regards to the community, which is the third area of concern in the implementation process. The community must become involved in community-oriented
policing in order for it to succeed to its greatest potential. There are most
assuredly a host of problems associated with the community's role in community-
oriented policing. These problems range from police departments leaving the
community out of the systemic approach (Goldstein 1987; Mastrofski 1988;
Rosenbaum 1988), and the inability to understand exactly what a "community" is
and how it is defined (Buerger 1994; Grinc 1994; Manning 1988; Riechers and
Roberg 1990; Skolnick and Bayley 1988), to the community not understanding its
role in community-oriented policing (Eck and Spelman 1987a; Goldstein 1987;
Grinc 1994), expecting too much from the programs (Skolnick and Bayley 1988),
and demonstrating high levels of apathy for both policy and programs (Grinc
1994; Ross 1995). All of these can be effectively dealt with by including all members of the community in the implementation process, from the preplanning
stages to the decision-making processes included within the three components
of community-oriented policing. Whether the community is a willing or non-
willing participant in the planning and implementation of community-oriented

policing, they must never be excluded from having the opportunity to become involved and they must consistently be kept informed of the methods utilized to address both the criminal and order maintenance issues a community faces. The goals of inclusion, communication, and demonstrating the realistic capabilities of the police should alleviate the majority of problems predicted to occur when dealing with the role of the community in community-oriented policing.

The fourth area of concern lies intrinsically in the organizational structure of the police department and in the related management style. Although the implementation of the three components that make up community-oriented policing are necessary for the policy implementation, it is imperative that the police department support these components through the decentralization of the police department. While the programs may thrive for some time without decentralizing the police department, a host of problems will surface because a centralized organizational structure will not support the goals and tenets of community-oriented policing, nor will it support the line officers, nor will it support the initiatives of the community. It is then critical to community-oriented policing that the organizational structure decentralize (Eck and Spelman 1987a; Eck and Spelman 1987b; Geller 1991; Goldstein 1987; Greene, Bergman, and McLaughlin 1994; Rosenbaum and Lurigio 1994; Rush 1992; Skogan 1994; Wilkinson and Rosenbaum 1994). It must not only decentralize by structure, but by geography and personnel as well, in order to fully implement community-oriented policing and to be completely successful in the endeavor. The police officers, who will bear the brunt of implementing the systemic approach, must be afforded the autonomy and the decision-making ability to handle problems at their level. If the police department retains any centralization, it will constrict the line officers' capabilities in performing their duties under the community-oriented approach, and it will create problems from a lack of support and growing frustration with their new role.

As community-oriented policing is a systemic approach to policing, there must be changes in every facet of the organizational structure. As a police department moves from the traditional style of policing to the community oriented, everything from recruiting (Metchik and Winton 1995; Moore 1992; Trojanowicz and Bucqueroux 1990a; Trojanowicz and Bucqueroux 1994), to training (Joseph 1994, Kelling, Wasserman, and Williams 1988; McLaughlin and Donahue 1995; Moore 1992; Worsnop 1993), to performance evaluations (Bureau of Justice Assistance, 1994; Eck and Spelman 1987a; Joseph 1994; Kelling, Wasserman, and Williams 1988; Manning 1988; Roberg 1994; Silverman 1995; Skolnick and Bayley 1988), to promotions (Eck and Spelman 1987a; Trojanowicz and Bucqueroux 1994) must change to complement the new philosophy, policy, and programs. No aspect of the police department should remain static during the implementation process and every facet of the police department must embody the philosophy of community-oriented policing.

Just as important in the process of moving a traditional police department to that of community-oriented policing is the necessity to not only change the organizational structure, but the management style as well. All of the previous styles that the police have utilized, ranging from the paramilitary to the bureaucratic model of policing, are not conducive to the systemic approach. It is important that police departments move toward a less authoritative/bureaucratic approach to management, either moving toward a corporate strategy (Andrews 1980; Freeman 1984; Moore and Trojanowicz 1988; Radelet and Carter 1994) or toward implementing Total Quality Management (TQM) (Couper 1991; Osborne and Gaebler 1992; Radelet and Carter 1994; Wycoff and Skogan 1994). In both of these cases, the style of management is conducive to all of the values and goals inherent within community-oriented policing as well as complementing the demand for decentralization. Without changing management style, the paramilitary and bureaucratic methods will cause extensive problems with the systemic approach to policing. The line police officers will not have the decision-making capabilities that are necessary at their level, the community will have no input into the process, thus negating the "community" aspects of community-oriented policing, and the decentralization of the organizational structure will not have a management style that is complementary to its purpose. Lacking any changes in the management style, community-oriented policing will fail to evolve beyond the confines of its programmatic application.

The last caveat with the implementation process resides in the many problems with evaluations. As was detailed in Chapter 12, it is critical that an incremental style of implementation be utilized when moving a police department from the traditional to the community oriented, allowing time for evaluations to be conducted, results obtained and interpreted, and changes made to the various programs. This prevents a multitude of problems from developing when a police department changes too quickly and fails to determine if the programs are effective, efficient, and equitable. Reliable and valid evaluations are critical to the success of community-oriented policing.

It is clear that the majority of problems police practitioners face occur during the implementation process. At every stage of implementing community-oriented policing, from planning to the full systemic approach, problems occur on a consistent basis. However, if the philosophy of policing, embodied in the systemic approach, is implemented in an incremental fashion, there should be ample time to make corrections to the various programs and implement changes. Incrementalism is the fail-safe device for bad policy and bad programs. As long as the problems are identified and alternative methods created and implemented, a healthy development of the philosophy, policy, and programs of community-oriented policing should become well entrenched in the daily functioning of the police department.

ANCILLARY CAVEATS

There are other caveats that both scholar and practitioner are concerned with in the systemic approach to policing. Although these problems are not directly related to the implementation problems discussed previously, they are ancillary issues that can quickly become insurmountable problems. It must not be taken for granted with the implementation of community-oriented policing that these problems will occur, but rather the predicted potential is high. A police chief implementing the systemic approach should then be aware of these types of problems, give them the consideration they deserve, and watch for them as potential problems that could detract or destroy all of the benefits derived from community-oriented policing. These issues consist of the problems of limited resources and the cost of implementing community-oriented policing, the potential for police corruption, and the negative interference of politics. Additional concerns are pseudo community-oriented policing police departments and what the future holds for the systemic approach.

The issue of limited resources and the excessive costs are often roadblocks to the implementation of community-oriented policing. The literature is filled with debate and concern over this particular issue (see Anderson 1988; Brown 1989; Kelling 1988; Moore 1992; Ross 1995; Sacco and Kennedy 1996; Silverman 1995; Skolnick and Bayley 1986; Skolnick and Bayley, 1988; Trojanowicz and Bucqueroux 1990a; Worsnop 1993). As Anderson (1988, 151) states, "Done right, community policing consumes significant manpower. Yet a department dare not let it drain resources from responding to emergency calls." However, as Lee P. Brown (1989, 10) argues, "because community policing is an operating style and not a new program, no additional officers are needed." In some cases, the cost of implementing community-oriented policing has been the downfall of the program (Kelling 1988; Trojanowicz 1982; Trojanowicz and Bucqueroux 1990b), while in many cases police departments have become overburdened attempting to hire new officers or by attempting to put more officers on the street (Silverman 1995; Worsnop 1993). In these particular cases, community-oriented policing was predominantly considered a program and not the philosophy to which Brown refers. In these cases, community-oriented policing was predestined to fail. A police department must not allow the concept of excessive cost and limited resources to either prevent the department from implementing the systemic approach to policing or to cause the community-oriented approach to fail.

COP IN ACTION
MAXIMIZING COMMUNITY RESOURCES, CAPE GIRARDEAU, MISSOURI

Community police officers need to be knowledgeable about their communities' resources. This awareness hit me like a ton of bricks when I was given the task of improving the quality of life in my assigned target area. A racially diverse neighborhood, my area is home to residents of a relatively low socioeconomic status and is known as the drug/crime area of the city. I discovered that many of the residents in my jurisdiction had no idea how or where to get help. There are many agencies and programs available to those in need, but it seems that few take advantage of these resources. Why? If Cape Girardeau is like other cities, it's probably because there are little to no outreach programs that get this information to citizens. As an officer, I know that law enforcement agencies are at the top of the list in terms of outreach capabilities. Helping to link those in need with resources should be a natural function of any law enforcement agency.

I have learned that informal neighborhood meetings are one of the most efficient ways to get to the heart of residents' concerns. And frequently, their concerns can be resolved with a simple phone call. For instance, I discovered that many of the residents in my area didn't know to call the parks department to have the neighborhood park mowed, or that the sanitation department will pick up trash left curbside for days, or that it's legitimate to complain to city departments about overgrown weeds and abandoned cars. I developed a resource card that my partner and I now distribute to every new resident we meet. The card lists phone numbers for such resources as shelters, clinics, family support, and food distribution centers. It includes a comprehensive list of city departments. With a quick glance at their card, residents are able to request services, register complaints, or contact their local municipal court, police station, or taxi company. The cards have effectively taught citizens how to utilize city services. The message is that city departments are one of the most valuable and overlooked resources available to police departments and citizens; we just need to help spread the word.

I also found that many of the individuals in my area have not completed their high school education. Fortunately, there is a GED program available through our local vocational-technical school. But unfortunately for the citizens in my target area, the campus is located several miles away and is not on a public transportation line. My partner contacted the coordinator of the GED program and asked if they could hold classes in an area convenient to the people we serve. That call resulted in a collaboration among the Salvation Army, Adult Basic Education and the police department to hold GED classes in a newly renovated Salvation Army building. This is a perfect example of how we, as officers, can help bring programs to the people who need them.

Another issue we helped our citizens deal with is employment. In our region, the unemployment rate is high, making work particularly difficult to find for those with limited skills and education. My partner and I established a working relationship with the local Private Industry Council (PIC). The PIC has a subsidized job-entry program but has had difficulty locating people eligible for their assistance. We were able to help both the PIC and citizens by identifying qualified persons and making referrals.

Finding people jobs, cleaning up the parks, and seeing that people get educated may not seem like "real" law enforcement to some. I believe, however, that helping citizens gain self-esteem and financial independence is the foundation for rebuilding our communities. For the police department of the '90s to succeed, it will have to be able to identify and maximize its use of community resources. The quest to restore order and quality of life can only be accomplished by first helping our citizens to get their lives together. Like it or not, local police departments must participate in this monumental task. The first step in climbing this mountain is to help others learn how to better their world by using the community's resources.

By Officer Charles Herbst

Source: Adapted with permission from Herbst, Charles. "Maximizing Community Resources." *Community Policing Exchange*, Washington, D.C.: The Community Policing Consortium, November/December 1995.

The primary reason that community-oriented policing should not cost any more than traditional policing is the fact that it is not an additional program that will draw on funds and resources, but rather it is a philosophy and a policy. If the police department implements the systemic approach as a program, it has already determined its outcome in the evaluation process. It will be deemed a failure. If community-oriented policing is implemented as a philosophy, the only changes that will occur lie in the area of the police perception of their job, how they perform their function, and integrating the community into their decision making.

A secondary reason that community-oriented policing should not cost more than traditional policing is the police should be utilizing their budget and resources in a more efficient manner. The police must become more efficient in their allocation of resources and begin to look at what programs are considered wasteful of time, resources, and funding and determine how they may be handled more efficiently, re-prioritized, or cut. Additionally, community policing becomes more cost-effective for two key reasons, according to Brown (1989, 10), "community participation in the crime-control function expands the amount of available resources, and the solving of problems (rather than responding again and again to the same ones) makes for a more efficient deployment of combined police and community resources." As one of the goals of community-oriented policing is to develop the relationship between the police and the community, this should make available resources that were previously undiscovered. The assistance of the community can come in many forms, ranging from volunteers for police mini stations to providing information and materials that will assist the police in the performance of their duties. And if the police and community work together to address and solve both the criminal and order maintenance problems in a neighborhood, the cost and resources that were repetitively directed at the problem can, in the future, be directed at other problems and concerns.

A tertiary method of dealing with the issue of cost and resources may come from a variety of other sources. Community-oriented policing must not be seen as making additional funds and resources necessary to implement the systemic approach; however, this is not to say that additional funding and resources should not be considered. As in traditional policing, if additional funds and resources are available, it can be beneficial to both the police and the community. As the movement toward community-oriented policing becomes a nationally supported endeavor, the federal government has made funds available supporting many of the programs that fall under neighborhood-oriented policing, and it has also made additional funds available for the hiring of an additional 100,000 police officers (Dilulio, Smith, and Saiger 1995; Marshall and Schram 1993). Additionally, one method of generating new funds for the community-oriented policing philosophy and assisting in the implementation of new programs may be derived through forfeiture dollars, specifically in the area of anti-drug initiatives (Trojanowicz and Bucqueroux, 1990b). A great deal of consideration should be made before implementing this option, as it is possible the forfeiture laws can have a negative impact on the police in regards to

St. Petersburg Police Department Marine Watch Community Resources Unit boat which was bought with drug seizure money. (Courtesy of St. Petersburg Police Dept., St. Pteresburg, Florida.)

public opinion. The police do not want to attract the image that the forfeiture laws exist so the police can confiscate property, sell it, and buy "new toys." And finally, it is possible that through the cooperation of the community and the local government, a tax increase of some form can assist in the implementation of community-oriented policing in many areas, such as personnel, programs, and training (Moore 1992; Trojanowicz 1982). However, since community-oriented policing is a long-term commitment, it is questionable as to whether or not this additional tax increase will have a negative effect on the implementation process at a later date (Silverman 1995). Great care and caution should be exercised whenever a department considers deriving additional funds and resources from any of the tertiary methods, for all of them can create problems for the concept of community-oriented policing if they are not handled in an equitable manner.

The second ancillary caveat that commands an equivalent amount of attention is the issue of community-oriented policing causing an increase in police corruption. The literature abounds with discussions over whether the systemic approach will cause corruption in the police departments or whether it will actually alleviate police corruption (Brown 1989; Dombrink 1994; Geller 1991; Goldstein 1987; Kelling 1988; Kelling, Wasserman and Williams 1988; Oliver 1994; Skolnick and Fyfe 1995; Wycoff 1988). The discussion focuses to a large degree on the increased power of the line officer and the decentralization of the police, making the argument that corruption will run rampant through the rank-and-file officers. On the other hand, the response is generally that closer ties to the community and working with a more educated police force, results of the systemic philosophy, will remove those situational factors that create and promote police. As one author explained the dilemma, "community policing exposes officers to different opportunities—for success and for corruption" (Geller 1991, 269).

In order to answer this dilemma, one must first understand that police corruption is defined as "acts involving the misuse of authority by a police officer in a manner designed to produce personal gain for himself or others" (Goldstein 1975, 3). The explanations for this type of behavior are extracted from a variety of sources including simple exposure to situations that may entice the officer, the authority and subculture of the police, and the style of policing that is employed by the police department (Barker and Carter 1994; Dempsey 1994; Goldstein 1975; Wilson 1968). Although it is apparently hard to determine why police corruption occurs, there is little doubt that it has a negative effect on not only the police department, but on the community as well (Barker and Carter 1994; Dempsey 1994). It is therefore extremely important that the question of police corruption and community-oriented policing be resolved, as no police chief will want to move his or her police department from the traditional approach to the systemic if police corruption will be part of the structural environment, fostered by the new approach, and allowed to run rampant for the sake of community-oriented policing.

As previously detailed, police corruption has been a problem that police chiefs have had to either face or fear since the inception of the police department, both in the United States and abroad. As police departments in the United States developed without much management or organization, they were often bastions of corruption. As Kelling explains (1988, 7), "early policing in the United States had been characterized by financial corruption, failure of police to protect the rights of all citizens, and zealotry. The police chiefs of the day, such as August Vollmer and O.W. Wilson, were placed in charge of organizations that were in poor shape in every aspect of the police department. It was their mission to "clean them up" and "straighten them out." This was essentially done through a process of centralizing the command of the police department to the charge of the police chief and removing much of the authority from the line police officers (Dempsey 1994; Geller 1991; Goldstein 1990). The ultimate goal at the time was to utilize scientific management theory (Peak 1995) and to "professionalize" the police (Goldstein 1990) in the hopes of creating a more effective and efficient police department to be less prone to corruption. With curious inquiry that one must now address, why move a police department backwards in management and organization to the days of rampant corruption? It is that direct relationship that poses the dilemma.

The direct relationship of decentralizing the police department, pushing the authority down the chain of command to the level at which the authority is necessary, and shifting the management style to one that is more participatory is not a movement backwards, but rather a movement forwards. Although the structural concepts appear on the surface to remain the same as the policing structure in the early twentieth century, the environment and quality of personnel are not. To equate early twentieth century police officers with the rank-and-file officers about to enter the twenty-first century is an exercise in futility. They are not the same and they never will be. The education level of the police has increased, technology has increased, and although many line officers would probably disagree, both pay and benefits have increased. Although they may share some of the same principles—foot patrol, decentralization, working with community—policing today is free of many of the elements that hindered policing in its infancy. Why then is there so much fear of police corruption in moving a traditional police department to the systemic approach? The answer lies in fear.

The fear of community-oriented policing is largely in the hands of the police chief. It is his or her fear of decentralization, losing control and authority, and sharing this power with the community that generates much of the animosity (Brown 1985; Kelling 1988; Kelling, Wasserman and Williams 1988). Although these may be legitimate concerns, they are not enough to prevent a police department from shifting to community-oriented policing. As Lee P. Brown (1989, 9) stated, "experience has not shown nor even suggested that community policing leads to corruption" and all of the literature from both scholar and practitioner since reflects this fact (Geller 1991; Goldstein 1987; Kelling 1988; Oliver 1994). This is not to say that the potential for corruption does not exist, as this is also recognized in much of the literature (Goldstein 1987; Kelling 1988; Oliver 1994; Wycoff 1988). Some also feel that community-oriented policing will reduce the occurrence of police corruption because of the organizational values and beliefs inherent within the philosophy, that reach far beyond the scope of policy, procedures, rules, and regulations (Kelling 1988; Kelling, Wasserman, and Williams 1988; Skolnick and Fyfe 1995). There is, however, one caveat to this belief.

The caveat lies in that a previously corrupt police department cannot utilize community-oriented policing as a panacea to its problems. Switching from the traditional to the community oriented is not a cure for police corruption (Dombrink 1994; Geller 1991). The police department will carry with it all of the previous problems it suffered under the traditional approach, but it will most likely have an even greater impact on the police department and the community as a result of the change. The community will expect more under community-oriented policing and if police corruption remains a problem, the community's beliefs in the benefits and all of the values inherent within the systemic approach will be destroyed. Public animosity will only be amplified and community-oriented policing will be deemed a failure.

Although it is apparent that police corruption in community-oriented policing is of great concern to both the scholar and practitioner, no basis of reality indicates that this has or will occur. Some believe that it will actually alleviate the occurrence of police corruption, but this too is merely subjective in nature. In any event, the potential for police corruption exists in any style of policing and must always be of concern to police management and police chiefs. Various methods of prevention should be utilized, such as an early warning system, and a strong disciplinary model should be maintained in the event of an incident. In any case, the fear of police corruption should not be utilized as an articulable fact for why a police department should not move to the systemic approach.

COP IN ACTION

THE EARLY WARNING SYSTEM

There is a relatively new concept, the "Early Warning System," which is a non-disciplinary management system for identifying potential problem officers. The Early Warning System is a computer database which tracks individual officers based on reportable elements of behavior. Each element in and of itself may not demonstrate any deficiency on the part of an individual officer, but numerous elements over short periods of time may indicate a behavioral problem. If this is the case, then the officer is "flagged."

Reportable elements include, but are not limited to, the following (as described by the International Association of Chiefs of Police IACP):

- Discharge of a firearm, whether accidental or duty related
- Excessive use-of-force reports
- Any motor vehicle damage
- Any loss of equipment
- "Injured on duty" reports
- Sick leave in excess of five days, or a regular pattern of using one or two sick-leave days over long periods
- All complaints, including supervisory reprimands and other disciplinary action.

The committee reviewing the Early Warning System must look into the incidents and attempt to discover the source of the problem. This may be clearly evident based on the information in the database presented before the committee. Analysis should include supervisory evaluations, awards, and commendations. Other considerations may include additional on-duty details, off-duty employment, marital status, number of dependents, extracurricular activities, and participation in fraternal organizations.

The Early Warning System, a proactive nondisciplinary system, is not for the purposes of punishment, in spite of the fact that intervention strategies may resemble punishment for various violations. The system is to intervene in an officer's career to prevent him from becoming a disciplinary problem and facing disciplinary charges and possible termination. This is but one method of assisting police managers in the retention of quality personnel.

The Early Warning System is not in widespread use yet, however many departments are switching to proactive forms of management with their implementation of community-oriented policing. This system demonstrates a shift in the philosophy of management, instead of away from an entrenched reactive mode and moving toward the proactive. If properly implemented, it can dramatically affect a department, decrease the number of complaints, and reduce police corruption.

Source: Adapted with permission from Oliver, Will. "The Early Warning System." *Law and Order*, September 1994, 182–183.

A third ancillary caveat, that can be closely linked to police corruption, is the issue of politics and community-oriented policing. As community-oriented policing necessitates a new role for the police chief in the community, specifically one that ties the two closer together, there is some concern that this may cause a politically ambitious chief to utilize this to his or her advantage (Wycoff 1988). There is equal concern that although police chiefs may not be politically ambitious, as a result of the role of the chief under community-oriented policing, the chief may become more of a figurehead than the local mayor or city manager, which may create political differences (Brown 1985). And finally, there are some genuine concerns that as a result of potential political conflicts, police chiefs may lose their ability to implement community-oriented policing or that there will be no political commitment to the systemic approach once a chief is asked to resign, is fired, or chooses to leave on his or her own volition (Manning 1988; Rush 1992).

In the area of politics and political leaders there also lies some concern with the implementation of community-oriented policing. Although community-oriented policing is largely a win–win situation for the political leadership (Skolnick and Bayley 1988) because crime, community, and community-oriented policing are all valence issues, the possibility exists that a mayor, city manager, or city council may turn on the philosophy if any negative publicity is attached to the systemic approach. Additionally, there is the possibility that as a result of the police attempting to deliver a more equitable form of policing, individuals and groups that once enjoyed high levels of police services may see a reduction in service, causing some concerns and political pressure on the community leaders (Trojanowicz and Bucqueroux 1990b). This in turn could have a negative effect on the systemic approach for it would not abide by one of the central criterion for community-oriented policing, equity.

The last area of political concern lies with the line officers. As they obtain more authority at their level and they attempt to solve community problems, they may become more politically involved or utilize solutions that move away from political neutrality (Riechers and Roberg 1990). If the police utilize this to their personal advantage or the advantage of their fellow officers, then this crosses over into police corruption. If they utilize this authority to solve problems, address community concerns, or set up neighborhood-oriented policing programs, it may result in a violation of their political neutrality, especially if citizens feel coerced into doing what the police officers suggest.

In all of these cases, there must be a political commitment to the systemic approach, just as there must be a line-officer commitment, a community commitment, and a government commitment. Once this commitment exists, the values and beliefs of the systemic approach must be adhered to in the political arena, as it is on the street. Just as there is potential for political abuses in the traditional police department, there are potentials for political abuses in the community-oriented policing department. It is critical that this concern be addressed at every step of the implementation process to ensure there are no violations, nor the appearance of any violations. Police chiefs, police officers,

Officer Lisa Marsh of the St. Petersburg Police Department, St. Petersburg, Florida teaching her fifth-grade DARE class with "Paul the Lion," a friend of the DARE mascot "Daren the Lion." (Courtesy of St. Petersburg Police Dept., St. Petersburg, Florida.)

and the police department as a whole, must do everything in their power to remain politically neutral and continue to serve at the discretion of not only the mayor or city manager, but the community as well.

The final ancillary caveat that community-oriented policing may face, and perhaps its most fatal problem, is the possibility of "look-a-likes" (Rush 1992, 50). As community-oriented policing becomes en vogue and police departments across the country begin to "implement" the systemic approach, if it is nothing more than a name change, community-oriented policing is predestined for failure. Herman Goldstein's explanation about problem-oriented policing can equally be applied to community-oriented policing:

> While the slightest progress toward focusing on substantive matters is commendable, concern about dilution of the concept is justified. Some accounts of claimed implementation of the problem-oriented policing contains very little that reflects any engagement with substantive problems and little understanding of the overall concept. Among police agencies, some have an uncanny knack for placing new labels on old prac-

tices—for claiming change without changing. I have seen elaborate but totally unrealistic schedules for "full implementation" that seem more appropriate to a military exercise than to implementing a complex, necessarily long-term plan for organizational change requiring a radical shift in the way in which employees view their job and carry it out. (Goldstein 1990, 178)

As the systemic approach to policing is evaluated by the media, by the community, by the police, and through reliable and valid evaluative research, if the police department has retained the traditional style of policing, but only changed the name, community-oriented policing will be declared a failure and will go the way of so many other attempts at improving the police function.

In similar regards, if community-oriented policing is implemented as a program, it will also see absolute failure. Community-oriented policing is a systemic approach to policing requiring department-wide implementation. All of the components of the concept must be implemented, all of the values and beliefs of the philosophy must be set into place, and every facet of the police department must see a move toward adopting the community-oriented policing philosophy. If the systemic approach is not implemented systematically, it will fail as a philosophy, it will fail as a program, and it will be just one more failed concept that police management attempted to implement. A large part of the success or failure lies in what happens to community-oriented policing in the future, and this will be addressed in the next chapter.

COP IN ACTION

POLICE CHIEF, ASSISTANT CITY MANAGER, AND BUDGET DIRECTOR FOCUS ON WHAT WORKS

Darrel Stephens, chief of police, St. Petersburg Police Department, St. Petersburg, Florida.

Q. Many city officials are not aware of how community policing benefits them and therefore do not see the need to become involved in the planning process. When you were developing your strategic plan to implement community policing, did you involve your mayor and other city leaders? If yes, at what point in the process did that occur and to what extent?

A. In St. Petersburg, both city officials and citizens were very involved in the city's efforts to plan and implement community policing. When we started back in 1991, a key issue that came up was the level of staffing that would be needed to implement this philosophy. There was concern that more officers would have to be added. Collectively, we thought community policing was right for St. Petersburg, but we knew the city was not in a position financially to hire any additional officers.

The department's approach was to create time by better managing the workload. We made a decision to implement new call management procedures after a broad-based community and political discussion took place.

The department developed and implemented a telephone call- and report-handling section that today routinely handles about 12 percent of the calls-for-service workload. In addition, we were able to change our procedures so that fewer reports were required. These measures, combined with some resource allocation decisions, provided a base of forty-four officers that were assigned to forty-four geographic areas in the city. All of this was done without adding a single officer to the department.

The collaborative efforts between the police department and city officials continue today as our community policing program continues to evolve. In 1993, St. Petersburg switched to a strong mayor-form of government. A mayor was elected who understands how important neighborhood safety is to meeting his overall goal of improving the city.

Q. In hindsight, how vital do you feel their contributions were to the success of your transition to community policing?

A. How vital are city leaders to making a successful transition to community policing? In my experience, they are critical to the effort. The mayor is committed to making our neighborhoods safe. Two years ago, he created "Operation Commitment," a program that pulls all city departments together to target a specific neighborhood for an intensive six-month improvement effort. It's this kind of involvement that helps to solve a community's problems.

John D. Hartman, Budget Director, city of Newport News, Virginia.

Q. It is the contention of some municipal leaders that community policing costs more than traditional policing. Can you respond to this concern for those chiefs and sheriffs who are interested in adopting this philosophy but need guidance about how this shift will affect their budgets? Based on your experience, does it cost more?

A. Does community policing cost more? Well, there are costs involved in decentralizing. Newport News is twenty-six-miles long, less than a mile wide at its narrowest point and has over 185,000 residents. Spreading resources over this type of geography is difficult to say the least. When we started community policing in 1992, we had the added cost of opening up "storefronts" from which the police officers operate, rent to pay in some cases, electricity, computers and so forth. We also had the added cost of additional personnel-like patrol officers and people to answer the phones at the neighborhood stations. These costs are quantifiable and can be compared with the cost of not implementing community policing.

But, it's not as simple to compare the operating and maintenance costs of your current public safety programs with the cost to do community policing. There's a little thing called "cost effectiveness" that needs to be thought out. In this situation, it's difficult to quantify, but it's there nonetheless. The cost effectiveness of the police department by having community policing probably is much better than the cost effectiveness of public safety by not having it. Let me explain.

In your home, if you lose power, you know the first place to go to look for the cause of the problem—the fuse box. When there's a problem in a neighborhood, the officers have a very good idea of the first places they should go to look for the "fuse box" or the cause of the problem. This is because they know the neighborhood, they know the people who live there, they're familiar with their homes and the cars they drive, they know the kids, they know their routines, and the citizens know them. This, I would think, makes them more efficient and productive in their work and therefore more cost effective than an officer having to come into the neighborhood without the benefit of that knowledge. The officers can go right to the "fuse box," or if they aren't sure where it is, many times someone in the neighborhood with whom they've developed a relationship with will lead them to it.

Does it cost more? It costs us less. Sure, we've had the initial costs of establishing the police presence in the neighborhoods. But, in the long-run, we've had to hire fewer officers because the ones in the neighborhoods are very effective in their jobs and that reduces the overall cost of policing city-wide.

Darryl Herring, Assistant City Manager, city of Springfield, Ohio.

Q. Do you think that most mayors and city managers are clear about the level of involvement needed from them in order to make community policing successful?

A. I can't speak for other mayors and city managers; all I can speak to is the process we went through here in Springfield. In 1991, our city commission adopted a goal of improving the image and responsiveness of our law enforcement. This goal gave us the opportunity to look into community policing. We conducted a pilot seminar on community policing that was sponsored by the International City/County Manager's Association (ICMA). We actually had representatives from as far away as Salinas, California, in attendance.

As a result of that seminar, we went back to our city commission and said that community policing was something that we should give serious consideration to. At that time [1991], our team consisted of the city manager, assistant city manager, chief of police, and his captains. After we expanded the team to include representatives from two police unions, we formally called ourselves an implementation team.

We invited ICMA to come back and talk to us again now that we had our team together. We also invited members of our community whom we knew would be impacted by the transition to community policing: ministers, county officials, city department heads, school board members, and leaders of neighborhood organizations. ICMA explained to all of US that community policing is a philosophy, not just a program.

Q. What mental stumbling blocks did you have to overcome before you recommended this philosophical shift to your community?

A. The biggest challenge we faced in this process was letting go of our top-down communication system and authorizing our street officers to directly contact other departmental field employees. The old system meant that an officer handling a citizen request would pass the information to a police department supervisor, who would in turn give the request to his or her employee. We knew those layers of communication had to go. We expedited the process by allowing officers to laterally contact field employees. Time, in a lot of instances, is paramount in dealing effectively with citizens' requests.

Q. Did you learn anything during the planning phase or implementation process that would be helpful to other city leaders?

A. One tactic I would encourage other city leaders to consider is to hold extended meetings between officers and the city employees they'll be working with. We wanted Springfield's officers to be aware of the process that city hall goes through to say, have a dilapidated, unsightly house demolished. We felt it was important for the officers to know the steps involved so they could pass this knowledge on to citizens. We also wanted the officers to know the people they would be working with on a first-name basis. Our solution was to put the officers through a week-long training session that incorporated the employees and procedures of the various city divisions.

One caution I would offer is to make sure citizens know that they are empowered to access the governmental systems. You don't want citizens to become too dependent, otherwise your officers will end up as glorified nuisance abatement officers. It's a weaning process; you take the citizens through the steps, teach them how to do it for themselves, and then you cut the umbilical cord.

Source: Adapted with permission from Stephens, Darrel, John D. Hartman, and Darryl Herring. "Giving Voice: Police Chief, Assistant City Manager and Budget Director Focus on What Works." *Community Policing Exchange*. Washington, D.C.: The Community Policing Consortium, November/December, 1995.

CONCLUSION

There is little doubt that community-oriented policing, as a new philosophy, a new policy, or a multitude of new programs, will generate problems for the police practitioner. This chapter has attempted to incorporate the concept of caveat emptor or "buyer beware" into police departments' adoption of the systemic approach. In order to address many of the potential problems the police department may face, it is important to understand past problems correlated to the implementation of the systemic approach. As the majority of these problems will most likely fall in the category of implementation problems, as with the implementation of any new policy, problems will need to be addressed, both prior to implementation and after they have been implemented. The programs that capture much of the community-oriented policing philosophy will generate problems that were previously unseen and unknown. These problems must be addressed every step of the way. The fail-safe device to ensure a police department has not wasted an excessive amount of their budget and resources on a problem program is to implement in an incremental fashion. By implementing in this manner, the police chief, police administration, and the line officers will be able to take the corrective action necessary to address the problem in an efficient and effective manner. If the implementation process is not incremental, generally the result will entail problems that are too large in scope to change, leaving only two viable options, continue the failed program with the problems or completely shut down the new program. Neither of these should be seen as healthy options.

The implementation problems that most likely will occur focus initially on the definition of community-oriented policing. The literature from both practitioner and scholar have difficulty in finding an agreeable consensus as to an all-encompassing definition. Therefore it is important to analyze the common themes among most community-oriented policing departments and generate a concrete definition (see Chapter 2). Once this definition is agreed upon, there will be a general focus for any traditional police department attempting to implement the systemic approach, and the policy will be understood by both police management and the line officers implementing community-oriented policing. Additionally, defining the roles of the police, community, and police chief are essential to avoiding problems under the systemic approach, as is understanding the changes that will be necessary in changing the management and organizational structures. And finally, it is important in the implementation process to continually evaluate the various programs implemented and both community and officer attitudes toward community-oriented policing and then make the incremental changes deemed necessary.

There are many other problems that may potentially occur under the systemic philosophy, just as they may occur under any other style of policing. These are ancillary problems that draw much concern from both practitioner and scholar, but are currently unfounded concerns. One of the most prevalent is a concern for additional funds and resources to implement community-oriented policing. However, because it is a philosophical change, it does not entail the expenditure of more money or more resources. This is not imperative for the systemic approach to work. The police must work within their means as they do in a traditional police department, although as a result of the changes in delivering their services, the police may see some money and resources become available as recurring problems are solved and as community involvement increases in addressing crime and order maintenance issues. The concern over police corruption and the police losing their political neutrality are both concerns raised in the literature, which should not be summarily dismissed. Although there is always potential that these two problems may surface, there exists no proof that this is a norm under the systemic philosophy. And finally, the concern of look-a-likes, traditional police departments changing to community-oriented policing in name only, is a concern for the systemic approach in the long term, which then creates a concern for analyzing the future of community-oriented policing, which will be done in more depth in the next chapter.

REFERENCES

Anderson, David C. *Crimes of Justice*. New York: Times Books, 1988.

Andrews, Kenneth R. *The Concept of Corporate Strategy*. Homewood, Il.: Richard D. Irwin, 1980.

Barker, Thomas and David L. Carter. *Police Deviance*. 3rd ed, ed. Thomas Barker and David L. Carter. Cincinnati: Anderson Publishing Company, 1994.

Bayley, David H. "Community Policing: A Report from the Devil's Advocate." In *Community Policing: Rhetoric or Reality,* ed. Jack R. Greene and Stephen D. Mastrofski. New York: Praeger Publishers, 1988.

Bayley, David H. "International Differences in Community Policing." In *The Challenge of Community Policing: Testing the Promises,* ed. Dennis P. Rosenbaum. Thousand Oaks, CA.: SAGE Publications, Inc., 1994.

Brown, Lee P. "Police-Community Power Sharing." In *Police Leadership in America: Crisis and Opportunity,* ed. William A. Geller. New York: American Bar Foundation, Praeger Publishers, 1985.

————. "Community Policing: A Practical Guide for Police Officials." In *Perspectives on Policing.* Washington, D.C.: National Institute of Justice and the Program in Criminal Justice Policy and Management, September 1989.

Buerger, Michael E. "A Tale of Two Targets: Limitations of Community Anticrime Actions." *Crime & Delinquency* 40, no. 3 (July 1994): 411–436.

Bureau of Justice Assistance. *Understanding Community Policing: A Framework for Action.* Washington, D.C.: National Institute of Justice, 1994.

Carter, David L., Allen D. Sapp, and Darrel W. Stephens. *The State of Police Education: Policy Directions for the 21st Century.* Washington, D.C.: Police Executive Research Forum, 1989.

Couper, David C. *Quality Policing: The Madison Experiment.* Washington, D.C.: Police Executive Research Forum, 1991.

Dempsey, John S. *Policing: An Introduction to Law Enforcement.* St. Paul, Minn.: West Publishing Company, 1994.

Dilulio, John J., Jr., Steven K. Smith, and Aaron J. Saiger. "The Federal Role in Crime Control." In *Crime,* ed. James Q. Wilson and Joan Petersilia. San Francisco: ICS Press, 1995.

Dolan, Harry P. "Coping with Internal Backlash." *The Police Chief,* March 1994, 28–32.

Dombrink, John. "The Touchables: Vice and Police Corruption in the 1980s." In *Police Deviance.* 3rd ed., ed. Thomas Barker and David L. Carter. Cincinnati: Anderson Publishing Company, 1994.

Eck, et. al. *Problem-Solving: Problem- Oriented Policing in Newport News.* Washington, D.C.: Police Executive Research Forum, 1987a.

Eck, John E. and William Spelman. "Who Ya Gonna Call? The Police as Problem Busters." *Crime & Delinquency* 33, no. 1 (January 1987b): 31–52.

Freeman, Edward R. *Strategic Management: A Stakeholder's Approach.* Marshall, MA.: Pittman, 1984.

Geller, William A. ed. *Local Government Police Management.* 3rd ed. Washington, D.C.: International City/County Management Association, 1991.

Goldstein, Herman. *Police Corruption: A Perspective on Its Nature and Control.* Washington, D.C.: The Police Foundation, 1975.

————. "Toward Community-Oriented Policing: Potential, Basic Requirements, and Threshold Questions." *Crime & Delinquency* 33, no. 1 (January 1987): 6–30.

————. *Problem-Oriented Policing.* New York: McGraw Hill Publishers. Co., 1990.

Greene, Jack R., William T. Bergman, and Edward J. McLaughlin. "Implementing Community Policing." In *The Challenge of Community Policing: Testing the Promises* ed. Dennis P. Rosenbaum. Thousand Oaks, CA.: SAGE Publications, Inc., 1994.

Greene, Jack R. and Stephen D. Mastrofski. "Preface." *Community Policing: Rhetoric or Reality?* ed. Jack R. Greene and Stephen D. Mastrofski. New York: Praeger Publishers, 1988.

Grinc, Randolph M. ""Angels in Marble": Problems in Stimulating Community Involvement in Community Policing." *Crime & Delinquency* 40, no. 3 (July 1994): 437–468.

Joseph, Thomas M. "Walking the Minefields of Community-Oriented Policing." *FBI Law Enforcement Bulletin,* September 1994, 8–12.

Kelling, George. "Police and Communities: the Quiet Revolution." *Perspectives on Policing.* Washington, D.C.: National Institute of Justice and the Program in Criminal Justice Policy and Management, June 1988.

Kelling, George L., Robert Wasserman, and Hubert Williams. "Police Accountability and Community Policing." *Perspectives on Policing.* Washington, D.C.: National Institute of Justice and the Program in Criminal Justice Policy and Management, November 1988.

Manning, Peter K. "Community Policing as a Drama of Control." In *Community Policing: Rhetoric or Reality,* ed. Jack R. Greene and Stephen D. Mastrofski. New York: Praeger Publishers, 1988.

Marshall, Will and Martin Schram. "Safer Streets and Neighborhoods." In *Mandate for Change.* New York: Berkley Books, 1993.

Mastrofski, Stephen D. "Community Policing as Reform: A Cautionary Tale." In *Community Policing: Rhetoric or Reality,* ed. Jack R. Greene and Stephen D. Mastrofski. New York: Praeger Publishers, 1988.

McLaughlin, Vance and Michael E. Donahue. "Training for Community-Oriented Policing." In *Issues in Community Policing,* ed. Peter C. Kratcoski and Duane Dukes. Cincinnati: Academy of Criminal Justice Sciences, Anderson Publishing Co., 1995.

Meese, Edwin III. "Community Policing and the Police Officer." *Perspectives on Policing.* Washington, D.C.: National Institute of Justice, Program in Criminal Justice Policy and Management, 1993.

Metchik, Eric and Ann Winton. "Community Policing and Its Implications for Alternative Models of Police Officer Selection." In *Issues in Community Policing,* ed. Peter C. Kratcoski and Duane Dukes. Cincinnati: Academy of Criminal Justice Sciences, Anderson Publishing Co., 1995.

Moore, Mark Harrison. "Problem-Solving and Community Policing." In *Criminal Justice: A Biannual Review of Research,* 15, ed. Michael Tonry and Norval Morris. Chicago, IL.: The University of Chicago, 1992.

Moore, Mark H. and Robert C. Trojanowicz. "Corporate Strategies for Policing." *Perspectives on Policing.* Washington, D.C.: National Institute of Justice and the Program in Criminal Justice Policy and Management, November 1988.

Murphy, Chris. "The Development, Impact, and Implications of Community Policing in Canada." In *Community Policing: Rhetoric or Reality,* ed. Jack R. Greene and Stephen D. Mastrofski. New York: Praeger Publishers, 1988.

Oliver, Will. "Corruption Potential in community-oriented policing." *Police Department Disciplinary Bulletin* 2, no. 12, December 1994.

Oliver, Willard M. "Community Policing Defined." *Law & Order,* August 1992, 46–58.

Osborne, David and Ted Gaebler. *Reinventing Government: How the Entrepreneurial Spirit is Transforming the Public Sector.* Reading, MA.: Addison-Wesley, 1992.

Peak, Kenneth. *Justice Administration:* Police, Courts and Corrections Management. Englewood Cliffs, N.J.: Prentice-Hall, Inc., 1995.

Radelet, Louis A. and David L. Carter. *The Police and the Community.* 5th ed. New York: Macmillan College Publishing Company, 1994.

Reuss-Iianni, Elizabeth and Francis A. J. Iianni. "Street Cops and Management Cops: The Two Cultures of Policing." In *Control in the Police Organization,* ed. Maurice Punch. Cambridge, MA.: MIT Press, 1983.

Riechers, Lisa M. and Roy R. Roberg. "Community Policing: A Critical Review of Underlying Assumptions." *Journal of Police Science and Administration* 17, no. 2 (1990): 105–114.

Roberg, Roy R. "Can Today's Police Organizations Effectively Implement Community Policing?" In *The Challenge of Community Policing: Testing the Promises,* ed. Dennis P. Rosenbaum. Thousand Oaks, CA.: SAGE Publications, Inc., 1994.

Rosenbaum, Dennis P. ed. *The Challenge of Community Policing: Testing the Promises,* Thousand Oaks, CA.: SAGE Publications, Inc., 1994.

Rosenbaum, Dennis P. and Arthur J. Lurigio. "an Inside Look at Community Policing Reform: Definitions, Organizational Changes, and Evaluation Findings," Crime and Delinquency 40, no. 3 (July 1994): 299–314.

Ross, Jeffrey Ian. "Confronting Community Policing: Minimizing Community Policing as Public Relations." In *Issues in Community Policing,* ed. Peter C. Kratcoski and Duane Dukes. Cincinnati: Academy of Criminal Justice Sciences, Anderson Publishing Company, 1995.

Rush, George E. "Community Policing: Overcoming the Obstacles." *The Police Chief,* October 1992, 50–55.

Sacco, Vincent F. and Leslie W. Kennedy. *The Criminal Event.* Belmont, CA.: Wadsworth Publishing Company, 1996

Silverman, Eli B. "Community Policing: The Implementation Gap." *Issues in Community Policing* ed. Peter C. Kratcoski and Duane Dukes. Cincinnati: Academy of Criminal Justice Sciences, Anderson Publishing Co., 1995.

Skogan, Wesley G. "The Impact of Community Policing on Neighborhood Residents." In *The Challenge of Community Policing: Testing the Promises,* ed. Dennis P. Rosenbaum. Thousand Oaks, CA.: SAGE Publications, Inc., 1994.

Skolnick, Jerome H. and David H. Bayley. *The New Blue Line: Police Innovation in Six American Cities.* New York: The Free Press, 1986.

———. "Theme and Variation in Community Policing." In *Criminal Justice: A Biannual Review of Research,* 10, ed. Michael Tonry and Norval Morris. Chicago, IL.: The University of Chicago Press, 1988.

Skolnick, Jerome H. and James J. Fyfe. "Community-Oriented Policing Would Prevent Police Brutality." In *Policing the Police.* San Diego, CA.: Greenhaven Press, Inc., 1995.

Sparrow, Malcolm K. "Implementing Community Policing." *Perspectives on Policing.* Washington, D.C.: National Institute of Justice and the Program in Criminal Justice Policy and Management, November 1988.

Trojanowicz, Robert. *An Evaluation of the Neighborhood Foot Patrol Program in Flint.* East Lansing, Mich.: National Neighborhood Foot Patrol Center, Michigan State University, 1982.

Trojanowicz, Robert and Bonnie Bucqueroux. *Community Policing: A Contemporary Perspective.* Cincinnati: Anderson Publishing Co., 1990a.

———. "The Community Policing Challenge." *PTM: Police Technology and Management* 1, no. 4 (November 1990b): 40–51.

———. *Community Policing: How to Get Started.* Cincinnati: Anderson Publishing Co., 1994.

Wilkinson, Deanna L. and Dennis P. Rosenbaum. "The Effects of Organizational Structure on Community Policing: A Comparison of Two Cities." In *The Challenge of Community Policing: Testing the Promises* ed. Dennis P. Rosenbaum. Thousand Oaks, CA.: SAGE Publications, Inc., 1994.

Wilson, James Q. *Varieties of Police Behavior: The Management of Law and Order in Eight Communities.* Cambridge, MA.: Harvard University Press, 1968.

Worsnop, Richard L. "Community Policing." *The CQ Researcher* 3, no. 5 (February 5, 1993): 97–120.

Wycoff, Mary Ann. "The Benefits of Community Policing: Evidence and Conjecture." In *Community Policing: Rhetoric or Reality,* ed. Jack R. Greene and Stephen D. Mastrofski. New York: Praeger Publishers, 1988.

Wycoff, Mary Ann and Wesley G. Skogan. "Community Policing in Madison." In *The Challenge of Community Policing: Testing the Promises:* An Analysis of Implementation and Impact, ed. Dennis P. Rosenbaum. Thousand Oaks, CA.: SAGE Publications, Inc., 1994.

CHAPTER 14

The Future

To believe in something not yet proved and to underwrite it with our lives:
it is the only way we can leave the future open.

-Lillian Smith-

Community-oriented policing is essentially a blending of the traditional principles of policing and the addition of some relatively new concepts. These concepts are what separate community-oriented policing from both the police–community relations era and from the traditional methods of policing. Although the core responsibilities of the police have changed little throughout the twentieth century, most of society, the environment, and crime has changed. It is this change that the systemic approach is attempting to move forward with and complement as the United States enters the twenty-first century.

As stated in Chapter 13, it is very difficult to predict what will occur in the future and we are often better served discussing what has occurred in the past and analyze what we currently know. However, this is not to say that looking at the future is not valuable. One can often look to these past occurrences and analyzie the present to project the future. An occasional foray into the future can be beneficial to most disciplines, but it may especially be helpful when it comes to policing and more importantly, community-oriented policing.

Since the systemic approach to policing is about the future, it is important to know all we can about the problems of the future so the organization can begin to prepare for any and every conceivable event. It is also important to explore the future benefits that will be derived from change, providing the incentives that may bear on successful implementation of the systemic approach today in order to achieve the benefits of the future. And finally, it is important to analyze the future of various factors that may impact or have dramatic effects within the community-oriented policing approach.

"CRIME FILES"

PREDICTING CRIMINALITY—PART 36

This edition of the "Crime Files" hosted by James Q. Wilson, features Peter Greenwood, from the Rand Corporation; Peter Hoffman, U.S. Parole Commission; and John Monahan, University of Virginia Law School. The discussion focuses on the efforts to protect the community by predicting future crimes by looking to potential repeat offenders. A key emphasis of the discussion revolves around the dilemmas posed by such predictions.

FUTURE RESEARCH

The police have traditionally given very little thought to the future of their discipline. The majority of police administrators and police officers are so busy with the details of the day that they often fail to project any further than a year ahead. In some cases, visionary police chiefs exist, but they find they can do little with these visions as they attend to the daily responsibilities of running a bureaucratic organization. In most cases, the futures research has been left to the scholar, and usually a special breed of scholar who, until recently, was considered to be exploring a world of fantasy and myth, based on current articulable facts—perhaps little different from the prognosticators of football. However, as the discipline of futures research has developed it has come to be accepted by many scholars as having some benefit (Tafoya 1991). The purpose and goal of futures research is "to accurately predict trends, incidents, and organizational policy in anticipation of future realities" (Gilbert 1993, 464). Community-oriented policing, as a new evolution in policing in its infancy stage, would benefit from utilizing futures research to assist in the implementation of change. An even greater benefit would be realized if both scholar and practitioner were able to combine their knowledge to derive a more accurate and useful model of what the future may entail for community-oriented policing. It has been said that those who shape the future of law enforcement can utilize, and essentially need, reliable and valid future-oriented data (Campbell 1990, 30; Gilbert 1993, 465). As police chiefs begin the process of implementing community-oriented policing, they are shaping the future. It is therefore only reasonable that they receive this reliable and valid future-oriented data.

FUTURE RESEARCH AND EVALUATION

In 1996, the National Institute of Justice surveyed 2,585 members of the criminal justice system, focusing largely on police chiefs and sheriffs. Those participating in the survey were asked to rank their priorities for future research and evaluation and the following were the top three responses by the police chiefs and sheriffs:

POLICE CHIEFS	SHERIFFS
Community policing	Community policing
Juvenile crime	Drugs
Violent crime	Juvenile crime

Source: Tom McEwen, *National Assessment Program: 1994 Survey Results*. Washington, D.C.: National Institute of Justice, 1996.

The key to understanding how one derives "reliable and valid future-oriented data" must begin with the distinction between a prediction and a forecast. A prediction is simply a guess into the future that something will occur and it is usually based on more of an instinctual reasoning, rather than an educated reasoning (see Joseph, 1974; Klofas and Stojkovic 1995; Rothermel 1982; Tafoya 1990). A prediction is attempting to look into a crystal ball and "predict" what is going to happen. On the other hand, forecasting is considered to be the purest form of futures research (Cornish 1977; Tafoya 1990). This is because in forecasting, the researcher is essentially forecasting what is likely to occur by looking ahead and reasoning the probable future. It is often analogized with the headlights of a car, where we do not see everything that lies ahead, but we see enough to allow us to proceed onward toward our destination (Rothermel 1982; Tafoya 1990; Tafoya 1991). There should be no doubt that this scanning ahead is beneficial to both the police and those in the academic fields. Instead of paying attention to what is going on within the confines of our car, we must look out the window and peer as far forward as our headlights will allow us to see.

There are many tools available to allow us this vision. They consist of a variety of methodologies that can provide the valid and reliable information we seek. In order to ensure these two qualities in futures research, a consensus has evolved regarding certain principles, premises, and priorities to which the futures researcher should adhere (Tafoya 1990). The three principles include "1) the unity of interconnectedness of reality, 2) the crucial importance of time, and 3) the significance of ideas" (Tafoya 1990, 201). The principles adhered to articulate that events do not happen in a random fashion, that since implementation today becomes reality in roughly five years the projection should be for more than five years, and that when discussing ideas, one must never abide by the status quo.

The three premises of the futurist consist of the consensual understanding that "1) the future is not predetermined, 2) the future is not predictable, and 3) future outcomes can be influenced by individual choices" (Tafoya 1990, 202). Once this understanding is reached, then the three priorities for future research become clear, and they consist of the goals that future research should "1) form perceptions of the future (the possible), 2) study likely alternatives (the probable), and 3) make choices to bring about particular events (the preferable)" (Tafoya 1990, 202). In regards to community-oriented policing, the goals are to then look to what is possible with the systemic approach, determine what is most probable for its implementation, and ultimately bring about its full systemic application, which is preferable.

The actual methods of forecasting the future fall into four distinct categories which include the use of 1) scenarios, 2) qualitative methods, 3) quantitative methods, and finally 4) the Delphi technique (Tafoya 1990). The scenario method of forecasting is one in which the writing of the future details the hypothetical in a summary format that analyzes the future subject through a factual basis in a multitude of ways (Cole 1995). Although multiple outcomes are possible, they usually describe the best-case scenario, the worst-case scenario, and the most probable-case scenario, all of which can be extremely beneficial in planning (Cole 1995; Tafoya 1990). The qualitative method is essentially analyzing the future by beginning with a time and place we want to be in the future

A future candidate for the Montgomery County Police Department, Montgomery County, Maryland, tests out the police motorcycle during "National Night Out." (Courtesy of the Montgomery County Dept. of Police, Montgomery County, Maryland.)

and working backward to understand how this can be obtained, a technique extremely beneficial in the planning of community-oriented policing to project the long-term implementation process (Tafoya 1990). The quantitative method consists of a mathematical model that analyzes past trends in order to forecast what the futures trends may entail (Tafoya 1990). This may be beneficial to the systemic approach because much of the information obtained for future numbers of crime and future demographics is generated in this fashion. And finally, the Delphi technique is perhaps one of the most sophisticated forecasting tools available in futures research. The Delphi technique utilizes a structured group process that moves members from individual responses toward a consensual agreement as to future events that will occur (Tafoya 1987; Tafoya 1990; Tafoya 1991). The personnel selected can consist of either scholars in the academic field, scholars in the research field, police practitioners, and police consultants. Essentially any individual with a knowledge base of the subject under consideration can be utilized. The responses are individualistic and obtained through a survey or through the use of computers, compiled together to form a consensus, at which time this consolidated information is provided back to the individual for further consideration. This may occur several times until a valid and reliable consensus is reached. It is then possible to articulate the consensus information in the form of a forecast of what is most likely to occur and when.

As policing in the United States moves into the twenty-first century the information provided through futures research can be beneficial to understanding the changes that are occurring. Futures research on community-oriented policing can provide the criminal justice scholar and the police practitioner with an understanding of what future problems may occur under the systemic approach in order to effectively deal with them before they occur. It can provide information on the future benefits of community-oriented policing that may provide the incentives and justification for implementing this evolutionary and systemic approach to policing. And finally, it can provide the forecast of community-oriented policing so that many of the pieces of the puzzle are answered, and it can promote thought on those pieces that we have yet to find.

PUBLIC SAFETY AND COMMUNITY POLICING GRANTS

THE COPS PROGRAM

Program Information

The COPS Program (Community-Oriented Policing Services) will provide competitive grants to states and localities to put 100,000 law enforcement officers on the streets.

Grants may be used to hire and train new officers, or to rehire officers that have been laid off due to budgetary reductions. In addition, some grants will be available to procure equipment, technology, or support systems, or to pay overtime, so long as the applicant can demonstrate that expenditures for such purposes will result in an increase in the number of officers deployed in Community-Oriented Policing. Funds will also be available for other related community policing activities.

Community policing grants are intended to substantially increase the number of law enforcement officers interacting directly with members of the community; to provide additional and more effective training to law enforcement officers to enhance their problem solving and other public service skills needed in interacting with members of the community; to encourage the development and implementation of innovative programs to permit members of the community to work with law enforcement agencies in the prevention of crime in the community; and to encourage the development of new technologies to assist law enforcement agencies in reorienting their emphasis from reacting to crime to preventing crime.

In addition, grants may be used: to increase law enforcement activities focused on interaction with the community; to enhance police participation in early intervention teams; to reduce the time officers spend out of the community and in court; to enhance proactive crime control; to enhance management and administration skills in community policing; to operate crime control programs; and to support the purchase of one service weapon per officer.

Source: U.S. Department of Justice, *Violent Crime Control and Law Enforcement Act of 1994: Briefing Book*, Washington D.C.: U.S. Dept. of Justice, 1995.

FUTURE PROBLEMS

The majority of problems that can be forecasted to occur with the systemic approach to policing have, to some degree, previously been covered. Many of the forecasts detail a difficult implementation process for community-oriented policing and detail many obstacles standing in the way to prevent the systemic approach from truly becoming the next evolution in policing. If past is prologue, then the lack of a consensual definition could pose enormous strain on the systemic approach as various agencies are naming a plethora of practices all under the guise of one name. Additional problems that have previously been detailed include the lack of involvement on the part of the police, community, and various government agencies. As Trojanowicz (1994, 262) so distinctly stated, "The future of community policing is in the hands and hearts of more than just the police." A very definitive forecast for community-oriented policing details much apathy, misunderstandings, and uninterested citizens when it comes to getting involved. We know this from human nature, we know this from many of the theories of collective action, and we know this from personal involvement in our own groups. It is hard to get a majority of fully committed people for any idea.

In returning to the last problem of community-oriented policing in Chapter 13, "look-a-likes," it is important to understand how they can affect the future of the systemic approach. As previously stated, many police departments have the uncanny ability to implement change without any change. If a police department subscribes to the latest philosophy and transforms to meet the latest standard without any substantive change, these departments defeat the purpose of ideas oriented on moving the police toward a more productive organization and if evaluated, destroy the very tool for determining whether or not the new concept works. Evaluating the look-a-likes creates an unreliable and invalid analysis of the systemic approach to policing and may cause irreparable harm to the concept by preventing a true evaluation.

The look-a-likes will most likely occur in four forms that are not conducive to the systemic approach that has been detailed in this book. The first will be those police departments who change the name, but do not change the department. Community-oriented policing will fail miserably in this setting, for the citizens and police officers will see no change, the new approach to policing will be deemed a failure, and none of the potential benefits will be actualized.

The second look-a-like is the department that implements community-oriented policing with no clear direction or concept of what the systemic approach entails. In some police departments this may be the implementation of foot and bike patrols, with no thought to strategic-oriented policing or problem-oriented policing. In other cases, the department may implement all three components, but may make no move toward decentralizing. In any of these cases, the forecast is bright for only several years, at which time any benefit derived from the concept will fade like a candle flame which has burnt itself out.

The third look-a-like forecasted to have problems in implementing community-oriented policing are those departments that implement the concept overnight. The forecast is predicated on so many other policing programs that the police chiefs have implemented without any concern for the police. Forced down from the top, these programs have failed to take hold because of the resistance by the line officers. Additionally, any program implemented overnight is sure to fail for lack of clarity. Implementing a concept that is at the same time a philosophy, a policy, a new management style, and a host of programs is absolutely sure to fail if there is no clarity.

And finally, the fourth type of look-a-like is revealed in the police department that implements community-oriented policing with misconceptions about what it can and cannot do. Perhaps the key forecast within the misconceptions is that many police departments will look for a stringent model of structural changes, programs to implement, and goals to achieve without any concern for the ideas behind the systemic approach. No formula exists for implementing community-oriented policing, only guidelines. Every community is different and therefore every community-oriented police department should be different as well. The three components of community-oriented policing and all of the other methods and changes are the clay that is to be molded by way of the consensual movement of the police, community, and various local government agencies.

The final forecasted problem for community-oriented policing lies in the arena of inflated expectations. The inflated expectations may come from anyone and everyone, but this can be divided into three categories: the community, the police, and the government. Regarding the community, community-oriented

Oceanside Police Officer from Oceanside, California, talks with a
local youth during the annual Community Relations Fair.
(Courtesy of Oceanside Police Dept., Oceanside, California.)

policing is not a panacea for all of its problems. In many scenarios, community-
oriented policing just will not solve or alleviate the problems that the community
identifies or demands addressed. It will also not change many of the core functions of the police that must continue to be implemented despite the fact there
will always be community opposition to its application. This may be as simple
as the continuation of writing traffic citations to responding in riot gear at a civil
disturbance. If the community believes these "things" will disappear under the
systemic approach to policing then they have been misinformed or have been
allowed to develop unrealistic expectations of what community-oriented policing is all about.

Equally possible in forecasting problems is the same inflated expectations
on the part of the police officer who may be led to believe that community-
oriented policing is a panacea or that it will be a simplistic approach to policing.
It will continue to be as difficult a job as it always has, and perhaps it will be
even more difficult as police officers are required to utilize skills not previously
required. They will have more authority, more responsibility, and finally they
will be required to process thought rather than process paperwork.

The inflated expectations can also occur on the part of the local government which can have an adverse affect on community-oriented policing.
Whether it is the mayor, city manager, or city council, the possibility that they
as the governing factor over the local jurisdiction may have inflated expectations for community-oriented policing is great. From their perception, community-oriented policing may well be the panacea for both criminal and order
maintenance issues, and without the dramatic changes desired, they may feel
the concept has failed. This can in turn be applied to all of the government
agencies that may have the expectations that the police can accomplish the
systemic approach without their assistance, and they may not wish to assist.

Regardless of whether we discuss the community, police, or government when it comes to inflated expectations, it is simply the case that the American mentality is often "we want it now." As in the case of the community-oriented police department that changes overnight, this is clearly a result of what so many want and what so many people expect. If the systemic approach to policing is to work in the long term, the fact that there is an inflated expectation for quick implementation and quick results must be dealt with during every stage of the implementation process. If the inflated expectations of the community, police, and local government are allowed to continue, the forecast shows that community-oriented policing will not be given the ample time it needs to become entrenched and the concept will be deemed a failure before it has time to develop.

FUTURE BENEFITS

In detailing many of the past problems of community-oriented policing to prevent potential problems from occurring, little time has been spent on the benefits of the systemic approach. As we have seen through most of the community-oriented policing evaluations over the past ten years, the response on the part of the community, police, and the police organization has been somewhat skeptical and cynical at first. After a period of time has passed, those opinions begin to change and everyone involved in the process, and to some degree those who are not, find community-oriented policing to be beneficial. Obviously if this were not the case, the concept would never have moved to the position in the literature and in the police departments that it now holds. However, one must ask the question, what are the future, long-term benefits of the systemic approach?

Some of the key literature in the area of community-oriented policing has laid the foundation for what benefits are being revealed in our forecasting headlights. The benefits lie in the same areas as the problems and can be broken down by analyzing the benefits to the community, the police, and the police organization.

COP IN ACTION

ENHANCING POLICE SERVICES WITH SENIOR VOLUNTEERS

The Newark Police Department, like many other police organizations, constantly struggles to enhance services without benefit of additional resources. Leaders are already challenged by managing their departments' existing budgets of tax dollars and city revenue. Our department found that it could enhance services and reduce some of the workload by using senior citizen volunteers to assist with the department's routine activities. In locations where communities are facing fiscal constraints, police volunteers are one of the few mechanisms for improving services without increasing citizens' taxes.

Newark was exposed to the idea of using senior volunteers through Triad. Prompted by information obtained from Triad, we linked up with the local Retired Seniors Volunteer Program (RSVP). RSVP is supported by federal dollars to enhance senior volunteerism in virtually every public service endeavor throughout the community. RSVP provides insurance that covers the volunteers from the time they leave their homes until the time they return and also reimburses them for mileage.

In six years, our program has expanded to fifteen volunteers who work in various divisions of the police department. We have come to value and rely on their services. We are quickly reminded how important their contributions are on those rare occasions when they are unable to work their scheduled hours. The volunteers perform a variety of tasks that assist with daily operations and the delivery of police services to Newark's citizens. Their responsibilities include:

* preparing a crime information bulletin that is distributed to all personnel twice weekly;
* capsulizing and documenting crime trends;
* assisting with centralized records by servicing citizen requests at the public information window, entering data from crime reports, processing requests for traffic accident reports, and filing reports in the central filing system;
* analyzing all false alarms, preparing follow-up correspondence, obtaining explanations for the false alarms and ensuring that corrective actions are taken to limit their frequency;
* reviewing 911 calls that are erroneously transferred to our system and taking action to ensure that future calls are transmitted to the appropriate 911 answering point;
* monitoring party, noise and disorderly conduct violations related to rental units and notifying landlords of the violations so that corrective action may be taken in conjunction with the city's ordinance; and
* assisting various units with data entry, evidence and property purges, mass mailings, and sorting and filing mug shots.

The volunteer program brings the citizens we serve into the police department and creates an environment for ongoing interaction between officers and the senior volunteers. Many of the volunteers say that the appreciation they receive is one of the primary reasons for volunteering with the police department. Officers have an opportunity to interact with caring and supportive citizens, and develop a greater sensitivity to senior citizen's concerns.

Advice for Departments Setting Up a Volunteer Program

Employees may be reluctant to allow "outsiders" into the working components of the police agency. They may have a natural fear that volunteers will eliminate or replace their positions. Therefore, it is important to reassure all employees that the volunteers are there to enhance services and to lessen the workload and increase efficiency. Agency personnel must be committed to train the volunteers to perform specific tasks. I have found that once volunteers have been properly screened and trained, they make for a highly professional and very dedicated group of individuals.

Agencies should conduct limited background investigations on the volunteers. It is also wise to get commitments about the frequency and number of hours volunteers are willing to devote.

I can't stress enough how important it is for police agencies to make certain the work given to volunteers is meaningful. Many of the volunteers who come into our department are well-educated, competent individuals who are looking for a challenge and want to know that they are truly contributing to the police operation.

It has been my experience that a volunteer program begins slowly, but if the police department is committed to the concept, it will grow both in terms of the number of volunteers and complexity of the assignments. As this evolution occurs, the services that volunteers provide will become indispensable; their contributions will benefit both the police agency and the citizens served.

By Chief William Hogan

Source: Adapted with permission from Chief William Hogan. "Enhancing Police Services with Senior Volunteers." *Community Policing Exchange*. Washington, D.C.: The Community Policing Consortium, November/December 1995.

The benefits to the community include unquestionably the crime prevention techniques the police are implementing that not only assist in preventing crime, but in reducing the public fear of crime as well (Skolnick and Bayley 1988a, 29; see also Brown 1989; Mastrofski 1988; Skolnick and Bayley 1988b; Wycoff 1988). Rather than maintaining the reactive stance of the traditional style of policing, community-oriented policing attempts to be proactive in nature in order to prevent crime and order maintenance issues. A second benefit to the community lies in the area of public scrutiny and public accountability (Brown 1989; Mastrofski 1988; Skolnick and Bayley 1988a; Skolnick and Bayley 1988b). Under the traditional forms of policing it was the "us versus them" mentality and the idea was that the police would take care of their own by hiding their problems from public view. Under the community-oriented policing approach, not only must the community play a role in the decision-making process for the allocation of police resources, they must also have a role in what the police do or fail to do. The police then must not only be accountable to the police organization, they must be accountable to the public. And finally, the benefit of community involvement with the police, with other members of the community, and the formation of community organizations are all benefits to reestablishing a healthy community (Brown 1989; Skolnick and Bayley 1988b). As people have migrated toward cities for the past 200 years to move closer to other people, they have actually moved further and further apart, as people have become strangers within their own communities. Pulling these people together to address the community's woes, having them communicate and work together, must assuredly be more beneficial then living as strangers.

The communication and commitment to work together not only benefits the community, but it benefits the police as well (Brown 1989; Cordner 1988; Skolnick and Bayley 1988a; Skolnick and Bayley 1988b; Wycoff 1988).

The Phoenix Police Department, Phoenix, Arizona, community-oriented policing bike patrol officers in the downtown area stop to say hello to a "little" citizen. (Courtesy of the Phoenix Police Dept., Phoenix, Arizona, and Mr. Bob Rink.)

Interaction between the community and the police can increase public knowledge about the role of the police, increase their respect, and most importantly increase their support for the police. The police know the community is behind them and supporting their efforts, thereby creating a healthy environment for the police officer, and most likely cultivating a more dedicated officer. Intrinsically tied to this support is the concept of shared responsibility for addressing criminal and order maintenance problems (Brown 1989; Skolnick and Bayley 1988a; Skolnick and Bayley 1988b; Wycoff 1988). If police officers see that the community not only supports their role in society, but are also willing to work with them toward eradicating the problems in the community, the police will, like the community, come to understand, increase their respect, and develop a more productive and healthy relationship.

Extremely unique to community-oriented policing, and certainly a benefit, is that the systemic approach enhances communication between the public and the police. However, it also enhances the communication from police to police and community to community. As the lines of communication open up between the police and the community, it requires, and sometimes forces, communication among these two groups. In order for line police officers to implement the various programs, they must communicate with other police officers and seek out their assistance to address problems, develop programs, and work alongside the community. Equally important is the fact that police find themselves communicating up the chain to first-line supervisors and beyond, while police management begins to communicate with line officers in a more dynamic way. Communication becomes a two-way street and the focus shifts to working together rather than the police officers and police management working against each other.

In addition to increased communication between the police, there is also greatly enhanced intercommunity communication. As the various programs under community-oriented policing grow and more and more people find themselves involved, relationships between community members tend to grow dramatically. Neighbors who once refused to go next-door to meet their neighbors, find themselves involved in many situations where they must work together. Once they are brought together, all pretenses, fears, and beliefs, are usually and quickly dismissed and a stronger community is forged through open communication. Communities truly begin to develop a sense of "community." This can be advantageous to the police, it can be advantageous to the individual citizens, but most importantly it is advantageous to the community at-large.

In addition to the benefits from open lines of communication, benefits are realized as the police department begins decentralizing the department's structure, changing the department's management style, and moving toward working together to address the community's needs. As a result of these changes, the police will have a better working environment, one where they are valued more, and thus greater job satisfaction will become the greatest benefit to the police (Brown 1989; Cordner 1988; Skolnick and Bayley 1988a; Skolnick and Bayley 1988b; Wycoff 1988). As a former police officer once explained, "it is sad when you have to quit because the stress of being a police officer comes from within the department, rather then from the elements on the street." The benefits to the police officer under community-oriented policing are clear and should the systemic approach be implemented, the forecast holds for a more satisfied police officer, and hence a more dedicated employee.

As community-oriented policing benefits the community and the line police officer, it benefits the police organization as well. The primary benefit to the police organization is increased job satisfaction among the line officers and the increased support derived from the community (Wycoff 1988). There is little doubt that a more satisfied employee will be a more productive worker, take less leave time, and will show a stronger attachment and dedication to the organization. Equally, if the community feels their police are doing a good job, and they support their efforts, the benefits to the police through resources, legitimacy, and status, are all beneficial to the police organization. A second benefit lies in the political arena, for community-oriented policing is a win–win situation for the police organization, which may explain why so many police departments are quick to adopt this new philosophy. As crime is a valence issue, no one supports crime, there can be little doubt that unfolding a new way to fight crime, will benefit the police organization politically. Although the police should remain politically neutral, there are often politics that cannot be avoided. In the case of community-oriented policing, there are no bad politics. And finally, little doubt exists that the police practices and procedures under the traditional approach to policing have failed to produce any true effect on crime and order maintenance problems, and therefore the mere implementation of the systemic approach may provide the opportunity to become the effective, efficient, equitable, and accountable police department desired by the public, and therefore it may be beneficial to the police organization.

COP IN ACTION

AUTOMATION FOR COMMUNITY POLICING

The use of advanced technology is rapidly gaining attention from crime fighters as they see a continuous success story of the reduction in citizen fear, neighborhood disorder, and crime. As this relationship between police and technology is strengthened, so too is the partnership between police and the community, commonly known as Community Policing (CP).

One of the components of CP that the Justice Department has identified as the result of employing advanced technology is the use of strategic analysis to complement the problem-oriented policing aspect of your overall plan. While tactical analyses are important in the forecasting of crime patterns, strategic analysis will assist in identifying the factors unique to your community that underlie the crime problems. Information gathering will center around interaction with the Neighborhood Watch Groups, schools, nonprofits and other groups, as well as conducting community surveys on citizen fear.

Modern computer-aided dispatch provides vital information to assist responding officers in the handling of a call for service and has been cited as providing vital information links between the community and police. "The argument was always that a common dispatcher for several towns could not possibly know enough about the entire area," Searcy said. "But with an effective CAD system, one dispatcher can pull up more information than any individual could possibly know, even if they worked in that town their whole life."

Organized information, drawn from both your department and your community, is an essential element in CP. A CP officer will find that department-wide computer bulletin boards or e-mail are effective means for information dissemination, capable of reaching all officers from all shifts. Feedback from meetings with community groups (such as minutes of the meeting, requests for changes in patrol routes, requests for overtime to monitor ethnic or church events or events held by the local chamber of commerce) should be made available on a department-wide basis.

In addition, intradepartmental communication facilitated by computerized communication allows for feedback from the officers themselves to the officers responsible for working directly with citizens. When departmental policy is being reviewed, the officers will have records of the fears, concerns, and recommendations made by members of the community before changes are implemented. Using citizen input to determine department policy is a critical component of CP that computer technology can facilitate.

These are just a few of the innovative uses to which technology can be put to assist departments with a department-wide CP philosophy and plan for citizen interaction. In order to be successful in obtaining federal COPS program funds, you must develop a CP strategy that is appropriate to and feasible for your department.

Source: Adapted with permission from Sweeney William. "Grant Writing for Technology." *Law and Order*, September 1995, 83–84.

The realization of these five criteria are also key benefits to the police department and the community. As the police department advances under the systemic approach to policing, these five criteria should be central to the department's philosophy and should be embodied in every policy and program enacted. The police will strive to be more effective in the delivery of their services to the public. They will work to be more efficient in how they utilize their available resources, and they will seek out new ways of delivering their services and tap into new resources available from within the police department, the business sector, and the community as a whole. They will always strive for equity by demonstrating that they are fair in the delivery of services, that they provide "equal protection under the law," and that they hold the principles of the Constitution as their highest concern, that which they have sworn to defend. They will be more accountable as police officers, as police managers, and as police chiefs, to the public, but more importantly, they will be more accountable as individuals. And finally, community-oriented policing is the impetuous for divesting authority in the police, as well as the community, for all things related to crime and social disorder. As the police adhere to these five criteria under the impetus of community-oriented policing, there should be little doubt of the benefits this will provide the community, which includes the police.

THE FUTURE

The future of community-oriented policing is very promising and the majority of the literature supports this fact. The advocates, both scholar and practitioner, have identified the systemic approach to policing as being, rather factually, the next evolution in policing. Although many agree the time is now to begin implementation, most also agree that as a standard in policing, community-oriented policing is still a decade away. Although the 1990s have been often deemed the decade of community-oriented policing, it would seem the first decade of the twenty-first century will be its decade of reality.

The majority of futures discussion of the systemic approach is laid out in the foundation of anecdotal evidence and through these advocates of community-oriented policing (Worsnop 1993). In other cases, there is such a vast amount of confidence in the systemic approach that it has been recommended as the answer to many departments' problems. This is especially true in Los Angeles, where the Christopher Commission's investigation in the aftermath of the Rodney King incident, called for community-oriented policing as the appropriate model to restore police and community relations (Christopher 1991). And in most cases, the forecasts of the future are positive, such as Bennett's statement (1989, 331) that "the social service functions of police will become more community-oriented." This is not to say, however, that everyone paints a rosy scenario when it comes to community-oriented policing.

Although there are in fact some scholars who are either opposed to community-oriented policing or are articulating extreme caution in implementing this style of policing (Bayley 1988; Klockars 1988; Riechers and Roberg 1990; Walker 1984), one futures research forecast articulates the concept will fail (Crank 1995). Crank (1995) forecasts that by the year 2000 the majority of police departments in the United States will have implemented community-oriented policing, but by the year 2010, as a result of two unpredictable incidents, the systemic approach will be called into question and eventually be deemed a failure. He also articulates that the "reorientation of patrol" will not work as intended, the costs of rapid response will pose problems, the decentralization and "civilianization" will fail, and that "the community-based policing movement failed to take into account historical and institutional features of the broader context in which policing occurred, and that context had profound effects on police organization and activity" (Crank 1995, p. 116). Although this surely paints a tragic end to the systemic approach, it can provide some information to the practitioner and scholars of today.

As the majority of these "problems" have previously been addressed, the key concern articulated by Crank is the possibility of a tragic event raising public awareness and public opinion of the community-oriented policing approach. These "historical shocks" as Crank (1995, 123) calls them, could pose potential problems for the systemic approach. The best analogy to one of these shocks and the difficulties community-oriented policing may face can be tied to the riots in the wake of the Rodney King incident. If the police department had previously shifted to the systemic approach and it was either in the implementation process or had seen full systemic implementation, would community-oriented policing have survived in its wake? The first response to this is that hopefully, under the systemic approach, this would never have happened, but that would prove too naive. If an isolated beating occurs, if a citizen is wounded or killed by the police, and if the police have to respond full force in a riot situation, will community-oriented policing be deemed a failure? There are no easy answers to this question, but understanding the potential for its occurrence, police departments implementing the systemic approach should give consideration to the appropriate community-oriented approach to this type of crisis situation.

Although all of these forecasts are beneficial to the literature revolving around community-oriented policing, there is a need for more futures research in this area. The majority of literature is not specifically directed toward the systemic approach except in anecdotal form. In order to turn to the core of the forecasting research, two key pieces of research provide some in-depth information that can be beneficial to the police practitioner. The first source is a Delphi forecast of the future in law enforcement and the second source details a list of external considerations that may have an effect on community-oriented policing.

The Delphi forecast was conducted by Dr. Tafoya (1991) during his doctoral dissertation, where he surveyed key scholars, police chiefs, scholar/practitioners, and finally key people in the professional criminal justice, criminology, and law enforcement societies. In three rounds of individual responses on various topics in law enforcement, these researchers reached consensus on many advancements in law enforcement along with a target date when they would occur (Tafoya 1991). The responses are most interesting for the discussion of community-oriented policing, as a variety of advancements are inherent within the systemic approach to policing.

The Delphi forecast, completed in 1986, was able to predict that by the year 1995, "community involvement and self-help in local policing [would become] common practice in more than 70 percent of the nation" (Tafoya 1991, 255). Additionally, Tafoya predicted (1991, 260) that in the same year "University/Professionally conducted research [would have] a direct and positive influence on crime reduction strategies." In both of these cases, the forecast has come true as the forecasted date has already arrived and proved to be largely accurate.

By the year 2005, Tafoya's (1991, 264) forecast states that "more than 50 percent of [all] police agencies [will] have personnel competent to conduct rigorous empirical research" As the evaluation of the various community-oriented policing programs becomes critical to determining the effectiveness, efficiency, and equity of these programs, this forecast is of critical importance to the systemic approach. As the evaluation process is an integral part of the concept of community-oriented policing, as detailed in Chapter 12, this forecast is good news in regard to future implementation.

And finally, the Delphi forecast states that by the year 2025, more than 70 percent of all police departments in the United States will have formal education as a "standard for entry and advancement" (Tafoya 1991, 261) and police executives will "adopt a non-traditional (proactive/goal oriented) leadership style" (Tafoya 1991, 262). As both of these are integral parts to the police officers' and police chiefs' roles under community-oriented policing (See Chapters 8 and 10), they provide a beneficial description of what is to come in our forecasting headlights. The Delphi forecast clearly articulates many of the fundamentals of community-oriented policing.

The second source of futures research that can provide some forecasting revolves around those forces that are likely to have an impact on the systemic approach, but lie outside of the police department's and community's capability to control. These four "drivers" as Cole (1995, 13) describes them, consist of 1) demographics, 2) economics, 3) technology, and 4) crime factors. Each of these will have either a direct or indirect impact on the systemic approach to policing, but all four should be taken into consideration when implementing community-oriented policing.

The first concern revolves around the changing demographics of the United States (Cole 1995; Enter 1991). As the three basic demographic variables include births, deaths, and migration (Farley 1994, 462), any shift in these three could change many of the criminal and order maintenance concerns of the police. Although the birth rates in the United States have decreased, the number of deaths at birth have decreased, causing a slight increase in the population. Equally important are the advancements in medicine which have prolonged life and advanced the average age of death. And finally, migration to the United States continues to see consistent growth. All of these factors play an impact on the demographics of America and will bring with it a host of variables that may impact crime and the police. The potential for an increase in "geriatric crimes" is already being addressed (Bennett 1989; Kercher 1987; Miller 1991; Steffensmeier 1987) as well as for an increase in their victimization rates.

The group that is of most concern in regards to aging is the "Baby Boomers," but an equally interesting trend is the coming of age of their children, the "Echo Baby-Boom" which will bring about an increase in juvenile crimes (McNulty 1995; Oliver 1996). The number of teenagers, based on this second wave of children, is projected to reach 11.5 million by the year 2010, and as most criminologists agree that age is a large factor in crime (Greenberg 1985; Hirschi and Gottfredson 1983), crime is projected to increase. However, what is more disturbing is the increasing number of violent crimes among this age group that may prove to have the biggest impact (McNulty 1995).

Whether it is the aging of America, the rising numbers of juveniles, or the influx of immigrants both legal and illegal, all of these fall under the application of demographics. The growing trends and the forecast of what is to come can provide essential data to understanding today what the police of tomorrow may face. This is critically important to community-oriented policing as the police of tomorrow will be community-oriented police officers.

The second concern falls in the arena of economics (Cole 1995, 13). It is here that the concern of economic viability on the part of the police is of great importance to the future of community-oriented policing. Although the systemic approach can be implemented without the addition of any new funds or resources, this is not to say that any cuts in the police department would not have detrimental effects on this new approach. Additionally, economic concerns can be applied to the local, state, and national level, for if the economy at any of these levels creates a depression or major disruption, regardless of the cause, there is a strong potential the crime rates may increase, the "community" may break down, and the police may be returned to a position that is reactive in nature. Obviously the economic factors of community-oriented policing should be taken into consideration.

The third concern lies in the area of technology (Cole 1995, 13). As the advancements in technology increase and the application to the police grow exponentially, a growing concern exists that the police may become more isolated from the public as a result (Radelet and Carter 1994, 518). There is also some genuine concern that the technology will not be utilized in an appropriate

Vienna police officer of the Vienna Police Department, Vienna, West Virginia, presents a stuffed lion to a local citizen for wearing her safetybelt and having her child in a car seat. (Courtesy of the Parkersburg Police Dept., Parkersburg, West Virginia, and Mr. David Bowie.)

manner and may drive a wedge between the public and the police, rather than bringing them together. In any event, a role for technology exists in community-oriented policing (Ricucci and McKeehan, 1993).

The final concern that will most likely impact community-oriented policing directly is the crime factor (Cole 1995, 13). Recent trends in crime point to different concerns that need to be addressed under community-oriented policing. As previously detailed, there will be a growing trend of "geriatric crimes" and violent crimes among juveniles. There is also a growing trend of women committing more crime, which may have profound effects on crime and policing (Silco 1993). In addition Tafoya's (1987, 18) Delphi forecast of an increase in terrorism by 1995, with the Oklahoma City bombing a prime example, has the potential of becoming a trend that will prove to be of great concern to policing. And finally, there is also the concern of the impact that the future trends of various crime-related issues may have on policing in the future, such as the legalization of drugs, gun control, euthanasia, capital punishment, domestic violence, the increasing prison population, and pornography (see Monk, 1996 for debates on these issues).

As community-oriented policing becomes the chosen method of policing in the United States and we move into the twenty-first century, there will be many factors that affect the systemic approach. Although it is relatively easy to understand what will impact the police internally, it is important that both scholar and practitioner understand what will impact the police externally. Comprehending

Stuffed lion presented to parents with children utilizing their
seatbelts by the Vienna Police Department, Vienna, West Virginia.
(Courtesy of the Parkersburg Police Dept., Parkersburg, West
Virginia, and Mr. David Bowie.)

the impact that these four areas of concern will have on community-oriented
policing can provide the police with the necessary forecast information, both
valid and reliable, that can assist in planning for the future, today.

CONCLUSION

The future of community-oriented policing has begun to arrive. Forecasting
that which lies just around the corner, whether a problem or a benefit, can
assist the police practitioner and police scholar today, in both planning and

implementation. It is important that this information is reliable and valid, and with the tools of research available, this has become a viable method of understanding what lies ahead in policy implementation. Although forecasting may not have the clarity of hindsight, nor may it be as real as the present, futures research can provide some posing questions, answers, and information to the systemic approach to policing.

REFERENCES

Bayley, David H. "Community Policing: A Report from the Devil's Advocate." In *Community Policing: Rhetoric or Reality*, ed. Jack R. Greene and Stephen D. Mastrofski. New York: Praeger Publishers, 1988.

Bennett, Georgette. *Crimewarps: The Future of Crime in America*. New York: Anchor Books, 1989.

Brown, Lee P. "Community Policing: A Practical Guide for Police Officials." *Perspectives on Policing*. Washington, D.C.: National Institute of Justice and the Program in Criminal Justice Policy and Management, September, 1989.

Campbell, John H. "Futures Research: Here and Abroad." *The Police Chief*, January 1990: 24–53.

Christopher, William et. al. "Summary Report." *Report of the Independent Commission on the Los Angeles Police Department*. Los Angeles, California: City of Los Angeles, 1991.

Cole, George F. "Criminal Justice in the Twenty-First Century: The Role of Futures Research." In *Crime and Justice in the Year 2010*, ed. John Klofas and Stan Stojkovic. Belmont, CA.: Wadsworth Publishing Company, 1995.

Cordner, Gary W. "A Problem-Oriented Approach to Community-Oriented Policing." In *Community Policing: Rhetoric or Reality*, ed. Jack R. Greene and Stephen D. Mastrofski. New York: Praeger Publishers, 1988.

Cornish, Edward. *The Study of the Future*. Washington, D.C.: World Future Society, 1977.

Crank, John. "The Community-Policing Movement of the Early Twenty-First Century: What We Learned." In *Crime and Justice in the Year 2010*, ed. John Klofas and Stan Stojkovic. Belmont, CA: Wadsworth Publishing Company, 1995.

Enter, Jack E. "Police Administration in the Future: Demographic Influence as they Relate to Management of Internal and External Environment." *American Journal of Police* 10, no. 4 (1991): 65–81.

Farley, John E. *Sociology*. 3rd ed. Englewood Cliffs, N.J.: Prentice Hall-Inc., 1994.

Gilbert, James N. *Criminal Investigation*. 3rd ed. New York: Macmillan Publishing Company, 1993.

Greenberg, David. "Age, Crime, and Social Explanations." *American Journal of Sociology*, vol. 91 (1985): 1–21.

Hirschi, Travis and Michael Gottfredson. "Age and Explanation of Crime." *American Journal of Sociology*, vol. 89 (1983): 552–584.

Joseph, Earl C. "An Introduction to Studying the Future." In *Futurism in Education: Methodologies*, ed. Stephen B. Hencley and James R. Yates. Berkeley, CA.: McCutchan, 1974.

Kercher, Kyle. "Causes and Correlates of Crime Committed by the Elderly." In *Critical Issues in Aging Policy*, ed. E. Borgatta and R. Montgomery. Beverly Hills: SAGE Publications, 1987.

Klockars, Carl B. "The Rhetoric of Community Policing." In *Community Policing: Rhetoric or Reality*, ed. Jack R. Greene and Stephen D. Mastrofski. New York: Praeger Publishers, 1988.

Klofas, John and Stan Stojkovic. *Crime and Justice in the Year 2010*. Belmont, CA.: Wadsworth Publishing Company, 1995.

McNulty, Paul J. "Natural Born Killers? Preventing the Coming Explosion of Teenage Crime." *Policy Review*, no. 71 (1995): 84–87.

Mastrofski, Stephen D. "Community Policing as Reform: A Cautionary Tale." In *Community Policing:Rhetoric or Reality*, ed. Jack R. Greene and Stephen D. Mastrofski: New York: Praeger Publishers, 1988.

Miller, William D. "The Graying of America: Implications Towards Policing." *Law and Order*, October 1991, 96–97.

Monk, Richard C. *Taking Sides: Clashing Views on Controversial Issues in Crime and Criminology*. 4th ed. Guilford, CT.: Dushkin Publishing Group, Brown & Benchmark Publishers, 1996.

Oliver, Willard M. "The Juvenile Justice System: A Road Paved with Good Intentions." Unpublished paper, 1996.

Radelet, Louis A. And David L. Carter. *The Police and the Community*. 5th ed. New York: Macmillan College Publishing Company, 1994.

Ricucci, Ronald A. and Michael W. McKeehan. "The Role of Technology in Community Policing." *The Police Chief*, May 1993, 41–42.

Riechers, Lisa M. And Roy R. Roberg. "Community Policing: A Critical Review of Underlying Assumptions." *Journal of Police Science and Administration* 17, no. 2, 1990: 105–114.

Rothermel, Terry W. "Forecasting Revisited." *Harvard Business Review* 60, no. 2 (March–April 1982):143–157.

Sileo, Chi Chi. "Crime Takes on a Feminine Face." *Insight*, December 20, 1993, 16–19.

Skolnick, Jerome H. and David H. Bayley. "Theme and Variation in Community Policing." In *Crime and Justice: A Biannual Review of Research*, ed. Michael Tonry and Norval Morris. Chicago, IL.: University of Chicago Press, 1988a.

————. *Community Policing: Issues and Practices Around the World*. Washington, D.C.: National Institute of Justice, 1988b.

Steffensmeier, Darrell. "The Invention of the 'New' Senior Citizen Criminal." *Research on Aging*, vol. 9 (1987): 281–311.

Tafoya, William L. "Into the Future...A Look at the 21st Century." *Law Enforcement Technology*, September/October 1987: 16–86.

————. "Futures Research: Implication for Criminal Investigations." In *Criminal Investigation: Essays and Cases*, ed. James N. Gilbert. Columbus, OH.: Merrill Publishing Company, 1990.

————. *A Delphi Forecast of the Future of Law Enforcement*. Ph.D. Dissertation. Ann Arbor, Michigan: University Microfilm International, 1991.

Trojanowicz, Robert C. "The Future of Community Policing." In *The Challenge of Community Policing: Testing the Promises*, ed. Dennis P. Rosenbaum. Thousand Oaks, CA.: SAGE Publications, Inc., 1994.

Walker, Samuel. "'Broken Windows' and Fractured History: The Use and Misuse of History in Recent Police Patrol Analysis." *Justice Quarterly*, no. 1 (1984): 75–90.

Worsnop, Richard L. "Community Policing." *CQ Researcher*. Washington, D.C.: Congressional Quarterly, Inc., 1993: 97–120.

Wycoff, Mary Ann. "The Benefits of Community Policing: Evidence and Conjecture." In *Community Policing: Rhetoric or Reality*, ed. Jack R. Greene and Stephen D. Mastrofski. New York: Praeger Publishers, 1988.

CHAPTER 15

The Systemic Approach

Greater than the tread of mighty armies is an idea whose time has come.

-Victor Hugo-

Community-oriented policing is an idea whose time has come. The idea is deeply rooted in many of the concepts of policing that have existed for nearly a century. Many of the ideas have come and gone, many are being brought back to life, while many others are new and innovative. An idea is rarely fresh and new among people, rather it is a culmination, a synthesis, and often a recombination of ideas that create new ideas. Community-oriented policing is one such human endeavor, aimed at addressing the crime and order maintenance issues of our time and of our indigenous communities.

The concept itself has generated an abundant amount of information, culminating, synthesizing, and recombining into a concept that is at the same time a philosophy and a practical application. It is a philosophy in the sense that it is a different thought process for the police than they have undertaken in the past. It is no longer an "us versus them" attitude, but one of two groups of people working toward the same goal. It is a practical application because of the numerous programs that have surfaced to assist police departments in implementing the philosophy. These programs range from the reestablishment of foot patrols, to community councils, to direct interaction with the children by the police officers. All of these combine to create the practical application of community-oriented policing.

A youth tries out a police helmet during the "National Night Out"
sponsored by the Montgomery County Police Department,
Montgomery County, Maryland. (Courtesy of the Montgomery
County Dept. of Police, Montgomery County, Maryland.)

This split, within the same concept, may explain why the academics find
the subject of community-oriented policing a little more murky, a little less
defined, and may treat the concept with some skepticism. While the practitioner
has also found the subject very murky, the majority of practitioners, police
chiefs, and administrators have come to embrace the concept with open arms,
regardless of whether they grasp the philosophy or not. It has become easier to
grasp the programs and implement them in a systematic manner as community-
oriented policing has grown and expanded, allowing for many departments to
forego any thought to the philosophy behind the concept. However, the key
here is not so much the fact the concept is unclear to so many, but that as the
concept has developed, it has managed to bridge the gap between the academicians and the police practitioners. Although, according to the literature, no consensus on how to define community-oriented policing has been agreed upon,
both the academicians and the practitioners articulate numerous common
themes that describe a definitive definition of the systemic approach to policing.
This consensus can then be defined in terms that capture all of the rhetoric, all
of the tenants, and all of the programs regarding community-oriented policing.
Therefore, the question posed should focus on how we arrived at this philo-
sophical-programmatic concept. How have we arrived at this consensus?

"CRIME FILES"

DRUGS: YOUTH GANGS—PART 8

This edition of the "Crime Files," hosted by James Q. Wilson, features Steve Valdivia, Executive Director, Community Youth Gang Services, Los Angeles; Lorne Kramer, Los Angeles Police Department Narcotics Group, California; and Malcolm Klein, Professor of Sociology, University of Southern California. The discussion centers on community-oriented policing methods for reducing crime and drug dealing by big-city youth gangs. The focus is primarily on Los Angeles, California, home of the Crips and the Bloods.

It is important to retrace the various social movements that spawned the evolution of the concept and then explore what has become the revolution in policing known as community-oriented policing. The importance of the fact that it is a systemic approach rather than a simplistic program or change in management style must then be explored to understand why the systemic approach is so important to policing in both the academic and practical sense. Fundamentally, we will explore why community-oriented policing is truly an idea whose time has come.

COP IN ACTION

COMMUNITY POLICING WORKS: THE CONCEPT IS LIMITED ONLY BY THOSE APPLYING IT

During a discussion about community policing, a fellow officer stated: "That's okay for a big city, but it will never work in a small community." His reasoning was that smaller agencies don't have sufficient manpower to commit to foot patrols. His idea of community policing was limited to neighborhood foot patrol; he had no concept of what the philosophy actually entailed. Unfortunately, many administrative officers suffer from similar misconceptions.

Community policing is often approached as a means of improving police–community relations, with major emphasis on the image of the police department. Implementation allows departments to be depicted as being concerned with the citizens and their plight, as being available to the individual on the street. Adoption of popular techniques such as neighborhood foot patrol, community precinct stations, bike patrol, etc., are quick methods of improving a department's image. All an administrator has to do is choose one and convince the community that this will solve the crime problems. A desperate community is likely to accept any promise of hope.

Community policing should be viewed as an ongoing process, not as patched-in programs. It is a philosophy; a way of identifying and addressing the real needs of a community. It is not a program that can be developed inside by the police and delivered to the neighborhood. It is a commitment on the part of the community's citizens and leaders and the police agency, working together in an ongoing process of identifying community needs/problems and appropriating community resources to improve the quality of life. Once a municipality has made a commitment to the concept, the work has just begun.

Community policing is based on the idea that crime prevention and apprehension are the responsibility of the whole community. Individuals who live in a neighborhood often have more knowledge about problems and offenders than do the police. Community agencies and leaders have access to resources and skills that police departments lack. In community policing, representatives from a neighborhood, community agencies, and the police are brought together to identify specific problems of the area and strategies to address them. Problems that are not within the sphere of the police are referred to appropriate agencies, and neighborhoods that are assisted in addressing problems successfully are altered or dropped and new ones are developed.

When viewed as a concept or philosophy, community policing is adaptable to any municipality. Large budgets and resources are not necessary. However, the agency must recognize that the community has resources and skills that are essential to dealing with its crime problems.

Source: Adapted with permission from Sgt. Bruce McVety. "Community Policing Works." *Law and Order*, February 1994, 71.

EVOLUTION

Community-oriented policing has evolved through factors and inputs that have combined to create the systemic approach to policing. Each has shaped the movement toward the concept in a unique form or fashion, and although everything affects the final synthesis of ideas, the following are the categories that are most important.

The first factor that truly shapes the concept exists outside of the government's or people's control, namely in the form of crime. The key to understanding the evolution of community-oriented policing lies in understanding the evolution of crime itself. The second influence has evolved as a result of other concepts from the social science fields that have created new methods and new ideas for improving the quality of life. This is essentially the accumulation of knowledge on the part of academicians, politicians, researchers, theorists, and those with the practical experience to either confirm or deny the plausible and practical use of this knowledge. The third influence has come from the public. Whether it exists in the form of public awareness and public opinion of the criminal justice system or of the police themselves, the pressure placed on both of these entities has demanded change. As the first and most visible arm of the criminal justice system, the police have long been blamed first for a broken system. In the event of police corruption, police brutality, rising crime rates, growing order maintenance issues, or simply a disrespectful police officer, the police have been blamed for allowing these problems to arise by a public demanding justice. The fourth factor has been a concern for the movement away from "community" as the United States has modernized.

There has been a decline in the small traditional community that so many citizens grew up in and many want a return to that sense of community for their children. And finally, the work of many police practitioners and academicians, with foresight and innovation, who have attempted to move the police to change and toward a better method of performing their critical function, have allowed the revolution to take place.

TABLE 15.1   RESPONDENTS RESPONDING THAT TOO LITTLE HAS BEEN SPENT ON HALTING THE RISING CRIME RATE IN THE UNITED STATES, 1973–1994.

1973	64%	1986	64%
1974	66%	1987	68%
1975	65%	1988	72%
1976	65%	1989	73%
1977	65%	1990	70%
1978	64%	1991	65%
1981	69%	1993	71%
1982	71%	1994	75%
1983	67%		
1984	68%		
1985	63%		

Source: Maguire, Kathleen, and Ann L. Pastore. *Bureau of Justice Statistics Sourcebook of Criminal Justice Statistics—994.* Washington, D.C.: Bureau of Justice Statistics, 1995.

In order to understand the evolution of community-oriented policing, it is important to understand crime and the maintenance of social order. As crime and order maintenance problems are a constant occurrence in every society, they must be dealt with in some manner. These problems are essentially public problems, falling to the people, in a collective sense, to deal with the crimes that are inevitably going to occur and with those things that detract from the quality of life. As it is generally most effective to place this responsibility in the hands of an organization that acts with the collective interest in mind, the role of policing society is placed in the hands of the government. It is then the role of the government, particularly the state and local governments, to determine its methods for addressing these problems.

In order to address the problem of crime, it is often helpful to understand why crime occurs in the first place. As we come to accept crime and social disorder as constants, we must explore why it is a constant. Why does crime occur? The answer is explored most heavily in the sociology field, through a sub-set of interest known as criminology. Although defined in a variety of ways, the sole premise is to determine why people commit crime. Although this should not be the sole basis for determining police practices and procedures, the criminological theories can be beneficial to understand what may work to address both the criminal and order maintenance issues.

In the event that choice theories are correct, and individuals choose to commit crime in the same manner that they choose what is for dinner, then the obvious response is to remove crime as an option or implement methods that make the choice less desirable. The goal is to then create a deterrence that would reduce a rational individual's propensity to commit crime. If, on the other hand, the biological and psychological theories of crime are accurate, then the deterrent factors will not work and other means of dealing with criminals must be addressed though prevention and intervention. However, if the social structure theories are correct, various factors such as socioeconomic status, race, ethnicity, our form of government, and other established structures in our society, are what cause people to commit crime, and hence the use of deterrents, prevention, and intervention will work to no avail unless the social structure is changed. A difficult task to say the least.

Another host of theories is categorized as social process theories, or theories that crime is caused by what is essentially human interaction. The impact that family, peers, education, and the media has on each individual may cause certain individuals to commit crime. Those with strong ties to their family and friends, who receive a good education and have a fundamental understanding of the media will grow to be productive citizens, while those without these ties or abilities will, as a result of the social process, resort to crime and commit deviant behaviors. Finally, the category of theories known as social conflict detail crime as a response by those who hold little power against the police who are considered a tool for those who wield both power and money. All of these are difficult theories for the police to address.

If all of the theories are taken into account, they still do not present an accurate picture of why people commit crime, but each in its own right addresses some of the fundamental reasons. They all seem to be right, but they all, even in a collective sense, do not paint the total picture. Despite this simplistic fault within the criminological theories, they are beneficial to the police and especially to the evolution of policing. As a result of the evolution in criminology, the police have been able to utilize many of their findings to address crime and social disorder. In the synthesis of community-oriented policing, the police can address choice theories by creating deterrents through crime prevention techniques. They can also work with other agencies to address the biological and psychological causation of crime by creating a working relationship with those agencies better capable of handling these types of criminals. If the social structure theories are correct, community-oriented policing addresses this by changing the social structure in relation to crime and order maintenance, by soliciting the help of the community and in some cases assisting in the formation of community where none exists. In answer to the social process theories, community-oriented policing moves toward providing many programs oriented toward both youths and adults that can improve their abilities and capabilities when it comes to strong family and peer relationships and a healthy atmosphere and respect toward education and the media. And finally, by making the police a more equitable institution and allowing for the community to become a buffer between government and the individual citizen, it addresses the conflict theories of crime. By placing the reasons that people commit crime into perspective, community-oriented policing has evolved to address each of these perspectives in its methods of dealing with crime and social disorder.

TABLE 15.2   ATTITUDES TOWARD GOVERNMENT SPENDING TO
REDUCE CRIME, 1994

Question: "In order to fight crime, the government can spend money in four different areas. The first is prevention, such as community education and youth programs. The second is enforcement, such as more police officers and tougher laws. The third is punishment, such as better courts and bigger jails, and the fourth is rehabilitation, such as education and work programs for former criminals. If the government could spend money in only one of these four areas to try to reduce crime in this country, do you feel the money should be spent on...?"

	Prevention	Punishment	Enforcement	Rehabilitation
National	41%	25%	19%	12%
Sex				
Male	41%	30%	16%	12%
Female	42%	20%	22%	12%
Race				
White	43%	26%	20%	9%
Black	37%	10%	11%	30%
Other	32%	33%	21%	12%
Age				
less than 35	41%	29%	17%	11%
35 to 54	45%	25%	19%	9%
55 & older	36%	18%	21%	17%

Source: Maguire, Kathleen, and Ann L. Pastore. *Bureau of Justice Statistics Sourcebook of Criminal Justice Statistics—1994*. Washington, D.C.: Bureau of Justice Statistics, 1995.

Understanding crime through the assistance of criminologists is one step toward understanding all of the issues of crime, but it also provides the first step toward understanding that the systemic approach to policing has resulted through a variety of disciplines that lie outside of the policing and criminal justice fields. Criminology is but one exogenous field and many others have offered their assistance in the evolution of community-oriented policing. The evolution of the management field has sponsored such methods as Total Quality Management (TQM) and has provided the impetus for mission-driven, customer-driven, and decentralized institutions to exist, thus clearing the way for the police. Another area that has provided for much of the movement has been the public administration field which has formed and advanced many of the understandings of how public institutions, specifically bureaucracies, either work or do not work. And, certainly not the last field, but one of the more important fields, is the political science field. The political science discipline provides the evolutionary background to understand government, its purpose, function and role in society, past, present, and future. It also provides the groundwork for exploring the role of the community and the role of the police in a civil society.

Although crime itself and the other disciplines have had a great impact on the evolution of policing, public opinion has played an equally important role. The public's awareness of crime and public opinion of crime have not always retained a high position of concern. Although crime and social disorder have always existed as important issues to each individual community, they have not always been held high as a national problem. Crime is a salient issue, pushed onto the public agenda often by politicians or as a result of a lack of other key issues facing the American population. In the Gallup polls exploring the question "What do you think is the most important problem facing the country today?" from 1964 to the present, the response has fluctuated with little correlation to the actual crime rates (see Beckett, 1994; Fairchild and Webb 1985; Gallup 1964–1994; Marion 1994; Oliver 1996; Scheingold, 1995; Scheingold, 1984). There are then other factors that push crime onto the public agenda, namely the media and, to a smaller degree, individual experience. However, even the actual perspective of crime held by the public is generally not in correlation with the actual crime rates. When asked if crime rates are increasing, decreasing, or holding steady, the majority answer to the effect that crime has increased or held steady (Maguire et al. 1995). This holds regardless of whether the actual crime rates are increasing or decreasing. Therefore, at any given time the public feels that crime is too high and they demand that something be done to address these issues.

The fourth influencing factor is the decline of the small, traditional community that once marked mainstream America, as a result of a steady movement toward modernization. As the United States has moved from an industrial age to an information age, the ability to rapidly move, communicate, and engage in various businesses nationwide, if not worldwide, have caused people to leave behind the small isolated communities. This modernity has essentially caused the "progressive weakening, if not destruction, of the concrete and relatively cohesive communities in which human beings have found solidarity and meaning throughout most of history" (Berger 1977, 72). Community-oriented policing is essentially a movement to recapture this lost sense of community through a coordinated effort to improve the quality of life in the various neighborhoods.

At the root of this return to community is an element of human life that has been long believed to be central to living the good life. The media consistently conjures up the debate over "family values" and "lost values" and their application to our current living status in the United States. It was Aristotle's *Politica* that was essentially a defense of values, which he believed made citizenship central to the good and rational life of mankind. Citizenship, and the responsibilities inherent within this concept, are those things often missing from present-day America. It is this sense of citizenship, a civic attachment and identity, one that goes far beyond limited or special interests, that community-oriented policing calls for every community member to promulgate.

TABLE 15.3   ATTITUDES TOWARD VARIOUS CRIME REDUCTION
                  PROPOSALS, 1994

Question: "Please tell me whether you would generally favor or oppose each of the following proposals which some people have made to reduce crime."

	Favor	Oppose
Prohibiting people under the age of 18 from being able to purchase a gun	88%	11%
A ban on the manufacture, sale, and possession of certain semi-automatic guns known as assault rifles	71%	26%
Requiring that if a sexual offender is released from prison, that the community where he lives be notified	89%	8%
Providing local communities with Federal tax money to hire more police officers	79%	18%
Passing a law called "three strikes and you're out," which requires that anyone convicted of three serious felonies be automatically sentenced to life in prison without parole	74%	21%
Providing local communities with Federal tax money to provide social programs and activities for low-income children, such as midnight basketball	65%	31%
Extending the death penalty for some serious crimes other than murder	60%	35%

Source: Maguire, Kathleen, and Ann L. Pastore. *Bureau of Justice Statistics Sourcebook of Criminal Justice Statistics—1994.* Washington, D.C.: Bureau of Justice Statistics, 1995.

This concept was central to our founding fathers and the principles of classical republican government. Thomas Paine argued that a republic can only flourish when the majority of citizens are virtuous and public-spirited and sacrifice their interests for the good of the community. However, Paine believed that community members had the most influential power in that "common interest regulates their concerns and forms their laws; and the laws which common usage ordains, have a greater influence than the laws of government." This was considered to be the mark of good citizenship and was necessary for the survival of civilization and to live the good life.

Tocqueville, in his writings on "Democracy in America," realized if society continued to advance and government continued to grow, citizens would lose their sense of identity and hence lose the power of common interest. Tocqueville recognized that strong democratic government needed a balance of authority and accountability between the state, the private citizen, and all those entities that attempt to mediate between the two, especially the police. It seems that Tocqueville effectively predicted America's future.

Community-oriented policing however, has attempted to restore the sense of citizenship and make it an integral part of the operation of government, in this case the police. This movement has been of great concern not only in the area of policing, but in the relationship of the public to all government agencies (see Bellah, et al. 1985; Green 1985; Marquand 1988; Sullivan, 1986). The goal is to restore the concept of citizenship to increase the commitment to family and community. Community-oriented policing is perhaps one step in this direction, but it is, without doubt, a good step.

THE CRIME BILL

PUBLIC SAFETY AND POLICING

The Crime Control Act of 1994 provides more than $13 billion dollars for federal, state, and local law enforcement officers, equipment, and various programs related to policing. One of the key goals of the Crime Bill was to add an additional 100,000 police officers nationwide to patrol the streets, both urban and rural. Nearly $9 billion of the $30.2 billion dollars allocated under the Crime Bill was directed toward this specific purpose. Police officers who have been laid off will be rehired, new officers will be hired and trained, and existing officers will be afforded the opportunity for additional training. Many of these officers are being added to police departments across the nation in order to implement and promote community-oriented policing.

Additional money has been set aside to fund the Police Corps program which would operate similar to the Reserve Officers Training Corps (ROTC). Students attending local colleges would be eligible for Federally funded college scholarships of up to $10,000 a year, of which they would then incur a four-year commitment to a state or local law enforcement agency upon their graduation. The act also takes into consideration those police officers who are already employed, but are looking to enhance their education by providing financial assistance to attend college. One final aspect of the act allocates additional funding for high school and college students interested in a career in law enforcement to work for a police department during the summer and part-time.

Over $2.5 billion has also been allocated specifically for Federal law enforcement agencies. Approximately half of these funds are going to the Immigration and Naturalization Service (INS) in order to increase the patrol along the United States southern border against illegal aliens, to apprehend illegal aliens who stay in the country beyond their visas, and to deport aliens convicted of serious felonies.

The final influencing factor in the evolution of community-oriented policing is of course in the policing arena. If not for forward-thinking individuals such as August Vollmer and O.W. Wilson, policing would not have evolved as quickly as it has in the twentieth century. These police chiefs, and many like them, began applying the lessons learned in other fields and listening to what the public wanted in their police, to create some of the finest police departments in the nation. By providing this base of excellence, other police chiefs and academicians have been able to build upon this foundation to move the police through the various eras. In moving the police from the political era and into the public relations era, police departments across the nation began to incorporate the public into their function, even if only in an advisory fashion. A great leap was made in relations with the police and community during the late-1950s and early-1960s in the police-community relations era, which paved the way for community-oriented policing.

These multiple factors—crime, various exogenous disciplines, the public, the desire for community through citizenship, and the police themselves—contributed heavily to the evolution of community-oriented policing. All of these factors have developed and built upon themselves to eventually provide the connection of information necessary to launch the revolution in policing known as community-oriented policing. As every era develops and refines its own public philosophy, the current era has developed a philosophy of community-oriented government, community partnerships, and most critical to the policing field, community-oriented policing. As the systemic approach becomes entrenched in police departments across the nation, one cannot deny that the revolution is upon us.

REVOLUTION

The revolution began oddly enough with the writings of three individuals, two in a collaborative effort via a theory, one with a distinct idea. In 1979, with the publication of "Improving Policing: A Problem-Oriented Approach" in the journal *Crime & Delinquency*, Herman Goldstein articulated the idea of problem-oriented policing which, despite the capability of seeing independent implementation, has become an integral part of community-oriented policing. In 1982, with the publication by two authors, one a political scientist, James Q. Wilson, and the other a former police officer and academic, George L. Kelling, entitled "Broken Windows" in the *The Atlantic Monthly*, the premise for the core of community-oriented policing was born. Wilson and Kelling later followed up their seminal work with "Broken Windows: Making Neighborhoods Safe" in the same monthly journal, further articulating the need for community-oriented policing.

The revolution of community-oriented policing, like most revolutions, began rather disjointedly and did not have a core focus as both the academic and practitioner debated over what was meant by this term. Arriving at a consensus was difficult, as many departments were implementing problem-oriented policing independent of community-oriented policing and not every community-oriented police department looked the same. The concept, meant to be a living and breathing idea, adaptable to any crime or order maintenance problem indigenous to a particular community, has sparked much debate as to how to define itself.

Officer Sandy Minor, the first female motorcycle officer of the
St. Petersburg Police Department, St. Petersburg, Florida, with her
nephew. (Courtesy of St. Petersburg Police Dept., St. Petersburg,
Florida.)

The model of community-oriented policing that this book articulates is a
synthesis of both the research and practical application of the concept,
attempting to arrive at a consensus to properly define and implement the philosophy, policy, and programs that have come to be defined as community-
oriented policing. It has combined the concept into three integral components:
strategic-oriented policing, neighborhood-oriented policing, and problem-oriented
policing to maintain the clarity of the different implementation methods that,
when combined, will weave a web of methods that will become the community-
oriented policing model. In addition, it has articulated that in order for the full
implementation to be realized, to support the three integral components, the
police department must decentralize by geography, personnel, and structure.
Only with the complementary and necessary decentralization of the police
department will community-oriented policing be realized.

However, there is more to the systemic approach than the complex implementation of the three components and decentralizing the police department.
Community-oriented policing must also take into consideration and change the
role of the police officer, the role of the community, and the role of the police
chief. The police officer must take on a different role under the systemic
approach in order for it to succeed. Line officers will not only have to maintain

and apply many of the traditional methods of policing, but they will have to learn to adapt to many of the new functions they may be asked to perform. They must also be provided the responsibility, authority, and decision-making power at their level that is so critical to community-oriented policing.

The role of the community will also change under the systemic approach as its citizens become more involved in the decision-making function that was once relegated to the city manager, city council, or the police chief. The community must take part in determining where the criminal and order maintenance problems are in their community and they must determine what is the most effective and efficient method for utilizing police resources. They must also work with the police to implement the policy and programs that will address their concerns and to provide the support necessary to accomplish these goals.

And finally, the police chief's role will also see some dramatic changes under community-oriented policing. The police chief will be required to become a more dynamic community figure under the systemic approach and will have to be the key proponent for community-oriented policing. Many principles will have to be adapted under the systemic approach, ranging from becoming the key ombudsmen for the police department when working with the community, other government agencies, and other police agencies, to adapting to the idea of sharing his or her role with the community. The chief will essentially become a member and a leader of the community and will set the standard for community values and community standards.

As police departments across the nation continue to adapt and implement community-oriented policing it is important to also understand that the systemic approach is not a "program" that can be implemented overnight. It is imperative that an incremental approach be taken with community-oriented policing and that those involved understand that although community-oriented policing can be quickly implemented with some of its concepts and ideas, true community-oriented policing will take many years, if not a decade or two to fully implement. Although no simplistic method exists for implementing the systemic approach to policing, because every community and police department is different, there are some fundamental stages that the police department should pass through. There must be a planning stage to determine the long-range goals and how the implementation process will proceed. A micro community-oriented policing stage is most beneficial to the police department to "test the waters" but the department must not leave it in place for very long. A transition stage is important to allow the entire police department the time to train, learn, and adapt to the systemic approach as it moves into the macro community-oriented policing stage. Only when the entire police department has come on line, and every facet of the department has witnessed a complete adaptation to the community-oriented approach, can the police department claim full legitimacy under community-oriented policing. Continual implementation in an incremental method, assessing all of the various programs implemented as well as community and police satisfaction, dealing quickly with any problems that may arise, and looking to the future, will be the four cornerstones for the successful implementation of community-oriented policing.

TABLE 15.4   THE CRIME BILL

Congressional appropriations for 1996 in the Violent Crime Control and Law Enforcement Act of 1994.*

Title 1 – Public safety and policing	$1.85 billion
Title 2 – Prisons	$1.07 billion
Title 3 – Crime prevention	$678 million
Title 4 – Violence against women	$274 million
Title 5 – Drug courts	$150 million
Title 6 – Death penalty	none
Title 7 – "Three strikes" legislation	none
Title 8 – Mandatory minimum penalties	none
Title 9 – Drug control	none
Title 10 – Drunk-driving provisions	none
Title 11 – Firearms	none
Title 12 – Terrorism	none
Title 13 — Criminal aliens & immigration	$332 million
Title 14 – Youth violence	none
Title 15 – Criminal street gangs	$1 million
Title 16 – Child pornography	none
Title 17 – Crimes against children	none
Title 18 – Rural crime	$37 million
Title 19 – Federal law enforcement	$145 million
Title 20 – Police corps and law enforcement officers training and education	$20 million
Title 21 – State & local law enforcement	$211 million
Title 22 – Motor vehicle theft protection	$1.5 million
Title 23 – Victims of crime	none
Title 24 – Protection for the elderly	$900,000
Title 25 – Senior citizens against marketing scams	$2 million
Title 26 – Commission membership and appointment	none
Title 27 – Presidential summit on violence & national commission on crime prevention & control	$1 million
Title 28 – Sentence provisions	none
Title 29 – Computer crime	none
Title 30 – Protection of privacy of information in state motor vehicle records	none
Title 31 – Violent crime reduction trust fund	$4.3 billion
Title 32 – Miscellaneous	none
Title 33 – Technical corrections	none
TOTAL APPROPRIATIONS FOR 1996	$9.07 billion

*Note: In the event of no expenditures ("none"), it is generally the case that either a new law was created or an old law was modified.

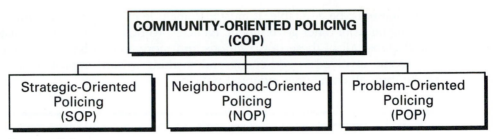

FIGURE 15.1

The revolution of community-oriented policing has arrived and the future of the systemic approach looks promising. The benefits to the police and community seem to far outweigh any negative considerations for implementation. As police departments across the nation begin to implement however, it is only the future that will reveal the success of the systemic approach. One of the keys to this potential success distinctly lies in the fact that it is a systemic approach. As this book has articulated this fact multiple times, it is essential that this statement be reviewed for its importance. Understanding what is meant by the systemic approach, and why it is important, is critical to a full understanding of community-oriented policing.

THE SYSTEMIC APPROACH

Community-oriented policing as a systemic approach to policing must incorporate more than the police. It must not be limited to the confines of the police department, but reach out to every member of the community, every social organization located in the community, every business, and every other government agency. It must also move beyond the concrete and into the abstract by touching many other aspects of society. It must begin to reach far into the cultural, economic, and social elements of a given community to truly touch every facet of both definitive and abstract elements of the community. And it cannot at any time leave anyone or anything untouched, for in the goals and tenets of community-oriented policing, all will be touched in some form or manner.

It is easy to articulate and clarify how the police will be affected by community-oriented policing. It is here that the police department has the most control and clarity in implementing the systemic philosophy. However, as the term alludes to, there must be a systemic change to the community. The community is the basis for the concept either through their inclusion in the decision-making process and allowing them to determine what problems are to be addressed in an active community, or by simply advising them of what has been implemented in their interest in a non-active community. It is therefore imperative that the systemic be actualized in this arena. The members of the community ranging from the rich to the poor, the employed to the unemployed, to those who enjoy the luxury of large homes to the homeless, everyone must receive the benefits of community-oriented policing, for the systemic

approach must be equitable. It must also include every type of organized interest ranging from other government agencies, to businesses, to homemakers, to
social clubs. All of these organizations and more should have the opportunity
to become involved in addressing and working toward improving the quality
of life through community-oriented policing.

COMMUNITY-ORIENTED POLICING DEFINED

A systemic approach to policing with the paradigm of instilling and fostering a sense of community, within a geographical neighborhood, to improve
the quality of life. It achieves this through the decentralization of the police
and the implementation of a synthesis of three key components: 1) strategic-
oriented policing—the redistribution of traditional police resources; 2) neighborhood-oriented policing—the interaction of police and all community
members to reduce crime and the fear of crime through indigenous proactive
programs; and 3) problem-oriented policing—a concerted effort to resolve
the causes of crime, rather than the symptoms.

It must then be understood that community-oriented policing is a systemic
approach that must see full implementation in all of these key police and community concepts. It cannot be implemented within a police department and
exclude the community. It cannot be implemented as a task force and not
throughout the entire police department. It cannot be implemented with strategic-oriented policing and neighborhood-oriented policing, while excluding
problem-oriented policing. It must be implemented at every step of the process
in a systemic manner.

As the systemic approach is implemented, it must move beyond merely
touching the police and community members and move into those abstract entities that exist in the philosophical arena of community-oriented policing. There
must be changes to the social factors of the community by way of improving the
quality of life, seeing community members come together to address that which
affects their lives in an adverse way, and forming a relationship of understanding
between the police and the community. But it must reach further still, into the
cultural aspects of the community through assisting those pockets of community
where the culture has grown used to high crime rates and poverty and has
developed an unhealthy culture in dealing with these problems without the support of the rest of the community or even the government. It must also reach
into the economic factors of a community through such programs as revitaliza-
tion and clean-up programs, which if complemented by more effective methods
of dealing with crime and reducing the fear a community feels, can increase the
economic prosperity of the community which is beneficial to all. And it must
continue to invade the legal, political, and other institutional factors to create a
complex relationship that can guide the community toward its choice of goals to
create the type of community in which its citizens wish to live.

In considering community-oriented policing as the next era of public policy, which has many relationships with other public policies being actualized, the systemic approach will most likely be infectious. The policy, however, must remain rooted in a constitutional context, rooted in the desires of

Police Officer Doug Bruce of the Phoenix Police Department, Phoenix, Arizona, assists a local citizen through a community contact. (Courtesy of Phoenix Police Dept., Phoenix, Arizona, and Mr. Bob Rink.)

the collective community, and guided by the goals and values that are so highly prized. It must be balanced among all of these aspects and it must remain equitable in its structure, it must remain equitable in its implementation and operation, and it must remain equitable by its very nature. Community-oriented policing is predicated in maintaining these key ideas within its conceptual understanding as a public policy, but more importantly as a philosophy.

Perhaps the most important question one could ask in reference to the systemic approach is "why?" Why must community-oriented policing be implemented as a system and not as a stand-alone program? What makes this approach to policing any more effective than those implemented in the past or than the traditional method of policing? There are perhaps multiple and complex answers to these questions, but there are some commonsense answers that perhaps speak best for the systemic approach.

First and foremost is the fact that the system currently in place is not equitable. The traditional form of police services does not provide benefits to all members of the community. The majority of time is spent with those members of the community who are considered the "least desirable" and with those who pay the most for police services. Many groups of people are overlooked that could benefit from police services, and who in turn may benefit the police. As the United States was founded on the principle of equity, articulating that it would not "deny to any person within its jurisdiction the equal protection of the laws," it is imperative that this key principle remain a guiding factor of the police, not to be overlooked. Traditional policing has often overlooked this principle. Community-oriented policing will not.

Second, there was a realization long ago that the police cannot deal with crime and order maintenance issues by themselves, but must elicit the help of the community. There are simply not enough police officers on the streets of America and there never will be. Yet it has long been the premise, deeply rooted in traditional policing, that the police should do their job and the public should leave them alone. Unfortunately this has been neither to the benefit of the police nor to the public, and has only managed to drive a wedge of misunderstanding between these two entities consisting of the same people, who rather than working against one another, should be working toward similar goals. Community-oriented policing recognizes that not only do the police need the assistance of the community, they need their full cooperation and support. Community coalitions must be formed, the community must have some decision-making power as the police work for the community, and there must be a cooperative effort if the problems that plague a community are ever to be truly addressed.

Third, the past eras of crime policy have not worked. The political era, where the police were closely tied to the political machines did not work, the public relations era created the gulf between police and community relations, and the police–community relations era has done little to foster solid police–community relations. Although each era has not been a complete failure because they have developed many of the tenets of community-oriented policing, they have not been largely successful in their own right either. Community-oriented policing is a policy which, if implemented correctly, will address many of the failures of the past and move crime policy toward a system that will work in an effective, efficient, and equitable manner. Continuation of past crime policy is not the answer, but, rather, moving forward to the policy and philosophy of community-oriented policing is.

Fourth, the key provision of centralization, embodied in traditional policing, has not been effective and has created an atmosphere of a military organization detached from the community. Although centralizing the police was implemented as a method of preventing political corruption amongst the police, policing as a profession has come a long way since the turn of the twentieth century. The decentralization of the police is the most effective way to improve police capability by providing not only more responsibility on the line officers, but also more authority. The return of police corruption and the political ties are not possible today with the benefits of communication, better management, and an understanding that supervision techniques have improved. This is not to say that community-oriented policing does not take into consideration the potential for corruption. However, it works toward preventing its possibility through proactive management measures. Finally, it is important to also point out that today, despite the strict centralization of the police, incidents of police corruption and police brutality are reported. The method implemented at the turn of the century has not effectively controlled these incidents. I is time to try another method. Community-oriented policing is the key.

Officer T. Pekin of the Montgomery County Police Department, Montgomery County, Maryland, has a heart-to-heart talk with a local youth during a dare event. (Courtesy of the Montgomery County Dept. of Police, Montgomery County, Maryland.)

When viewed in the systemic approach to policing, it is clear that community-oriented policing is the key to a better police department. Ranging from the results of a more effective and efficient police department to more satisfied citizens and line officers, the benefits of community-oriented policing far outweigh anything that may detract from the philosophy. The systemic approach can be rewarding to everyone within the community as it provides for an equitable method of delivering police services. It is a system that has transformed the police and will continue to do so well into the twenty-first century. It is a system that, once fully implemented, will have far-reaching capabilities to affect every fabric of the community. And it is a system that will provide for the reduction of crime, address those order maintenance issues that affect the community, and promote a better quality of life for all of the community members, which includes those members of the community known as the police.

REFERENCES

Beckett, Katherine. "Setting the Public Agenda: "Street Crime" and Drug Use in American Politics." *Social Problems* 41, (1994): 425–447.

Bellah, Robert N., Richard Madsen, William M. Sullivan, Ann Swindler, and Steven M. Tipton. *Habits of the Heart*. New York: Harper & Row, 1985.

Berger, Peter L. *Facing up to Modernity: Excursions in Society, Politics, and Religion*. New York, New York, Basic Books, 1977.

Fairchild, Erika S. and Vincent J. Webb. *The Politics of Crime and Criminal Justice*. Beverly Hills: SAGE Publications, 1985.

Gallup, George. *The Gallup Poll: Public Opinion*. Wilmington, Delaware: Scholarly Resources Inc., 1964–1994.

Green, P. *Retrieving Democracy*. Totowa, N.J.: Rowman and Allanheld, 1985.

Maguire, Kathleen, et al. *Sourcebook of Criminal Justice Statistics—1994*. Washington, D.C.: U.S. GPO, 1995.

Marion, Nancy E. *A History of Federal Crime Control Initiatives, 1960-1993*. Westport, CT.: Praeger Publishers, 1994.

Marquand, D. "Preceptoral Politics, Yeoman Democracy and the Enabling State." *Government and Opposition*, vol.23 (1988): 261–275.

Paine, Thomas. *Common Sense*. ed. Isaac Kramnick. New York: Penguin Books, 1976.

Scheingold, Stuart A. *Politics of Law and Order*. New York: Longman, Inc., 1984.

————. "Politics, Public Policy, and Street Crime." *Annals of the American Academy of Political and Social Science*. 539 (1995): 155–168.

Sullivan, William M. *Reconstructing Public Philosophy*. Berkeley, CA.: University of California Press, 1986.

Wilson, James Q. and George L. Kelling. "Broken Windows: The Police and Neighborhood Safety." *The Atlantic Monthly*. March 1982: 29-38.

————."Broken Windows: Making Neighborhoods Safe." *The Atlantic Monthly*. February 1989: 46-52.

BIBLIOGRAPHY

Abella, Mary. "Law Camps: A New Twist on an Old Favorite." *Law and Order*, December 1994, 30–32.

Aeilts, Tony. "Crime Suppression: A Multi-Agency Approach." *Law and Order*, September 1993, 121–122.

Ahrens, Michael K. "School Resources Officers." *Law and Order*, July 1995, 81–83.

Albritton, James S. "The Technique of Community-Oriented Policing: an Alternative Explanation." In *Issues in Community Policing*, ed. Peter C. Kratcoski and Duane Dukes. Cincinnati: Academy of Criminal Justice Sciences, Anderson Publishing Company, 1995.

Alpert, Geoffrey P. and Roger G. Dunham. *Policing Urban America*. 2nd ed. Prospect Heights, IL.: Waveland Press Inc., 1992.

Anderson, David C. *Crimes of Justice*. New York: Times Books, 1988.

Andrews, Allen H. Jr. "Structuring the Political Independence of the Police Chief." In *Police Leadership in America,* ed. William A. Geller. New York: American Bar Foundation, Praeger Publishers, 1985.

Andrews, Kenneth R. *The Concept of Corporate Strategy*. Homewood, IL.: Richard D. Irwin, 1980.

Austin, Dave and Jane Bratten. "Turning Lives Around: Portland Youth Find a New PAL." *The Police Chief,* May 1991, 36–38.

Austin, David. "Community Policing: the Critical Partnership." *Public Management,* July 1992, 3–9.

Banton, Michael. *The Police in the Community*. New York: Basic Books, 1964.

Barker, Thomas and David L. Carter. *Police Deviance*. 3rd ed., ed. Thomas Barker and David L. Carter. Cincinnati: Anderson Publishing Company, 1994.

Bassett, Adele. "Community-Oriented Gang Control." *The Police Chief*. February 1993, 20–23.

Bassett, Nicholas. "Total quality Management in the Public Sector." Unpublished Paper. June 1995.

Bayley, David H. "Community Policing: A Report from the Devil's Advocate." In *Community Policing: Rhetoric or Reality,* ed. Jack R. Greene and Stephen D. Mastrofski. New York: Praeger Publishers, 1988.

Bayley, David H. *A Model of Community Policing: The Singapore Force Story*. Washington, D.C.: National Institute of Justice, 1989.

Bayley, David H. "International Differences in Community Policing." In *The Challenge of Community Policing: Testing the Promises*. ed. Dennis P. Rosenbaum. Thousand Oaks, CA.: SAGE Publications, Inc., 1994.

Beckett, Katherine. "Setting the Public Agenda: "Street Crime" and Drug Use in American Politics." *Social problems* 41 (1994): 425–447.

Begovich, Ray. "Cracking Down on Crack." *Law and Order,* October 1995, 80–81.

Bellah, Robert N., Richard Madsen, William M. Sullivan, Ann Swindler, and Steven M. Tipton. *Habits of the Heart*. New York: Harper & Row, 1985.

Bennett, Charles W. Jr. "The Last Taboo of Community Policing." *The Police Chief* 60, no. 8 (1993): 86.

Bennett, Georgette. *Crimewarps: The Future of Crime in America*. New York: Anchor Books, 1989.

Bennett, Georgette. "Cultural Lag in Law Enforcement: Preparing Police for the Crimewarps of the Future." *American Journal of Police* 9, 1990: 79–86.

Bennett, Richard and Theodore Greenstein. "The Police Personality: A Test of the Predispositional Model." *Journal of Police Science and Administration,* No. 3 (1975): 439–445.

Bennett, Susan F. and Paul J. Lavrakas. "Community-Based Crime Prevention: An Assessment of the Eisenhower Foundation's Neighborhood Program." *Crime & Delinquency* 35, no. 3, (July 1989): 345–364.

Bennett, Trevor. "Community Policing on the Ground." In *The Challenge of Community Policing: Testing the Promises*. ed. Dennis P. Rosenbaum. Thousand Oaks, CA.: SAGE Publications, Inc., 1994.

Berg, Gregory R. "Promises vs. Reality in Community Policing." *Law and Order,* September 1995, 147–148.

Berger, Peter L. *Facing Up to Modernity: Excursions in Society, Politics, and Religion*. New York: Basic Books, 1977.

Berger, William B., Linda Mertes, and Alan Graham. "A Blueprint for Police-Community Partnerships." *The Police Chief* 61, no. 5 (1994): 20–25.

Bloom, Lynda. "Community Policing Nips Gang Problem In The Bud." *Law & Order,* September 1992, 67–70.

Bondurant, Elizabeth, "Citizen Response Questionnaire: A Valuable Evaluation Tool." *The Police Chief,* November 1991, 74–76.

Booth, Walter S. "Integrating COP into Selection and Promotional Systems." *The Police Chief,* March 1995, 19–24.

Bowers, W. J. and J. H. Hirsch. "The Impact of Foot Patrol Staffing on Crime and Disorder in Boston: An Unmet Promise." *American Journal of Police* 6, no. 1 (1987): 17–44.

Boydstun, John E. *San Diego Field Interrogations: Final Report*. Washington, D.C.: The Police Foundation, 1975.

Bragg, Mike. "Restaurants as Police Outposts." *Law and Order*. October 1995: 77–78.

Braiden, Chris. *Community Policing: Nothing New Under the Sun*.Edmonton, Canada: Edmonton Police Department, 1987.

Braiden, Chris. "Enriching Traditional Police Roles." *Police Management: Issues and Perspectives*. Washington, D.C.: Police Executive Research Forum, 1992.

Brandstatter, A. F. and Louis A. Radelet. *Police and Community Relations: A Sourcebook*. Beverly Hills: Glencoe Press, 1968.

Bratton, William J. "William J. Bratton: Police Training for Youth." *Policy Review*, March/April 1996, 26–27.

Brown, Lee P. "Police-Community Power Sharing." In *Police Leadership in America: Crisis and Opportunity*. ed. William A. Geller. New York: American Bar Foundation, Praeger Publishers, 1985.

Brown, Lee P. and Mary Ann Wycoff. "Policing Houston: Reducing Fear and Improving Service." *Crime & Delinquency* 33, no. 1 (January 1987): 71–89.

Brown, Lee P. "Community Policing: A Practical Guide for Police Officials." *Perspectives on Policing*. Washington, D.C.: National Institute of Justice and the Program in Criminal Justice Policy and Management, September 1989.

Brown, Lee P. "The Police-Community Partnership." *The Police Chief*. December 1990, 8.

Brown, Lee P. "Community Policing: Its Time has Come." *The Police Chief*. September, 1991: 6.

Brown, Lee P. *Policing New York City in the 1990s: The Strategy for Community Policing*. New York: New York City Police Department, 1991.

Brown, Lee P. "Violent Crime and Community Involvement." *FBI Law Enforcement Bulletin*, May 1992, 2–5.

Brown, Lee P. "Community Policing: A Partnership with Promise." *The Police Chief,* (October 1992): 45–48.

Bruns, Bill. "Operation Bootstrap: Opening Corporate Classrooms to Police Managers." *National Institute of Justice Research in Action*. Washington, D.C.: National Institute of Justice, August 1989.

Brzeczek, Richard J. "Chief-Mayor Relations: The View from the Chief's Chair." In *Police Leadership in America,* ed. William A. Geller. New York: American Bar Foundation, Praeger Publishers, 1985.

Bucqueroux, Bonnie. "Community Policing is Alive and Well." *Community Policing Exchange*. Washington, D.C.: The Community Policing Consortium, May/June 1995.

Buerger, Michael E. "The Limits of Community." In *The Challenge of Community Policing: Testing the Promises,* ed. Dennis P. Rosenbaum. Thousand Oaks, CA.: SAGE Publications, Inc., 1994.

Buerger, Michael E. "A Tale of Two Targets: Limitations of Community Anticrime Actions." *Crime & Delinquency* 40 no. 3 (July 1994): 411–436.

Burden, Ordway P. "Citizens Spur Community-Based Policing." *Law Enforcement News*, (March 15, 1992): 5–6.

Bureau of Justice Assistance. *Weed & Seed*. Washington, D.C.: U.S. Department of Justice, October 1991.

Bureau of Justice Assistance. *An Introduction to DARE: Drug Abuse Resistance Education.* Washington, D.C.: U.S. Department of Justice, Bureau of Justice Administration, 1992.

Bureau of Justice Assistance. *A Police Guide to Surveying Citizens and Their Environment.* Washington, D.C.: U.S. Department of Justice, Bureau of Justice Administration, 1993.

Bureau of Justice Assistance. "The Systems Approach to Crime and Drug Prevention: A Path to Community Policing." *Bulletin: Bureau of Justice Assistance.* Washington, D.C.: Bureau of Justice Assistance, U.S. Department of Justice, September 1993.

Bureau of Justice Assistance. *Problem-Oriented Drug Enforcement: A Community-Based Approach for Effective Policing.* Washington, D.C.: Bureau of Justice Assistance, U.S. Department of Justice, October 1993.

Bureau of Justice Assistance. *Unleashing Community Policing.* Washington, D.C.: Bureau of Justice Assistance, U.S. Department of Justice, August 1994.

Bureau of Justice Assistance. *Neighborhood-Oriented Policing in Rural Communities: A Program Planning Guide.* Washington, D.C.: Bureau of Justice Assistance, U.S. Department of Justice, 1994a.

Bureau of Justice Statistics. *Drugs, Crime, and the Justice System.* Washington, D.C.: U.S. Department of Justice, 1992.

Bureau of Justice Statistics. *Report to the Nation on Crime and Justice.* 2nd ed. Washington, D.C.: U.S. Department of Justice, 1988.

Byrt, Frank. "A Kids' Interview Room." *Law and Order.* October 1995: 100–101.

Campbell, John H. "Futures Research: Here and Abroad." *The Police Chief,* January 1990.

Capezio, P. and Morehouse, D. *A Practical Guide to Total Quality Management.* Hawthorne, N.J.: Career Press, 1993.

Capowich, George E. and Janice A. Roehl. "Problem-Oriented Policing: Actions and Effectiveness in San Diego." In *The Challenge of Community Policing: Testing the Promises.* ed. Dennis P. Rosenbaum. Thousand Oaks, CA.: SAGE Publications Inc., 1994.

Caradelli, Albert P. and Jack McDevitt. "Toward a Conceptual Framework for Evaluating Community Policing." In *Issues in Community Policing*, ed. Peter C. Kratcoski and Duane Dukes. Cincinnati: Academy of Criminal Justice Sciences, Anderson Publishing Company, 1995.

Carter, David L. *An Overview of Research in Support of the Community Policing Concept.* Quantico, Virginia: FBI National Academy, 1988.

Carter, David L. and Allen D. Sapp. "Making the Grade." *Police Technology and Management,* December 1990, 39–43.

Carter, David L., Allen D. Sapp, and Darrel W. Stephens. *The State of Police Education: Policy Directions for the 21st Century.* Washington, D.C.: Police Executive Research Forum, 1989.

Chaiken, Jan M. *Local Police Departments 1993.* Washington, D.C.: U.S. Department of Justice, April 1995.

Champion, Dean J. *Research Methods for Criminal Justice and Criminology.* Englewood Cliffs, N.J.: Prentice-Hall Inc., 1993.

Christopher, William et. al. "Summary Report." *Report of the Independent Commission on the Los Angeles Police Department.* Los Angeles, California: City of Los Angeles, 1991.

Clark, Jacob R. "Does Community Policing Add Up?' *Law Enforcement News*, 20, no. 399: 1–8.

Coffey, Alan, Edward Eldefonso, and Walter Hartinger. *Human Relations: Law Enforcement in a Changing Community.* 3rd ed. Englewood Cliffs, N.J.: Prentice Hall, Inc., 1982.

Cohen, Steven and Ronald Brand. *Total quality Management in Government*. San Francisco, CA.: Jossey-Bass, 1993.

Cohn, Alvin W. *The Future of Policing*. Beverly Hills: SAGE Publications, Inc., 1978.

Cohn, Alvin W. and Emilio C. Viano, eds. *Police Community Relations: Images, Roles, Realities*. Philadelphia: Lippincott, 1976.

Cole, Allen W. "Non-Traditional Problem Solving." *Law and Order*, August 1993, 59–64.

Cole, Allen W. "Better Customer Focus: TQM & Law Enforcement." *The Police Chief*, December 1993: 23–26.

Cole, Allen W. and David Kelley. "Non Traditional Problem Solving: Barricades Eliminate Drug Dealing, Restore Neighborhood." *Law & Order*, August 1993, 59–64.

Cole George F. *The American System of Criminal Justice*. 7th ed. Belmont, CA.: The Wadsworth Publishing Company, 1995.

Cole, George F. "Criminal Justice in the Twenty-First Century: The Role of Futures Research." In *Crime and Justice in the Year 2010*, ed. John Klofas and Stan Stojkovic. Belmont, CA.: Wadsworth Publishing Company, 1995.

Communicare. *Community Policing Video Site Visit Series*. Austin, Texas Police Department. Westerville, Ohio: Communicare Educational Video Productions, 1995.

Communicare. *Community Policing Video Site Visit Series*. Boca Raton, Florida Police Department. Westerville, Ohio: Communicare Educational Video Productions, 1995.

Communicare. *Community Policing Video Site Visit Series*. Fort Worth, Texas Police Department. Westerville, Ohio: Communicare Educational Video Productions, 1995.

Communicare. *Community Policing Video Site Visit Series*. Lansing, Michigan Police Department. Westerville, Ohio: Communicare Educational Video Productions, 1995.

Communicare. *Community Policing Video Site Visit Series*. Lumberton, North Carolina Police Department. Westerville, Ohio: Communicare Educational Video Productions, 1995.

Communicare. *Community Policing Video Site Visit Series*.Portland, Oregon Police Bureau. Parts I and II. Westerville, Ohio: Communicare Educational Video Productions, 1995

Communicare. *Community Policing Video Site Visit Series*. St. Petersburg, Florida Police Department. Parts I and II. Westerville, Ohio: Communicare Educational Video Productions, 1995.

Communicare. *Community Policing Video Site Visit Series*. San Diego, California Police Department. Parts I and II. Westerville, Ohio: Communicare Educational Video Productions, 1995.

Communicare. *Community Policing Video Site Visit Series*. Sedgwick County, Kansas Sheriff's Department. Westerville, Ohio: Communicare Educational Video Productions, 1995.

Community Policing Consortium. *Understanding Community Policing: A Framework for Action*. Washington, D.C.: U.S. Department of Justice, 1994.

Cordner, Gary W. *The Baltimore County Citizen Oriented Police Enforcement (COPE) Project: Final Evaluation*. New York: Florence V. Burden Foundation, 1985.

Cordner, Gary W. "The Effects of Directed Patrol: A Natural Quasi-Experiment in Pontiac." In *Contemporary Issues in Law Enforcement*. ed. James J. Fyfe. Beverly Hills: Sage Publications, 1981: 242–261.

Cordner, Gary W. "A Problem-Oriented Approach to Community-Oriented Policing." In *Community Policing: Rhetoric or Reality*, ed. Jack R. Greene and Stephen D. Mastrofski. New York: Praeger Publishers, 1988.

Cordner, Gary W. "Fear of Crime and the Police: An Evaluation of a Fear-Reduction Strategy." *Journal of Police Science and Administration* 14, no. 3 (1987): 223–233.

Cordner, Gary W. "Foot Patrol Without Community Policing: Law and Order in Public Housing." In *The Challenge of Community Policing: Testing the Promises* ed. Dennis P. Rosenbaum. Thousand Oaks, CA.: SAGE Publications Inc., 1994.

Cordner, Gary W. and Michael A. Jones. "The Effects of Supplementary Foot Patrol on Fear of Crime and Attitudes Toward the Police." In *Issues in Community Policing*, ed. Peter C. Kratcoski and Duane Dukes. Cincinnati: Academy of Criminal Justice Sciences and Anderson Publishing Company, 1995.

Cordner, Gary W. and Robert C. Trojanowicz. "Patrol." In *What Works in Policing? Operation and Administration Examined*. ed. Gary W. Cordner and Donna C. Hale. Cincinnati: Anderson Publishing, 1992.

Cornish, Edward. *The Study of the Future*. Washington, D.C.: World Future Society, 1977.

Corter, Walter., Richard Whelan, and James J. Lynch. "Solving Problems Through Teamwork." *Law and Order*, August 1993, 64–66.

Couper, David C. *Quality Policing: The Madison Experiment*. Washington, D.C.: Police Executive Research Forum, 1991.

Couper, David C. and Sabine H. Lobitz. "The Customer is Always Right: Applying Vision, Leadership, and Problem-Solving Methods to Community Policing." *The Police Chief*, September 1991, 16–23.

Couper, David C. and Sabine H. Lobitz. *Quality Policing: The Madison Experience*. Washington, D.C.: Police Executive Research Forum, 1991.

Cox, Steven M. and Jack D. Fitzgerald. *Police in Community Relations*. 3rd ed. Guilford, CT.: Brown and Benchmark Publishers, 1996.

Crank, John. "The Community-Policing Movement of the Early Twenty-First Century: What We Learned." In *Crime and Justice in the Year 2010*. ed. John Klofas and Stan Stojkovic. Belmont, CA.: Wadsworth Publishing Company, 1995: 107–126.

Cummings, D. Brian. "Problem-Oriented Policing and Crime Specific Planning." *The Police Chief*, March 1990, 63–64.

Danner, Morgan L. "Dial-A-Cop Brings Officers Closer to the Community." *Law and Order* 40, no. 6, 1992: 43–44.

Davis, Raymond C. "Organizing the Community for Improved Policing." In *Police Leadership in America: Crisis and Opportunity*. ed. William A. Geller. New York: American Bar Foundation, Praeger Publishers, 1985.

DeLong, Rhonda K. "Police-Community Partnerships: Neighborhood Watch and the Neighborhood Liaison Officer Program in Kalamazoo, Michigan." In *Issues in Community Policing,* ed. Peter Kratcoski and Duane Dukes. Cincinnati: Academy of Criminal Justice Sciences, Anderson Publishing Company, 1995.

Deming, W. Edwards. *Quality, Productivity, and Competitive Position*. Cambridge, Massachusetts: Massachusetts Institute of Technology, Center for Advanced Engineering Study, 1982.

Deming, W. Edwards. *Out of the Crisis*. Cambridge, MA.: MIT Press, 1986.

Dempsey, John S. *Policing: An Introduction to Law Enforcement*. St. Paul, Minn.: West Publishing Company, 1994.

Denhardt, Robert B. *Theories of Public Organization*. 2nd ed. Belmont, CA.: Wadsworth Publishing Company, 1993.

Denhardt, Robert B. *Public Administration: An Action Orientation.* 2nd ed. Belmont, CA.: Wadsworth, 1995.

Dilulio, John J., Jr. "Arresting Ideas." *Policy Review.* no. 74 (Fall 1995): 12–16.

Dilulio, John J., Jr., Steven K. Smith, and Aaron J. Saiger. "The Federal Role in Crime Control." In *Crime,* ed. James Q. Wilson and Joan Petersilia. San Francisco: ICS Press, 1995.

Dolan, Harry P. "Coping with Internal Backlash." *The Police Chief,* March 1994, 28–32.

Dombrink, John. "The Touchables: Vice and Police Corruption in the 1980s." In *Police Deviance.* 3rd ed., ed. Thomas Barker and David L. Carter. Cincinnati: Anderson Publishing Company, 1994.

Donahue, Michael E. "A Comprehensive Program to Combat Violent Crime: The Savannah Experience." *The Police Chief,* September 1993, 12–22.

Donsi, Joseph M. "Police Practices: Ft. Lauderdale's Code Enforcement Team." *FBI Law Enforcement Bulletin,* March 1992, 24–25.

Douthit, Nathan. "August Vollmer." *Thinking about Police: Contemporary Readings.* 2nd ed., ed. Carl B. Klockars and Stephen D. Mastrofski. New York: McGraw-Hill, Inc., 1991.

Dudley, William. ed. *Police Brutality.* San Diego: Greenhaven Press, Inc., 1991.

Dye, Thomas R. *Understanding Public Policy.* 6th ed. Englewood Cliffs, N.J.: Prentice-Hall, Inc., 1987.

Earle, Howard H. *Police-Community Relations: Crisis in Our Times.* Springfield, IL.: Charles C. Thomas, Publishers, 1967.

Eck, John E. *Solving Crimes: The Investigation of Burglary and Robbery.* Washington, D.C.: Police Executive Research Forum, 1982.

Eck, John E. "Alternative Futures for Policing." In *Police Innovation and Control of the Police.* Edited by David Weisburd and C. Uchida. New York: Springer, 1993.

Eck, John E. and Dennis P. Rosenbaum. "The New Police Order." In *The Challenge of Community Policing: Testing the Promises.* ed. Dennis P. Rosenbaum. Thousand Oaks, CA.: SAGE Publications, Inc., 1994.

Eck, John E. and William Spelman. *Problem-Solving: Problem-Oriented Policing in Newport News.* Washington, D.C.: Police Executive Research Forum, 1987.

Eck, John E. and William Spelman. "Who Ya Gonna Call? The Police as Problem Busters." *Crime & Delinquency* 33 no. 1 (January 1987): 31–52.

Eck, John E. and William Spelman. "A Problem-Oriented Approach to Police Service Delivery." In *Police and Policing: Contemporary Issues,* ed. Dennis Jay Kenney. New York: Praeger Publishers, 1989.

Eck, John E., William Spelman, Diane Hill, Darrel W. Stephens, John R. Stedman and Gerard R. Murphy. *Problem-Solving: Problem-Oriented Policing in Newport News.* Washington, D.C.: Police Executive Research Forum, 1987.

Eggers, William D. and John O'Leary. "The Beat Generation." *Policy Review* no. 74 (Fall 1995): 4–11.

Enns, Tracy. "Citizens' Police Academies: The Farmington Experience." *The Police Chief,* April 1995, 133–135.

Enter, Jack E. "Police Administration in the Future: Demographic Influence as they Relate to Management of Internal and External Environment." *American Journal of Police* 10, no. 4 (1991): 65–81.

Ebenson, F. "Foot Patrol: of What Value?" *American Journal of Police.* 6, no. 1 (1987): 45–66.

Fairchild, Erika S. and Vincent J. Webb. *The Politics of Crime and Criminal Justice*. Beverly Hills: SAGE Publications, 1985.

Farley, John E. *Sociology*. 3rd ed. Englewood Cliffs, N.J.: Prentice Hall, Inc., 1994.

Farley, William J. "Policing in Tough Budgetary Times: Gaston County Finds New Methods Increase Service." *Law & Order*. August 1993: 53–57.

Farrell, Michael J. "The Development of the Community Patrol Officer Program: Community-Oriented Policing in the New York City Police Department." In *Community Policing: Rhetoric or Reality*, ed. Jack R. Greene and Stephen D. Mastrofski. New York: Praeger Publishers, 1988.

Feins, J.D. *Partnerships For Neighborhood Crime Prevention*. Washington, D.C.: The National Institute of Justice, 1983.

Fleissner, Dan, Nicholas Fedan, David Klinger, and Ezra Stotland. "Community Policing in Seattle: A Model Partnership Between Citizens and Police." *National Institute of Justice: Research in Brief*. Washington, D.C.: National Institute of Justice, August 1992.

Fogelson, Robert. *Big-City Police*. Cambridge, MA.: Harvard University Press, 1977.

Fosdick, Raymond B. *American Police Systems*. Montclair, N.J.: Patterson Smith, 1969.

Fowler, Floyd J., Jr. and Thomas W. Mangione. "A Three-Pronged Effort to Reduce Crime and Fear of Crime: The Hartford Experiment." In *Community Crime Prevention: Does It Work?* ed. Dennis P. Rosenbaum. Beverly Hills, SAGE Publications Inc., 1986: 87–108.

Francis, Charles E. "Charleston Tries Voluntary Program." *Community Policing Exchange*. Washington, D.C.: The Community Policing Consortium, January/February 1996.

Freeman, Edward R. *Strategic Management: A Stakeholder's Approach*. Marshall, MA.: Pittman, 1984.

Friedman, Warren. "The Community Role in Community Policing." In *The Challenge of Community Policing: Testing the Promises*, ed. Dennis P. Rosenbaum. Thousand Oaks, CA.: SAGE Publications, Inc., 1994.

Friedmann, Robert R. "Community Policing: Promises and Challenges." *Journal of Contemporary Criminal Justice* 6 (May 1990): 79–88.

Fyfe, James, J. *Police Practices in the '90's: Key Management Issues*. Washington, D.C.: International City/County Management Association, 1989.

Gaines, Larry. "Community-Oriented Policing: Management Issues, Concerns, and Problems." *Journal of Contemporary Criminal Justice* 10, no. 1 (March 1994): 17–35.

Gaines, Larry K., Victor E. Kappeler, and Joseph B. Vaughn. *Policing in America*. Cincinnati: Anderson Publishing Company, 1994.

Gallup, George: *The Gallup Poll: Public Opinion*. Wilmington, Delaware: Scholarly Resources Inc., 1964–1994.

Garafalo, James and Maureen McLeod. "Improving the Use and Effectiveness of Neighborhood Watch Programs." *National Institute of Justice/Research in Action*. Washington, D.C.: The National Institute of Justice, April 1988.

Geller, William A. ed. *Police Leadership in America: Crisis and Opportunity*. New York: American Bar Foundation/Praeger Publishers, 1985.

Geller, William A. ed. *Local Government Police Management*. 3rd ed. Washington, D.C.: International City/County Management Association, 1991.

Geller, William A. and Michael S. Scott. *Deadly Force: What We Know*. Washington, D.C.: Police Executive Research Forum, 1992.

Gentile, John R. "Community Policing: a Philosophy—Not a Program." *Community Policing Exchange*. Washington, D.C.: The Community Policing Consortium, November/December 1995, 2.

Getz, Ronald J. "A Cops Show of Your Own." *Law and Order*, February 1995, 43–49.

Gilbert, James N. *Criminal Investigation*. 2nd ed. Columbus, OH.: Charles E. Merrill Publishing Company, 1986.

Gilbert, James N. *Criminal Investigation*. 3rd ed. New York: Macmillan Publishing Company, 1993.

Gleason, Richard. "Community Policing: Give Citizens the Policing They Want." *The Police Chief*, August 1987.

Goldstein, Herman. *Police Corruption: A Perspective on Its Nature and Control*. Washington, D.C.: The Police Foundation, 1975.

Goldstein, Herman. *Policing a Free Society*. Cambridge, MA.: Ballinger, 1977.

Goldstein, Herman. "Improving Policing: A Problem-Oriented Approach." *Crime & Delinquency*. 25, no. 2 (1979): 236–258.

Goldstein, Herman. "Toward Community-Oriented Policing: Potential, Basic Requirements, and Threshold Questions." *Crime & Delinquency*. 33, no. 1, (January 1987): 6–30.

Goldstein, Herman. *Problem-Oriented Policing*. New York: McGraw Hill Publisher. Co., 1990.

Goldstein, Herman. "Foreword." In *The Challenge of Community Oriented Policing: Testing the Promises*. ed. Dennis P. Rosenbaum. Thousand Oaks, CA.: SAGE Publications, Inc., 1994.

Goldstein, Herman. "Police Policy Formulation: A Proposal for Improving Police Performance." *Michigan Law Review*. 65 (1967): 1123–1146.

Goodstein, Laurie. "New Philosophy of Policing."*Washington Post* (December 23, 1991): A1–A7.

Greenberg, David. "Age, Crime, and Social Explanations." *American Journal of Sociology*, 91 (1985): 1–21.

Greenburg, Reuben and Arthur Gordon. *Let's Take Back Our Streets!* Chicago: Contemporary Books, Inc., 1989.

Greene, Jack R. "Foot Patrol and Community Policing: Past Practices and Future Prospects." *American Journal of Police* 6, no. 1 (1987): 1–15.

Greene, Jack R. "Police and Community Relations: Where Have We Been and Where Are We Going?" In *Critical Issues in Policing*, ed. R.G. Dunham and G. P. Alpert. Prospect Heights IL.: Waveland Press, 1989: 349–368.

Greene, Jack R. "Police Officer Job Satisfaction and Community Perceptions: Implications for Community-Oriented Policing." *Journal of Research in Crime and Delinquency* 26, (1989): 168–184.

Greene, Jack R., William T. Bergman, and Edward J. McLaughlin. "Implementing Community Policing." In *The Challenge of Community Policing: Testing the Promises*, ed. Dennis P. Rosenbaum. Thousand Oaks, CA.: SAGE Publications, Inc., 1994.

Greene, Jack R. and S.H. Decker. "Police and Community Perception of the Community Role in Policing: The Philadelphia Perspective." *The Howard Journal* (28) 1989: 105–123.

Greene, Jack R. and Carl B. Klockars. "What Police Do." *Thinking About Police*. 2nd ed., ed. Carl B. Klockars and Stephen D. Mastrofski. New York: McGraw Hill, 1991.

Greene, Jack R. and Stephen D. Mastrofski. *Community Policing: Rhetoric or Reality?* New York: Praeger Publishers, 1988.

Greene, Jack R. and Stephen D. Mastrofski. eds. "Preface." *Community Policing: Rhetoric or Reality?* New York: Praeger Publishers, 1988.

Greene, Jack R. and Ralph B. Taylor. "Community-Based Policing and Foot Patrol: Issues of Theory and Evaluation." In *Community Policing: Rhetoric or Reality?* ed. Jack R. Greene and Stephen D. Mastrofski. New York: Praeger Publishers, 1988.

Greenwood, Peter W. and Joan Petersilia. *The Criminal Investigation Process—Volume I: Summary and Policy Implications.* Santa Monica, CA.: Rand Corporation, 1975.

Greenwood, Peter W., Joan Petersilia, and J. Chaiken. *The Criminal Investigation Process.* Lexington, MA.: Heath Publishing, 1977.

Griffith, Douglas L. "Citizen Feedback Line." *Law and Order.* December 1993: 37–40.

Grinc, Randolph M. "'Angels in Marble': Problems in Community Involvement in Community Policing." *Crime & Delinquency* 40, No. 3 (July 1994): 437–468.

Guyot, Dorothy. "Bending Granite: Attempts to Change the Rank Structure of American Police Departments." *Journal of Police Science and Administration* 7, no. 3 (1979): 253–384.

Guyot, Dorothy. "Policing as Though People Matter." *Philadelphia: Temple University Press,* 1991.

Guyot, Dorothy. "Problem-Oriented Policing Shines in the Stats." *PM: Public Management* 73, no. 9 (1991): 12–16.

Hageman, Mary Jeanette. *Police-Community Relations.* Beverly Hills: SAGE Publications Inc., 1985.

Hamilton, Sandra. "The Saskatoon Experience." *Law & Order,* December 1993, 20–26.

Hayeslip, D. W., Jr. and Gary W. Cordner. "The Effects of Community-Oriented Patrol on Police Officer Attitudes." *American Journal of Police* 6, no. 1 (1987): 95–119.

Herbst, Charles. "Maximizing Community Resources." *Community Policing Exchange.* Washington, D.C.: The Community Policing Consortium, November/December 1995.

Hersey, Paul and Kenneth H. Blanchard. *Management of Organizational Behavior.* 6th ed. Englewood Cliffs, N.J.: Prentice-Hall, Inc., 1993.

Higdon, Richard Kirk and Phillip G. Huber. *How to Fight Fear: The Citizen Oriented Police Enforcement Program Package.* Washington, D.C.: Police Executive Research Forum, 1987.

Hirschi, Travis. *Causes of Delinquency.* Berkeley, CA.: University of California Press, 1969.

Hirschi, Travis and Michael Gottfredson. "Age and Explanation of Crime." *American Journal of Sociology,* vol. 89 (1983): 552–584.

Hogan, William. "Enhancing Police Services with Senior Volunteers." *Community Policing Exchange.* Washington, D.C.: The Community Policing Consortium, November/December 1995.

Holcomb, Richard L. *The Police and the Public.* Springfield, IL.: Charles C. Thomas Publishing, 1954.

Holden, Richard N. *Modern Police Management.* Englewood Cliffs, N.J.: Prentice-Hall, Inc., 1986.

Hornick, Joseph P., Barry N. Leighton, and Barbara A. Burrows. "Evaluating Community Policing: The Edmonton Project." In *Evaluating Justice: Canadian Policies and Programs,* ed. Julian V. Roberts and Joe Hudson. Toronto, Canada: Thompson Educational Publishing Inc., 1993.

Inkster, Norman D. "The Essence of Community Policing." *The Police Chief,* March 1992, 28–31.

International City/County Management Association. *Community-Oriented Policing: An Alternative Strategy, Sourcebook*. Washington, D.C.: International City/County Management Association, 1992.

Johnson, Thomas A., Gordon E. Misner, and Lee P. Brown. *The Police and Society: An Environment for Collaboration and Confrontation*. Englewood Cliffs, N.J.: Prentice-Hall, Inc., 1981.

Joseph, Earl C. "An Introduction to Studying the Future." In *Futurism in Education: Methodologies*, ed. Stephen B. Hencley and James R. Yates. Berkeley, CA.: McCutchan, 1974.

Joseph, Thomas M. "Walking the Minefields of Community-Oriented Policing." *FBI Law Enforcement Bulletin*, September 1994, 8–12.

Kansas City Police Department. *Response Time Analysis: Volume II-Part I, Crime Analysis*. Washington, D.C.: U.S. Government Printing Office, 1980.

Kappeler, Victor E., Richard D. Sluder, and Geoffrey P. Alpert. *Forces of Deviance*. Prospect Heights, IL.: Waveland Press, 1994.

Kelling, George L. "Acquiring A Taste for Order: The Community and the Police." *Crime and Delinquency* 33, no. 1 (1987): 90–102.

Kelling, George L. "Order Maintenance, the Quality of Urban Life, and Police: A Line of Argument." In *Police Leadership In America*, ed. William A. Geller. New York: American Bar Foundation, 1985.

Kelling, George. *Foot Patrol*. Washington, D.C.: The National Institute of Justice, 1987.

Kelling, George L. "Police and Communities: the Quiet Revolution." *Perspectives on Policing*. No. 1. Washington, D.C.: U.S. Department of Justice, June 1988.

Kelling, George L. "Measuring What Matters: A New Way of Thinking about Crime and Public Order." *The City Journal*. Spring 1992, 21–33.

Kelling, George L. and William J. Bratton. "Implementing Community Policing: The Administrative Problem." *Perspectives on Policing*. Washington, D.C.: U.S. Department of Justice and the Program in Criminal Justice Policy and Management, John F. Kennedy School of Government, Harvard University, July 1993.

Kelling, George L. and David Fogel. "Police Patrol—Some Future Directions." In *The Future of Policing*, ed. Alvin W. Cohn. Beverly Hills: SAGE Publications, Inc., 1978.

Kelling, George L. and Mark H. Moore. "From Political to Reform to Community: The Evolving Strategy of Police." In *Community Policing: Rhetoric or Reality*, ed. Jack R. Greene and Stephen D. Mastrofski. New York: Praeger Publishing Company, 1988.

Kelling, George L., Tony Pate, Suzane Dieckman, and Charles E. Brown. *The Kansas City Preventive Patrol Experiment: A Summary Report*. Washington, D.C.: Police Foundation, 1974.

Kelling, George L., Tony Pate, Suzane Dieckman, and Charles E. Brown. *The Kansas City Preventive Patrol Experiment: A Technical Report*. Washington, D.C.: Police Foundation, 1975.

Kelling, George, Robert Wasserman, and Hubert Williams. "Police Accountability and Community Policing." *Perspectives on Policing*. Washington, D.C.: National Institute of Justice and the John F. Kennedy School of Government, Harvard University, 1988.

Kennedy, David M. "The Strategic Management of Police Resources." *Perspectives on Policing*. Washington, D.C.: National Institute of Justice and the John F. Kennedy School of Government, Harvard University, January 1993.

Kercher, Kyle. "Causes and Correlates of Crime Committed by the Elderly." In *Critical Issues in Aging Policy*, ed. E. Borgatta and R. Montgomery. Beverly Hills: SAGE Publications, 1987.

Kerstetter, Wayne A. "Who Disciplines the Police? Who Should?" In *Police Leadership in America: Crisis and Opportunity*, ed. William A. Geller. New York: American Bar Foundation, 1985.

Kessler, David A. "Integrating Calls for Service With Community-and Problem-Oriented Policing: A Case Study." *Crime & Delinquency* 39, no. 4 (October 1993): 485–508.

Klein, Malcolm W. and Katherine S. Tielmann. eds. *Handbook of Criminal Justice Evaluation*. Beverly Hills: SAGE Publications Inc., 1980.

Klockars, Carl B. *The Idea of Police*. Beverly Hills: SAGE Publications Inc., 1985.

Klockars, Carl B. "The Rhetoric of Community Policing." In *Community Policing: Rhetoric or Reality*, ed. Jack R. Greene and Stephen D. Mastrofski. New York: Praeger Publishers, 1988.

Klockars, Carl B. "Order Maintenance, the quality of Urban Life, and Police: A Different Line of Argument." In *Police Leadership in America: Crisis and Opportunity*, ed. William A. Geller. New York: Praeger Publishers: 309–321.

Klofas, John and Stan Stojkovic. *Crime and Justice in the Year 2010*. Belmont, CA.: Wadsworth Publishing Company, 1995.

Kratcoski, Peter C. and Robert B. Blair. "Dynamics of Community Policing in Small Communities." In *Issues in Community Policing*, ed. Peter C. Kratcoski and Duane Dukes. Cincinnati: The Academy of Criminal Justice Sciences and Anderson Publishing Company, 1995.

Kratcoski, Peter C. and Duane Dukes. "Activity Time Allocation of Community Policing Officers." In *Issues in Community Policing*, ed. Peters C. Kratcoski and Duane Dukes. Cincinnati: Academy of Criminal Justice Sciences, Anderson Publishing Company, 1995.

Kratcoski, Peter C. and Duane Dukes. *Issues in Community Policing*. ed. Peter C. Kratcoski and Duane Dukes. Cincinnati: Anderson Publishing Company, 1995.

Kratcoski, Peter C. and Duane Dukes. "Perspectives on Community Policing." In *Issues in Community Policing*, ed. Peter C. Kratcoski and Duane Dukes. Cincinnati: Academy of Criminal Justice Sciences and Anderson Publishing Co., 1995.

Kratcoski, Peter C., Duane Dukes, and Sandra Gustavson. "An Analysis of Citizens' Responses to Community Policing in a Large Midwestern City." In *Issues in Community Policing*, ed. Peter C. Kratcoski and Duane Dukes. Cincinnati: The Academy of Criminal Justice Sciences and Anderson Publishing Company, 1995.

Kratcoski, Peter C. and Susan B. Noonan. "An Assessment of Police Officers' Acceptance of Community Policing." In *Issues in Community Policing*, ed. Peter C. Kratcoski and Duane Dukes. Cincinnati: Academy of Criminal Justice Sciences, Anderson Publishing Company, 1995.

Krieble, James H. "Community-Oriented Policing: Selection, Training and Evaluation Ensure Success." *The Police Chief*, 61, no. 5 (1994): 20–23.

Lacayo, Richard. "Law and Order." *Time*, January 15, 1996, 48–54.

Larson, Richard C. "What Happened to Patrol Operations in Kansas City? A Review of the Kansas City Preventive Patrol Experiment." *Journal of Criminal Justice* 3, no. 4, (1975): 267–297.

Lasley, James R. "The Impact of the Rodney King Incident on Citizen Attitudes Toward Police." *Policing and Society* 3 (1993): 20–35.

Lasley, James R., Robert L. Vernon, and George M. Dery III. "Operation Cul-De-Sac: LAPD's 'Total Community' Policing Program." In *Issues in Community Policing*, ed. Peter C. Kratcoski and Duane Dukes. Cincinnati: Anderson Publishing Company, 1995.

Lavrakas, Paul J. "Evaluating Police-Community Anticrime Newsletters: The Evanston, Houston, and Newark Field Studies." In *Community Crime Prevention: Does It Work?* ed. Dennis P. Rosenbaum. Beverly Hills: SAGE Publications Inc., 1986.

Lavrakas, Paul J. and James W. Kushmuk. "Evaluating Crime Prevention through Environmental Design: The Portland Commercial Demonstration Project." In *Community Crime Prevention: Does It Work?* ed. Dennis P. Rosenbaum. Beverly Hills: SAGE Publications Inc., 1986.

Leal, Carolyn V. "Cop Cards." *Law and Order*, October 1992, 63–64.

Lee-Sammons, Lynette. "Beyond Neighborhood Watch: The Role of the Community in Community Policing." *Community Policing Exchange*. Washington, D.C.: The Community Policing Consortium, September/October 1995.

Leighton, Barry N. "Community Policing in Canada: An Overview of Experiences and Evaluations." In *The Challenge of Community Policing: Testing the Promises*, ed. Dennis P. Rosenbaum. Thousands Oaks, CA.: SAGE Publications, Inc., 1994

Lesce, Tony. "Code Enforcement Teams." *Law and Order*, September 1995, 93–95.

Lewis, R. G., Jack R. Greene, and Steven M. Edwards. *Special Police Units in Michigan: An Evaluation*. East Lansing, Mich.: Criminal Justice Systems Center, Michigan State University, 1977.

Lewis, Dan A. and Greta Salem. "Community Crime Prevention: An analysis of a Developing Strategy." *Crime and Delinquency* 27, (1988): 405–421.

Lindbloom, Charles E. "The Science of Muddling Through." *Public Administration Review*, no. 19 (Spring 1959): 79–88.

Lipsky, Michael. *Street-Level Bureaucracy*. New York: Russell Sage Foundation, 1980.

Lurigio, Arthur J. and Dennis P. Rosenbaum. "The Impact of Community Policing on Police Personnel." In *The Challenge of Community Policing: Testing the Promises*. ed. Dennis P. Rosenbaum. Thousand Oaks, CA.: SAGE Publications, Inc., 1994.

Lurigio, Arthur J. and Wesley G. Skogan. "Winning the Hearts and Minds of Police Officers: An Assessment of Staff Perceptions of Community Policing in Chicago." *Crime & Delinquency* 40, no. 3 (July 1994): 315–330.

Lynch, Ronald G. *Police Manger*. 4th ed. Cincinnati: Anderson Publishing Company, 1995.

Manning, Peter K. "Community Policing." *American Journal of Police* 3, (1984): 205–227.

Manning, Peter K. "Community Policing." In *Critical Issues in Policing: Contemporary Readings*, ed. Roger G. Dunham and Geoffrey P. Alpert. Prospect, IL.: Waveland Press, 1989.

Manning, Peter K. "Community Policing as a Drama of Control." In *Community Policing: Rhetoric or Reality?*, ed. Jack R. Greene and Stephen D. Mastrofski. New York: Praeger Publishers, 1988.

Marion, Nancy E. *A History of Federal Crime Control Initiatives, 1960-1993*. Westport, CT.: Praeger Publishers, 1994.

Marquand, Barbara. "How Are We Doing?" *Law and Order*, December 1994, 41–43.

Marquand, Barbara. "How to Save Money." *Law and Order*, December 1994, 44.

Marquand, D. "Perceptoral Politics, Yeoman Democracy and the Enabling State." *Government and Opposition* 23 (1988): 261–275.

Marshall, Will and Martin Schram, eds. "Safer Streets and Neighborhoods." In *Mandate for Change*. New York: Berkeley Books, 1993.

Martin, Susan E. "Policing Career Criminal: An Examination of an Innovative Crime Control Program." *Journal of Criminal Law and Criminology* 77 (Winter 1986): 1159–1182.

Martin, Susan E. and Lawrence W. Sherman. "Selective Apprehension: A Police Strategy for Repeat Offenders." *Criminology* 24 (February 1986): 155–173.

Maslow, Abraham H. *Motivation and Personality*. 2nd ed. New York: Harper and Collins, 1970.

Mastrofski, Stephen D. "Community Policing as Reform: A Cautionary Tale." In *Community Policing: Rhetoric or Reality?* ed. Jack R. Greene and Stephen D. Mastrofski. New York: Praeger Publishers, 1988.

Mastrofski, Stephen D. "What Does Community Policing Mean for Daily Police Work?" *National Institute of Justice Journal*, no. 225 (August 1992): 23–27.

Mastrofski, Stephen D. and Jack R. Greene. "Community Policing and the Rule of Law." In *The Changing Focus of Police Innovation: Problems of Law, Order, and Community*, ed. David Weisburd and C. Uchida. New York: Praeger Publishers, 1991.

Mastrofski, Stephen D., Robert E. Worden, and Jeffrey B. Snipes. "Law Enforcement in a Time of Community Policing." *Criminology* 33, no. 4 (1995): 539–563.

Matthews, John. "Community Policing: Department-Wide versus 'Task Force' Implementation." *Law and Order*. December 1995, 34–37.

Maxfield, Michael G. and Earl Babbie. *Research Methods for Criminal Justice and Criminology*. Belmont, CA.: Wadsworth Publishing Company, 1995.

Mayhall, Pamela D., Thomas Barker, and Ronald D. Hunter. *Police-Community Relations and the Administration of Justice*. 4th ed. Englewood Cliffs, N.J.: Prentice-Hall, Inc., 1995.

McElroy, Jerome E., Colleen A. Cosgrove, and Susan Sadd. *COP: The Research*. New York: The Vera Institute of Justice, 1990.

McElroy, Jerome E., Colleen A. Cosgrove, and Susan Sadd. *Community Policing: The CPOP in New York*. Newbury Park, CA.: SAGE Publications, Inc., 1993.

McEwen, Tom. "National Assessment Program: 1994 Survey Results." *National Institute of Justice Research in Brief*. Washington, D.C.: National Institute of Justice, May 1995.

McLaughlin, Vance and Michael E. Donahue. "Training for Community-Oriented Policing." In *Issues in Community Policing*, ed. Peter C. Kratcoski and Duane Dukes. Cincinnati: Academy of Criminal Justice Sciences, Anderson Publishing Co., 1995.

McNulty, Paul J. "Natural Born Killers? Preventing the Coming Explosion of Teenage Crime." *Policy Review*, no. 71 (1995): 84–87.

McPherson, Nancy. "Solution-Driven Partnerships: Just Six Steps Away." *Community Policing Exchange*. Washington, D.C.: The Community Policing Consortium, September/October 1995.

McVety, Bruce. "Community policing Works." *Law and Order*, February 1994, 71.

Meese, Edwin III. "Community Policing and the Police Officer." *Perspectives on Policing*. Washington, D.C.: National Institute of Justice and the John F. Kennedy School of Government, Harvard University, January 1993.

Metchik, Eric and Ann Winton. "Community Policing and Its Implications for Alternative Models of Police Officer Selection." In *Issues in Community Policing*, ed. Peter C. Kratcoski and Duane Dukes. Cincinnati: Academy of Criminal Justice Sciences, Anderson Publishing Co., 1995.

Miller, Linda S. and Karen M. Hess. *Community Policing: Theory and Practice*. St. Paul, Minn.: West Publishing Company, 1994.

Miller, William D. "The Graying of America: Implications Towards Policing." *Law and Order*, October 1991, 96–97.

Monk, Richard C. *Taking Sides: Clashing Views on Controversial Issues in Crime and Criminology*. 4th ed. Guilford, CT.: Dushkin Publishing Group, Brown & Benchmark Publishers, 1996.

Moore, Harry W. and W. Fred Wegner. *Effective Police Supervision*. 2nd ed. Cincinnati: Anderson Publishing Company, 1996.

Moore, Mark H. "Research Synthesis and Policy Implications." In *the Challenge of Community Policing: Testing the Promises*, ed. Dennis P. Rosenbaum. Thousand Oaks, CA.: SAGE Publications, Inc., 1994.

Moore, Mark Harrison. "Problem-Solving and Community Policing." *Criminal Justice: A Review of Research*, vol. 15, ed. Michael Tonry and Norval Morris. Chicago, IL.: The University of Chicago, 1992.

Moore, Mark H. and George L. Kelling. "'To Serve and Protect': Learning from Police History." *The Public Interest* 70 (Winter 1983): 49–65.

Moore, Mark H. and Darrel Stephens. *Beyond Command and Control: The Strategic Management of Police Departments*. Washington, D.C.: Police Executive Research Forum, 1991.

Moore, Mark H. and Robert C. Trojanowicz. "Corporate Strategies for Policing." *Perspectives on Policing*. Washington, D.C.: National Institute of Justice and the Program in Criminal Justice Policy and Management, November 1988.

Moore, Mark H. and Robert C. Trojanowicz. "Policing and the Fear of Crime." *Perspectives on Policing*. Washington, D.C.: National Institute of Justice and the Program in Criminal Justice Policy and Management, June 1988.

Moore, Mark H., Robert C. Trojanowicz, and George L. Kelling. "Crime and Policing." *Perspectives on Policing* 2. Washington, D.C.: National Institute of Justice, June 1988.

Muehleisen, Tom. "Community Problem Solving." *Law & Order*, June 1995, 31–32.

Murphy, Chris. "The Development, Impact, and Implications of Community Policing in Canada." In *Community Policing: Rhetoric or Reality?* ed. Jack R. Greene and Stephen D. Mastrofski. New York: Praeger Publishers, 1988.

Murphy, Christopher. "Community Problems, Problem Communities, and Community Policing in Toronto." *Journal of Research in Crime and Delinquency* 25 (1988): 392–410.

Murphy, Patrick. "Foreword." In *The State of Police Education: Policy Directions for the 21st Century*, by Carter, David L. Allen D. Sapp, and Darrel W. Stephens. Washington, D.C.: Police Executive Research Forum, 1989.

National Institute of Justice. *Solicitation for an Impact Evaluation of Operation Weed and Seed*. Washington, D.C.: U.S. Department of Justice, April 1995.

Nelligan, Peter J. and Robert W. Taylor. "Ethical Issues in Community Policing." *Journal of Contemporary Criminal Justice* 10, no. 1 (March 1994): 59–66.

Nila, Michael J. "Defining the Police Mission: A Community/Police Perspective." *The Police Chief*, October 1990, 43–47.

O'Brien, John T. "Public Attitudes Toward the Police." *Journal of Police Science and Administration* 6, no. 3 (1978): 34–47.

Oettmeier, Timothy and Lee P. Brown. "Developing a Neighborhood- Oriented Policing Style." In *Community Policing: Rhetoric or Reality?* ed. Jack R. Greene and Stephen D. Mastrofski. New York: Praeger Publishers, 1988.

Oliver, Will. "The Early Warning System." *Law and Order*, September 1994, 182–183.

Oliver, Will. "Disciplinary Exceptions to the Rule: Reserve, Auxiliary, and Seasonal Officers." *Police Department Disciplinary Bulletin*, October 1994, 4–5.

Oliver, Will. "The Changing Role of the Police Chief in Community Policing." *Law & Order*, March 1993, 85–86.

Oliver, Will. "Corruption Potential in Community Oriented Policing." *Police Department Disciplinary Bulletin* 2, no. 12 (December 1994). 2–5

Oliver, Will. "Higher Education and Discipline." *Police Department Disciplinary Bulletin* Boston, Mass.: Quinlan Publishing Company, May 1995, 2–3.

Oliver, Willard M. "Community Policing Defined." *Law & Order*. August 1992, 46, 56–58.

Oliver, Willard M. "The Juvenile Justice System: A Road Paved with Good Intentions." Unpublished paper, 1996.

Osborne, David. *Laboratories of Democracy*. Cambridge, MA.: Harvard Business School Press, 1990.

Osborne, David and Ted Gaebler. *Reinventing Government: How the Entrepreneurial Spirit is Transforming the Public Sector*. Reading, MA.: Addison-Wesley, 1992.

O'Shaughnessy, Leslie. "Hawaii Innovations." *Law and Order*, September 1994, 50–52.

Overman, Richard. "The Case for Community Policing." *The Police Chief*, March 1994, 20–23.

Paine, Thomas. *Common Sense*, ed. Issac Kramnick. New York: Penguin Books, 1976.

Painter, Ellen. "The Secrets of Their Success." *Community Policing Exchange*. Washington, D.C.: The Community Policing Consortium, May/June 1995.

Painter, Ellen. "Tragedy Sparks Community Policing in Spokane, Washington." *Community Policing Exchange*. Washington, D.C.: The Community Policing Consortium, May/June 1995.

Pate, Antony M. "Experimenting with Foot Patrol: The Newark Experience." In *Community Crime Prevention: Does it Work?* ed. Dennis P. Rosenbaum. Beverly Hills: SAGE Publications Inc., 1986.

Pate, Antony M. "Community-Oriented Policing in Baltimore." In *Police and Policing: Contemporary Issues*, ed. D. J. Kenney. New York: Praeger Publishers, 1989.

Pate, Antony M. and Penny Shtull. "Community Policing Grows in Brooklyn: An Inside View of the New York City Police Department's Model Precinct." *Crime & Delinquency* 40 no. 3 (July 1994): 384–410.

Pate, Anthony M., Mary Ann Wycoff, Wesley G. Skogan, and Lawrence Sherman. *Reducing Fear of Crime in Houston and Newark: A Summary Report*. Washington, D.C.: The Police Foundation, 1986.

Patton, Michael Quinn. *Utilization-Focused Evaluation*. 2nd ed. Beverly Hills: SAGE Publications, Inc., 1986.

Patton, Michael Quinn. *How to use Qualitative Methods in Evaluation*. Newbury Park, CA.: SAGE Publications Inc., 1987.

Peak, Kenneth. *Justice Administration: Police, Courts, and Corrections Management*. Englewood Cliffs, N.J.: Prentice-Hall, Inc., 1995.

Peak, Ken, Robert V. Bradshaw, and Ronald W. Glensor. "Improving Citizen Perceptions of the Police: 'Back to the Basics' with a Community Policing Strategy." *Journal of Criminal Justice* 20, no. 1 (1992): 25–40.

Peak, Kenneth J. and Ronald W. Glensor. *Community Policing & Problem Solving: Strategies and Practices*. Upper Saddle River, N.J.: Prentice-Hall Inc., 1996.

Pegels, C. Carl. *Total Quality Management: A Survey of Its Important Aspects*. Danvers, MA.: Boyed and Fraser, 1995.

Perez, Marta Brito. "IACP Offers Training in Community-Oriented Policing." *The Police Chief*, May 1993, 39–40.

Petersilia, Joan. "The Influence of Research on Policing." In *Critical Issues in Policing; Contemporary Readings*, ed. Roger C. Dunham and Geoffrey P. Alpert. Prospect Heights, IL.: Waveland Press, 1989: 230–247.

Petersilia, Joan, Allan Abrahamse, and James Q. Wilson. "A Summary of RAND's Research on Police Performance, Community Characteristics, and Case Attrition." *Journal of Police Science and Administration* 17, no. 3 (1990): 219–226.

Pomrenke, Norman E. *Police Community Relations*. Norman E. Pomrenke, ed. Chapel Hill, N.C.: University of North Carolina Press, 1966.

Pooley, Eric. "One Good Apple." *Time*, January 15, 1996, 54–56.

Potter, Tom. "How to Plan Strategically for your Community." *Community Policing Exchange*. Washington, D.C.: The Community Policing Consortium, November/December 1995.

Quinn, James Brian. *Strategies for Change: Logical Incrementalism*. Homewood, IL: Irwin, 1980.

Quinn, James Brian. "Managing Innovation: Controlled Chaos." *Harvard Business Review*, no. 3 (May-June 1985): 73–84.

Radelet, Louis A. *The Police and the Community*. Beverly Hills: Glencoe Press, 1973.

Radelet, Louis A. and David L. Carter. *The Police and the Community*. 5th ed. Englewood Cliffs, N.J.: Prentice Hall, 1994.

Redlinger, Lawrence J. "Community Policing and Changes in the Organizational Structure." *Journal of Contemporary Criminal Justice* 10, no. 1 (March 1994): 36–58.

Reiss, Albert J. Jr. "Crime Control and the Quality of Life." *American Behavioral Scientist* 27, September/October 1983: 43–58.

Reiss, Albert J. Jr. "Shaping and Serving the Community: The Role of the Police Chief Executive." In *Police Leadership in America*. New York, New York: American Bar Foundation, Praeger Publishers, 1985.

Reiss, Albert J. Jr. *The Police and the Public*. New Haven, Connecticut: Yale University Press, 1985.

Reuss-Iianni, Elizabeth and Francis A. J. Iianni. "Street Cops and Management Cops: The Two Cultures of Policing." In *Control in the Police Organization*, ed. Maurice Punch. Cambridge, MA.: MIT Press, 1983.

Ricucci, Ronald A. and Michael W. McKeehan. "The Role of Technology in Community Policing." *The Police Chief*, May 1993, 41–42.

Riechers, Lisa M. and Roy R. Roberg. "Community Policing: A Critical Review of Underlying Assumptions." *Journal of Police Science and Administration* 17, no. 2 (1990): 105–114.

Roberg, Roy. "Can Today's Police Organizations Effectively Implement Community Policing?" *The Challenge of Community Policing: Testing the Promises*. ed. Dennis P. Rosenbaum. Thousand Oaks, CA.: SAGE Publications, Inc., 1994.

Roberg, Roy R. and Jack Kuykendall. *Police & Society*. Belmont, California: Wadsworth Publishing Company, 1993.

Roneck, Dennis and Pamela Maier. "Bars, Blocks, and Crime Revisited: Linking the Theory of Routine Activities to the Empiricism of 'Hot Spots.'" *Criminology* 29, 1991: 725–753.

Rosenbaum, Dennis P. *Community Crime Prevention: Does it Work?* Beverly Hills, California: SAGE Publications Inc., 1986.

Rosenbaum, Dennis P. "Community Crime Prevention: A Review and Synthesis of the Literature." *Justice Quarterly* 5 no. 3 (September 1988): 323–395.

Rosenbaum, Dennis P. *The Challenge of Community Policing: Testing The Promises*. ed. Dennis P. Rosenbaum. Thousand Oaks, CA.: SAGE Publications, Inc., 1994.

Rosenbaum, Dennis P. "The Theory and Research Behind Neighborhood Watch: Is It a Sound Fear and Crime Reduction Strategy?" *Crime & Delinquency* 33, no. 1 (January 1987): 103–134.

Rosenbaum, Dennis, Robert Flewelling, Susan Bailey, Chris Ringwalt, and Deanna Wilkinson. "Cops in the Classroom: A Longitudinal Evaluation of Drug Abuse Resistance Education (DARE)." *Journal of Research in Crime and Delinquency* 31 (1994): 3–31.

Rosenbaum, Dennis P. and Arthur J. Lurigio. "An Inside Look at Community Policing Reform: Definitions, Organizational Changes, and Evaluation Findings." *Crime & Delinquency* 40, no. 3 (July 1994): 299–314.

Rosenbaum, Dennis P., Sandy Yeh, and Deanna L. Wilkinson. "Impact of Community Policing on Police Personnel: A Quasi- Experimental Test." *Crime & Delinquency* 40, no. 3 (July 1994):" 331–353.

Ross, Jeffrey Ian. "Confronting Community Policing: Minimizing Community Policing as Public Relations." In *Issues in Community Policing*, ed. Peter C. Kratcoski and Duane Dukes. Cincinnati: Academy of Criminal Justice Sciences, Anderson Publishing Company, 1995.

Rossiter, Clinton. *The Federalist Papers*. New York: New American Library, 1961.

Rothermel, Terry W. "Forecasting Revisited." *Harvard Business Review* 60, no. 2 (March–April 1982): 143*157.

Rush, George E. "Community Policing: Overcoming the Obstacles." *The Police Chief*, October 1992, 50–55.

Rush, George E. *The Dictionary of Criminal Justice*. 4th ed. Guilford, CT.: The Dushkin Publishing Group, Inc., 1994.

Ryan, Joseph F. "Community Policing: Tends, Policies, Programs and Definitions." In *Critical Issues in Crime and Justice*. ed. Albert R. Roberts. Thousand Oaks, CA.: SAGE Publications Inc., 1994.

Sacco, Vincent F. and Leslie W. Kennedy. *The Criminal Event*. Belmont, CA.: Wadsworth Publishing Company, 1996

Sadd, Susan and Randolph M. Grinc. "Implementation Challenges in Community Policing." *National Institute of Justice Research in Brief*. Washington, D.C.: National Institute of Justice, February 1996.

Sadd, Susan and Randolph Grinc. "Innovative Neighborhood Oriented Policing." In *The Challenge of Community Policing: Testing the Promises*, ed. Dennis P. Rosenbaum. Thousand Oaks, CA.: SAGE Publications Inc., 1994.

Sadd, Susan and Randloph Grinc. *Issues in Community Policing: An Evaluation of Eight Innovative Neighborhood Oriented Policing Projects*. New York: Vera Institute of Justice, 1993.

Sampson, Robert and Jacqueline Cohen. "Deterrent Effects of the Police on Crime: A Replication and Theoretical Extension." *Law and Society Review* 22, 1988: 163–191.

Schaefer, Richard T. and Robert P. Lamm. *Sociology*. 4th ed. New York: McGraw-Hill, Inc., 1992.

Scheingold, Stuart A. "Politics, Public Policy, and Street Crime." *Annals of the American Academy of Political and Social Science*. 539 (1995): 155–158.

Scheingold, Stuart A. *Politics of Law and Order*. New York: Longman, Inc., 1984.

Schmalleger, Frank. *Criminal Justice Today*. 3rd ed. Englewood Cliffs, N.J.: Prentice-Hall Inc., 1995.

Schmitt, Sheila, "ROPE: The Resident Officer Program of Elgin." *Law and Order*, May 1995, 52–58.

Schnelle, John F., Robert E. Kirchner, Jr., J. R. Lawler, and M. Patrick McNees. "Social Evaluation Research: The Evaluation of Two Police Patrol Strategies." *Journal of Applied Behavioral Analysis*, no. 8 (1975): 232–240.

Schwab, William A. *The Sociology of Cities*. Englewood Cliffs, N.J.: Prentice-Hall, Inc., 1992.

Scott, Eric J. *Calls for Service: Citizen Demand and Initial Police Response*. Washington, D.C.: U.S. Government Printing Office, 1981.

Sharp, Arthur. "Pedaling Not Hard to Peddle." *Law and Order*, July 1995, 35–40.

Sherman, Lawrence. *Scandal and Reform: Controlling Police Corruption*. Berkeley, California: University of California Press, 1978.

Sherman, Lawrence. "The Police Executive as Statesman." In *Police Leadership in America*, ed. William A. Geller. New York: American Bar Foundation, Praeger Publishers, 1985.

Sherman, Lawrence. "Policing Communities: What Works." In *Crime and Justice: A Review of Research*. vol 8. ed. A.J. Reiss and Michael Tonry. Chicago: University of Chicago Press, 1986: 366–379.

Sherman, Lawrence. "Police Crackdowns: Initial and Residual Deterrence." In *Crime and Justice: A Review of Research*. vol. 12. ed. Michael Tonry and Norval Morris. Chicago: University of Chicago Press, 1990b: 1–48.

Sherman, Lawrence. "Police Crackdowns." *National Institute of Justice Reports*, March/April, 1990a.

Sherman, Lawrence, "Police and Crime Control." *Modern Policing*. ed. Michael Tonry and Norval Morris. Chicago: The University of Chicago Press, 1992.

Sherman, Lawrence. "The Police." *Crime*. ed. James Q. Wilson and Joan Petersilia. San Francisco: ICS Press, 1995.

Sherman, Lawrence W. "Middle Management and Democratization: A Reply to John E. Angell." *Criminology* 12, no. 4 (1975): 363–377.

Sherman, Lawrence, W., Catherine H. Milton, and Thomas V. Kelly. *Team Policing: Seven Case Studies*. Washington, D.C.: Police Foundation, 1973.

Siegel, Jeff. "The East Dallas Police Storefront." *Law and Order*, May 1995, 53–55.

Siegel, Larry, J. *Criminology*. 5th ed. St. Paul: West Publishing Company, 1995.

Sileo, Chi Chi. "Crime Takes on a Feminine Face." *Insight*, December 20, 1993, 16–19.

Silverman, Eli B. "Community Policing: The Implementation Gap." In *Issues in Community Policing*, ed. Peter C. Kratcoski and Duane Dukes. Cincinnati: Academy of Criminal Justice Sciences, Anderson Publishing Co., 1995.

Simonsen, Clifford and Douglas Arnold. "TQM: Is it Right for Law Enforcement?" *The Police Chief*, December 1993, 20–22.

Skogan, Wesley G. "Communities, Crime, and Neighborhood Organization." *Crime and Delinquency*, Vol. 35, (1990): 437–457.

Skogan, Wesley G. *Disorder and Decline: Crime and the Spiral of Decay in American Neighborhoods*. New York: The Free Press, 1990.

Skogan, Wesley G. "Fear of Crime and Neighborhood Change." In *Criminal Justice: A Review of Research Communities and Crime*, ed. Albert J. Reiss and Michael Tonry. Chicago, Illinois: The University of Chicago Press vol. 8 (1986): 203–230.

Skogan, Wesley G. "The Impact of Community Policing on Neighborhood Residents: A Cross-Site Analysis." In *The Challenges of Community Policing: Testing the Promises*, ed. Dennis P. Rosenbaum. Thousand Oaks, CA.: SAGE Publications, Inc., 1994.

Skogan, Wesley G. "The Impact of Victimization on Fear." *Crime & Delinquency* 33, no. 1 (January 1987): 135–154

Skogan, Wesley G. and M.G. Maxfield. *Coping with Crime: Individual and Neighborhood Reactions*. Beverly Hills: SAGE Publications, Inc., 1981.

Skogan, Wesley G. and Mary Ann Wycoff. "Storefront Police Officers: The Houston Field Test." In *Community Crime prevention: Does it Work?* ed. Dennis P. Rosenbaum. Beverly Hills, California: SAGE Publications Inc., 1986: 179–199.

Skolnick, Jerome H. and David H. Bayley. *The New Blue Line: Police Innovation in Six American Cities*. New York: The Free Press, 1986.

Skolnick, Jerome H. and David H. Bayley. *Community Policing: Issues and Practices Around the World*. Washington, D.C.: National Institute of Justice, 1988.

Skolnick, Jerome H. and David H. Bayley. "Theme and Variation in Community Policing." In *Crime and Justice: A Biannual Review of Research* 10, ed. Michael Tonry and Norval Morris. Chicago, IL.: The University of Chicago Press, 1988.

Skolnick, Jerome H. and James J. Fyfe. "Community-Oriented Policing Would Prevent Police Brutality." In *Policing the Police*. San Diego: Greenhaven Press, Inc., 1995.

Smith, Bruce. *Police Systems in the United States*. New York: Harper and Brothers, 1960.

Smith, Michael R. "integrating Community Policing and the Use of Force: Public Education, Involvement, and Accountability." *American Journal of Police* 12, no. 4, 1994: 1–21.

Smith, William J. "Investigation at the Local Level." *Law and Order*, September 1994, 63–65.

Sparrow, Malcolm K. "Implementing Community Policing." *Perspective on Policing*. Washington, D.C.: National Institute of Justice and the Program in Criminal Justice Policy and Management (November 1988).

Sparrow, Malcolm K., Mark H. Moore, and David H. Kennedy. *Beyond 911: A New Era for Policing*.

Spelman, William and Dale K. Brown. *Calling the Police: Citizen Reporting of Serious Crime*. Washington, D.C.: U.S. Government Printing Office, 1984.

Spelman, William and John E. Eck. "Newport News Tests Problem- Oriented Policing." *National Institute of Justice: Research in Action*. Washington, D.C.: National Institute of Justice, January/February, 1987a.

Spelman, William and John E. Eck. "Problem-Oriented Policing." *National Institute of Justice: Research in Brief*. Washington, D.C.: National Institute of Justice, January 1987b.

Spelman, William and John E. Eck. "The Police and Delivery of Local Government Services: A Problem Oriented Approach." *Police Practices in the 90's: Key Management Issues*. ed. James Fyfe. Washington D.C.: International City/COUNTY Management Association, 1989.

Stedman, Robert F. *The Police and the Community*. Baltimore, Maryland: the John Hopkins University Press, 1972.

Steffensmeier, Darrell. "The Invention of the 'New' Senior Citizen Criminal." *Research on Aging*, vol. 9 (1987): 281–311.

Stephens, Darrel W. "Policing in the Future." *American Journal of Police* 9, 1990: 151–157.

Stephens, Darrel W., John D. Hartman, and Darryl Herring. "Giving Voice: The Police Chief, Assistant City Manger and Budget Director Focus on What Works." *Community Policing Exchange*. Washington, D.C.: The Community Policing Consortium, November/December 1995.

Sullivan, John L. *Introduction to Police Science*. 3rd ed. New York: McGraw-Hill, Inc., 1977.

Sullivan, William M. *Reconstructing Public Philosophy*. Berkeley, California: University of California Press, 1986.

Sweeney, William. "Grant Writing for Technology." *Law and Order*. September 1995: 83–84.

Swiss, James. "Adapting Total Quality Management (TQM) to Government." *Public Administration Review* 52 (1992): 356–362.

Sykes, Gary W. "Accreditation and Community Policing: Passing Fads or Basic Reforms?" *Journal of Contemporary Criminal Justice* 10, no. 1, March 1994: 1–16.

Tafoya, William L. "Into the Future . . . A Look at the 21st Century." *Law Enforcement Technology*, September/October 1987.

Tafoya, William L. *A Delphi Forecast of the Future of Law Enforcement*. Ph.D. Dissertation. Ann Arbor, Michigan: University Microfilm International, 1991.

Tafoya, William L. "Futures Research: Implication for Criminal Investigations." In *Criminal Investigation: Essays and Cases*, ed. James N. Gilbert. Columbus, OH: Merrill Publishing Company, 1990.

Taft, Philip B., Jr. *Fighting Fear: The Baltimore County C.O.P.E. Project*. Washington, D.C.: The Police Executive Research Forum, 1986.

Thurman, Quint C., Andrew Giacomazzi, and Phil Bogen. "Research Note: Cops, Kids, and Community Policing—An Assessment of a Community Policing Demonstration Project." *Crime & Delinquency* 39, no. 4, October 1993: 554–564.

Tien, James M. and Thomas F. Rich. "The Hartford COMPASS Program: Experiences With a Weed and Seed-Related Program." *The Challenge of Community Policing: Testing the Promises*, ed. Dennis P. Rosenbaum. Thousand Oaks, CA.: SAGE Publications Inc., 1994.

Tien, James M., James W. Simon, and Richard C. Larson. *An Alternative Approach in Police Patrol: The Wilmington Split-Force Experiment*. Cambridge, MA.: Public Systems Evaluation, 1977.

Toch, Hans and J. Douglas Grant. *Police as Problem Solvers*. New York: Plenum Press, 1991.

Trojanowicz, Robert C. *An Evaluation of the Neighborhood Foot Patrol Program in Flint*. East Lansing, Mich.: National Neighborhood Foot Patrol Center, Michigan State University, 1982.

Trojanowicz, Robert C. "Community-Policing Is Not Police-Community Relations." *FBI Law Enforcement Bulletin*. October 1990: 6–11.

Trojanowicz, Robert C. "Evaluating a Neighborhood Foot Patrol Program: The Flint Michigan Project." In *Community Crime Prevention: Does it Work?* ed. Dennis P. Rosenbaum. Beverly Hills: Sage Publications, 1986.

Trojanowicz, Robert C. "The Future of Community Policing." In *The Challenge of Community Policing: Testing the Promises*, ed. Dennis P. Rosenbaum. Thousand Oaks, CA.: SAGE Publications, Inc., 1994.

Trojanowicz, Robert C. and Bonnie Bucqueroux. *Community Policing: A Contemporary Perspective*. Cincinnati: Anderson Publishing Company, 1989.

Trojanowicz, Robert C. and Bonnie Bucqueroux. *Community Policing: How to Get Started*. Cincinnati: Anderson Publishing Co., 1994.

Trojanowicz, Robert C. and Bonnie Bucqueroux. "The Community Policing Challenge." *PTM: Police Technology and Management* 1 no. 4 (November 1990b): 40–51.

Trojanowicz, Robert C. and David Carter. *The Philosophy and Role of Community Policing.* East Lansing, Mich.: Michigan State University, 1988.

Trojanowicz, Robert C. and Samuel L. Dixon. *Criminal Justice and the Community.* Englewood Cliffs, N.J.: Prentice-Hall, Inc., 1974.

Trojanowicz, Robert C., John M. Trojanowicz, and Forrest M. Moss. *Community Based Crime Prevention.* Pacific Palisades, California: Goodyear Publishing Com., 1975.

Turner, Robyne and Michael D. Wiatrowski. "Community Policing and Community Innovation: The 'New Institutionalism' in American Government." In *Issues in Criminal Justice*, ed. Peter C. Kratcoski and Duane Dukes. Cincinnati, Ohio: Academy of Criminal Justice Sciences, Anderson Publishing Company, 1995.

Uchida, Craig D., Brian Forst, and Sampson O. Annan. *Modern Policing and the Control of Illegal Drugs: Testing New Strategies in Two American Cities.* Washington, D.C.: National Institute of Justice and the Police Foundation, May 1992.

U.S. Department of Justice. Office of Justice Programs. *Drugs, Crime, and the Justice System.* Washington, D.C.: GPO, December 1992.

U.S. Department of Justice. *Operation Weed and Seed Implementation Manual.* Washington, D.C.: U.S. Department of Justice, 1992.

Vaughn, Jerald R. "Community Oriented Policing . . . You Can Make It Happen." *Law and Order.* June 1991: 35–39.

Vold, George B. and Thomas J. Bernard. *Theoretical Criminology.* 3rd ed. New York: Oxford University Press, 1986.

Vollmer, August. "Police Progress in the Past Twenty-Five Years." *Journal of Criminal Law and Criminology* 24 no. 1 (1933): 161–175.

Wagner, W.F. *An Evaluation of a Police Patrol Experiment.* Pullman, Wash.: Washington State University, 1978.

Walinsky, Adam. "The Crisis of Public Order." *The Atlantic Monthly.* July 1995, 39–54.

Walker, Samuel. *A Critical History of Police Reform: The Emergence of Professionalism.* Lexington, MA.: Lexington Books, 1977.

Walker, Samuel. *Popular Justice: History of American Criminal Justice.* New York: Oxford University Press, 1980.

Walker, Samuel. "'Broken Windows' and Fractured History: The Use and Misuse of History in Recent Police Patrol Analysis." *Justice Quarterly*, no. 1 (1984): 75–90.

Walker, Samuel. *Sense and Nonsense about Crime and Drugs: A Policy Guide.* 3rd ed. Belmont, CA.: Wadsworth Publishing Company, 1994.

Walsh, William F. "Analysis of the Police Supervisor's Role in Community Policing." *Issues in Community Policing.* ed. Peter C. Kratcoski and Duane Dukes. Cincinnati, Ohio: Academy of Criminal Justice Sciences, Anderson Publishing Company, 1995.

Walters, Paul M. "Community-Oriented Policing: A Blend of Strategies." FBI Law Enforcement Bulletin 62, no. 11 (1993): 20–23.

Warren, J.W., M.L. Forst, and M. M. Estrella. "Directed Patrol: An Experiment That Worked." *The Police Chief,* July 1979, 48–49.

Wasserman, Robert and Mark H. Moore. "Values in Policing." *Perspectives on Policing.* Washington, D.C.: National Institute of Justice and John F. Kennedy School of Government, Harvard University, 1988.

Watson, Nelson A. *Police-Community Relations*. Washington, D.C.: International Association of Chiefs of Police, 1966.

Weatheritt, Mollie. "Community Policing: Rhetoric or Reality?" In *Community Policing: Rhetoric or Reality?*, ed. Jack R. Greene and Stephen D. Mastrofski. New York: Praeger Publishers, 1988.

Webber, Alan M. "Crime and Management: An Interview with New York City Police Commissioner Lee P. Brown." *Harvard Business Review*, May–June 1991, 111–126.

Webster, Barbara and Edward F. Connors. *Community Policing: Identifying Problems*. Alexandria, VA.: Institute for Law and Justice, March 1991.

Weisburd, David. "Evaluating Community Policing: Role Tensions Between Practitioners and Evaluators." In *The Challenge of Community Policing: Testing the Promises*. ed. Dennis P. Rosenbaum. Thousand Oaks, CA.: SAGE Publications, Inc., 1994.

Weisburd, David and Jerome E. McElroy. "Enacting the CPO Role: Findings From the New York City Pilot Program in Community Policing." In *Community Policing: Rhetoric or Reality?*, ed. Jack R. Greene and Stephen D. Mastrofski. New York: Praeger Publishers, 1988.

Weisburd, David, Jerome E. McElroy, and Patricia Hardyman. "Challenges to Supervision in Community Policing: Observations on a Pilot Project." *American Journal of Police* 7 no. 2 (1988): 29–50.

Weisel, Deborah Lamm. "Playing the Home Field: A Problem-Oriented Approach to Drug Control." *American Journal of Police* 9, 1990.

Weisel, Deborah Lamm and John E. Eck. "Toward a Practical Approach to Organizational Change: Community Policing Initiatives in Six Cities." In *The Challenge of Community Policing: Testing the Promises*. ed. Dennis P. Rosenbaum. Thousand Oaks, CA.: SAGE Publications Inc., 1994.

Weisheit, Ralph A., L. Edward Wells, and David N. Falcone. "Community Policing in Small Town and Rural America." *Crime & Delinquency* 40, no. 4 (October 1994): 549–567.

West, Marty. "Police and Private Security." *Law and Order*, July 1994, 86–88.

West, Marty. "POP in Fresno: Effective Problem-Solving Techniques." *The Police Chief*, March 1995, 37–43.

White, Mervin F. and Ben A. Menke. "A Critical Analysis on Public Opinion Toward Police Agencies." *Journal of Police Science and Administration*. Vol. 6, 1978: 204–218.

Whiteley, Richard C. *The Customer-Driven Company*. Reading, MA.: Addison-Wesley, 1991.

Whitman, Sylvia. "Police Academies for Citizens." *Law and Order*, June 1993, 66–71.

Wiatrowski, Michael D. "Community Policing in Delray Beach." In *Issues in Community Policing*, ed. Peters C. Kratcoski and Duane Dukes. Cincinnati: Academy of Criminal Justice Sciences and Anderson Publishing Company, 1995.

Wiauowski, M. and J. Vardalis. "Community Policing and a Model of Crime Prevention in the Community." *Criminal Psychology*, October 1994: 53–57.

Wilkinson, Deanna L. and Dennis P. Rosenbaum. "The Effects of Organizational Structure on Community Policing." In *The Challenge of Community Policing: Testing the Promises*. ed. Dennis P. Rosenbaum. Thousand Oaks, CA.: SAGE Publications Inc., 1994.

Williams, Hubert. "Retrenchment, the Constitution, and Policing." In *Police Leadership in America*. ed. William A. Geller. Chicago: American Bar Foundation, 1985.

Williams, Hubert and Antony M. Pate. "Returning to First Principles: Reducing the Fear of Crime in Newark." *Crime & Delinquency*, 33, no. 1 (January 1987): 53–70.

Wilson, Deborah G. and Susan F. Bennett. "Officers' Response to Community Policing: Variations on a Theme." *Crime & Delinquency* 40, no. 3 (July 1994): 354–370.

Wilson, James Q. *Bureaucracy*. New York: Basic Books, Inc., 1989.

Wilson, James Q. "Just Take Away Their Guns." *The New York Times Sunday Magazine*, March 20, 1994.

Wilson, James Q. *Thinking About Crime*. New York: Vintage Books, 1975.

Wilson, James Q. *Varieties of Police Behavior: The Management of Law and Order in Eight Communities*. Cambridge, MA.: Harvard University Press, 1968.

Wilson, James Q. "What Makes a Better Policeman?" *The Atlantic Monthly*. March 1969.

Wilson, James Q. and Barbara Boland. *The Effects of Police on Crime*. Washington, D.C.: U.S. Government Printing Office, 1979

Wilson, James Q. and Barbara Boland. "The Effect of Police on Crime." *Law and Society Review*, 12, 1978: 367–384.

Wilson, James Q. and George L. Kelling. "Broken Windows: The Police and Neighborhood Safety." *The Atlantic Monthly*, March 1982, 29–38.

Wilson, James Q. and George L. Kelling. "Broken Windows: Making Neighborhoods Safe." *The Atlantic Monthly*, February 1989, 46–52.

Wilson, James Q. and Joan Petersilia. *Crime*. ed. James Q. Wilson. San Francisco, CA.: ICS Press, 1995.

Wilson, Laurie J. "Placing Community-Oriented Policing in the Broader Realm of Community Cooperation." *The Police Chief*, April 1995, 127–128.

Wilson, O. W. *Municipal Police Administration*. Washington, D.C.: International City Management Association, 1941.

Wilson, O. W. *Police Administration*. New York: McGraw-Hill, 1950.

Witkin, Gordon. "Police Chiefs at War." *U.S. News and World Report*, June 8, 1992.

Witkin, Gordon and Dan McGraw. "Beyond 'Just the Facts, Ma'am'." *U.S. News and World Report*, August 2, 1993, 28–30.

Worden, Robert E. "A Badge and a Baccalaureate: Policies, Hypotheses, and Further Evidence." *Justice Quarterly* 7, no. 3: 565–592.

Worrell, Ann. "Officers 'Love Our Kids'." *Law and Order*, September 1993, 109–110.

Worrell, Ann. "Operation Blue: Cops Become Bankers to aid Elderly Citizens." *Law and Order*, December 1993, 32–35.

Worrell, Ann. "Police Museums Offer Opportunities To Teach, Recruit." *Law and Order*, December 1993, 32–35.

Worsnop, Richard L. "Community Policing." *The CQ Researcher* 3, no. 5, (February 5, 1993): 97–120.

Wycoff, Mary Ann. "Community Policing in Madison." In *The Challenges of Community Policing: Testing the Promises*, ed. Dennis P. Rosenbaum. Thousand Oaks, CA.: SAGE Publications, 1994.

Wycoff, Mary Ann. "The Benefits of Community Policing: Evidence and Conjecture." In *Community Policing: Rhetoric or Reality?*, ed. Jack R. Greene and Stephen D. Mastrofski. New York: Praeger Publishers, 1988.

Wycoff, Mary Ann. *The Role of Municipal Police Research as a Prelude to Changing It*. Washington, D.C.: Police Foundation, 1982.

Wycoff, Mary Ann and Wesley G. Skogan. *Community Policing in Madison: Quality from the Inside Out*. An Evaluation of Implementation and Impact. Washington, D.C.: Police Foundation, 1993.

Wycoff, Mary Ann and Wesley G. Skogan. "Community Policing in Madison: An Analysis of Implementation and Impact." In *The Challenge of Community Policing: Testing the Promises*, ed. Dennis P. Rosenbaum. Thousand Oaks, CA.: SAGE Publications, Inc., 1994.

Wycoff, Mary Ann and Wesley G. Skogan. "The Effect of a Community Policing Management Style on Officers' Attitudes." *Crime & Delinquency* 40, no. 3, (July 1994): 371–383.

Yin, Robert K. "Community Crime Prevention: A Synthesis of Eleven Evaluations." In *Community Crime Prevention: Does It Work?* ed. Dennis P. Rosenbaum. Beverly Hills: SAGE Publications Inc., 1986: 294–308.

Younce, Thomas C. "'Broken Window' Stops Drug Sales." *Law & Order*, April 1992, 67–70.

Zimmer, Lynn. "Proactive Policing Against Street-Level Drug Trafficking." *American Journal of Police* 9, 1990: 43–65.

INDEX

Strategic planning, 270
Strategic policing, 41, 55-57, 61
Sullivan, J. L., 3-5, 10, 23, 301, 335
Sullivan, W. M., 394, 404
Supreme Court, U.S., 11
Surveys, 310, 320-26, 329
Systems management, 242
Systemic approach, 18-19
Systemic considerations, 181
Sweeney, W., 376
Swiss, J., 175, 184

T

Tafoya, W. L., 363-66, 380, 383
Targeting, 57-60, 78, 137
Taylor, A., 102
Taylor, F. W., 239
Taylor, R. B., 82, 89, 98, 303-5, 323, 333
Taxi connection, 57
Team policing, 16-17
Technology, 10
Theoretical framework, 2
Thurman, Q. C., 153, 328, 335
Tien, J. M., 57, 61, 74, 227, 235
Tithing, 3
Tithingman, 3
Tocqueville, A., 393
Total quality management, 156, 173-82, 254-55, 299-300, 343, 391
Trading cards, 93, 195
Training, 168, 202, 293, 295-96
Traditional policing, 11-12, 18, 35, 38, 40, 48, 54, 186-87, 192
Traffic checkpoints, 37
Trenton, NJ PD, 80
Trojanowicz, R., 16, 19, 23, 29-31, 36, 46, 53, 56, 62, 73, 76, 83, 98, 101, 125, 193, 210, 266, 298, 342-44, 346-47, 351, 360, 367, 378, 383
Twentieth century, 10
Twenty-first Amendment, 10
Tzu, S., 154

U

Uchide, C. D., 322, 335
Uniform Crime Reports, 301
U.S. Department of Justice, 13, 41, 53, 159, 177-78, 367
U.S. Military, 78-80
University of Wisconsin in Madison, 100

V

Valdiva, S., 387
Values, 156-57, 159, 168, 180-81, 269-70
Vera Institute, 91, 199
Vernon, R. L., 226, 235, 328
Veterans of Foreign Wars, 225, 231
VFW Magazine, 232
Viano, E. C., 16, 22
Victimization, 35, 84
Vienna, WV PD, 380-81
Violent Crime Control and Law Enforcment Act, 367, 394, 398
Vision statement, 145, 276
Vitelli, M., 231
Vold, G. B., 98
Volmer, A., 11, 161, 239-40, 260-61, 348, 394
Volstead Act, 10
Volunteer Corp., 215

W

Wagman, D., 231
Wagner, W. F., 303, 335
Walinsky, A., 214, 235
Walker, S., 9, 23, 26,53, 161, 184, 377, 384
Ward, B., 141-42
Washington D.C. PD, 68-69
Washington Redskins, 93
Washington State Institute for Community-Oriented Policing, 146
Washington State University, 148
Wasserman, R., 157, 183, 342, 347, 349, 359
Watch and Ward, 4

Y

Z